Strategy Six

Strategy Six

By

Sun Tzu

Julius Caesar

Einhard

Niccolò Machiavelli

Carl von Clausewitz

Ardant du Picq

Enhanced Media
2017

The Art of War by Sun Tzu. Translated by Lionel Giles. First published in 1910.

The Gallic Wars: Commentarii de Bello Gallico by Julius Caesar. Translated by Thomas Holmes. First published in 1908.

The Life of Charlemagne by Einhard. Translated by Samuel Epes Turner. First published in 1880.

The Prince by Niccolò Machiavelli. Translated by William Kenaz Marriott. First published in 1908.

On War by Carl von Clausewitz. Translated by J. J. Graham. First published in 1873.

Battle Studies: Ancient and Modern Battle by Ardant Du Picq. Translated by John Nesmith Greely and Robert Christie Cotton. First published in 1921.

Strategy Six ©2017 Enhanced Media Publishing.

First Printing: 2017.

ISBN: 9781549795244.

Contents

The Art of War by Sun Tzu

Introduction

Ssu-ma Ch`ien gives the following biography of Sun Tzu:

Sun Tzu Wu was a native of the Ch`i State. His *Art Of War* brought him to the notice of Ho Lu, King of Wu. Ho Lu said to him:

"I have carefully perused your thirteen chapters. May I submit your theory of managing soldiers to a slight test?"

Sun Tzu replied: "You may."

Ho Lu asked: "May the test be applied to women?"

The answer was again in the affirmative, so arrangements were made to bring one hundred and eighty ladies out of the Palace. Sun Tzu divided them into two companies, and placed one of the King's favorite concubines at the head of each. He then bade them all take spears in their hands, and addressed them thus:

"I presume you know the difference between front and back, right hand and left hand?"

The girls replied: Yes.

Sun Tzu went on:

"When I say "Eyes front," you must look straight ahead. When I say "Left turn," you must face towards your left hand. When I say "Right turn," you must face towards your right hand. When I say "About turn," you must face right round towards your back."

Again the girls assented. The words of command having been thus explained, he set up the halberds and battle-axes in order to begin the drill. Then, to the sound of drums, he gave the order "Right turn." But the girls only burst out laughing. Sun Tzu said:

"If words of command are not clear and distinct, if orders are not thoroughly understood, then the general is to blame."

So he started drilling them again, and this time gave the order "Left turn," whereupon the girls once more burst into fits of laughter. Sun Tzu:

"If words of command are not clear and distinct, if orders are not thoroughly understood, the general is to blame. But if his orders *are* clear, and the soldiers nevertheless disobey, then it is the fault of their officers."

So saying, he ordered the leaders of the two companies to be beheaded.

Now the king of Wu was watching the scene from the top of a raised pavilion; and when he saw that his favorite concubines were about to be executed, he was greatly alarmed and hurriedly sent down the following message: "We are now quite satisfied as to our general's ability to handle troops. If We are bereft of these two concubines, our meat and drink will lose their savor. It is our wish that they shall not be beheaded." Sun Tzu replied:

"Having once received His Majesty's commission to be the general of his forces, there are certain commands of His Majesty which, acting in that capacity, I am unable to accept."

Accordingly, he had the two leaders beheaded, and straightway installed the pair next in order as leaders in their place. When this had been done, the drum was sounded for the drill once more; and the girls went through all the evolutions, turning to the right or to the left, marching ahead or wheeling back, kneeling or standing, with perfect accuracy and precision, not venturing to utter a sound.

Then Sun Tzu sent a messenger to the King saying:

"Your soldiers, Sire, are now properly drilled and disciplined, and ready for your majesty's inspection. They can be put to any use that their sovereign may desire; bid them go through fire and water, and they will not disobey." But the King replied:

"Let our general cease drilling and return to camp. As for us, We have no wish to come down and inspect the troops." Thereupon Sun Tzu said:

"The King is only fond of words, and cannot translate them into deeds."

After that, Ho Lu saw that Sun Tzu was one who knew how to handle an army, and finally appointed him general. In the west, he defeated the Ch'u State and forced his way into Ying, the capital; to the north he put fear into the States of Ch'i and Chin, and spread his fame abroad amongst the feudal princes. And Sun Tzu shared in the might of the King.

I. LAYING PLANS

1. Sun Tzu said: The art of war is of vital importance to the State.

2. It is a matter of life and death, a road either to safety or to ruin. Hence it is a subject of inquiry which can on no account be neglected.

3. The art of war, then, is governed by five constant factors, to be taken into account in one's deliberations, when seeking to determine the conditions obtaining in the field.

4. These are: (1) The Moral Law; (2) Heaven; (3) Earth; (4) The Commander; (5) Method and discipline.

5, 6. The MORAL LAW causes the people to be in complete accord with their ruler, so that they will follow him regardless of their lives, undismayed by any danger.

7. HEAVEN signifies night and day, cold and heat, times and seasons.

8. EARTH comprises distances, great and small; danger and security; open ground and narrow passes; the chances of life and death.

9. The COMMANDER stands for the virtues of wisdom, sincerity, benevolence, courage and strictness.

10. By METHOD AND DISCIPLINE are to be understood the marshaling of the army in its proper subdivisions, the graduations of rank among the officers, the maintenance of roads by which supplies may reach the army, and the control of military expenditure.

11. These five heads should be familiar to every general: he who knows them will be victorious; he who knows them not will fail.

12. Therefore, in your deliberations, when seeking to determine the military conditions, let them be made the basis of a comparison, in this wise: —

13. (1) Which of the two sovereigns is imbued with the Moral law?

(2) Which of the two generals has most ability?

(3) With whom lie the advantages derived from Heaven and Earth?

(4) On which side is discipline most rigorously enforced?

(5) Which army is stronger?

(6) On which side are officers and men more highly trained?

(7) In which army is there the greater constancy both in reward and punishment?

14. By means of these seven considerations I can forecast victory or defeat.

15. The general that hearkens to my counsel and acts upon it, will conquer: — let such a one be retained in command! The general that hearkens not to my counsel nor acts upon it, will suffer defeat: —let such a one be dismissed!

16. While heading the profit of my counsel, avail yourself also of any helpful circumstances over and beyond the ordinary rules.

17. According as circumstances are favorable, one should modify one's plans.

18. All warfare is based on deception.

19. Hence, when able to attack, we must seem unable; when using our forces, we must seem inactive; when we are near, we must make the enemy believe we are far away; when far away, we must make him believe we are near.

20. Hold out baits to entice the enemy. Feign disorder, and crush him.

21. If he is secure at all points, be prepared for him. If he is in superior strength, evade him.

22. If your opponent is of choleric temper, seek to irritate him. Pretend to be weak, that he may grow arrogant.

23. If he is taking his ease, give him no rest.

24. Attack him where he is unprepared, appear where you are not expected.

25. These military devices, leading to victory, must not be divulged beforehand.

26. Now the general who wins a battle makes many calculations in his temple ere the battle is fought. The general who loses a battle makes but few calculations beforehand. Thus do many calculations lead to victory, and few calculations to defeat: how much more no calculation at all! It is by attention to this point that I can foresee who is likely to win or lose.

II. WAGING WAR

1. Sun Tzu said: In the operations of war, where there are in the field a thousand swift chariots, as many heavy chariots, and a hundred thousand mail-clad soldiers, with provisions enough to carry them a thousand *li*, [2.78 modern *li* go to a

mile. The length may have varied slightly since Sun Tzu's time.] the expenditure at home and at the front, including entertainment of guests, small items such as glue and paint, and sums spent on chariots and armor, will reach the total of a thousand ounces of silver per day. Such is the cost of raising an army of 100,000 men.

2. When you engage in actual fighting, if victory is long in coming, then men's weapons will grow dull and their ardor will be damped. If you lay siege to a town, you will exhaust your strength.

3. Again, if the campaign is protracted, the resources of the State will not be equal to the strain.

4. Now, when your weapons are dulled, your ardor damped, your strength exhausted and your treasure spent, other chieftains will spring up to take advantage of your extremity. Then no man, however wise, will be able to avert the consequences that must ensue.

5. Thus, though we have heard of stupid haste in war, cleverness has never been seen associated with long delays.

6. There is no instance of a country having benefited from prolonged warfare.

7. It is only one who is thoroughly acquainted with the evils of war that can thoroughly understand the profitable way of carrying it on.

8. The skillful soldier does not raise a second levy, neither are his supply-wagons loaded more than twice.

[Once war is declared, he will not waste precious time in waiting for reinforcements, nor will he return his army back for fresh supplies, but crosses the enemy's frontier without delay.]

9. Bring war material with you from home, but forage on the enemy. Thus the army will have food enough for its needs.

10. Poverty of the State exchequer causes an army to be maintained by contributions from a distance. Contributing to maintain an army at a distance causes the people to be impoverished.

11. On the other hand, the proximity of an army causes prices to go up; and high prices cause the people's substance to be drained away.

12. When their substance is drained away, the peasantry will be afflicted by heavy exactions.

13, 14. With this loss of substance and exhaustion of strength, the homes of the people will be stripped bare, and three-tenths of their income will be dissipated; while government expenses for broken chariots, worn-out horses, breast-plates and helmets, bows and arrows, spears and shields, protective mantles, draught-oxen and heavy wagons, will amount to four-tenths of its total revenue.

15. Hence a wise general makes a point of foraging on the enemy. One cart-load of the enemy's provisions is equivalent to twenty of one's own, and likewise a single *picul* of his provender is equivalent to twenty from one's own store.

[Because twenty cartloads will be consumed in the process of transporting one cartload to the front. A *picul* is a unit of measure equal to 133.3 pounds (65.5 kilograms).]

16. Now in order to kill the enemy, our men must be roused to anger; that there may be advantage from defeating the enemy, they must have their rewards.

17. Therefore in chariot fighting, when ten or more chariots have been taken, those should be rewarded who took the first. Our own flags should be substituted for those of the enemy, and the chariots mingled and used in conjunction with ours. The captured soldiers should be kindly treated and kept.

18. This is called, using the conquered foe to augment one's own strength.

19. In war, then, let your great object be victory, not lengthy campaigns.

20. Thus it may be known that the leader of armies is the arbiter of the people's fate, the man on whom it depends whether the nation shall be in peace or in peril.

III. ATTACK BY STRATAGEM

1. Sun Tzu said: In the practical art of war, the best thing of all is to take the enemy's country whole and intact; to shatter and destroy it is not so good. So, too, it is better to recapture an army entire than to destroy it, to capture a regiment, a detachment or a company entire than to destroy them.

[The equivalent to an army corps, according to Ssu-ma Fa, consisted nominally of 12500 men; according to Ts`ao Kung, the equivalent of a regiment contained 500 men, the equivalent to a detachment consists from any number between 100 and 500, and the equivalent of a company contains from 5 to 100 men. For the last two, however, Chang Yu gives the exact figures of 100 and 5 respectively.]

2. Hence to fight and conquer in all your battles is not supreme excellence; supreme excellence consists in breaking the enemy's resistance without fighting.

3. Thus the highest form of generalship is to balk the enemy's plans; the next best is to prevent the junction of the enemy's forces; the next in order is to attack the enemy's army in the field; and the worst policy of all is to besiege walled cities.

4. The rule is, not to besiege walled cities if it can possibly be avoided. The preparation of mantlets, movable shelters, and various implements of war, will take up three whole months; and the piling up of mounds over against the walls will take three months more.

[These were great mounds or ramparts of earth heaped up to the level of the enemy's walls in order to discover the weak points in the defense, and also to destroy the fortified turrets mentioned in the preceding note.]

5. The general, unable to control his irritation, will launch his men to the assault like swarming ants, with the result that one-third of his men are slain, while the town still remains untaken. Such are the disastrous effects of a siege.

6. Therefore the skillful leader subdues the enemy's troops without any fighting; he captures their cities without laying siege to them; he overthrows their kingdom without lengthy operations in the field.

7. With his forces intact he will dispute the mastery of the Empire, and thus, without losing a man, his triumph will be complete. This is the method of attacking by stratagem.

8. It is the rule in war, if our forces are ten to the enemy's one, to surround him; if five to one, to attack him; if twice as numerous, to divide our army into two.

9. If equally matched, we can offer battle; if slightly inferior in numbers, we can avoid the enemy; if quite unequal in every way, we can flee from him.

10. Hence, though an obstinate fight may be made by a small force, in the end it must be captured by the larger force.

11. Now the general is the bulwark of the State; if the bulwark is complete at all points; the State will be strong; if the bulwark is defective, the State will be weak.

12. There are three ways in which a ruler can bring misfortune upon his army:—

13. (1) By commanding the army to advance or to retreat, being ignorant of the fact that it cannot obey. This is called hobbling the army.

14. (2) By attempting to govern an army in the same way as he administers a kingdom, being ignorant of the conditions which obtain in an army. This causes restlessness in the soldier's minds.

15. (3) By employing the officers of his army without discrimination, [That is, he is not careful to use the right man in the right place.] through ignorance of the military principle of adaptation to circumstances. This shakes the confidence of the soldiers.

16. But when the army is restless and distrustful, trouble is sure to come from the other feudal princes. This is simply bringing anarchy into the army, and flinging victory away.

17. Thus we may know that there are five essentials for victory: (1) He will win who knows when to fight and when not to fight.

(2) He will win who knows how to handle both superior and inferior forces.

(3) He will win whose army is animated by the same spirit throughout all its ranks.

(4) He will win who, prepared himself, waits to take the enemy unprepared.

(5) He will win who has military capacity and is not interfered with by the sovereign.

18. Hence the saying: If you know the enemy and know yourself, you need not fear the result of a hundred battles. If you know yourself but not the enemy, for every victory gained you will also suffer a defeat. If you know neither the enemy nor yourself, you will succumb in every battle.

IV. TACTICAL DISPOSITIONS

1. Sun Tzu said: The good fighters of old first put themselves beyond the possibility of defeat, and then waited for an opportunity of defeating the enemy.

2. To secure ourselves against defeat lies in our own hands, but the opportunity of defeating the enemy is provided by the enemy himself.

3. Thus the good fighter is able to secure himself against defeat, but cannot make certain of defeating the enemy.

4. Hence the saying: One may *know* how to conquer without being able to *do* it.

5. Security against defeat implies defensive tactics; ability to defeat the enemy means taking the offensive.

6. Standing on the defensive indicates insufficient strength; attacking, a superabundance of strength.

7. The general who is skilled in defense hides in the most secret recesses of the earth; he who is skilled in attack flashes forth from the topmost heights of heaven. Thus on the one hand we have ability to protect ourselves; on the other, a victory that is complete.

8. To see victory only when it is within the ken of the common herd is not the acme of excellence.

9. Neither is it the acme of excellence if you fight and conquer and the whole Empire says, "Well done!"

10. To lift an autumn hair is no sign of great strength; to see the sun and moon is no sign of sharp sight; to hear the noise of thunder is no sign of a quick ear.

11. What the ancients called a clever fighter is one who not only wins, but excels in winning with ease.

12. Hence his victories bring him neither reputation for wisdom nor credit for courage.

13. He wins his battles by making no mistakes. Making no mistakes is what establishes the certainty of victory, for it means conquering an enemy that is already defeated.

14. Hence the skillful fighter puts himself into a position which makes defeat impossible, and does not miss the moment for defeating the enemy.

15. Thus it is that in war the victorious strategist only seeks battle after the victory has been won, whereas he who is destined to defeat first fights and afterwards looks for victory.

16. The consummate leader cultivates the moral law, and strictly adheres to method and discipline; thus it is in his power to control success.

17. In respect of military method, we have, firstly, Measurement; secondly, Estimation of quantity; thirdly, Calculation; fourthly, Balancing of chances; fifthly, Victory.

18. Measurement owes its existence to Earth; Estimation of quantity to Measurement; Calculation to Estimation of quantity; Balancing of chances to Calculation; and Victory to Balancing of chances.

19. A victorious army opposed to a routed one, is as a pound's weight placed in the scale against a single grain.

20. The onrush of a conquering force is like the bursting of pent-up waters into a chasm a thousand fathoms deep.

V. ENERGY

1. Sun Tzu said: The control of a large force is the same principle as the control of a few men: it is merely a question of dividing up their numbers.

2. Fighting with a large army under your command is nowise different from fighting with a small one: it is merely a question of instituting signs and signals.

3. To ensure that your whole host may withstand the brunt of the enemy's attack and remain unshaken - this is effected by maneuvers direct and indirect.

4. That the impact of your army may be like a grindstone dashed against an egg - this is effected by the science of weak points and strong.

5. In all fighting, the direct method may be used for joining battle, but indirect methods will be needed in order to secure victory.

6. Indirect tactics, efficiently applied, are inexhaustible as Heaven and Earth, unending as the flow of rivers and streams; like the sun and moon, they end but to begin anew; like the four seasons, they pass away to return once more.

7. There are not more than five musical notes, yet the combinations of these five give rise to more melodies than can ever be heard.

8. There are not more than five primary colors (blue, yellow, red, white, and black), yet in combination they produce more hues than can ever been seen.

9 There are not more than five cardinal tastes (sour, acrid, salt, sweet, bitter), yet combinations of them yield more flavors than can ever be tasted.

10. In battle, there are not more than two methods of attack - the direct and the indirect; yet these two in combination give rise to an endless series of maneuvers.

11. The direct and the indirect lead on to each other in turn. It is like moving in a circle - you never come to an end. Who can exhaust the possibilities of their combination?

12. The onset of troops is like the rush of a torrent which will even roll stones along in its course.

13. The quality of decision is like the well-timed swoop of a falcon which enables it to strike and destroy its victim.

14. Therefore the good fighter will be terrible in his onset, and prompt in his decision.

15. Energy may be likened to the bending of a crossbow; decision, to the releasing of a trigger.

16. Amid the turmoil and tumult of battle, there may be seeming disorder and yet no real disorder at all; amid confusion and chaos, your array may be without head or tail, yet it will be proof against defeat.

17. Simulated disorder postulates perfect discipline, simulated fear postulates courage; simulated weakness postulates strength.

18. Hiding order beneath the cloak of disorder is simply a question of subdivision; concealing courage under a show of timidity presupposes a fund of latent energy; masking strength with weakness is to be effected by tactical dispositions.

19. Thus one who is skillful at keeping the enemy on the move maintains deceitful appearances, according to which the enemy will act. He sacrifices something, that the enemy may snatch at it.

20. By holding out baits, he keeps him on the march; then with a body of picked men he lies in wait for him.

21. The clever combatant looks to the effect of combined energy, and does not require too much from individuals.

Hence his ability to pick out the right men and utilize combined energy.

22. When he utilizes combined energy, his fighting men become as it were like unto rolling logs or stones. For it is the nature of a log or stone to remain motionless on level ground, and to move when on a slope; if four-cornered, to come to a standstill, but if round-shaped, to go rolling down.

23. Thus the energy developed by good fighting men is as the momentum of a round stone rolled down a mountain thousands of feet in height. So much on the subject of energy.

VI. WEAK POINTS AND STRONG

1. Sun Tzu said: Whoever is first in the field and awaits the coming of the enemy, will be fresh for the fight; whoever is second in the field and has to hasten to battle will arrive exhausted.

2. Therefore the clever combatant imposes his will on the enemy, but does not allow the enemy's will to be imposed on him.

3. By holding out advantages to him, he can cause the enemy to approach of his own accord; or, by inflicting damage, he can make it impossible for the enemy to draw near.

4. If the enemy is taking his ease, he can harass him; if well supplied with food, he can starve him out; if quietly encamped, he can force him to move.

5. Appear at points which the enemy must hasten to defend; march swiftly to places where you are not expected.

6. An army may march great distances without distress, if it marches through country where the enemy is not.

7. You can be sure of succeeding in your attacks if you only attack places which are undefended.

You can ensure the safety of your defense if you only hold positions that cannot be attacked.

8. Hence that general is skillful in attack whose opponent does not know what to defend; and he is skillful in defense whose opponent does not know what to attack.

9. O divine art of subtlety and secrecy! Through you we learn to be invisible, through you inaudible; and hence we can hold the enemy's fate in our hands.

10. You may advance and be absolutely irresistible, if you make for the enemy's weak points; you may retire and be safe from pursuit if your movements are more rapid than those of the enemy.

11. If we wish to fight, the enemy can be forced to an engagement even though he be sheltered behind a high rampart and a deep ditch. All we need do is attack some other place that he will be obliged to relieve.

12. If we do not wish to fight, we can prevent the enemy from engaging us even though the lines of our encampment be merely traced out on the ground. All we need do is to throw something odd and unaccountable in his way.

13. By discovering the enemy's dispositions and remaining invisible ourselves, we can keep our forces concentrated, while the enemy's must be divided.

14. We can form a single united body, while the enemy must split up into fractions. Hence there will be a whole pitted against separate parts of a whole, which means that we shall be many to the enemy's few.

15. And if we are able thus to attack an inferior force with a superior one, our opponents will be in dire straits.

16. The spot where we intend to fight must not be made known; for then the enemy will have to prepare against a possible attack at several different points; and his forces being thus distributed in many directions, the numbers we shall have to face at any given point will be proportionately few.

17. For should the enemy strengthen his van, he will weaken his rear; should he strengthen his rear, he will weaken his van; should he strengthen his left, he will weaken his right; should he strengthen his right, he will weaken his left. If he sends reinforcements everywhere, he will everywhere be weak.

18. Numerical weakness comes from having to prepare against possible attacks; numerical strength, from compelling our adversary to make these preparations against us.

19. Knowing the place and the time of the coming battle, we may concentrate from the greatest distances in order to fight.

20. But if neither time nor place be known, then the left wing will be impotent to succor the right, the right equally impotent to succor the left, the van unable to relieve the rear, or the rear to support the van. How much more so if the furthest portions of the army are anything under a hundred *li* apart, and even the nearest are separated by several *li*!

21. Though according to my estimate the soldiers of Yueh exceed our own in number, that shall advantage them nothing in the matter of victory. I say then that victory can be achieved.

22. Though the enemy be stronger in numbers, we may prevent him from fighting. Scheme so as to discover his plans and the likelihood of their success.

23. Rouse him, and learn the principle of his activity or inactivity.

Force him to reveal himself, so as to find out his vulnerable spots.

24. Carefully compare the opposing army with your own, so that you may know where strength is superabundant and where it is deficient.

25. In making tactical dispositions, the highest pitch you can attain is to conceal them; conceal your dispositions, and you will be safe from the prying of the subtlest spies, from the machinations of the wisest brains.

26. How victory may be produced for them out of the enemy's own tactics—that is what the multitude cannot comprehend.

27. All men can see the tactics whereby I conquer, but what none can see is the strategy out of which victory is evolved.

28. Do not repeat the tactics which have gained you one victory, but let your methods be regulated by the infinite variety of circumstances.

29. Military tactics are like unto water; for water in its natural course runs away from high places and hastens downwards.

30. So in war, the way is to avoid what is strong and to strike at what is weak.

31. Water shapes its course according to the nature of the ground over which it flows; the soldier works out his victory in relation to the foe whom he is facing.

32. Therefore, just as water retains no constant shape, so in warfare there are no constant conditions.

33. He who can modify his tactics in relation to his opponent and thereby succeed in winning, may be called a heaven- born captain.

34. The five elements (water, fire, wood, metal, earth) are not always equally predominant; There are short days and long; the moon has its periods of waning and waxing.

VII. MANEUVERING

1. Sun Tzu said: In war, the general receives his commands from the sovereign.

2. Having collected an army and concentrated his forces, he must blend and harmonize the different elements thereof before pitching his camp.

3. After that, comes tactical maneuvering, than which there is nothing more difficult. The difficulty of tactical maneuvering consists in turning the devious into the direct, and misfortune into gain.

4. Thus, to take a long and circuitous route, after enticing the enemy out of the way, and though starting after him, to contrive to reach the goal before him, shows knowledge of the artifice of *deviation*.

5. Maneuvering with an army is advantageous; with an undisciplined multitude, most dangerous.

6. If you set a fully equipped army in march in order to snatch an advantage, the chances are that you will be too late. On the other hand, to detach a flying column for the purpose involves the sacrifice of its baggage and stores.

7. Thus, if you order your men to roll up their buff-coats, and make forced marches without halting day or night, covering double the usual distance at a stretch, doing a hundred *li* in order to wrest an advantage, the leaders of all your three divisions will fall into the hands of the enemy.

8. The stronger men will be in front, the jaded ones will fall behind, and on this plan only one-tenth of your army will reach its destination.

9. If you march fifty *li* in order to outmaneuver the enemy, you will lose the leader of your first division, and only half your force will reach the goal.

10. If you march thirty *li* with the same object, two-thirds of your army will arrive.

11. We may take it then that an army without its baggage-train is lost; without provisions it is lost; without bases of supply it is lost.

12. We cannot enter into alliances until we are acquainted with the designs of our neighbors.

13. We are not fit to lead an army on the march unless we are familiar with the face of the country—its mountains and forests, its pitfalls and precipices, its marshes and swamps.

14. We shall be unable to turn natural advantage to account unless we make use of local guides.

15. In war, practice dissimulation, and you will succeed.

16. Whether to concentrate or to divide your troops, must be decided by circumstances.

17. Let your rapidity be that of the wind, your compactness that of the forest.

18. In raiding and plundering be like fire, in immovability like a mountain.

19. Let your plans be dark and impenetrable as night, and when you move, fall like a thunderbolt.

20. When you plunder a countryside, let the spoil be divided amongst your men; when you capture new territory, cut it up into allotments for the benefit of the soldiery.

21. Ponder and deliberate before you make a move.

22. He will conquer who has learnt the artifice of deviation. Such is the art of maneuvering.

23. The Book of Army Management says: On the field of battle, the spoken word does not carry far enough: hence the institution of gongs and drums. Nor can ordinary objects be seen clearly enough: hence the institution of banners and flags.

24. Gongs and drums, banners and flags, are means whereby the ears and eyes of the host may be focused on one particular point.

25. The host thus forming a single united body, is it impossible either for the brave to advance alone, or for the cowardly to retreat alone. This is the art of handling large masses of men.

26. In night-fighting, then, make much use of signal-fires and drums, and in fighting by day, of flags and banners, as a means of influencing the ears and eyes of your army.

27. A whole army may be robbed of its spirit; a commander-in-chief may be robbed of his presence of mind.

28. Now a soldier's spirit is keenest in the morning; by noonday it has begun to flag; and in the evening, his mind is bent only on returning to camp.

29. A clever general, therefore, avoids an army when its spirit is keen, but attacks it when it is sluggish and inclined to return. This is the art of studying moods.

30. Disciplined and calm, to await the appearance of disorder and hubbub amongst the enemy:—this is the art of retaining self-possession.

31. To be near the goal while the enemy is still far from it, to wait at ease while the enemy is toiling and struggling, to be well-fed while the enemy is famished:—this is the art of husbanding one's strength.

32. To refrain from intercepting an enemy whose banners are in perfect order, to refrain from attacking an army drawn up in calm and confident array:—this is the art of studying circumstances.

33. It is a military axiom not to advance uphill against the enemy, nor to oppose him when he comes downhill.

34. Do not pursue an enemy who simulates flight; do not attack soldiers whose temper is keen.

35. Do not swallow bait offered by the enemy. Do not interfere with an army that is returning home.

36. When you surround an army, leave an outlet free. Do not press a desperate foe too hard.

37. Such is the art of warfare.

VIII. VARIATION IN TACTICS

1. Sun Tzu said: In war, the general receives his commands from the sovereign, collects his army and concentrates his forces.

2. When in difficult country, do not encamp. In country where high roads intersect, join hands with your allies. Do not linger in dangerously isolated positions. In hemmed-in situations, you must resort to stratagem. In a desperate position, you must fight.

3. There are roads which must not be followed, armies which must be not attacked, towns which must not be besieged, positions which must not be contested, commands of the sovereign which must not be obeyed.

4. The general who thoroughly understands the advantages that accompany variation of tactics knows how to handle his troops.

5. The general who does not understand these, may be well acquainted with the configuration of the country, yet he will not be able to turn his knowledge to practical account.

6. So, the student of war who is unversed in the art of war of varying his plans, even though he be acquainted with the Five Advantages, will fail to make the best use of his men.

7. Hence in the wise leader's plans, considerations of advantage and of disadvantage will be blended together.

8. If our expectation of advantage be tempered in this way, we may succeed in accomplishing the essential part of our schemes.

9. If, on the other hand, in the midst of difficulties we are always ready to seize an advantage, we may extricate ourselves from misfortune.

10. Reduce the hostile chiefs by inflicting damage on them; and make trouble for them, and keep them constantly engaged; hold out specious allurements, and make them rush to any given point.

11. The art of war teaches us to rely not on the likelihood of the enemy's not coming, but on our own readiness to receive him; not on the chance of his not attacking, but rather on the fact that we have made our position unassailable.

12. There are five dangerous faults which may affect a general: (1) Recklessness, which leads to destruction; (2) cowardice, which leads to capture; (3) a hasty temper, which can be provoked by insults; (4) a delicacy of honor which is sensitive to shame; (5) over-solicitude for his men, which exposes him to worry and trouble.

13. These are the five besetting sins of a general, ruinous to the conduct of war.

14. When an army is overthrown and its leader slain, the cause will surely be found among these five dangerous faults. Let them be a subject of meditation.

IX. THE ARMY ON THE MARCH

1. Sun Tzu said: We come now to the question of encamping the army, and observing signs of the enemy. Pass quickly over mountains, and keep in the neighborhood of valleys.

2. Camp in high places, [Not on high hills, but on knolls or hillocks elevated above the surrounding country.] facing the sun. Do not climb heights in order to fight. So much for mountain warfare.

3. After crossing a river, you should get far away from it.

4. When an invading force crosses a river in its onward march, do not advance to meet it in mid-stream. It will be best to let half the army get across, and then deliver your attack.

5. If you are anxious to fight, you should not go to meet the invader near a river which he has to cross.

6. Moor your craft higher up than the enemy, and facing the sun. Do not move up-stream to meet the enemy. So much for river warfare.

7. In crossing salt-marshes, your sole concern should be to get over them quickly, without any delay.

8. If forced to fight in a salt-marsh, you should have water and grass near you, and get your back to a clump of trees. So much for operations in salt-marches.

9. In dry, level country, take up an easily accessible position with rising ground to your right and on your rear, so that the danger may be in front, and safety lie behind. So much for campaigning in flat country.

10. These are the four useful branches of military knowledge [Those, namely, concerned with (1) mountains, (2) rivers, (3) marshes, and (4) plains. Compare Napoleon's "Military Maxims," no. 1.] which enabled the Yellow Emperor to vanquish four several sovereigns.

11. All armies prefer high ground to low and sunny places to dark.

12. If you are careful of your men, and camp on hard ground, the army will be free from disease of every kind, and this will spell victory.

13. When you come to a hill or a bank, occupy the sunny side, with the slope on your right rear. Thus you will at once act for the benefit of your soldiers and utilize the natural advantages of the ground.

14. When, in consequence of heavy rains up-country, a river which you wish to ford is swollen and flecked with foam, you must wait until it subsides.

15. Country in which there are precipitous cliffs with torrents running between, deep natural hollows, tangled thickets, quagmires and crevasses, should be left with all possible speed and not approached.

16. While we keep away from such places, we should get the enemy to approach them; while we face them, we should let the enemy have them on his rear.

17. If in the neighborhood of your camp there should be any hilly country, ponds surrounded by aquatic grass, hollow basins filled with reeds, or woods with thick undergrowth, they must be carefully routed out and searched; for these are places where men in ambush or insidious spies are likely to be lurking.

18. When the enemy is close at hand and remains quiet, he is relying on the natural strength of his position.

19. When he keeps aloof and tries to provoke a battle, he is anxious for the other side to advance.

20. If his place of encampment is easy of access, he is tendering a bait.

21. Movement amongst the trees of a forest shows that the enemy is advancing. The appearance of a number of screens in the midst of thick grass means that the enemy wants to make us suspicious.

22. The rising of birds in their flight is the sign of an ambuscade. Startled beasts indicate that a sudden attack is coming.

23. When there is dust rising in a high column, it is the sign of chariots advancing; when the dust is low, but spread over a wide area, it betokens the approach of infantry. When it branches out in different directions, it shows that parties have been sent to collect firewood. A few clouds of dust moving to and fro signify that the army is encamping.

24. Humble words and increased preparations are signs that the enemy is about to advance. Violent language and driving forward as if to the attack are signs that he will retreat.

25. When the light chariots come out first and take up a position on the wings, it is a sign that the enemy is forming for battle.

26. Peace proposals unaccompanied by a sworn covenant indicate a plot.

27. When there is much running about [Every man hastening to his proper place under his own regimental banner.] and the soldiers fall into rank, it means that the critical moment has come.

28. When some are seen advancing and some retreating, it is a lure.

29. When the soldiers stand leaning on their spears, they are faint from want of food.

30. If those who are sent to draw water begin by drinking themselves, the army is suffering from thirst.

31. If the enemy sees an advantage to be gained and makes no effort to secure it, the soldiers are exhausted.

32. If birds gather on any spot, it is unoccupied. Clamor by night betokens nervousness.

33. If there is disturbance in the camp, the general's authority is weak. If the banners and flags are shifted about, sedition is afoot. If the officers are angry, it means that the men are weary.

34. When an army feeds its horses with grain and kills its cattle for food, [In the ordinary course of things, the men would be fed on grain and the horses chiefly on grass.] and when the men do not hang their cooking-pots over the camp- fires,

showing that they will not return to their tents, you may know that they are determined to fight to the death.

35. The sight of men whispering together in small knots or speaking in subdued tones points to disaffection amongst the rank and file.

36. Too frequent rewards signify that the enemy is at the end of his resources; too many punishments betray a condition of dire distress.

37. To begin by bluster, but afterwards to take fright at the enemy's numbers, shows a supreme lack of intelligence.

38. When envoys are sent with compliments in their mouths, it is a sign that the enemy wishes for a truce.

39. If the enemy's troops march up angrily and remain facing ours for a long time without either joining battle or taking themselves off again, the situation is one that demands great vigilance and circumspection.

40. If our troops are no more in number than the enemy, that is amply sufficient; it only means that no direct attack can be made.

What we can do is simply to concentrate all our available strength, keep a close watch on the enemy, and obtain reinforcements.

41. He who exercises no forethought but makes light of his opponents is sure to be captured by them.

42. If soldiers are punished before they have grown attached to you, they will not prove submissive; and, unless submissive, then will be practically useless. If, when the soldiers have become attached to you, punishments are not enforced, they will still be useless.

43. Therefore soldiers must be treated in the first instance with humanity, but kept under control by means of iron discipline. This is a certain road to victory.

44. If in training soldiers commands are habitually enforced, the army will be well-disciplined; if not, its discipline will be bad.

45. If a general shows confidence in his men but always insists on his orders being obeyed, the gain will be mutual.

X. TERRAIN

1. Sun Tzu said: We may distinguish six kinds of terrain, to wit: (1) Accessible ground; (2) entangling ground; (3) temporizing ground; (4) narrow passes; (5) precipitous heights; (6) positions at a great distance from the enemy.

2. Ground which can be freely traversed by both sides is called ACCESSIBLE.

3. With regard to ground of this nature, be before the enemy in occupying the raised and sunny spots, and carefully guard your line of supplies. Then you will be able to fight with advantage.

4. Ground which can be abandoned but is hard to re-occupy is called *entangling*.

5. From a position of this sort, if the enemy is unprepared, you may sally forth and defeat him. But if the enemy is prepared for your coming, and you fail to defeat him, then, return being impossible, disaster will ensue.

6. When the position is such that neither side will gain by making the first move, it is called *temporizing* ground.

7. In a position of this sort, even though the enemy should offer us an attractive bait, it will be advisable not to stir forth, but rather to retreat, thus enticing the enemy in his turn; then, when part of his army has come out, we may deliver our attack with advantage.

8. With regard to *narrow passes*, if you can occupy them first, let them be strongly garrisoned and await the advent of the enemy.

9. Should the army forestall you in occupying a pass, do not go after him if the pass is fully garrisoned, but only if it is weakly garrisoned.

10. With regard to *precipitous heights*, if you are beforehand with your adversary, you should occupy the raised and sunny spots, and there wait for him to come up.

11. If the enemy has occupied them before you, do not follow him, but retreat and try to entice him away.

12. If you are situated at a great distance from the enemy, and the strength of the two armies is equal, it is not easy to provoke a battle, and fighting will be to your disadvantage.

13. These six are the principles connected with Earth. The general who has attained a responsible post must be careful to study them.

14. Now an army is exposed to six several calamities, not arising from natural causes, but from faults for which the general is responsible. These are: (1) Flight; (2) insubordination; (3) collapse; (4) ruin; (5) disorganization; (6) rout.

15. Other conditions being equal, if one force is hurled against another ten times its size, the result will be the *flight* of the former.

16. When the common soldiers are too strong and their officers too weak, the result is *insubordination*. When the officers are too strong and the common soldiers too weak, the result is *collapse*.

17. When the higher officers are angry and insubordinate, and on meeting the enemy give battle on their own account from a feeling of resentment, before the commander-in-chief can tell whether or no he is in a position to fight, the result is *ruin*.

18. When the general is weak and without authority; when his orders are not clear and distinct;

19. When a general, unable to estimate the enemy's strength, allows an inferior force to engage a larger one, or hurls a weak detachment against a powerful one, and neglects to place picked soldiers in the front rank, the result must be *rout*.

20. These are six ways of courting defeat, which must be carefully noted by the general who has attained a responsible post.

21. The natural formation of the country is the soldier's best ally; but a power of estimating the adversary, of controlling the forces of victory, and of shrewdly calculating difficulties, dangers and distances, constitutes the test of a great general.

22. He who knows these things, and in fighting puts his knowledge into practice, will win his battles. He who knows them not, nor practices them, will surely be defeated.

23. If fighting is sure to result in victory, then you must fight, even though the ruler forbid it; if fighting will not result in victory, then you must not fight even at the ruler's bidding.

24. The general who advances without coveting fame and retreats without fearing disgrace, whose only thought is to protect his country and do good service for his sovereign, is the jewel of the kingdom.

25. Regard your soldiers as your children, and they will follow you into the deepest valleys; look upon them as your own beloved sons, and they will stand by you even unto death.

26. If, however, you are indulgent, but unable to make your authority felt; kind-hearted, but unable to enforce your commands; and incapable, moreover, of quelling disorder: then your soldiers must be likened to spoilt children; they are useless for any practical purpose.

27. If we know that our own men are in a condition to attack, but are unaware that the enemy is not open to attack, we have gone only halfway towards victory.

28. If we know that the enemy is open to attack, but are unaware that our own men are not in a condition to attack, we have gone only halfway towards victory.

29. If we know that the enemy is open to attack, and also know that our men are in a condition to attack, but are unaware that the nature of the ground makes fighting impracticable, we have still gone only halfway towards victory.

30. Hence the experienced soldier, once in motion, is never bewildered; once he has broken camp, he is never at a loss.

31. Hence the saying: If you know the enemy and know yourself, your victory will not stand in doubt; if you know Heaven and know Earth, you may make your victory complete.

XI. THE NINE SITUATIONS

1. Sun Tzu said: The art of war recognizes nine varieties of ground: (1) Dispersive ground; (2) facile ground; (3) contentious ground; (4) open ground; (5) ground of intersecting highways; (6) serious ground; (7) difficult ground; (8) hemmed-in ground; (9) desperate ground.

2. When a chieftain is fighting in his own territory, it is dispersive ground.

3. When he has penetrated into hostile territory, but to no great distance, it is facile ground.

4. Ground the possession of which imports great advantage to either side, is contentious ground.

5. Ground on which each side has liberty of movement is open ground.

6. Ground which forms the key to three contiguous states, so that he who occupies it first has most of the Empire at his command, [The belligerent who holds this dominating position can constrain most of them to become his allies.] is a ground of intersecting highways.

7. When an army has penetrated into the heart of a hostile country, leaving a number of fortified cities in its rear, it is serious ground.

8. Mountain forests, rugged steeps, marshes and fens—all country that is hard to traverse: this is difficult ground.

9. Ground which is reached through narrow gorges, and from which we can only retire by tortuous paths, so that a small number of the enemy would suffice to crush a large body of our men: this is hemmed in ground.

10. Ground on which we can only be saved from destruction by fighting without delay, is desperate ground.

11. On dispersive ground, therefore, fight not. On facile ground, halt not. On contentious ground, attack not.

12. On open ground, do not try to block the enemy's way. On the ground of intersecting highways, join hands with your allies.

13. On serious ground, gather in plunder. In difficult ground, keep steadily on the march.

14. On hemmed-in ground, resort to stratagem. On desperate ground, fight.

15. Those who were called skillful leaders of old knew how to drive a wedge between the enemy's front and rear; to prevent co-operation between his large and small divisions; to hinder the good troops from rescuing the bad, the officers from rallying their men.

16. When the enemy's men were united, they managed to keep them in disorder.

17. When it was to their advantage, they made a forward move; when otherwise, they stopped still.

18. If asked how to cope with a great host of the enemy in orderly array and on the point of marching to the attack, I should say: "Begin by seizing something which your opponent holds dear; then he will be amenable to your will."

19. Rapidity is the essence of war: take advantage of the enemy's unreadiness, make your way by unexpected routes, and attack unguarded spots.

20. The following are the principles to be observed by an invading force: The further you penetrate into a country, the greater will be the solidarity of your troops, and thus the defenders will not prevail against you.

21. Make forays in fertile country in order to supply your army with food.

22. Carefully study the well-being of your men, and do not overtax them. Concentrate your energy and hoard your strength.

23. Throw your soldiers into positions whence there is no escape, and they will prefer death to flight. If they will face death, there is nothing they may not achieve. Officers and men alike will put forth their uttermost strength.

24. Soldiers when in desperate straits lose the sense of fear. If there is no place of refuge, they will stand firm. If they are in hostile country, they will show a stubborn front. If there is no help for it, they will fight hard.

25. Thus, without waiting to be marshaled, the soldiers will be constantly on the *qui vive*; without waiting to be asked, they will do your will; without restrictions, they will be faithful; without giving orders, they can be trusted.

26. Prohibit the taking of omens, and do away with superstitious doubts. Then, until death itself comes, no calamity need be feared.

27. If our soldiers are not overburdened with money, it is not because they have a distaste for riches; if their lives are not unduly long, it is not because they are disinclined to longevity.

28. On the day they are ordered out to battle, your soldiers may weep, those sitting up bedewing their garments, and those lying down letting the tears run down their cheeks. But let them once be brought to bay, and they will display the courage of a Chu or a Kuei.

29. The skillful tactician may be likened to the *shuai-jan*. Now the *shuai-jan* is a snake that is found in the Ch`ang mountains. Strike at its head, and you will be attacked by its tail; strike at its tail, and you will be attacked by its head; strike at its middle, and you will be attacked by head and tail both.

30. Asked if an army can be made to imitate the *shuai-jan*, I should answer, Yes. For the men of Wu and the men of Yueh are enemies; yet if they are crossing a river in the same boat and are caught by a storm, they will come to each other's assistance just as the left hand helps the right.

31. Hence it is not enough to put one's trust in the tethering of horses, and the burying of chariot wheels in the ground.

32. The principle on which to manage an army is to set up one standard of courage which all must reach.

33. How to make the best of both strong and weak—that is a question involving the proper use of ground.

34. Thus the skillful general conducts his army just as though he were leading a single man, willy-nilly, by the hand.

35. It is the business of a general to be quiet and thus ensure secrecy; upright and just, and thus maintain order.

36. He must be able to mystify his officers and men by false reports and appearances, and thus keep them in total ignorance.

37. By altering his arrangements and changing his plans, [Wang Hsi thinks that this means not using the same stratagem twice.] he keeps the enemy without definite knowledge. By shifting his camp and taking circuitous routes, he prevents the enemy from anticipating his purpose.

38. At the critical moment, the leader of an army acts like one who has climbed up a height and then kicks away the ladder behind him. He carries his men deep into hostile territory before he shows his hand.

39. He burns his boats and breaks his cooking-pots; like a shepherd driving a flock of sheep, he drives his men this way and that, and nothing knows whither he is going.

40. To muster his host and bring it into danger:—this may be termed the business of the general.

41. The different measures suited to the nine varieties of ground; the expediency of aggressive or defensive tactics; and the fundamental laws of human nature: these are things that must most certainly be studied.

42. When invading hostile territory, the general principle is, that penetrating deeply brings cohesion; penetrating but a short way means dispersion.

43. When you leave your own country behind, and take your army across neighborhood territory, you find yourself on critical ground. When there are means of communication on all four sides, the ground is one of intersecting highways.

44. When you penetrate deeply into a country, it is serious ground. When you penetrate but a little way, it is facile ground.

45. When you have the enemy's strongholds on your rear, and narrow passes in front, it is hemmed-in ground. When there is no place of refuge at all, it is desperate ground.

46. Therefore, on dispersive ground, I would inspire my men with unity of purpose. On facile ground, I would see that there is close connection between all parts of my army.

47. On contentious ground, I would hurry up my rear.

48. On open ground, I would keep a vigilant eye on my defenses. On ground of intersecting highways, I would consolidate my alliances.

49. On serious ground, I would try to ensure a continuous stream of supplies. On difficult ground, I would keep pushing on along the road.

50. On hemmed-in ground, I would block any way of retreat. On desperate ground, I would proclaim to my soldiers the hopelessness of saving their lives.

51. For it is the soldier's disposition to offer an obstinate resistance when surrounded, to fight hard when he cannot help himself, and to obey promptly when he has fallen into danger.

52. We cannot enter into alliance with neighboring princes until we are acquainted with their designs. We are not fit to lead an army on the march unless we are familiar with the face of the country—its mountains and forests, its pitfalls and precipices, its marshes and swamps. We shall be unable to turn natural advantages to account unless we make use of local guides.

53. To be ignored of any one of the following four or five principles does not befit a warlike prince.

54. When a warlike prince attacks a powerful state, his generalship shows itself in preventing the concentration of the enemy's forces. He overawes his opponents, and their allies are prevented from joining against him.

55. Hence he does not strive to ally himself with all and sundry, nor does he foster the power of other states. He carries out his own secret designs, keeping his antagonists in awe. Thus he is able to capture their cities and overthrow their kingdoms.

56. Bestow rewards without regard to rule, issue orders without regard to previous arrangements; and you will be able to handle a whole army as though you had to do with but a single man.

57. Confront your soldiers with the deed itself; never let them know your design. When the outlook is bright, bring it before their eyes; but tell them nothing when the situation is gloomy.

58. Place your army in deadly peril, and it will survive; plunge it into desperate straits, and it will come off in safety.

59. For it is precisely when a force has fallen into harm's way that is capable of striking a blow for victory.

60. Success in warfare is gained by carefully accommodating ourselves to the enemy's purpose.

61. By persistently hanging on the enemy's flank, we shall succeed in the long run in killing the commander-in-chief.

62. This is called ability to accomplish a thing by sheer cunning.

63. On the day that you take up your command, block the frontier passes, destroy the official tallies, and stop the passage of all emissaries.

64. Be stern in the council-chamber, so that you may control the situation.

65. If the enemy leaves a door open, you must rush in.

66. Forestall your opponent by seizing what he holds dear, and subtly contrive to time his arrival on the ground.

67. Walk in the path defined by rule, and accommodate yourself to the enemy until you can fight a decisive battle.

68. At first, then, exhibit the coyness of a maiden, until the enemy gives you an opening; afterwards emulate the rapidity of a running hare, and it will be too late for the enemy to oppose you.

XII. THE ATTACK BY FIRE

1. Sun Tzu said: There are five ways of attacking with fire. The first is to burn soldiers in their camp; the second is to burn stores; the third is to burn baggage trains; the fourth is to burn arsenals and magazines; the fifth is to hurl dropping fire amongst the enemy.

2. In order to carry out an attack, we must have means available. The material for raising fire should always be kept in readiness.

3. There is a proper season for making attacks with fire, and special days for starting a conflagration.

4. The proper season is when the weather is very dry; the special days are those when the moon is in the constellations of the Sieve, the Wall, the Wing or the Cross-bar; for these four are all days of rising wind.

5. In attacking with fire, one should be prepared to meet five possible developments:

6. (1) When fire breaks out inside to enemy's camp, respond at once with an attack from without.

7. (2) If there is an outbreak of fire, but the enemy's soldiers remain quiet, bide your time and do not attack.

[The prime object of attacking with fire is to throw the enemy into confusion. If this effect is not produced, it means that the enemy is ready to receive us. Hence the necessity for caution.]

8. (3) When the force of the flames has reached its height, follow it up with an attack, if that is practicable; if not, stay where you are.

9. (4) If it is possible to make an assault with fire from without, do not wait for it to break out within, but deliver your attack at a favorable moment.

10. (5) When you start a fire, be to windward of it. Do not attack from the leeward.

11. A wind that rises in the daytime lasts long, but a night breeze soon falls.

12. In every army, the five developments connected with fire must be known, the movements of the stars calculated, and a watch kept for the proper days.

13. Hence those who use fire as an aid to the attack show intelligence; those who use water as an aid to the attack gain an accession of strength.

14. By means of water, an enemy may be intercepted, but not robbed of all his belongings.

15. Unhappy is the fate of one who tries to win his battles and succeed in his attacks without cultivating the spirit of enterprise; for the result is waste of time and general stagnation.

16. Hence the saying: The enlightened ruler lays his plans well ahead; the good general cultivates his resources.

[Tu Mu quotes the following from the *San Lueh*, ch. 2: "The warlike prince controls his soldiers by his authority, kits them together by good faith, and by rewards makes them serviceable. If faith decays, there will be disruption; if rewards are deficient, commands will not be respected."]

17. Move not unless you see an advantage; use not your troops unless there is something to be gained; fight not unless the position is critical.

18. No ruler should put troops into the field merely to gratify his own spleen; no general should fight a battle simply out of pique.

19. If it is to your advantage, make a forward move; if not, stay where you are.

20. Anger may in time change to gladness; vexation may be succeeded by content.

21. But a kingdom that has once been destroyed can never come again into being; nor can the dead ever be brought back to life.

22. Hence the enlightened ruler is heedful, and the good general full of caution. This is the way to keep a country at peace and an army intact.

XIII. THE USE OF SPIES

1. Sun Tzu said: Raising a host of a hundred thousand men and marching them great distances entails heavy loss on the people and a drain on the resources of the State. The daily expenditure will amount to a thousand ounces of silver. There will be commotion at home and abroad, and men will drop down exhausted on the highways. As many as seven hundred thousand families will be impeded in their labor.

2. Hostile armies may face each other for years, striving for the victory which is decided in a single day. This being so, to remain in ignorance of the enemy's condition simply because one grudges the outlay of a hundred ounces of silver in honors and emoluments, is the height of inhumanity.

3. One who acts thus is no leader of men, no present help to his sovereign, no master of victory.

4. Thus, what enables the wise sovereign and the good general to strike and conquer, and achieve things beyond the reach of ordinary men, is *foreknowledge*.

5. Now this foreknowledge cannot be elicited from spirits; it cannot be obtained inductively from experience, cannot be gained by reasoning nor by any deductive calculation.

6. Knowledge of the enemy's dispositions can only be obtained from other men.

7. Hence the use of spies, of whom there are five classes: (1) Local spies; (2) inward spies; (3) converted spies; (4) doomed spies; (5) surviving spies.

8. When these five kinds of spy are all at work, none can discover the secret system. This is called "divine manipulation of the threads." It is the sovereign's most precious faculty.

9. Having *local spies* means employing the services of the inhabitants of a district.

10. Having *inward spies*, making use of officials of the enemy.

11. Having *converted spies*, getting hold of the enemy's spies and using them for our own purposes.

12. Having *doomed spies*, doing certain things openly for purposes of deception, and allowing our spies to know of them and report them to the enemy.

13. *Surviving spies*, finally, are those who bring back news from the enemy's camp.

14. Hence it is that which none in the whole army are more intimate relations to be maintained than with spies. None should be more liberally rewarded. In no other business should greater secrecy be preserved.

15. Spies cannot be usefully employed without a certain intuitive sagacity.

16. They cannot be properly managed without benevolence and straightforwardness.

17. Without subtle ingenuity of mind, one cannot make certain of the truth of their reports.

18. Be subtle! be subtle! and use your spies for every kind of business.

19. If a secret piece of news is divulged by a spy before the time is ripe, he must be put to death together with the man to whom the secret was told.

20. Whether the object be to crush an army, to storm a city, or to assassinate an individual, it is always necessary to begin by finding out the names of the attendants, the aides-de- camp, and door-keepers and sentries of the general in command. Our spies must be commissioned to ascertain these.

21. The enemy's spies who have come to spy on us must be sought out, tempted with bribes, led away and comfortably housed. Thus they will become converted spies and available for our service.

22. It is through the information brought by the converted spy that we are able to acquire and employ local and inward spies.

23. It is owing to his information, again, that we can cause the doomed spy to carry false tidings to the enemy.

24. Lastly, it is by his information that the surviving spy can be used on appointed occasions.

25. The end and aim of spying in all its five varieties is knowledge of the enemy; and this knowledge can only be derived, in the first instance, from the converted spy. Hence it is essential that the converted spy be treated with the utmost liberality.

26. Of old, the rise of the Yin dynasty was due to I Chih who had served under the Hsia. Likewise, the rise of the Chou dynasty was due to Lu Ya who had served under the Yin.

27. Hence it is only the enlightened ruler and the wise general who will use the highest intelligence of the army for purposes of spying and thereby they achieve great results. Spies are a most important element in war, because on them depends an army's ability to move.

The Gallic Wars by Julius Caesar

BOOK I

CAMPAIGNS AGAINST THE HELVETII AND ARIOVISTUS

Gaul, taken as a whole, is divided into three parts, one of which is inhabited by the Belgae, another by the Aquitani, and the third by a people who call themselves Celts and whom we call Gauls. These peoples differ from one another in language, institutions, and laws. The Gauls are separated from the Aquitani by the river Garonne, from the Belgae by the Marne and the Seine. Of all these peoples the bravest are the Belgae; for they are furthest removed from the civilization and refinement of the Province, traders very rarely visit them with the wares which tend to produce moral enervation, and they are nearest to the Germans, who dwell on the further side of the Rhine, and are constantly at war with them. For the same reason the Helvetii also are braver than the other Gauls; they are fighting almost daily with the Germans, either trying to keep them out of their own country or making raids into theirs. That part of the whole country which, as we have said, is occupied by the Gauls, begins at the river Rhone, and is bounded by the Garonne, the Ocean, and the country of the Belgae. It extends, moreover, in the region occupied by the Sequani and the Helvetii, to the Rhine; and its trend is towards the north. The territory of the Belgae, commencing from the most distant frontier of Gaul, extends to the lower Rhine, and has a northerly and easterly aspect. Aquitania extends from the Garonne to the Pyrenees and that part of the Ocean which is off the coast of Spain; and its outlook is towards the north-west.

Pre-eminent among the Helvetii in rank and wealth was Orgetorix. In the consulship of Marcus Messala and Marcus Piso he organized a conspiracy among the nobles in the hope of making himself king, and persuaded the community to undertake a national emigration, as, being the most warlike of all the Gallic peoples, they could easily achieve dominion over the whole of Gaul. He had no difficulty in convincing them, because their country is limited everywhere by natural features, on one side by the Rhine, a broad deep river, which separates the Helvetian territory from the Germans; on another by the lofty range of the Jura, between the Helvetii and the Sequani; on a third by the Lake of Geneva and the Rhone, which separates our Province from the Helvetii. These Hermits restricted their movements and made it comparatively difficult for them to attack their neighbours; and, being a warlike people, they chafed under this restraint. Moreover, considering their numbers and their renown as valiant warriors, they felt that their territories —only two hundred and forty miles long by one hundred and eighty broad—were too small.

Impelled by these motives and swayed by Orgetorix, they determined to emigrate into Gaul: buying up all the draught cattle and wagons that they could obtain, bringing all available lands under cultivation, with the object of securing an abundance of grain for the journey, and establishing relations of peace and amity with the neighbouring tribes. They believed that two years would be sufficient to complete these preparations, and passed an enactment fixing their departure for the third year. Orgetorix was chosen as leader, and undertook a mission to the several tribes. In the course of his tour he persuaded a Sequanian named Casticus, whose father, Catamantaloedes, had for many years held sovereignty over the Sequani, and had been honoured by the Roman Senate with the title of Friend, to seize the royal power, which his father had held before him, over his own tribe; he also persuaded Dumnorix, an Aeduan, brother of Diviciacus, who at that time held the principal power in his own country, and was very popular with the masses, to make a similar attempt, and gave him his daughter in marriage. He convinced them that it would be quite easy to achieve their purpose, as he was going to seize sovereignty over his own tribe; the Helvetii were undoubtedly the strongest people in the whole of Gaul; and he affirmed that by his wealth and his armed force he would secure them the possession of their thrones. Enthralled by his eloquence, they swore mutual fidelity; and they hoped that, once they had secured their thrones, they would be able, backed by three powerful and stable peoples, to make themselves masters of the whole of Gaul.

The scheme was made known to the Helvetii by informers. In accordance with national Helvetian custom, they insisted that Orgetorix should plead suicide. If he were condemned, his inevitable punishment would be death at the stake. On the day fixed for the pleading he made all his slaves from all parts, numbering ten thousand, come to the trial, and marched thither at the head of all his retainers and debtors, who were very numerous. With their protection he escaped trial. Exasperated at this defiance, the community endeavoured to assert their rights by force, and the authorities summoned a posse from the districts, when Orgetorix died; and there is some reason to suspect (so the Helvetii believe) that he died by his own hand.

After his death the Helvetii in no way relaxed their efforts to carry out their intended emigration. As soon as they believed themselves ready for the enterprise, they set fire to all their strongholds, of which there were twelve, their villages, numbering four hundred, and the remaining buildings, which belonged to individuals; and burned the whole of their grain, except what they were going to take with them, that they might have no hope of returning home, and so be more ready to face every danger. Every man was directed to take a supply of flour from his house for three months for his own use. They induced their neighbours, the Rauraci, the Tulingi and the Latobrigi, to join their enterprise, burn their strongholds and villages, and emigrate along with them; at the same time they formed a close alliance with the Boii, who had formerly dwelt on the further bank of the Rhine, and had migrated into Noricum and taken Noreia.

There were only two routes by which it was possible for them to leave their country. One, a march leading through the country of the Sequani, passing between the Jura and the Rhone, was so narrow and difficult that carts could barely pass along it one at a time, while a lofty mountain overhung it, so that a handful of men could easily stop them; the other, leading through our Province, is much easier and more convenient, for the Rhone, which flows between the country of the Helvetii and that of the Allobroges, who had recently been subdued, is, at certain points, fordable. Geneva, the most remote town belonging to the Allobroges, is connected by a bridge with the country of the Helvetii, to which it is quite close. The Helvetii believed that they could either induce the Allobroges to let them pass through their country, as they were not yet apparently well disposed towards the Romans, or could compel them to do so. When everything was ready for their departure, they fixed the 28th of March, in the consulship of Lucius Piso and Aulus Gabinius, for the general muster on the banks of the Rhone.

As soon as Caesar was informed that they were attempting to march through the Province, he promptly quit the capital, pushed on as fast as he could possibly travel into Further Gaul, and made his way to the neighbourhood of Geneva. As the entire force in Further Gaul amounted only to one legion, he ordered as many troops as possible to be raised throughout the Province, and directed that the bridge at Geneva should be broken down. The Helvetii, on being informed of his approach, sent an embassy to him, composed of their most illustrious citizens, headed by Nammeius and Verucloetius, to say that they purposed, with his consent, to march through the Province, as there was no other route open to them, but that they would do no harm. Caesar, remembering that Lucius Cassius, when consul, had been slain by the Helvetii, and his army defeated and forced to pass under the yoke, was not disposed to grant their request; and he was of opinion that men of hostile temper were not likely to refrain from outrage and mischief. Still, in order to gain time for his levies to assemble, he told the envoys that he would take some days for consideration: if they had any favour to ask, they might return on the 13th of April.

Meantime, employing the legion which he had with him and the troops which had assembled from the Province, he constructed a rampart sixteen feet high and a trench from the Lake of Helvetii to Geneva, which overflows into the Rhone, to the passage Jura, which separates the territory of the Sequani from the Helvetii—a distance of nineteen miles. When these works were finished he constructed redoubts to enable him to repel the Helvetii, in case they attempted to force a passage. When the appointed day came round, and the envoys returned, he told them that he could not, consistently with the established usage of the Roman People, allow any one to march through the Province; and he warned them that, if they attempted to use force, he would stop them. The disappointed Helvetii lashed barges together and made a number of rafts, while others forded the Rhone at the shallowest parts, sometimes in the day, but oftener at night, and tried to break through; but, foiled by the entrenchments, the rapid concentration of the troops, and their volleys of missiles, they abandoned their attempt.

There remained only the route through to the Sequani; and it was so narrow that they could not advance if the Sequani objected. Being unable to win their consent by their own efforts, they sent envoys to the Aeduan, Dumnorix, hoping, by his intercession, to gain their object. Dumnorix had great influence with the Sequani from his personal popularity and lavish bribery, and was well disposed towards the

Helvetii, having married a daughter of Orgetorix, who belonged to that tribe: more-over, his desire of royal power made him eager for revolution, and he wished to lay as many tribes as possible under obligations to himself. Accordingly he undertook the mission. He induced the Sequani to allow the Helvetii to pass through their territory, and effected an exchange of hostages between the two peoples, the Sequani undertaking not to obstruct the march of the Helvetii, the Helvetii to abstain from mischief and outrage.

Caesar was informed that the Helvetii intended to march through the country of the Sequani and the Aedui into the territories of the Santones, which are not far distant from those boundaries of the Tolosates, which is a state in the Province. If this took place, he saw that it would be attended with great danger to the Province to have warlike men, enemies of the Roman people, bordering upon an open and very fertile tract of country. For these reasons he placed Titus Labienus, one of his generals, in charge of the entrenchments which he had constructed; hastened to Italy by forced marches; raised two legions there; withdrew three from their winter quarters in the neighbourhood of Aquileia; and advanced rapidly with all five by the shortest road leading over the Alps into Further Gaul. The Ceutrones, Graioceli, and Caturiges seized the Alpine heights and tried to stop the advance of the army. Beating them off in several combats, he made his way in seven days from Ocelum, the extreme point of the Cisalpine Province, into the territory of the Vocontii in the Further Province: thence he led the army into the country of the Allobroges, and from their country into that of the Segusiani, the first people outside the Province, beyond the Rhone.

The Helvetii had by this time threaded their forces over through the narrow defile and the territories of the Sequani, and had arrived at the territories of the Aedui, and were ravaging their lands. The Aedui, unable to defend themselves or their property against their attacks, sent a deputation to Caesar to ask for help, pleading that they had at all times deserved well of the Roman People, and it was not right that their lands should be ravaged, their children carried off into slavery, and their towns captured almost under the eyes of our army. At the same time the Ambarri, who were connected with the Aedui by friendship and blood, informed Caesar that their lands had been laid waste, and that it was more than they could do to repel the enemy's attacks upon their towns. The Allobroges also, who possessed villages and estates on the further side of the Rhone, fled to Caesar, alleging that they had nothing left except the bare soil. For these reasons Caesar decided that it would be unwise to wait till his allies had lost all that they possessed, and the Helvetii reached the country of the Santoni.

A river called the Saone flows through the territories of the Aedui and Sequani into the Rhone with such incredible slowness, that it cannot be determined by the eye in which direction it flows. This the Helvetii were crossing by rafts and boats joined together. Learning from his patrols that about one-fourth were still on the near side of the river, while three-fourths had passed over, Caesar started from his camp in the third watch, with three legions, and came up with the division which had not yet crossed. Attacking them unexpectedly while their movements were impeded, he destroyed a great many: the rest took to flight and concealed themselves in the neighbouring woods. The clan in question was called the Tigurini, the entire Helvetian community being divided into four clans. This clan, acting independently, had emigrated within the memory of our fathers, and made the army of the consul, Lucius Cassius, who was himself killed, pass under the yoke. Thus, either by accident or divine providence, that section of the Helvetian community which had brought a signal disaster upon the Roman People was the first to pay the penalty. In this action Caesar avenged a family wrong as well as the wrongs of his country; for a general named Lucius Piso, the grandfather of his father-in-law, Lucius Piso, had perished in the same battle as Cassius at the hands of the Tigurini.

After fighting this action, Caesar bridged the Saone with the object of pursuing the rest of the Helvetian force, and thereby conveyed his army across. The Helvetii, seeing that he had effected in a single day the passage of the river, which they had accomplished with the greatest difficulty in twenty days, and alarmed by his unexpected advance, sent an embassy to meet him, headed by Divico, who had commanded in the campaign against Cassius. He addressed Caesar in the following terms:—if the Roman People would make peace with the Helvetii, they would go wherever Caesar fixed their abode, and would remain there; but if he persisted in his hostile attitude, he would do well to remember the disaster which had befallen the Roman People in the past and the ancient valour of the Helvetii. Granted that he had surprised one clan at a moment when their countrymen had crossed the river and could not help them, he need not therefore exaggerate his own prowess, or look down upon them. The lesson they had learned from their fathers and their forefathers was to fight like men, and not to rely upon trickery or ambuscade. Let him not, then, suffer the place where they stood to derive its name from a Roman reverse and from the annihilation of an army, or bequeath the remembrance thereof to posterity.

Caesar replied that he had no reason to hesitate, because he well remembered the events which the Helvetian envoys had recounted; and he remembered them with indignation, for the Roman People had not deserved what had befallen them. If they had been conscious of wrong-doing it would have been easy to take precautions; but they had been deceived because they were not conscious of having done anything to justify alarm, and saw no necessity for taking alarm without reason. Even if he were willing to forget an old affront, how could he banish the recollection of fresh outrages,—their attempt to force a passage through the Province in despite of him, and their raids upon the Aedui, the Ambarri, and the Allobroges? The insolence with which they boasted of their victory, their astonishment at his having so long put up with their outrages, pointed to the same conclusion. For it was the wont of the immortal gods sometimes to grant prosperity and long impunity to men whose crimes they were minded to punish in order that a complete reverse of fortune might make them suffer more bitterly. Still, notwithstanding this, if they would give hostages to satisfy him that they intended to fulfil their promises, and if they would recompense the Aedui for the wrongs which they had done to them and likewise the Allobroges, he would make peace with them. Divico replied that, as the Roman People could testify, the Helvetii, following the maxims of their ancestors, were in the habit of receiving hostages, not of giving them. With this rejoinder he withdrew.

Next day the Helvetii quitted their march up the valley campment. Caesar did the same, and sent on ahead all his cavalry, amounting to four thousand, which he had raised from the whole Province, from the Aedui, and from their allies, to see in what direction the enemy were going. Following the rearguard too eagerly, they engaged the Helvetian cavalry on unfavourable ground, and a few of our men fell. Elated at having repulsed such a numerous body of cavalry with five hundred horsemen, the Helvetii more than once halted boldly, their rearguard challenging our men. Caesar would not allow his men to fight, and for the time he thought it enough to prevent the enemy from looting, foraging, and ravaging the country. The two armies marched in close company for about a fortnight, the enemy's rear and our van never being more than five or six miles apart.

Meanwhile Caesar daily called upon the Aedui for the grain which, as he reminded them, they had promised in the name of their Government. Gaul being situated, as the narrative has shown, beneath a northern sky, the climate is cold, and therefore not only was the standing corn unripe, but there was not even a sufficient supply of fodder; while Caesar was unable to use the grain which he had brought up the Saone in barges, because the Helvetii had struck off from that river, and he was unwilling to move away from them. From day to day the Aedui kept him on the expectant, affirming that the grain was being collected—was on the way—was just at hand. When the day on which the men's rations would be due was near, feeling that his patience had been tried too long, he assembled their leading men, of whom he had a large number in camp; amongst others Diviciacus and Liscus, the chief magistrate — the Vergobret, as the Aedui call him—who is elected annually, and possesses the power of life and death over his countrymen. Caesar took them seriously to task for not helping him in this critical conjuncture, when the enemy were near and it was impossible either to buy corn or to get it from the fields, especially as he had undertaken the campaign in compliance with the entreaties of many of their own representatives. But what he complained of more seriously still was that they had played him false.

Then at length Liscus, moved by Caesar's speech, disclosed what he had hitherto kept secret. There were certain individuals, he said, who had great influence with the masses, and unofficially had more power than the magistrates themselves. These men made seditious and violent speeches, and worked upon the fears of the people to prevent them from contributing their due quota of grain. It would be better, they argued, supposing that the Aedui could not for the moment win supremacy over Gaul, to have Gauls for their masters than Romans; and they had no doubt that, if the Romans overpowered the Helvetii, they would deprive the Aedui of their liberty, along with the rest of Gaul. These men kept the enemy informed of our plans, and of all that was going on in camp, and they were beyond his control. What was more, he knew that, in making these revelations to Caesar, which he had only done under pressure, he had acted at great personal risk, and for that reason he had kept silent as long as he could.

Caesar perceived that Liscus's remarks pointed to Dumnorix, the brother of Diviciacus; but, as he did not want these matters to be talked about with a number of people present, he promptly dismissed the assembly, only detaining Liscus.

When they were alone, he questioned him about what he had said in the meeting. Liscus spoke unreservedly and boldly. Caesar put the same questions to others separately, and found that what Liscus said was true. The individual referred to was Dumnorix, a man of boundless audacity, extremely popular with the masses from his open-handedness, and an ardent revolutionary. For many years he had farmed at a low rate and monopolized the Aeduan tolls and all the other taxes, as, when he made a bid, no one dared to bid against him. In this way he had increased his fortune and amassed large sums to expend in bribery; he permanently maintained at his own expense a large body of horsemen, whom he kept in attendance upon him; he possessed great influence not only in his own country, but also with the surrounding tribes; and, to strengthen this influence, he had arranged a marriage for his mother with a Biturigian of the highest rank and the greatest authority, while his own wife was a Helvetian, and he had arranged marriages for his sister on the mother's side and his female relations among other tribes. From his connection with the Helvetii, he was a partisan of theirs and well disposed towards them and he also personally detested Caesar and the Romans, because their coming had lessened his power and restored his brother, Diviciacus, to his former influential and honourable position. If anything should befall the Romans, he saw great reason to hope that, by the aid of the Helvetii, he would secure the throne; while, so long as the Roman People were supreme, he despaired not only of making himself king, but even of retaining his existing influence. Caesar also found, in the course of his inquiries, that, in the disastrous cavalry combat a few days before, it was Dumnorix with his troopers (for he commanded the auxiliary cavalry which the Aedui had sent to Caesar) who had set the example of flight, and that, on their flight, the rest of the cavalry had taken alarm.

After learning these circumstances, since to these suspicions the most unequivocal facts were added, viz., that he had led the Helvetii through the territories of the Sequani; that he had provided that hostages should be mutually given; that he had done all these things, not only without any orders of his [Caesar's] and of his own state's, but even without their [the Aedui] knowing anything of it themselves; that he [Dumnorix] was reprimanded by the [chief] magistrate of the Aedui; he [Caesar] considered that there was sufficient reason why he should either punish him himself, or order the state to do so. There was one objection. Caesar had come to know that Diviciacus, Dumnorix's brother, felt the utmost devotion to the Roman People and the utmost goodwill towards himself, and that his loyalty, equity, and good sense were quite exceptional; in fact, he was afraid of offending Diviciacus by punishing his brother. Accordingly, before taking any definite step, he sent for Diviciacus, and, dismissing the ordinary interpreters, conversed with him through the medium of Gaius Valerius Troucillus, a leading Provincial and an intimate friend of his own, whom he trusted absolutely in all matters. Reminding Diviciacus of what had been said about Dumnorix at the meeting, when he was present, and at the same time telling him what everyone had separately said about him when alone with himself, he urgently requested him to consent to his either personally trying Dumnorix and passing judgement upon him, or else calling upon the state to do so, and not to take offence.

Bursting into tears, Diviciacus embraced but accepted Caesar and entreated him not to take severe measures against his brother. Caesar knew, he said, that the story was true, and no one suffered more under his brother's conduct than himself; for at a time when his own influence was paramount with his countrymen and in the rest of Gaul, and his brother, on account of his youth, was powerless, the latter had risen through his support; and the resources and strength which he thus acquired he used not only to weaken his influence, but almost to ruin him. Public opinion as well as fraternal affection had weight with him. If Dumnorix were severely dealt with by Caesar, then, considering his own friendly relations with the latter, no one would believe that he was not responsible; and the result would be that the feeling of the whole country would turn against him. He continued pleading at great length and with tears when Caesar grasped his hand, reassured him, and begged him to say no more, telling him that he valued his friendship so highly that, out of regard for his loyalty and his intercession, he would overlook both political injury and personal grievance. He then called Dumnorix, keeping his brother, by; pointed out what he had to find fault with in his conduct; stated what he knew about him, and the complaints which his own countrymen brought against him; warned him to avoid giving any ground for suspicion in the future; and told him that he would overlook the past for his brother Diviciacus's sake. Nevertheless he placed Dumnorix under surveillance, in order to ascertain what he was doing and who were his associates.

On the same day Caesar was informed by his patrols that the enemy had encamped at the foot of a hill eight miles from his own camp, and accordingly sent a party to reconnoiter the hill and find out what the ascent was like from the rear. They reported that it was quite practicable. In the third watch he explained his plans to Titus Labienus, his second-in-command, and ordered him to ascend to the summit of the hill with two legions, taking the party who had ascertained the route as guides. In the fourth watch he marched in person against the enemy, following the route by which they had advanced and sending on all the cavalry in front. Publius Considius, who was considered a thorough soldier, and had served in the army of Lucius Sulla and afterwards in that of Marcus Crassus, was sent on in advance with patrols.

At daybreak Labienus was in possession of the summit of the hill, while Caesar was not more than a mile and a half from the enemy's camp, and, as he afterwards learned from prisoners, his own approach and that of Labienus were alike unknown, when Considius rode up to him at full gallop, and stated that the hill which he had desired Labienus to occupy was in possession of the enemy, as he could tell from the arms and crests being Gallic. Caesar withdrew his troops to a hill close by, and formed them in line of battle. Labienus, acting on Caesar's order not to engage until he saw his force close to the enemy's camp, so that they might be attacked on all sides at once, kept possession of the hill, waiting for the appearance of our men, and declined an engagement. At length, late in the day, Caesar learned from his patrols that the hill was in the possession of his own troops, that the Helvetii had moved off, and that Considius from panic had reported as a fact actually seen what he had not seen at all. The same day Caesar followed the enemy at the usual interval, and pitched his camp three miles from theirs.

Next day, as the rations of the army would be due in just forty-eight hours, and Caesar was not more than eighteen miles from Bibracte —by far the wealthiest and most important town of the Aedui—he thought it time to secure his supplies, and accordingly struck off from the route followed by the Helvetii and marched rapidly for Bibracte. The move was reported to the enemy by deserters from Lucius Aemilius, who commanded a troop of Gallic cavalry. The Helvetii, believing that the Romans were moving away because they were afraid of them (especially as on the day before, though they had occupied a position of vantage, they had declined an action), or confident of being able to cut them off from supplies, altered their plans, reversed their march, and began to hang upon our rearguard and harass them.

Observing this, Caesar withdrew his troops on to a hill close by and sent his cavalry to stem the enemy's attack. Meanwhile he formed his four veteran legions in three lines half-way up the hill, posting the two which he had recently levied in Cisalpine Gaul and all the auxiliaries above on the ridge, and thus occupying the whole hill; at the same time he ordered the men's packs to be collected and the space which they covered to be entrenched by the troops posted on the high ground. The Helvetii, following with all their wagons, parked their baggage, repulsed our cavalry with their dense array, and, forming a phalanx, moved up against our first line.

Caesar sent first his own charger and then the chargers of all the officers out of sight, in order, by putting all on an equality, to banish the idea of flight; then he harangued his men, and the battle began. The legionaries, throwing their javelins from their commanding position, easily broke the enemy phalanx, and, having destroyed their formation, drew their swords and charged. The Gauls were greatly hampered in action by the fact that in many cases several shields were transfixed and pinned together by the impact of one javelin, and, as the iron bent, they could not pull the javelins out or fight properly with their left arms encumbered, so that many, after repeated jerks, preferred to drop their shields and fight bare. At length, enfeebled by wounds, they began to fall back and retreat towards a hill about a mile off. They had gained the hill and the Romans were following after them, when the Boii and Tulingi, some fifteen thousand strong, who closed the enemy's column and served as the rearguard, marched up, immediately attacked the Romans on their exposed flank, and lapped round them; observing this, the Helvetii who had retreated to the hill began to press forward again and renewed the battle. The Romans effected a change of front and advanced in two divisions, the first and second lines to oppose the enemy when they had beaten and driven off; the third to withstand the new-comers.

Thus two battles went on at once, and the fighting was prolonged and fierce. When the enemy could no longer withstand the onslaughts of the Romans, one division drew back, up the hill, while the other withdrew to their baggage and wagons,—withdrew, not fled, for throughout the whole of this battle, though the fighting lasted from the seventh hour till evening, none could see an enemy in flight. Till far into the night fighting actually went on by the baggage; for the enemy had made a rampart of their wagons, and from their commanding position hurled missiles against our men as they came up, while some got between the wagons and behind the wheels and threw darts and javelins, which wounded our men. After a long struggle our men took possession of the baggage. Orgetorix's daughter and one of his sons were captured on the spot. About one hundred and thirty thousand souls survived the battle and fled without halting throughout the whole of that night. Three days later they reached the country of the Lingones, for our troops remained on the field for three days, out of consideration for their wounded and to bury the dead, and therefore were unable to pursue. Caesar sent dispatches and messages to the Lingones, warning them not to supply the fugitives with corn or otherwise assist them, and threatening that, if they did so, he would treat them as he had treated the Helvetii. After an interval of three days he started with his whole force in pursuit.

The Helvetii, under stress of utter destitution, sent envoys to Caesar to propose surrender. The envoys met him on the march, prostrated themselves before him, and in suppliant terms besought him with tears for peace. He told them that the fugitives must remain where they were and await his arrival; and they promised obedience. When Caesar reached the spot, he required the Helvetii to give hostages and to surrender their arms and the slaves who had deserted to them. While the hostages and deserters were being searched for and the arms collected, night came on, and about six thousand men, belonging to the clan known as the Verbigeni, quitted the Helvetian encampment in the early part of the night and pushed on for the Rhine and the territory of the Germans. Either they were afraid that after surrendering their arms they would be punished, or they hoped to get off scot-free, believing that, as the number which had surrendered was so vast, their flight might escape detection or even remain entirely unnoticed. When Caesar discovered this, he ordered the peoples through whose territories they had gone to hunt them down and bring them back if they wished him to hold them guiltless. When they were brought back he treated them as Aedui enemies; but all the rest, after they had delivered up hostages, arms, and deserters, he admitted to surrender. He ordered the Helvetii, Tulingi, and Latobrigi to return to their own country, whence they had come; and, as all their corn and pulse were gone, and they had not in their own country the means of satisfying their hunger, he directed the Allobroges to supply them with corn, and ordered them to rebuild the towns and villages which they had burned. His chief reason for doing this was that he did not wish the region which the Helvetii had abandoned to remain uninhabited, lest the Germans, who dwelt on the further side of the Rhine, might be induced by the fertility of the land to migrate from their own country into theirs, and establish themselves in proximity to the Province of Gaul, and especially to the Allobroges. The Aedui begged to be allowed to find room for the Boii within their own country, as they were a people of eminent and proved courage; and Caesar granted their request. The Aedui assigned them lands, and afterwards admitted them to the enjoyment of rights and liberties on an equality with their own.

Documents, written in Greek characters, were found in the encampment of the Helvetii and brought to Caesar. They contained a schedule, giving the names of individuals, the, number of emigrants capable of bearing arms, and likewise, under separate heads, the numbers of old men, women, and children. The aggregate amounted to two hundred and sixty-three thousand Helvetii, thirty-six thousand Tulingi, thirteen thousand Latobrigi, twenty-three thousand Rauraci, and thirty-two thousand Boii. The number capable of bearing arms was ninety-two thousand, and the grand total three hundred and sixty-eight thousand. A census was taken, by Caesar's orders, of those who returned home; and the number was found to be one hundred and ten thousand.

Envoys from almost every part of Gaul, the leading men of their respective tribes, convened a camp to congratulate Caesar. They were aware, they said, that, if he had exacted atonement from the Helvetii by the sword for the wrongs they had done in the past to the Roman People, yet his action was just as much to the advantage of Gaul as of the Romans; for, though the Helvetii were perfectly well off, they had quitted their own abode with the intention of attacking the whole of Gaul, usurping dominion, selecting for occupation out of numerous tracts the one which they deemed the most suitable and the most fertile in the whole country, and making the other tribes their tributaries. The envoys begged to be allowed to convene, with Caesar's express sanction, a Pan-Gallic council for a particular day, representing that they had certain favours to ask of him after their substance was unanimously agreed upon. Their request being granted, they fixed a date for the council, and bound themselves mutually by oath not to disclose its proceedings without official sanction.

After the council had broken up, the tribal leaders who had been closeted with Caesar before returned, and asked permission to discuss with him privately, in a place secluded from observation, matters which concerned their own and the common weal. Their request being acceded to, they all prostrated themselves with tears at Caesar's feet. They told him that it was their aim and endeavour to prevent what they said from being disclosed no less than to obtain the favours they desired; because they saw that if it were disclosed, they would incur the most cruel punishment. Their spokesman was the Aeduan Diviciacus. Gaul, he said, comprised, as a whole, two rival groups, the Aedui being the overlords of one and the Arverni of the other. The two tribes had been struggling hard for supremacy for many years, when it happened that the Arverni and the Sequani hired Germans to join them. About fifteen thousand had crossed the Rhine in the first instance; but the rude barbarians conceived a passion for the lands, the civilization, and the wealth of the Gauls, and afterwards more crossed over, the number at that time in Gaul amounting to twenty thousand. The Aedui and their dependents had encountered them repeatedly, had been beaten, and had suffered a great disaster, losing all their men of rank, all their council, and all their knighthood. Overwhelmed by these disastrous defeats, they, whose prowess and whose hospitable and amicable relations with the Roman People had before made them supreme in Gaul, had been forced to give as hostages to the Sequani their most illustrious citizens, and to bind the tribe by oath not to attempt to recover the hostages, or to solicit aid from the Roman People, and to remain forever without demur beneath the sovereign power of their conquerors. He himself was the only man of the whole Aeduan community who could not be prevailed upon to take the oath or to give his children as hostages. He had therefore fled from his country and gone to Rome to claim assistance from the Senate, because he alone was not bound either by oath or surrender of hostages. A worse fate, however, had befallen the victorious Sequani than the beaten Aedui, for Ariovistus, king of the Germans, had settled in their country and seized one-third of the Sequanian territory,—the best land in the whole of Gaul; and now he insisted that the Sequani should quit another third, because a few months previously twenty-four thousand Harudes had joined him, and he had to find a place for them to settle in. Within a few years the whole population of Gaul would be expatriated, and the Germans would all cross the Rhine; for there was no comparison between the land of the Gauls and that of the Germans, or between the standard of living of the former and that of the latter. Ariovistus, having defeated the united Gallic forces in one battle, which took place at Magetobriga, was exercising his authority with arrogance and cruelty, demanding from every man of rank his children as hostages, and inflicting upon them all kinds of cruel punishments if the least intimation of his will were not obeyed. The man was a ferocious headstrong savage; and it was impossible to endure his dictation any longer. Unless Caesar and the Roman People could help them, the Gauls must all do as the Helvetii had done,—leave house and home, seek another abode, other settlements out of reach of the Germans, and take their chance of whatever might befall them. If his words were reported to Ariovistus, he had no doubt that he would inflict the heaviest penalty upon all the hostages in his keeping. Caesar, by his prestige and that of his army, or by his late victory, or by the weight of the Roman name, could deter any fresh host of Germans from crossing the Rhine, and protect the whole of Gaul from the outrageous conduct of Ariovistus.

After Diviciacus had made this speech, all who were present began to weep bitterly and to entreat Caesar for help. He noticed that the Sequani alone did not behave like the rest, but remained mournfully looking down, with heads bowed. In astonishment he asked them what was the reason of this behaviour. The Sequani made no reply, but remained, without uttering, in the same mournful mood. After he had questioned them repeatedly without being able to get a single word out of them, the Aeduan, Diviciacus, again answered: the lot of the Sequani, he explained, was more pitiable and more grievous than that of the others, because they alone dared not, even in secret, complain or implore help; and though Ariovistus was away, they dreaded his cruelty just as much as if he were there, confronting them; for, while the others had at any rate the chance of escape, the Sequani, having admitted Ariovistus within their territories, and all their strongholds being in his power, would have to submit to every form of cruel punishment.

On learning these facts, Caesar reassured the Gauls and promised to give the matter his attention, remarking that he had every hope that Ariovistus, in return for his kindness and in deference to his authority, would cease his outrages. When he had finished speaking, he dismissed the assembly. Besides these considerations, indeed, many circumstances forced upon him the conviction that this problem must be faced and solved. First of all, there was the fact that the Aedui, who had repeatedly been recognized as Brethren, indeed kinsmen, by the Senate, were held in subjection under the sway of the Germans, while their hostages, as he knew, were detained by Ariovistus and the Sequani; and this, considering the great power of the Roman People, he regarded as an extreme disgrace to himself and his country. Besides, that the Germans should insensibly form the habit of crossing the Rhine, and enter Gaul in large numbers was, he saw, fraught with danger to the Roman People. He believed, too, that, being fierce barbarians, they would not stop short when they had taken possession of the whole of Gaul, but would pass into the Province, as the Cimbri and Teutoni had done before them, and thence push on into Italy, especially as the Sequani were only separated from our Province by the Rhone; and he thought it essential to obviate this danger at the earliest possible moment. Moreover, Ariovistus himself had assumed an inflated and arrogant demeanour, which made him quite insufferable.

Accordingly Caesar decided to send envoys to Ariovistus, requesting him to name some spot, midway between their respective quarters, for a proposal for conference, and saying that he wished to discuss with him political affairs and matters of the utmost importance to both parties. Ariovistus told the envoys in reply that, if he had wanted anything from Caesar, he would have gone to him in person, and if Caesar wanted anything from him, he must come to him. Besides, he could not venture to go without his army into the districts occupied by Caesar, and he could not concentrate his army without collecting a large quantity of stores, which would involve great labour. Moreover, he was at a loss to understand what business Caesar, or for that matter the Roman People, had in his part of Gaul, which he had conquered by the sword.

When this reply was conveyed to Caesar, he again sent envoys to Ariovistus with the following message:—Ariovistus had been treated with great kindness by himself and by the Roman People, having, in his consulship, received from the Senate the titles of King and Friend. Since he showed his gratitude to himself and the Roman People by raising objections when invited to a conference, and refusing to make any statement or to inform himself about matters which concerned them both, these were Caesar's demands:— first, he must not bring any additional body of men across the Rhine into Gaul; secondly, he must restore the hostages belonging to the Aedui, and authorize the Sequani to restore theirs; furthermore, he must not provoke the Aedui by outrages or attack them or their allies. If he complied, Caesar and the Roman People would be bound to him by lasting goodwill and amity. If not, then, in accordance with the resolution which the Senate had passed in the consulship of Marcus Messala and Marcus Piso—that the Governor of Gaul for the time being should, so far as the public interest would permit, protect the Aedui and the other friends of the Roman People—Caesar would not suffer the wrongs of the Aedui to go unavenged.

Ariovistus replied that the rights of war entitled conquerors to dictate their own terms to the conquered. The Roman People acted on the same principle: they regularly dealt with conquered peoples, not in obedience to the mandate of a third party, but according to their own judgement. If he did not dictate to the Roman People how they should exercise their rights, the Roman People ought not to interfere with him in the exercise of his. The Aedui had become his tributaries because they tempted the fortune of war, fought, and suffered defeat. Caesar was doing him a serious injury; for his coming depreciated the tribute. He would not restore the Aedui their hostages; but neither would he attack them or their allies wantonly if they abided by their agreement and paid their tribute annually. If not, much good would the title of "Brethren of the Roman People" do them! As for Caesar's threat, that he would not suffer the wrongs of the Aedui to go unavenged, no man had ever fought Ariovistus and escaped destruction. Let Caesar come on when he liked: he would then appreciate the mettle of Germans who had never known defeat, whose lives had been passed in war, and who, for fourteen years, had never sheltered beneath a roof.

Simultaneously with the delivery of this message envoys came to Caesar from the Aedui against Ario and the Treveri; the Aedui to complain that the Harudes, who had recently migrated into Gaul, were devastating their territory, and that even the surrender of hostages had failed to purchase the forbearance of Ariovistus, while the Treveri announced that one hundred clans of the Suevi, commanded by two brothers, Nasua and Cimberius, had established themselves on the banks of the Rhine, intending to attempt a passage. Caesar was seriously alarmed. He considered it necessary to act at once, lest, if a fresh horde of Suevi joined Ariovistus's veteran force, it might be harder to cope with him. Accordingly he arranged as quickly as possible for a supply of grain, and advanced against Ariovistus by forced marches.

After a march of three days he received news that Ariovistus was hurrying with all his forces to seize Vesontio, the largest town of the Sequani, and had advanced three days' journey beyond his own frontier. Caesar felt it necessary to make a great effort to forestall him, for the town was well provided with military material of every kind; and its natural strength made it a most valuable military position, the river Doubs winding round in a course that might have been traced with a compass, and almost surrounding the stronghold. The remaining space, not more than sixteen hundred feet, where the river left a gap, was occupied by a hill of great elevation, the banks of the river on either side touching the base of the hill. The hill itself was converted into a citadel by a wall, which surrounded it and connected it with the town. Caesar pushed on by forced marches night and day, took possession of, and garrisoned the town. While he was halting for a few days to collect corn and other supplies, a violent panic suddenly seized the whole army, completely paralysing every one's judgement and nerve. It arose from the inquisitiveness of our men and the chatter of the Gauls and the traders, who affirmed that the Germans were men of huge stature, incredible valour, and practised skill in war: many a time they had themselves come across them, and had not been able even to look them in the face or meet the glare of their piercing eyes. The panic began with the tribunes, the auxiliary officers, and others who had left the capital to follow Caesar in the hope of winning his favour, and had little experience in war. Some of them applied for leave of absence, alleging various urgent reasons for their departure, though a good many, anxious to avoid the imputation of cowardice, stayed behind for very shame. They were unable, however, to assume an air of unconcern, and sometimes even to restrain their tears; shutting themselves up in their tents, they bemoaned their own fate or talked dolefully with their intimates of the peril that threatened the army. All over the camp men were making their wills. Gradually even legionaries, centurions, and cavalry officers, who had long experience of campaigning, were unnerved by these alarmists. Those who did not want to be thought cowards said that it was not the enemy they were afraid of, but the narrow roads and the huge forests which separated them from Ariovistus, or the difficulty of bringing up grain. Some actually told

Caesar that when he gave the order to strike the camp and advance, the men would not obey, and would be too terrified to move.

Observing the state of affairs, Caesar called a meeting, to which the centurions of all offices and grades were summoned, and rated them severely for presuming to suppose that it was their business to inquire or even to consider where they were going, or on what errand. When he was consul, Ariovistus had eagerly solicited the friendship of the Roman People. Why, then, should any one suppose that he would abandon his loyal attitude in this hare-brained way? For his own part, he was convinced that when he came to know his demands and realized the fairness of his terms, he would not reject his friendship or that of the Roman People. But supposing he were carried away by mad passion and went to war, what on earth was there to fear? Or why should they distrust their own courage or his generalship? The measure of their enemy had been taken at a time which their fathers could remember, when the Cimbri and Teutoni were defeated by Gaius Marius, and the army confessedly earned no less credit than their commander; and again in recent years in Italy during the Slave War, although the slaves were, in some measure, helped by the experience and discipline which they had learned from us. This war enabled one to appreciate the value of steadfastness; for the men whom the Romans had long dreaded without reason, while they were without arms, they afterwards overcame when they were armed and flushed with victory. Finally, these Germans were the same whom the Helvetii had many times encountered, not only in their own but in German territory, and generally beaten: yet the Helvetii were no match for our army. Those who were alarmed by the defeat and rout of the Gauls could ascertain, if they inquired, that the Gauls were tired out by the long duration of the war, and that Ariovistus, after keeping himself shut up for many months in an encampment protected by marshes without giving them a chance of attacking him, suddenly fell upon them when they had dispersed in despair of bringing him to action, and beat them by craft and stratagem rather than by valour. Ariovistus himself could not expect that Roman armies were to be trapped by the craft for which there had been an opening against the simple natives. Those who pretended that their cowardice was only anxiety about supplies and the narrow roads were guilty of presumption; for it was evident that they either had no confidence in their general's sense of duty or meant to lecture him. These things were his business. The Sequani, the Leuci, and the Lingones were providing grain, and the corn in the fields was already ripe: about the road they would shortly judge for themselves. As to the report that they did not intend to obey orders and advance, that did not trouble him at all; for he knew that generals whose armies mutinied were either bunglers whose luck had deserted them, or had been detected in some scandalous crime, and thereby convicted of avarice. The whole tenor of his life proved his integrity, and the war with the Helvetii his good fortune. Accordingly he intended to do at once what he would otherwise have postponed: on the following night, in the fourth watch, he should strike his camp, so as to find out as soon as possible whether honour and duty or cowardice were the stronger motive with them. If no one else would follow him, he would go on alone with the 10th legion, in which he had full confidence; and it should be his bodyguard. This legion Caesar had always treated with special favour, and, on account of its soldierly spirit, he trusted it in the highest degree.

After this speech a marvellous change came over the temper of all ranks, and the utmost of them. The 10th legion, taking the initiative, miles away from them, conveyed their thanks to Caesar through their tribunes for having expressed such a high opinion of them, and declared themselves perfectly ready to take the field. Following their lead, the other legions deputed their tribunes and chief centurions to make their apologies to Caesar, protesting that they had never hesitated or been afraid, and that they recognized that it was the general's business and not theirs to direct the campaign. Their excuses were accepted. By the aid of Diviciacus, in whom he had more confidence than in any of the other Gauls, Caesar had discovered a route which, though it would involve making a detour of more than fifty miles, would enable him to march through open country. He kept his word, and started in the fourth watch. After a continuous march of seven days, he was informed by his patrols that Ariovistus's forces were twenty-four miles from ours.

On learning of Caesar's arrival, Ariovistus sent envoys to say that, since he had come nearer, and his own safety would probably not be imperilled, he would not oppose his original request for an interview. Caesar did not spurn his offer, believing that he was now returning to reason, as he offered, of his own accord, to do what he had refused before when he was asked; and he entertained a strong hope that when he learned his demands, he would, in consideration of the great favours conferred upon him by himself and the Roman People, abandon his stubborn attitude.

The interview was fixed for the fourth day following. Meanwhile envoys were frequently passing to and fro between the two generals. Ariovistus insisted that Caesar should not bring any infantry to the conference, as he was afraid he might treacherously surround him; they must each come with a mounted escort, otherwise he would not come at all. Caesar, not wishing any obstacle to stand in the way and stop the conference, and fearing to trust his life to Gallic cavalry, decided that his best plan would be to dismount all the Gallic troopers and mount the infantry of the 10th legion, in whom he had the greatest confidence, on their horses, so that, in case it were necessary to act, he might have an escort on whose devotion he could absolutely rely. On this, one of the soldiers of the 10th remarked with a touch of humour, "Caesar is better than his word; he promised to make the 10th his bodyguard, and now he's knighting us."

There was a great plain, in which was an earthen mound of considerable size about equidistant from the camps of Ariovistus and of Caesar. To this spot they came, as agreed, to hold the conference. Caesar posted the mounted legion, which he had brought with him, four hundred paces from the mound; and Ariovistus's horsemen took up a position at the same distance. Ariovistus stipulated that he and Caesar should confer on horseback, each accompanied by ten men. When they reached the spot Caesar began by recalling the kindness with which he himself and the Senate had treated Ariovistus,—the Senate had conferred upon him the titles of Wing and Friend, and the handsomest presents had been sent to him. Such a mark of favour, he told him, had fallen to the lot of few, and was usually bestowed only as a reward for great services. Ariovistus had no right to approach the Senate and no title to claim anything; and it was to the kindness and generosity of himself and the Senate that he owed these distinctions. Caesar explained further that between the Romans and the Aedui there were longstanding and solid grounds of intimacy; senatorial resolutions, couched in the most complimentary terms, had repeatedly been passed in their favour, and at all times, even before they sought our friendship, the Aedui had held the foremost position in the whole of Gaul! As a matter of settled policy, the Roman People desired their allies and friends not only to lose nothing by the connection, but to be gainers in influence, dignity, and consideration; who, then, could suffer them to be robbed of what they already possessed when they sought the friendship of the Roman People? Caesar then repeated the demands which he had charged his envoys to present,—that Ariovistus should not make war upon the Aedui or upon their allies; that he should restore the hostages; and that, if he were unable to send back any of the Germans to their own country, he should at all events not suffer any more to cross the Rhine.

Ariovistus said little in reply to Caesar's demands, but spoke at great length about his own merits. He said that he had not crossed the Rhine spontaneously, but in response to the urgent request of the Gauls; he had not left home and kinsmen without great expectations and great inducements; the possessions which he occupied in Gaul had been ceded to him by Gauls; their hostages had been given voluntarily; while by the rights of war he made them pay the tribute which conquerors habitually exacted from the conquered. He had not made war upon the Gauls; the Gauls had made war upon him. The tribes of Gaul had all come to attack him, and kept the field against him; and he had beaten the whole host in a single battle and crushed them. If they wanted to try again, he was ready for another fight; if they wanted peace, it was not fair of them to refuse their tribute, which they had hitherto paid of their own free will. The friendship of the Roman People ought to be a distinction and a protection, not a drawback; and it was with that expectation that he had sought it. If through their interference his tribute were stopped and those who had surrendered to him withdrawn from his control, he would be just as ready to discard their friendship as he had been to ask for it. If he continued to bring Germans in large numbers into Gaul, he did so not for aggression but in self-defence; the proof was that he had not come till he was asked, and that he had not attacked but only repelled attack. He had come to Gaul before the Romans. Never till now had a Roman army stirred outside the frontier of the Province of Gaul. What did Caesar mean by invading his dominions? This part of Gaul was his province, just as the other was ours. If he made a raid into our territory, we should be wrong to give in to him; similarly, it was unjust of us to obstruct him in his rightful sphere. Caesar said that the Aedui had been given the title of Brethren by the Senate; but he was not such an oaf, he was not so ignorant of the world as not to know that in the late war with the Allobroges the Aedui had not helped the Romans, and that in the struggle which the Aedui had had with himself and the Sequani, they had not had the benefit of Roman aid. He was bound to suspect that Caesar, under the mask of friendship, was keeping his army in Gaul to ruin him. Unless he took his departure and withdrew his army from the neighbourhood, he should treat him not as a friend but as an enemy; in fact, if he put him to death, he should be doing an acceptable service to many of the nobles and leading men of Rome. This he knew as a fact, for he had it through their agents from their own lips; and he could purchase the gratitude and friendship of them all by killing him. If, on the other hand, he withdrew and left him in undisturbed possession of Gaul, he would reward him handsomely; and whenever he had occasion to go to war, he would fight all his battles for him and save him all trouble and risk.

Caesar spoke at considerable length, the gist of his speech being that he could not abandon his undertaking; that his own principles and those of the Roman People would not allow him to forsake deserving allies; and that he could not admit that Gaul belonged to Ariovistus any more than to the Roman People. The Arverni and the Ruteni had been conquered by Quintus Fabius Maximus; but the Roman People had granted them an amnesty, and had not annexed their country or imposed tribute upon them. If priority of occupation were to be considered, the title of the Roman People to dominion in Gaul was unimpeachable; if they were to abide by the decision of the Senate, Gaul had a right to independence, for the Senate, although it had conquered Gaul, had granted it autonomy.

While these questions were being argued Caesar was informed that Ariovistus's horsemen were moving nearer the mound, riding towards the conference and our men and throwing stones and other missiles at them. Caesar ceased speaking, went back to his men, and ordered them not to retaliate; for although he saw that the legion of his choice would run no risk in engaging the cavalry, he did not choose, by beating the enemy, to let it be said that he had pledged his word and then surrounded them while a conference was going on. When the news spread to the ranks that Ariovistus, in the course of the conference, had arrogantly denied the right of the Romans to be in Gaul, and that his cavalry had attacked our troops, thereby breaking off the conference, the army was inspired with an intenser enthusiasm and eagerness for battle.

Two days later Ariovistus sent envoys to Caesar, saying that he desired to confer with him on the questions which they had begun to discuss without reaching any conclusion: let Caesar confer with Ariovistus, either name another day for a conference, or, if he were disinclined to do that, send one of his men to represent him. Caesar saw no reason for further discussion, especially as on the preceding day the Germans could not be prevented from throwing missiles at our men; while to send a representative would be very dangerous, and would be placing him at the mercy of savages. The best course appeared to be to send Gaius Valerius Procillus, son of Gaius Valerius Caburus, a young man of the highest character and a true gentleman, whose father had been enfranchised by Gaius Valerius Flaccus. He selected him because he could be thoroughly trusted, and because he knew Gallic, which Ariovistus, from long practice, now spoke fluently, and also because, in his case, the Germans had no motive for foul play. With him he sent Marcus Metius, who was on friendly terms with Ariovistus. Their instructions were to hear what Ariovistus had to say and report to him. When Ariovistus caught sight of them, close by, in his camp, he roared out before the troops, "What are you coming to me for? To play the spy?" When they attempted to speak, he silenced them and put them in irons.

On the same day he advanced and took a position six miles from Caesar's camp, at the foot of a hill. The following day he marched his force past Caesar's camp and encamped two miles beyond, with the intention of cutting him off from the corn and other supplies which were being brought up from the territories of the Sequani and the Aedui. On each of the five following days Caesar regularly led out his troops in front of his camp, and kept them in line of battle, to give Ariovistus the chance of fighting if he wished. During all this time Ariovistus kept his army shut up in camp, but skirmished daily with his cavalry. The mode of fighting practised by the Germans was as follows. They had six thousand cavalry, with the same number of infantry, swift runners of extraordinary courage, each one of whom had been selected by one of the cavalry out of the whole host for his own protection. The cavalry were accompanied by them in action, and regularly fell back upon their support. In case of a check, they flocked to the rescue; whenever a trooper was severely wounded and fell from his horse, they rallied round him; and they had acquired such speed by training that if it was necessary to make a forced march or retreat rapidly, they supported themselves by the horses' manes and kept pace with them.

Seeing that Ariovistus meant to keep Caesar within his camp, and being resolved to reopen communication with his envoys without delay, Caesar selected a suitable position for a camp about twelve hundred paces beyond the spot where the Germans were encamped, and advanced to this position in three columns. Keeping the first and second under arms, he ordered the third to construct a camp. The site, as I have said, was about twelve hundred paces from the enemy. Ariovistus sent about sixteen thousand light infantry with all his cavalry to overawe our men and prevent them from completing the entrenchment. Nevertheless, Caesar, adhering to his original resolve, ordered the first two lines to keep the enemy at bay, while the third finished the entrenchment. When the camp was entrenched, he left two legions and a detachment of auxiliaries to hold it, and withdrew the remaining four to the larger camp.

The next day Caesar, according to his regular superstition practice, made his troops move out of both camps, and, advancing a short distance from the larger one, formed a line of battle and gave the enemy an opening for attack. Seeing that they would not come out even then, he withdrew his army into camp about midday. Then at last Ariovistus sent a detachment to attack the smaller camp. Fighting was kept up with spirit on both sides till evening. At sunset Ariovistus led back his forces, which had inflicted heavy loss upon the Romans and suffered heavily themselves, into camp. On inquiring from prisoners why he would not fight a decisive battle, Caesar found that the reason was this:—among the Germans it was customary for the matrons to tell by lots and divinations whether it would be advantageous to fight or not, and their decision was that it was not fated that the Germans should gain the victory if they fought before the new moon.

Next day Caesar left detachments of adequate strength to guard the two camps; posted all his auxiliaries, in view of the enemy, in front of the smaller one, with the object of creating a moral effect, as his regular infantry, compared with the enemy, were numerically rather weak; and, forming his army in three lines, advanced right up to the enemy's camp. Then at last the Germans perforce led their troops out of camp, formed them up at equal intervals in tribal groups —Harudes, Marcomanni, Triboci, Vangiones, Nemetes, Sedusii, and Suevi—and closed their whole line with wagons and carts, to do away with all hope of escape. In the wagons they placed their women, who, as they were marching out to battle, stretched out their hands and besought them with tears not to deliver them into bondage to the Romans.

Caesar placed each of his generals and his quaestor in command of a legion, so that every man might feel that his courage would be recognized, and engaged with the right wing, which he commanded in person, for he observed that the troops which faced it were the weakest part of the enemy's line. When the signal was given, our men charged the enemy with such vigour, and the enemy dashed forward so suddenly and so swiftly that there was no time to hurl the javelins at them. The men therefore dropped their javelins and fought hand to hand with swords. The Germans, however, rapidly formed in a phalanx—their usual order—and thus sustained the impact of the swords. Many of our men actually leaped on to the phalanx, tore the shields out of their enemies' hands, and stabbed them from above. On the left wing the enemy's line was beaten and put to flight; but on the right their great numbers enabled them to press our line very hard. Noticing this, the younger Publius Crassus, who commanded the cavalry, and was more free to observe and act than the officers who were engaged in the actual fighting, sent the third line to the relief of our hard-pressed troops.

Thus the battle was restored, and the enemy all turned tail and did not cease their flight until they reached the Rhine, about five miles from the battlefield. A few, trusting to their strong limbs, struck out and swam across; a few found boats and saved themselves. Among the latter was Ariovistus, who found a skiff moored by the bank, and escaped in it. All the rest were hunted down by our cavalry and slain. Ariovistus had two wives, one a Suevan by birth, whom he had brought with him from his own country, the other a Norican, a sister of King Voccio, who had been sent to him by her brother, and whom he had married in Gaul. Both of them perished in the rout. He also had two daughters, one of whom was killed and the other captured. Gaius Valerius Procillus was being dragged along among the fugitives by his warders, fettered with three chains, when he fell in with Caesar, who was leading the cavalry in pursuit of the enemy. To see this excellent Provincial, his own familiar friend, rescued from the enemy's clutches and restored to him, and to feel that Fortune had not brought upon him any calamity that could lessen the pleasure of a victory upon which he might fairly congratulate himself—these things gave Caesar no less pleasure than the victory itself. Procillus said that, in his own presence, they had cast lots three times to see whether he should be burned alive at once or kept for execution later; and happily the lots had so fallen that he was safe. Marcus Metius also was found and brought back to Caesar.

When the result of the battle was known beyond the Rhine, the Suevi, who had reached the banks of the river, turned homewards. The Ubii, who live in the immediate neighbourhood of the Rhine, seeing their alarm, pursued them and killed a large number. Having finished two important campaigns in a single summer, Caesar led his army back to winter in the country of the Sequani a little before the usual time, and, placing Labienus in command of the camp, started for Cisalpine Gaul to hold the assizes.

BOOK II

THE FIRST CAMPAIGN AGAINST THE BELGAE

While Caesar, as we have mentioned above, was in Cisalpine Gaul, frequent rumours reached him, which were confirmed by dispatches from Labienus, that the Belgae, whose territory, as we have remarked, forms a third part of Gaul, were all conspiring against the Roman People and exchanging hostages. The motives of the conspiracy, it appeared, were these: first, the Belgae were afraid that, as the whole of Gaul was tranquillized, our army might advance against them. Secondly, they were egged on by sundry Gauls, some of whom, just as they had objected to the continued presence of the Germans in Gaul, were irritated by the Roman army wintering in the country and settling there, while others, from instability and fickleness of temperament, hankered after a change of masters; and also by powerful individuals, especially those who had the means of hiring mercenaries, who, as often happened in Gaul, had been wont to usurp royal authority, and found it less easy to achieve this end under our dominion.

Alarmed by these messages and dispatches Caesar raised two new legions in Cisalpine Gaul and directed Quintus Pedius, one of his generals, to lead them, at the beginning of the fine weather, into Further Gaul. As soon as forage began to be plentiful he joined the army in person, and charged the Senones and the other Gauls who were conterminous with the Belgae to find out what was going on in their country and keep him informed. They all agreed in reporting that levies were being raised and that an army was concentrating. Caesar now thought it his duty to march against them without hesitation. After arranging for a supply of grain, he broke up his camp and reached the Belgic frontier in about a fortnight.

He arrived unexpectedly and sooner than any one had anticipated. The Remi— the nearest of the Belgae to Gaul—sent Iccius and Andecumborius, the leading men of the tribe, as envoys, to say that they would place their lives and all that they possessed under the protection and at the disposal of the Roman People; that they had not shared the counsels of the other Belgae or joined their conspiracy against the Roman People, and that they were prepared to give hostages, to obey orders, to admit the Romans into their strongholds, and to supply them with corn and other necessaries; that all the other Belgae were in arms, and that the Germans who dwelt on the near side of the Rhine had joined them; and that they were all possessed by such frenzy that the Remi could not deter even the Suessiones, their own kith and kin, who had the same rights and laws as themselves, and jointly owned the authority of one and the same magistrate, from taking their side.

On inquiring from the envoys the names of the belligerent tribes, their size, and their military strength, Caesar collected the following information. Most of the Belgae were of German origin, and had crossed the Rhine at a remote period and settled in Gaul on account of the fertility of the land. They had driven out the Gallic inhabitants, and were the only people who, at the time within the memory of our fathers, when the whole of Gaul was devastated, prevented the Teutoni and the Cimbri from invading their country. Inspired by the memory of that achievement, they arrogated to themselves great authority, and assumed the air of a great military power. With regard to their numbers the Remi professed to have full information, for, being allied to them by blood and intermarriage, they had ascertained the strength of the contingent which each tribe had promised in the general council of the Belgae for the impending war. The Bellovaci, who, from their valour, prestige, and numbers, were the most powerful of all, and could muster one hundred thousand armed men, had promised sixty thousand picked troops, and claimed the general direction of the campaign. The Suessiones were their own neighbours, and their territory was very extensive and very fertile. Within the memory of men still living, their king had been Diviciacus, the most powerful prince in the whole of Gaul, who was overlord not only of a large part of the Belgic territory, but also of Britain. The reigning king was Galba, who, on account of his integrity and sound judgement, was unanimously entrusted with the chief command. The Suessiones possessed twelve strongholds, and promised fifty thousand armed men. The same number was promised by the Nervii, who were considered by the Belgae themselves as the fiercest of them all, and who were the most remote. The Atrebates promised fifteen thousand; the Ambiani ten thousand; the Menapii seven thousand; the Caleti ten thousand; the Veliocasses and the Viromandui jointly the same number; the Aduatuci nineteen thousand; the Condrusi, the Eburones, the Caeroesi, and the Paemani (who are known by the common appellation of Germans promised), so the Remi believed, about forty thousand.

Caesar addressed the Remi in encouraging and gracious terms, and ordered their entire council to meet him and the children of the leading men to be brought to him as hostages. All these orders they carefully and punctually obeyed. He then earnestly impressed upon the Aeduan, Diviciacus, that it was most important, in the interest of the Republic, and indeed of Aeduans and Romans alike, to break up the enemy's forces, so as to avoid the necessity of engaging such a powerful host at once. The object could be attained if the Aedui marched into the country of the Bellovaci and proceeded to devastate their lands. With this injunction he dismissed Diviciacus. Finding that all the Belgic forces had concentrated and were marching against him, and learning from the reconnoitering parties which he had sent out and from the Remi that they were now not far off, he pushed on rapidly, crossed the Aisne, which flows through the most distant part of the country of the Remi, and encamped near its banks. This movement northern protected one side of his camp by the banks of the river, secured his rear, and enabled his supplies to be brought up without danger by the Remi and the other tribes. The river was spanned by a bridge, at the head of which he established a strong post, while on the other side of the river he left six cohorts under one of his generals, Titurius Sabinus. At the same time he ordered a camp to be constructed, with a rampart twelve feet high and a trench eighteen feet wide.

Eight miles from the camp there was a town belonging to the Remi called Bibrax. The rax! Belgae attacked it furiously on their march; and the garrison had difficulty in holding out that day. The following method of attacking forts is practised by Gauls and Belgae alike. Surrounding the whole circuit of the fortifications with a multitude of men, they proceed to hurl stones from all sides against the wall, and when they have cleared it, they lock their shields over their heads, advance right up to the gates, and undermine the wall. In this case the operation was easily performed, for with such a huge host hurling stones and other missiles no man had a chance of keeping his footing on the wall. When night stopped the attack, Iccius, a Roman of the highest rank, and very popular with his countrymen, who was acting as governor of the town, one of the envoys who had come to Caesar to sue for peace, sent him word that, unless a force were sent to his relief, he could hold out no longer.

About midnight Caesar, employing as guides the messengers who had come from Diviciacus, sent Numidian and Cretan archers and Balearic slingers to Bibrax, to relieve the inhabitants. On their arrival, the Remi, inspired by the hope of repelling the attack, became eager to take the offensive; and for the same reason the enemy abandoned the hope of taking the town. Accordingly, after lingering a short time in the neighbourhood, ravaging the lands of the Remi, and burning all the villages and homesteads within reach, they pushed on with all their forces towards Caesar's camp, and encamped barely two miles off. Judging by the smoke and watch-fires, their camp extended more than eight miles in width. Caesar determined, in the first instance, to avoid an action, on account of the great numbers of the enemy and of their extraordinary reputation for valour: still, he daily tested the mettle of the enemy and the daring of our troops, and found that the latter were a match for them. The ground in front of his camp was naturally just suited for forming a line of battle. The hill on which the camp stood, rising gradually from the plain, extended, facing the enemy, over the exact space which the line would occupy: on either flank its sides descended abruptly, while in front it gradually merged in the plain by a gentle slope. On either side of the hill Caesar drew a trench athwart, about eight hundred paces long, and at the end of each trench erected a redoubt, in which he posted artillery to prevent the enemy, when he had formed his line, from taking advantage of their great numerical superiority to attack his men in flank and surround them. Having done this, he left his two newly-raised legions in camp, so that they might be available at any point as a reserve, and drew up the remaining six in line of battle in front of the camp. The enemy likewise had marched their forces out of camp and formed them in line.

There was a morass of no great size between our army and that of the enemy. The ford the enemy waited to see whether our men would order to cross it; while our men, weapons in hand, were Caesar's ready to attack them in case they crossed first, when their movements would be impeded. Meanwhile a skirmish of horse was going on between the two lines. Neither side would cross first, and, the skirmish resulting in favour of our men, Caesar withdrew his infantry into camp. Forthwith the enemy moved rapidly from their position to gain the river Aisne, which, as the narrative has shown, was in the rear of our camp. There they discovered a ford, and endeavoured to throw a part of their force across, intending, if possible, to storm the redoubt commanded by the general, Quintus Titurius, and break down the bridge; or, failing this, to devastate the lands of the Remi, who were very useful to us in the campaign, and to cut off our troops from supplies.

Caesar, on receiving information from Titurius, took the whole of his cavalry, his light-armed Numidians, slingers, and archers across the bridge, and pushed on rapidly against them.

A fierce combat took place at the spot where they were crossing. Our men attacked the enemy in the river, while their movements were impeded, and killed a great number of them: the rest made a most daring attempt to get across over their dead bodies, but were beaten back by a shower of missiles; while the leading division, who had crossed already, were surrounded by the cavalry and killed. The enemy realized that they had deceived themselves in expecting to storm the stronghold and cross the river: they saw that the Romans would not advance and fight on an unfavourable position; and their supply of grain was beginning to run short. They therefore called a council of war, and decided that the best course would be for the several contingents to return home, and rally from all parts to the defence of the people whose country the Roman army invaded first: they would thus fight in their own and not in foreign territory, and have the benefit of homegrown supplies. Among other reasons, they were led to adopt this resolution by the knowledge that Diviciacus and the Aedui were approaching the country of the Bellovaci, and the latter could not be induced to remain any longer and refrain from helping their own people.

Their departure resembled a rout. Caesar was promptly informed of what they had done by scouts. Fearing an ambuscade (for he did not yet clearly see the reason for their departure), he kept his army, including the cavalry, in camp. At daybreak the report was confirmed by patrols; and Caesar sent on ahead the whole of his cavalry, commanded by two generals, Quintus Pedius and Lucius Aurunculeius Cotta, to retard the rearguard, at the same time ordering Titus Labienus to follow in support with three legions. This force attacked the rearguard and pursued them for many miles, killing a large number of the fugitives; for while the rearmost ranks, when overtaken, made a stand and gallantly resisted the attack of our infantry, the van, fancying themselves out of reach of danger and not being restrained by necessity or discipline, broke their ranks when they heard the distant cries and ran for their lives. Thus our men slaughtered them in numbers, without any risk to themselves, as long as daylight lasted: towards sunset they left off, and returned, in obedience to instructions, to camp.

On the day following, before the enemy could recover from their panic flight, Caesar led the army into the country of the Suessiones, who were conterminous with the Kemi, and Noviodu of Noviodunum. Hearing that it was undefended, he attempted, immediately after his arrival, to storm it; but the moat was so broad and the wall so high that, notwithstanding the small numbers of the garrison, he was unable to carry the position. After entrenching his camp, he proceeded to form a line of sheds, and to make the necessary preparations, for a siege. On the following night, before he could resume operations, the whole host of the fugitive Suessiones thronged into the town. The sheds were speedily brought up, earth was shot and towers were erected; and the Gauls, alarmed by the magnitude of the works, which they had never seen or even heard of before, and also by the swift energy of the Romans, sent envoys to Caesar, proposing to surrender. The Remi interceded for their lives; and their prayer was granted.

Caesar took the leading men of the tribe, as well as two of King Galba's own sons, as hostages; and, after all the arms in the town had been delivered up, he accepted the surrender of the Suessiones, and marched into the country of the Bellovaci, who threw themselves with all their belongings into the stronghold of Bratuspantium. When Caesar and his army were about five miles off, the older men all came out, stretched out their hands to him, and declared that they were ready to place themselves under his protection and in his power, and that they were not in arms against the Roman People. In like manner, when he had approached the stronghold and was encamping on its outskirts, the women and children stretched out their hands from the wall in the native fashion, and begged the Romans for peace.

Diviciacus, who, after the retreat of the Belgae, had disbanded the Aeduan forces and returned to Caesar, interceded for the suppliants. The Bellovaci, he said, had at all times been dependents of the Aedui, and in amicable relations with them; but, at the instigation of their leaders, who said that the Aedui had been enslaved by Caesar and had to put up with ill-usage and insult of every kind, they had abandoned their connection with them and taken up arms against the Roman People. The ringleaders, realizing the magnitude of the disaster which they had brought upon their country, had escaped to Britain. Not only the Bellovaci, but also the Aedui on their behalf, would beg Caesar to treat them with the forbearance and humanity for which he was distinguished. By doing so he would increase the authority of the Aedui among the Belgae generally, for the Aedui commonly relied on their assistance and resources to carry on any wars in which they happened to be engaged.

Caesar said that he would spare their lives and take them under his protection out of respect for Diviciacus and the Aedui; but, as the tribe ranked high among the Belgae and had a very large population, he required six hundred hostages. After they had been delivered over and all the arms brought out of the town and piled, Caesar marched from Bratuspantium to the territory of the Ambiani, who surrendered unreservedly without delay. Their territory was conterminous with that of the Nervii. Caesar made inquiries about the character, manners, and customs of this people, and collected the following information. Traders were not allowed to enter their country; they would not permit the importation of anything in the shape of wine or other luxuries, believing that courage was enfeebled by these indulgences and manly vigour enervated; they were a fierce, brave people; and, railing at the other Belgae and accusing them of having surrendered to the Romans and made shipwreck of their ancestral valour, they vowed that they would not send envoys or accept peace on any terms. After marching for three days through their territory, Caesar learned from prisoners that Nervii had all encamped on the further side of a river called the Sambre, which was not more than ten miles from his camp, and were there awaiting the arrival of the Romans, along with their neighbours, the

Atrebates and the Viromandui, both of whom they had persuaded to share with them the fortune of war. They were waiting for the force of the Aduatuci, which was marching to join them and they had hastily transferred their women and all who were disqualified by age for fighting to a spot which was rendered inaccessible for an army by marshes.

On learning this, Caesar sent on ahead a reconnoitering party and centurions to choose a good position for a camp. A considerable number of the Belgae who had surrendered and other Gauls had followed him, and were marching in his train. Some of them, as was afterwards ascertained from prisoners, having observed the order in which our army marched during the first three days, made their way to the Nervii in the night, and explained to them that each legion was followed by a great quantity of baggage, and that when the foremost legion reached camp and the rest were a long way off, there would be no difficulty in attacking it while the men were burdened with their packs: when it was beaten and its baggage plundered, the rest would not venture to make a stand. One circumstance favoured the plan recommended by the men who gave this information. In times past the Nervii, having no cavalry (to this day they pay no attention to that arm, their whole strength being in infantry), devised the following method of checking their neighbours' cavalry, when they made plundering raids into their territory. Lopping off the tops of young saplings and bending them over, so that their branches shot out thickly sideways, they planted brambles and briers between, the hedges thus formed making a barrier like a wall, which it was impossible not only to penetrate, but even to see through. As the march of our column was delayed by these obstacles, the Nervii felt that the proffered advice was worth following.

Caesar had sent on his cavalry in advance, and was following with all his forces; but the troops' column was formed on a different principle from that which the Belgae had described to the Nervii. Six of Caesar's legions, according to his usual practice when he was approaching an enemy, were advancing in light marching order; behind them was the baggage-train of the entire army, followed by the two newly-raised legions, which closed the rear and protected the baggage. Our cavalry, along with the slingers and archers, crossed the river and engaged the enemy's horse.

The latter fell back repeatedly into the woods on the support of their comrades, and again emerging, charged our men, who dared not pursue them, when they retreated, beyond the fringe of the open ground. Meanwhile the six legions which had come up first proceeded to entrench the camp along the lines which had been marked out.

The camp was almost certainly on the heights of Neuf-Mesnil, on the left bank of the Sambre, opposite the camp.

When the head of our baggage-train was ambushed in the woods—the moment which they had agreed upon for beginning the battle—suddenly, in the exact order in which, with mutual exhortations, they had formed their line within, the whole force darted forth and swooped down upon our cavalry. Sending them flying in disorder without an effort, they rushed down to the stream with such incredible swiftness that it seemed as if almost at the same instant they were at the woods, in the river, and now at sword's point with our men. As swiftly they pressed up the hill to attack our camp and the men who were engaged in entrenching it.

Caesar had to arrange everything at once,— the red flag, the signal for arming; sound the trumpet; recall the men from the trenches; send for those who had gone further afield in search of wood; form the line; harangue the troops; and give the signal for battle. Want of time and the enemy's onset prevented much of this from being done. Two things, however, served to lighten his difficulties,—first, the knowledge and experience of the soldiers, who, as seasoned campaigners, were able to decide for themselves what ought to be done as well as others could tell them; and secondly, the fact that he had forbidden his marshals to leave the works and their respective legions till the camp was entrenched. As the enemy were so close and coming up so fast, they did not wait for orders from Caesar, but made the arrangements which they thought right on their own responsibility.

Caesar, after giving indispensable orders, hurried down at haphazard to encourage the soldiers, and came to the 10th legion. He spoke briefly, merely urging the men to remember their ancient valour, keep cool, and sustain resolutely the enemy's rush; then, as the enemy were within range, he gave the signal for action. Going on to another part of the field to encourage the men, he found them already engaged. Time was so short, and the enemy were so ready and eager for battle that there was not a moment even for putting on helmets and pulling the covers off shields, much less for fitting on crests. Each man, as he came down from the trenches, fell in by the standard he first caught sight of, wherever he happened to find himself, not wishing to waste the time for action in looking for the men of his company.

The army was drawn up as well as time permitted, according to the requirements of the ground and the slope of the hill rather than the formation prescribed by tactical rules. The legions were separated and making head against the enemy at different points; while the view was interrupted, as we have explained before, by hedges of extraordinary thickness. It was therefore impossible to post reserves at fixed points, or to foresee what would be wanted at each and every part of the field; nor could one man give all the necessary orders. With such adverse conditions, then, the vicissitudes of fortune were naturally various.

The men of the 9th and 10th legions were posted on the left of the line. With a volley of javelins they drove the Atrebates—the division which they had encountered—who were breathless and tired from their rapid charge and enfeebled by wounds, from the high ground to the river, and when they attempted to cross, pressed after them sword in hand, and killed a great many while their movements were impeded. Crossing themselves without hesitation, and pushing on though the slope was against them, when the enemy rallied they renewed the combat and routed them. Similarly in another part of the field two legions, the 11th and 8th, which were separated from one another, encountered the Viromandui, drove them from the higher ground, and maintained the combat right on the banks of the river. Nearly the whole camp, however, in front and on the left, was exposed; and, the 12th legion and at no great distance the 7th being posted on the right wing, the whole of the Nervii, formed in a compact column and led by Boduognatus, the commander-in-chief, advanced rapidly against the position; and while some of them began to move round the legions on their exposed flank, others made for the summit of the hill, on which the camp stood.

At the same time our cavalry and the light-armed foot associated with them, who were routed, as I have said, by the enemy's first charge, were retreating to the camp, when they came full upon the enemy and again took to flight in another direction; and the servants, who from the rear-gate, situated on the crest of the ridge, had seen our victorious troops cross the river and had gone out to plunder, looked back and, seeing the enemy moving about in the camp, precipitately fled. Simultaneously a babel of voices arose from the men who were coming up with the baggage, and they rushed panic-stricken in different directions. A body of horsemen belonging to the Treveri, whose courage is proverbial among the Gauls, had been sent by their tribe, as an auxiliary force, to join Caesar. Alarmed by all these signs of panic, seeing that our camp was thronged by the enemy, that the legions were hard pressed and all but hemmed in, that servants, horsemen, slingers, and Numidians had parted company and scattered and were flying in all directions, they despaired of our success, hastened homewards, and told their countrymen that the Romans were disastrously defeated, and that the enemy had captured their camp and baggage.

Caesar, after haranguing the 10th legion, had gone off to the right wing. He saw that his troops were hard pressed and that the men of the 12th legion, their standards closely massed, were crowded together and preventing each other from fighting: all the centurions of the 4th cohort, as well as the standard-bearer, were killed; the standard was lost; almost all the centurions of the other cohorts were either killed or wounded, including the chief centurion, Publius Sextius Baculus, the bravest of the brave, who was so exhausted by a number of severe wounds that he could no longer keep his feet; the men had lost all dash, and some in the rear ranks had abandoned their posts and were slinking away from the field and getting out of range; while the enemy were coming up in front in an unbroken stream from below, and closing in on both flanks: in short, the situation was critical and there was no reserve, available. Seeing all this, Caesar, who had come up without a shield, took one from a soldier in the rear rank, stepped forward into the front rank, and, addressing the centurions by name, encouraged the men and told them to advance, opening their ranks so that they might be able to use their swords more readily. His coming inspired them with hope and gave them new heart; and as everyone, even in his extremest peril, was anxious to do his utmost under the eyes of his general, the enemy's onset was in some measure checked.

Noticing that the 7th legion, which stood close by, was likewise hard pressed by the enemy, Caesar told the tribunes to make the legions gradually approach one another, face the enemy on all sides, and advance. This was done; and, as the men now gave each other mutual support and were not afraid of being taken in rear, they began to offer a more confident resistance and to fight with more resolution. Meanwhile the men of the two legions which had brought up the rear and guarded the baggage, having received news of the action, had quickened their pace and were descried on the brow of the hill by the enemy; and Titus Labienus, who had captured the enemy's camp and observed from the high ground what was going on in ours, sent the 10th legion to the assistance of our men. Realizing from the flight of the cavalry and servants how-matters stood, and seeing that camp, legions, and general were in great peril, they put forth their utmost speed.

Their arrival wrought such a complete change that, on our side, even men who had lain down severely wounded learned on their shields and renewed the fight: the servants, noticing the enemy's alarm, rushed upon them, unarmed against armed; while the cavalry, anxious to wipe out the disgrace of their flight by gallant deeds, out vied the legionaries at every point. But the enemy, even in their despair, displayed such heroic courage that, when their foremost ranks had fallen, the next mounted upon their prostrate comrades and fought standing on their bodies; and when they too were struck down and the corpses littered in a heap, the survivors hurled as from a mound their missiles against our men, and picked up and flung back their javelins. We are not to think, then, that it was in vain that these gallant men dared to cross a broad river, to climb high banks, and to assail a formidable position. These things, in themselves most difficult, had been made easy by their heroism.

The battle was over and the Nervian people, nay their very name, was brought to the verge of extinction. On hearing the news, the old people, who, as we have said, had taken refuge, along with the women and children, in tidal creeks and in swamps, believing that there was nothing to stop the victors and no security for the vanquished, sent envoys to Caesar with the consent of all the survivors, and surrendered; and, recounting the calamity which had befallen their country, they affirmed that their council had been reduced from six hundred to three, and the number of men capable of bearing arms from sixty thousand to a bare five hundred. Caesar, wishing to establish his character for mercy towards unfortunate suppliants, was careful to shield them from harm, authorized them to retain possession of their territories and strongholds, and commanded their neighbours to abstain and to make their dependents abstain from maltreating or molesting them.

The Aduatuci, whose movements we have already described, were coming with all their refuge in forces to the assistance of the Nervii, when, on the announcement of the battle, they turned without halting and went home. Abandoning all their other strongholds and fortified posts, they removed all their belongings into one fortress of extraordinary natural strength. All round, it presented a line of high rocks and steep declivities, which at one point left a gently sloping approach, not more than two hundred feet wide. This place the garrison had fortified with a double wall of great height, upon which, as a further protection, they were laying stones of great weight and sharp-pointed beams. The Aduatuci were descended from the Cimbri and Teutoni, who, on their march for our Province and Italy, left the stock and baggage which they were unable to drive or carry with them, on this side of the Rhine, with some of their number to look after them and six thousand men to protect them. After the fate of their countrymen this band was for many years harassed by the neighbouring peoples, sometimes attacking, at other times repelling attack: at length they made peace, and with the consent of all the other tribes selected this district as their abode.

Immediately after the arrival of our army, the Aduatuci made a series of sorties from the town and engaged in skirmishes with our troops; afterwards, however, finding themselves shut in by a rampart twelve feet high and three miles in extent, with numerous redoubts, they kept inside the stronghold. A line of sheds was formed and a terrace constructed; and seeing a tower in process of erection some way off, they at first jeered and made abusive remarks from the wall at the idea of such a huge machine being erected at such a distance. Did those pygmy Romans, with their feeble hands and puny muscles (the Gauls, as a rule, despise our short stature, contrasting it with their own great height), believe themselves able to mount such a ponderous tower on the wall?

When, however, they saw it in motion and actually approaching the walls, the strange and unwanted spectacle alarmed them, and they sent envoys to Caesar to sue for peace. The envoys, saying that Roman warriors were evidently not left unaided by the gods, since they could propel such towering engines at such a rate, declared themselves ready to surrender unreservedly. One thing only they would beg him not to do—if haply in his mercy and forbearance, of which they heard from other peoples, he had decided to spare the Aduatuci — not to deprive them of their arms. Almost all their neighbours were their bitter enemies and jealous of their prowess, and if they surrendered their arms, they could not defend themselves against them. If they were reduced to the alternative, it would be better for them to suffer any fate at the hands of the Romans rather than to be tortured to death by men among whom they were accustomed to hold sway.

To this appeal Caesar replied that he would spare the tribe, not because they deserved mercy, but because it was his wont to be merciful, provided they surrendered before the ram touched the wall; but the question of surrender could not be entertained unless they gave up their arms. He would act as he had acted in the case of the Nervii, and order their neighbours not to molest those who had surrendered to the Roman People. The envoys, after reporting his decision to their principals, professed themselves ready to obey his commands. A great quantity of arms was pitched down from the wall into the trench in front of the town, the heap almost reaching the top of the wall and of the terrace; and yet, as was afterwards discovered, about one-third was concealed and kept in the town. The gates were then thrown open; and on the same day the garrison entered upon the enjoyment of peace.

Towards evening Caesar ordered the gates to be shut and the soldiers to leave the town, for fear the inhabitants should suffer any injury at their hands in the night. They had evidently prearranged a plan. Believing that, after the capitulation, our troops would withdraw their piquets, or at any rate be less vigilant in maintaining them, and taking the arms which they had kept back and concealed, as well as shields made of bark or wattle-work, which, being pressed for time, they had hastily covered with skins, they made a sudden sortie in the third watch with their whole force at the point where the slope leading up to our entrenchments appeared easiest. The alarm was promptly given, in obedience to orders which Caesar had issued in anticipation, by fire-signals; and troops hurried to the point from the nearest redoubts. The enemy's whole hope of safety depended upon courage alone; and they fought with the fierce energy that was to be expected from brave men, fighting on a forlorn hope, on unfavourable ground, against opponents who were hurling their missiles from rampart and towers. About four thousand were killed, and the rest driven back into the town. Next day, as there was no longer any resistance, the gates were burst open; the soldiers were sent in; and Caesar sold by auction, in one lot, all the booty of war found in the town. The purchasers reported the number of individuals as fifty-three thousand.

At the same time Caesar was informed by Publius Crassus, whom he had sent with a single legion to the territories of the Veneti, Osismi, Coriosolites, Esuvii, Aulerci, and Redones — maritime tribes whose country reaches the Ocean—that all of them had been brought completely under the dominion of the Roman People.

These operations resulted in the pacification of the whole of Gaul; and the natives were so impressed by the story of the campaign which reached them, that the peoples who dwelt beyond the Rhine sent envoys to Caesar, promising to give hostages and fulfil his commands. Being anxious to get to Italy and Illyricum without delay, he ordered the envoys to return to him at the commencement of the following summer. Quartering his legions for the winter in the territories of the Carnutes, Andes, Turoni, and other tribes which were near the theatre of the recent campaign, he started for Italy. On the receipt of his dispatches, a thanksgiving service of fifteen days was appointed to celebrate his achievements,—an honour which had not hitherto fallen to the lot of any one.

BOOK III

GALBA'S CAMPAIGN IN THE VALAIS – CAMPAIGNS AGAINST THE MARITIME TRIBES AND THE AQUITANI

When Caesar was starting for Italy, he sent Servius Galba with the 12th legion and a detachment of cavalry to the country belonging to the Nantuates, Veragri, and Seduni, which extends from the frontier of the Allobroges, the Lake of Geneva, and the Rhone to the crest of the Alps, being anxious to open up the route over the Alps, by which traders usually travelled at great risk and with the obligation of paying heavy tolls. Galba was authorized to quarter his legion in the district for the winter, if he thought it necessary. After he had gained several victories and taken a number of forts belonging to the tribesmen, they sent envoys to him from all parts, gave hostages, and made peace; whereupon he determined to quarter two cohorts in the country of the Nantuates, and to winter with the remaining cohorts of the legion in a village, belonging to the Veragri, called Octodurus. The village, which is situated in a valley, and adjoined by a plain of moderate extent, is walled in on every side by lofty mountains. It was divided by a stream into two parts, one of which he allowed the Gauls to occupy, while he reserved the vacant part for the winter quarters of the cohorts, and fortified the position with a rampart and trench.

Several days had been spent in camp, and Galba had ordered grain to be brought in, when suddenly he was informed by his patrols that during the night the

Gauls had all quitted the part of the village which he had allotted to them, and that the overhanging mountains were occupied by a numerous host of Seduni and Veragri. Various reasons had led the Gauls to form the sudden resolution of renewing hostilities and overpowering the legion. First, the legion was numerically so weak that they despised it; it had not been at its full strength originally, and two cohorts, as well as numerous individuals who had been sent out to get supplies, had been withdrawn. Again, as the Romans had the worst of the ground, while they would themselves hurl their missiles, charging down into the valley from the hills, they were confident that their first onslaught would be irresistible. Besides, they resented their children being taken from them as hostages; and they were convinced that the Romans were trying to occupy the commanding points of the Alps, and to annex the district to the neighbouring Province, not merely in order to open up communication, but to secure permanent possession.

Octodurus was between Martigny-la-Ville and the more southerly Martigny-Bourg, on the left bank of the Rhone, near the point where it bends northward towards the Lake of Geneva. Galba's camp was on the left bank of the Dranse, a tributary of the Rhone, which then flowed in a different channel down the middle of the valley. The work of entrenching the camp was not yet quite completed, and corn and other supplies war had not been provided in sufficient quantity, for Galba had concluded that, as the enemy had submitted and he had received their hostages, there was no reason to fear hostilities: accordingly, on receiving the news, he promptly called a council of war, and invited opinions. A great peril had befallen suddenly and unexpectedly, already, indeed, almost all the heights were seen to be swarming with armed men; the roads were blocked, and therefore it was impossible for relief to arrive or for supplies to be brought up; and safety was deemed all but hopeless: some, therefore, expressed the opinion that they ought to abandon the baggage, make a sortie, and try to reach a place of safety by the same route by which they had come. The majority, however, decided to reserve this plan to the last, and meanwhile to defend the camp and await developments. After a short interval, which barely gave time for making the dispositions and carrying out the arrangements which had been resolved upon, the enemy rushed down at a given signal from every side, and hurled stones and javelins on to the rampart. At first, while our men were still fresh, they resisted stoutly, not a missile which they threw from their commanding position missing its mark; and when any part of the camp that was inadequately manned appeared to be hard pressed, men hurried to the rescue: but what told against them was that when the enemy were exhausted by prolonged fighting they went out of action, and fresh men took their places, while our men, owing to their slender numbers, could not follow their example; and not only was it impossible for a man to go out of action when he was tired, but even if wounded he could not leave his post and recover himself.

For more than six hours the fighting had been incessant: not only the strength of our men, but even their missiles were failing; the enemy were pressing on with increased energy, and, as our men grew feebler, they began to fill up the trenches and demolish the rampart. In this extremity Publius Sextius Baculus, the chief centurion, who, as we have said, had received several severe wounds in the battle with the Nervii, ran to Galba, accompanied by Gains Volusenus, a tribune of great judgement and courage, and pointed out that the only chance of safety was to try a forlorn hope and make a sortie. Galba therefore summoned the centurions, and quickly made the men understand that they were to leave off fighting for a little, only parrying the enemy's missiles, rest after their exertions, and afterwards, when the signal was given, charge out of camp and trust for safety to sheer courage.

The order was carried out. Suddenly they charged out of all the gates, and never gave the enemy a chance of divining their intention or of closing their ranks. Fortune had changed sides. The assailants, who had actually hoped to take the camp, were surrounded and slain. More than a third of the entire native force that had assailed the camp, which was known to number over thirty thousand men, were killed; the rest were sent flying in panic; and the Romans would not suffer them to rally even on the heights. Having thus routed the entire hostile force and taken their arms, they returned to their entrenchments.

After fighting this battle, Galba had no wish to tempt fortune any more: he reflected that the circumstances with which he had had to contend were at variance with the purpose for which he had taken up his quarters; and the scarcity of corn and other supplies caused him great anxiety. Next day, therefore, he fired all the buildings in the village and hastened to return to the Province; and, as no enemy attempted to stop him or opposed his march, he brought the legion back safely into the country of the Nantuates, and thence into that of the Allobroges, where he passed the winter. After these operations everything led Caesar to believe that Gaul was tranquillized, for the revolted. Belgae were overpowered, the Germans driven out, and the Seduni defeated in the Alps: accordingly he had started, at the beginning of winter, for Illyricum, being anxious to visit the tribes there as well as those of Gaul, and to make himself acquainted with their country, when suddenly war broke out in Gaul, for the following reason.

The younger Publius Crassus, who was wintering with the 7th legion among the Andes, near the Ocean, finding that corn was scarce in the district, sent a number of auxiliary officers and tribunes to the neighbouring tribes to arrange for a supply. Amongst others, Titus Terrasidius was sent to the Esuvii, Marcus Trebius Gallus to the Coriosolites.

The last named tribe is by far the most influential of all the maritime peoples in that part of the country. They possess numerous ships, in which they regularly sail to Britain; they excel in knowledge of navigation and in seamanship; and, the sea being very stormy and open, with only a few scattered harbours, which they keep under their control, they compel almost all who sail those waters to pay toll. They took the initiative by detaining Silius and Velanius, believing that they would be able to use them to get back the hostages whom they had given to Crassus. Their neighbours, influenced by their example, and making up their minds, like true Gauls, suddenly and without consideration, detained Trebius and Terrasidius for the same reason; hurriedly dispatched envoys, and, through the medium of their leaders, pledged themselves to do nothing without official sanction, and to stand by one another in victory or defeat; and called upon the other tribes to resolve to hold fast to the liberty which they had received from their forefathers, and not to submit to the yoke of the Romans. They speedily gained over all the maritime tribes, and jointly sent an embassy to Publius Crassus, calling upon him, if he wished to recover his officers, to restore their hostages. When Caesar was informed of these events, he was a long way off, and accordingly gave orders that ships of war should be built, before his return, on the Loire, which flows into their ocean.

Oarsmen were raised from the Province, and seamen and pilots assembled. These orders were promptly executed; and, as soon as the season permitted, he [Caesar] hastened to join the army. On hearing of his approach, the Veneti, and also the other tribes, being aware that they had committed a heinous offence in detaining and imprisoning envoys, whose office had always, among all peoples, been held sacred and inviolable, proceeded to make preparations for war — and especially to provide for the equipment of their ships—on a scale commensurate with the magnitude of the danger; and they worked with a hopefulness which was increased by their faith in the natural strength of their country. They knew that the roads were interrupted by estuaries, and that navigation was rendered difficult by the want of topographical information and the scarcity of harbours; they were confident that our armies would not be able to remain long in their country, for want of grain; and, even if all their calculations were upset, they had command of the sea, while the Romans were ill supplied with ships and had no knowledge of the theatre of the approaching war, — the shoals, harbours, and islands; finally, they saw that navigation in a land-locked sea and in the open, boundless ocean were very different things. After forming their plans, they fortified their strongholds, stored them with grain from the country districts, and assembled as many ships as possible in Venetia, where it was known that Caesar would open the campaign. They secured the alliance of the Osismi, Namnetes, Ambiliati and Morini.

The difficulties above mentioned which beset the campaign were serious but nevertheless Caesar had many urgent motives for undertaking it - the violation of international law in detaining Roman knights; the fact that the tribes after submission had renewed hostilities, and revolted although they had given hostages; the wide extension of the conspiracy; and, above all, the danger that, if this district were left unpunished, the other peoples would fancy that they might offend in the same way. Knowing, therefore, that the Gauls were almost all politically restless, and that their warlike passions were easily and swiftly roused, and moreover that all men are naturally fond of freedom and hate to be in subjection, he thought it best, before more tribes had time to join the movement, to break up his army and distribute it over a wider area.

Accordingly he sent Titus Labienus with a body of cavalry into the country of the Treveri, near the Rhine, with orders to visit the Aquitanians, and the other Belgic peoples and keep them obedient; and in case the Germans, whose assistance was said to have been solicited by the Belgae, attempted to force a passage in boats of his fleet across the river, to stop them. Publius Crassus was directed to march with twelve legionary cohorts and a strong body of cavalry for Aquitania, in order to prevent the dispatch of reinforcements to Gaul from the peoples of that country and the junction of two powerful races. Quintus Titurius Sabinus, one of the generals, was sent with three legions into the country of the Venelli, Coriosolites, and Lexovii, to keep that section of the rebels isolated. The younger Decimus Brutus was placed in command of the fleet and of the Gallic ships which Caesar had ordered to assemble from the ports of the Pictones and Santoni and from the other settled districts, with orders to sail, as soon as possible, for the country of the Veneti. Caesar marched thither in person with the land forces.

The strongholds were generally situated on the ends of spits or headlands that it was impossible to approach them on foot, when the tide came rushing in from the open sea (which regularly happens every twelve hours), or to sail up to them, because at the ebb the ships would have been injured in the shallow water. Both of these causes interfered with the siege of the strongholds. The besiegers kept out the sea by building dykes, and by this means got on a level with the walls of the town; but when the besieged, overmatched by the magnitude of the works, began to lose confidence, they brought up a large number of ships, of which they had an unlimited supply, removed all their property, and withdrew to the nearest strongholds, where they again defended themselves by the same advantages of position. These tactics they found it easy to keep up during a great part of the summer, because our ships were detained by stormy weather, and navigation was very difficult in a vast open sea, where the tides were strong and harbours few and far between, indeed practically non-existent.

Their own ships were built and fitted out in the following way. They were a good deal more flat-bottomed than ours, to adapt them to the conditions of shallow water and ebbing tides. Bows and sterns alike were very lofty, being thus enabled to resist heavy seas and severe gales. The hulls were built throughout of oak, in order to stand any amount of violence and rough usage. The cross-timbers, consisting of beams a foot thick, were riveted with iron bolts as thick as a man's thumb. The anchors were secured with iron chains instead of ropes. Hides or leather dressed fine were used instead of sails, either because flax was scarce and the natives did not know how to manufacture it, or, more probably, because they thought it difficult to make head against the violent storms and squalls of the Ocean, and to manage vessels of such burden with ordinary sails. When these ships encountered our fleet, the latter had the advantage only in speed and in being propelled by oars; in other respects the former, from their more suitable construction, were better adapted to the conditions of the coast and the force of the storms. They were so solidly built that our ships could not injure them by ramming; owing to their height, it was not easy to throw javelins onto them; and for the same reason it was difficult to seize them with grappling irons. Moreover, when it began to blow hard and they were running before the wind, they could weather the storm more easily; they could lie up more safely in shallow water; and when they were left aground by the ebb, they had nothing to fear from a stony bottom and sharp rocks; whereas our ships were in great danger from all these contingencies. After taking several strongholds, Caesar saw that all his labour was being expended in vain, and that, by merely capturing their forts, he could neither prevent the enemy from escaping nor cripple them. He decided, therefore, that it would be best to wait for his fleet. As soon as it arrived and was sighted by the enemy, their ships, numbering about two hundred and twenty, ready for sea and fully equipped, stood out of harbour and ranged opposite ours. Brutus, who commanded the fleet, and the tribunes and centurions, each of whom had been entrusted with a single ship, did not quite know what to do, or what tactics to adopt. They had ascertained that it was impossible to injure the enemy's ships by ramming. The turrets were run up; but even then they were overtopped by the lofty sterns, so that, from the lower position, it was impossible to throw javelins with effect, while the missiles thrown by the Gauls fell with increased momentum.

Our men, however, had a very effective contrivance ready, namely, hooks, sharpened at the ends and fixed to long poles, shaped somewhat like grappling-hooks. By means of these the halyards were seized and pulled taut: the galley rowed hard; and the ropes snapped. When they were cut, the yards of course fell down; and as the efficiency of the Gallic ships depended altogether upon their sails and rigging, when they were gone the ships were no longer of any use. Thenceforward the struggle turned upon sheer courage, in which our soldiers easily had the advantage, especially as the fighting went on under the eyes of Caesar and the whole army, so that no act of courage at all remarkable could escape notice; for all the cliffs and high ground which commanded a near view over the sea were occupied by the army.

When, as we have said, the yards tumbled down, the Roman ships, two or three at a time, closed round one of the enemy's; and the legionaries clambered aboard with the utmost vigour. Several ships had been captured, when the natives, seeing what was happening and realizing that there was no help for it, hastened to save themselves by flight. And now, just as the ships had been put before the wind, there was suddenly a dead calm, and they could not stir. This was just what was wanted to make the victory complete. Our men gave chase and captured the ships one after another, with the result that, after a battle lasting from about the fourth hour till sunset, only a very few of the whole armada managed, when night stopped the pursuit, to make the land.

This battle brought the war with the Veneti and all the coast tribes to an end; for all the fighting men, and indeed all the seniors of any standing or whose counsels had any weight, had taken part in it: they had brought every one of their ships into action; and now that they were lost, the survivors had no place to escape to and no means of defending their strongholds. They surrendered, therefore, to Caesar unreservedly. He determined to inflict upon them a signal punishment, in order to make the natives respect the rights of ambassadors more carefully in future. Accordingly he put to death the entire council, and sold the rest of the population into slavery.

While these events were passing in the country of the Veneti, Quintus Titurius Sabinus made his way with the troops assigned to him by Caesar into the country of the Venelli. Their leader was Viridovix, who was also commander-in-chief of all the insurgent tribes, and had raised from them an army and large irregular levies. Within the few days that followed Sabinus's arrival, the Aulerci, Eburovices and the Lexovii massacred their senators because they refused to sanction the war, shut their gates, and joined Viridovix; and a host of desperadoes and brigands had also assembled from all parts of Gaul, to whom the hope of plunder and love of fighting were more attractive than farming and regular work. Sabinus, who occupied a position in all respects excellent, remained obstinately in camp; while Viridovix, who had encamped opposite him, two miles off, led out his troops every day and offered battle. The result was that Sabinus not only incurred the contempt of the enemy, but was actually the object of some abuse from his own troops; and he let the enemy become so convinced of his timidity that they presently ventured to approach close to the rampart. His motive was that he felt bound, as a subordinate, especially in the absence of his chief, to avoid engaging such a numerous enemy unless he had the best of the ground or some favourable opportunity presented itself.

Now that they were convinced of his timidity, he selected from his auxiliaries a quick-witted Gaul, the very man for his purpose, induced him by liberal rewards and promises to go over to the enemy, and explained his object. The man came to them in the guise of a deserter; described the terror of the Romans; and explained that Caesar himself was hard pressed by the Veneti, and that Sabinus would march his army stealthily out of camp not later than the following night and go to his assistance. On hearing this, they all cried that the chance of striking a decisive blow was not to be lost: they must attack the camp. Many circumstances combined to impel them to this decision,—the recent inaction of Sabinus, the assurances of the deserter, want of supplies (for which they had made scant provision), the hope that the Veneti would succeed in their campaign, and lastly, the fact that what men desire they are generally prone to believe. Influenced by these motives, they would not suffer Viridovix and the other leaders to leave the assembly until they had agreed to let them arm and make a dash for the camp. When they were allowed to have their way they were as exultant as if victory were certain, and, collecting brushwood and faggots to fill up the Roman trenches, they advanced against the camp.

The camp stood on rising ground, which sloped gently from its base for about a mile. The Gauls hurried up at a great pace, in order to give the Romans the least possible time for falling into line and arming, and arrived breathless. Sabinus harangued his men, and gave the signal which they were eagerly awaiting. As the enemy were hampered by their loads, he ordered a sudden sortie from two of the gates. Thanks to the favourable position, the courage of the legionaries and the experience which they had gained in previous combats, and their own want of skill and exhaustion, the enemy instantly turned tail without standing a single charge from our men. They were in no condition to escape, and our troops, who were fresh for pursuit, killed a great number of them. The rest were hunted down by the cavalry, who allowed few to get away. Thus Sabinus heard of the sea-fight and Caesar of Sabinus's victory at the same time; and all the tribes immediately submitted to Titurius. For, while the Gallic temperament is impetuous and warlike, their character is irresolute and has little power of bearing up against disaster.

About the same time Crassus arrived in Aquitania, which, as the narrative has shown, may be regarded, in area and population, as one-third of Gaul. Knowing that he had to fight in a country where, a few years before, a Roman general, Lucius Valerius Praeconinus, had been killed and his army defeated, and from which a proconsul, Lucius Manlius, had retreated in disorder with the loss of his baggage, he saw that he would have to exercise no ordinary care. Accordingly he provided for a supply of grain, raised auxiliaries and cavalry, and also called out individually a large number of excellent soldiers from Tolosa, Carcaso, and Narbo—states in the Province, adjacent to Aquitania — and marched his army into the country of the Sotiates. On becoming aware of his approach, they raised a large force, including cavalry (being very strong in that arm), and attacked our column on its march. The battle began with a combat of horse. Their cavalry were repulsed and ours were pursuing them, when suddenly they unmasked their infantry, which they had stationed in ambush in a valley. The latter fell upon our disordered troops and renewed the action.

The fighting was prolonged and fierce; for the Sotiates relied upon their past victories and felt that the fate of all Aquitania depended upon their courage; while our men were eager that the world should see what they could achieve under their youthful leader, without the chief and the other legions. At length the enemy, having suffered heavy loss, turned and fled. Many of them were slain; and Crassus, advancing to the chief town of the Sotiates, at once proceeded to lay siege to it. As the garrison offered a stout resistance, he brought up sheds and towers. The garrison first attempted a sortie, then drove galleries in the direction of the terrace and sheds (the Aquitanians are very skilled in operations of this kind, as mining works exist in many parts of their country); but finding that, owing to the vigilance of our troops, they could affect nothing by these devices, they sent envoys to Crassus, asking him to accept their surrender. Their request was granted; and, in obedience to his command, they laid down their arms. But all was not over. Our men were all intently watching what was going on, when Adiatunnus, who was in command, attempted a sortie from another part of the town with six hundred devoted followers, whom the natives call soldurity —men who, while life lasts, share all good things with the friends to whom they have attached themselves, on the understanding that, if any violence befall them, they are either to share their fate or to die by their own hands; and within the memory of man no one has ever been known to shrink from death when his friend and leader was slain. With these men Adiatunnus attempted a sortie; but when the roar of battle arose from that part of the entrenchment, the soldiers ran to arms, and, after hard fighting, Adiatunnus was driven back into the town. Notwithstanding, he prevailed upon Crassus to allow him to surrender on the original terms.

On receiving the arms and hostages, Crassus started for the country of the Vocates tribes and Tarusates. And now, learning that a fortified town of great natural strength had been captured a few days after the arrival of the besiegers, the natives were thoroughly alarmed and began to send envoys in all directions, to swear mutual fidelity, to exchange hostages, and to raise troops. Envoys were also sent to the tribes of Higher Spain, near Aquitania, with a request for reinforcements and leaders, whose arrival enabled them to undertake the campaign with great prestige and to put a large number of men in the field. The leaders chosen had served from first to last with Quintus Sertorius, and were believed to possess great military skill. Adopting Roman methods, they proceeded to select positions, to entrench their camp, and to cut off our convoys. Crassus, reflecting that his own force was too small to be readily divided, that the enemy, while scouring the country and blocking the roads, were able to leave a sufficient force to protect their camp, which made it difficult to bring up corn and other supplies, and that their numbers were daily increasing, thought it best to- fight a decisive battle without delay. He referred the question to a council of war, and, finding that everyone agreed with him, determined to fight on the morrow.

At daybreak he moved out the whole force, formed them in two lines with the auxiliaries in the centre, and awaited the development of the enemy's plans. Although, relying on their numbers, their established military reputation, and the weakness of our force, they considered it safe to fight, they nevertheless thought it safer to gain a bloodless victory by blocking the roads and cutting off our supplies; while, in case the Romans began to retreat from want of food, their idea was to attack them on the march, when their movements were impeded and they had their packs to carry and were dispirited. The plan was approved by their leaders; and accordingly when the Roman army moved out they remained shut up in camp. Crassus divined their intention. Their inaction, which produced the belief that they were cowed, had stimulated the ardour of our troops for battle, and all were overheard saying that the camp ought to be attacked without further delay; so Crassus, haranguing his men, who were all in great heart, advanced rapidly against the enemy's camp.

Some filled up the trenches; others drove the defenders from the rampart and fortifications with volleys of missiles; and the auxiliaries, in whose soldierly qualities Crassus had not much faith, kept the combatants supplied with stones and other missiles, brought up sods for filling the trench, and thus made a decent show of fighting. The enemy, too, fought steadily and with no lack of courage; and the missiles which they threw from their commanding position did good execution. Meanwhile some troopers rode round the enemy's camp and reported to Crassus that on the side of the rear gate it was not entrenched so carefully as elsewhere and offered easy entrance.

Crassus urged his cavalry officers to stimulate their men by liberal rewards and promises, and explained his object. In obedience to orders, they marched out the cohorts which had been left to protect the camp and had had nothing to tire them; made a wide detour, to avoid being observed from the enemy's camp; and, while everybody was intent upon the action and noticed nothing else, rapidly gained the part of the entrenchments which we have mentioned, demolished them, and made good their footing in the camp before the enemy could clearly see them or make out what was going on. And now, when our troops heard the shouting from that part of the camp, their strength returned, as generally happens when soldiers feel confident of victory, and they fought with redoubled energy.

Finding themselves surrounded, the enemy in utter despair hastened to throw themselves over the entrenchments and ran for their lives. The cavalry hunted them over the broad open plains; out of fifty thousand who were known to have come from Aquitania and the land of the Cantabri, barely a fourth escaped them; and late at night they returned to camp.

On hearing the result of the battle, the bulk of the population of Aquitania, including the Tarbelli, Bigerriones, Ptianii, Vocates, Tarusates, Elusates, Gates, Ausci, Garumni, Sibusates, and Cocosates, submitted to Crassus and voluntarily sent hostages. A few distant tribes trusted to the lateness of the season, as winter was coming on, and neglected to follow their example.

About the same time Caesar led his army against the Morini and the Menapii, in the belief that the campaign could be soon finished. The summer was nearly over; but, while all the rest of Gaul was tranquillized, they remained in arms, and had never sent envoys to him to sue for peace. Their tactics were quite different from those of the other Gauls. Being aware that the strongest tribes which had fought in the open field had been completely defeated, they took refuge, with all their belongings, in their continuous forests and marshes. On reaching the outskirts of the forests, Caesar proceeded to entrench his camp. No enemy had so far appeared, and the men were working in scattered groups, when suddenly the enemy rushed out of the forest from all sides and attacked them. The men quickly seized their weapons and drove them back into the forest with considerable loss; but, pursuing them too far over very difficult ground, lost a few of their own number.

Caesar now proceeded to clear the forest, and continued doing so day after day. To prevent the soldiers from being attacked in flank while they were unarmed and off their guard, he regularly laid the timber as it was felled in the direction of the enemy, and piled it as a barricade on both flanks. A large space was cleared with incredible speed in a few days, by which time the enemy's cattle and the rear portion of their baggage were in our hands, while they were making for the denser parts of the forest: but such stormy weather followed that the work had to be discontinued; and, owing to continuous rains, it was impossible to keep the soldiers longer under tents. Accordingly, after ravaging but is forced all the enemy's fields and burning their hamlets and homesteads, Caesar withdrew his troops and quartered them for the winter in the territories of the Aulerci, the Lexovii, and the other tribes which had recently been in arms.

BOOK IV

THE FATE OF THE USIPETES AND TENCTERI— CAESAR'S FIRST INVASION OF BRITAIN

In the following winter—the year in which Cn. Pompey and M. Crassus were consuls—a German tribe, the Usipetes, accompanied by the Tencteri, crossed the Rhine in large numbers, not far from the point where it enters the sea. Their motive was that for several years they had been subject to harassing attacks from the Suevi, and prevented from tilling the land. The Suevi are by far the most numerous and warlike of all the German peoples. They are said to comprise a hundred clans, each of which annually sends a thousand armed men on a military expedition beyond the frontier. The rest of the population remain at home, and support the expeditionary force as well as themselves. Next year they take up arms in their turn, and the others remain at home. Thus agriculture goes on uninterruptedly along with theoretical and practical training in war. Private property in land, however, does not exist; and no one is allowed to remain for farming in one spot longer than a year. Not much corn, indeed, is consumed; the people live principally on milk and flesh-meat, and spend much time in hunting. This, combined with the nature of their food, their constant exercise and freedom from restraint (for they have never, from childhood, been made to obey or subjected to discipline, and never do anything against their inclination), fosters their bodily vigour and produces a race of gigantic stature. Moreover, they have trained themselves to wear no clothing, even in the coldest districts, except skins, which leave a large part of the body bare, and to bathe in the rivers.

Traders are allowed to enter their country, not because they want to import anything but that they may find purchasers for their booty. Even horses, of which the Gauls are extremely fond, and to procure which they go to great expense, are not imported by the Germans. The native horses are undersized and ugly, but by constant exercise they develop in them extraordinary powers of endurance. In cavalry combats they often dismount and fight on foot, training their horses to stand still, and quickly remounting when necessary. According to their notions, nothing is more shameful or unmanly than the use of saddles; and so, however small their numbers, they are ready to encounter any number of cavalry who use them. They will not allow wine to be imported at all, considering that its use enfeebles a man's power of endurance and makes him effeminate.

The communities as such pride themselves on keeping the land round their own borders uninhabited as far as possible, regarding it as a proof that many tribes are unable to cope with them. Thus it is said that on one side of the Suevan territory there is an uninhabited tract extending about six hundred miles. On the opposite side, their neighbours are the Ubii, who were once a considerable, and, according to German standards, flourishing tribe. They are in fact rather more civilized than the rest of the nation; for they are near the Rhine, their country is much frequented by traders, and, from propinquity, they have become familiarized with Gallic customs. The Suevi, after many campaigns and frequent attempts, had found them too numerous and powerful to be dispossessed; but they made them tributary and reduced them to comparative insignificance and weakness. The Usipetes and Tencteri, mentioned above, were in the same position. For several years they withstood the pressure of the Suevi; but at length they were dispossessed, and, after wandering three years through many parts of Germany, came to the Rhine. The Menapii inhabited that region, and owned lands, homesteads, and villages on both banks of the river; but alarmed by the incursion of this huge host, they abandoned their dwellings on the further bank, established outposts on this side of the Rhine, and determined to prevent the Germans from crossing. The latter tried every expedient; but being unable to force a passage from want of boats or to get across unobserved because of the Menapian patrols, pretended to return to the district where they had settled, marched on for three days, and then turned back again. Their cavalry made the whole journey in a single night, and swooped down upon the Menapii, who, knowing nothing of their movements, were off their guard, and, having been informed by their patrols that they had gone off, had fearlessly recrossed the Rhine and returned to their villages. The Germans slaughtered them; seized their boats; crossed the river before the Menapii on this side of the Rhine could tell what they were about; took possession of all their buildings; and for the rest of the winter lived on their stores.

The unstable character of the Gauls caused Caesar anxiety, for they do not abide by their decisions, and are generally prone to revolution: accordingly, when he learned the facts, he thought it best not to rely upon them at all. It is a custom of theirs to detain travellers, even against their will, and question them individually about what they have heard or ascertained on this or that topic; and in the towns the people cluster round traders and make them, say where they come from and tell them the news. Influenced by these reports, even when they are merely hearsay, they often embark upon the most momentous enterprises; and, as they trust blindly to vague gossip, and their informants generally tell lies and frame their answers to please them, they naturally repent of their plans as soon as they are formed.

Caesar was aware of this custom, and, to avoid having a serious war on his hands, he started to rejoin his army earlier than usual. On his arrival he found that his forebodings were justified: embassies had been sent by more than one tribe to the Germans, inviting them to quit the neighbourhood of the Rhine, and promising to supply all their requirements. Allured by this prospect, they were now wandering further afield and had reached the territories of the Eburones and Condrusi,—both dependents of the Treveri. Caesar summoned the Gallic notables, and, thinking it well to dissemble what he knew, addressed them in soothing and reassuring terms, directed them to furnish cavalry, and announced his intention of taking the field against the Germans.

After arranging for a supply of grain and selecting troopers from the several contingents, he began his march towards the districts in which he heard that the Germans were encamped. When he was within a few days' march from them, their envoys arrived, and addressed him as follows:—the Germans were not the aggressors, but, if they were provoked, they would not shrink from a contest with the Roman People; for it was a principle of theirs, handed down by their forefathers, to resist all who attacked them, and not to sue for mercy. Still, this much they would say,—they had come reluctantly, because they had been driven from their country. If the Romans cared for their goodwill, their friendship might be of use to them: let the Romans either assign them lands or suffer them to retain those which they had won by the sword. They acknowledged the superiority of the Suevi alone, for even the immortal gods were no match for them; and there was no other people upon earth whom they could not overcome.

Caesar made a suitable reply. The upshot of his speech was that there could be no friendship between him and the Germans if they remained in Gaul. It was not reasonable for land of the people who could not defend their own territories to take possession of those of others; and besides, there were no unoccupied lands in Gaul which could be made over to any people, least of all to one so numerous, without injustice. Still, they might settle, if they wished, in the country of the Ubii, whose envoys were with him, complaining of the ill-treatment of the Suevi and asking for his aid; and he would order the Ubii to receive them.

The envoys said that they would refer this offer to their principals, and, after it had been considered, would return to Caesar in three days; meanwhile they requested him not to move nearer. Caesar told them that it was impossible for him to make even this concession. He had ascertained that a large detachment of their cavalry had been sent across the Meuse some days before to the country of the Ambivariti, to plunder and forage; and he believed that they were waiting for their return, and that that was their motive for trying to gain time.

The Meuse rises in the Vosges mountains, which are in the territory of the Lingones, receives an affluent called the Waal from the Rhine, thereby forming the island of the Batavi, and not more than eighty miles from that point flows into the Ocean. The Rhine rises in the country of the Lepontii, who inhabit the Alps, and flows swiftly for a long distance through the territories of the Nantuates, Helvetii, Sequani, Mediomatrici, Triboci, and Treveri: as it approaches the sea it branches off into several channels, and forms numerous large islands, many of which are inhabited by fierce rude tribes, some of whom are supposed to live on fish and birds' eggs, and discharges itself by numerous outlets into the ocean.

When Caesar was not more than twelve miles from the enemy, their envoys returned to see him, according to agreement, and meeting him earnestly entreated him to advance no further. As they could not induce him to comply, they begged him to send word to the cavalry, which had gone on in advance of the column, forbidding them to fight, and to let them send envoys to the Ubii; declaring that if their council and chiefs swore to keep faith with them, they would avail themselves of the terms which he offered, and asking him to give them three days to complete the arrangements. Caesar believed that all these stipulations had the same object,— to secure three days' delay for the return of the absent cavalry; still, he said that he would advance four miles and no more that day, to get water; on the morrow as many of them as could come were to assemble at his halting-place, that he might take cognizance of their requests. Meanwhile he sent messengers to tell the cavalry officers, who had gone on in front with their whole force, not to attack the enemy, and, in case they were attacked themselves, to remain on the defensive till he came up with the rest of the army.

Our cavalry, who numbered five thousand, felt no anxiety, as the German envoys had asked for an armistice for that day, and had only just left Caesar. The moment the enemy caught sight of them, although they had not more than eight hundred horse, those who had crossed the Meuse to forage not having yet returned, they charged and speedily threw them into confusion; and when they rallied, the enemy, following their regular practice, sprang to the ground, stabbed the horses in the belly and unhorsed a number of our men, sent the rest flying, and swept them along in such panic that they never drew rein till they came in sight of our column. Seventy-four of our troopers were killed in the affair, including Piso, a gallant Aquitanian of most illustrious family, whose grandfather had been honoured by the Senate with the title of Friend, and had held sovereignty in his own tribe. His brother was surrounded by the enemy, but he went to his assistance and rescued him, and though his horse was wounded, and he was thrown, he resisted most gallantly as long as he could: surrounded and covered with wounds, he fell, when his brother, who had by this time got away from the press and was some distance off, saw what had happened, and putting spurs to his horse, rode straight against the enemy and perished.

After this combat, Caesar no longer felt bound to listen to the envoys, or to entertain the proposals of a people who, after asking for peace, instantly had made a treacherous, insidious, and unprovoked attack. On the other hand, he thought that it would be the height of folly to wait till the enemy were reinforced by the return of their cavalry: from his knowledge of the unstable character of the Gauls, he realized that the enemy, by a single victory, had already gained great prestige with them; and he thought it best to give them no time to form their plans. Having come to this decision, he communicated to his quaestor and generals his determination not to lose a day in forcing on a battle, when a most fortunate event occurred. Next day, early in the morning, a numerous deputation of the Germans, comprising all the leading men and all those of mature age, came to the camp, in the same spirit of treachery and deceit, to wait upon him. Their ostensible object was to clear themselves from complicity in the attack which had taken place the day before, contrary to the agreement which they had themselves asked for; at the same time they intended, if possible, to gain an extension of the armistice on some pretext. Caesar was delighted that they had put themselves in his power, and ordered them to be detained: he then marched out of camp at the head of his whole force, ordering the cavalry, whom he believed to be demoralized by the recent combat, to bring up the rear. Forming the army in three lines, he made a rapid march of eight miles, and reached the enemy's camp before the Germans could realize what was going to happen. The rapidity of our advance and the absence of their leaders suddenly and completely unnerved them; there was no time to consider or to arm; and they were too distracted to know whether it was best to throw their strength against the enemy, to defend the camp, or to fly for their lives. Their terror was manifested by cries and hurried movements, and the soldiers, exasperated by the treachery of the previous day, burst into the camp. Those who were quick enough to seize their weapons made a brief stand there against our men, fighting under cover of their wagons and baggage: but the host of women and children (for they had left their country and crossed the Rhine with all their belongings) began to flee in all directions; and Caesar sent his cavalry to hunt them down.

The Germans heard the shrieks behind, and, seeing that their kith and kin were being slaughtered, threw away their weapons, abandoned their standards, and rushed out of the camp. When they reached the confluence of the Moselle and the Rhine great numbers were already killed; and the rest, giving up all hope of escape, plunged into the stream and there perished, overcome by terror, weariness, and the force of the current. Our men had anxiously anticipated an arduous struggle, for the enemy's numbers had amounted to four hundred and thirty thousand; but all to a man returned safe to camp with only a very few wounded. Caesar gave the prisoners whom he had detained in camp the option of going free; but, as they were afraid of being punished and tortured by the Gauls whose lands they had ravaged, they said that they would prefer to remain with him, and he permitted them to do so.

The campaign against the Germans being concluded, Caesar thought it advisable for many reasons to cross the Rhine. The most cogent reason was this:— observing that the Germans were so ready to invade Gaul, he desired to make them feel alarm on their own account, and realize that the army of the Roman People could and would cross the Rhine. There was another consideration. That division of the cavalry of the Usipetes and Tencteri which, as I have already related, had crossed the Meuse to plunder and forage and had taken no part in the action, had recrossed the Rhine after the rout of their countrymen, taken refuge in the territory of the Sugambri, and joined forces with them. When Caesar sent envoys to the Sugambri, calling upon them to deliver up the fugitives on the ground that they had made war upon him and upon Gaul, they replied that the Rhine was the limit of Roman dominion: if Caesar thought that the Germans had no right to cross over into Gaul without his permission, how could he claim any authority or power beyond the Rhine? The Ubii, on the other hand, who, alone among these peoples, had sent envoys to Caesar, entered into friendly relations with him, and given hostages, earnestly entreated him to help them, as they were hard pressed by the Suevi, or, if he were prevented from doing so by reasons of state, merely to throw his army across the Rhine, which would be sufficient to support them and assure their prospects for the future. The name and fame which his army had gained, even with the most distant German peoples, by defeating Ariovistus and by this recent victory, were so great that they could safely rely on the prestige and friendship of the Roman People. At the same time they promised to provide a large flotilla of boats for the passage of the army.

Caesar was determined to cross the Rhine for the reasons which I have mentioned; but he thought it hardly safe to cross in boats, and considered that to do so would not be consistent with his own dignity or that of the Roman People. Therefore, although the construction of a bridge presented great difficulties on account of the breadth, swiftness, and depth of the stream, he nevertheless thought it best to make the attempt, or else not to cross at all. The principle upon which he designed the bridge was as follows. He took a couple of piles a foot and a half thick, had them sharpened to a point from a little above the lower end and adapted in length to the varying depth of the river, and fastened them together at an interval of two feet. These piles he caused to be lowered into the river by means of floats, fixed, and driven home with pile-drivers, not vertically, like ordinary piles, but leaning forward in the same plane, so that they followed the direction of the current; then he had another couple of piles, similarly joined together, planted opposite them on the lower side, at a distance of forty feet, against the force and rush of the current. Beams two feet wide, fitting into the interval between the piles of each couple, were laid across; and the two couples were kept apart by a pair of braces on either side at the extremity. The couples being thus kept apart, and on the other hand held firmly in place, the strength of the structure was so great and its principle so ordered that, the greater the force of the current, the more closely were the piles locked together. The series of piles and transverse beams was connected by timbers laid in the direction of the bridge, which were floored with poles and fascines. Finally, notwithstanding the existing strength of the structure, piles were also driven in diagonally on the down-stream side, which were connected with the entire structure and planted below like a buttress, so as to break the force of the stream. Other piles were likewise planted a little above the bridge, so that in case the natives floated down trunks of trees or barges to demolish the structure, their force might be weakened by these bulwarks, and they might not injure the bridge.

Within ten days after the collection of the timber began, the whole work was finished, and the army crossed over. Caesar left a strong force at both ends of the bridge, and marched rapidly for the country of the Sugambri. Meanwhile envoys came in from several tribes; and Caesar replied graciously to their prayer for peace and friendship and directed them to bring him hostages. The Sugambri, on the contrary, from the moment when the construction of the bridge began, acting on the advice of the refugees from the Tencteri and Usipetes whom they were entertaining, had prepared for flight, left their country with all their belongings, and hidden themselves in the recesses of the forests.

Caesar remained a few days in their country, burned all their villages and homesteads, cut down their corn, and returned to the territory of the Ubii. Promising to help them in case they were molested by the Suevi, he ascertained from them that the latter, on learning from their scouts that the bridge was being made, had called a council according to their custom, and sent messengers in all directions, bidding the people to abandon the strongholds, convey their wives and children and all their belongings into the forests, and assemble— all of them who could bear arms—at a fixed place, nearly in the centre of the region occupied by the Suevi; here they were awaiting the arrival of the Romans, and here they had determined to fight a decisive battle. Caesar had achieved every object for which he had determined to lead his army across,—overawed the Germans, punished the Sugambri, and relieved the Ubii from hostile pressure: he felt that honour was satisfied and that he had served every useful purpose. When, therefore, he heard the news about the Suevi, he returned to Gaul, having spent just eighteen days on the further side of the Rhine, and destroyed the bridge.

Only a small part of the summer remained, and in these parts, the whole of Gaul having a northerly trend, winter sets in early: nevertheless Caesar made active preparations for an expedition to Britain; for he knew that in almost all the operations in Gaul our enemies had been reinforced from that country. Besides, if there were not time for a campaign, he thought that it would be well worth his while merely to visit the island, see what the people were like, and make himself acquainted with the features of the country, the harbours, and the landing-places; for of all this the Gauls knew practically nothing. No one, indeed, readily undertakes the voyage to Britain except traders; and even they know nothing of it except the coast and the parts opposite the different regions of Gaul. Accordingly, though Caesar summoned traders from all parts to meet him, he could not ascertain the extent of the island, what tribes dwelt therein, their strength, their method of fighting, their manners and customs, or what harbours were capable of accommodating a large flotilla.

To procure information on these points before risking the attempt, he sent Gaius Volusenus, whom he considered perfectly competent, with a galley, instructing him to make a thorough reconnaissance and return as soon as possible. At the same time he marched with his whole force for the country of the Morini, as the shortest passage to Britain was from their coast, and ordered ships to assemble there from all the adjacent districts, as well as the fleet which he had built in the previous summer for the war with the Veneti. Meanwhile his envoys reported by traders to the Britons, whereupon envoys came to him from several tribes of the island, promising to give hostages and to submit to the authority of the Roman People. On hearhearing what they had to say, Caesar graciously reassured them, and sent them home, enjoining them to abide by their resolve. Along with them he sent Commius, whom, after the overthrow of the Atrebates, he had set up as king over that people,—a man of whose energy and judgement he had a high opinion, whom he believed to be loyal, and who was reputed to have great influence in the country. He instructed him to visit all the tribes he could, to urge them to trust to the good faith of the Roman People, and to announce that Caesar would soon arrive. Volusenus reconnoitered all the features of the coast, as far as he could get the chance, for he could not venture to disembark and trust himself to the natives, and in five days returned to Caesar and reported his observations.

While Caesar was waiting in these parts to get his ships ready for sea, envoys came from a large section of the Morini to apologize for their recent conduct in attacking the Roman People and promise obedience to his commands, pleading that they were uncivilized and knew nothing of our ways. Caesar regarded this as most opportune, for he had no wish to leave an enemy in his rear; owing to the time of year, he had no means of undertaking a campaign; and he did not think it wise to postpone his expedition to Britain for trivia. Accordingly he ordered the envoys to furnish a large number of hostages, and on their arrival admitted the Morini to terms. About eighty transports, which he considered sufficient to convey two legions, were collected and assembled; the galleys which he had besides he assigned to the quaestor, the generals, and the auxiliary officers. Besides these there were eighteen transports, eight miles off, which were prevented from making the same harbour by contrary winds: these he assigned to the cavalry. Placing the rest of the army under the command of two generals, Quintus Titurius Sabinus and Lucius Aurunculeius Cotta, with orders to march against the Menapii and those clans of the Morini from which no envoys had come, he directed another general, Publius Sulpicius Rufus, to hold the port with a force which he considered adequate.

The arrangements were now complete; and, taking advantage of favourable weather, he set sail about the third watch, directing the cavalry to march to the further harbour, embark there, and follow him. They were rather dilatory in getting through their work; but Caesar, with the leading ships, reached Britain about this fourth hour; and there, standing in full view on all the heights, he saw an armed force of the enemy. The formation of the ground was peculiar, the sea being so closely walled in by abrupt heights that it was possible to throw a missile from the ground above on to the shore. Caesar thought the place most unsuitable for landing, and accordingly remained till the ninth hour, waiting at anchor for the other ships to join him. Meanwhile he assembled the generals and tribunes, told them what he had learned from Volusenus, and explained his own plans, charging them to bear in mind the requirements of war and particularly of seamanship, involving as it did rapid and irregular movements, and to see that all orders were carried out smartly and at the right moment. The officers dispersed; and, getting wind and tide together in his favour, Caesar gave the signal, weighed anchor, and, sailing on about seven miles further, ran the ships aground on an open and shelving shore.

The natives knew what the Romans intended. Sending on ahead their cavalry and charioteers—a kind of warriors whom they habitually employ in action—they followed with the rest of their force and attempted to prevent our men from disembarking. It was very difficult to land, for these reasons. The size of the ships made it impossible for them to ground except in deep water; the soldiers did not know the ground, and with their hands loaded, and weighted by their heavy, cumbrous armour, they had to jump down from the ships, keep their foothold in the surf, and fight the enemy all at once; while the enemy had all their limbs free, they knew the ground perfectly, and standing on dry land or moving forward a little into the water, they threw their missiles boldly and drove their horses into the sea, which they were trained to enter. Our men were unnerved by the situation; and having no experience of this kind of warfare, they did not show the same dash and energy that they generally did in battles on land.

Caesar, noticing this, ordered the galleys, with the look of which the natives were not familiar, and which were easier to handle, to sheer off a little from the transports, row hard and range alongside of the enemy's flank, and slingers, archers, and artillery to shoot from their decks and drive the enemy out of the way. This manoeuvre was of great service to our men; for the natives, alarmed by the build of the ships, the motion of the oars, and the strangeness of the artillery, stood still, and then drew back a little. And now, as our soldiers were hesitating, chiefly because of the depth of the water, the standard-bearer of the 10th, praying that his attempt might redound to the success of the legion, cried, "Leap down, men, unless you want to abandon the eagle to the enemy: I, at all events, shall have done my duty to my country and my general." Uttering these words in a loud voice, he threw himself overboard, and advanced, bearing the eagle, against the enemy. Then, calling upon each other not to suffer such a disgrace, the men leaped all together from the ship. Seeing this, their comrades in the nearest ships followed them, and advanced close up to the enemy.

Both sides fought with spirit; but the Romans, being unable to keep their ranks unbroken or get firm foothold or follow their respective standards, and, as they came from this or that ship, joining any standard they met, became greatly confused; while the enemy knew all the shallows, and when from their standpoint on shore they saw a few men disembarking one by one, urged on their horses, and, surrounding the little group in numbers, attacked them before they were ready; others again got on the exposed flank of an entire company and plied them with missiles. Caesar, noticing this, ordered the men-of-war's boats and also the scouts to be manned, and, whenever he saw any of his men in difficulties, sent them to the rescue. Our men, as soon as they got upon dry land, followed by all their comrades, charged the enemy and put them to flight, but could not pursue them far because the cavalry had not been able to keep their course and make the island. This was the only drawback to Caesar's usual good fortune.

The beaten enemy at once sent envoys to Caesar to sue for peace, promising to give hostages and to obey his commands. The envoys were accompanied by the

Atrebatian, Commius, who, as I have already related, had been sent on by Caesar to Britain in advance. He had just landed, and, in the character of an envoy, was conveying Caesar's mandates to the Britons, when they seized him and loaded him with chains; but now, after the battle, they sent him back, and, while suing for peace, laid the blame of the outrage upon the rabble, and begged that it might be overlooked in consideration of their ignorance. Caesar complained that, after the Britons had spontaneously sent envoys to the continent and asked him for peace, they had attacked him without provocation, but said that he would pardon their ignorance, and demanded hostages. Part of the required number they handed over at once, saying that they had to fetch the rest from long distances, and would deliver them in a few days. Meanwhile they ordered their followers to go back to their districts, while chiefs began to come in from all parts and place themselves and their tribes under Caesar's protection.

Peace had been thus established, when, dispersed by three days after the expedition reached Britain, the eighteen ships, mentioned above, which had taken the cavalry on board, sailed from the upper port with a light breeze. They were getting close to Britain and were seen from the camp, when such a violent storm suddenly arose that none of them could keep their course, but some were carried back to the point from which they had started, while the others were swept down in great peril to the lower and more westerly part of the island. They anchored notwithstanding, but as they were becoming waterlogged, were forced to stand out to sea in the face of night and make for the continent.

The same night it happened to be full moon, which generally causes very high tides in the Ocean, a fact of which our men were not aware. The result was that the galleys, in which Caesar had brought over troops, and which he had drawn up on dry land, were waterlogged, while the transports, which were at anchor, were damaged by the storm, and the men were unable to be of any service or go to their assistance. Several ships were wrecked; the rest were rendered useless by the loss of their rigging, anchors, and other fittings; and naturally the whole army was seized by panic. There were no other ships to take them back; everything required for repairing ships was lacking; and, as the troops all understood that they would have to winter in Gaul, no corn for the winter had been provided on the spot.

When this became known, the British chiefs who had waited on Caesar after the battle took counsel together. They knew that the Romans had neither cavalry nor ships nor grain; and they gathered that their troops were few from the smallness of the camp, which, as Caesar had taken over the legions without heavy baggage, was extraordinarily contracted. They therefore concluded that their best course would be to renew hostilities, cut off our men from corn and other supplies, and protract the campaign till winter, being confident that, if they overpowered them or prevented their return, no invader would ever again come over to Britain. Accordingly they renewed their oaths of mutual fidelity, and began to move away one by one from the camp and to fetch their tribesmen secretly from the districts.

Caesar was not yet aware of their plans; but from what had happened to his ships and from the fact that the chiefs had left off sending hostages, he guessed what was coming. Accordingly he prepared for all contingencies. He had corn brought in daily from the fields into camp; utilized the timber and bronze belonging to the ships that had been most severely damaged to repair the rest; and ordered everything required for the purpose to be brought over from the continent. The men worked with hearty goodwill; and, thus although twelve ships were lost, he managed to have the rest made tolerably seaworthy.

Meanwhile a legion, the 7th, was sent out in the ordinary course to fetch corn. So far no one had suspected that hostilities were brewing; for some of the natives still remained in the districts, while others were actually passing in and out of the camp; but the troops on guard in front of the gates of the camp reported to Caesar that an unusual amount of dust was to be seen in the direction in which the legion had gone. Suspecting (with good reason, as it happened) that the natives had hatched some scheme, Caesar ordered the cohorts on guard to accompany him in the direction indicated, two of the others to relieve them, and the rest to arm and follow him immediately. He had advanced some little distance from the camp when he observed that his troops were hard pressed by the enemy and could barely hold their own, the legion being huddled together and missiles hurled in from all sides. All the corn had been cut except in this one spot; and the enemy, anticipating that the Romans would come here, had lain in wait in the woods during the night; then, when the troops had laid aside their weapons and were dispersed and busy reaping, they had suddenly fallen upon them. A few were killed; the rest, whose ranks were not properly formed, were thrown into confusion; and the enemy's horse and war-chariots had at the same time encompassed them.

First of all the charioteers drive all over the field, the warriors hurling missiles; and generally they throw the enemy's ranks into confusion by the mere terror inspired by their horses and the clatter of the wheels. As soon as they have penetrated between the troops of cavalry, the warriors jump off the chariots and fight on foot. The drivers meanwhile gradually withdraw from the action, and range the cars in such a position that, if the warriors are hard pressed by the enemy's numbers, they may easily get back to them. Thus they exhibit in action the mobility of cavalry combined with the steadiness of infantry; and they become so efficient from constant practice and training that they will drive their horses at full gallop, keeping them well in hand, down a steep incline, check and turn them in an instant, run along the pole, stand on the yoke, and step backwards again to the cars with the greatest nimbleness.

Our men were unnerved by these movements, because the tactics were new to them; and Caesar came to their support in the nick of time. When he came up the enemy stood still, and our men recovered from their alarm. Thinking, however, that the moment was not favourable for challenging the enemy and forcing on a battle, he simply maintained his position, and after a short interval withdrew the legions into camp. During these operations our people were all busy, and the rest of the Britons, who were still in their districts, left them. Stormy weather followed for several days running, which kept the troops in camp and prevented the enemy from attacking. Meantime the natives sent messengers in all directions, telling their tribesmen that our troops were few, and pointing out that they had an excellent opportunity for plundering and establishing their independence for good by driving the

Romans from their camp. By these representations they speedily got together a large body of horse and foot, and advanced against the camp.

Caesar foresaw that what had happened on previous days would happen again,—even if the enemy were beaten, their mobility would enable them to get off scot free; however, he luckily obtained about thirty horsemen, whom the Atrebatian, Commius, already mentioned, had taken over with him, and drew up the legions in front of the camp. A battle followed; and the enemy, unable to stand long against the onset of our troops, turned and fled. The troops pursued them as far as their speed and endurance would permit, and killed a good many of them; then, after burning all the buildings far and wide, they returned to camp.

On the same day the enemy sent envoys who came to Caesar to sue for peace. He ordered them to find twice as many hostages as before and take them across to the continent; for the equinox was near, and, as his ships were unsound, he did not think it wise to risk a stormy passage. Taking advantage of favourable weather, he set sail a little after midnight. All the ships reached the continent in safety; but two transports were unable to make the same harbours as the rest, and drifted a little further down.

About three hundred infantry had landed from these two vessels and were making the best of their way to camp, when the Morini, who had troops whom had been quite submissive when Caesar left them on attacked by hope of plunder, and told them, if they did not want to be killed, to lay down their arms. The Morini were not very numerous at first; but when the soldiers formed square and defended themselves, about six thousand, hearing the uproar, quickly assembled. On receiving the news, Caesar sent all his cavalry from camp to rescue his men. Meanwhile our soldiers sustained the enemy's onslaught and fought most gallantly for more than four hours; a few of them were wounded, but they killed many of their assailants. After our cavalry came in sight, the enemy threw away their arms and fled, and a large number of them were cut to pieces.

Next day Caesar sent Titus Labienus, in command of the legions which he had brought back from Britain, to punish the rebellious Morini. The marshes, which had served them as a refuge in the previous year, were dried up; and having no place to escape to, almost all of them fell into the hands of Labienus. Quintus Titurius and Lucius Cotta, the generals who had led the other legions into the country of the Menapii, finding that they had all taken refuge in the thickest parts of their forests, ravaged all their lands, cut their corn, burned their homesteads, and returned to Caesar, who quartered all the legions for the winter in the country of the Belgae. Thither no more sent hostages: the rest neglected to do so. In honour of these achievements, the Senate, on receiving Caesar's dispatches, appointed a thanksgiving service of twenty days.

BOOK V

CAESAR'S SECOND INVASION OF BRITAIN—THE DISASTER AT ADUATUCA—QUINTUS CICERO AT BAY –THE DOOM OF INDUTIOMARUS

When Caesar, according to his yearly custom, was leaving his winter quarters for Italy, in the consulship of Lucius Domitius and Appius Britain, he ordered the generals whom he had placed in command of the legions to have as many ships as possible built during the winter and the old ones repaired. He explained the principle and indicated the lines on which they were to be built. To enable them to be loaded rapidly and hauled up on shore, he had them made a little shallower than those which are habitually used in the Mediterranean, (especially as he had found that, owing to the frequent ebb and flow of the tides, the waves there are comparatively small). On the other hand, to carry stores as well as the numerous horses, he built them a little wider than those which we use in other waters. All these vessels he ordered to be constructed both for rowing and sailing, which was greatly facilitated by their low freeboard, and the tackle required for fitting them out to be imported from Spain. After finishing the assizes in Cisalpine Gaul, he started for Illyricum, hearing that the Pirustae were making devastating raids upon the adjacent part of the province. On his arrival, he levied troops from the tribes and ordered them to concentrate at a prescribed place. The Pirustae, on hearing of this, sent envoys to tell him that the authorities were not responsible for anything that had occurred, and declared themselves ready to make full reparation. After listening to what the envoys had to say, Caesar ordered them to furnish hostages, who were to be brought to him by a fixed date, warning them that, in default of compliance, he would attack the tribe. The hostages were brought punctually, in obedience to his orders; and he appointed umpires to weigh the matters in dispute between the several tribes and settle the fines.

After disposing of these affairs and finishing the assizes, Caesar returned to Cisalpine Gaul, and thence started to join the army. On his arrival, he inspected all the camps, and found that, thanks to the extraordinary energy of the troops, and notwithstanding the extreme deficiency of resources, about six hundred ships of the class described above and twenty-eight galleys had been built, and would be ready for launching in a few days. Heartily commending the soldiers and the officers who had superintended the work, he gave the necessary instructions, and ordered all the ships to assemble at the harbour, from which he had ascertained that the passage to Britain was most convenient,—the run from the continent being about thirty miles. Leaving an adequate number of troops to effect this movement, he started with four legions in light marching order and eight hundred horse for the country of the Treveri, as they would not attend his councils or submit to his authority, and were said to be making overtures to the Germans.

This tribe possesses by far the most power in the whole of Gaul, as well as numerous infantry; and, as we have remarked above, its territory reaches the Rhine. Two rivals, Indutiomarus and Cingetorix, were engaged in a struggle for supremacy.

The latter, as soon as the approach of Caesar and his legions was known, presented himself before him, gave an assurance that he and all his followers would remain staunch and not break off their friendship with the Romans, and told him what was going on among the Treveri. Indutiomarus, on the other hand, proceeded to levy horse and foot and to make preparations for war, while he sent those who were not of an age to bear arms into the Ardennes, a forest of vast extent, which stretches from the Rhine through the heart of the Treveran territory to the frontier of the Remi. Some leading men, however, of the former tribe, influenced by friendship for Cingetorix and alarmed by the arrival of our army, came to Caesar and, feeling unable to do anything for their country, began to proffer petitions on their own behalf. Thereupon Indutiomarus, afraid of being left in the lurch, sent envoys to Caesar to say that he had only refrained from leaving his followers and presenting himself before him in order to keep the tribe loyal, lest, if all the men of rank left them, the masses, in their ignorance, might fall away. Accordingly the people were under his control, and, if Caesar would allow him, he would wait upon him in his camp and entrust his own interests and those of the community to his protection.

He spoke to him kindly and urged him to remain staunch. Nevertheless he summoned the leading men of the Treveri, and called upon them individually to support Cingetorix. He felt that Cingetorix deserved this service at his hands, and at the same time he thought it most important that a man of whose remarkable good-will towards himself he had clear evidence should, as far as possible, command the respect of his own countrymen. Indutiomarus bitterly resented this action as diminishing his own credit; and, whereas he had already been ill-disposed towards us, this grievance kindled his indignation into a fiercer flame.

After settling these affairs, Caesar moved with the legions to the Italian harbour. There he learned that sixty ships, which had been built in the country of the Meldi, had been driven back by stress of weather, and, failing to keep their course, had returned to the point from which they had started: the rest he found completely fitted out and ready for sea. Some four thousand cavalry from the whole of Gaul and the leading men from all the tribes assembled at the same place. A few of them, of whose fidelity he was assured, he had determined to leave in Gaul, taking the rest with him as hostages, as he was afraid that, during his absence, there would be disturbances in the country.

Amongst the other hostages was Dumnorix, of whom we have already spoken. Caesar had determined to keep this man particularly under his eye, because he knew him to be an ardent revolutionary, fond of power, a man of masterful character, and possessing great influence with the Gauls. Moreover, Dumnorix had stated in the Aeduan council that Caesar was going to confer upon him the sovereignty over the tribe; and the Aedui were seriously offended at this remark, and yet did not venture to send envoys to Caesar to protest or to deprecate his intention. Caesar had learned this from natives who were his friends. Dumnorix at first earnestly prayed for leave to remain in Gaul; partly on the ground that he was not accustomed to being on board ship and dreaded the sea, partly, as he alleged, because he was debarred by religious obligations. Finding that his request was steadily refused and that there was no hope of getting Caesar's consent, he began to importune the Gallic magnates, taking them aside one by one and urging them to remain on the continent: he wrought upon their fears; he told them that there was some strong reason for robbing Gaul of all her men of rank; Caesar shrank from putting them to death under the eyes of their countrymen, but his purpose was to take them all over to Britain and there murder them. He made them promise to stay, and called upon them to swear that they would unite in carrying out the policy which they saw to be for the interest of Gaul. These intrigues were reported to Caesar by numerous informants. Having learned the facts, he determined, inasmuch as it was his policy to treat the Aedui with special distinction, that it was his duty to coerce and intimidate Dumnorix by every means in his power; and, as his frenzy was evidently passing all bounds, to see that he did no injury to himself personally or to the public interest.

For about twenty-five days he was kept waiting in the port, because the northwest wind, which commonly blows throughout a great part of the year on these coasts, made it impossible to sail. Accordingly he did his best to keep Dumnorix steady, but at the same time to acquaint himself with all his plans: at length, taking advantage of favourable weather, he ordered the infantry and cavalry to embark. While everybody's attention was distracted, Dumnorix, accompanied by the Aeduan cavalry, left the camp without Caesar's knowledge, and started for his own country. On receiving the news, Caesar broke off his departure, postponed all his arrangements, and sending a strong detachment of cavalry to pursue Dumnorix, ordered him to be brought back, and, in case he resisted and refused to submit, to be put to death; for he thought that a man who disregarded his authority when he was present would not behave rationally in his absence. When called upon to return he resisted, defended himself with vigour, and adjured his retainers to be true to him, crying loudly and repeatedly that he was a free man and belonged to a free people. The cavalry, in obedience to orders, surrounded the fellow and put him to death; the Aeduan cavalry all returned to Caesar.

Having disposed of this business, Caesar, leaving Labienus on the continent with three legions and two thousand cavalry to protect the ports, provide for a supply of corn, to ascertain what was passing in Gaul, and act as the circumstances of the moment might dictate, set sail towards sunset with five legions and the same number of cavalry as he had left behind. A light southwesterly breeze wafted him on his way: but about midnight the wind dropped; he failed to keep his course; and, drifting far away with the tide, he descried Britain at daybreak lying behind on the port quarter. Then, following the turn of the tide, he rowed hard to gain the part of the island where, as he had learned in the preceding summer, it was best to land. The energy shown by the soldiers on this occasion was most praiseworthy; rowing hard without a break they kept up in their heavily-laden transports with the ships of war. The ships all reached Britain about midday, but no enemy was visible: large numbers, as Caesar found out afterwards from prisoners, had assembled at the spot, but, alarmed by the great number of the ships, more than eight hundred of which, counting those of the preceding year and the private vessels which individuals had built for their own convenience, were visible at once, they had quitted the shore and withdrawn to the higher ground. Caesar disembarked the army and chose a suitable spot for a camp. Having ascertained from prisoners where the enemy's forces were posted, he left ten cohorts and three hundred cavalry near the sea to protect the ships, and marched against the enemy about the third watch. He felt little anxiety for the ships, as, he was leaving them at anchor on a nice open shore. The ships and the detachment which protected them were placed under the command of Quintus Atrius.

After a night march of about twelve miles Caesar descried the enemy's force. Advancing with their cavalry and chariots from higher ground towards a river, they attempted to check our men and force on an action. Beaten off by the cavalry, they fell back into the woods and occupied a well-fortified post of great natural strength, which they had apparently prepared for defence some time before with a view to intestine war, for all the entrances were blocked by felled trees laid close together. Fighting in scattered groups, they threw missiles from the woods, and tried to prevent our men from penetrating within the defences; but the soldiers of the 7th legion, locking their shields over their heads, and piling up lumber against the defences, captured the position and drove them out of the woods at the cost of a few wounded. Caesar, however, forbade them to pursue the fugitives far, partly because he had no knowledge of the ground, partly because much of the day was spent and he wished to leave time for entrenching his camp.

On the following morning he sent a light force of infantry and cavalry, in three columns, to pursue the fugitives. They had advanced a considerable distance, the rearguard being just in sight, when some troopers from Quintus Atrius came to Caesar with the news that there had been a great storm on the preceding night, and that almost all the ships had been damaged and gone ashore, as the anchors and cables did not hold, and the seamen and their captains could not cope with the force of the storm. The collisions between different vessels had therefore caused heavy loss. On receiving this information, Caesar recalled the legions and cavalry, ordering them to damage, defend themselves as they marched, and went back himself to the ships. He saw with his own eyes much the same as he had learned from the messengers and the dispatch which they brought: about forty ships were lost, but it seemed possible to repair the rest, though at the cost of considerable trouble. Accordingly he selected skilled workmen from the legions and ordered others to be sent for from the continent, at the same time writing to tell Labienus to build as many ships as possible with the legions under his command. Although it involved great trouble and labour, he decided that the best plan would be to have all the ships hauled up and connected with the camp by one entrenchment. About ten days were spent in these operations, the troops not suspending work even in the night. As soon as the ships were hauled up and the camp strongly fortified, Caesar left the same force as before to protect them, and advanced to the point from which he had returned. By the time that he arrived reinforcements of Britons had assembled on the spot from all sides. The chief command and the general direction of the campaign had been entrusted by common consent to Cassivellaunus, whose territories are separated from those of the maritime tribes by a river called the Thames, under about eighty miles from the sea. He had before been incessantly at war with the other tribes; but in their alarm at our arrival the Britons had made him commander-in-chief.

The island is triangular in shape, one side being opposite Gaul. One corner of this side, by Kent—the landing-place for almost all ships from Gaul—has an easterly, and the lower one a southerly aspect. The extent of this side is about five hundred miles. The second trends westward towards Spain: off the coast here is Ireland, which is considered only half as large as Britain, though the passage is equal in length to that between Britain and Gaul. Half-way across is an island called Man; and several smaller islands also are believed to be situated opposite this coast, in which, according to some writers, there is continuous night, about the winter solstice, for thirty days. Our inquiries could elicit no information on the subject, but by accurate measurements with a water-clock we could see that the nights were shorter than on the continent. The length of this side, according to the estimate of the natives, is seven hundred miles. The third side has a northerly aspect, and no land lies opposite it; its corner, however, looks, if anything, in the direction of Germany. The length of this side is estimated at eight hundred miles. Thus the whole island is two thousand miles in circumference.

By far the most civilized of all the natives are the inhabitants of Kent—a purely maritime district—whose culture does not differ much from that of the Gauls. The people of the interior do not, for the most part, cultivate grain, but live on milk and flesh-meat and clothe themselves with skins. All the Britons, without exception, stain themselves with woad, which produces a blueish tint; and this gives them a wild look in battle. They wear their hair long, and shave the whole of their body except the head and the upper lip. Groups of ten or twelve men have wives in common, brothers generally sharing with each other and fathers with their sons; the offspring of these unions are counted as the children of the man to whose home the mother, as a virgin, was originally taken.

The enemy's horsemen and charioteers kept up a fierce running fight with our cavalry, the latter, however, getting the best of it at all points, and driving the enemy into the woods and on to the hills: they killed a good many, but, pursuing too eagerly, lost some of their own number. After a time, while our men were off their guard and occupied in entrenching their camp, the enemy suddenly dashed out of the woods, swooped down upon the outpost in front of the camp, and engaged in a hot combat; and when Caesar sent two cohorts—the first of their respective legions—to the rescue, which were separated from each other by a very small interval, our men were unnerved by tactics which were new to them, and they boldly charged between the two and got back unhurt. Quintus Laberius Durus, a military tribune, was killed that day. After additional cohorts had been sent up, the enemy were beaten off.

Throughout this peculiar combat, which was fought in full view of every one and actually in front of the camp, it was clear that the infantry, owing to the weight of their armour, were ill fitted to engage an enemy of this kind; for they could not pursue him when he retreated, and they dared not abandon their regular formation: also that the cavalry fought at great risk, because the enemy generally fell back on purpose, and, after drawing our men a little distance away from the legions, leaped down from their chariots and fought on foot with the odds in their favour. On the other hand, the mode in which their cavalry fought exposed the Romans, alike in retreat and in pursuit, an exactly similar danger. Besides, the Britons never fought in masses, but in groups separated by wide intervals; they posted reserves and relieved each other in succession, fresh vigorous men taking the places of those who were tired.

Next day the enemy occupied a position on the heights at a distance from the camp, and began to show themselves in scattered groups and harass our cavalry, but with less vigour than the day before. At midday, however, Caesar having sent three legions and all his cavalry on a foraging expedition under one of his generals, Gains Trebonius, they suddenly swooped down from all points on the foragers, not hesitating to attack the ordered ranks of the legions. The men charged them vigorously, beat them off, and continued to pursue them until the cavalry, relying upon the support of the legions, which they saw behind them, drove them headlong: they killed a great many of them and never allowed them to rally or make a stand or get down from their chariots. After this rout the reinforcements, which had assembled from all sides, immediately dispersed; and from that time the enemy never encountered us in a general action.

Having ascertained the enemy's plans, Caesar led his army to the Thames, into the territories of Cassivellaunus. The river can only be forded at one spot, and there with difficulty. On the passage reaching this place, he observed that the enemy were drawn up in great force near the opposite bank of the river. The bank was fenced by sharp stakes planted along its edge; and similar stakes were fixed under water and concealed by the river. Having learned these facts from prisoners and deserters, Caesar sent his cavalry on in front, and ordered the legions to follow them speedily; but the men advanced with such swiftness and dash, though they only had their heads above water, that the enemy, unable to withstand the combined onset of infantry and cavalry, quitted the bank and fled.

Cassivellaunus, abandoning, as we have remarked above, all thoughts of regular combat, disbanded the greater part of his force, retaining only about four thousand charioteers; watched our line of march; and, moving a little away from the track, concealed himself in impenetrable wooded spots, and removed the cattle and inhabitants from the open country into the woods in those districts through which he had learned that we intended to march. Whenever our cavalry made a bold dash into the country to plunder and devastate, he sent his charioteers out of the woods (for he was familiar with every track and path), engaged the cavalry to their great peril, and by the fear which he thus inspired prevented them from moving far afield. Caesar had now no choice but to forbid them to move out of touch with the column of infantry, and, by ravaging the country and burning villages, to injure the enemy as far as the legionaries' powers of endurance would allow.

Meanwhile the Trinovantes — about the strongest tribe in that part of the country—sent envoys to Caesar, promising to surrender and obey his commands. Mandubracius, a young chief of this tribe, whose father had been their king and had been put to death by Cassivellaunus, but who had saved his own life by flight, had gone to the continent to join Caesar, and thrown himself upon his protection. The Trinovantes begged Caesar to protect Mandubracius from harm at the hands of Cassivellaunus, and to send him to rule over his own people with full powers. Caesar sent Mandubracius, but ordered them to furnish forty hostages and grain for his army. They promptly obeyed his commands, sending hostages to the number required and also the grain.

As the Trinovantes had been granted protection and immunity from all injury on the part of the soldiers, the Cenimagni, Segontiaci, Ancalites, Japtire of Bibroci, and Cassi sent embassies to Caesar and surrendered. He learned from the envoys that the stronghold of Cassivellaunus, which was protected by woods and marshes, was not far off, and that a considerable number of men and of cattle had assembled in it. The Britons apply the name of stronghold to any woodland spot, difficult of access and fortified with a rampart and trench, to which they are in the habit of resorting in order to escape a hostile raid. Caesar marched to the spot indicated with his legions, and found that the place was of great natural strength and well-fortified; nevertheless he proceeded to assault it on two sides. The enemy stood their ground a short time, but could not sustain the onset of our infantry, and fled precipitately from another part of the stronghold. A great quantity of cattle was found in the place, and many of the garrison were captured as they were trying to escape, and killed.

While the operations above mentioned were going on in this district, Cassivellaunus sent envoys to Kent, which, as we have remarked above, is close to the sea, ordering Cingetonix, Carvilius, Taximagulus, and Segovax, the four kings who ruled over the country, to collect all their forces, make a sudden descent upon the naval camp, and attack it. When they reached the camp, the officers made a sortie, killed many of them, captured their leader Lugotorix, a man of rank, and withdrew their men without loss. On receiving news of the action, Cassivellaunus, who was greatly alarmed by the defection of the tribes, following the numerous disasters which he had sustained and the ravaging of his country, availed himself of the mediation of the Atrebatian, Commius, and sent envoys to Caesar to propose surrender. Caesar had resolved to winter on the continent, because disturbances were likely to break out suddenly in Gaul: not much of the summer remained, and the enemy, as, he knew, could easily spin out the time. Accordingly he ordered hostages to be given, and fixed the tribute which Britain was to pay annually to the Roman People, at the same time strictly forbidding Cassivellaunus to molest Mandubracius or the Trinovantes.

On receiving the hostages, he led back the army to the sea, where he found the ships repaired. When they were launched, he arranged to take the army back in two trips, as he had a large number of prisoners and some ships had been destroyed by the storm. It so happened that of all this numerous fleet, after so many voyages, not a single vessel conveying troops was lost either in this or in the preceding year; while of the ships that were empty, comprising those which had landed troops after the first trip and were sent back to Caesar from the continent, and sixty others which Labienus had constructed after the wreck, only a very few reached their destination, nearly all the rest being driven back. Caesar waited for them a considerable time in vain; and then, for fear the lateness of the season (just before the equinox) should prevent his sailing, he was obliged to pack the troops rather closely. A dead calm followed, and unmooring at the beginning of the second watch, he reached land at dawn and brought all the ships safe ashore.

The harvest that year in Gaul had been scanty on account of drought; and accordingly, after beaching the ships and holding a council of quarters over the Gallic deputies at Samarobriva, Caesar was compelled to quarter the army for the winter on a different principle from that which he had followed in former years, distributing the legions among several tribes. He assigned one of them to Gaius Fabius, one of his generals, another to Quintus Cicero, and a third to Lucius Roscius, with orders to march them into the countries of the Morini, the Nervii, and the Esuvii respectively; quartered the fourth under Titus Labienus in the country of the Remi, just on the frontier of the Treveri; and stationed three in Belgium under the command of the quaestor, Marcus Crassus, and two generals, Lucius Munatiis Plancus and Gaius Trebonius. A single legion, which he had recently raised north of the Po, was sent, along with five cohorts, into the country of the Eburones, a people ruled by Ambiorix and Catuvolcus, the greater part of whose territory is between the Meuse and the Rhine. Quintus Titurius Sabinus and Aurunculeius Cotta were ordered to take command of these troops. This method of distributing the legions Caesar regarded as the easiest way of remedying the scarcity of corn. And in fact the quarters of all the legions, except the one which he had sent under Lucius Roscius into a perfectly tranquil and undisturbed district, were enclosed within an area whose extreme points were only one hundred miles apart. Caesar determined to remain himself in Gaul until he ascertained that the legions were in their several positions and their camps entrenched.

Among the Carnutes was a man of noble birth, named Tasgetius, whose ancestors had held sovereignty in their own country, and to whom Caesar, in recognition of his energy and devotion (for in all his campaigns he had found his services exceptionally valuable), had restored their position. He was now in the third year of his reign when his enemies, with the avowed sanction of many of the citizens, assassinated him. The crime was reported to Caesar. Fearing that, as many were implicated, the tribe might be impelled by them to revolt, he ordered Lucius Plancus to march rapidly with his legion from Belgium into the country of the Carnutes, winter there, and arrest the individuals whom he found responsible for Tasgetius's death. Meanwhile he was informed by all the officers under whose command he had placed the legions, that they had reached their respective quarters and that the positions were entrenched.

About fifteen days after the positions had been taken up a sudden and alarming revolt was voiced, started by Ambiorix and Catuvolcus. They had waited upon Sabinus and Cotta at the frontier of their kingdom and conveyed the corn to the camp when, egged on by emissaries from the Sabinus, roused their tribesmen, suddenly overpowered a party who were cutting wood, and came with a large force to attack the camp. Our men speedily armed and mounted the rampart; some Spanish horse were sent out from one side and came off victorious in a cavalry combat; and the enemy, seeing the futility of their attempt, called off their troops. Then, after the manner of their nation, they shouted for some one on our side to go out and parley with them, declaring that they had something to say, affecting both sides, which, they hoped, might settle disputes.

Gaius Arpineius, a Roman knight, who was intimate with Quintus Titunus, was sent to confer with them, accompanied by one Quintus Ambiorix Junius, a Spaniard, who had been in the habit of visiting as Caesar's representative, troops to Ambiorix addressed them in the following terms. He would admit that he was deeply indebted to Caesar for various acts of kindness, having by his good offices been relieved of tribute which he had regularly paid to his neighbours, the Aduatuci, while his own son and his brother's, who had been sent to them as hostages and by them enslaved and imprisoned, had been sent back by Caesar; moreover, in attacking the camp, he had not acted spontaneously or on his own judgement, but under the compulsion of the tribe, his sovereignty being so far limited that the multitude had no less power over him than he over them. Furthermore, the tribe had only taken up arms because it was unable to resist a sudden conspiracy on the part of the Gauls. This he could easily prove from his own insignificance; for he was not so ignorant of affairs as to imagine that his troops could get the better of the Roman People. Gaul, however, was unanimous: that very day had been fixed for a general attack on Caesar's camps, to prevent any one legion from assisting another. It was not easy for Gauls to refuse help to their countrymen, especially as the object of the movement was, of course, to recover national liberty. However, having done his duty to them on the score of patriotism, he now thought of what he owed to Caesar for his favours; he therefore urged, nay, implored, Titurius, as a friend whose salt he had eaten, to consider his own and his soldiers' safety. A large force of German mercenaries had crossed the Rhine, and would be at hand in a couple of days. It was for the Roman generals to decide whether they would withdraw their troops from camp before the neighbouring tribes could find out, and transfer them either to Cicero or to Labienus, the former of whom was about fifty miles off, the latter rather more. He would solemnly promise on oath to grant them a safe-conduct through his territory. In so doing he was acting in the interests of his tribe, which would be relieved from the burden of the camp, and showing his gratitude for Caesar's services. After this speech Ambiorix withdrew.

Arpineius and Junius reported to the generals what they had heard. The suddenness of the news made them anxious; and although it came from an enemy, they did not think it wise to disregard it. What most alarmed them was that it seemed hardly credible that an obscure and insignificant tribe like the Eburones would have ventured to make war upon the Roman People on their own account. Accordingly they referred the question to a council of war, and a violent dispute arose between them. Lucius Aurunculeius and many of the tribunes and chief centurions held that it would not be right to take any step without due consideration or to leave the camp without authority from Caesar. They pointed out that, as the camp was fortified, it was possible to hold out against any force, even of Germans. Experience proved this; for they had resolutely sustained the enemy's first onslaught and inflicted heavy loss upon him into the bargain; they were not pressed for supplies; and reinforcements would arrive in time from the nearest camp and from Caesar himself: finally, what could be more puerile or more unsoldierlike than to make a momentous decision on the advice of an enemy.

In opposition to these arguments, Titurius loudly insisted that it would be too late to act when the enemy's reinforcements had arrived with their German allies, or the nearest camp had suffered a disaster. The time for deliberation was short. Caesar, so he believed, had started for Italy; otherwise the Carnutes would not have dreamed of putting Tasgetius to death; nor, if Caesar had been at hand, would the Eburones have held our men so cheap as to attack the camp. It was not to the enemy that he looked for guidance, but to facts. The Rhine was close by. The Germans were embittered by the death of Ariovistus and our earlier victories; Gaul was ablaze with indignation at all the indignities she had suffered, at her subjection to the dominion of the Roman People, and at the eclipse of her former military renown. Finally, who could persuade himself that Ambiorix had ventured upon an enterprise like this without solid support? His advice was safe either way: if nothing untoward happened, they would get to the nearest legion without any danger; if the whole of Gaul were in league with the Germans, their only safety was in prompt action. As to Cotta and those who took the opposite view, what would be the result of following their counsel? It involved, if not immediate danger, at all events the prospect of a long blockade accompanied by famine.

Such were the arguments on both sides; and, as Cotta and the chief centurions continued to oppose him vehemently, Sabinus, raising his voice, so that a large number of the soldiers might hear, cried, "Have your own way, if you like. Death has no more terrors for me than for you. The men will judge; and if any disaster happens, they'll call you to account for it; whereas if you, Cotta, would consent, on the day after tomorrow they would join their comrades in the nearest camp and share the fortune of war with them, instead of perishing by the sword or by famine, like outcasts far removed from their fellows."

The assembled officers stood up. Sabinus took the two generals by the hand and implored them not to precipitate a disaster by quarrelling and obstinacy; go or stay, everything could be managed if only they were all unanimous; but no good, that they could see, would come from quarrelling. The dispute dragged on till midnight. At length Cotta, overborne by superior authority, gave way: Sabinus's view prevailed. An order was issued that the troops were to march at daybreak. The men stayed up for the rest of the night, every one looking about to see what he could take with him, what part of his winter's kit he would be forced to leave behind. Men thought of every argument to persuade themselves that they could not remain without danger, and that the danger would be increased by protracted watches and consequent exhaustion. At dawn they marched out of camp.

The enemy, perceiving from the hum of Ambiorix's voices in the night and the Romans remanning the column, stationed themselves in ambush in two divisions in the woods, in a convenient position, screened from observation, about two miles off, to await their arrival; and when the bulk of the column had moved down into a large defile, they suddenly showed themselves on either side of it, hustled forward the rearguard, checked the ascent of the van, and forced on a combat on a spot most unfavourable for our men.

And now Titurius, having exercised no forethought, lost all nerve, ran from place to place, and tried to get the cohorts into formation; but he did this nervously and in such a way that one could see he was at his wits' end, as indeed generally happens to men who are forced to decide on the spur of the moment. Cotta, on the other hand, who had foreseen, that these things might happen on the march, and for that reason had declined to sanction the movement, was fully equal to the occasion : he performed a general's part in calling upon the men and encouraging them, and in action he did the work of a private soldier. Owing to the length of the column, it was not easy for the generals to look to everything themselves and make the necessary arrangements for every part of the field; they therefore ordered the word to be given to abandon the baggage and form in a square. Although, in the circumstances, the plan cannot be condemned, its effect was nevertheless disastrous; for, as it would evidently not have been resorted to but for extreme anxiety and despair, it made our soldiers despondent and stimulated the enemy's ardour for battle. Moreover, as was inevitable, soldiers were everywhere abandoning their companies, every one hurrying to the baggage-train to look for his most cherished possessions and carry them off; while the whole field was a scene of weeping and uproar.

The natives, on their part, showed no lack of resource. Their leaders ordered the word to be passed along the line that no man was to stir from his post: the booty was their prize, and whatever the Romans left was to be kept for them. They were to remember, then, that everything depended upon victory. Our men were as brave as they and not overmatched in point of numbers: forsaken by their leader and by fortune, they trusted for safety to courage alone; and as often as a cohort charged, there many of the enemy fell. Observing this, Ambiorix ordered the word to be given for the tribesmen to throw their missiles from a distance and not go too close; wherever the Romans charged, they were to fall back: being lightly armed and in constant training, they could not suffer; when the Romans attempted to rejoin their companies, they were to pursue.

The order was carefully obeyed. Whenever a cohort left the square and charged, the enemy ran swiftly away. Meanwhile the cohort was necessarily exposed, and missiles fell on its unshielded flank. When the men began to return to the position they had left, they were surrounded by the enemy who stood near them as well as by those who had fallen back: if, on the other hand, they chose to hold their ground, there was no room for courage; and, being crowded together, they could not avoid the missiles hurled by that huge host. Yet, harassed by all these disadvantages and in spite of heavy loss, they held out; and throughout a combat which lasted the greater part of the day, from dawn till the eighth hour, they did nothing unworthy of themselves. At this moment Titus Balventius, who, in the previous year, had been chief centurion of his legion—a brave and highly-respected man— had both his thighs pierced by a javelin; Quintus Lucanius, an officer of the same rank, while trying to save his son, who had been surrounded, was killed, fighting most gallantly; and Lucius Cotta, while cheering on all the cohorts and centuries, was struck full in the face by a stone from a sling.

Quintus Titurius was greatly agitated at the aspect of affairs; and descrying Ambiorix some way off haranguing his men, he sent his interpreter, Gnaeus Pompeius, to ask for quarter for himself and the troops. In reply to this appeal, Ambiorix said that Titurius might speak to him if he liked; he hoped that the host might be induced to consent as far as the safety of the troops was concerned: Titurius, at all events, should come to no harm, and for that he would pledge his word. Sabinus consulted the wounded Cotta, proposing that, if he approved, they should withdraw from the action and together confer with Ambiorix, who might, he hoped, be induced to spare both them and the troops. Cotta replied that he would not meet an armed enemy; and to this resolve he adhered.

Sabinus ordered the tribunes and centurions whom he had round him at the moment to follow him. On approaching Ambiorix, he was ordered to lay down his arms, and obeyed, telling his officers to do the same. The principals were discussing about terms, and Ambiorix was purposely making a long speech, when Sabinus was gradually surrounded and slain. Then, in the native fashion, they shouted "Victory," and with a loud yell dashed into our ranks and broke them. Lucius Cotta fell fighting where he stood, and the bulk of the men with him. The rest retreated to the camp, whence they had come. Lucius Petrosidius, the standard-bearer, finding himself beset by a multitude of enemies, threw his eagle inside the rampart, and, fighting most gallantly in front of the camp, was slain. His comrades with difficulty sustained the onslaught till night: then, seeing that hope was gone, they all slew each other to the last man. A few, who had slipped away from the battle, made their way by the woodland tracks to the quarters of Titus Labienus and told him what had occurred.

Ambiorix was in high glee at his victory. Bidding his infantry follow him, he started at once with his cavalry for the country of the Aduatuci, who were conterminous with his kingdom, and pushed on throughout the night and the next day. Having related what had happened and roused the Aduatuci, he reached the country of the Nervii next day, and urged them not to lose the chance of establishing their independence for good and taking vengeance upon the Romans for the wrongs which they had suffered. Two generals, he told them, were killed, and a great part of the army had perished: there would be no difficulty in surprising the legion that was wintering under Cicero and destroying it. He promised to help in the attack, and the Nervii were readily persuaded by his words.

Accordingly they at once sent off messengers to the Ceutrones, Grudii, Levaci, Pleumoxii, and Geidumni, all of whom are under their sway, raised as large a force as they could, and swooped down unexpectedly upon Cicero's camp before the news of Titunus's death reached him. In his case too the inevitable result was that some soldiers who had gone off into the forests to fetch wood for fortification were cut off by the sudden arrival of the cavalry and surrounded; and the Eburones, Nervii, and Aduatuci, accompanied by all their allies and dependents, attacked the legion in great force. Our men flew to arms and mounted the rampart. They could barely hold out that day, for the enemy staked all their hopes upon swift action; and they were confident that if they were victorious on this occasion, their victory would be lasting.

Cicero instantly sent dispatches to Caesar, offering large rewards to the messengers if they succeeded in delivering them; but all the roads were blocked, and the messengers were intercepted. In the night as many as one hundred and twenty towers were run up with incredible speed out of the timber which the men had collected for fortification; and the defects in the works were made good. Next day the enemy, who had been largely reinforced, renewed their attack on the camp, and filled up the trench. Our men resisted in the same way as the day before; and day after day the course of events was the same. Work went on without a break throughout the night: neither the sick nor the wounded could get a chance of rest. Everything necessary for repelling the next day's attack was got ready in the night: numerous stakes, burnt and hardened at the ends, and a large number of heavy pikes were prepared; the towers were furnished with platforms, and embattled breastworks of wattle-work were fastened to them. Cicero himself, though he was in very poor health, would not allow himself to rest even in the nighttime; so that the soldiers actually thronged round him and by their remonstrances constrained him to spare himself.

And now the commanders and chieftains of the Nervii, who had some claim to address Cicero and were on friendly terms with him, expressed the wish to have an interview. Their request being granted, they repeated the same tale that Ambiorix had told in dealing with Titurius: the whole of Gaul was in arms; the Germans had crossed the Rhine; Caesar's camp and the camps of the other officers were beleaguered. They also mentioned the death of Sabinus, and pointed to Ambiorix to gain credit for their story. The Romans, they said, were mistaken if they expected any help from men who were themselves desperate. However, they had no quarrel with Cicero and the Roman People, except that they objected to winter camps and did not want the custom to become established: they might leave their camp in safety, as far as they were concerned, and go wherever they liked, without fear. To these arguments Cicero simply replied that it was not the habit of the Roman People to accept terms from an armed enemy: if the Gauls would lay down their arms, they could send envoys to Caesar and avail themselves of his intercession; Caesar was just, and he hoped that they would obtain what they asked.

After this rebuff the Nervii invested the Roman siege camp with a rampart ten feet high and a trench fifteen feet wide. They had learned the secret from observing our methods in former years; and they also got hints from prisoners whom they had taken, belonging to our army: but, as they had no supply of iron tools suitable for the purpose, they were obliged to cut the sods with their swords, and take up the earth with their hands and in their cloaks. From this one could form an estimate of their vast numbers; for in less than three hours they completed a contravallation three miles in extent; and during the next few days they proceeded, after due preparation, to construct towers proportioned to the height of the Roman rampart, grappling-hooks, and sappers' huts, which the prisoners had also taught them how to make.

On the seventh day of the siege a great a desperate gale sprang up; and the besiegers began to sling resolutely red-hot bullets made of plastic clay and to throw burning darts at the huts, which, in the Gallic fashion, were thatched. The huts quickly took fire, and, owing to the force of the wind, the flames spread all over the camp. The enemy cheered loudly, as if victory were already certain, and began to move forward their towers and huts and to escalade the rampart. But so great was the courage of the legionaries, and such was their presence of mind, that, although they were everywhere scorched by the flames and harassed by a hail of missiles, and knew that all their baggage and everything that belonged to them was on fire, not only did none of them abandon his post on the rampart, but hardly a man even looked round; and in that hour all fought with the utmost dash and resolution. This was far the most trying day for our men; but nevertheless the result was that a very large number of the enemy were killed or wounded, for they had crowded right under the rampart, and the rear ranks would not allow those in front to fall back. The fire abating a little, a tower was pushed up at one point and brought into contact with the rampart, when the centurions of the 3rd cohort stepped back from the spot where they were standing, withdrew all their men, and began to challenge the enemy, by voice and gesture, to come on if they liked; but not one of them dared to advance. Then they were sent flying by showers of stones from every side; and the tower was set on fire.

In this legion there were two centurions, Pullo and Vorenus, who, by dint of extraordinary courage, were getting close to the first grade. They were forever disputing as to which was the better man; and every year they contended for promotion with the greatest acrimony. When the fighting at the entrenchment was at its hottest, "Vorenus," cried Pullo, "why hesitate? What better chance can you want of proving your courage? This day shall settle our disputes." With these words he walked outside the entrenchment, and where the enemy's ranks were thickest dashed in. Vorenus of course did not keep inside the rampart: afraid of what every one would think, he followed his rival. At a moderate distance, Pullo threw his javelin at the enemy and struck one of them as he was charging out of the throng: he fainted from the blow, and the enemy protected him with their shields, and all together hurled their missiles at his assailant and cut off his retreat. Pullo's shield was transfixed, and the dart stuck in his sword-belt. The blow knocked his scabbard round, so that his hand was hampered as he tried to draw his sword; and in his helpless state the enemy thronged round him. His rival, Vorenus, ran to his rescue, and helped him in his stress. In a moment the whole multitude left Pullo, believing that the dart had killed him, and turned upon Vorenus. Sword in hand, Vorenus fought at bay, killed one of his assailants, and forced the rest a little way back; but pressing on too eagerly, he ran headlong down a slope and fell. He was in his turn surrounded, but Pullo succoured him, and the two men slew several of the enemy and got back, safe and sound and covered with glory, into the entrenchment. Thus Fortune made them her puppets in rivalry and combat, rival helping rival and each saving the other, so that it was impossible to decide which was to be deemed the braver man.

Day by day the perils and the hardships of the siege increased, for this reason above all, a dispatch to that, many of the soldiers being enfeebled by wounds, few were now available for defence; and day by day messengers were sent off with dispatches to Caesar in more and more rapid succession. Some of them were caught and tortured to death in sight of our soldiers. There was a solitary Nervian in the camp, named Vertico, a man of good birth, who at the beginning of the siege had taken refuge with Cicero, and had done him loyal service. This man induced his slave, by the hope of freedom and by large rewards, to take a dispatch to Caesar. The slave carried the dispatch tied to a javelin, and, being a Gaul himself, went among the Gauls without exciting any suspicion, and made his way to Caesar, who learned from him the perils that encompassed Cicero and the legion.

Caesar received the dispatch about the eleventh hour. He at once sent a messenger the rescue, to Marcus Crassus, the quaestor, whose camp was twenty-five miles off, ordering his legion to march at midnight and join him speedily. Crassus left on receiving the message. Caesar sent another messenger to Gaius Fabius, bidding him march his legion into the country of the Atrebates, through which he knew that he would himself have to go, and wrote to Labienus, directing him, if he could do so consistently with the public interest, to move with his legion to the country of the Nervii. As the rest of the army was rather too far off, he did not think it wise to wait for it; but he got together about four hundred horsemen from the nearest camps.

About the third hour he learned from the scouting parties of Crassus's advanced guard that he was coming, and on the same day marched twenty miles. He left Crassus in command at Samarobriva, and assigned him a legion, as he was leaving behind the heavy baggage of the army, the hostages of the various tribes, the state papers, and the whole of the grain which he had brought there to last the winter. Fabius obeyed orders, and, without any serious delay, joined Caesar on the march with his legion. Labienus was aware of the fate of Sabinus and the massacre of his cohorts; the whole host of the Treveri was upon him; and he was afraid that, if he quitted his camp like a runaway, he would not be able to sustain the enemy's attack, especially as he knew that they were elated by their recent success; accordingly he sent a dispatch to Caesar, telling him that it would be very dangerous for him to withdraw his legion from its quarters, describing what had happened in the country of the Eburones, and explaining that the whole host of the Treveri, horse and foot, had taken up a position three miles from his camp.

Caesar approved his decision; and although he had only two legions instead of the three which he had expected, he saw that success was just possible with speed. By forced marches he advanced into the Nervian territory, where, learning from prisoners what was going on at Cicero's camp, and realizing the extreme peril of his position, he induced one of his Gallic horsemen to carry a letter to him. He wrote it in Greek characters, for fear it might be intercepted and his plans become known to the enemy, and advised the man, if he could not get into the camp, to tie the letter to the thong of a javelin and throw it inside the entrenchment. He said that he had started with his legions and would soon arrive, and exhorted Cicero to be true to himself. The Gaul, dreading the risk of detection, threw his javelin, as he had been directed. It chanced to lodge in a tower and was not noticed by our men for two days; but on the third day a soldier observed it, took it down, and brought it to Cicero. After perusing the letter, he paraded the troops and read it aloud, to their intense delight. And now the smoke of distant fires was seen; and all doubt about the coming of the legions was dispelled.

The Gauls, on hearing the news from their patrols, raised the siege, and marched to the valley.

Cavalry skirmishes took place that day by the water-side, but the two armies maintained their respective positions, the Gauls waiting for reinforcements, which had not yet come up, while Caesar hoped that he might perhaps succeed, by feigning fear, in enticing the enemy over to his position, and thus be able to fight on the near side of the valley, in front of his camp; or, failing that, might reconnoitre the roads and so cross valley and rivulet with less risk. At daybreak the enemy's horse came close up to the camp and engaged ours. Caesar deliberately ordered his cavalry to give way and fall back into the camp, at the same time directing the troops to increase the height of the rampart on all sides and block up the gateways, and in doing so to move about as hurriedly as possible and do their work with a pretence of fear.

Lured on by all these devices, the enemy crossed over and formed up on unfavourable ground; and as our men were actually withdrawn from the rampart, they ventured nearer, and threw missiles from all sides into the entrenchment, sending round criers with orders to announce that if any one, Gaul or Roman, cared to come over and join them before the third hour, he might safely do so, but that after that time the permission would be withdrawn. The gates were blocked, but merely for show, with a single row of sods; and, fancying that they could not break through that way, some of them, in their contempt for our men, began to demolish the rampart with their bare hands, and others to fill up the ditches. Then, while the infantry rushed out from all the gates, Caesar let loose the cavalry and quickly sent the enemy flying, not a man standing to strike one blow. Many were slain, and all had to drop their arms.

Caesar was afraid to continue the pursuit, because there were woods and marshes in the way, and he could see no chance of inflicting the smallest loss upon the fugitives; but he reached Cicero on the same day without the loss of a man. He surveyed with admiration the towers which the enemy had erected, their sappers' huts, and earthworks: when the legion was paraded, he found that not one man in ten had got off unwounded; and from all these things he appreciated the danger and the resolution with which the defence had been conducted. Warmly commending Cicero for his services, and also the legion, he addressed individually the centurions and tribunes, who, as he learned from Cicero's report, had shown distinguished gallantry. Having obtained correct information from prisoners about the fate of Sabinus and Cotta, he paraded the legion next day, described what had happened, and cheered and reassured the men:—the culpable rashness of a general officer had entailed a disaster; but they must take it calmly, for the blessing of the immortal gods and their own valour had repaired the loss; and the enemy had as little cause for lasting exultation as they for inordinate grief.

Meanwhile the news of Caesar's victory was brought to Labienus with incredible rapidity: he was sixty miles from Cicero's camp, and it was past the ninth hour when Caesar arrived there; yet before midnight a shout arose at the gates of his camp, announcing a victory and conveying the congratulations of the Remi. When the news reached the Treveri, Indutiomarus, who had determined to attack Labienus's camp on the following day, made off in the night and withdrew his whole force into their country. Caesar sent back Fabius and his legion to camp, intending to winter himself with three legions in three separate camps near Samarobriva; and, as such serious disturbances had broken out in Gaul, he determined to remain with the army the whole winter. When the news of Sabinus's calamitous death spread abroad, almost all the tribes of Gaul began to form warlike projects, sending messages and embassies in all directions, trying to ascertain each other's plans and see who would take the initiative, and holding meetings by night in lonely places. Caesar indeed had hardly any respite all through the winter from the harassing expectation of hearing news about schemes and outbreaks on the part of the Gauls. Among the reports which reached him was one from Lucius Roscius, whom he had placed in command of the 13th legion, announcing that large numbers of Gauls had assembled from the Armorican tribes, as they are called, to attack him, and had been within eight miles of his camp, but that, on receiving the announcement of Caesar's victory, they had made off like runaways.

Caesar summoned the leading men of each tribe to his presence; frightened some by letting them know that he was aware of what was going on; encouraged others; and thus managed to keep a large part of Gaul obedient. The government of the Senones, however, an extremely powerful tribe, who have great influence among the Gauls, attempted to put to death Cavarinus, whom Caesar had set over them as king, and whose brother, Moritasgus, had held sovereignty when Caesar came to Gaul, and his ancestors before him. Cavarinus, anticipating their design, had fled. They pursued him as far as the frontier, dethroned and banished him, and then sent envoys to Caesar to explain. He ordered the whole council to appear before him; but they refused to obey. The mere fact that leaders had been found to strike the first blow had so much weight with the ignorant natives, and wrought such a complete change in the temper of all, that, except the Aedui and the Remi, whom Caesar always treated with special distinction— the former in consideration of their long-standing and steady loyalty to the Roman People, the latter for their recent services in the war—there was hardly a single tribe that we did not suspect. And indeed I am inclined to think that their conduct was quite natural, for this reason among many others:—the Gauls were once the most warlike of all people; and it was most bitterly mortifying to them to have so completely lost that reputation as to be forced to submit to the domination of the Roman People through the winter, without intermission. The Treveri and Indutiomarus continued sending envoys across the Rhine, making overtures to tribes, promising them money, and assuring them that the greater part of our army had been destroyed and that the existent was insignificant. Not a single German tribe, however, could be induced to cross the Rhine: they said that they had tried twice—in the war with Ariovistus and the migration of the Tencteri— and would not tempt fortune any more. Not-withstanding this disappointment, Indutiomarus proceeded to raise forces and drill them, to procure horses from the neighbouring peoples, and by large rewards to induce exiles and condemned criminals from the whole of Gaul to join him. Indeed, he had now acquired such prestige in the country by these measures that embassies poured in from all quarters, soliciting his countenance and alliance both privately and with the authority of their respective governments.

Finding that advances were being spontaneously made to him, that on one side there were the Senones and Carnutes, stimulated by consciousness of guilt, on the other the Nervii and Aduatuci, preparing to attack the Romans, and that once he made a forward movement outside his frontier, he would have no lack of volunteers, he gave notice of a muster in arms. This, by Gallic usage is tantamount to a declaration of war. By intertribal law all adult males are obliged to attend the muster under arms; and the last comer is tortured to death in sight of the host. At this gathering Indutiomarus passed judgement upon Cingetorix, the leader of the rival party, his own son-in-law (who, as we have already observed, had thrown in his lot with Caesar and had not failed him), declaring him a public enemy, and confiscated his property. After this step, he announced before the assembled host that he had been invited by the Senones, the Carnutes, and several other tribes to join them, and intended to march through the territory of the Remi, ravaging their lands, but first of all to attack the camp of Labienus. He then gave the necessary orders. Labienus, who was ensconced in a strongly fortified camp of great natural strength, felt no anxiety for himself or his legion: his only care was not to lose any chance of striking a decisive blow. Accordingly, having ascertained from Cingetorix and his relations the drift of Indutiomarus's speech at the gathering, he sent messengers to the neighbouring tribes and summoned cavalry from all sides, naming a date for their arrival. Meanwhile Indutiomarus rode up and down almost every day close under the rampart of the camp, sometimes to examine the position, sometimes to converse with or intimidate the soldiers; while all his troopers generally threw missiles inside the rampart. Labienus steadily kept his men within the entrenchment, and did everything in his power to foster the belief that he was cowed.

Day after day Indutiomarus moved up to the camp with growing contempt. Labienus made the cavalry, which he had summoned from all the neighbouring tribes, enter the entrenchment in a single night, and was so careful to keep all his troops inside under guard that it was quite impossible for their arrival to be made public or reach the knowledge of the Treveri. Meanwhile Indutiomarus, according to his daily custom, came up to the camp and spent a great part of the day there, his troopers throwing missiles and challenging our men in the most insulting terms to fight. The men made no reply; and towards evening, thinking it time to be off, they broke up and dispersed. Suddenly Labienus sent out orders that when the enemy were panic-stricken and routed, as he rightly foresaw would happen, all ranks were to look out for Indutiomarus, and not a man strike a blow till he saw Indutiomarus killed; for he resolved that he should not gain time to escape by delay with the rest. He set a heavy price upon his head, and sent a number of cohorts to support the cavalry. Fortune justified the general's plans. With every man on his track, Indutiomarus was caught and killed in the act of fording a river, and his head brought back to camp. The cavalry on their way back pursued and killed all they could. On learning what had happened, the forces of the Eburones and Nervii which had assembled all went off; and thenceforward Caesar found Gaul somewhat more peaceable.

BOOK VI

CONTINUED DISTURBANCES IN NORTH-EASTERN GAUL – CAESAR'S SECOND PASSAGE OF THE RHINE – MANNERS AND CUSTOMS, RELIGIONS AND INSTITUTIONS OF THE GAULS AND GERMANS – ILL-OMENED ADUATUCA – EXTERMINATION OF THE EBURONES

Anticipating, for many reasons, increased disturbances in Gaul, Caesar determined to employ his lieutenants, Marcus Silanus, Gaius Antistius Reginus, and Titus Sextius, in raising troops. At the same time he requested Gnaeus Pompeius, then proconsul, who, though vested with the command of an army, remained, on public grounds, in the neighbourhood of the capital, to order the recruits from Cisalpine Gaul whom he had sworn in, when consul, to join their standards and repair to his quarters; for, looking to the future as well as the present, he thought it essential, with a view to impressing public opinion in Gaul, that the resources of Italy should appear sufficient not only to repair speedily any disaster in the field, but actually to increase the original army. Pompeius acceded to this request from motives of patriotism as well as of friendship: the levy was speedily completed by Caesar's officers; and thus before the close of winter three legions were organized and mobilized, making double the number of the cohorts lost under Quintus Titurius. By this swift display of armed force he showed what could be effected by the organization and resources of the Roman People.

After the death of Indutiomarus, already described, his command was transferred to his relations, who tried persistently to gain the support of the neighbouring German rebellious peoples by promises of money. Failing to obtain the Nervii, a favourable answer from their neighbours, they made overtures to the more distant tribes, and found some compliant. The parties mutually confirmed the alliance by oath, and hostages were given as security for the money; at the same time the Treveri made a formal alliance with Ambiorix. On learning this, Caesar felt it necessary to take the field at once, for he saw that warlike preparations were afoot on all sides. The Nervii, the Aduatuci, and the Menapii, combined with all the local Germans, were in arms; the Senones refused to attend at his bidding, and were in communication with the Carnutes and the neighbouring peoples; while the Treveri were sending embassies in rapid succession to solicit the aid of the Germans.

Accordingly, before the winter was over, Caesar assembled the four nearest legions, made an unexpected raid into the country of the Nervii, and, before they could either concentrate or flee, captured a large number of cattle and also of men, handed over this booty to the troops, ravaged the country, and compelled the Nervii to surrender and give hostages. This affair rapidly disposed of, he withdrew the legions once more into winter quarters. In the early spring he convened a Gallic council, as usual. All the delegates, except the Senones, Carnutes, and Treveri, attended; and, regarding their absence as the first step in rebellion, he determined to mark his sense of its paramount importance, and accordingly transferred the council to Lutetia, a town belonging to the Parisii. The Parisii were conterminous with the

Senones, and the two had, within recent times, formed one state; but on this occasion were believed to have dissociated themselves from the Senones. After announcing the adjournment from the front of the tribunal in his camp, Caesar started on the same day with his legions for the country of the Senones, and made his way thither by forced marches. The ringleader of the conspiracy, on learning his approach, directed the populace to assemble in the forts. They endeavoured to obey; but before they could do so the arrival of the Romans was announced. Compelled to abandon their intention, they sent envoys to entreat Caesar's forbearance, who were introduced by the Aedui, under whose protection their tribe had been from time immemorial. At the request of the Aedui, Caesar readily pardoned them and accepted their excuses, feeling that the summer-time should be devoted to the impending war, not to investigation. He ordered them, however, to find a hundred hostages, whom he handed over to the custody of the Aedui. The Carnutes likewise sent envoys and hostages to Caesar's quarters, availing themselves of the intercession of the Remi, whose dependents they were, and received the same answer. Caesar then finished the business of the council, and directed the tribes to furnish cavalry.

Having tranquillized this part of Gaul, he devoted himself, heart and soul, to the campaign against the Treveri and Ambiorix. He directed Cavarinus to take the cavalry of the Senones and accompany him, for fear any disturbance should arise among the tribe from his resentment or from the odium which he had brought upon himself. After making these arrangements, he endeavoured to fathom Ambiorix's intentions, for he regarded it as certain that he did not intend to fight. Close to the country of the Eburones, and protected by continuous marshes and forests, were the Menapii, the only people in Gaul who had never sent envoys to Caesar to sue for peace. He knew that they were on friendly terms with Ambiorix; and he had ascertained that they had also, through the medium of the Treveri, come to an understanding with the Germans. His idea was to deprive Ambiorix of the support of these tribes before attacking him, lest, in despair, he should take refuge in the country of the Menapii, or be driven to join the peoples beyond the Rhine. Having decided upon this plan, he sent the heavy baggage of the whole army into the country of the Treveri, to Labienus, and ordered two legions to join him; while he started in person with five legions in light marching order for the country of the Menapii. They had not assembled any force, but, relying upon the strength of their country, took refuge in the forests and marshes and transferred their belongings thither.

Caesar placed Gaius Fabius and the quaestor, Marcus Crassus, in command of divisions, and, rapidly constructing causeways, advanced with the three columns, burned homesteads and hamlets, and captured a large number of cattle and also of men. Yielding to this pressure, the Menapii sent envoys to him to sue for peace. He took hostages, from them, and warned them that he would treat them as enemies if they admitted either Ambiorix or his agents within their territories. After settling these affairs, he left the Atrebatian, Commius, with a body of cavalry as a warden among the Menapii, and marched in person for the country of the Treveri.

While Caesar was engaged in these operations, the Treveri, who had assembled a large force of infantry and cavalry, were preparing to attack Labienus and the single legion which was wintering in their country. They were within two days' march of his position when they learned that the two legions dispatched by Caesar had arrived. Encamping fifteen miles off, they determined to wait for reinforcements from the Germans. Labienus ascertained their intention, and, hoping that their rashness would give him an opportunity for bringing them to action, left five cohorts to guard his baggage, marched against the enemy with twenty-five cohorts and a large body of cavalry, and encamped within a mile of them. Between him and the enemy there was a river with steep banks, which was difficult to cross. He had no intention of crossing it himself, and did not think it likely that the enemy would do so. Their prospects of obtaining reinforcements were daily improving. Labienus remarked openly in a council of war that, as the Germans were said to be approaching, he would not risk his own reputation and the safety of his army, but would strike his camp next morning at dawn. His words rapidly reached the enemy; for out of a large body of Gallic cavalry it was naturally inevitable that some should sympathize with the Gallic cause. In the night Labienus called together the tribunes and chief centurions, explained his plans, and, with the view of making the enemy believe that he was afraid of them, ordered the camp to be struck with more noise and bustle than is customary with Romans. By this means he contrived that his departure should resemble a flight. This also was reported to the enemy by their patrols before daybreak; for the two camps were very close together. The rearguard had barely got outside the entrenchment when the Gauls told each other not to let the hoped-for prize slip from their grasp: it would be waste of time to wait for German aid when the Romans were panic-stricken; and it was humiliating, with their huge host, to shrink from attacking a handful of men, especially as they were running away and hampered by their baggage. With this encouragement, they did not hesitate to cross the river and force on an action on unfavourable ground. Labienus had divined that this would happen, and hoping to lure them all across the stream, he kept quietly moving on, feigning, as before, that he was marching away. Then, sending on the baggage a little way and parking it on a knoll, "Soldiers," he said, "you have got your chance. You have the enemy in your grasp: he is in a bad position, where he is not free to act. Show the same courage under my command that you have shown many a time under the chief: imagine that he is here, watching what is going on." With these words he ordered the column to wheel into line of battle and advance, and, sending a few troops of horse to protect the baggage, posted the rest on the flanks. The men raised a cheer and swiftly launched their javelins against the enemy. Seeing the runaways unexpectedly advancing to attack them, they could not even sustain their charge, but the moment they closed, fled precipitately to the nearest woods. Labienus hunted them down with his cavalry, killed a large number, took numerous prisoners, and a few days afterwards received the submission of the tribe; for the Germans, who were on their way to reinforce the Treveri, hearing of their rout, went back home. The relations of Indutiomarus, who had started the revolt, followed in their train and fled the country. The chief authority was transferred to Cingetorix, who, as we have explained, had from the outset remained steadily loyal.

After his march from the country of the Menapii to that of the Treveri, Caesar determined to cross the Rhine, for two reasons:—first, because Caesar again had sent the Treveri reinforcements; and secondly, to prevent allies of Ambiorix from finding an asylum in their country. Accordingly he proceeded to construct a bridge a little above the spot where he had crossed before. The principle of construction was perfectly familiar; and by great energy on the part of the men, the work was completed in a few days. Leaving a strong guard by the bridge in the country of the Tre-Treveri, to prevent any sudden outbreak on their part, he transported the remaining forces, including the cavalry, across the river. The Ubii, who had previously given hostages and submitted, wishing to clear themselves, sent envoys to him to explain that no reinforcements had been sent from their country into that of the Treveri, and that they had not been guilty of disaffection: they earnestly begged him to spare them, and not to make the innocent suffer for the guilty through indiscriminate animosity against the Germans, promising to give more hostages, if he required them. On making inquiry he found that the reinforcements had been sent by the Suevi; accordingly he accepted the explanations of the Ubii and asked for particulars about the routes leading into the country of the Suevi.

A few days later he was informed by the Ubii that the Suevi were all concentrating their forces and warning the tribes under their sway to send their contingents of horse and foot. On receiving this information he arranged for a supply of grain and selected a suitable spot for a camp.

At the same time he directed the Ubii to withdraw their flocks and herds and transfer all their belongings from the open country into their strongholds, hoping that the ignorant barbarians might be tempted by want of food to fight a battle in unfavourable conditions; and he instructed them to send numerous scouts into the country of the Suevi and to ascertain what they were about. The Ubii fulfilled their instructions, and, after the lapse of a few days, reported that all the Suevi, on the arrival of messengers with trustworthy information about the Roman army, had retreated with all their forces and those which they had raised from their allies to the furthest extremity of their country, where there was an immense forest called Bacenis, stretching far into the heart of the continent, and, like a natural wall, protecting the Cherusci from the raids of the Suevi, and the Suevi from those of the Cherusci. On the outskirts of this forest the Suevi had determined to await the arrival of the Romans.

At the stage which this narrative has reached, it will not, I think, be irrelevant to describe the manners and customs of the Gauls and the Germans, and the points wherein the two peoples differ one from the other. Factions exist in Gaul, not only among all the tribes and in all the smaller communities and subdivisions, but, one may almost say, in separate households: the leaders of the rival factions are those who are popularly regarded as possessing the greatest influence; and accordingly to their judgement belongs the final decision on all questions and political schemes. This custom seems to have been established at a remote period in order that none of the common people might lack protection against the strong; for the rival leaders will not suffer their followers to be oppressed or overreached; otherwise they do not command their respect. The same principle holds good in Gaul regarded in its entirety, the tribes as a whole being divided into two groups.

When Caesar arrived in Gaul, one faction was headed by the Aedui, the other by the Sequani. The latter, being in themselves the weaker (for the supremacy had from time immemorial been vested in the Aedui, who possessed extensive dependencies), had secured the alliance of the Germans under Ariovistus, gaining their adhesion by lavish expenditure and promises. As a result of several victories, in which all the Aedui men of rank were killed, they had far outstripped their rivals in power, annexing a large proportion of their dependencies, taking the sons of their leading men as hostages, making the authorities swear to form no designs hostile to the Sequani, seizing and occupying a part of their territory near the common frontier, and establishing supremacy over the whole of Gaul. Yielding to the inevitable, Diviciacus had undertaken a journey to Rome, to solicit aid from the Senate, but had returned unsuccessful. On the arrival of Caesar, the situation was completely changed; the Aedui recovered their hostages, regained power supremacy; over their former dependents, and gained new ones through the influence of Caesar,—for the tribes who had allied themselves to them found that they were better off and more equitably treated than before,—while in other respects their influence and prestige were increased. The Sequaui, on the other hand, had lost their supremacy. Their place was taken by the Remi; and, as it was known that they stood as high in Caesar's favour as the Aedui, the tribes who could not be induced, on account of old feuds, to join the latter ranged themselves among the dependents of the Remi. The Remi took care to protect them, and thus secured the new authority which they had suddenly acquired. The situation at that time was this: the Aedui ranked far the highest in general estimation, while the Remi stood next to them in importance.

Everywhere in Gaul two classes only alone possess or enjoy any distinction; the masses are regarded almost as slaves, never venture to act on their own initiative, and are not admitted to any council. Generally, when masses, crushed by debt or heavy taxation or ill-treated by powerful individuals, they bind themselves to serve men of rank, who exercise over them all the rights that masters have over their slaves. One of the two classes consists of the Druids, the other of the Knights.

The former officiate at the worship of the gods, regulate sacrifices, private as well as public, and expound questions power of religion. Young men resort to them in large numbers for study, and the people hold them in great respect. They are judges in nearly all disputes, whether between tribes or individuals; and when a crime is committed, when a murder takes place, when a dispute arises about inherited property or boundaries, they settle the matter and fix the awards and fines. If any litigant, whether an individual or a tribe, does not abide by their decision, they excommunicate the offender, — the heaviest punishment which they can inflict. Persons who are under such a sentence are looked upon as impious monsters: everybody avoids them, everybody shuns their approach and conversation, for fear of incurring pollution; if they appear as plaintiffs, they are denied justice; nor have they any share in the offices of state. The Druids are all under one head, who commands the highest respect among the order. On his death, if any of the rest is of higher standing than his fellows, he takes the vacant place: if there are several on an equality, the question of supremacy is decided by the votes of the Druids, and sometimes actually by force of arms. The Druids hold an annual session on a settled date at a hallowed spot in the country of the Carnutes,—the reputed centre of Gaul. All litigants assemble here from all parts and abide by their decisions and awards.

The Druids, as a rule, take no part in war, and do not pay taxes conjointly with other people: they enjoy exemption from military service and immunity from all burdens. Attracted by these great privileges, many persons voluntarily come to learn from them, while many are sent by their parents and relatives. During their novitiate it is said that they learn by heart a great number of verses; and accordingly some remain twenty years in a state of pupilage. It is against the principles of the Druids to commit their doctrines to writing, though, for most other purposes, such as public and private documents, they use Greek characters. Their motive, I take it, is two-fold: they are unwilling to allow their doctrine to become common property, or their disciples to trust to documents and neglect to cultivate their memories; for most people find that, if they rely upon documents, they become less diligent in study and their memory is weakened. The doctrine which they are most earnest in inculcating is that the soul does not perish, but that after death it passes from one body to another: this belief they regard as a powerful incentive to valour, as it inspires a contempt for death. They also hold long discussions about the heavenly bodies and their motions, the size of the universe and of the earth, the origin of all things, the power of the gods and the limits of their dominion, and instruct their young scholars accordingly.

The second of the two classes consists of the Knights. On occasion, when war breaks out, as happened almost every year before Caesar's arrival, the Knights either attacking or repelling attack, they all take the field, and surround themselves with as many armed servants and retainers as their birth and resources permit. This is the only mark of influence and power which they recognize.

The Gallic people, in general, are remarkably addicted to religious observances; and for human sacrifices. For this reason persons suffering from serious maladies and those whose lives are danger offer or vow to offer human sacrifices, and employ Druids to perform the sacrificial rites; for they believe that unless the life of man be duly offered, the divine spirit cannot be propitiated. They also hold regular state sacrifices of the same kind. They have, besides, colossal images, the limbs of which, made of wicker-work, they fill with living men and set on fire; and the victims perish, encompassed by the flames.

They regard it as more acceptable to the gods to punish those who are caught in the commission of theft, robbery, or any other crime; but, in default of criminals, they actually resort to the sacrifice of the innocent.

The god whom they most reverence is Mercury, whose images abound. He is regarded as the inventor of all arts and the pioneer and guide of travellers; and he is believed to be all-powerful in promoting commerce and the acquisition of wealth. Next to him they reverence Apollo, Mars, Jupiter, and Minerva. Their notions about these deities are much the same as those of other peoples: Apollo they regard as the dispeller of disease, Minerva as the originator of industries and handicrafts, Jupiter as the suzerain of the celestials, and Mars as the lord of war. To Mars, when they have resolved upon battle, they commonly dedicate the spoils: after victory they sacrifice the captured cattle, and collect the rest of the booty in one spot. In the territories of many tribes are to be seen heaps of such spoils reared on consecrated ground; and it has rarely happened that any one dared, despite religion, either to conceal what he had captured or to remove what had been consecrated. For such an offence the law prescribes the heaviest punishment with torture.

The Gauls universally describe themselves as descendants of Dis Pater, affirming that this is the Druidical tradition. For this reason they measure all periods of time not by days but by nights, and reckon birthdays, the first of the month, and the first of the year on the principle that day comes after night. As regards the other customs of daily life, about the only point a peculiar in which they differ from the rest of mankind is this,—they do not allow their children to come near them openly until they are old enough for military service; and they regard it as unbecoming for a son, while he is still a boy, to appear in public where his father can see him.

It is the custom for married men to take dowries from their own property an amount equivalent, according to valuation, to the sum which they have received from their wives as dowry, and lump the two together. The whole property is jointly administered and the interest saved; and the joint shares of husband and wife, with the interest of past years, go to the survivor. Husbands have power of life and death over status of their wives as well as their children: on the death of the head of a family of high birth, his relations assemble, and, if his death gives rise to suspicion, examine his wives under torture, like slaves, and, if their guilt is proved, burn them to death with all kinds of tortures. Funerals, considering the Gallic standard of living, are splendid and costly: everything, even including animals, which the departed are supposed to have cared for when they were alive, is consigned to the flames; and shortly before our time slaves and retainers who were known to have been beloved by their masters were burned along with them after the conclusion of the regular obsequies.

The tribes which are regarded as comparatively well-governed have a legal enactment to the effect that if any one hears any political rumour or intelligence from the neighbouring peoples, he is to inform the magistrate and not communicate it to any one else, as experience has proved that headstrong persons, who know nothing of affairs, are often alarmed by false reports and impelled to commit crimes and embark on momentous enterprises. The magistrates suppress what appears to demand secrecy, and publish what they deem it expedient for the people to know. The discussion of politics, except in a formal assembly, is forbidden.

The manners and customs of the Germans differ widely from those just described. They have no Druids to preside over public worship. The Germans care nothing for sacrifices. The only deities whom they recognize are those whom they can see, and from whose power they derive manifest benefit, namely, Sun, Moon, and Fire: the rest they have not even heard of. Their lives are passed entirely in hunting and warlike pursuits; and from infancy they are inured to toil and hardship. Those who preserve their virginity longest are most respected by their fellows, for it is considered that by such continence stature and strength are developed and nerve invigorated: indeed, to have connection with a woman before her twentieth year is thought most disgraceful. Concealment is impossible, as they bathe promiscuously in rivers and only wear hides or small cloaks of reindeer skin, leaving a large part of the body bare.

The Germans are not an agricultural people, and live principally upon milk, cheese and meat. Nobody possesses any landed estate and have no or private demesne: the authorities and chieftains annually assign to the several clans and groups of kinsmen assembled at the time as much land as they think proper, in whatever quarter they please, and in the following year compel them to remove to another place. Many reasons are assigned for this custom:—that men may not become slaves of habit, lose their zest for war, and take to agriculture instead; that the strong may not aim at the acquisition of large estates and dispossess those of low degree; that they may not build with elaboration, to avoid cold and heat; to prevent the growth of avarice, which gives birth to party-spirit and dissension; and to keep the masses contented and therefore quiet by letting every one see that he is as well off as the most powerful.

The greatest distinction which a tribe can have is to be surrounded by as wide a belt as possible of waste and desert land. They regard it as a tribute to their valour that the neighbouring peoples should be dispossessed and retreat, and that no one should venture to settle in their vicinity; at the same time they count on gaining additional security by being relieved from the fear of sudden raids. When a tribe has to repel or to make an attack, officers are chosen to conduct the campaign and invested with powers of life and death. In time of peace there is no central magistracy: the chiefs of the various districts and hundreds administer justice and settle disputes among their own people. No discredit attaches to predatory expeditions outside the tribal boundary; and the people tell you that they are undertaken in order to keep the young men in training and to prevent laziness. Whenever any of the chiefs announces his intention in the assembly of leading an expedition, and calls for volunteers, those who approve the enterprise and the leader stand up and promise to help, and the whole gathering applaud them: those who do not follow their leader are counted as deserters and traitors, and thenceforth they are no longer trusted. To ill-treat a guest is regarded as a crime: those who visit them, from whatever motive, they shield from injury and regard their persons as sacred; every man's house is open to them, and they are welcomed at meals.

Once there was a time when Gauls were more warlike than Germans, actually invading their country and, on account of their dense population and insufficient territory, sending colonies across the Rhine. Thus they occupied the most fertile districts of Germany round the mans: their present Hercynian forest (which, I find, was known by degeneracy, name to Eratosthenes and other Greeks, who called it Orcynia), and there settled. To this day the people in question, who enjoy the highest reputation for fair dealing and warlike prowess, continue to occupy this territory. The Germans still live the same life of poverty, privation, and patient endurance as before, and their food and physical training are the same; while the Gauls, from the proximity of the provinces and familiarity with sea-borne products, are abundantly supplied with luxuries and articles of daily consumption. Habituated, little by little, to defeat, and beaten in numerous combats, they do not even pretend themselves to be as brave as their neighbours.

The Hercynian forest, above mentioned, extends over an area which a man travelling without encumbrance requires nine days to traverse. There is no other way of defining its extent, and the natives have no standards of measurement. Starting from the frontiers of the Helvetii, Nemetes, and Rauraci, it extends right along the line of the Danube to the frontiers of the Dacians and Anartes; then, bending to the left and passing through a country remote from the river, it borders (so vast is its extent) upon the territories of many peoples; and no one in Western Germany can say that he has got to the end of the forest, even after travelling right on for sixty days, or has heard whereabouts it begins. It is known to produce many kinds of wild animals which have never been seen elsewhere. The following, on account of their strongly marked characteristics, seem worthy of mention.

There is a species of ox, shaped like a stag, with a single horn standing out between its ears from the middle of its forehead, higher and straighter than horns as we know them spread out wide from the top, like hands and branches. The characteristics of the male and the female are identical, and so are the shape and size of their horns.

Again, there are elks, so-called, which resemble goats in shape and in having piebald coats, but are rather larger. They have blunt horns, and their legs have no knots or joints. They do not lie down to sleep; and if by any chance they are knocked down, they cannot stand up again, or even raise themselves. Their resting-places are trees, against which they lean, and thus rest in a partially recumbent position. Hunters mark their usual lair from their tracks, and uproot or cut deep into all the trees in the neighbourhood, so that they just look as if they were standing. The animals lean against them as usual, upset the weakened trunks by their mere weight, and fall down along with them.

There is a third species, called aurochs, a little smaller than elephants, having the appearance, colour, and shape of bulls. They are very strong and swift, and attack every man and beast they catch sight of. The natives sedulously trap them in pits and kill them. Young men engage in the sport, hardening their muscles by the exercise; and those who kill the largest head of game exhibit the horns as a trophy, and thereby earn high honour. These animals, even when caught young, cannot be domesticated and tamed. Their horns, in size, shape, and appearance, differ widely from those of our oxen. The natives, who are fond of collecting them, mount them round the rim with silver and use them as drinking-cups at grand banquets.

After ascertaining from the Ubian scouts that the Suevi had retreated into their forests, Caesar determined to advance no further. Germans, as we have explained above, pay very little attention to agriculture, and he was therefore afraid of running short of corn. Still, to avoid releasing the natives altogether from the fear of his return, and to delay their reinforcements, after withdrawing the army he broke down the end of the bridge, for the length of two hundred feet, which touched the Ubian bank, erected a tower with four stories on its extremity, and posted a detachment of twelve cohorts to protect the bridge, fortifying the position with strong works. A young officer, Gaius Volcacius Tullus, was placed in command, and charged with the defence of the position. Now that the crops were beginning to ripen, Caesar started in person to conduct the campaign against Ambiorix, taking the route through the Ardennes, the largest forest in the whole of Gaul, which extends from the banks of the Rhine — the Treveran frontier—to the country of the Nervii —a distance of more than five hundred miles. He sent on ahead Lucius Minucius Basilus with all the cavalry, in the hope that by marching rapidly and so arriving in good time he might be able to strike an effective blow; enjoined him not to allow fires to be lighted in his camp, that there might be no distant sign of his approach; and promised to follow him immediately.

Basilus carried out his instructions. Making a rapid march, which upset all calculations, he surprised and seized a large number of men in the open country, and, following their directions, hastened to a place where Ambiorix himself with a few horsemen was said to be staying. Fortune is a great power in war, as in all other affairs. By a rare chance Basilus came upon Ambiorix himself when he was still off his guard and unprepared, and they all saw him coming before his approach was rumoured or announced; and by great good luck, although all the equipment which he had with him was looted and his carriages and horses seized, Ambiorix himself escaped death. His escape, however, was partly due to the fact that his house, like the dwellings of the Gauls in general, was surrounded by a wood (for, in order to escape the heat, they generally look for sites near woods and rivers); and accordingly his retainers and friends resisted for a time, in this confined space, the onslaught of our horsemen. While they were fighting, one of his followers mounted him on horseback; and the woods covered his flight. Thus Fortune had much to do both with his peril and with his escape.

Whether Ambiorix deliberately stopped from collecting his forces in the belief that it would be unwise to fight, or whether his inaction was due to want of time and the sudden arrival of the cavalry, which made him believe that the rest of the army was following; is doubtful. At all events he sent out messengers over the countryside, bidding every man shift for himself. Some fled into the Ardennes, others to unbroken stretches of morass; those who lived nearest the Ocean hid themselves in districts periodically insulated by the tides. Many quitted their own country and trusted their lives and all that they possessed to utter strangers. Catuvolcus, who joined in the enterprise of Ambiorix, and was now a worn-out old man, unable to stand the hardships of campaigning or of flight, heartily cursed Ambiorix for having planned the enterprise, and poisoned himself with yew, a tree which grows abundantly in Gaul and Germany. The Segni and Condrusi, who are Germans by race and are reckoned among that people, and in charge of who dwell between the Eburones and the Treveri, sent envoys to Caesar, begging him not to count them as enemies or assume that all the Germans were associated, and assuring him that they had never dreamed of war, and had sent no reinforcements to Ambiorix. Caesar, after testing their statements by examining prisoners, ordered them to hand over to him any Eburonian fugitives who joined them, and promised not to molest their country if they obeyed. He then broke up his forces into three divisions, and transferred the heavy baggage of all the legions to Aduatuca (the name denotes a fort), in which Titurius and Aurunculeius had established themselves for the winter, and which is nearly in the centre of the territory of the Eburones. Amongst other reasons, Caesar had selected the position in order to spare the soldiers fatigue, as the fortifications made in the preceding year were still standing. Leaving the 14th legion, one of the three which he had brought from Italy, where they had recently been raised, to protect the baggage, he entrusted Quintus Tullius Cicero with the command of it and the defence

After dividing the army, he ordered Titus and Labienus to move towards the Ocean with three legions into the districts bordering upon the country of the Menapii, and sent Gaius Trebonius with the same number, to devastate the region adjacent to the country of the Aduatuci; while he determined to march himself with the remaining three towards the river Scheldt, which flows into the Meuse, and the most distant parts of the Ardennes, whither he heard that Ambiorix had gone with a few horsemen. On his departure, he announced his intention of returning at the end of a week, when, as he was aware, the rations of the legions left on guard would be due. He enjoined Labienus and Trebonius to return by that day, if they could do so consistently with the public interest, so that, after comparing notes anew and ascertaining the enemy's methods, they might be able to form a fresh plan of campaign.

As we have remarked above, there was no organized body, no stronghold, and no force capable of armed resistance: the population was dispersed in all directions. Every one had taken up his abode in any remote glen or wooded spot or impenetrable morass that offered him a chance of defending himself or of saving his life. The people near these places knew the ground; and great care was required, not indeed in protecting the army as a whole, for while the troops were massed no danger could befall them from a panic-stricken and scattered enemy, but to secure the safety of individual soldiers; and yet this in some measure concerned the safety of the whole army.

Lust for plunder led many far afield; and the woods with their ill-defined and dusky paths defied compact bodies to enter them. If Caesar meant to finish his task outright and slaughter the whole brood of scoundrels, he must send out numerous parties and break up the troops into detachments; if he chose to keep his companies in formation, according to the established and familiar system of the Roman army, the natives were protected by the nature of the country, and individuals among them had courage enough to lie in ambush and cut off scattered parties. In these difficult circumstances all possible care and forethought were exercised; for it was determined to forgo some advantage in punishing the enemy, although all were burning for revenge, rather than to punish him at the cost of any loss to the men.

Caesar sent messengers to the neighbouring tribes, holding out to all the hope of plunder and inviting them to harry the Eburones; for Gauls should risk their lives in the forests and not his legionaries, and at the same time to surround the people with a mighty host, and, in requital for their signal villainy, to destroy them, root, branch, and name. Large numbers speedily assembled from every side. While these events were passing in all parts of the Eburonian territory, the last day of the week was approaching, by which time Caesar had determined to return to the legion that guarded his baggage. Now occurred an instance of the power which Fortune wields in war and of the hazards with which Fortune is fraught. The enemy, as we have pointed out, were scattered and panic-stricken, and there was no force to give the slightest ground for alarm. The rumour made its way across the Rhine to the Germans that the Eburones were being harried, and, what was more, that all comers were invited to plunder them. The Sugambri, who dwell in the immediate neighbourhood of the Rhine, and who, as we have stated above, sheltered the Tencteri and Usipetes after their flight, raised two thousand horse; crossed the Rhine in barges and on rafts thirty miles below the spot where Caesar had built his bridge and had left a garrison; invaded the nearest part of the Eburonian territory; captured a large number of scattered fugitives; and seized a great quantity of cattle, which uncivilized peoples greatly prize. Lured on by the hope of plunder, they advanced further; and these born warriors and freebooters were not to be stopped by marsh or forest. They asked their prisoners whereabouts Caesar was; found that he had gone far away; and satisfied themselves that his whole army had quitted the neighbourhood. Thereupon one of the prisoners asked, "Why go after this wretched, worthless loot when in a twinkling you can make your fortunes? In three hours you can get to Aduatuca, where the Roman army have stored all their belongings: the garrison are a mere handful, unable even to man the wall, and not a soul dares stir out of the entrenchments." Here was a chance. The Germans concealed and left behind the booty they had got, and pushed on for Aduatuca, guided by the man from whom they had learned the news.

Cicero, in obedience to Caesar's instructions, had been most careful to keep his troops every day in camp, not even allowing a single servant to stir outside the entrenchment. On the seventh day, however, hearing more than once that Caesar had advanced to a great distance, and not receiving any intimation of his return, he was afraid that he would not keep his appointment; at the same time he was disquieted by the remarks of the men, who said that, if one mightn't even leave the camp, what he called patience was virtually submission to blockade; and with nine legions and a powerful body of cavalry in the field, and an enemy scattered and all but annihilated, he never expected such a contingency as a disaster within three miles of camp. Accordingly he sent five cohorts to reap the nearest crops, which were only separated from the camp by a solitary hill. Many invalids belonging to the various legions had been left in camp. About three hundred of these, who had recovered in the course of the week, were sent out with the cohorts under a separate command; and a large number of servants got permission to go as well, with a great quantity of baggage cattle which had been stabled in the camp.

Just at this critical moment up came the German horsemen, and, riding right on without slackening speed, tried to break into the camp at the rear gate: woods obstructed the view on that side, and they were not seen till they were getting close to the camp, so that the traders, whose tents were at the foot of the rampart, had no chance of retreating. Our men, being off their guard, were startled by the suddenness of the attack, and the cohort on duty barely withstood the first shock. The enemy spread round the other sides, to see if they could find an entrance. Our men with difficulty defended the gates; but the strength of the position as well as the entrenchments forbade any attempt to enter elsewhere. The whole camp was a scene of confusion, every man asking his neighbour the reason of the uproar; and there was no attempt to determine where the troops should advance or at what point the men were to fall in. One declared that the camp was already taken; another insisted that the natives had come, flushed with victory, from destroying the army and the chief; nearly all, remembering where they were, conceived superstitious fancies and pictured to themselves the disaster that had befallen Cotta and Titurius, who, as they imagined, had perished in the same fort. All being thus panic-stricken, the barbarians were confirmed in the notion, derived from their prisoner, that there was no force within. Striving to break through, they exhorted each other not to let such a chance slip from their grasp.

Publius Sextius Baculus, who had served Bacuius under Caesar's command as principal centurion and who has been mentioned in connection with earlier engagements, had been left invalided in the garrison, and had not tasted food for five days. Feeling anxious for his own safety and that of his comrades, he walked unarmed out of his tent, and, seeing the menacing attitude of the enemy and the extreme peril of the situation, borrowed weapons from the men nearest him and planted himself in the gateway. The centurions of the cohort on guard followed him, and for a short space they sustained the brunt of the fight together. Severely wounded, Sextius fainted and was with difficulty saved by being passed along from hand to hand. The breathing-space thus gained enabled the rest to pluck up courage enough to man the fortifications and make a show of defence.

Meanwhile our soldiers heard the din from afar. The horsemen rode on ahead, and learned the gravity of the danger. There was no entrenchment here to shelter the men in their terror: raw recruits, with no experience of war, they turned to their tribune and centurions, waiting for orders. Not one of them had the courage to keep cool in the face of the unexpected. The barbarians descried the standards in the distance and abandoned their attack. At first they believed that the legions, which, as they had learned from their prisoners, had gone on a distant expedition, had returned; but afterwards, seeing that they were a mere handful, they charged them on every side.

The servants ran forward to a knoll close by. They were speedily dislodged and rushed pell-mell into the maniples as they stood in line, thereby increasing the terror of the soldiers. Some voted for forming in a wedge and making a rapid dash through the enemy, urging that, as the camp was so near, most of them could escape even if a few were cut off and killed; others for standing firm upon the hill and all taking their chance together. The veterans, who, as we have stated, had gone out with the rest under a separate command, disapproved of this suggestion. Accordingly, led by Gains Trebonius, a Roman knight, who had been placed in command of them, they charged, with mutual exhortations, through the midst of the enemy, and reached camp without the loss of a man. The servants and cavalry, following close behind, joined in the charge of the infantry and owed their escape to their courage. Those, however, who had taken their stand upon the hill, and who even now had not learned what fighting meant, could neither abide by their own resolution and defend themselves on their position of vantage, nor imitate the swift energy which, as they saw, was the salvation of the others, but, in their attempt to get back to camp, abandoned the advantage of their position. The centurions, some of whom had been promoted for valour from the lower grades of the other legions to the higher grades of this, determined not to forfeit the credit they had earned in the field, and died fighting with the greatest gallantry. Their brave stand compelling the enemy to fall back, some of the soldiers unexpectedly reached camp in safety; the rest were surrounded by the natives and perished.

The Germans, seeing that our men had by this time manned the works, abandoned the camp and recrossed the Rhine with the booty which they had left in the woods. Even after they had gone, the panic was so great that Gaius Volusenus, who had been sent on with the cavalry, on arriving in camp that night, could not make the men believe that Caesar was close by and the army with him, safe and sound. Fear had so completely taken possession of them that they were almost beside themselves, and maintained that the whole force must have been annihilated and that the cavalry had alone escaped the rout; for, they insisted, if the army had been safe, the Germans would not have attacked the camp. Caesar's arrival, however, dispelled the panic.

Caesar was well aware that in war it is the unexpected that happens. On his return, therefore, he made no complaint except that the cohorts had been allowed to leave their proper place in the garrison, remarking that no opening should have been left even for the slightest accident; and he considered that Fortune had shown her great power in the enemy's sudden arrival, and still more in having repelled the natives when they had all but gained the rampart and the gates of the camp. The most remarkable point in the whole incident was that the Germans, having crossed the Rhine with the object of ravaging the territories of Ambiorix, had been led to attack the Roman camp, and had thereby done Ambiorix the greatest service that he could desire.

Caesar set out once more to harry the enemy, and, having got together a great horde from the neighbouring tribes, let them loose in every direction. Every hamlet, every building that was to be seen was fired; cattle were driven in from all parts; and the corn was not only devoured by the immense multitude of horses and men, but also laid by the autumnal rains. In fact, it seemed certain that even if any of the inhabitants concealed themselves for the time, they must perish, after the withdrawal of the army, from utter destitution. The cavalry, which was very numerous, was sent out in all directions. Often success was all but in their grasp, for prisoners, who had just descried Ambiorix making Escape of off, looked round and insisted that he was barely out of sight; so that his pursuers, seeing a chance of running him down, made herculean efforts and, in the expectation of winning Caesar's favour, showed almost superhuman zeal; but always they seemed just to miss complete success: the quarry broke away from wooded glade or other lair, and, hiding in the night, made for another part of the country. His only escort was four horsemen, to whom alone he ventured to trust his life.

After ravaging the districts in this way, Caesar led back his army, with the loss of two cohorts, to Durocortorum in the country of the Remi, at which place he convened a Gallic council and proceeded to hold an inquiry into the conspiracy of the Senones and Carnutes. He pronounced the extreme sentence on Acco, the author of the movement, and executed him in the time-honoured Roman fashion. Some of the conspirators, fearing to be brought to trial, fled and Caesar interdicted them from fire and water. Having quartered two legions for the winter close to the Treveran frontier, two among the Lingones, and the remaining six at Agedincum in the country of the Senones, and arranged for a supply of corn for the army, he set out, according to his custom, for Italy, to hold the assizes.

BOOK VII

THE REBELLION OF VERCINGETORIX

Gaul was now tranquillized; and Caesar, in accordance with his determination, started for Italy to hold the assizes. There he was informed at Rome of the murder of Clodius; and, learning that the Senate had decreed that all Italians eligible for service should be sworn in, he proceeded to levy troops throughout the whole Province. The news of these events speedily made its way into Transalpine Gaul. The Gauls amplified and embellished the story as the facts seemed to warrant, spreading rumours that Caesar was detained by the disturbances in the capital, and that, while these fierce conflicts were raging, he could not rejoin his army. The opportunity stimulated the Gauls. They were already smarting under their subjection to the Roman People; and they now began, unreservedly and boldly, to form projects for war. The leading men of Gaul mutually arranged meetings in secluded woodland spots. They spoke bitterly of the death of Acco, telling their hearers that the same fate might befall them; and, deploring the fortune that oppressed the whole country, they made promises and offered rewards of every kind to induce volunteers to strike the first blow and risk their lives to restore the liberty of Gaul. The first step was to contrive a plan for cutting off Caesar from his army before their secret designs could get abroad. This could be easily done; for the legions would not venture to leave their quarters in the general's absence, and the general would not be able to get to the legions without an escort. Finally, it was better to die in battle than to fail in recovering their old military renown and the freedom which was their heritage from their forefathers. At the close of the debate the Carnutes declared that they would shrink from no peril for the common weal, and promised to strike the first blow; and as, in the circumstances, it was impossible to give mutual security by exchanging hostages, for fear they should get abroad, they demanded that the confederates should make a sheaf of their military standards —an act which, according to Gallic custom, involves a most awful rite—and bind themselves by solemn oath, as a pledge that, after they had begun the war, the others should not leave them in the lurch. The Carnutes were loudly cheered; all who were present took the oath; a date was fixed for the enterprise; and then the assembly dispersed.

When the appointed day came round and the signal was given, the Carnutes, led by two desperadoes named Cotuatus and Conconnetodumnus, swooped down upon Cenabum; killed the Roman citizens who had settled in the place for trade — amongst others Gaius Cita, a Roman knight of good position, whom Caesar had placed in charge of the commissariat —and plundered their stores. The news spread swiftly to all the tribes of Gaul; for whenever an event of signal importance occurs, the people make it known by loud cries over the countryside, and others in turn take up the cry and pass it on to their neighbours. So it happened on this occasion. The events which had occurred at Cenabum at sunrise were heard of in the country of the Arverni before the close of the first watch, the distance being about one hundred and sixty miles.

In this country dwelt Vercingetorix, son of Celtillus, a young Arvernian of commanding influence, whose father had held the foremost position numerous in all Gaul, and had been put to death by his elected tribe for trying to make himself king. Following the lead of the conspirators, he called his retainers together, and easily inflamed their passions. On learning his design, men flew to arms. Gobannitio, his father's brother, and the other chiefs, who thought that this was no occasion for tempting fortune, frowned upon his enterprise and expelled him from Gergovia: still he did not abandon his purpose, but raised a posse of needy and desperate men in the rural districts. Master of this force, he won over every tribesman whom he approached, and urged them to take up arms in the cause of national freedom; and raising a numerous host, he drove his opponents, by whom he had himself just before been banished, to leave the country. His adherents saluted him as king. He sent out envoys in every direction, adjuring the confederates to remain true. He quickly secured the adhesion of the Senones, Parisii, Pictones, Cadurci, Turoni, Aulerci, Lemovices, Andi, and all the other maritime tribes; and the chief command was conferred upon him unanimously. Armed with this power, he ordered all these tribes to give hostages and bring him speedily a definite quota of troops. He fixed a date by which each tribe was to turn out a specified quantity of arms from its own workshops, and devoted special attention to his cavalry. With the utmost diligence he combined the utmost severity in the exercise of his command, coercing waverers by heavy penalties. Thus he punished serious misdemeanours by death at the stake with all kinds of tortures, while he sent home minor offenders with their ears lopped off or eye gouged out, that they might serve as a warning to the rest and that the severity of their punishment might make others quail.

By these stern measures he speedily raised insurrection. He sent a Cadurcan, named Lucterius, a man of the greatest daring, with a detachment into the country of the Ruteni; while he marched in person for the country of the Bituriges. On his approach the Bituriges sent envoys to the Aedui, whose overlordship they acknowledged, asking for aid to enable them to offer a better resistance to the enemy's force. The Aedui, acting on the advice of the generals whom Caesar had left with the army, sent a force of cavalry and infantry to their assistance. When they reached the Loire—the boundary between the Bituriges and the Aedui—they lingered there a few days, and then turned back without venturing to cross the river. They told the generals that they had returned from fear of treachery on the part of the Bituriges, as they had found out that it was their intention, if they crossed the river, to hem them in on one side, while the Arverni hemmed them in on the other. Whether they acted for the reason which they stated to the generals or from motives of treachery we have no certain knowledge, and therefore do not think it right to make any positive statement. On their departure the Bituriges immediately joined the Arverni.

By the time that news of these events reached Caesar in Italy, he was aware that the situation in the capital had improved, and accordingly started for Transalpine Gaul. On his arrival he found it very difficult to devise a plan for getting to his army. He realized that if he summoned the legions to the Province they would fight a battle on the march without his being present; if, on the other hand, he pushed on alone to join the army, he saw that he could not prudently trust his safety, at such a crisis, even to the tribes which were apparently peaceable.

Meanwhile the Cadurcan, Lucterius, who had been sent into the country of the Ruteni, induced that tribe to join the Arverni. Advancing into the territories of the Nitiobroges and Gabali, he took hostages from both, and, collecting a large force, attempted to make a raid into the Province, in the direction of Narbo. On receiving news of this, Caesar deemed it imperative, before doing anything else, to march for Narbo. Arriving there, he encouraged the faint-hearted detachments among the Provincial Ruteni, the Volcae Arecomici, the Tolosates, and in the districts round Narbo which were in proximity to the enemy, and ordered a part of the Provincial troops and a fresh draft which he had brought from Italy to concentrate in the country of the Helvii, which is conterminous with that of the Arverni.

As a result of these measures, Lucterius was checked and in fact forced to retire, for he thought it hazardous to venture within the chain of posts; and accordingly Caesar started for the country of the Helvii. It was the most rigorous season of the year, and the Cevennes, which separates the Arverni from the Helvii, was covered by snow of extraordinary depth, which made marching difficult; but the snow, which was six feet deep, was shovelled aside, and, the roads being thus cleared by prodigious exertion on the part of the men, he made his way to the country of the Arverni. They were taken completely by surprise, for they had always supposed that the Cevennes protected them like a wall, and at that time of the year the tracks had never been practicable even for solitary travellers. Caesar ordered his cavalry to scour the country far and wide, and do their utmost to strike terror into the enemy. The news travelled swiftly by rumour and dispatches to Vercingetorix; and the Arverni in great alarm all thronged round him and besought him to have some consideration for them and not let them be pillaged by the enemy, for he must see that the whole brunt of the war had been shifted on to them. Yielding to their entreaties, he moved from the country of the Bituriges towards that of the Arverni.

Caesar had anticipated that this would happen with Vercingetorix; therefore, after remaining a couple of days in the district, he left the army on the pretext of having to concentrate the new draft and the cavalry, and placed the younger Brutus in command of the troops, charging him to make the cavalry scour the country in all directions, far and wide, and announcing that he would do his best not to stay away from camp more than three days. Having settled these matters, he made his way, as fast as he could possibly travel, to Vienna, before his troops expected him; picked up his cavalry there, which he had sent on a considerable time before, in good condition; and pushed on through the country of the Aedui, marching night and day, so that in case they had any intention of molesting him he might be too quick for them, till he reached the country of the Lingones, where two legions were wintering. On his arrival he sent word to the remaining legions, and concentrated them all before news of his arrival could reach the Arverni. Vercingetorix, on hearing what he had done, led his army back into the country of the Bituriges, and moving thence, proceeded to besiege Gorgobina, a stronghold of the Boii, whom Caesar had established there after their defeat in the battle with the Helvetii, and had placed in dependence on the Aedui.

Caesar was greatly embarrassed by this move. If he kept his legions concentrated for the rest of the winter, and the tributaries of the Aedui were overpowered, the whole of Gaul, seeing that he could not be relied upon to protect his friends, might simultaneously fall away: if, on the other hand, he prematurely withdrew the army from its quarters, he might be pressed for supplies owing to the difficulties of transport. Still, it seemed better to face every difficulty than to alienate all who were on his side by submitting to an indignity like this. Accordingly he charged the Aedui to forward supplies, and sent on messengers to let the Boii know that he was coming and to urge them to remain faithful and sustain the enemy's attack with fortitude. Then, leaving two legions and the heavy baggage of the whole army at Agedincum, he set out to join the Boii.

Next day he reached Vellaunodunum, a stronghold of the Senones. In order to avoid leaving an enemy in his rear and so expedite supply, he proceeded to besiege the town, and in a couple of days surrounded it. On the third day envoys were sent out to propose surrender. Caesar ordered the garrison to pile arms, bring out their horses, and give six hundred hostages. He left Gaius Trebonius to give effect to these orders, and, being anxious to finish his march as soon as possible, pushed on for Cenabum in the country of the Carnutes. Believing that the siege of Vellaunodunum, news of which had only just reached them, would be protracted, they were beginning to collect troops to send to the protection of Cenabum. Caesar reached the town in a couple of days. He encamped before it; but, as recaptures it was late in the day and he was prevented from beginning the siege, he postponed it till the morrow, ordering the troops to make all needful preparations; and, as there was a bridge over the Loire in contact with the town and he feared that the garrison might escape in the night, he directed two legions to remain under arms. Shortly before midnight the townspeople moved silently out of Cenabum and began to cross the river. The movement was reported to Caesar by his patrols, whereupon he fired the gates, sent in the legions which he had ordered to remain in readiness, and took possession of the town. Very few of the enemy escaped capture; for the narrowness of the bridge and streets prevented the throng from getting away. Caesar plundered and burned the town; gave the booty to the soldiers; threw his army across the Loire, and made his way into the country of the Bituriges.

When Vercingetorix learned that Caesar and captures was approaching, he abandoned the siege and marched to encounter him. Caesar had prepared to besiege a stronghold of the Bituriges, called Noviodunum, situated upon his line of march. Envoys came from the town to beg him to pardon them and to spare their lives; and, in order to finish the campaign as rapidly as he had begun it, he ordered the garrison to pile their arms, bring out their horses, and give hostages. Some of the hostages had been delivered up and the other arrangements were in progress, the centurions and a few soldiers having been sent into the town to collect the arms and cattle, when the enemy's cavalry, which had gone on in advance of Vercingetorix's column, were seen in the distance. The moment the townspeople caught sight of them, they realized that there was a chance of relief; and with a yell they seized their arms, shut the gates,, and manned the walls. The centurions in the town, understanding from the behaviour of the Gauls that they meant mischief, drew their swords, took possession of the gates, and withdrew all their men in safety.

Caesar ordered his cavalry out of camp, and forced on an engagement: presently, his men being in difficulties, he sent about four hundred German horse, whom he had regularly entertained from the first, to the rescue. The Gauls, unable to sustain their charge, were put to flight, and fell back, with heavy loss, upon the main body. On their defeat, the townsmen again took alarm, and, seizing the individuals whom they believed to have been instrumental in stirring up the rabble, took them to Caesar and surrendered. This affair disposed of, Caesar marched for Avaricum, the largest and strongest town in the against country of the Bituriges, which is situated in a very fertile tract, for he was confident that by the recovery of this stronghold he would re-establish his authority over the tribe.

Having sustained these successive disasters, at Vellaunodunum, Cenabum, and Noviodunum, Vercingetorix called his followers to a council, and ordered them that the campaign must thence forward be conducted on widely different lines. The object was by every means to prevent the Romans from foraging and getting supplies. This object could easily be attained; for their side was strong in cavalry, and the season was in their favour. No grass could be cut; the enemy must perforce disperse and get fodder from the barns; and the cavalry could destroy all these detachments from day to day. Moreover, in the public interest, personal convenience must be disregarded: all round the road, as far as the country was accessible for forage, the hamlets and homesteads should be burned. They were well off for supplies themselves, as they could draw upon the resources of the people whose territory was the theatre of the war: but the Romans would either succumb to their privations or would have to move far from their camp at great risk; and it made no difference whether they killed them or took their baggage, for, if it were lost, they could not keep the field. Moreover, it would be well to burn those towns which were not rendered impregnable by fortification and a naturally strong position, for fear they should serve their own side as refuges for shirking military duty, and tempt the Romans to pillage them and plunder their stores. If this sounded hard or cruel, they should consider how much harder it was for their wives and children to be carried off into slavery while they were themselves put to death; and if they were beaten, this would be inevitable.

This view was unanimously approved; and in a single day more than twenty towns belonging to the Bituriges were set ablaze. The same thing happened in the territories of the other tribes: the whole country was a scene of conflagration; and although all felt this a grievous trial, they consoled themselves with the assurance that victory was practically in their grasp and that they would soon recover what they had lost. The question was debated in a general assembly, whether Avaricum should be burned or defended. The Bituriges knelt before their countrymen, begging that they might not be forced to fire with their own hands the town which was wellnigh the finest in the whole of Gaul,—the bulwark and the pride of their people: it was naturally so strong that they would easily defend it; for it was almost entirely surrounded by running water and marshy ground, and could only be approached at one place, which was very narrow. Their prayer was granted. Vercingetorix at first opposed them, but afterwards gave way, in deference to their entreaties and the general sympathy that was shown them. Capable officers were selected to defend the town.

Vercingetorix, following Caesar, selected for his encampment a spot, protected by marshes and woods, sixteen miles from Avaricum. He hourly kept himself informed, by organized patrols, of what was going on at Avaricum, and issued his orders accordingly. He watched all our expeditions for forage and corn, attacked our men when they were scattered—for they were obliged to go far afield—and inflicted on them considerable loss, although they took every precaution that ingenuity could devise to baffle him, starting at odd times and in different directions.

Caesar encamped on the side of the town siege of which, as we have mentioned above, was undefended by running water and marshy ground, and was approached by a narrow neck of land. As the lie of the country made it impossible to invest the position, he proceeded to build a terrace, form lines of sheds, and erect two towers. He urged the Boii and the Aedui unceasingly to keep him supplied with grain: but the latter, being halfhearted, were of little service; while the former, a small and feeble tribe, whose resources were slender, soon used up what they had. Owing to the poverty of the Boii, the slackness of the Aedui, and the burning of the granaries, the army was in the greatest straits for supplies, insomuch that for several days the men were without grain, and only kept famine at bay by driving in the cattle from distant villages: yet not a word were they heard to utter unworthy of the majesty of the Roman People and their own record of victory. Nor was this all. Caesar spoke to the legions singly while they were at work, and told them that, if they found their privations too hard to bear, he would abandon the siege; but with one voice they begged him not to do so: they had served under his command for several years without disgrace, and had never abandoned any operation which they had undertaken. They would feel it a disgrace to abandon the siege, having once begun it; and it was better to put up with every hardship than fail in avenging the Romans who had fallen at Cenabum by Gallic treachery. They said the same to the centurions and tribunes, charging them to repeat it to Caesar.

The towers were now getting close to the wall. Caesar learned from prisoners that Vercingetorix, having consumed his provender, had moved closer to Avaricum, and gone off himself with his cavalry and the light-armed foot who regularly fight along with the cavalry, intending to lie in ambush at the spot where he believed that our men would go to forage on the following day. Acting on this information, Caesar started quietly at midnight and reached the enemy's encampment in the morning. They were informed of his approach by their patrols, and, swiftly removing their carts and baggage into the densest parts of the woods, drew up all their forces on open rising ground. On receiving this report Caesar ordered the troops to pile their packs promptly and get their arms ready.

The hill sloped gently upward from its base, and was almost entirely surrounded by marshy ground, difficult to cross, but not more than fifty feet wide. The Gauls had broken down the causeways and remained obstinately on the hill, confident in the strength of the position; formed up in tribal groups, they held all the fords and the thickets that bordered the marsh, determined, if the Romans attempted to force a passage, to attack them from their commanding position while they were bogged in the slush. Seeing the proximity of the two forces, one would have thought that the Gauls were ready to fight and that the chances were nearly even; but any one who detected the disparity in the conditions would have known that their defiant attitude was mere bravado. The legionaries, indignant that the enemy behind that paltry barrier had the hardihood to look them in the face, clamoured for the signal for action: but Caesar made them understand that victory could only be gained at a heavy cost and by the sacrifice of many brave men; he could see that for his honour their hearts were steeled to face any peril, and for that reason he should deserve to be called the most heartless of men if he did not hold their lives dearer than his own reputation. In this way he soothed the men's feelings, and, leading them back the same day to camp, proceeded to complete his arrangements for the siege of the town.

Vercingetorix, on returning to his troops, was accused of treachery. The charge was that he had moved nearer the Romans; that he had taken all the cavalry with him; that he had left his numerous forces without a head; and that on his departure the Romans had rapidly advanced at the opportune moment. These things could not all have happened by accident: they must have been deliberately planned; and evidently he would rather reign over Gaul as Caesar's creature than by the favour of his countrymen. In reply to these charges Vercingetorix said that if he had shifted his camp, he had done so because forage was scarce and at their own instigation; if he had moved nearer to the Romans, it was because he was attracted by a favourable position, whose natural features were its own defence; while cavalry ought not to have been required on marshy ground, and were useful in the place to which they had actually gone. When he left them he had deliberately refrained from delegating the command to any one, for fear his substitute might be driven by the impetuosity of the host to fight; for he could see that that was what they all wanted, because they were infirm of purpose and incapable of prolonged exertion. If the arrival of the Romans in his absence was accidental, they ought to thank Fortune; if they had come on the invitation of a spy, they ought to thank him for having enabled them to ascertain from their commanding position the smallness of their numbers, and to see how despicable was the spirit of men who dared not fight, but slunk back ignominiously to their camp. For himself, he did not want to get from Caesar by treachery a power which he could secure by victory,—victory which was already in his grasp and in that of the whole Gallic people. No! he would give them back their gift if they imagined that they were conferring a favour upon him instead of owing their safety to him.

"To satisfy yourselves," he continued, "that what I say is true, listen to Roman soldiers!"

He made some slaves step forward, whom he had captured foraging a few days before, and had kept in chains on starvation diet. They had been carefully taught beforehand what to say when questioned. They said that they were legionaries: hunger and want had led them to steal out of camp to see whether they could find any corn or cattle in the fields; the whole army was in the same straits, and not a man was now strong enough to stand the strain of his daily work. The General had therefore resolved to withdraw the army in three days unless he made some real progress in the siege of the town.

"These benefits," said Vercingetorix, "you owe to me,—me, whom you falsely accuse of treachery: thanks to my efforts, without shedding a drop of your blood you see this mighty, this victorious army well-nigh starved; and I have taken care that, when it seeks safety in ignominious flight, not one tribe shall grant it refuge."

The whole multitude cheered loudly and receive clashed their weapons in the native fashion; for acclamation. Gauls generally do this when they are pleased with what an orator says. Vercingetorix, they declared, was the greatest of leaders: his loyalty was above suspicion; and it was impossible to carry on the war with greater judgement They determined to throw ten thousand men, selected from all the contingents, into the town, not thinking it wise to trust the national safety to the Bituriges alone; for they realized that if the Bituriges succeeded in holding the town, the whole victory would be theirs.

The extraordinary valour of our soldiers found its match in the manifold devices of the Gauls; for they are a most ingenious people, and always show the greatest aptitude in borrowing and giving effect to ideas which they get from any one. They pulled aside the grappling-hooks with nooses, and when they had got hold of them hauled them inside the town by means of windlasses. They also undermined and dragged away the material of the terrace, performing the operation very adroitly, because there are large iron-mines in their country, and they are thoroughly familiar with every kind of underground gallery. Moreover, they had covered the whole wall at every point with towers, provided with platforms, and protected by hides. Again, they made frequent sorties by day and night, setting fire to the terrace or attacking the troops at their work: as the terrace, daily rising, raised our towers to a higher level, they lashed together the uprights of their own towers, and gave them a corresponding elevation; and opening into the Roman mines, they prevented them, with beams sharpened and hardened in the fire, boiling pitch, and heavy stones, from approaching the wall.

Gallic walls are always constructed on the following or some similar plan. Balks of timber are laid upon the ground, at right angles to the line of the intended wall and in unbroken succession along its length, at regular intervals of two feet. These balks are made fast on the inner side and thickly coated with rubble; while the intervals above mentioned are tightly packed in front with large stones. When the balks are fixed in their places and fastened together, a fresh row is laid on the top of them in such a way that the same interval is kept, and the balks do not touch each other, but are separated by similar intervals, into each of which a stone is thrust, and thus are kept firmly in position. Thus, step by step, the whole fabric is constructed until the wall reaches its proper height. While the structure, with its alternate balks and stones, which preserve their regular succession in straight lines, presents a variegated aspect which is not unsightly, it is also extremely serviceable and adapted for the defence of towns; for the stone secures it against fire, and the woodwork, which is braced on the inner side by beams generally forty feet long running right across, and so can neither be broken through nor pulled to pieces, protects it against the ram.

All the above-mentioned causes impeded the siege, and the men were hampered all the time by cold and continual rain; yet by unremitting toil they overcame all these difficulties, and in twenty-five days erected a terrace three hundred and thirty feet broad and eighty feet high. The terrace was almost in contact with the enemy's wall, and Caesar was, as usual, bivouacking at the works, urging the men not to suspend labour for a moment, when, a little before the third watch, it was noticed that the terrace was smoking. The enemy had undermined and set it on fire. At the same moment a cheer arose all along the wall and troops came pouring out of the two gates on either side of the towers, while others flung down torches and dry wood from their commanding position on the wall on to the terrace, and shot pitch and other inflammable material; so that it was scarcely possible to decide where to strike a counter blow or what point to reinforce. But Caesar's practice was to have two legions regularly bivouacking in front of the camp, while a larger number, which took duty in turns, were constantly at work; so that a number of men soon checked the sortie, while others drew back the towers and dragged asunder the timbers of the terrace, and the whole multitude from the camp came thronging to extinguish the flames.

The rest of the night passed by; and still the fight was going on at every point. The enemy's hope of victory continually revived, for they saw that the breastworks of the towers were burnt, and that it was not easy to advance and support a threatened position without cover; in their own ranks fresh men were continually relieving those who were tired, and they felt that on that moment depended the salvation of Gaul:—just then we witnessed an episode which seemed worthy of remembrance and we have therefore thought ought not to be passed over. A Gaul, standing in front of one of the gates of the town, was throwing lumps of fat and pitch, passed to him from hand to hand, into the fire opposite one of the towers. A bolt from a small catapult pierced him on the right side, and he dropped dead. One of the men nearest him stepped across his prostrate body and continued the work; a shot from the catapult killed him in the same way, and a third man took his place, and a fourth the place of the third; nor was the post abandoned by the defenders until the fire on the terrace was put out, the enemy everywhere repulsed, and the fighting at an end.

The Gauls had tried every expedient; and next day, as nothing had succeeded, they took the urgent advice of Vercingetorix and determined to escape from the town. By making the attempt in the stillness of night they hoped to succeed without much loss; for Vercingetorix's camp was not far from the town, and the continuous marsh which intervened would make it difficult for the Romans to pursue. It was night and they were preparing for their attempt, when suddenly the matrons came running into the open and, weeping and flinging themselves at their husbands' feet, passionately entreated them not to give them up and the children who were their common possession to the tender mercies of the enemy; for natural bodily weakness prevented them from making their escape. When they saw that their resolve was immovable—for often in extremity of peril fear leaves no room for compassion—

they began to scream and gesticulate, to warn the Romans of the intended flight. The Gauls were terrified by this, fearing that the Roman cavalry would seize the roads, and abandoned their resolve.

Next day, Caesar advanced one of his towers; and the works which he had begun were completed. A heavy storm of rain came on, and he thought the opportunity a good one for maturing his plans. Observing that the guards were rather carelessly posted on the wall, he ordered his own men to go about their work with a show of listlessness, and explained his intention. The legions, unobserved, got ready for action under the cover of the sheds. Caesar told them that now was the moment to repay themselves for their herculean toils and grasp the prize of victory; and, offering rewards to the men who should first mount the wall, he gave the troops the signal. Suddenly they darted forth from every point and swiftly lined the wall.

The enemy, panic-stricken by this unexpected move, were driven from the wall and towers, but formed in wedge-shaped masses in the market-place and open spaces, determined, if they were attacked, to fight it out, shoulder to shoulder. Seeing that no one would come down on to the level, but that men were swarming all along the wall on every side, they feared that all chance of escape would be gone, and, flinging away their arms, made a rush for the furthest quarter of the town. There some of them, jostling one another in the narrow gateways, were slaughtered by the infantry, and others, after they had got clear of the gates, by the cavalry. Not a man reeked of plunder. Exasperated by the massacre at Cenabum and the toil of the siege, they spared not the aged, nor women, nor children. Of the entire garrison, numbering about forty thousand, a bare eight hundred, who had fled precipitately from the town on hearing the first outcry, escaped unhurt to Vercingetorix. Late at night he received the fugitives in silence. Fearing that, as they came thronging in, the sympathies of the host might be aroused and a riot ensue in the camp, he stationed his trusted associates and the tribal leaders some distance off on the road, and had the fugitives conveyed separately to join their comrades in the sections of the camp which had been allotted originally to each tribe.

Next day he called a council of war and consoled his followers, bidding them not be unduly disheartened or disquieted by the disaster. Romans had not beaten them by superior courage or in fair fight, but by a kind of trickery and by their knowledge of siege-work, of which they themselves had no experience. It was a mistake to expect invariable success in war. They could testify that he had never approved of defending Avaricum: this reverse was due to the short-sightedness of the Bituriges and the undue complaisance of the other tribes. However, he would soon repair it by successes greater still. By good management he would gain over the dissentient tribes and make the whole of Gaul of one mind; and when Gaul was united, the whole world could not stand against her. This object, indeed, he had already nearly attained. Meanwhile he had a right to expect, in the name of the common weal, that they would take to fortifying their camps, so as to withstand sudden attacks more readily.

This speech made a good impression upon the Gauls. What pleased them most was that, despite a signal disaster, Vercingetorix had not lost heart or concealed himself or shrunk from facing the multitude; and they gave him all the more credit for foresight and prescience because, before the event, he had voted, first for the burning of Avaricum and afterwards for its abandonment. And so, while a reverse weakens the authority of commanders in general, his prestige, on the contrary, in consequence of the disaster, waxed daily greater. At the same time, relying upon his assurance, they entertained the hope of gaining over the other tribes. Gauls now for the first time began to fortify their camps; and they were so thoroughly frightened that, unused though they were to labour, they felt constrained to submit to every order.

Vercingetorix was as good as his word, and exercised his ingenuity to gain over the other tribes, tempting their chiefs by presents and offers of reward. He chose agents qualified for the purpose, selecting them for the persuasive power which they could exercise by plausible speech or good-fellowship. He made it his business to provide those who had escaped on the fall of Avaricum with arms and clothing; at the same time, in order to make good his losses, he levied a definite number of recruits from the tribes, fixing the strength of each contingent and the date by which he required them to arrive at headquarters; and he gave orders that all the archers in Gaul—a very numerous body—should be searched for and sent to him. By these measures the losses at Avaricum were speedily repaired. Meanwhile Teutomatus, king of the Nitiobroges, whose father had received from our Senate the title of Friend, joined him with a large body of his own cavalry and of others from Aquitania whom he had hired.

Caesar remained several days at Avaricum, where he found an abundance of grain and other stores, and thus enabled the army to recover from their labour and privation. Winter was now nearly over: the propitious season bade him take the field; and he had determined to march against the enemy in the hope of being able to lure him out of the marshes and forests or to keep him under close blockade, when the Aeduan magnates came as envoys to beg him to help their country in a serious emergency. The situation, they pleaded, was extremely critical. From remote antiquity the chief magistrates had regularly been appointed one at a time and held sovereign power for one year; now, however, there were two in office, each of whom asserted that his appointment was legal. One of them was Convictolitavis, a young man of influence and distinction; the other Cotus, a scion of a very old family, and, moreover, a man of commanding position and powerful family connections, whose brother, Valetiacus, had held the same office in the preceding year. The people were all up in arms: the council and the commonalty were divided; and the rivals were each supported by their own retainers. If the dispute were prolonged, the result would be civil war. It rested with Caesar to prevent this by his energy and influence.

Caesar considered it detrimental to leave the theatre of war and suspend his operations against the enemy; but he was aware that great disasters commonly arise from civil strife. The Aedui were a powerful tribe, bound by the closest ties to the Roman People: he had always promoted their interests and distinguished them by every mark of favour; and he regarded it as his first duty to prevent them from coming to blows, and the weaker party from applying for aid to Vercingetorix. As the holder of the chief magistracy was forbidden by Aeduan law to leave the country, he determined, in order to avoid the semblance of slighting their rights or their laws, to go in person to their country, and accordingly summoned the whole council and the disputants themselves to meet him at Decetia. There almost all the citizens of note assembled. Caesar was informed that a few persons had been secretly called together, and that one of the rivals had been declared elected by his own brother, in a wrong place and at a wrong time; whereas the law not only forbade two members of one family to be appointed while both were alive, but actually prohibited them from sitting in the council. He therefore compelled Cotus to resign, and authorized Convictolitavis, who had been appointed by the priests, in accordance with tribal custom in a period of interregnum, to continue to hold office.

Having stopped the dispute by this decision, Caesar counselled the Aedui to forget their disputes and dissensions, and, putting aside everything else, to devote themselves to the campaign, and look forward to receiving from him the reward which would be their due when Gaul was finally conquered: they were to send him quickly the whole of their cavalry and ten thousand foot, that he might distribute them for the protection of his convoys. He then divided the army into two parts. Assigning part of the cavalry to Labienus and retaining the rest, he gave him four legions, with which he was to march against the Senones and the Parisii, and advanced in person at the head of the remaining six towards the country of the Arverni, in the direction of the stronghold of Gergovia, following the bridges over the river, and marched up the opposite bank. The two armies were in full view of one another, and each encamped almost parallel with the camp of the other: patrols were thrown out to prevent the Romans from making a bridge anywhere and throwing their troops across; and thus Caesar was in a very difficult position, for he was in danger of being barred by the river for the greater part of the summer, as the Allier is not generally fordable before the autumn. To prevent this, he encamped in a wooded spot opposite which Vercingetorix had broken down, and next day remained there in concealment with two legions; the rest of the force he sent on as usual with all the baggage, breaking up some of the cohorts, so that the number of the legions might appear unchanged. He ordered them to march on as far as possible; and when he inferred from the time of day that they had reached camp, he proceeded to repair the bridge, making use of the original piles, the lower part of which was still entire. The work was rapidly finished; the legions crossed over; and, selecting a suitable spot for his camp, he recalled the other troops. When Vercingetorix found out what had happened, he pushed on ahead by forced marches, in order to avoid being compelled to fight against his will.

From the point where he had halted Caesar made his way to Gergovia in five marches. On the day of his arrival a cavalry skirmish took place. The town, situated upon a lofty hill, was difficult of access on all sides. After making a reconnaissance, Caesar concluded that a regular siege would be hopeless; and he resolved not to attempt a blockade until he had secured his supplies. Vercingetorix had encamped near the town and grouped the contingents of the several tribes at moderate distances from one another and round his own quarters. His force occupied all the high points of the mountain mass commanding a view over the plain, and presented a formidable appearance. He ordered the tribal chieftains, whom he had chosen to share his counsels, to come to him every morning at daybreak, to communicate intelligence or make arrangements for the defence; and there was hardly a day on which he missed sending his cavalry into action with archers scattered among their ranks, so as to test the mettle and the soldierly qualities of every man. Opposite the town, and at the very foot of the mountain, there was a hill of great natural strength and scarped on every side. If our troops could occupy it, they would probably be able to cut off the enemy from a principal source of their water-supply and harass their foragers; but they held the place, though with an inadequate force. Notwithstanding, Caesar moved out of his camp in the stillness of night, and before relief could arrive from the town, expelled the garrison, took possession of the place, and posted two legions to hold it. From the larger camp to the smaller he drew a pair of trenches, each twelve feet broad, to enable the men to come and go, even one at a time, secure from any sudden attack.

While these events were passing at Gergovia, Convictolitavis, the Aeduan, upon whom, as we have related, Caesar had conferred the chief magistracy, was bribed by the Arverni to join them. He communicated with a number of young men, the most prominent of whom were Litaviccus and his brothers, who belonged to a very illustrious family. Sharing the money with them, he urged them to bear in mind that they were free men, born to command. The Aedui, and they alone, prevented Gaul from making sure of success: their influence kept the other tribes in check; and if it were thrown into the opposite scale, the Romans would have no footing in Gaul. Personally, he was under some obligation to Caesar, though he had fully deserved to win his case; but obligation was outweighed by regard for the national liberty. Why, indeed, should the Aedui submit their rights and laws to the arbitration of Caesar any more than the Romans to that of the Aedui? The young men were speedily won by the magistrate's eloquence and his gold, and promised even to take the lead in his enterprise; and they tried to think of some method of accomplishing it, feeling doubtful whether the community could be lightly induced to embark on war. It was decided that Litaviccus should take command of the ten thousand who were to be sent to Caesar to take part in the campaign, and undertake the duty of leading them, and that his brothers should hurry on in advance to join Caesar. At the same time they arranged the rest of their programme.

Litaviccus took command of the army. About thirty miles from Gergovia he suddenly paraded the troops.

"Soldiers," he said, with a burst of tears, "All our cavalry, all our men of rank have perished. Two of our leading citizens, Eporedorix and Aeduan Viridomarus, have been falsely charged with treason and put to death by the Romans without trial. Learn the facts from these men, who have fled straight from the massacre; for my brothers and all my kinsfolk are slain, and grief prevents me from telling what has happened."

Some men whom he had schooled in their parts came forward, and repeated to the host the tale which Litaviccus had told. All the Aeduan cavalry, they said, had been massacred on the rumour that they had been in communication with the Arverni; they had themselves hidden in the crowd of soldiers and escaped from the midst of the slaughter. With one voice the Aedui adjured Litaviccus to consider their safety.

"As if," he cried, "it were a case for consideration! As if we were not bound to hurry on to Gergovia and join the Arverni! Can we doubt that the Romans, after the shameful deed they have done, are even now hastening to slay us? Therefore, if we have a spark of courage in us, let us avenge the deaths of our countrymen who have been most foully murdered, and kill these brigands."

Then, pointing to some Roman citizens who had accompanied him in reliance upon his escort, he seized a quantity of corn and other stores belonging to them, cruelly tortured them, and put them to death. Sending messengers throughout the length and breadth of the Aeduan territory, he stirred up the populace by the same lying tale of the massacre of cavalry and chiefs, and urged them to follow his example and avenge their wrongs.

Eporedorix, a young Aeduan of noble birth and commanding influence in his own country, and Viridomarus, a man of the same age and equally popular, but of lower birth, had been summoned expressly by Caesar, and had taken the field with the cavalry. Diviciacus had recommended Viridomarus to Caesar; and Caesar had raised him from a humble position to the highest dignity. He and Eporedorix were rivals for power; and in the struggle between the magistrates Eporedorix had been a strong partisan of Convictolitavis, and Viridomarus of Cotus. On learning Litaviccus's design, Eporedorix went to Caesar about midnight and told him the story. He begged him not to suffer the tribe to fall away from its friendship with the Roman People through the misguided counsels of raw youths; telling him that he foresaw that this would happen if such a numerous force joined the enemy, for their kinsmen could not disregard their safety or the tribe treat it as insignificant.

The news caused Caesar great anxiety; for he had always shown especial favour to the Aeduan community. Without a moment's hesitation, therefore, he left camp at the head of four legions in light marching order and the whole of the cavalry. There was no time at such a crisis to reduce the size of the camp, for success plainly depended upon prompt action; and he left Gaius Gergovia. Fabius to guard it with two legions. He ordered Litaviccus's brothers to be arrested, but found that they had escaped to the enemy a short time before. Addressing the men, he urged them not to mind a hard march at so critical a conjuncture. They were all in great heart; and, after a march of twenty-five miles, Caesar descried the Aeduan column, and, sending on his cavalry, delayed and finally stopped their advance, at the same time strictly forbidding all ranks to kill a single man, and telling Eporedorix and Viridomarus, who were supposed by the Aedui to have been killed, to move about among the troopers and speak to their countrymen. As soon as they were recognized and the Aedui saw that Litaviccus had deceived them, they stretched out their hands in token of surrender, grounding their arms and begging for their lives. Litaviccus escaped to Gergovia, accompanied by his retainers; for Gallic custom brands it as shameful for retainers to desert their lords even when all is lost.

Caesar sent messengers to the Aedui to explain that, as an act of favour, he had spared men whom the rights of war would have entitled him to put to death; and, after giving the army three hours in the night to rest, he moved on towards Gergovia. About half-way, some horsemen, sent by Fabius, met him and reported that the camp had been in imminent danger. The entire force of the enemy, they said, had attacked it, fresh men frequently relieving their comrades when they were tired, and wearing out our troops by incessant toil, as, on account of its great extent, they had to keep constantly on the rampart without relief Many had been wounded by showers of arrows and missiles of every kind; but the artillery had been of great use in enabling them to hold out. When the enemy retired, Fabius was blocking up all the gates except two, strengthening the rampart with breastworks, and preparing to meet a similar attack on the morrow. On receiving this intelligence, Caesar pushed on, and, thanks to the extraordinary energy of the men, reached camp before sunrise.

While these events were passing at Gergovia, the Aedui received Litaviccus's first message. Leaving themselves no time to find out the truth, they were impelled, some by greed, others by anger and rashness—an innate quality of the race —to take an idle rumour for an ascertained fact. They plundered Roman citizens; murdered them; kidnapped and enslaved them. Convictolitavis added fuel to the flame, and hounded on the masses to frenzy, in the hope that, once committed, they would feel ashamed to return to reason. Marcus Aristius, a military tribune, was on his way to join his legion. They promised him a safe conduct, and made him quit the town of Cabillonum, compelling the Romans who had settled there for trade to depart also. Forthwith they fell upon them on the road and robbed them of all their baggage. The Romans resisted, and their assailants beset them all day and the following night. Many were killed on both sides; and the assailants roused numbers to arm.

Meanwhile news arrived that all their infantry were in Caesar's power. Hurrying to Aristius, they explained that the government was not responsible for anything; and ordering an inquiry about the plundered property, they confiscated the goods of Litaviccus and his brothers, and sent envoys to make their excuses to Caesar. Their motive was to get their countrymen restored; but, stained with crime, fascinated by the profits of plunder (for many had had a hand in the outrages), and dreading retribution, they began to make secret preparations for war, and sent embassies to gain over the other tribes. Caesar was aware of their designs; nevertheless he spoke to their envoys with all possible gentleness, assuring them that he would not judge the whole people harshly because of the ignorant folly of the masses, or abate his goodwill towards the Aedui. Anxiety that the insurrection in Gaul would spread, and desiring to avoid being surrounded by all the tribes, he began to think out a plan for withdrawing from the neighbourhood of Gergovia and once more concentrating the whole army in such a way that his departure might not be attributed to fear of a general defection and resemble a flight.

While he was meditating on this problem, he thought he saw an opportunity of striking a telling blow. Going to the smaller camp to inspect the works, he noticed that a hill in the possession of the enemy was completely deserted whereas before it could hardly be discerned for their number. In astonishment, he inquired of the deserters, who daily flocked to join him in great numbers, what was the reason. They were all agreed—and Caesar had already found out the same thing for himself through his patrols—that the ridge to which the hill belonged was nearly level, but where it gave access to the further side of the town wooded and narrow. The Gauls were intensely anxious for the safety of this place; and, one hill being already held by the Romans, they now felt sure that, if they lost the other, they would be all but surrounded, fairly cut off from all egress, and prevented from foraging. Every man, therefore, had been called away by Vercingetorix to fortify the position.

On learning this, Caesar sent several squadrons of cavalry thither about midnight, ordering them to rove all over the country and make a good deal of noise. At daybreak he ordered a large number of pack-horses and mules to be taken out of camp, the pack-saddles to be taken off, and the drivers to put on helmets, so as to look like troopers, and ride round over the hills. He sent a few regular cavalry with them, with orders to wander further afield, so as to increase the effect. All were to make a wide circuit and head towards the same goal. These movements could be seen, far off, from the town, as Gergovia commanded a view of the camp; but it was impossible, at such a distance, to make out exactly what they mean. A single legion was sent along the same chain; and after it had advanced a little way it was stationed on lower ground and concealed in the woods. The suspicions of the Gauls were intensified; and they transferred all their forces to the threatened point to help in the work of fortification. Noticing that the enemy's camps were deserted, Caesar made his soldiers cover their crests and hide their standards, and move, a few at a time, to avoid being observed from the town, from the larger to the smaller camp. At the same time he explained his plans to his generals, each of whom he had placed in command of a legion, warning them above all to keep the men in hand, and not let them advance too far from over-eagerness for fighting or lust for plunder. He pointed out that the unfavourable ground placed them at a disadvantage, which could only be avoided by moving quickly; it was a case for a surprise, not a regular battle. Having made these instructions clear, he gave the signal, at the same time sending the Aedui up the hill by another path on the right.

The wall of the town was nine furlongs in a straight line from the plain, where the ascent began, without reckoning any bend; the turns that were necessary for easing the slope added outer line of so much to the length of the climb. About halfway up, running lengthways in the direction indicated by the formation of the mountain, the Gauls had built a wall six feet high, of large stones, to check any attack by our men. All the space below was left unoccupied; but the higher part of the hill up to the wall of the town was thickly covered by their camps. When the signal was given, the men rapidly gained the outer line of defence, clambered over it, and took possession of three camps. They did this so quickly that Teutomatus, king of the Nitiobroges, was surprised in his tent, where he was taking his siesta, and only just broke away, naked to the waist and with his horse wounded, from the clutches of the plundering soldiers. Having achieved his purpose, Caesar ordered the recall to be sounded, and immediately halted the legion, which he commanded in person. The men of the other legions did not hear the sound of the trumpet, as a considerable valley intervened; still the tribunes and the generals, in obedience to Caesar's command, tried to keep them in hand. Elated, however, by the expectation of a speedy triumph, by the enemy's flight, and by the recollection of past victories, they fancied that nothing was too difficult for their valour to achieve, and pressed on in pursuit till they got close to the wall and gates of the fortress. Then a cry arose from every part of the town; and those who were some way off, panic-stricken by the sudden uproar, and believing that the enemy were inside the gates, rushed pell-mell out of the stronghold. Matrons flung down clothes and money from the wall, and, leaning over with breasts bare, stretched forth their hands and besought the Romans to spare them, and to refuse quarter even to women and children, as they had done at Avaricum; while some were let down from the walls and gave themselves up to the soldiers. Lucius Fabius, a centurion of the 8th legion, who was known to have said that day, in the hearing of his men, that he was fired by the recollection of the rewards that had been offered at Avaricum, and would suffer no man to mount the wall before him, got three men of his company, and, being hoisted up by them, clambered up the wall; then in turn hauling them up one by one, he lifted them on to it.

Meanwhile the men who, as we have pointed out above, had assembled near the other end of the town to fortify the position, heard the outcry, and presently, stimulated by a succession of messages, telling that the town was in the hands of the Romans, sent on horsemen ahead, and hurried up at a great pace. Each man, as he successively arrived, took his stand under the wall and swelled the number of his comrades. And now a great multitude had assembled, and the matrons, who a moment before had been holding out their hands to the Romans from the wall, began to adjure their men-folk and displayed their streaming locks, as Gallic women do, and brought out their children for all to see. It was no fair fight for the Romans. The ground was unfavourable; their numbers were inferior; and, tired out by their rapid climb and the protracted combat, they could not well hold their own against men who had just come fresh into action.

Caesar, seeing that the fight was not on a fair field, and that the enemy's force was increasing became anxious for the safety of his men, and sent an order to Titus Sextius, the general whom he had left in charge of the smaller camp, to take his cohorts out quickly and form them up at the foot of the hill, on the enemy's right flank, so as to check their pursuit in case he saw our men driven from their position. Advancing a little with his own legion from the position which he had taken up, he awaited the issue of the combat.

Fierce fighting was going on, the enemy relying upon position and numbers, our men upon valour, when suddenly the Aedui, whom Caesar had sent up by another path on the right, to create a diversion, were descried on our exposed flank. Being armed like Gauls, they caused a violent panic among our men; and although it was noticed that their right shoulders were bare—the recognized symbol of peace—yet the soldiers fancied that they were foes and had done this on purpose to deceive them. At the same moment the centurion, Lucius Fabius, and the men who had climbed the wall along with him, were surrounded and killed, and their bodies pitched down from the wall. Marcus Petronius, a centurion of the same legion, made an attempt to hew down the gates, but, overwhelmed by numbers, desperate, and covered with wounds, he said to the men of his company who had followed him, "Since I cannot save myself and you, I will, at all events, try to save your lives, for it was I, in my lust for glory, who brought you into danger. You have your chance: use it!" With these words he dashed in among the enemy, killed two of them, and forced the rest back a little way from the gate. His men attempted to help him. "It's useless," he cried, "for you to try to save my life, for blood and strength are ebbing. Go, then, while you have the chance, and return to your legion." So he fought, and soon fell; and so he saved his men.

Overborne at every point, the Romans were driven from their position with the loss of forty-six centurions. The Gauls were relentlessly pursuing when the 10th legion, which had taken post in reserve on comparatively favourable ground, checked them; and the 10th was in its turn supported by the cohorts of the 13th, which had quitted the smaller camp under Titus Sextius, and occupied a commanding position. The moment the legions reached the plain they halted and showed a bold front to the enemy; and Vercingetorix withdrew his men from the foot of the hill into his entrenchments. Nearly seven hundred men were lost that day.

Next day Caesar paraded his troops, and reprimanded them for the rashness and impetuosity which they had shown in judging for themselves how far they were to advance and what they were to do, not halting when the signal was given for recall, and refusing to submit to the control of the tribunes and the generals. He explained that an unfavourable position made a serious difference; he had experienced this himself at Avaricum, when, though he had the enemy in his grasp without their general and without their cavalry, he had an assured triumph for fear the unfavourable ground should entail a loss, however slight, in the action. He heartily admired their heroic spirit, which entrenched camp and high mountain and walled fortress were powerless to daunt; but just as heartily he reprobated their contempt for discipline and their presumption in imagining that they knew how to win battles and forecast results better than their general. He required from his soldiers obedience and self-control just as much as courage and heroism. After this harangue Caesar, in conclusion, encouraged the men, telling them not to let an incident like this trouble them, and not to ascribe losses to the enemy's courage a result which had been brought about by the unfavourable nature of the ground. His intention of abandoning Gergovia being unchanged, he led the legions out of camp, and formed them in line of battle on a good position. Still Vercingetorix did not venture down on to the level. A cavalry skirmish followed, which resulted in favour of the Romans; and Caesar then withdrew his army into camp. Next day he fought a similar action; and then, thinking that he had done enough to humble the vainglory of the Gauls and to restore the confidence of his soldiers, he marched for the country of the Aedui. Even then the enemy did not pursue. Two days later Caesar repaired a bridge over the Allier and threw his army across.

At this Stage the Aeduans, Viridomarus and Eporedorix, approached and accosted him. He learned that Litaviccus had gone off with all the cavalry to work upon the Aedui. It was essential, they urged, that they should be beforehand, in order to keep the tribe steady. By this time Caesar saw clearly from many signs that the Aedui were traitors, and he was of opinion that the departure of these men would hasten their defection: still he did not think it right to detain them; for he desired to avoid the semblance of injustice and not lay himself open to the suspicion of fear. As they were leaving he told them briefly what he had done for the Aedui, pointing out how they were situated and how low they had fallen when his connection with them began, — driven into their strongholds, their lands confiscated, and their allies all taken from them, tribute imposed upon them and hostages wrung from them with the grossest insults; then how he had raised them to such prosperity and power that they not only regained their former position but acquired, in the sight of all, a prestige and influence which they had never enjoyed before. With this reminder he let them go.

There was an Aeduan town, advantageously situated on the banks of the Loire, called Noviodunum. Thither Caesar had conveyed all the hostages of Gaul, his grain, the public monies, and a large portion of his own baggage and that of the army: thither, too, he had sent a large number of horses, which he had purchased in Italy and Spain for the war. On reaching the town, Eporedorix and Viridomarus ascertained the attitude of their tribe: Litaviccus had been received by the Aedui at Bibracte, the most influential town in the country; Convictolitavis, the first magistrate, and a large proportion of the council had assembled to meet him; and envoys had been officially dispatched to Vercingetorix to effect a friendly understanding. An opportunity like this, they thought, was not to be missed. Accordingly they massacred the guard at Noviodunum and the individuals who had settled there for trade, and divided the treasure and the horses; arranged for the conveyance of the hostages of the several tribes to the magistrate at Bibracte; burned the town, which they considered it impossible to hold, to prevent its being of use to the Romans; carried away in barges as much grain as they could hurriedly stow away; and threw the rest into the river or burned it. They then proceeded to raise forces from the neighbouring districts, establishing detachments and piquets along the banks of the Loire, and throwing out cavalry in all directions to terrorize the Romans, in the hope of being able to prevent them from getting corn or to drive them, under stress of destitution, to make for the Province. It was a strong point in their favour that the Loire was swollen from the melting of the snow, so that, to all appearance, it was quite unfordable.

On learning this, Caesar decided that he must act at once, in case it should be necessary to take the risk of bridging the river, he might be able to fight before reinforcements came up. To change his whole plan of campaign and march for the Province,—that, he deemed, was a course to which he ought not to allow even the pressure of fear to force him; for the disgrace and the humiliation of retreat, the barrier interposed by the Cevennes, and the condition of the roads forbade him to attempt it; and above all he was intensely anxious for Labienus, who was separated from him, and for the legions which he had placed under his command. Accordingly he made a series of extraordinary marches by day and night; reached the Loire before any one had expected him; and discovered a ford by the help of the cavalry, which was good enough for an emergency (the men being just able to keep their arms and shoulders above water, to carry their weapons). The cavalry were formed in line to break the force of the current; and, the enemy flying in confusion at the first sight of the army, he brought it safely across. Having satisfied its wants with corn and large numbers of cattle, which he found in the district, he pushed on for the country of the Senones.

While Caesar was engaged in these operations, Labienus marched for Lutetia with his four legions, leaving the draft which had recently arrived from Italy at Agedincum, to protect the heavy baggage. Lutetia is a town belonging to the Parisii, situated on an island in the river Seine. When the enemy became aware of his approach, large forces assembled from the neighbouring tribes. The chief command was conferred upon an Aulercan, named Camulogenus, who, though old and worn, was called to this high place because of his uncommon knowledge of war. Observing that there was a continuous marsh, which drained into the Seine and rendered the whole country in its neighbourhood impassable, Labienus at first formed a line of sheds and attempted to fill up the marsh with fascines and other material and thus make a causeway to march across. Finding this scarcely practicable, he silently quitted his camp in the third watch, and made his way, by the route by which he had advanced, to Metiosedum, a town belonging to the Senones, situated, like Lutetia, of which we have just spoken, on an island in the Seine. Labienus seized about fifty barges, rapidly lashed them together, and threw the troops on to them: the townspeople, many of whom had been summoned into the field, were paralysed with astonishment and fear; and Labienus took the town without a blow. After repairing the bridge, which the enemy had recently broken down, he made the army cross over, and marched on, following the course of the stream, in the direction of Lutetia. The enemy, informed of what he had done by fugitives from Metiosedum, gave orders that Lutetia should be burned and its bridges broken down: then, moving away from the marsh, they encamped on the banks of the Seine, opposite Lutetia and over against the camp of Labienus.

By this time it was known that Caesar had abandoned his position at Gergovia: by this. time too rumours were arriving about the defection of the Aedui and the success of the Gallic insurrection; and the Gauls affirmed that Caesar was prevented from pursuing his march and from crossing the Loire, and that want of corn had forced him to make a dash for the Province. The Bellovaci, moreover, who were already and spontaneously disaffected, on learning that the Aedui had gone over, began to raise troops and to make overt preparations for war. Now that the situation had so completely changed, Labienus saw that he must completely alter his original plan: what he thought of now was not how to gain some positive advantage and force the enemy to an engagement, but how to get his army safely back to Agedincum. On one side he was menaced by the Bellovaci, who have the greatest reputation for fighting as any tribe in Gaul; on the other Camulogenus held the field with a well-found army, ready for action; while a great river separated the legions from their baggage and the troops which protected it. With these formidable difficulties suddenly confronting him, he saw that he must look for aid to the force of his own character.

Towards evening he assembled his officers, and, charging them to carry out his orders to the letter, placed one of the Roman knights in charge of each of the barges which he had brought down from Metiosedum, and ordered them to move silently four miles downstream at the end of the first watch, and wait for him there. Leaving five cohorts, which he believed to be the least steady in action, to hold the camp, he ordered the remaining five of the same legion to move up the river about midnight with the whole baggage-train, and make a great noise. He also procured a number of small boats, and sent them in the same direction, the rowers making a great splash with their oars. Soon afterwards he silently moved out of camp with three legions, and made for the spot to which he had ordered the barges to be rowed.

When the legions reached the spot, the enemy's patrols were surprised at their posts all along the river by our troops—for a great storm had sprung up suddenly—and cut down. Infantry and cavalry were swiftly ferried across under the superintendence of the Roman knights, whom Labienus had charged with the duty. Just before dawn and almost simultaneously the enemy were informed that an unusual commotion was going on in the Roman camp; that a large column was moving up the river, and the sound of oars audible in the same direction; and that troops were being ferried across a little lower down. On hearing this, they imagined that the legions were crossing at three places, and that the Romans, in alarm at the defection of the Aedui, were all preparing for flight. Accordingly they made a corresponding distribution of their own troops. Leaving a force opposite the Roman camp, and sending a small body in the direction of Metiosedum, with orders to advance as far as the boats had gone, they led the rest of their troops against Labienus.

By daybreak the whole of our troops were ferried across and the enemy's line was discernible. Labienus, bidding the soldiers remember their ancient valour and their many splendid victories, and imagine that Caesar, under whose command they had many times beaten the enemy, was present in person, gave the signal for action. At the first onset, the right wing, where the 7th legion stood, drove back the enemy and put them to flight. The 12th legion occupied the left. There the enemy's foremost ranks fell, transfixed by javelins: but the other ranks vigorously resisted; and not a man laid himself open to the suspicion of cowardice. Camulogenus, the enemy's commander, supported his men by his presence and cheered them on. And now, when victory was still doubtful, the tribunes of the 7th legion, who had been told of what was passing on the left wing, made the legion show itself on the enemy's rear, and charged. Even in that moment not a man quitted his post; but all were surrounded and slain. Camulogenus shared their fate. The detachment which had been left on guard opposite Labienus's camp, on hearing that the battle had begun, went to the support of their comrades and occupied a hill; but they could not withstand the onset of our victorious soldiery. Mingling with their flying comrades, they were slain—all who failed to find shelter in the woods and on the hills—by the Roman cavalry. Labienus's task was accomplished. He returned to Agedincum, where he had left the heavy baggage of the whole army, and thence made his way, with his entire force, to the quarters of Caesar.

When the defection of the Aedui became known the gravity of the war increased. Embassies were dispatched in all directions, the Aedui exerting all their influence, prestige, and pecuniary resources to win over the tribes; and, having in their power the hostages whom Caesar had left in their country, they intimidated waverers by threatening to kill them. They requested Vercingetorix to visit them and concert with them a plan of campaign; and when he complied, they insisted that the supreme control should be transferred to them. The demand was disputed; and a Pan-Gallic council was convened at Bibracte. Delegates flocked thither in numbers.

The question was put to the vote; and the delegates unanimously confirmed the appointment of Vercingetorix as commander-in-chief. The Remi, Lingones, and Treveri were not represented in the council,—the two former because they adhered to their friendship with the Romans; the Treveri because they were far away and were themselves hard pressed by the Germans, for which reason they kept aloof all through the war and remained neutral. The Aedui, bitterly chagrined at being ousted from the supremacy, lamented their change of fortune and sorely missed Caesar's favour; yet, having taken up arms, they dared not sever themselves from the other tribes. Reluctantly those ambitious young leaders, Eporedorix and Viridomarus, obeyed Vercingetorix.

The commander-in-chief ordered the newly joined tribes to give hostages, fixing a date for their arrival, and directed all the cavalry, numbering fifteen thousand, to assemble speedily. He announced that he would content himself with the infantry which he had already, and would not tempt fortune by fighting a battle, for, as he was strong in cavalry, it would be quite easy to prevent the Romans from getting corn and forage: only let the patriots destroy their own corn and burn their homesteads in the certainty that by this personal sacrifice they were securing independence and liberty for evermore, Having made these arrangements, he ordered the Aedui and the Segusiavi, who are conterminous with the Province, to furnish ten thousand infantry, which he reinforced by eight hundred cavalry, and, placing Eporedorix's brother in command, directed him to attack the Allobroges. In another quarter, he sent the Gabali and the Arvernian clans nearest to the Helvii to attack that people, and the Ruteni and Cadurci to devastate the territory of the Volcae Arecomici. At the same time he attempted by secret emissaries and embassies to gain over the Allobroges, promising money to the leading men, and to the tribe dominion over the whole Province; for he hoped that they had not yet forgotten the late war.

To meet these emergencies there were detachments in readiness, amounting to twenty-two cohorts, which had been raised by Lucius from the whole Province, and were posted to meet every attack. The Helvii, who encountered the neighbouring clans on their own, were defeated with the loss of Gaius Valerius Domnotaurus, the first magistrate, and many others, and forced to take refuge in strongholds and behind walls. The Allobroges posted a chain of piquets along the Rhone, and defended their own territory with great care and vigilance. Caesar, being aware of the enemy's superiority in cavalry, and unable to get any assistance from the Province and Italy as all the roads were blocked, sent across the Rhine to the tribes of Germany which he had subdued in former years, and called into the field cavalry with the light-armed foot which habitually fight in their rank's. On their arrival, as their horses were unserviceable, he took those of the tribunes and other Roman knights and also of the time-expired volunteers, and assigned them to the Germans.

During these operations the enemy's forces and the cavalry levied from Vercingetorix were assembling to attack him. Vercingetorix collected a large number of these troops, and while Caesar was marching through the most distant part of the country of the Lingones which was furthest from his [Caesar's] starting-point in the direction in which he was going, that is, towards the country of the Sequani, that he might be in a better position for reinforcing the Province, took post in three camps about ten miles from the Romans. Summoning his cavalry officers to a council of war, he told them that the hour of victory had come: the Romans were retreating to the Province and abandoning Gaul. This would secure liberty for the time: but for lasting peace and tranquillity the gain was small; for they would come back in increased force and continue the war indefinitely. The cavalry, then, must attack them on the march, while they were helpless. If the infantry stopped to support their comrades, they could not continue their march: if, as he thought more likely, they abandoned their baggage and tried to save themselves, they would lose indispensable materiel as well as prestige. As for the enemy's cavalry, they at any rate ought not to doubt that not a man of them would dare so much as stir outside the column. To encourage them in their attack, he would post all his troops in front of the camps and overawe the enemy. With one voice the knights exclaimed that every man must be sworn by a solemn oath to ride twice through the enemy's column, or never be admitted beneath a roof, never come nigh unto children, or parents, or wife.

The proposal was approved; and every man was sworn. Next day the cavalry were divided into three sections, two of which made a demonstration on either flank, while the third checked the advance of the vanguard. When the movement was reported, Caesar in turn divided his cavalry into three parts, and ordered them to advance against the enemy. The combat became general. The column halted; and the baggage was brought into the intervals between the legions. When, at any point, our men appeared to be in difficulties or actually overmatched, Caesar made the infantry advance in their direction and form in line. These tactics prevented the enemy from following up their advantage, and encouraged our men by the assurance of support. At length the Germans occupied the summit of a ridge on the right flank, dislodged the enemy, and drove them in rout with heavy loss to a stream where Vercingetorix had taken post with his infantry. Observing this, the rest of the cavalry were afraid of being surrounded, and took to flight. The whole field was a scene of carnage. Three Aeduans of the highest rank were brought prisoners to Caesar,— Cotus, commandant of the cavalry, who had disputed the claims of Convictolitavis at the recent election; Cavarillus, who had taken command of the infantry after the defection of Litaviccus; and Eporedorix, who had commanded the Aedui in their war with the Sequani before Caesar's arrival.

After the total defeat of his cavalry, Vercingetorix withdrew his infantry from the position which he had taken up in front of the fortress camps, and, ordering his baggage-train to leave camp quickly and follow him, marched forthwith for Alesia, a stronghold of the Mandubii. Caesar removed his baggage to a hill close by, and, leaving two legions to guard it, kept up the pursuit as long as daylight permitted, killing about three thousand of the enemy's rearguard, and encamped next day in the neighbourhood of Alesia. The enemy were cowed by the defeat of their cavalry, the arm in which they had the greatest confidence; accordingly, after reconnoitering the position, he called upon the soldiers to brace themselves for an effort and proceeded to form a contravallation.

The fortress stood on the top of a hill, in a very commanding position, being apparently impregnable except by blockade. The base of the hill was washed on two sides by two streams. In front of the town extended a plain about three miles in length; and on every other side it was surrounded, at a moderate distance, by hills of elevation equal to its own. Below the wall, on the side of the hill which looked towards the east, the whole space was crowded with the Gallic troops, who had fortified it with a ditch and a wall of loose stones, six feet high. The perimeter of the works which the Romans were about to construct covered eleven miles. Camps were established in convenient positions; and in their neighbourhood twenty-three redoubts were constructed, in which piquets were posted during the day, to prevent any sudden sortie, while at night they were guarded by strong bivouacs. After the commencement of the works a cavalry combat took place in the plain which, as we have explained above, formed a gap in the hills, extending three miles in length. Both sides fought their hardest. As our men were in difficulties, Caesar sent the Germans to support them, and drew up the legions in front of the camps to prevent any sudden attack by the enemy's infantry. Supported by the legions, our men gathered confidence: the enemy were put to flight, and, hampered by their own numbers, got jammed in the gateways, which had been left too narrow. The Germans hotly pursued them right up to the entrenchments. The carnage was great, and some of the fugitives dismounted and tried to cross the ditch and climb over the wall. Caesar ordered the legions which he had drawn up in front of the ramparts to advance a little. The Gauls inside the entrenchments were not less terrified than the fugitives, and, believing that they would speedily be attacked, shouted "To arms"; while some rushed panic-stricken into the town. Vercingetorix ordered the gates to be shut, to prevent the camp from being deserted; and the Germans, having killed a great many men and captured a number of horses, returned.

Vercingetorix now determined to send away all his cavalry in the night before the Romans had time to complete the entrenchments. As they were moving off, he bade them go, every man to his own country, and make all who were of an age to bear arms take the field. Reminding them of his own services, he adjured them to have some regard for his safety and not to give up one who had served so well the cause of national liberty to be tortured by the enemy. If they did not bestir themselves, he told them, eighty thousand picked men would perish with him. He calculated that he had corn enough to last barely thirty days: but by reducing the rations it might be possible to hold out a little longer. With these instructions he silently sent out the cavalry through a gap in the works. He ordered all the grain to be brought to him, giving notice that those who disobeyed should be put to death; distributed the livestock, of which a great quantity had been driven in by the Mandubii, individually among the garrison; made arrangements for doling out the grain gradually; and withdrew into the town all the forces which he had posted in front of it. In this way he prepared to fight on and await the Gallic reinforcements.

Being informed of what had passed by deserters and prisoners, Caesar planned defensive works of the following kind. Constructing a trench twenty feet wide with vertical sides, the width at the bottom being exactly equal to the distance between its upper edges, he traced out all the remaining works eight hundred paces behind it, his object being, as he was obliged to cover such a vast extent of ground and it was not easy to man the whole system of works with an unbroken ring of troops, to prevent the enemy from swooping down unexpectedly upon the lines in force at night, or in the day-time discharging missiles at the men while they were at work. Leaving this interval, he dug two trenches of equal depth, each fifteen feet wide, and filled the inner one, where it crossed the plain and the low ground, with water drawn from the stream. Behind the trenches he constructed a rampart and palisade twelve feet high, which he strengthened by an embattled breastwork, with large forked branches projecting along the line where the breastwork joined the rampart, to check the ascent of the enemy; and erected towers on the entire circuit of the works at intervals of eighty feet.

While these vast fortifications were being constructed, it was necessary to fetch timber and corn; and the troops, having to move considerable distances from camp, were unavoidably weakened. Sometimes, indeed, the Gauls attempted to storm our works and made furious sallies from the town by several gates. Caesar therefore thought it necessary to strengthen the works still further, in order to render the lines defensible by a smaller force. Accordingly trees or very stout branches were cut down and their ends stripped of their bark and sharpened to a point; continuous trenches were then dug, five feet deep, in which the logs were planted and fastened down at the bottom to prevent their being dragged out, while the boughs projected above. There were five rows in each trench, connected with one another and interlaced; and all who stepped in would impale themselves on the sharp stakes. The men called them "grave-stones." In front of them, arranged in slanting rows in the form of a quincunx, pits were dug, three feet deep, which tapered gradually towards the bottom. Smooth logs, as thick as a man's thigh, sharpened at the top and hardened by fire, were planted in them, projecting not more than four fingers above the ground. At the same time the earth was trampled down to the depth of one foot above the bottom, to keep them firmly in position; while the rest of the pit was covered with twigs and brushwood to hide the trap. There were eight rows of this kind, three feet apart. The men called them lilies, from their resemblance to that flower. In front of them blocks of wood a foot long, with barbed iron spikes let into them, were completely buried in the earth and scattered about in all directions at moderate intervals. The men called them "spurs."

When these defences were completed, Caesar constructed, along the most suitable tracts which the lie of the country enabled him to follow, embracing a circuit of fourteen miles, corresponding works of the same kind, facing the opposite way, to repel the enemy from without, so as to prevent the troops who defended the lines from being hemmed in by any force, however numerous; and, in order to avoid the danger of having to leave camp, he directed all the troops to provide themselves with fodder and corn for thirty days.

While this was going on at Alesia, the Gauls convened a council of their leading men, who decided not to adopt Vercingetorix's plan of assembling all who could bear arms, but to levy a definite contingent from each tribe; for they were afraid that with such a vast multitude crowding together they would not be able to control their respective contingents or keep them apart, or to organize any system for providing grain. The Aedui with their dependents, the Segusiavi, Ambivareti, and Aulerci Bran-novices, were ordered to find thirty-five thousand men; the Arverni, along with the Eleuteti, Cadurci, Gabali, and Vellavii, who are habituated to their sway, the same number; the Sequani, Senones, Bituriges, Santoni, Ruteni, and Carnutes, each twelve thousand; the Bellovaci, ten thousand, and the Lemovices the same; the Pictones, Turoni, Parisii, and Helvetii, each eight thousand; the Andes, Ambiani, Mediomatrici, Petrocorii, Nervii, Morini, and Nitiobroges, each six thousand; the Aulerci Cenomani, five thousand, and the Atrebates the same; the Vellocasses, four thousand; the Aulerci Eburovices three thousand; the Rauraci and Boii, each two thousand; and all the maritime tribes conjointly, which the Gauls usually call Armorican, including the Coriosolites, Redones, Ambibarii, Caletes, Osismi, Veneti, Lemovices, and Venelli, thirty thousand. The Bellovaci did not furnish their proper contingent, saying that they would fight the Romans on their own account, just as they pleased, and not submit to the dictation of any one; however, at the request of Commius, and in consideration of their friendly relations with him, they sent two thousand men along with the rest.

Caesar, as we have already mentioned, had found Commius a loyal and serviceable agent in former years in Britain; and, in acknowledgment of these services, he had granted his tribe immunity from taxation, restored to it its rights and laws, and placed the Morini under his authority. Yet so intense was the unanimous determination of the entire Gallic people to establish their liberty and recover their ancient military renown that no favours, no recollection of former friendship, had any influence with them, but all devoted their energies and resources to the prosecution of the war. Eight thousand horse and about two hundred and fifty thousand foot were raised. They were reviewed and numbered in the country of the Aedui, and their officers appointed. The Atrebatian, Commius, the two Aeduans, Viridomarus and Eporedorix, and Vercassivellaunus, an Arvernian and kinsman of Vercingetorix, were entrusted with the command. Delegates from the various tribes were associated with them, in accordance with whose advice they were to conduct the campaign. All started for Alesia in high spirits and full of confidence; and there was not one of them who did not believe that the mere appearance of so vast a host would be irresistible especially as the fighting would be on two fronts, the besieged sallying forth from the town, while without would be conspicuous those huge hosts of cavalry and infantry.

But the besieged in Alesia knew nothing of what was going on in the country of the Aedui; cannibalism, which they had expected their countrymen to succour them was past; and their grain was all consumed. A council of war was therefore convened; and they considered what was to become of them. Various opinions were mooted. Some advised surrender; others a sortie while their strength held out; but Critognatus, an Arvernian of noble family and acknowledged influence, made a speech, which, in view of its singular and atrocious cruelty, ought not, I think, to be passed over. "I do not intend," he said, "to notice the view of those who dignify the most abject slavery by the title of surrender; for I hold that they ought not to be counted as citizens or admitted to a council. I am only concerned with those who are in favour of a sortie; for, as you are all agreed, in their counsel is to be recognized the memory of our ancient valour. To be unable to bear privation for a short span,— that I call weakness, not manly resolution. It is easier to find men who will affront death than men who will patiently endure suffering. And yet I would give my sanction to this view—so highly do I respect the authority of its advocates—if I saw no evil involved in it save the sacrifice of our own lives; but in forming our plans we must have regard to the whole of Gaul, for we have called upon the whole of Gaul to help us. If eighty thousand men fall on one field, what, think you, will be the feelings of our friends and kinsmen, when they are constrained to fight almost on the very corpses of the slain? To save you, they have counted their personal danger as nothing; do not, then, rob them of your aid; do not, by your folly and rashness or lack of resolution, ruin the whole of Gaul and subject it to perpetual slavery. Can it be that, because they have not arrived punctually to the day, you doubt their good faith and resolution? What then? Do you suppose that the Romans are toiling day after day on those outer lines, simply to amuse themselves? If the messengers of your countrymen cannot reassure you because all ingress is barred, accept Roman testimony that their coming is near: dread of that event keeps them busy upon their works night and day. What, then, is my counsel I counsel you to do what our fathers did in their war with the Cimbri and Teutoni,—a war in no way comparable to this: forced into their strongholds and brought low, like us, by famine, they kept themselves alive by feeding upon the flesh of those whose age disqualified them for war; but they did not surrender to the enemy. And if we had no precedent for this, still, in the name of liberty, I would hold it a most glorious precedent to create and bequeath to posterity. For what resemblance was there between that war and this? The Cimbri devastated Gaul and brought upon her grievous calamity; but they did at last leave our country and seek other lands; they did leave us our rights, our laws, our lands, our liberty. But the Romans, what aim, what purpose have they but this,—from mere envy to settle in the lands and tribal territories of a people whose renown and warlike prowess they have come to know, and to fasten upon them the yoke of everlasting slavery? Never have they made war on any other principle. If you know not what is going on among distant peoples, look at the Gaul on your border: reduced to a province, its rights and laws revolutionized, prostrate beneath the lictor's axe, it is crushed by perpetual slavery."

The votes were recorded. It was decided that those whose age or infirmity disqualified them for fighting should leave the town; that the rest should try every expedient before having recourse to Critognatus's proposal; but that, if circumstances were too strong and the reinforcements delayed, they should adopt it rather than stoop to accept terms of surrender or peace. The Mandubii, who had admitted them into the town, were compelled to leave with their wives and children. When they reached the lines, they earnestly entreated the Romans with tears to receive them as slaves,—only give them something to eat. But Caesar posted guards on the rampart, and forbade them admission from our entrenchments. Next day they moved their cavalry out of camp, occupied the whole plain which, as we have shown, extends three miles in length, and, drawing back their infantry a little, posted them on the high ground. The town of Alesia commanded a view over the plain. Descrying the reinforcements, the besieged crowded together and congratulated each other; and all were joyfully excited. Leading their forces to the front, they took post before the town, filled up the nearest trench with fascines covered with earth, and made ready for a sortie and for every hazard.

Disposing his whole force on both lines of entrenchment, so that every man might know his cavalry. proper place and keep it, ready for emergencies, Caesar ordered the cavalry to move out of camp and engage. All the camps which crowned the surrounding heights commanded a view of the field; and all the soldiers were intently awaiting the issue of the combat. Here and there among their cavalry the Gauls had scattered archers and active light-armed foot, to support their comrades in case they gave way, and withstand the charges of our cavalry. A good many men were wounded by these troops, whose attack they had not foreseen, and left the field. Feeling sure that their countrymen were winning, and observing that our men were being overpowered by numbers, the beleaguered Gauls, as well as those who had come to rescue them, cheered and yelled on every side to encourage their comrades. As the fighting was going on in full view of every one, and no gallant deed, no cowardice, could escape notice, love of glory and fear of disgrace stimulated both sides to valour. From noon till near sunset the fight went on; and still the issue was doubtful. At length the Germans massed their squadrons at one point, and charged and forced back the enemy; and on their flight the archers were surrounded and slain. The other divisions likewise falling back, our men gave them no chance of rallying, but pursued them right up to their encampment. The besieged, who had sallied forth from Alesia, well-nigh despairing of success, sadly retreated into the town.

An interval of one day followed, during which the Gauls made a great quantity of fascines, ladders, and grappling-hooks fixed to long poles. At midnight they moved silently out of camp and advanced to the entrenchments in the plain. Suddenly they raised a shout to inform the besieged of their approach, and began to throw their fascines, to drive the Romans from the rampart with slings, arrows, and stones, and in every other way to press the attack. Simultaneously Vercingetorix, hearing the distant cry, sounded the trumpet and led his men out of the town. Our troops moved up to the entrenchments, in the places which had been severally allotted to them beforehand, and drove back the Gauls with slings throwing large stones and sharp stakes which they had laid at intervals on the rampart, and with bullets. The darkness made it impossible to see clearly, and on both sides many were wounded; while missiles were hurled in showers by the artillery. Two generals, Mark Antony and Gains Trebonius, who had been charged with the defence of this part of the lines, withdrew troops from the distant redoubts, and reinforced our men at every point where they saw them overmatched.

So long as the Gauls kept at a distance from the entrenchment, the number of their missiles gave them the advantage; but when they came closer, some trod unawares upon the "spurs," others tumbled into the pits and impaled themselves, while others were transfixed by heavy pikes from the rampart and towers, and perished. Everywhere they suffered heavy loss, and at no point did they break the lines. Towards daybreak, fearing that they might be attacked from the higher camps on their exposed flank and surrounded, they fell back and rejoined their comrades. The besieged lost much time in bringing out the implements which Vercingetorix had prepared for the sortie, and in filling up the nearer trench; and finding, before they could approach the contravallation, that their comrades had withdrawn, they went back unsuccessful to the town.

Having been twice repulsed with heavy loss, the Gauls considered what was to be done. They called in natives who were familiar with the ground, and ascertained from them the position of the higher camps and the nature of their fortifications. There was a hill on the north which had such a wide sweep that the Romans had not been able to include it within the circumvallation, and were obliged to make the camp there on a gentle slope, which gave an assailant a slight advantage. This camp was garrisoned by two legions under the command of two generals, Gaius Antistius Reginus and Gaius Caninius Rebilus. After making a reconnaissance, the hostile leaders selected from the whole force sixty thousand men belonging to the tribes which had the highest reputation for valour, secretly decided on their plan of operations, and fixed the attack for noon. Vercassivellaunus, an Arvernian, one of the four generals and a relation of Vercingetorix, was placed in command of the force. He left camp in the first watch: towards daybreak he had almost finished his march; and, concealing himself behind the hill, he ordered his soldiers to rest after the toil of the night. Towards noon he pushed on for the camp mentioned above; and simultaneously the cavalry began to move towards the entrenchments in the plain, while the rest of the host made a demonstration in front of their camp.

Descrying his countrymen from the citadel of Alesia, Vercingetorix moved out of the town, taking from the camp the long pikes, sappers, grappling-hooks, and other implements which he had prepared for the sortie. Fighting went on simultaneously at every point; and the besieged tried every expedient, concentrating their strength on the weakest points. The Roman forces, being strung out over lines of vast extent, found it hard to move to several points at once. The shouts of the combatants in their rear had a serious effect in unnerving the men, who saw that their own lives were staked upon the courage of others; for men are generally disquieted most by the unseen.

Caesar found a good position, from which he observed all the phases of the action and reinforced those who were in difficulties. Both sides saw that now was the moment for a supreme effort: the Gauls utterly despaired of safety unless they could break the lines; the Romans, if they could but hold their ground, looked forward to the end of all their toils. The struggle was most severe at the entrenchments on the high ground, against which, as we have remarked, Vercassivellaunus had been sent. The unfavourable downward slope told heavily. Some of the assailants showered in missiles, while others locked their shields above their heads, and advanced to the assault; and when they were tired, fresh men took their places. The entire force shot earth against the fortifications, which at once enabled the Gauls to ascend and buried the obstacles which the Romans had hidden in the ground. And now weapons, and strength to use them were failing our men.

On learning the state of affairs, Caesar sent Labienus with six cohorts to rescue the hard-pressed garrison, telling him, in case he could not hold on, to lead out the cohorts and charge, but only as a forlorn hope. Visiting the other divisions in person, he adjured them not to give in: on that day, he told them, on that hour was staked the prize of all past combats. The besieged, abandoning the hope of forcing the formidable works in the plain, took the implements which they had prepared and attempted to storm a steep ascent. With a hail of missiles they drove off the men who defended the towers, filled up the trenches with earth and fascines, and with their grappling-hooks tore down the rampart and breastworks.

Caesar first sent the younger Brutus with a number of cohorts, and afterwards Gaius Fabius with others: finally, as the fighting grew fiercer, he led a fresh detachment in person to the rescue. Having restored the battle and beaten off the enemy, he hastened to the point to which he had dispatched Labienus, withdrawing four cohorts from the nearest redoubt, and ordering part of the cavalry to follow him and part to ride round the outer lines and attack the enemy in the rear. Labienus, finding that neither rampart nor trench could check the enemy's onslaught, massed eleven cohorts, which he was fortunately able to withdraw from the nearest piquets, and sent messengers to let Caesar know what he intended. Caesar hastened to take part in the action.

The enemy knew that he was coming from the colour of his cloak, which he generally wore in action to mark his identity, and, catching sight of the cohorts and troops of cavalry which he had ordered to follow him, descending the incline, which was plainly discernible from their commanding position, began the attack. Both sides raised a cheer, and the cheering was taken up along the rampart and the whole extent of the lines. Our men dropped their javelins and plied their swords. Suddenly the cavalry was seen on the enemy's rear: the fresh cohorts came up; the enemy turned tail; and the cavalry charged the fugitives. The carnage was great. Sedulius, commander and chieftain of the Lemovices, was slain; Vercassivellaunus, the Arvernian, was taken alive as he was trying to escape: seventy-four standards were brought to Caesar; and few of that mighty host got safely back to camp. Descrying from the town the slaughter and the rout of their countrymen, the besieged in despair recalled their troops from the entrenchments. Hearing this, the Gauls in camp forthwith fled; and if the soldiers had not been tired out by frequent supporting movements and by the whole day's toil, the enemy's entire host might have been annihilated. The cavalry were dispatched about midnight, and hung upon the rearguard. A large number were captured and slain; the rest escaped and went off to their respective tribes.

Next day Vercingetorix called a council. He explained that he had undertaken the war, not for private ends, but in the cause of national freedom; and, since they must needs bow to fortune, he would submit to whichever alternative they preferred,—either to appease the Romans by putting him to death or to surrender him alive. Envoys were sent to refer the question to Caesar. He ordered the arms to be surrendered and the leaders brought out. The officers were conducted to the entrenchment in front of his camp, where he was seated. Vercingetorix surrendered, and the arms were grounded. Caesar allotted one prisoner by way of prize to every man in the army, making an exception in favour of the Aedui and Arverni, as he hoped by restoring them to win back the two tribes.

These arrangements completed, he started for the country of the Aedui, and received the sent envoys, promising to obey his orders; and he ordered them to furnish a large number of hostages. The legions were sent into winter quarters, and about twenty thousand prisoners restored to the Aedui and Arverni. He directed Titus Labienus to march with two legions and. a detachment of cavalry into the country of the Sequani, placing Marcus Sempronius Rutilus under his command; stationed Gaius Fabius and Lucius Minucius Basilus with two legions in the country of the Remi, to protect them from injury at the hands of their neighbours, the Bellovaci; dispatched Gaius Antistius Reginus into the country of the Ambivareti, Titus Sextius into that of the Bituriges, and Gaius Caninius Rebilus into that of the Ruteni,— each in command of a legion; and quartered Quintus Tullius Cicero and Publius Sulpicius in the country of the Aedui at Cabillo and Matisco on the Saone, to collect grain.

He decided to winter himself at Bibracte. When the results of the campaign were made known by his dispatches, a thanksgiving service of twenty days was held at Rome.

The Life of Charlemagne by Einhard

The Merovingian Family

The Merovingian family, from which the Franks used to choose their kings, is commonly said to have lasted until the time of Childeric [III] who was deposed, shaved, and thrust into the cloister by command of the Roman Pontiff Stephen [II (or III)]. But although, to all outward appearance, it ended with him, it had long since been devoid of vital strength, and conspicuous only from bearing the empty epithet Royal; the real power and authority in the kingdom lay in the hands of the chief officer of the court, the so-called Mayor of the Palace, and he was at the head of affairs. There was nothing left the King to do but to be content with his name of King, his flowing hair, and long beard, to sit on his throne and play the ruler, to give ear to the ambassadors that came from all quarters, and to dismiss them, as if on his own responsibility, in words that were, in fact, suggested to him, or even imposed upon him. He had nothing that he could call his own beyond this vain title of King and the precarious support allowed by the Mayor of the Palace in his discretion, except a single country seat, that brought him but a very small income. There was a dwelling house upon this, and a small number of servants attached to it, sufficient to perform the necessary offices. When he had to go abroad, he used to ride in a cart, drawn by a yoke of oxen driven, peasant-fashion, by a Ploughman; he rode in this way to the palace and to the general assembly of the people, that met once a year for the welfare of the kingdom, and he returned him in like manner. The Mayor of the Palace took charge of the government and of everything that had to be planned or executed at home or abroad.

Charlemagne's Ancestors

At the time of Childeric's deposition, Pepin, the father of King Charles, held this office of Mayor of the Palace, one might almost say, by hereditary right; for Pepin's father, Charles [Martel], had received it at the hands of his father, Pepin, and filled it with distinction. It was this Charles that crushed the tyrants who claimed to rule the whole Frank land as their own, and that utterly routed the Saracens, when they attempted the conquest of Gaul in two great battles, one in Aquitania, near the town of Poitiers, and the other on the River Berre, near Narbonne-and compelled them to return to Spain. This honor was usually conferred by the people only upon men eminent from their illustrious birth and ample wealth. For some years, ostensibly under King the father of King Charles, Childeric, Pepin, shared the duties inherited from his father and grandfather most amicably with his brother, Carloman. The latter, then, for reasons unknown, renounced the heavy cares of an earthly crown and retired to Rome. Here he exchanged his worldly garb for a cowl, and built a monastery on Mt. Oreste, near the Church of St. Sylvester, where he enjoyed for several years the seclusion that he desired, in company with certain others who had the same object in view. But so many distinguished Franks made the pilgrimage to Rome to fulfill their vows, and insisted upon paying their respects to him, as their former lord, on the way, that the repose which he so much loved was broken by these frequent visits, and he was driven to change his abode. Accordingly when he found that his plans were frustrated by his many visitors, he abandoned the mountain, and withdrew to the Monastery of St. Benedict, on Monte Cassino, in the province of Samnium, and passed the rest there in the exercise of religion.

Charlemagne's Accession

Pepin, however, was raised by decree of the Roman pontiff, from the rank of Mayor of the Palace to that of King, and ruled alone over the Franks for fifteen years or more. He died of dropsy [Sept. 24] in Paris at the close of the Aquitanian War, which he had waged with William, Duke of Aquitania, for nine successive years, and left his two sons, Charles and Carloman, upon whim, by the grace of God, the succession devolved.

The Franks, in a general assembly of the people, made them both kings [Oct 9] on condition that they should divide the whole kingdom equally between them, Charles to take and rule the part that had to belonged to their father, Pepin, and Carloman the part which their uncle, Carloman had governed. The conditions were accepted, and each entered into the possession of the share of the kingdom that fell to him by this arrangement; but peace was only maintained between them with the greatest difficulty, because many of Carloman's party kept trying to disturb their good understanding, and there were some even who plotted to involve them in a war with each other. The event, however, which showed the danger to have been rather imaginary than real, for at Carloman's death his widow [Gerberga] fled to Italy with her sons and her principal adherents, and without reason, despite her husband's brother put herself and her children under the protection of Desiderius, King of the Lombards. Carloman had succumbed to disease after ruling two years [in fact more than three] in common with his brother and at his death Charles was unanimously elected King of the Franks.

Plan of This Work

It would be folly, I think, to write a word concerning Charles' birth and infancy, or even his boyhood, for nothing has ever been written on the subject, and there is no one alive now who can give information on it. Accordingly, I determined to pass that by as unknown, and to proceed at once to treat of his character, his deed, and such other facts of his life as are worth telling and setting forth, and shall first give an account of his deed at home and abroad, then of his character and pursuits, and lastly of his administration and death, omitting nothing worth knowing or necessary to know.

Aquitanian War

His first undertaking in a military way was the Aquitanian War, begun by his father but not brought to a close; and because he thought that it could be readily carried through, he took it up while his brother was yet alive, calling upon him to render aid. The campaign once opened, he conducted it with the greatest vigor, notwithstanding his broth withheld the assistance that he had promised, and did not desist or shrink from his self-imposed task until, by his patience and firmness, he had completely gained his ends. He compelled Hunold, who had attempted to seize Aquitania after Waifar's death, and renew the war then almost concluded, to abandon Aquitania and flee to Gascony. Even here he gave him no rest, but crossed the River Garonne, built the castle of Fronsac, and sent ambassadors to Lupus, Duke of Gascony, to demand the surrender of the fugitive, threatening to take him by force unless he were promptly given up to him. Thereupon Lupus chose the wiser course, and not only gave Hunold up, but submitted himself, with the province which he ruled, to the King.

Lombard War

After bringing this war to an end and settling matters in Aquitania (his associate in authority had meantime departed this life), he was induced, by the prayers and entreaties of Hadrian [I], Bishop of the city of Rome, to wage war on the Lombards. His father before him had undertaken this task at the request of Pope Stephen [II or III], but under great difficulties, for certain leading Franks, of whom he usually took counsel, had so vehemently opposed his design as to declare openly that they would leave the King and go home. Nevertheless, the war against the Lombard King Astolf had been taken up and very quickly concluded. Now, although Charles seems to have had similar, or rather just the same grounds for declaring war that his father had, the war itself differed from the preceding one alike in its difficulties and its issue. Pepin, to be sure, after besieging King Astolf a few days in Pavia, had compelled him to give hostages, to restore to the Romans the cities and castles that he had taken, and to make oath that he would not attempt to seize them again: but Charles did not cease, after declaring war, until he had exhausted King Desiderius by a long siege, and forced him to surrender at discretion; driven his son Adalgis, the last hope of the Lombards, not only from his kingdom, but from all Italy; restored to the Romans all that they had lost; subdued Hruodgaus, Duke of Friuli, who was plotting revolution; reduced all Italy to his power, and set his son Pepin as king over it.

At this point I should describe Charles' difficult passage over the Alps into Italy, and the hardships that the Franks endured in climbing the trackless mountain ridges, the heaven-aspiring cliffs and ragged peaks, if it were not my purpose in this work to record the manner of his life rather than the incidents of the wars that he waged. Suffice it to say that this war ended with the subjection of Italy, the banishment of King Desiderius for life, the expulsion of his son Adalgis from Italy, and the restoration of the conquests of the Lombard kings to Hadrian, the head of the Roman Church.

Saxon War

At the conclusion of this struggle, the Saxon war, that seems to have been only laid aside for the time, was taken up again. No war ever undertaken by the Frank nation was carried on with such persistence and bitterness, or cost so much labor, because the Saxons, like almost all the tribes of Germany, were a fierce people, given to the worship of devils, and hostile to our religion, and did not consider it dishonorable to transgress and violate all law, human and divine. Then there were peculiar circumstances that tended to cause a breach of peace every day. Except in a few places, where large forests or mountain ridges intervened and made the bounds certain, the line between ourselves and the Saxons passed almost in its whole extent through an open country, so that there was no end to the murders thefts and arsons on both sides. In this way the Franks became so embittered that they at last resolved to make reprisals no longer, but to come to open war with the Saxons. Accordingly war was begun against them, and was waged for thirty-three successive years with great fury; more, however, to the disadvantage of the Saxons than of the Franks. It could doubtless have been brought to an end sooner, had it not been for the faithlessness of the Saxons. It is hard to say how often they were conquered, and, humbly submitting to the King, promised to do what was enjoined upon them, without hesitation the required hostages, gave and received the officers sent them from the King. They were sometimes so much weakened and reduced that they promised to renounce the worship of devils, and to adopt Christianity, but they were no less ready to violate these terms than prompt to accept them, so that it is impossible to tell which came easier to them to do; scarcely a year passed from the beginning of the war without such changes on their part. But the King did not suffer his high purpose and steadfastness - firm alike in good and evil fortune - to be wearied by any fickleness on their part, or to be turned from the task that he had undertaken, on the contrary, he never allowed their faithless behavior to go unpunished, but either took the field against them in person, or sent his counts with an army to wreak vengeance and exact righteous satisfaction. At last, after conquering and subduing all who had offered resistance, he took ten thousand of those that lived on the banks of the Elbe, and settled them, with their wives and children, in many different bodies here and there in Gaul and Germany. The war that had lasted so many years was at length ended by their acceding to the terms offered by the King; which were renunciation of their national religious customs and the worship of devils, acceptance of the sacraments of the Christian faith and religion, and union with the Franks to form one people.

Charles himself fought but two pitched battles in this war, although it was long protracted one on Mount Osning, at the place called Detmold, and again on the bank of the river Hase, both in the space of little more than a month. The enemy were so routed and overthrown in these two battles that they never afterwards ventured to take the offensive or to resist the attacks of the King, unless they were protected by a strong position. A great many of the Frank as well as of the Saxon nobility, men occupying the highest posts of honor, perished in this war, which only came to an end after the lapse of thirty-two years. So many and grievous were the wars that were declared against the Franks in the meantime, and skillfully conducted by the King, that one may reasonably question whether his fortitude or his good fortune is to be more admired. The Saxon war began two years before the Italian war; but although it went on without interruption, business elsewhere was not neglected, nor was t ere any shrinking from other equally arduous contests. The King, who excelled all the princes of his time in wisdom and greatness of soul, did not suffer difficulty to deter him or danger to daunt him from anything that had to be taken up or carried through, for he-had trained himself to bear and endure whatever came, without yielding in adversity, or trusting to the deceitful favors of fortune in prosperity.

Spanish Expedition

In the midst of this vigorous and almost uninterrupted struggle with the Saxons, he covered the frontier by garrisons at the proper points, and marched over the Pyrenees into Spain at the head of all the forces that he could muster. All the towns and castles that he attacked surrendered. and up to the time of his homeward march he sustained no loss whatever; but on his return through the Pyrenees he had cause to rue the treachery of the Gascons. That region is well adapted for ambuscades by reason of the thick forests that cover it; and as the army was advancing in the long line of march necessitated by the narrowness of the road, the Gascons, who lay in ambush on the top of a very high mountain, attacked the rear of the baggage train and the rear guard in charge of it, and hurled them down to the very bottom of the valley [at Roncevalles, later celebrated in the Song of Roland]. In the struggle that ensued they cut them off to a man; they then plundered the baggage, and dispersed with all speed in every direction under cover of approaching night. The lightness of their armor and the nature of the battle ground stood the Gascons in good stead on this occasion, whereas the Franks fought at a disadvantage in every respect, because of the weight of their armor and the unevenness of the ground. Eggihard, the King's steward; Anselm, Count Palatine; and Roland, Governor of the March of Brittany, with very many others, fell in this engagement. This ill turn could not be avenged for the nonce, because the enemy scattered so widely after carrying out their plan that not the least clue could be had to their whereabouts.

Submission of the Bretons and Beneventans

Charles also subdued the Bretons, who live on the sea coast, in the extreme western part of Gaul. When they refused to obey him, he sent an army against them, and compelled them to give hostages, and to promise to do his bidding. He afterwards entered Italy in person with his army, and passed through Rome to Capua, a city in Campania, where he pitched his camp and threatened the Beneventans with hostilities unless they should submit themselves to him. Their duke, Aragis, escaped the danger by sending his two sons, Rumold and Grimold, with a great sum of money to meet the King, begging him to accept them as hostages, and promising for himself and his people compliance with all the King's commands, on the single condition that his personal attendance should not be required. The King took the welfare of the people into account rather than the stubborn disposition of the Duke, accepted the proffered hostages, and released him from the obligation to appear before him in consideration of his handsome gift. He retained the younger son only as hostage, and sent the elder back to his father, and returned to Rome, leaving commissioners with Aragis to exact the oath of allegiance, and administer it to the Beneventans. He stayed in Rome several days in order to pay his devotions at the holy places, and then came back to Gaul.

Tassilo and the Bavarian Campaign

At this time, on a sudden, the Bavarian war broke out, but came to a speedy end. It was due to the arrogance and folly of Duke Tassilo. His wife [Liutberga], a daughter of King Desiderius, was desirous of avenging her father's banishment through the agency of her husband, and accordingly induced him to make a treaty with the Huns, the neighbors of the Bavarians on the east, and not only to leave the King's commands unfulfilled, but to challenge him to war. Charles' high spirit could not brook Tassilo's insubordination, for it seemed to him to pass all bounds; accordingly he straightway summoned his troops from all sides for a campaign against Bavaria and appeared in person with a great army on the river Lech , which forms the boundary between the Bavarians and the Alemanni. After Pitching his camp upon its banks, he determined to put the Duke's disposition to the test by an embassy before entering the province. Tassilo did not think that it was for his own or his people's good to persist, so he surrendered himself to the King, gave the hostages demanded, among them his own son Theodo, and promised by oath not to give ear to any one who should attempt to turn him from his allegiance; so this war, which bade fair to be very grievous, came very quickly to an end. Tassilo, however, was afterward summoned to the King's presence, and not suffered to depart, and the government of the province that he had had in charge was no longer intrusted to a duke, but to counts.

Slavic War

After these uprisings had been thus quelled, war was declared against the Slavs who are commonly known among us as Wilzi, but properly, that is to say in their own tongue, are called Welatabians. The Saxons served in this campaign as auxiliaries among the tribes that followed the King's standard at his summons, but their obedience lacked sincerity and devotion. War was declared because the Slavs kept harassing the Abodriti, old allies of the Franks, by continual raids, in spite of all commands to the contrary. A gulf [i.e. the Baltic Sea] of unknown length, but nowhere more than a hundred miles wide, and in many parts narrower, stretches off towards the east from the Western Ocean. Many tribes have settlements on its shores; the Danes and Swedes, whom we call Northmen, on the northern shore and all the adjacent islands; but the southern shore is inhabited by the Slava and the Aïsti [from whom derive the modern name of "Estonia"]; and various other tribes. The Welatabians, against whom the King now made war, were the chief of these; but in a single campaign, which he conducted in person, he so crushed and subdued them that they did not think it advisable thereafter to refuse obedience to his commands.

War with the Huns

The war against the Avars, or Huns, followed, and, except the Saxon war, was the greatest that he waged; he took it up with more spirit than any of his other wars, and made far greater preparations for it. He conducted one campaign in person in Pannonia, of which the Huns then had possession. He entrusted all subsequent operations to his son, Pepin, and the governors of the provinces, to counts even, and lieutenants. Although they most vigorously prosecuted the war, it only came to a conclusion after a seven years' struggle. The utter depopulation of Pannonia, and the site of the Khan's palace, now a desert, where not a trace of human habitation is visible bear witness how many battles were fought in those years, and how much blood was shed. The entire body of the Hun nobility perished in this contest, and all its glory with it. All the money and treasure that had been years amassing was seized, and no war in which the Franks have ever engaged within the memory of man brought them such riches and such booty. Up to that time the Huns had passed for, a poor people, but so much gold and silver was found in the Khan's palace, and so much valuable spoil taken in battle, that one may well think that the Franks took justly from the Huns what the Huns had formerly taken unjustly from other nations. Only two of the chief men of the Franks fell in this war - Eric, Duke of Friuli, who was killed in Tarsatch, a town on the coast of Liburnia by the treachery of the inhabitants; and Gerold, Governor of Bavaria, who met his death in Pannonia, slain, with two men that were accompanying him, by an unknown hand while he was marshaling his forces for battle against the Huns, and riding up and down the line encouraging his men. This war was otherwise almost a bloodless one so far as the Franks were concerned, and ended most satisfactorily, although by reason of its magnitude it was long protracted.

Danish War

The Saxon war next came to an end as successful as the struggle had been long. The Bohemian and Linonian wars that next broke out could not last long; both were quickly carried through under the leadership of the younger Charles. The last of these wars was the one declared against the Northmen called Danes. They began their career as pirates, but afterward took to laying waste the coasts of Gaul and

Germany with their large fleet. Their King Godfred was so puffed with vain aspirations that he counted on gaining empire overall Germany, and looked upon Saxony and Frisia as his provinces. He had already subdued his neighbors the Abodriti, and made them tributary, and boasted that he would shortly appear with a great army before Aix-la-Chapelle [Aachen - Charlemagne's capital], where the King held his court. Some faith was put in his words, empty as they sound, and it is supposed that he would have attempted something of the sort if he had not been prevented by a premature death. He was murdered by one of his own bodyguard, and so ended at once his life and the war that he had begun.

Extent of Charlemagne's Conquests

Such are the wars, most skillfully planned and successfully fought, which this most powerful king waged during the forty-seven years of his reign. He so largely increased the Frank kingdom, which was already great and strong when he received it at his father's hands, that more than double its former territory was added to it. The authority of the Franks was formerly confined to that part of Gaul included between the Rhine and the Loire, the Ocean and the Balearic Sea; to that part of Germany which is inhabited by the so-called Eastern Franks, and is bounded by Saxony and the Danube, the Rhine and the Saale-this stream separates the Thuringians from the Sorabians; and to the country of the Alemanni and Bavarians. By the wars above mentioned he first made tributary Aquitania, Gascony, and the whole of the region of the Pyrenees as far as the River Ebro, which rises in the land of the Navarrese, flows through the most fertile districts of Spain, and empties into the Balearic Sea, beneath the walls of the city of Tortosa. He next reduced and made tributary all Italy from Aosta to Lower Calabria, where the boundary line runs between the Beneventans and the Greeks, a territory more than a thousand miles" long; then Saxony, which constitutes no small part of Germany, and is reckoned to be twice as wide as the country inhabited by the Franks, while about equal to it in length; in addition, both Pannonias, Dacia beyond the Danube, and Istria, Liburnia, and Dalmatia, except the cities on the coast, which he left to the Greek Emperor for friendship's sake, and because of the treaty that he had made with him. In fine, he vanquished and made tributary all the wild and barbarous tribes dwelling in Germany between the Rhine and the Vistula, the Ocean and the Danube, all of which speak very much the same language, but differ widely from one another in customs and dress. The chief among them are the Welatabians, the Sorabians, the Abodriti, and the Bohemians, and he had to make war upon these; but the rest, by far the larger number, submitted to him of their own accord.

Foreign Relations

He added to the glory of his reign by gaining the good will of several kings and nations; so close, indeed, was the alliance that he contracted with Alfonso [II] King of Galicia and Asturias, that the latter, when sending letters or ambassadors to Charles, invariably styled himself his man. His munificence won the kings of the

Scots also to pay such deference to his wishes that they never gave him any other title than lord or themselves than subjects and slaves: there are letters from them extant in which these feelings in his regard are expressed. His relations with Aaron [i.e. Harun Al-Rashid], King of the Persians, who ruled over almost the whole of the East, India excepted, were so friendly that this prince preferred his favor to that of all the kings and potentates of the earth, and considered that to him alone marks of honor and munificence were due. Accordingly, when the ambassadors sent by Charles to visit the most holy sepulcher and place of resurrection of our Lord and Savior presented themselves before him with gifts, and made known their master's wishes, he not only granted what was asked, but gave possession of that holy and blessed spot. When they returned, he dispatched his ambassadors with them, and sent magnificent gifts, besides stuffs, perfumes, and other rich products of the Eastern lands.. A few years before this, Charles had asked him for an elephant, and he sent the only one that he had. The Emperors of Constantinople, Nicephorus [I], Michael [I], and Leo [V], made advances to Charles, and sought friendship and alliance with him by several embassies; and even when the Greeks suspected him of designing to wrest the empire from them, because of his assumption of the title Emperor, they made a close alliance with him, that he might have no cause of offense. In fact, the power of the Franks was always viewed by the Greeks and Romans with a jealous eye, whence the Greek proverb "Have the Frank for your friend, but not for your neighbor."

Public Works

This King, who showed himself so great in extending his empire and subduing foreign nations, and was constantly occupied with plans to that end, undertook also very many works calculated to adorn and benefit his kingdom, and brought several of them to completion. Among these, the most deserving of mention are the basilica of the Holy Mother of God at Aix-la-Chapelle, built in the most admirable manner, and a bridge over the Rhine at Mayence, half a mile long, the breadth of the river at this point. This bridge was destroyed by fire [May] the year before Charles died, but, owing to his death so soon after, could not be repaired, although he had intended to rebuild it in stone. He began two palaces of beautiful workmanship - one near his manor called Ingelheim, not far from Mayence; the other at Nimeguen, on the Waal, the stream that washes the south side of the island of the Batavians. But, above all, sacred edifices were the object of his care throughout his whole kingdom; and whenever he found them falling to ruin from age, he commanded the priests and fathers who had charge of them to repair them , and made sure by commissioners that his instructions were obeyed. He also fitted out a fleet for the war with the Northmen; the vessels required for this purpose were built on the rivers that flow from Gaul and Germany into the Northern Ocean. Moreover, since the Northmen continually overran and laid waste the Gallic and German coasts, he caused watch and ward to be kept in all the harbors, and at the mouths of rivers large enough to admit the entrance of vessels, to prevent the enemy from disembarking; and in the

South, in Narbonensis and Septimania, and along the whole coast of Italy as far as Rome, he took the same precautions against the Moors, who had recently begun their piratical practices. Hence, Italy suffered no great harm in his time at the hands of the Moors, nor Gaul and Germany from the Northmen, save that the Moors got possession of the Etruscan town of Civita Vecchia by treachery, and sacked it, and the Northmen harried some of the islands in Frisia off the German coast.

Private Life

Thus did Charles defend and increase as well, as beautify his, kingdom, as is well known; and here let me express my admiration of his great qualities and his extraordinary constancy alike in good and evil fortune. I will now forthwith proceed to give the details of his private and family life.

After his father's death, while sharing the kingdom with his brother, he bore his unfriendliness and jealousy most patiently, and, to the wonder of all, could not be provoked to be angry with him. Later he married a daughter of Desiderius, King of the Lombards, at the instance of his mother; but he repudiated her at the end of a year for some reason unknown, and married Hildegard, a woman of high birth, of Suabian origin. He had three sons by her - Charles, Pepin and Louis -and as many daughters - Hruodrud, Bertha, and Gisela. He had three other daughters besides these- Theoderada, Hiltrud, and Ruodhaid - two by his third wife, Fastrada, a woman of East Frankish (that is to say, of German) origin, and the third by a concubine, whose name for the moment escapes me. At the death of Fastrada, he married Liutgard, an Alemannic woman, who bore him no children. After her death [Jun4] he had three concubines - Gersuinda, a Saxon by whom he had Adaltrud; Regina, who was the mother of Drogo and Hugh; and Ethelind, by whom he lead Theodoric. Charles' mother, Berthrada, passed her old age with him in great honor; he entertained the greatest veneration for her; and there was never any disagreement between them except when he divorced the daughter of King Desiderius, whom he had married to please her. She died soon after Hildegard, after living to three grandsons and as many granddaughters in her son's house, and he buried her with great pomp in the Basilica of St. Denis, where his father lay. He had an only sister, Gisela, who had consecrated herself to a religious life from girlhood, and he cherished as much affection for her as for his mother. She also died a few years before him in the nunnery where she passed her life.

The plan that he adopted for his children's education was, first of all, to have both boys and girls instructed in the liberal arts, to which he also turned his own attention. As soon as their years admitted, in accordance with the custom of the Franks, the boys had to learn horsemanship, and to practise war and the chase, and the girls to familiarize themselves with cloth-making, and to handle distaff and spindle, that they might not grow indolent through idleness, and he fostered in them every virtuous sentiment. He only lost three of all his children before his death, two sons and one daughter, Charles, who was the eldest, Pepin, whom he had made King of Italy, and Hruodrud, his oldest daughter. whom he had betrothed to Constantine [VI], Emperor of the Greeks. Pepin left one son, named Bernard, and five daughters, Adelaide, Atula, Guntrada, Berthaid and Theoderada. The King gave a striking proof of his fatherly affection at the time of Pepin's death: he appointed the grandson to succeed Pepin, and had the granddaughters brought up with his own daughters. When his sons and his daughter died, he was not so calm as might have been expected from his remarkably strong mind, for his affections were no less strong, and moved him to tears. Again, when he was told of the death of Hadrian, the Roman Pontiff, whom he had loved most of all his friends, he wept as much as if he had lost a brother, or a very dear son. He was by nature most ready to contract friendships, and not only made friends easily, but clung to them persistently, and cherished most fondly those with whom he had formed such ties. He was so careful of the training of his sons and daughters that he never took his meals without them when he was at home, and never made a journey without them; his sons would ride at his side, and his daughters follow him, while a number of his body-guard, detailed for their protection, brought up the rear. Strange to say, although they were very handsome women, and he loved them very dearly, he was never willing to marry any of them to a man of their own nation or to a foreigner, but kept them all at home until his death, saying that he could not dispense with their society. Hence, though other-wise happy, he experienced the malignity of fortune as far as they were concerned; yet he concealed his knowledge of the rumors current in regard to them, and of the suspicions entertained of their honor.

Conspiracies Against Charlemagne

By one of his concubines he had a son, handsome in face, but hunchbacked, named Pepin, whom I omitted to mention in the list of his children. When Charles was at war with the Huns, and was wintering in Bavaria, this Pepin shammed sickness, and plotted against his father in company with some of the leading Franks, who seduced him with vain promises of the royal authority. When his deceit was discovered, and the conspirators were punished, his head was shaved, and he was suffered, in accordance with his wishes, to devote himself to a religious life in the monastery of Prüm. A formidable conspiracy against Charles had previously been set on foot in Germany, but all the traitors were banished, some of them without mutilation, others after their eyes had been put out. Three of them only lost their lives; they drew their swords and resisted arrest, and, after killing several men, were cut down, because they could not be otherwise overpowered. It is supposed that the cruelty of Queen Fastrada was the primary cause of these plots, and they were both due to Charles' apparent acquiescence in his wife's cruel conduct, and deviation from the usual kindness and gentleness of his disposition. All the rest of his life he was regarded by everyone with the utmost love and affection, so much so that not the least accusation of unjust rigor was ever made against him.

Charlemagne's Treatment of Foreigners

He liked foreigners, and was at great pains to take them under his protection. There were often so many of them, both in the palace and the kingdom, that they might reasonably have been considered a nuisance; but he, with his broad humanity, was very little disturbed by such annoyances, because he felt himself compensated for these great inconveniences by the praises of his generosity and the reward of high renown.

Personal Appearance

Charles was large and strong, and of lofty stature, though not disproportionately tall (his height is well known to have been seven times the length of his foot); the upper part of his head was round, his eyes very large and animated, nose a little long, hair fair, and face laughing and merry. Thus his appearance was always stately and dignified, whether he was standing or sitting; although his neck was thick and somewhat short, and his belly rather prominent; but the symmetry of the rest of his body concealed these defects. His gait was firm, his whole carriage manly, and his voice clear, but not so strong as his size led one to expect. His health was excellent, except during the four years preceding his death, when he was subject to frequent fevers; at the last he even limped a little with one foot. Even in those years he consulted rather his own inclinations than the advice of physicians, who were almost hateful to him, because they wanted him to give up roasts, to which he was accustomed, and to eat boiled meat instead. In accordance with the national custom, he took frequent exercise on horseback and in the chase, accomplishments in which scarcely any people in the world can equal the Franks. He enjoyed the exhalations from natural warm springs, and often practised swimming, in which he was such an adept that none could surpass him; and hence it was that he built his palace at Aixla-Chapelle, and lived there constantly during his latter years until his death. He used not only to invite his sons to his bath, but his nobles and friends, and now and then a troop of his retinue or body guard, so that a hundred or more persons sometimes bathed with him.

Dress

He used to wear the national, that is to say, the Frank, dress-next his skin a linen shirt and linen breeches, and above these a tunic fringed with silk; while hose fastened by bands covered his lower limbs, and shoes his feet, and he protected his shoulders and chest in winter by a close-fitting coat of otter or marten skins. Over all he flung a blue cloak, and he always had a sword girt about him, usually one with a gold or silver hilt and belt; he sometimes carried a jewelled sword, but only on great feast-days or at the reception of ambassadors from foreign nations. He despised foreign costumes, however handsome, and never allowed himself to be robed in them, except twice in Rome, when he donned the Roman tunic, chlamys, and shoes; the first time at the request of Pope Hadrian, the second to gratify Leo, Hadrian's successor. On great feast-days he made use of embroidered clothes, and shoes bedecked with precious stones; his cloak was fastened by a golden buckle, and he appeared crowned with a diadem of gold and gems: but on other days his dress varied little from the common dress of the people.

Habits

Charles was temperate in eating, and particularly so in drinking, for he abominated drunkenness in anybody, much more in himself and those of his household; but he could not easily abstain from food, and often complained that fasts injured his health. He very rarely gave entertainments, only on great feast-days, and then to large numbers of people. His meals ordinarily consisted of four courses, not counting the roast, which his huntsmen used to bring in on the spit; he was more fond of this than of any other dish. While at table, he listened to reading or music. The subjects of the readings were the stories and deeds of olden time: he was fond, too, of St. Augustine's books, and especially of the one entitled "The City of God." He was so moderate in the use of wine and all sorts of drink that he rarely allowed himself more than three cups in the course of a meal. In summer after the midday meal, he would eat some fruit, drain a single cup, put off his clothes and shoes, just as he did for the night, and rest for two or three hours. He was in the habit of awaking and rising from bed four or five times during the night. While he was dressing and putting on his shoes, he not only gave audience to his friends, but if the Count of the Palace told him of any suit in which his judgment was necessary, he had the parties brought before him forthwith, took cognizance of the case, and gave his decision, just as if he were sitting on the Judgment-seat. This was not the only business that he transacted at this time, but he performed any duty of the day whatever, whether he had to attend to the matter himself, or to give commands concerning it to his officers.

Studies

Charles had the gift of ready and fluent speech, and could express whatever he had to say with the utmost clearness. He was not satisfied with command of his native language merely, but gave attention to the study of foreign ones, and in particular was such a master of Latin that he could speak it as well as his native tongue; but he could understand Greek better than he could speak it. He was so eloquent, indeed, that he might have passed for a teacher of eloquence. He most zealously cultivated the liberal arts, held those who taught them in great esteem, and conferred great honors upon them. He took lessons in grammar of the deacon Peter of Pisa, at that time an aged man. Another deacon, Albin of Britain, surnamed Alcuin, a man of Saxon extraction, who was the greatest scholar of the day, was his teacher in other branches of learning. The King spent much time and labour with him studying rhetoric, dialectics, and especially astronomy; he learned to reckon, and used to investigate the motions of the heavenly bodies most curiously, with an intelligent scrutiny. He also tried to write, and used to keep tablets and blanks in bed under his pillow, that at leisure hours he might accustom his hand to form the letters; however, as he did not begin his efforts in due season, but late in life, they met with ill success.

Piety

He cherished with the greatest fervor and devotion the principles of the Christian religion, which had been instilled into him from infancy. Hence it was that he built the beautiful basilica at Aix-la-Chapelle, which he adorned with gold and silver and lamps, and with rails and doors of solid brass. He had the columns and marbles for this structure brought from Rome and Ravenna, for he could not find such as were suitable elsewhere. He was a constant worshipper at this church as long as his health permitted, going morning and evening, even after nightfall, besides attending mass; and he took care that all the services there conducted should be administered with the utmost possible propriety, very often warning the sextons not to let any improper or unclean thing be brought into the building or remain in it. He provided it with a great number of sacred vessels of gold and silver and with such a quantity of clerical robes that not even the doorkeepers who fill the humblest office in the church were obliged to wear their everyday clothes when in the exercise of their duties. He was at great pains to improve the church reading and psalmody, for he was well skilled in both although he neither read in public nor sang, except in a low tone and with others.

Generosity

He was very forward in succoring the poor, and in that gratuitous generosity which the Greeks call alms, so much so that he not only made a point of giving in his own country and his own kingdom, but when he discovered that there were Christians living in poverty in Syria, Egypt, and Africa, at Jerusalem, Alexandria, and Carthage, he had compassion on their wants, and used to send money over the seas to them. The reason that he zealously strove to make friends with the kings beyond seas was that he might get help and relief to the Christians living under their rule.

He cherished the Church of St. Peter the Apostle at Rome above all other holy and sacred places, and heaped its treasury with a vast wealth of gold, silver, and precious stones. He sent great and countless gifts to the popes; and throughout his whole reign the wish that he had nearest at heart was to re-establish the ancient authority of the city of Rome under his care and by his influence, and to defend and protect the Church of St. Peter, and to beautify and enrich it out of his own store above all other churches. Although he held it in such veneration, he only repaired to Rome to pay his vows and make his supplications four times during the whole forty-seven years that he reigned.

Charlemagne Crowned Emperor

When he made his last journey thither, he also had other ends in view. The Romans had inflicted many injuries upon the Pontiff Leo, tearing out his eyes and cutting out his tongue, so that he had been comp lied to call upon the King for help [Nov 24, 800]. Charles accordingly went to Rome, to set in order the affairs of the

Church, which were in great confusion, and passed the whole winter there. It was then that he received the titles of Emperor and Augustus [Dec 25, 800], to which he at first had such an aversion that he declared that he would not have set foot in the Church the day that they were conferred, although it was a great feast-day, if he could have foreseen the design of the Pope. He bore very patiently with the jealousy which the Roman emperors showed upon his assuming these titles, for they took this step very ill; and by dint of frequent embassies and letters, in which he addressed them as brothers, he made their haughtiness yield to his magnanimity, a quality in which he was unquestionably much their superior.

Reforms

It was after he had received the imperial name that, finding the laws of his people very defective (the Franks have two sets of laws, very different in many particulars), he determined to add what was wanting, to reconcile the discrepancies, and to correct what was vicious and wrongly cited in them. However, he went no further in this matter than to supplement the laws by a few capitularies, and those imperfect ones; but he caused the unwritten laws of all the tribes that came under his rule to be compiled and reduced to writing. He also had the old rude songs that celebrate the deeds and wars of the ancient kings written out for transmission to posterity. He began a grammar of his native language. He gave the months names in his own tongue, in place of the Latin and barbarous names by which they were formerly known among the Franks. He likewise designated the winds by twelve appropriate names; there were hardly more than four distinctive ones in use before. He called January, Wintarmanoth; February, Hornung; March, Lentzinmanoth; April, Ostarmanoth; May, Winnemanoth; June, Brachmanoth; July, Heuvimanoth; August, Aranmanoth; September, Witumanoth; October, Windumemanoth; Novemher, Herbistmanoth; December, Heilagmanoth. He styled the winds as follows; Subsolanus, Ostroniwint; Eurus, Ostsundroni, Euroauster, Sundostroni; Auster, Sundroni; Austro-Africus, Sundwestroni; Africus, Westsundroni; Zephyrus, Westroni; Caurus, Westnordroni; Circius, Nordwestroni; Septentrio, Nordroni; Aquilo, Nordostroni; Vulturnus, Ostnordroni.

Coronation of Louis - Charlemagne's Death

Toward the close of his life, when he was broken by ill-health and old age, he summoned Louis, Kigi of Aquitania, his only surviving son by Hildegard, and gathered together all the chief men of the whole kingdom of the Franks in a solemn assembly. He appointed Louis, with their unanimous consent, to rule with himself over the whole kingdom and constituted him heir to the imperial name; then, placing the diadem upon his son's head, he bade him be proclaimed Emperor and is step was hailed by all present favor, for it really seemed as if God had prompted him to it for the kingdom's good; it increased the King's dignity, and struck no little terror into foreign nations. After sending his son back to Aquitania, although weak from age he set out to hunt, as usual, near his palace at Aix-la-Chapelle, and passed the rest of the autumn in the chase, returning thither about the first of November. While wintering there, he was seized, in the month of January, with a high fever Jan 22], and took to his bed. As soon as he was taken sick, he prescribed for himself abstinence from food, as he always used to do in case of fever, thinking that the disease could be driven off , or at least mitigated, by fasting. Besides the fever, he suffered from a pain in the side, which the Greeks call pleurisy; but he still persisted in fasting, and in keeping up his strength only by draughts taken at very long intervals. He died January twenty-eighth, the seventh day from the time that he took to his bed, at nine o'clock in the morning, after partaking of the holy communion, in the seventy-second year of his age and the forty-seventh of his reign [Jan 28].

Burial

His body was washed and cared for in the usual manner, and was then carried to the church, and interred amid the greatest lamentations of all the people. There was some question at first where to lay him, because in his lifetime he had given no directions as to his burial; but at length all agreed that he could nowhere be more honorably entombed than in the very basilica that he had built in the town at his own expense, for love of God and our Lord Jesus Christ, and in honor of the Holy and Eternal Virgin, His Mother. He was buried there the same day that he died, and a gilded arch was erected above his tomb with his image and an inscription. The words of the inscription were as follows: "In this tomb lies the body of Charles, the Great and Orthodox Emperor, who gloriously extended the kingdom of the Franks, and reigned prosperously for forty-seven years. He died at the age of seventy, in the year of our Lord 814, the 7th Indiction, on the 28th day of January."

Omens of Death

Very many omens had portended his approaching end, a fact that he had recognized as well as others. Eclipses both of the sun and moon were very frequent during the last three years of his life, and a black spot was visible on the sun for the space of seven days. The gallery between the basilica and the palace, which he had built at great pains and labor, fell in sudden ruin to the ground on the day of the Ascension of our Lord. The wooden bridge over the Rhine at Mayence, which he had caused to be constructed with admirable skill, at the cost of ten years' hard work, so that it seemed as if it might last forever, was so completely consumed in three hours by an accidental fire that not a single splinter of it was left, except what was under water. Moreover, one day in his last campaign into Saxony against Godfred, King of the Danes, Charles himself saw a ball of fire fall suddenly from the heavens with a great light, just as he was leaving camp before sunrise to set out on the march. It rushed across the clear sky from right to left, and everybody was wondering what was the meaning of the sign, when the horse which he was riding gave a sudden plunge, head foremost, and fell, and threw him to the ground so heavily that his cloak buckle was broken and his sword belt shattered; and after his servants had hastened to him and relieved him of his arms, he could not rise without their assistance. He happened to have a javelin in his hand when he was thrown, and this was struck from his grasp with such force that it was found lying at a distance of twenty feet or more from the spot. Again, the palace at Aix-la-Chapelle frequently trembled, the roofs of whatever buildings he tarried in kept up a continual crackling noise, the basilica in which he was afterwards buried was struck by lightning, and the gilded ball that adorned the pinnacle of the roof was shattered by the thunderbolt and hurled upon the bishop's house adjoining. In this same basilica, on the margin of the cornice that ran around the interior, between the upper and lower tiers of arches, a legend was inscribed in red letters, stating who was the builder of the temple, the last words of which were Karolus Princeps. The year that he died it was remarked by some, a few months before his decease, that the letters of the word Princeps were so effaced as to be no longer decipherable. But Charles despised, or affected to despise, all these omens, as having no reference whatever to him.

Will

It had been his intention to make a will, that he might give some share in the inheritance to his daughters and the children of his concubines; but it was begun too late and could not be finished. Three years before his death, however, he made a division of his treasures, money, clothes, and other movable goods in the presence of his friends and servants, and called them to witness it, that their voices might insure the ratification of the disposition thus made. He had a summary drawn up of his wishes regarding this distribution of his property, the terms and text of which are as follows:

"In the name of the Lord God, the Almighty Father, Son, and Holy Ghost. This is the inventory and division dictated by the most glorious and most pious Lord Charles, Emperor Augustus, in the 811th year of the Incarnation of our Lord Jesus Christ, in the 43d year of his reign in France and 37th in Italy, the 11th of his empire, and the 4th Indiction, which considerations of piety and prudence have determined him, and the favor of God enabled him, to make of his treasures and money ascertained this day to be in his treasure chamber. In this division he is especially desirous to provide not only that the largess of alms which Christians usually make of their possessions shall be made for himself in due course and order out of his wealth, but also that his heirs shall be free from all doubt, and know clearly what belongs to them, and be able to share their property by suitable partition without litigation or strife. With this intention and to this end he has first divided all his substance and movable goods ascertained to be in his treasure chamber on the day aforesaid in gold, silver, precious stones, and royal ornaments into three lots and has subdivided and set off two of the said lots into twenty-one parts, keeping the third entire. The first two lots have been thus subdivided into twenty one parts because there are in his kingdom twenty-one" recognized metropolitan cities, and in order that each archbishopric may receive by way of alms, at the hands of his heirs and friends, one of the said parts, and that the archbishop who shall then administer its affairs shall take the part given to it, and share the same with his suffragans in such manner that one third shall go to the Church, and the remaining two thirds be divid-

162

ed among the suffragans. The twenty-one parts into which the first two lots are to be distributed, according to the number of recognized metropolitan cities, have been set apart one from another, and each has been put aside by itself in a box labeled with the name of the city for which it is destined. The names of the cities to which this alms or largess is to be sent are as follows: Rome, Ravenna, Milan, Friuli, Grado, Cologne, Mayence, Salzburg, Treves, Sens, Besançon, Lyons, Rouen, Rheims, Arles, Vienne, Moutiers-en-Tarantaise, Embrun, Bordeaux, Tours, and Bourges. The third lot, which he wishes to be kept entire, is to be bestowed as follows: While the first two lots are to be divided into the parts aforesaid, and set aside under seal, the third lot shall be employed for the owner's daily needs, as property which he shall be under no obligation to part with in order to the fulfillment of any vow, and this as long as he shall be in the flesh, or consider it necessary for his use. But upon his death, or voluntary-renunciation of the affairs of this world, this said lot shall be divided into four parts, and one thereof shall be added to the aforesaid twenty-one parts; the second shall be assigned to his sons and daughters, and to the sons and daughters of his sons, to be distributed among them in just and equal partition; the third, in accordance with the custom common among Christians, shall be devoted to the poor; and the fourth shall go to the support of the men servants and maid servants on duty in the palace. It is his wish that to this said third lot of the whole amount, which consists, as well as the rest, of gold and silver shall be added all the vessels and utensils of brass iron and other metals together with the arms, clothing, and other movable goods, costly and cheap, adapted to divers uses, as hangings, coverlets, carpets, woolen stuffs leathern articles, pack-saddles, and whatsoever shall be found in his treasure chamber and wardrobe at that time, in order that thus the parts of the said lot may be augmented, and the alms distributed reach more persons. He ordains that his chapel-that is to say, its church property, as well that which he has provided and collected as that which came to him by inheritance from his father shall remain entire, and not be dissevered by any partition whatever. If, however, any vessels, books or other articles be found therein which are certainly known not to have been given by him to the said chapel, whoever wants them shall have them on paying their value at a fair estimation. He likewise commands that the books which he has collected in his library in great numbers shall be sold for fair prices to such as want them, and the money received therefrom given to the poor. it is well known that among his other property and treasures are three silver tables, and one very large and massive golden one. He directs and commands that the square silver table, upon which there is a representation of the city of Constantinople, shall be sent to the Basilica of St. Peter the Apostle at Rome, with the other gifts destined therefor; that the round one, adorned with a delineation of the city of Rome, shall be given to the Episcopal Church at Ravenna; that the third, which far surpasses the other two in weight and in beauty of workmanship, and is made in three circles, showing the plan of the whole universe, drawn with skill and delicacy, shall go, together with the golden table, fourthly above mentioned, to increase that lot which is to be devoted to his heirs and to alms.

This deed, and the dispositions thereof, he has made and appointed in the presence of the bishops, abbots, and counts able to be present, whose names are hereto subscribed: Bishops - Hildebald, Ricolf, Arno, Wolfar, Bernoin, Laidrad, John, Theodulf, Jesse, Heito, Waltgaud. Abbots - Fredugis, Adalung, Angilbert, Irmino. Counts Walacho, Meginher, Otulf, Stephen, Unruoch Burchard Meginhard, Hatto, Rihwin, Edo, Ercangar, Gerold, Bero, Hildiger, Rocculf."

Charles' son Louis who by the grace of God succeeded him, after examining this summary, took pains to fulfill all its conditions most religiously as soon as possible after his father's death.

The Prince by Niccolò Machiavelli

To the Magnificent Lorenzo Di Piero De' Medici:

Those who strive to obtain the good graces of a prince are accustomed to come before him with such things as they hold most precious, or in which they see him take most delight; whence one often sees horses, arms, cloth of gold, precious stones, and similar ornaments presented to princes, worthy of their greatness.

Desiring therefore to present myself to your Magnificence with some testimony of my devotion towards you, I have not found among my possessions anything which I hold more dear than, or value so much as, the knowledge of the actions of great men, acquired by long experience in contemporary affairs, and a continual study of antiquity; which, having reflected upon it with great and prolonged diligence, I now send, digested into a little volume, to your Magnificence.

And although I may consider this work unworthy of your countenance, nevertheless I trust much to your benignity that it may be acceptable, seeing that it is not possible for me to make a better gift than to offer you the opportunity of understanding in the shortest time all that I have learnt in so many years, and with so many troubles and dangers; which work I have not embellished with swelling or magnificent words, nor stuffed with rounded periods, nor with any extrinsic allurements or adornments whatever, with which so many are accustomed to embellish their works; for I have wished either that no honour should be given it, or else that the truth of the matter and the weightiness of the theme shall make it acceptable.

Nor do I hold with those who regard it as a presumption if a man of low and humble condition dare to discuss and settle the concerns of princes; because, just as those who draw landscapes place themselves below in the plain to contemplate the nature of the mountains and of lofty places, and in order to contemplate the plains place themselves upon high mountains, even so to understand the nature of the people it needs to be a prince, and to understand that of princes it needs to be of the people.

Take then, your Magnificence, this little gift in the spirit in which I send it; wherein, if it be diligently read and considered by you, you will learn my extreme desire that you should attain that greatness which fortune and your other attributes promise. And if your Magnificence from the summit of your greatness will sometimes turn your eyes to these lower regions, you will see how unmeritedly I suffer a great and continued malignity of fortune.

I — HOW MANY KINDS OF PRINCIPALITIES THERE ARE, AND BY WHAT MEANS THEY ARE ACQUIRED

All states, all powers, that have held and hold rule over men have been and are either republics or principalities.

Principalities are either hereditary, in which the family has been long established; or they are new.

The new are either entirely new, as was Milan to Francesco Sforza, or they are, as it were, members annexed to the hereditary state of the prince who has acquired them, as was the kingdom of Naples to that of the King of Spain.

Such dominions thus acquired are either accustomed to live under a prince, or to live in freedom; and are acquired either by the arms of the prince himself, or of others, or else by fortune or by ability.

II — CONCERNING HEREDITARY PRINCIPALITIES

I will leave out all discussion on republics, inasmuch as in another place I have written of them at length, and will address myself only to principalities. In doing so I will keep to the order indicated above, and discuss how such principalities are to be ruled and preserved.

I say at once there are fewer difficulties in holding hereditary states, and those long accustomed to the family of their prince, than new ones; for it is sufficient only not to transgress the customs of his ancestors, and to deal prudently with circumstances as they arise, for a prince of average powers to maintain himself in his state, unless he be deprived of it by some extraordinary and excessive force; and if he should be so deprived of it, whenever anything sinister happens to the usurper, he will regain it.

We have in Italy, for example, the Duke of Ferrara, who could not have withstood the attacks of the Venetians in '84, nor those of Pope Julius in '10, unless he had been long established in his dominions. For the hereditary prince has less cause and less necessity to offend; hence it happens that he will be more loved; and unless extraordinary vices cause him to be hated, it is reasonable to expect that his subjects will be naturally well disposed towards him; and in the antiquity and duration of his rule the memories and motives that make for change are lost, for one change always leaves the toothing for another.

III — CONCERNING MIXED PRINCIPALITIES

But the difficulties occur in a new principality. And firstly, if it be not entirely new, but is, as it were, a member of a state which, taken collectively, may be called composite, the changes arise chiefly from an inherent difficulty which there is in all new principalities; for men change their rulers willingly, hoping to better themselves, and this hope induces them to take up arms against him who rules: wherein they are deceived, because they afterwards find by experience they have gone from bad to worse. This follows also on another natural and common necessity, which always causes a new prince to burden those who have submitted to him with his soldiery and with infinite other hardships which he must put upon his new acquisition.

In this way you have enemies in all those whom you have injured in seizing that principality, and you are not able to keep those friends who put you there because of your not being able to satisfy them in the way they expected, and you cannot take strong measures against them, feeling bound to them. For, although one may be very strong in armed forces, yet in entering a province one has always need of the goodwill of the natives.

For these reasons Louis the Twelfth, King of France, quickly occupied Milan, and as quickly lost it; and to turn him out the first time it only needed Lodovico's own forces; because those who had opened the gates to him, finding themselves deceived in their hopes of future benefit, would not endure the ill-treatment of the new prince. It is very true that, after acquiring rebellious provinces a second time, they are not so lightly lost afterwards, because the prince, with little reluctance, takes the opportunity of the rebellion to punish the delinquents, to clear out the suspects, and to strengthen himself in the weakest places. Thus to cause France to lose Milan the first time it was enough for the Duke Lodovico to raise insurrections on the borders; but to cause him to lose it a second time it was necessary to bring the whole world against him, and that his armies should be defeated and driven out of Italy; which followed from the causes above mentioned.

Nevertheless Milan was taken from France both the first and the second time. The general reasons for the first have been discussed; it remains to name those for the second, and to see what resources he had, and what any one in his situation would have had for maintaining himself more securely in his acquisition than did the King of France.

Now I say that those dominions which, when acquired, are added to an ancient state by him who acquires them, are either of the same country and language, or they are not. When they are, it is easier to hold them, especially when they have not been accustomed to self-government; and to hold them securely it is enough to have destroyed the family of the prince who was ruling them; because the two peoples, preserving in other things the old conditions, and not being unlike in customs, will live quietly together, as one has seen in Brittany, Burgundy, Gascony, and Normandy, which have been bound to France for so long a time: and, although there may be some difference in language, nevertheless the customs are alike, and the people will easily be able to get on amongst themselves. He who has annexed them, if he wishes to hold them, has only to bear in mind two considerations: the one, that the family of their former lord is extinguished; the other, that neither their laws nor their taxes are altered, so that in a very short time they will become entirely one body with the old principality.

But when states are acquired in a country differing in language, customs, or laws, there are difficulties, and good fortune and great energy are needed to hold them, and one of the greatest and most real helps would be that he who has acquired them should go and reside there. This would make his position more secure and durable, as it has made that of the Turk in Greece, who, notwithstanding all the other measures taken by him for holding that state, if he had not settled there, would not have been able to keep it. Because, if one is on the spot, disorders are seen as they spring up, and one can quickly remedy them; but if one is not at hand, they are heard of only when they are great, and then one can no longer remedy them. Besides this, the country is not pillaged by your officials; the subjects are satisfied by prompt recourse to the prince; thus, wishing to be good, they have more cause to love him, and wishing to be otherwise, to fear him. He who would attack that state from the outside must have the utmost caution; as long as the prince resides there it can only be wrested from him with the greatest difficulty.

The other and better course is to send colonies to one or two places, which may be as keys to that state, for it is necessary either to do this or else to keep there a great number of cavalry and infantry. A prince does not spend much on colonies, for with little or no expense he can send them out and keep them there, and he offends a minority only of the citizens from whom he takes lands and houses to give them to the new inhabitants; and those whom he offends, remaining poor and scattered, are never able to injure him; whilst the rest being uninjured are easily kept quiet, and at the same time are anxious not to err for fear it should happen to them as it has to those who have been despoiled. In conclusion, I say that these colonies are not costly, they are more faithful, they injure less, and the injured, as has been said, being poor and scattered, cannot hurt. Upon this, one has to remark that men ought either to be well treated or crushed, because they can avenge themselves of lighter injuries, of more serious ones they cannot; therefore the injury that is to be done to a man ought to be of such a kind that one does not stand in fear of revenge.

But in maintaining armed men there in place of colonies one spends much more, having to consume on the garrison all the income from the state, so that the acquisition turns into a loss, and many more are exasperated, because the whole state is injured; through the shifting of the garrison up and down all become acquainted with hardship, and all become hostile, and they are enemies who, whilst beaten on their own ground, are yet able to do hurt. For every reason, therefore, such guards are as useless as a colony is useful.

Again, the prince who holds a country differing in the above respects ought to make himself the head and defender of his less powerful neighbours, and to weaken the more powerful amongst them, taking care that no foreigner as powerful as himself shall, by any accident, get a footing there; for it will always happen that such a one will be introduced by those who are discontented, either through excess of ambition or through fear, as one has seen already. The Romans were brought into Greece by the Aetolians; and in every other country where they obtained a footing they were brought in by the inhabitants. And the usual course of affairs is that, as soon as a powerful foreigner enters a country, all the subject states are drawn to him, moved by the hatred which they feel against the ruling power. So that in respect to those subject states he has not to take any trouble to gain them over to himself, for the whole of them quickly rally to the state which he has acquired there. He has only to take care that they do not get hold of too much power and too much authority, and then with his own forces, and with their goodwill, he can easily keep down the more powerful of them, so as to remain entirely master in the country.

And he who does not properly manage this business will soon lose what he has acquired, and whilst he does hold it he will have endless difficulties and troubles.

The Romans, in the countries which they annexed, observed closely these measures; they sent colonies and maintained friendly relations with the minor powers, without increasing their strength; they kept down the greater, and did not allow any strong foreign powers to gain authority. Greece appears to me sufficient for an example. The Achaeans and Aetolians were kept friendly by them, the kingdom of Macedonia was humbled, Antiochus was driven out; yet the merits of the Achaeans and Aetolians never secured for them permission to increase their power, nor did the persuasions of Philip ever induce the Romans to be his friends without first humbling him, nor did the influence of Antiochus make them agree that he should retain any lordship over the country. Because the Romans did in these instances what all prudent princes ought to do, who have to regard not only present troubles, but also future ones, for which they must prepare with every energy, because, when foreseen, it is easy to remedy them; but if you wait until they approach, the medicine is no longer in time because the malady has become incurable; for it happens in this, as the physicians say it happens in hectic fever, that in the beginning of the malady it is easy to cure but difficult to detect, but in the course of time, not having been either detected or treated in the beginning, it becomes easy to detect but difficult to cure. This it happens in affairs of state, for when the evils that arise have been foreseen (which it is only given to a wise man to see), they can be quickly redressed, but when, through not having been foreseen, they have been permitted to grow in a way that every one can see them, there is no longer a remedy. Therefore, the Romans, foreseeing troubles, dealt with them at once, and, even to avoid a war, would not let them come to a head, for they knew that war is not to be avoided, but is only to be put off to the advantage of others; moreover they wished to fight with Philip and Antiochus in Greece so as not to have to do it in Italy; they could have avoided both, but this they did not wish; nor did that ever please them which is for ever in the mouths of the wise ones of our time:—Let us enjoy the benefits of the time—but rather the benefits of their own valour and prudence, for time drives everything before it, and is able to bring with it good as well as evil, and evil as well as good.

King Louis was brought into Italy by the ambition of the Venetians, who desired to obtain half the state of Lombardy by his intervention. I will not blame the course taken by the king, because, wishing to get a foothold in Italy, and having no friends there—seeing rather that every door was shut to him owing to the conduct of Charles—he was forced to accept those friendships which he could get, and he would have succeeded very quickly in his design if in other matters he had not made some mistakes. The king, however, having acquired Lombardy, regained at once the authority which Charles had lost: Genoa yielded; the Florentines became his friends; the Marquess of Mantua, the Duke of Ferrara, the Bentivogli, my lady of Forli, the Lords of Faenza, of Pesaro, of Rimini, of Camerino, of Piombino, the Lucchese, the Pisans, the Sienese—everybody made advances to him to become his friend. Then could the Venetians realize the rashness of the course taken by them, which, in order that they might secure two towns in Lombardy, had made the king master of two-thirds of Italy.

Let any one now consider with what little difficulty the king could have maintained his position in Italy had he observed the rules above laid down, and kept all his friends secure and protected; for although they were numerous they were both weak and timid, some afraid of the Church, some of the Venetians, and thus they would always have been forced to stand in with him, and by their means he could easily have made himself secure against those who remained powerful. But he was no sooner in Milan than he did the contrary by assisting Pope Alexander to occupy the Romagna. It never occurred to him that by this action he was weakening himself, depriving himself of friends and of those who had thrown themselves into his lap, whilst he aggrandized the Church by adding much temporal power to the spiritual, thus giving it greater authority. And having committed this prime error, he was obliged to follow it up, so much so that, to put an end to the ambition of Alexander, and to prevent his becoming the master of Tuscany, he was himself forced to come into Italy.

And as if it were not enough to have aggrandized the Church, and deprived himself of friends, he, wishing to have the kingdom of Naples, divides it with the King of Spain, and where he was the prime arbiter in Italy he takes an associate, so that the ambitious of that country and the malcontents of his own should have somewhere to shelter; and whereas he could have left in the kingdom his own pensioner as king, he drove him out, to put one there who was able to drive him, Louis, out in turn.

The wish to acquire is in truth very natural and common, and men always do so when they can, and for this they will be praised not blamed; but when they cannot do so, yet wish to do so by any means, then there is folly and blame. Therefore, if France could have attacked Naples with her own forces she ought to have done so; if she could not, then she ought not to have divided it. And if the partition which she made with the Venetians in Lombardy was justified by the excuse that by it she got a foothold in Italy, this other partition merited blame, for it had not the excuse of that necessity.

Therefore Louis made these five errors: he destroyed the minor powers, he increased the strength of one of the greater powers in Italy, he brought in a foreign power, he did not settle in the country, he did not send colonies. Which errors, had he lived, were not enough to injure him had he not made a sixth by taking away their dominions from the Venetians; because, had he not aggrandized the Church, nor brought Spain into Italy, it would have been very reasonable and necessary to humble them; but having first taken these steps, he ought never to have consented to their ruin, for they, being powerful, would always have kept off others from designs on Lombardy, to which the Venetians would never have consented except to become masters themselves there; also because the others would not wish to take Lombardy from France in order to give it to the Venetians, and to run counter to both they would not have had the courage.

And if any one should say: "King Louis yielded the Romagna to Alexander and the kingdom to Spain to avoid war," I answer for the reasons given above that a blunder ought never to be perpetrated to avoid war, because it is not to be avoided, but is only deferred to your disadvantage. And if another should allege the pledge which the king had given to the Pope that he would assist him in the enterprise, in exchange for the dissolution of his marriage and for the cap to Rouen, to that I reply what I shall write later on concerning the faith of princes, and how it ought to be kept.

Thus King Louis lost Lombardy by not having followed any of the conditions observed by those who have taken possession of countries and wished to retain them. Nor is there any miracle in this, but much that is reasonable and quite natural. And on these matters I spoke at Nantes with Rouen, when Valentino, as Cesare Borgia, the son of Pope Alexander, was usually called, occupied the Romagna, and on Cardinal Rouen observing to me that the Italians did not understand war, I replied to him that the French did not understand statecraft, meaning that otherwise they would not have allowed the Church to reach such greatness. And in fact it has been seen that the greatness of the Church and of Spain in Italy has been caused by France, and her ruin may be attributed to them. From this a general rule is drawn which never or rarely fails: that he who is the cause of another becoming powerful is ruined; because that predominancy has been brought about either by astuteness or else by force, and both are distrusted by him who has been raised to power.

IV — WHY THE KINGDOM OF DARIUS, CONQUERED BY ALEXANDER, DID NOT REBEL AGAINST THE SUCCESSORS OF ALEXANDER AT HIS DEATH

Considering the difficulties which men have had to hold to a newly acquired state, some might wonder how, seeing that Alexander the Great became the master of Asia in a few years, and died whilst it was scarcely settled (whence it might appear reasonable that the whole empire would have rebelled), nevertheless his successors maintained themselves, and had to meet no other difficulty than that which arose among themselves from their own ambitions.

I answer that the principalities of which one has record are found to be governed in two different ways; either by a prince, with a body of servants, who assist him to govern the kingdom as ministers by his favour and permission; or by a prince and barons, who hold that dignity by antiquity of blood and not by the grace of the prince. Such barons have states and their own subjects, who recognize them as lords and hold them in natural affection. Those states that are governed by a prince and his servants hold their prince in more consideration, because in all the country there is no one who is recognized as superior to him, and if they yield obedience to another they do it as to a minister and official, and they do not bear him any particular affection.

The examples of these two governments in our time are the Turk and the King of France. The entire monarchy of the Turk is governed by one lord, the others are his servants; and, dividing his kingdom into sanjaks, he sends there different administrators, and shifts and changes them as he chooses. But the King of France is placed in the midst of an ancient body of lords, acknowledged by their own subjects, and beloved by them; they have their own prerogatives, nor can the king take these away except at his peril. Therefore, he who considers both of these states will recognize great difficulties in seizing the state of the Turk, but, once it is conquered, great ease in holding it. The causes of the difficulties in seizing the kingdom of the Turk are that the usurper cannot be called in by the princes of the kingdom, nor can he hope to be assisted in his designs by the revolt of those whom the lord has around him. This arises from the reasons given above; for his ministers, being all slaves and bondmen, can only be corrupted with great difficulty, and one can expect little advantage from them when they have been corrupted, as they cannot carry the people with them, for the reasons assigned. Hence, he who attacks the Turk must bear in mind that he will find him united, and he will have to rely more on his own strength than on the revolt of others; but, if once the Turk has been conquered, and routed in the field in such a way that he cannot replace his armies, there is nothing to fear but the family of this prince, and, this being exterminated, there remains no one to fear, the others having no credit with the people; and as the conqueror did not rely on them before his victory, so he ought not to fear them after it.

The contrary happens in kingdoms governed like that of France, because one can easily enter there by gaining over some baron of the kingdom, for one always finds malcontents and such as desire a change. Such men, for the reasons given, can open the way into the state and render the victory easy; but if you wish to hold it afterwards, you meet with infinite difficulties, both from those who have assisted you and from those you have crushed. Nor is it enough for you to have exterminated the family of the prince, because the lords that remain make themselves the heads of fresh movements against you, and as you are unable either to satisfy or exterminate them, that state is lost whenever time brings the opportunity.

Now if you will consider what was the nature of the government of Darius, you will find it similar to the kingdom of the Turk, and therefore it was only necessary for Alexander, first to overthrow him in the field, and then to take the country from him. After which victory, Darius being killed, the state remained secure to Alexander, for the above reasons. And if his successors had been united they would have enjoyed it securely and at their ease, for there were no tumults raised in the kingdom except those they provoked themselves.

But it is impossible to hold with such tranquillity states constituted like that of France. Hence arose those frequent rebellions against the Romans in Spain, France, and Greece, owing to the many principalities there were in these states, of which, as long as the memory of them endured, the Romans always held an insecure possession; but with the power and long continuance of the empire the memory of them passed away, and the Romans then became secure possessors. And when fighting afterwards amongst themselves, each one was able to attach to himself his own parts of the country, according to the authority he had assumed there; and the family of the former lord being exterminated, none other than the Romans were acknowledged.

When these things are remembered no one will marvel at the ease with which Alexander held the Empire of Asia, or at the difficulties which others have had to keep an acquisition, such as Pyrrhus and many more; this is not occasioned by the little or abundance of ability in the conqueror, but by the want of uniformity in the subject state.

V — CONCERNING THE WAY TO GOVERN CITIES OR PRINCIPALITIES WHICH LIVED UNDER THEIR OWN LAWS BEFORE THEY WERE ANNEXED

Whenever those states which have been acquired as stated have been accustomed to live under their own laws and in freedom, there are three courses for those who wish to hold them: the first is to ruin them, the next is to reside there in person, the third is to permit them to live under their own laws, drawing a tribute, and establishing within it an oligarchy which will keep it friendly to you. Because such a government, being created by the prince, knows that it cannot stand without his friendship and interest, and does it utmost to support him; and therefore he who would keep a city accustomed to freedom will hold it more easily by the means of its own citizens than in any other way.

There are, for example, the Spartans and the Romans. The Spartans held Athens and Thebes, establishing there an oligarchy, nevertheless they lost them. The Romans, in order to hold Capua, Carthage, and Numantia, dismantled them, and did not lose them. They wished to hold Greece as the Spartans held it, making it free and permitting its laws, and did not succeed. So to hold it they were compelled to dismantle many cities in the country, for in truth there is no safe way to retain them otherwise than by ruining them. And he who becomes master of a city accustomed to freedom and does not destroy it, may expect to be destroyed by it, for in rebellion it has always the watchword of liberty and its ancient privileges as a rallying point, which neither time nor benefits will ever cause it to forget. And whatever you may do or provide against, they never forget that name or their privileges unless they are disunited or dispersed, but at every chance they immediately rally to them, as Pisa after the hundred years she had been held in bondage by the Florentines.

But when cities or countries are accustomed to live under a prince, and his family is exterminated, they, being on the one hand accustomed to obey and on the other hand not having the old prince, cannot agree in making one from amongst themselves, and they do not know how to govern themselves. For this reason they are very slow to take up arms, and a prince can gain them to himself and secure them much more easily. But in republics there is more vitality, greater hatred, and more desire for vengeance, which will never permit them to allow the memory of their former liberty to rest; so that the safest way is to destroy them or to reside there.

VI — CONCERNING NEW PRINCIPALITIES WHICH ARE ACQUIRED BY ONE'S OWN ARMS AND ABILITY

Let no one be surprised if, in speaking of entirely new principalities as I shall do, I adduce the highest examples both of prince and of state; because men, walking almost always in paths beaten by others, and following by imitation their deeds, are yet unable to keep entirely to the ways of others or attain to the power of those they imitate. A wise man ought always to follow the paths beaten by great men, and to imitate those who have been supreme, so that if his ability does not equal theirs, at least it will savour of it. Let him act like the clever archers who, designing to hit the mark which yet appears too far distant, and knowing the limits to which the strength of their bow attains, take aim much higher than the mark, not to reach by their strength or arrow to so great a height, but to be able with the aid of so high an aim to hit the mark they wish to reach.

I say, therefore, that in entirely new principalities, where there is a new prince, more or less difficulty is found in keeping them, accordingly as there is more or less ability in him who has acquired the state. Now, as the fact of becoming a prince from a private station presupposes either ability or fortune, it is clear that one or other of these things will mitigate in some degree many difficulties. Nevertheless, he who has relied least on fortune is established the strongest. Further, it facilitates matters when the prince, having no other state, is compelled to reside there in person.

But to come to those who, by their own ability and not through fortune, have risen to be princes, I say that Moses, Cyrus, Romulus, Theseus, and such like are the most excellent examples. And although one may not discuss Moses, he having been a mere executor of the will of God, yet he ought to be admired, if only for that favour which made him worthy to speak with God. But in considering Cyrus and others who have acquired or founded kingdoms, all will be found admirable; and if their particular deeds and conduct shall be considered, they will not be found inferior to those of Moses, although he had so great a preceptor. And in examining their actions and lives one cannot see that they owed anything to fortune beyond opportunity, which brought them the material to mould into the form which seemed best to them. Without that opportunity their powers of mind would have been extinguished, and without those powers the opportunity would have come in vain.

It was necessary, therefore, to Moses that he should find the people of Israel in Egypt enslaved and oppressed by the Egyptians, in order that they should be disposed to follow him so as to be delivered out of bondage. It was necessary that Romulus should not remain in Alba, and that he should be abandoned at his birth, in order that he should become King of Rome and founder of the fatherland. It was necessary that Cyrus should find the Persians discontented with the government of the Medes, and the Medes soft and effeminate through their long peace. Theseus could not have shown his ability had he not found the Athenians dispersed. These opportunities, therefore, made those men fortunate, and their high ability enabled them to recognize the opportunity whereby their country was ennobled and made famous.

Those who by valorous ways become princes, like these men, acquire a principality with difficulty, but they keep it with ease. The difficulties they have in acquiring it rise in part from the new rules and methods which they are forced to introduce to establish their government and its security. And it ought to be remembered that there is nothing more difficult to take in hand, more perilous to conduct, or more uncertain in its success, than to take the lead in the introduction of a new order of things, because the innovator has for enemies all those who have done well under the old conditions, and lukewarm defenders in those who may do well under the new. This coolness arises partly from fear of the opponents, who have the laws on their side, and partly from the incredulity of men, who do not readily believe in new things until they have had a long experience of them. Thus it happens that whenever those who are hostile have the opportunity to attack they do it like partisans, whilst the others defend lukewarmly, in such wise that the prince is endangered along with them.

It is necessary, therefore, if we desire to discuss this matter thoroughly, to inquire whether these innovators can rely on themselves or have to depend on others: that is to say, whether, to consummate their enterprise, have they to use prayers or can they use force? In the first instance they always succeed badly, and never compass anything; but when they can rely on themselves and use force, then they are rarely endangered. Hence it is that all armed prophets have conquered, and the unarmed ones have been destroyed. Besides the reasons mentioned, the nature of the people is variable, and whilst it is easy to persuade them, it is difficult to fix them in that persuasion. And thus it is necessary to take such measures that, when they believe no longer, it may be possible to make them believe by force.

If Moses, Cyrus, Theseus, and Romulus had been unarmed they could not have enforced their constitutions for long—as happened in our time to Fra Girolamo Savonarola, who was ruined with his new order of things immediately the multitude believed in him no longer, and he had no means of keeping steadfast those who believed or of making the unbelievers to believe. Therefore such as these have great difficulties in consummating their enterprise, for all their dangers are in the ascent, yet with ability they will overcome them; but when these are overcome, and those who envied them their success are exterminated, they will begin to be respected, and they will continue afterwards powerful, secure, honoured, and happy.

To these great examples I wish to add a lesser one; still it bears some resemblance to them, and I wish it to suffice me for all of a like kind: it is Hiero the Syracusan. This man rose from a private station to be Prince of Syracuse, nor did he, either, owe anything to fortune but opportunity; for the Syracusans, being oppressed, chose him for their captain, afterwards he was rewarded by being made their prince. He was of so great ability, even as a private citizen, that one who writes of him says he wanted nothing but a kingdom to be a king. This man abolished the old soldiery, organized the new, gave up old alliances, made new ones; and as he had his own soldiers and allies, on such foundations he was able to build any edifice: thus, whilst he had endured much trouble in acquiring, he had but little in keeping.

VII — CONCERNING NEW PRINCIPALITIES WHICH ARE ACQUIRED EITHER BY THE ARMS OF OTHERS OR BY GOOD FORTUNE

Those who solely by good fortune become princes from being private citizens have little trouble in rising, but much in keeping atop; they have not any difficulties on the way up, because they fly, but they have many when they reach the summit. Such are those to whom some state is given either for money or by the favour of him who bestows it; as happened to many in Greece, in the cities of Ionia and of the Hellespont, where princes were made by Darius, in order that they might hold the cities both for his security and his glory; as also were those emperors who, by the corruption of the soldiers, from being citizens came to empire. Such stand simply elevated upon the goodwill and the fortune of him who has elevated them—two most inconstant and unstable things. Neither have they the knowledge requisite for the position; because, unless they are men of great worth and ability, it is not reasonable to expect that they should know how to command, having always lived in a private condition; besides, they cannot hold it because they have not forces which they can keep friendly and faithful.

States that rise unexpectedly, then, like all other things in nature which are born and grow rapidly, cannot leave their foundations and correspondencies fixed in such a way that the first storm will not overthrow them; unless, as is said, those who unexpectedly become princes are men of so much ability that they know they have to be prepared at once to hold that which fortune has thrown into their laps, and that those foundations, which others have laid BEFORE they became princes, they must lay AFTERWARDS.

Concerning these two methods of rising to be a prince by ability or fortune, I wish to adduce two examples within our own recollection, and these are Francesco Sforza and Cesare Borgia. Francesco, by proper means and with great ability, from being a private person rose to be Duke of Milan, and that which he had acquired with a thousand anxieties he kept with little trouble. On the other hand, Cesare Borgia, called by the people Duke Valentino, acquired his state during the ascendancy of his father, and on its decline he lost it, notwithstanding that he had taken every measure and done all that ought to be done by a wise and able man to fix firmly his roots in the states which the arms and fortunes of others had bestowed on him.

Because, as is stated above, he who has not first laid his foundations may be able with great ability to lay them afterwards, but they will be laid with trouble to the architect and danger to the building. If, therefore, all the steps taken by the duke be considered, it will be seen that he laid solid foundations for his future power, and I do not consider it superfluous to discuss them, because I do not know what better precepts to give a new prince than the example of his actions; and if his dispositions were of no avail, that was not his fault, but the extraordinary and extreme malignity of fortune.

Alexander the Sixth, in wishing to aggrandize the duke, his son, had many immediate and prospective difficulties. Firstly, he did not see his way to make him master of any state that was not a state of the Church; and if he was willing to rob the Church he knew that the Duke of Milan and the Venetians would not consent, because Faenza and Rimini were already under the protection of the Venetians. Besides this, he saw the arms of Italy, especially those by which he might have been assisted, in hands that would fear the aggrandizement of the Pope, namely, the Orsini and the Colonnesi and their following. It behoved him, therefore, to upset this state of affairs and embroil the powers, so as to make himself securely master of part of their states. This was easy for him to do, because he found the Venetians, moved by other reasons, inclined to bring back the French into Italy; he would not only not oppose this, but he would render it more easy by dissolving the former marriage of King Louis. Therefore the king came into Italy with the assistance of the Venetians and the consent of Alexander. He was no sooner in Milan than the Pope had soldiers from him for the attempt on the Romagna, which yielded to him on the reputation of the king. The duke, therefore, having acquired the Romagna and beaten the Colonnesi, while wishing to hold that and to advance further, was hindered by two things: the one, his forces did not appear loyal to him, the other, the goodwill of France: that is to say, he feared that the forces of the Orsini, which he was using, would not stand to him, that not only might they hinder him from winning more, but might themselves seize what he had won, and that the king might also do the same. Of the Orsini he had a warning when, after taking Faenza and attacking Bologna, he saw them go very unwillingly to that attack. And as to the king, he learned his mind when he himself, after taking the Duchy of Urbino, attacked Tuscany, and the king made him desist from that undertaking; hence the duke decided to depend no more upon the arms and the luck of others.

For the first thing he weakened the Orsini and Colonnesi parties in Rome, by gaining to himself all their adherents who were gentlemen, making them his gentlemen, giving them good pay, and, according to their rank, honouring them with office and command in such a way that in a few months all attachment to the factions was destroyed and turned entirely to the duke. After this he awaited an opportunity to crush the Orsini, having scattered the adherents of the Colonna house. This came to him soon and he used it well; for the Orsini, perceiving at length that the aggrandizement of the duke and the Church was ruin to them, called a meeting of the Magione in Perugia. From this sprung the rebellion at Urbino and the tumults in the Romagna, with endless dangers to the duke, all of which he overcame with the help of the French. Having restored his authority, not to leave it at risk by trusting either to the French or other outside forces, he had recourse to his wiles, and he knew so well how to conceal his mind that, by the mediation of Signor Pagolo—whom the duke did not fail to secure with all kinds of attention, giving him money, apparel, and horses—the Orsini were reconciled, so that their simplicity brought them into his power at Sinigalia. Having exterminated the leaders, and turned their partisans into his friends, the duke laid sufficiently good foundations to his power, having all the Romagna and the Duchy of Urbino; and the people now beginning to appreciate their prosperity, he gained them all over to himself. And as this point is worthy of notice, and to be imitated by others, I am not willing to leave it out.

When the duke occupied the Romagna he found it under the rule of weak masters, who rather plundered their subjects than ruled them, and gave them more cause for disunion than for union, so that the country was full of robbery, quarrels, and every kind of violence; and so, wishing to bring back peace and obedience to authority, he considered it necessary to give it a good governor. Thereupon he pro- promoted Messer Ramiro d'Orco, a swift and cruel man, to whom he gave the fullest power. This man in a short time restored peace and unity with the greatest success. Afterwards the duke considered that it was not advisable to confer such excessive authority, for he had no doubt but that he would become odious, so he set up a court of judgment in the country, under a most excellent president, wherein all cities had their advocates. And because he knew that the past severity had caused some hatred against himself, so, to clear himself in the minds of the people, and gain them entirely to himself, he desired to show that, if any cruelty had been practised, it had not originated with him, but in the natural sternness of the minister. Under this pretence he took Ramiro, and one morning caused him to be executed and left on the piazza at Cesena with the block and a bloody knife at his side. The barbarity of this spectacle caused the people to be at once satisfied and dismayed.

But let us return whence we started. I say that the duke, finding himself now sufficiently powerful and partly secured from immediate dangers by having armed himself in his own way, and having in a great measure crushed those forces in his vicinity that could injure him if he wished to proceed with his conquest, had next to consider France, for he knew that the king, who too late was aware of his mistake, would not support him. And from this time he began to seek new alliances and to temporize with France in the expedition which she was making towards the kingdom of Naples against the Spaniards who were besieging Gaeta. It was his intention to secure himself against them, and this he would have quickly accomplished had Alexander lived.

Such was his line of action as to present affairs. But as to the future he had to fear, in the first place, that a new successor to the Church might not be friendly to him and might seek to take from him that which Alexander had given him, so he decided to act in four ways. Firstly, by exterminating the families of those lords whom he had despoiled, so as to take away that pretext from the Pope. Secondly, by winning to himself all the gentlemen of Rome, so as to be able to curb the Pope with their aid, as has been observed. Thirdly, by converting the college more to himself. Fourthly, by acquiring so much power before the Pope should die that he could by his own measures resist the first shock. Of these four things, at the death of Alexander, he had accomplished three. For he had killed as many of the dispossessed lords as he could lay hands on, and few had escaped; he had won over the Roman gentlemen, and he had the most numerous party in the college. And as to any fresh acquisition, he intended to become master of Tuscany, for he already possessed Perugia and Piombino, and Pisa was under his protection. And as he had no longer to study France (for the French were already driven out of the kingdom of Naples by the Spaniards, and in this way both were compelled to buy his goodwill), he pounced down upon Pisa. After this, Lucca and Siena yielded at once, partly through hatred and partly through fear of the Florentines; and the Florentines would have had no remedy had he continued to prosper, as he was prospering the year that Alexander died, for he had acquired so much power and reputation that he would have stood by himself, and no longer have depended on the luck and the forces of others, but solely on his own power and ability.

But Alexander died five years after he had first drawn the sword. He left the duke with the state of Romagna alone consolidated, with the rest in the air, between two most powerful hostile armies, and sick unto death. Yet there were in the duke such boldness and ability, and he knew so well how men are to be won or lost, and so firm were the foundations which in so short a time he had laid, that if he had not had those armies on his back, or if he had been in good health, he would have overcome all difficulties. And it is seen that his foundations were good, for the Romagna awaited him for more than a month. In Rome, although but half alive, he remained secure; and whilst the Baglioni, the Vitelli, and the Orsini might come to Rome, they could not effect anything against him. If he could not have made Pope him whom he wished, at least the one whom he did not wish would not have been elected. But if he had been in sound health at the death of Alexander, everything would have been different to him. On the day that Julius the Second was elected, he told me that he had thought of everything that might occur at the death of his father, and had provided a remedy for all, except that he had never anticipated that, when the death did happen, he himself would be on the point to die.

When all the actions of the duke are recalled, I do not know how to blame him, but rather it appears to be, as I have said, that I ought to offer him for imitation to all those who, by the fortune or the arms of others, are raised to government. Because he, having a lofty spirit and far-reaching aims, could not have regulated his conduct otherwise, and only the shortness of the life of Alexander and his own sickness frustrated his designs. Therefore, he who considers it necessary to secure himself in his new principality, to win friends, to overcome either by force or fraud, to make himself beloved and feared by the people, to be followed and revered by the soldiers, to exterminate those who have power or reason to hurt him, to change the old order of things for new, to be severe and gracious, magnanimous and liberal, to destroy a disloyal soldiery and to create new, to maintain friendship with kings and princes in such a way that they must help him with zeal and offend with caution, cannot find a more lively example than the actions of this man.

Only can he be blamed for the election of Julius the Second, in whom he made a bad choice, because, as is said, not being able to elect a Pope to his own mind, he could have hindered any other from being elected Pope; and he ought never to have consented to the election of any cardinal whom he had injured or who had cause to fear him if they became pontiffs. For men injure either from fear or hatred. Those whom he had injured, amongst others, were San Pietro ad Vincula, Colonna, San Giorgio, and Ascanio. The rest, in becoming Pope, had to fear him, Rouen and the Spaniards excepted; the latter from their relationship and obligations, the former from his influence, the kingdom of France having relations with him. Therefore, above everything, the duke ought to have created a Spaniard Pope, and, failing him, he ought to have consented to Rouen and not San Pietro ad Vincula. He who believes that new benefits will cause great personages to forget old injuries is deceived. Therefore, the duke erred in his choice, and it was the cause of his ultimate ruin.

VIII — CONCERNING THOSE WHO HAVE OBTAINED A PRINCIPALITY BY WICKEDNESS

Although a prince may rise from a private station in two ways, neither of which can be entirely attributed to fortune or genius, yet it is manifest to me that I must not be silent on them, although one could be more copiously treated when I discuss republics. These methods are when, either by some wicked or nefarious ways, one ascends to the principality, or when by the favour of his fellow-citizens a private person becomes the prince of his country. And speaking of the first method, it will be illustrated by two examples—one ancient, the other modern—and without entering further into the subject, I consider these two examples will suffice those who may be compelled to follow them.

Agathocles, the Sicilian, became King of Syracuse not only from a private but from a low and abject position. This man, the son of a potter, through all the changes in his fortunes always led an infamous life. Nevertheless, he accompanied his infamies with so much ability of mind and body that, having devoted himself to the military profession, he rose through its ranks to be Praetor of Syracuse. Being established in that position, and having deliberately resolved to make himself prince and to seize by violence, without obligation to others, that which had been conceded to him by assent, he came to an understanding for this purpose with Amilcar, the Carthaginian, who, with his army, was fighting in Sicily. One morning he assembled the people and the senate of Syracuse, as if he had to discuss with them things relating to the Republic, and at a given signal the soldiers killed all the senators and the richest of the people; these dead, he seized and held the princedom of that city without any civil commotion. And although he was twice routed by the Carthaginians, and ultimately besieged, yet not only was he able to defend his city, but leaving part of his men for its defence, with the others he attacked Africa, and in a short time raised the siege of Syracuse. The Carthaginians, reduced to extreme necessity, were compelled to come to terms with Agathocles, and, leaving Sicily to him, had to be content with the possession of Africa.

Therefore, he who considers the actions and the genius of this man will see nothing, or little, which can be attributed to fortune, inasmuch as he attained preeminence, as is shown above, not by the favour of any one, but step by step in the military profession, which steps were gained with a thousand troubles and perils, and were afterwards boldly held by him with many hazardous dangers. Yet it cannot be called talent to slay fellow-citizens, to deceive friends, to be without faith, without mercy, without religion; such methods may gain empire, but not glory. Still, if the courage of Agathocles in entering into and extricating himself from dangers be considered, together with his greatness of mind in enduring and overcoming hardships, it cannot be seen why he should be esteemed less than the most notable captain. Nevertheless, his barbarous cruelty and inhumanity with infinite wickedness do not permit him to be celebrated among the most excellent men. What he achieved cannot be attributed either to fortune or genius.

In our times, during the rule of Alexander the Sixth, Oliverotto da Fermo, having been left an orphan many years before, was brought up by his maternal uncle, Giovanni Fogliani, and in the early days of his youth sent to fight under Pagolo Vitelli, that, being trained under his discipline, he might attain some high position in the military profession. After Pagolo died, he fought under his brother Vitellozzo, and in a very short time, being endowed with wit and a vigorous body and mind, he became the first man in his profession. But it appearing a paltry thing to serve under others, he resolved, with the aid of some citizens of Fermo, to whom the slavery of their country was dearer than its liberty, and with the help of the Vitelleschi, to seize Fermo. So he wrote to Giovanni Fogliani that, having been away from home for many years, he wished to visit him and his city, and in some measure to look upon his patrimony; and although he had not laboured to acquire anything except honour, yet, in order that the citizens should see he had not spent his time in vain, he desired to come honourably, so would be accompanied by one hundred horsemen, his friends and retainers; and he entreated Giovanni to arrange that he should be received honourably by the Fermians, all of which would be not only to his honour, but also to that of Giovanni himself, who had brought him up.

Giovanni, therefore, did not fail in any attentions due to his nephew, and he caused him to be honourably received by the Fermians, and he lodged him in his own house, where, having passed some days, and having arranged what was necessary for his wicked designs, Oliverotto gave a solemn banquet to which he invited Giovanni Fogliani and the chiefs of Fermo. When the viands and all the other entertainments that are usual in such banquets were finished, Oliverotto artfully began certain grave discourses, speaking of the greatness of Pope Alexander and his son Cesare, and of their enterprises, to which discourse Giovanni and others answered; but he rose at once, saying that such matters ought to be discussed in a more private place, and he betook himself to a chamber, whither Giovanni and the rest of the citizens went in after him. No sooner were they seated than soldiers issued from secret places and slaughtered Giovanni and the rest. After these murders Oliverotto, mounted on horseback, rode up and down the town and besieged the chief magistrate in the palace, so that in fear the people were forced to obey him, and to form a government, of which he made himself the prince. He killed all the malcontents who were able to injure him, and strengthened himself with new civil and military ordinances, in such a way that, in the year during which he held the principality, not only was he secure in the city of Fermo, but he had become formidable to all his neighbours. And his destruction would have been as difficult as that of Agathocles if he had not allowed himself to be overreached by Cesare Borgia, who took him with the Orsini and Vitelli at Sinigalia, as was stated above. Thus one year after he had committed this parricide, he was strangled, together with Vitellozzo, whom he had made his leader in valour and wickedness.

Some may wonder how it can happen that Agathocles, and his like, after infinite treacheries and cruelties, should live for long secure in his country, and defend himself from external enemies, and never be conspired against by his own citizens;

seeing that many others, by means of cruelty, have never been able even in peaceful times to hold the state, still less in the doubtful times of war. I believe that this follows from severities being badly or properly used. Those may be called properly used, if of evil it is possible to speak well, that are applied at one blow and are necessary to one's security, and that are not persisted in afterwards unless they can be turned to the advantage of the subjects. The badly employed are those which, notwithstanding they may be few in the commencement, multiply with time rather than decrease. Those who practise the first system are able, by aid of God or man, to mitigate in some degree their rule, as Agathocles did. It is impossible for those who follow the other to maintain themselves.

Hence it is to be remarked that, in seizing a state, the usurper ought to examine closely into all those injuries which it is necessary for him to inflict, and to do them all at one stroke so as not to have to repeat them daily; and thus by not unsettling men he will be able to reassure them, and win them to himself by benefits. He who does otherwise, either from timidity or evil advice, is always compelled to keep the knife in his hand; neither can he rely on his subjects, nor can they attach themselves to him, owing to their continued and repeated wrongs. For injuries ought to be done all at one time, so that, being tasted less, they offend less; benefits ought to be given little by little, so that the flavour of them may last longer.

And above all things, a prince ought to live amongst his people in such a way that no unexpected circumstances, whether of good or evil, shall make him change; because if the necessity for this comes in troubled times, you are too late for harsh measures; and mild ones will not help you, for they will be considered as forced from you, and no one will be under any obligation to you for them.

IX — CONCERNING A CIVIL PRINCIPALITY

But coming to the other point—where a leading citizen becomes the prince of his country, not by wickedness or any intolerable violence, but by the favour of his fellow citizens—this may be called a civil principality: nor is genius or fortune altogether necessary to attain to it, but rather a happy shrewdness. I say then that such a principality is obtained either by the favour of the people or by the favour of the nobles. Because in all cities these two distinct parties are found, and from this it arises that the people do not wish to be ruled nor oppressed by the nobles, and the nobles wish to rule and oppress the people; and from these two opposite desires there arises in cities one of three results, either a principality, self-government, or anarchy.

A principality is created either by the people or by the nobles, accordingly as one or other of them has the opportunity; for the nobles, seeing they cannot withstand the people, begin to cry up the reputation of one of themselves, and they make him a prince, so that under his shadow they can give vent to their ambitions. The people, finding they cannot resist the nobles, also cry up the reputation of one of themselves, and make him a prince so as to be defended by his authority. He who obtains sovereignty by the assistance of the nobles maintains himself with more difficulty than he who comes to it by the aid of the people, because the former finds himself with many around him who consider themselves his equals, and because of this he can neither rule nor manage them to his liking. But he who reaches sovereignty by popular favour finds himself alone, and has none around him, or few, who are not prepared to obey him.

Besides this, one cannot by fair dealing, and without injury to others, satisfy the nobles, but you can satisfy the people, for their object is more righteous than that of the nobles, the latter wishing to oppress, while the former only desire not to be oppressed. It is to be added also that a prince can never secure himself against a hostile people, because of their being too many, whilst from the nobles he can secure himself, as they are few in number. The worst that a prince may expect from a hostile people is to be abandoned by them; but from hostile nobles he has not only to fear abandonment, but also that they will rise against him; for they, being in these affairs more far-seeing and astute, always come forward in time to save themselves, and to obtain favours from him whom they expect to prevail. Further, the prince is compelled to live always with the same people, but he can do well without the same nobles, being able to make and unmake them daily, and to give or take away authority when it pleases him.

Therefore, to make this point clearer, I say that the nobles ought to be looked at mainly in two ways: that is to say, they either shape their course in such a way as binds them entirely to your fortune, or they do not. Those who so bind themselves, and are not rapacious, ought to be honoured and loved; those who do not bind themselves may be dealt with in two ways; they may fail to do this through pusillanimity and a natural want of courage, in which case you ought to make use of them, especially of those who are of good counsel; and thus, whilst in prosperity you honour them, in adversity you do not have to fear them. But when for their own ambitious ends they shun binding themselves, it is a token that they are giving more thought to themselves than to you, and a prince ought to guard against such, and to fear them as if they were open enemies, because in adversity they always help to ruin him.

Therefore, one who becomes a prince through the favour of the people ought to keep them friendly, and this he can easily do seeing they only ask not to be oppressed by him. But one who, in opposition to the people, becomes a prince by the favour of the nobles, ought, above everything, to seek to win the people over to himself, and this he may easily do if he takes them under his protection. Because men, when they receive good from him of whom they were expecting evil, are bound more closely to their benefactor; thus the people quickly become more devoted to him than if he had been raised to the principality by their favours; and the prince can win their affections in many ways, but as these vary according to the circumstances one cannot give fixed rules, so I omit them; but, I repeat, it is necessary for a prince to have the people friendly, otherwise he has no security in adversity.

Nabis, Prince of the Spartans, sustained the attack of all Greece, and of a victorious Roman army, and against them he defended his country and his government; and for the overcoming of this peril it was only necessary for him to make himself secure against a few, but this would not have been sufficient had the people been hostile. And do not let any one impugn this statement with the trite proverb that "He who builds on the people, builds on the mud," for this is true when a private citizen makes a foundation there, and persuades himself that the people will free him when he is oppressed by his enemies or by the magistrates; wherein he would find himself very often deceived, as happened to the Gracchi in Rome and to Messer Giorgio Scali in Florence. But granted a prince who has established himself as above, who can command, and is a man of courage, undismayed in adversity, who does not fail in other qualifications, and who, by his resolution and energy, keeps the whole people encouraged—such a one will never find himself deceived in them, and it will be shown that he has laid his foundations well.

These principalities are liable to danger when they are passing from the civil to the absolute order of government, for such princes either rule personally or through magistrates. In the latter case their government is weaker and more insecure, because it rests entirely on the goodwill of those citizens who are raised to the magistracy, and who, especially in troubled times, can destroy the government with great ease, either by intrigue or open defiance; and the prince has not the chance amid tumults to exercise absolute authority, because the citizens and subjects, accustomed to receive orders from magistrates, are not of a mind to obey him amid these confusions, and there will always be in doubtful times a scarcity of men whom he can trust. For such a prince cannot rely upon what he observes in quiet times, when citizens have need of the state, because then every one agrees with him; they all promise, and when death is far distant they all wish to die for him; but in troubled times, when the state has need of its citizens, then he finds but few. And so much the more is this experiment dangerous, inasmuch as it can only be tried once. Therefore a wise prince ought to adopt such a course that his citizens will always in every sort and kind of circumstance have need of the state and of him, and then he will always find them faithful.

X — CONCERNING THE WAY IN WHICH THE STRENGTH OF ALL PRINCIPALITIES OUGHT TO BE MEASURED

It is necessary to consider another point in examining the character of these principalities: that is, whether a prince has such power that, in case of need, he can support himself with his own resources, or whether he has always need of the assistance of others. And to make this quite clear I say that I consider those who are able to support themselves by their own resources who can, either by abundance of men or money, raise a sufficient army to join battle against any one who comes to attack them; and I consider those always to have need of others who cannot show themselves against the enemy in the field, but are forced to defend themselves by sheltering behind walls. The first case has been discussed, but we will speak of it again should it recur. In the second case one can say nothing except to encourage such princes to provision and fortify their towns, and not on any account to defend the country. And whoever shall fortify his town well, and shall have managed the other concerns of his subjects in the way stated above, and to be often repeated, will never be attacked without great caution, for men are always adverse to enterprises where difficulties can be seen, and it will be seen not to be an easy thing to attack one who has his town well fortified, and is not hated by his people.

The cities of Germany are absolutely free, they own but little country around them, and they yield obedience to the emperor when it suits them, nor do they fear this or any other power they may have near them, because they are fortified in such a way that every one thinks the taking of them by assault would be tedious and difficult, seeing they have proper ditches and walls, they have sufficient artillery, and they always keep in public depots enough for one year's eating, drinking, and firing. And beyond this, to keep the people quiet and without loss to the state, they always have the means of giving work to the community in those labours that are the life and strength of the city, and on the pursuit of which the people are supported; they also hold military exercises in repute, and moreover have many ordinances to uphold them.

Therefore, a prince who has a strong city, and had not made himself odious, will not be attacked, or if any one should attack he will only be driven off with disgrace; again, because that the affairs of this world are so changeable, it is almost impossible to keep an army a whole year in the field without being interfered with. And whoever should reply: If the people have property outside the city, and see it burnt, they will not remain patient, and the long siege and self-interest will make them forget their prince; to this I answer that a powerful and courageous prince will overcome all such difficulties by giving at one time hope to his subjects that the evil will not be for long, at another time fear of the cruelty of the enemy, then preserving himself adroitly from those subjects who seem to him to be too bold.

Further, the enemy would naturally on his arrival at once burn and ruin the country at the time when the spirits of the people are still hot and ready for the defence; and, therefore, so much the less ought the prince to hesitate; because after a time, when spirits have cooled, the damage is already done, the ills are incurred, and there is no longer any remedy; and therefore they are so much the more ready to unite with their prince, he appearing to be under obligations to them now that their houses have been burnt and their possessions ruined in his defence. For it is the nature of men to be bound by the benefits they confer as much as by those they receive. Therefore, if everything is well considered, it will not be difficult for a wise prince to keep the minds of his citizens steadfast from first to last, when he does not fail to support and defend them.

XI — CONCERNING ECCLESIASTICAL PRINCIPALITIES

It only remains now to speak of ecclesiastical principalities, touching which all difficulties are prior to getting possession, because they are acquired either by capacity or good fortune, and they can be held without either; for they are sustained by the ancient ordinances of religion, which are so all-powerful, and of such a character that the principalities may be held no matter how their princes behave and live. These princes alone have states and do not defend them; and they have subjects and do not rule them; and the states, although unguarded, are not taken from them, and the subjects, although not ruled, do not care, and they have neither the desire nor the ability to alienate themselves. Such principalities only are secure and happy. But being upheld by powers, to which the human mind cannot reach, I shall speak no more of them, because, being exalted and maintained by God, it would be the act of a presumptuous and rash man to discuss them.

Nevertheless, if any one should ask of me how comes it that the Church has attained such greatness in temporal power, seeing that from Alexander backwards the Italian potentates (not only those who have been called potentates, but every baron and lord, though the smallest) have valued the temporal power very slightly—yet now a king of France trembles before it, and it has been able to drive him from Italy, and to ruin the Venetians—although this may be very manifest, it does not appear to me superfluous to recall it in some measure to memory.

Before Charles, King of France, passed into Italy, this country was under the dominion of the Pope, the Venetians, the King of Naples, the Duke of Milan, and the Florentines. These potentates had two principal anxieties: the one, that no foreigner should enter Italy under arms; the other, that none of themselves should seize more territory. Those about whom there was the most anxiety were the Pope and the Venetians. To restrain the Venetians the union of all the others was necessary, as it was for the defence of Ferrara; and to keep down the Pope they made use of the barons of Rome, who, being divided into two factions, Orsini and Colonnesi, had always a pretext for disorder, and, standing with arms in their hands under the eyes of the Pontiff, kept the pontificate weak and powerless. And although there might arise sometimes a courageous pope, such as Sixtus, yet neither fortune nor wisdom could rid him of these annoyances. And the short life of a pope is also a cause of weakness; for in the ten years, which is the average life of a pope, he can with difficulty lower one of the factions; and if, so to speak, one people should almost destroy the Colonnesi, another would arise hostile to the Orsini, who would support their opponents, and yet would not have time to ruin the Orsini. This was the reason why the temporal powers of the pope were little esteemed in Italy.

Alexander the Sixth arose afterwards, who of all the pontiffs that have ever been showed how a pope with both money and arms was able to prevail; and through the instrumentality of the Duke Valentino, and by reason of the entry of the French, he brought about all those things which I have discussed above in the actions of the duke. And although his intention was not to aggrandize the Church, but the duke, nevertheless, what he did contributed to the greatness of the Church, which, after his death and the ruin of the duke, became the heir to all his labours.

Pope Julius came afterwards and found the Church strong, possessing all the Romagna, the barons of Rome reduced to impotence, and, through the chastisements of Alexander, the factions wiped out; he also found the way open to accumulate money in a manner such as had never been practised before Alexander's time. Such things Julius not only followed, but improved upon, and he intended to gain Bologna, to ruin the Venetians, and to drive the French out of Italy. All of these enterprises prospered with him, and so much the more to his credit, inasmuch as he did everything to strengthen the Church and not any private person. He kept also the Orsini and Colonnesi factions within the bounds in which he found them; and although there was among them some mind to make disturbance, nevertheless he held two things firm: the one, the greatness of the Church, with which he terrified them; and the other, not allowing them to have their own cardinals, who caused the disorders among them. For whenever these factions have their cardinals they do not remain quiet for long, because cardinals foster the factions in Rome and out of it, and the barons are compelled to support them, and thus from the ambitions of prelates arise disorders and tumults among the barons. For these reasons his Holiness Pope Leo found the pontificate most powerful, and it is to be hoped that, if others made it great in arms, he will make it still greater and more venerated by his goodness and infinite other virtues.

XII — HOW MANY KINDS OF SOLDIERY THERE ARE, AND CONCERNING MERCENARIES

Having discoursed particularly on the characteristics of such principalities as in the beginning I proposed to discuss, and having considered in some degree the causes of their being good or bad, and having shown the methods by which many have sought to acquire them and to hold them, it now remains for me to discuss generally the means of offence and defence which belong to each of them.

We have seen above how necessary it is for a prince to have his foundations well laid, otherwise it follows of necessity he will go to ruin. The chief foundations of all states, new as well as old or composite, are good laws and good arms; and as there cannot be good laws where the state is not well armed, it follows that where they are well armed they have good laws. I shall leave the laws out of the discussion and shall speak of the arms.

I say, therefore, that the arms with which a prince defends his state are either his own, or they are mercenaries, auxiliaries, or mixed. Mercenaries and auxiliaries are useless and dangerous; and if one holds his state based on these arms, he will stand neither firm nor safe; for they are disunited, ambitious, and without discipline, unfaithful, valiant before friends, cowardly before enemies; they have neither the fear of God nor fidelity to men, and destruction is deferred only so long as the attack is; for in peace one is robbed by them, and in war by the enemy. The fact is, they have no other attraction or reason for keeping the field than a trifle of stipend, which is not sufficient to make them willing to die for you. They are ready enough to be your soldiers whilst you do not make war, but if war comes they take themselves off or run from the foe; which I should have little trouble to prove, for the ruin of Italy has been caused by nothing else than by resting all her hopes for many years on mercenaries, and although they formerly made some display and appeared valiant amongst themselves, yet when the foreigners came they showed what they were. Thus it was that Charles, King of France, was allowed to seize Italy with chalk in hand; and he who told us that our sins were the cause of it told the truth, but they were not the sins he imagined, but those which I have related. And as they were the sins of princes, it is the princes who have also suffered the penalty.

I wish to demonstrate further the infelicity of these arms. The mercenary captains are either capable men or they are not; if they are, you cannot trust them, because they always aspire to their own greatness, either by oppressing you, who are their master, or others contrary to your intentions; but if the captain is not skilful, you are ruined in the usual way.

And if it be urged that whoever is armed will act in the same way, whether mercenary or not, I reply that when arms have to be resorted to, either by a prince or a republic, then the prince ought to go in person and perform the duty of a captain; the republic has to send its citizens, and when one is sent who does not turn out satisfactorily, it ought to recall him, and when one is worthy, to hold him by the laws so that he does not leave the command. And experience has shown princes and republics, single-handed, making the greatest progress, and mercenaries doing nothing except damage; and it is more difficult to bring a republic, armed with its own arms, under the sway of one of its citizens than it is to bring one armed with foreign arms. Rome and Sparta stood for many ages armed and free. The Switzers are completely armed and quite free.

Of ancient mercenaries, for example, there are the Carthaginians, who were oppressed by their mercenary soldiers after the first war with the Romans, although the Carthaginians had their own citizens for captains. After the death of Epaminondas, Philip of Macedon was made captain of their soldiers by the Thebans, and after victory he took away their liberty.

Duke Filippo being dead, the Milanese enlisted Francesco Sforza against the Venetians, and he, having overcome the enemy at Caravaggio, allied himself with them to crush the Milanese, his masters. His father, Sforza, having been engaged by Queen Johanna of Naples, left her unprotected, so that she was forced to throw herself into the arms of the King of Aragon, in order to save her kingdom. And if the Venetians and Florentines formerly extended their dominions by these arms, and yet their captains did not make themselves princes, but have defended them, I reply that the Florentines in this case have been favoured by chance, for of the able captains, of whom they might have stood in fear, some have not conquered, some have been opposed, and others have turned their ambitions elsewhere. One who did not conquer was Giovanni Acuto, and since he did not conquer his fidelity cannot be proved; but every one will acknowledge that, had he conquered, the Florentines would have stood at his discretion. Sforza had the Bracceschi always against him, so they watched each other. Francesco turned his ambition to Lombardy; Braccio against the Church and the kingdom of Naples. But let us come to that which happened a short while ago. The Florentines appointed as their captain Pagolo Vitelli, a most prudent man, who from a private position had risen to the greatest renown. If this man had taken Pisa, nobody can deny that it would have been proper for the Florentines to keep in with him, for if he became the soldier of their enemies they had no means of resisting, and if they held to him they must obey him. The Venetians, if their achievements are considered, will be seen to have acted safely and gloriously so long as they sent to war their own men, when with armed gentlemen and plebians they did valiantly. This was before they turned to enterprises on land, but when they began to fight on land they forsook this virtue and followed the custom of Italy. And in the beginning of their expansion on land, through not having much territory, and because of their great reputation, they had not much to fear from their captains; but when they expanded, as under Carmignuola, they had a taste of this mistake; for, having found him a most valiant man (they beat the Duke of Milan under his leadership), and, on the other hand, knowing how lukewarm he was in the war, they feared they would no longer conquer under him, and for this reason they were not willing, nor were they able, to let him go; and so, not to lose again that which they had acquired, they were compelled, in order to secure themselves, to murder him. They had afterwards for their captains Bartolomeo da Bergamo, Roberto da San Severino, the count of Pitigliano, and the like, under whom they had to dread loss and not gain, as happened afterwards at Vaila, where in one battle they lost that which in eight hundred years they had acquired with so much trouble. Because from such arms conquests come but slowly, long delayed and inconsiderable, but the losses sudden and portentous.

And as with these examples I have reached Italy, which has been ruled for many years by mercenaries, I wish to discuss them more seriously, in order that, having seen their rise and progress, one may be better prepared to counteract them. You must understand that the empire has recently come to be repudiated in Italy, that the Pope has acquired more temporal power, and that Italy has been divided up into more states, for the reason that many of the great cities took up arms against their nobles, who, formerly favoured by the emperor, were oppressing them, whilst the Church was favouring them so as to gain authority in temporal power: in many others their citizens became princes. From this it came to pass that Italy fell partly into the hands of the Church and of republics, and, the Church consisting of priests and the republic of citizens unaccustomed to arms, both commenced to enlist foreigners.

The first who gave renown to this soldiery was Alberigo da Conio, the Romagnian. From the school of this man sprang, among others, Braccio and Sforza, who in their time were the arbiters of Italy. After these came all the other captains who till now have directed the arms of Italy; and the end of all their valour has been, that she has been overrun by Charles, robbed by Louis, ravaged by Ferdinand, and insulted by the Switzers. The principle that has guided them has been, first, to lower the credit of infantry so that they might increase their own. They did this because, subsisting on their pay and without territory, they were unable to support many soldiers, and a few infantry did not give them any authority; so they were led to employ cavalry, with a moderate force of which they were maintained and honoured; and affairs were brought to such a pass that, in an army of twenty thousand soldiers, there were not to be found two thousand foot soldiers. They had, besides this, used every art to lessen fatigue and danger to themselves and their soldiers, not killing in the fray, but taking prisoners and liberating without ransom. They did not attack towns at night, nor did the garrisons of the towns attack encampments at night; they did not surround the camp either with stockade or ditch, nor did they campaign in the winter. All these things were permitted by their military rules, and devised by them to avoid, as I have said, both fatigue and dangers; thus they have brought Italy to slavery and contempt.

XIII — CONCERNING AUXILIARIES, MIXED SOLDIERY, AND ONE'S OWN

Auxiliaries, which are the other useless arm, are employed when a prince is called in with his forces to aid and defend, as was done by Pope Julius in the most recent times; for he, having, in the enterprise against Ferrara, had poor proof of his mercenaries, turned to auxiliaries, and stipulated with Ferdinand, King of Spain, for his assistance with men and arms. These arms may be useful and good in themselves, but for him who calls them in they are always disadvantageous; for losing, one is undone, and winning, one is their captive.

And although ancient histories may be full of examples, I do not wish to leave this recent one of Pope Julius the Second, the peril of which cannot fail to be perceived; for he, wishing to get Ferrara, threw himself entirely into the hands of the foreigner. But his good fortune brought about a third event, so that he did not reap the fruit of his rash choice; because, having his auxiliaries routed at Ravenna, and the Switzers having risen and driven out the conquerors (against all expectation, both his and others), it so came to pass that he did not become prisoner to his enemies, they having fled, nor to his auxiliaries, he having conquered by other arms than theirs.

The Florentines, being entirely without arms, sent ten thousand Frenchmen to take Pisa, whereby they ran more danger than at any other time of their troubles.

The Emperor of Constantinople, to oppose his neighbours, sent ten thousand Turks into Greece, who, on the war being finished, were not willing to quit; this was the beginning of the servitude of Greece to the infidels.

Therefore, let him who has no desire to conquer make use of these arms, for they are much more hazardous than mercenaries, because with them the ruin is ready made; they are all united, all yield obedience to others; but with mercenaries, when they have conquered, more time and better opportunities are needed to injure you; they are not all of one community, they are found and paid by you, and a third party, which you have made their head, is not able all at once to assume enough authority to injure you. In conclusion, in mercenaries dastardy is most dangerous; in auxiliaries, valour. The wise prince, therefore, has always avoided these arms and turned to his own; and has been willing rather to lose with them than to conquer with the others, not deeming that a real victory which is gained with the arms of others.

I shall never hesitate to cite Cesare Borgia and his actions. This duke entered the Romagna with auxiliaries, taking there only French soldiers, and with them he captured Imola and Forli; but afterwards, such forces not appearing to him reliable, he turned to mercenaries, discerning less danger in them, and enlisted the Orsini and Vitelli; whom presently, on handling and finding them doubtful, unfaithful, and dangerous, he destroyed and turned to his own men. And the difference between one and the other of these forces can easily be seen when one considers the difference there was in the reputation of the duke, when he had the French, when he had the Orsini and Vitelli, and when he relied on his own soldiers, on whose fidelity he could always count and found it ever increasing; he was never esteemed more highly than when every one saw that he was complete master of his own forces.

I was not intending to go beyond Italian and recent examples, but I am unwilling to leave out Hiero, the Syracusan, he being one of those I have named above. This man, as I have said, made head of the army by the Syracusans, soon found out that a mercenary soldiery, constituted like our Italian condottieri, was of no use; and it appearing to him that he could neither keep them not let them go, he had them all cut to pieces, and afterwards made war with his own forces and not with aliens.

I wish also to recall to memory an instance from the Old Testament applicable to this subject. David offered himself to Saul to fight with Goliath, the Philistine champion, and, to give him courage, Saul armed him with his own weapons; which David rejected as soon as he had them on his back, saying he could make no use of them, and that he wished to meet the enemy with his sling and his knife. In conclusion, the arms of others either fall from your back, or they weigh you down, or they bind you fast.

Charles the Seventh, the father of King Louis the Eleventh, having by good fortune and valour liberated France from the English, recognized the necessity of being armed with forces of his own, and he established in his kingdom ordinances concerning men-at-arms and infantry. Afterwards his son, King Louis, abolished the infantry and began to enlist the Switzers, which mistake, followed by others, is, as is now seen, a source of peril to that kingdom; because, having raised the reputation of the Switzers, he has entirely diminished the value of his own arms, for he has destroyed the infantry altogether; and his men-at-arms he has subordinated to others, for, being as they are so accustomed to fight along with Switzers, it does not appear that they can now conquer without them. Hence it arises that the French cannot stand against the Switzers, and without the Switzers they do not come off well against others. The armies of the French have thus become mixed, partly mercenary and partly national, both of which arms together are much better than mercenaries alone or auxiliaries alone, but much inferior to one's own forces. And this example proves it, for the kingdom of France would be unconquerable if the ordinance of Charles had been enlarged or maintained.

But the scanty wisdom of man, on entering into an affair which looks well at first, cannot discern the poison that is hidden in it, as I have said above of hectic fevers. Therefore, if he who rules a principality cannot recognize evils until they are upon him, he is not truly wise; and this insight is given to few. And if the first disaster to the Roman Empire should be examined, it will be found to have commenced only with the enlisting of the Goths; because from that time the vigour of the Roman Empire began to decline, and all that valour which had raised it passed away to others.

I conclude, therefore, that no principality is secure without having its own forces; on the contrary, it is entirely dependent on good fortune, not having the valour which in adversity would defend it. And it has always been the opinion and judgment of wise men that nothing can be so uncertain or unstable as fame or power not founded on its own strength. And one's own forces are those which are composed either of subjects, citizens, or dependents; all others are mercenaries or auxiliaries. And the way to make ready one's own forces will be easily found if the rules suggested by me shall be reflected upon, and if one will consider how Philip, the father of Alexander the Great, and many republics and princes have armed and organized themselves, to which rules I entirely commit myself.

XIV — THAT WHICH CONCERNS A PRINCE ON THE SUBJECT OF THE ART OF WAR

A prince ought to have no other aim or thought, nor select anything else for his study, than war and its rules and discipline; for this is the sole art that belongs to him who rules, and it is of such force that it not only upholds those who are born princes, but it often enables men to rise from a private station to that rank. And, on the contrary, it is seen that when princes have thought more of ease than of arms they have lost their states. And the first cause of your losing it is to neglect this art; and what enables you to acquire a state is to be master of the art. Francesco Sforza, through being martial, from a private person became Duke of Milan; and the sons, through avoiding the hardships and troubles of arms, from dukes became private persons. For among other evils which being unarmed brings you, it causes you to be despised, and this is one of those ignominies against which a prince ought to guard himself, as is shown later on. Because there is nothing proportionate between the armed and the unarmed; and it is not reasonable that he who is armed should yield obedience willingly to him who is unarmed, or that the unarmed man should be secure among armed servants. Because, there being in the one disdain and in the other suspicion, it is not possible for them to work well together. And therefore a prince who does not understand the art of war, over and above the other misfortunes already mentioned, cannot be respected by his soldiers, nor can he rely on them. He ought never, therefore, to have out of his thoughts this subject of war, and in peace he should addict himself more to its exercise than in war; this he can do in two ways, the one by action, the other by study.

As regards action, he ought above all things to keep his men well organized and drilled, to follow incessantly the chase, by which he accustoms his body to hardships, and learns something of the nature of localities, and gets to find out how the mountains rise, how the valleys open out, how the plains lie, and to understand the nature of rivers and marshes, and in all this to take the greatest care. Which knowledge is useful in two ways. Firstly, he learns to know his country, and is better able to undertake its defence; afterwards, by means of the knowledge and observation of that locality, he understands with ease any other which it may be necessary for him to study hereafter; because the hills, valleys, and plains, and rivers and marshes that are, for instance, in Tuscany, have a certain resemblance to those of other countries, so that with a knowledge of the aspect of one country one can easily arrive at a knowledge of others. And the prince that lacks this skill lacks the essential which it is desirable that a captain should possess, for it teaches him to surprise his enemy, to select quarters, to lead armies, to array the battle, to besiege towns to advantage.

Philopoemen, Prince of the Achaeans, among other praises which writers have bestowed on him, is commended because in time of peace he never had anything in his mind but the rules of war; and when he was in the country with friends, he often stopped and reasoned with them: "If the enemy should be upon that hill, and we should find ourselves here with our army, with whom would be the advantage? How should one best advance to meet him, keeping the ranks? If we should wish to retreat, how ought we to pursue?" And he would set forth to them, as he went, all the chances that could befall an army; he would listen to their opinion and state his, confirming it with reasons, so that by these continual discussions there could never arise, in time of war, any unexpected circumstances that he could not deal with.

But to exercise the intellect the prince should read histories, and study there the actions of illustrious men, to see how they have borne themselves in war, to examine the causes of their victories and defeat, so as to avoid the latter and imitate the former; and above all do as an illustrious man did, who took as an exemplar one who had been praised and famous before him, and whose achievements and deeds he always kept in his mind, as it is said Alexander the Great imitated Achilles, Caesar Alexander, Scipio Cyrus. And whoever reads the life of Cyrus, written by Xenophon, will recognize afterwards in the life of Scipio how that imitation was his glory, and how in chastity, affability, humanity, and liberality Scipio conformed to those things which have been written of Cyrus by Xenophon. A wise prince ought to observe some such rules, and never in peaceful times stand idle, but increase his resources with industry in such a way that they may be available to him in adversity, so that if fortune chances it may find him prepared to resist her blows.

XV — CONCERNING THINGS FOR WHICH MEN, AND ESPECIALLY PRINCES, ARE PRAISED OR BLAMED

It remains now to see what ought to be the rules of conduct for a prince towards subject and friends. And as I know that many have written on this point, I expect I shall be considered presumptuous in mentioning it again, especially as in discussing it I shall depart from the methods of other people. But, it being my intention to write a thing which shall be useful to him who apprehends it, it appears to me more appropriate to follow up the real truth of the matter than the imagination of it; for many have pictured republics and principalities which in fact have never been known or seen, because how one lives is so far distant from how one ought to live, that he who neglects what is done for what ought to be done, sooner effects his ruin than his preservation; for a man who wishes to act entirely up to his professions of virtue soon meets with what destroys him among so much that is evil.

Hence it is necessary for a prince wishing to hold his own to know how to do wrong, and to make use of it or not according to necessity. Therefore, putting on one side imaginary things concerning a prince, and discussing those which are real, I say that all men when they are spoken of, and chiefly princes for being more highly placed, are remarkable for some of those qualities which bring them either blame or praise; and thus it is that one is reputed liberal, another miserly, using a Tuscan term (because an avaricious person in our language is still he who desires to possess by robbery, whilst we call one miserly who deprives himself too much of the use of his own); one is reputed generous, one rapacious; one cruel, one compassionate; one faithless, another faithful; one effeminate and cowardly, another bold and brave; one affable, another haughty; one lascivious, another chaste; one sincere, another cunning; one hard, another easy; one grave, another frivolous; one religious, another unbelieving, and the like. And I know that every one will confess that it would be most praiseworthy in a prince to exhibit all the above qualities that are considered good; but because they can neither be entirely possessed nor observed, for human conditions do not permit it, it is necessary for him to be sufficiently prudent that he may know how to avoid the reproach of those vices which would lose him his state; and also to keep himself, if it be possible, from those which would not lose him it; but this not being possible, he may with less hesitation abandon himself to them. And again, he need not make himself uneasy at incurring a reproach for those vices without which the state can only be saved with difficulty, for if everything is considered carefully, it will be found that something which looks like virtue, if followed, would be his ruin; whilst something else, which looks like vice, yet followed brings him security and prosperity.

XVI — CONCERNING LIBERALITY AND MEANNESS

Commencing then with the first of the above-named characteristics, I say that it would be well to be reputed liberal. Nevertheless, liberality exercised in a way that does not bring you the reputation for it, injures you; for if one exercises it honestly and as it should be exercised, it may not become known, and you will not avoid the reproach of its opposite. Therefore, any one wishing to maintain among men the name of liberal is obliged to avoid no attribute of magnificence; so that a prince thus inclined will consume in such acts all his property, and will be compelled in the end, if he wish to maintain the name of liberal, to unduly weigh down his people, and tax them, and do everything he can to get money. This will soon make him odious to his subjects, and becoming poor he will be little valued by any one; thus, with his liberality, having offended many and rewarded few, he is affected by the very first trouble and imperilled by whatever may be the first danger; recognizing this himself, and wishing to draw back from it, he runs at once into the reproach of being miserly.

Therefore, a prince, not being able to exercise this virtue of liberality in such a way that it is recognized, except to his cost, if he is wise he ought not to fear the reputation of being mean, for in time he will come to be more considered than if liberal, seeing that with his economy his revenues are enough, that he can defend himself against all attacks, and is able to engage in enterprises without burdening his people; thus it comes to pass that he exercises liberality towards all from whom he does not take, who are numberless, and meanness towards those to whom he does not give, who are few.

We have not seen great things done in our time except by those who have been considered mean; the rest have failed. Pope Julius the Second was assisted in reaching the papacy by a reputation for liberality, yet he did not strive afterwards to keep it up, when he made war on the King of France; and he made many wars without imposing any extraordinary tax on his subjects, for he supplied his additional expenses out of his long thriftiness. The present King of Spain would not have undertaken or conquered in so many enterprises if he had been reputed liberal. A prince, therefore, provided that he has not to rob his subjects, that he can defend himself, that he does not become poor and abject, that he is not forced to become rapacious, ought to hold of little account a reputation for being mean, for it is one of those vices which will enable him to govern.

And if any one should say: Caesar obtained empire by liberality, and many others have reached the highest positions by having been liberal, and by being considered so, I answer: Either you are a prince in fact, or in a way to become one. In the first case this liberality is dangerous, in the second it is very necessary to be considered liberal; and Caesar was one of those who wished to become pre-eminent in Rome; but if he had survived after becoming so, and had not moderated his expenses, he would have destroyed his government. And if any one should reply: Many have been princes, and have done great things with armies, who have been considered very liberal, I reply: Either a prince spends that which is his own or his subjects' or else that of others. In the first case he ought to be sparing, in the second he ought not to neglect any opportunity for liberality. And to the prince who goes forth with his army, supporting it by pillage, sack, and extortion, handling that which belongs to others, this liberality is necessary, otherwise he would not be followed by soldiers. And of that which is neither yours nor your subjects' you can be a ready giver, as were Cyrus, Caesar, and Alexander; because it does not take away your reputation if you squander that of others, but adds to it; it is only squandering your own that injures you.

And there is nothing wastes so rapidly as liberality, for even whilst you exercise it you lose the power to do so, and so become either poor or despised, or else, in avoiding poverty, rapacious and hated. And a prince should guard himself, above all things, against being despised and hated; and liberality leads you to both. Therefore it is wiser to have a reputation for meanness which brings reproach without hatred, than to be compelled through seeking a reputation for liberality to incur a name for rapacity which begets reproach with hatred.

XVII — CONCERNING CRUELTY AND CLEMENCY, AND WHETHER IT IS BETTER TO BE LOVED THAN FEARED

Coming now to the other qualities mentioned above, I say that every prince ought to desire to be considered clement and not cruel. Nevertheless he ought to take care not to misuse this clemency. Cesare Borgia was considered cruel; notwithstanding, his cruelty reconciled the Romagna, unified it, and restored it to peace and loyalty. And if this be rightly considered, he will be seen to have been much more merciful than the Florentine people, who, to avoid a reputation for cruelty, permitted Pistoia to be destroyed. Therefore a prince, so long as he keeps his subjects united and loyal, ought not to mind the reproach of cruelty; because with a few examples he will be more merciful than those who, through too much mercy, allow disorders to arise, from which follow murders or robberies; for these are wont to injure the whole people, whilst those executions which originate with a prince offend the individual only.

And of all princes, it is impossible for the new prince to avoid the imputation of cruelty, owing to new states being full of dangers. Hence Virgil, through the mouth of Dido, excuses the inhumanity of her reign owing to its being new, saying:

"Res dura, et regni novitas me talia cogunt
Moliri, et late fines custode tueri."

Nevertheless he ought to be slow to believe and to act, nor should he himself show fear, but proceed in a temperate manner with prudence and humanity, so that too much confidence may not make him incautious and too much distrust render him intolerable.

Upon this a question arises: whether it be better to be loved than feared or feared than loved? It may be answered that one should wish to be both, but, because it is difficult to unite them in one person, it is much safer to be feared than loved, when, of the two, either must be dispensed with. Because this is to be asserted in general of men, that they are ungrateful, fickle, false, cowardly, covetous, and as long as you succeed they are yours entirely; they will offer you their blood, property, life, and children, as is said above, when the need is far distant; but when it approaches they turn against you. And that prince who, relying entirely on their promises, has neglected other precautions, is ruined; because friendships that are obtained by payments, and not by greatness or nobility of mind, may indeed be earned, but they are not secured, and in time of need cannot be relied upon; and men have less scruple in offending one who is beloved than one who is feared, for love is preserved by the link of obligation which, owing to the baseness of men, is broken at every opportunity for their advantage; but fear preserves you by a dread of punishment which never fails.

Nevertheless a prince ought to inspire fear in such a way that, if he does not win love, he avoids hatred; because he can endure very well being feared whilst he is not hated, which will always be as long as he abstains from the property of his citizens and subjects and from their women. But when it is necessary for him to proceed against the life of someone, he must do it on proper justification and for manifest cause, but above all things he must keep his hands off the property of others, because men more quickly forget the death of their father than the loss of their patrimony. Besides, pretexts for taking away the property are never wanting; for he who has once begun to live by robbery will always find pretexts for seizing what belongs to others; but reasons for taking life, on the contrary, are more difficult to find and sooner lapse. But when a prince is with his army, and has under control a multitude of soldiers, then it is quite necessary for him to disregard the reputation of cruelty, for without it he would never hold his army united or disposed to its duties.

Among the wonderful deeds of Hannibal this one is enumerated: that having led an enormous army, composed of many various races of men, to fight in foreign lands, no dissensions arose either among them or against the prince, whether in his bad or in his good fortune. This arose from nothing else than his inhuman cruelty, which, with his boundless valour, made him revered and terrible in the sight of his soldiers, but without that cruelty, his other virtues were not sufficient to produce this effect. And short-sighted writers admire his deeds from one point of view and from another condemn the principal cause of them. That it is true his other virtues would not have been sufficient for him may be proved by the case of Scipio, that most excellent man, not only of his own times but within the memory of man, against whom, nevertheless, his army rebelled in Spain; this arose from nothing but his too great forbearance, which gave his soldiers more license than is consistent with military discipline. For this he was upbraided in the Senate by Fabius Maximus, and called the corrupter of the Roman soldiery. The Locrians were laid waste by a legate of Scipio, yet they were not avenged by him, nor was the insolence of the legate punished, owing entirely to his easy nature. Insomuch that someone in the Senate, wishing to excuse him, said there were many men who knew much better how not to err than to correct the errors of others. This disposition, if he had been continued in the command, would have destroyed in time the fame and glory of Scipio; but, he being under the control of the Senate, this injurious characteristic not only concealed itself, but contributed to his glory.

Returning to the question of being feared or loved, I come to the conclusion that, men loving according to their own will and fearing according to that of the prince, a wise prince should establish himself on that which is in his own control and not in that of others; he must endeavour only to avoid hatred, as is noted.

XVIII — CONCERNING THE WAY IN WHICH PRINCES SHOULD KEEP FAITH

Every one admits how praiseworthy it is in a prince to keep faith, and to live with integrity and not with craft. Nevertheless our experience has been that those princes who have done great things have held good faith of little account, and have known how to circumvent the intellect of men by craft, and in the end have overcome those who have relied on their word. You must know there are two ways of contesting, the one by the law, the other by force; the first method is proper to men, the second to beasts; but because the first is frequently not sufficient, it is necessary to have recourse to the second. Therefore it is necessary for a prince to understand how to avail himself of the beast and the man. This has been figuratively taught to princes by ancient writers, who describe how Achilles and many other princes of old were given to the Centaur Chiron to nurse, who brought them up in his discipline; which means solely that, as they had for a teacher one who was half beast and half man, so it is necessary for a prince to know how to make use of both natures, and that one without the other is not durable. A prince, therefore, being compelled knowingly to adopt the beast, ought to choose the fox and the lion; because the lion cannot defend himself against snares and the fox cannot defend himself against wolves. Therefore, it is necessary to be a fox to discover the snares and a lion to terrify the wolves. Those who rely simply on the lion do not understand what they are about. Therefore a wise lord cannot, nor ought he to, keep faith when such observance may be turned against him, and when the reasons that caused him to pledge it exist no longer. If men were entirely good this precept would not hold, but because they are bad, and will not keep faith with you, you too are not bound to observe it with them. Nor will there ever be wanting to a prince legitimate reasons to excuse this non-observance. Of this endless modern examples could be given, showing how many treaties and engagements have been made void and of no effect through the faithlessness of princes; and he who has known best how to employ the fox has succeeded best.

But it is necessary to know well how to disguise this characteristic, and to be a great pretender and dissembler; and men are so simple, and so subject to present necessities, that he who seeks to deceive will always find someone who will allow himself to be deceived. One recent example I cannot pass over in silence. Alexander the Sixth did nothing else but deceive men, nor ever thought of doing otherwise, and he always found victims; for there never was a man who had greater power in asserting, or who with greater oaths would affirm a thing, yet would observe it less; nevertheless his deceits always succeeded according to his wishes, because he well understood this side of mankind.

Therefore it is unnecessary for a prince to have all the good qualities I have enumerated, but it is very necessary to appear to have them. And I shall dare to say this also, that to have them and always to observe them is injurious, and that to appear to have them is useful; to appear merciful, faithful, humane, religious, upright, and to be so, but with a mind so framed that should you require not to be so, you may be able and know how to change to the opposite.

And you have to understand this, that a prince, especially a new one, cannot observe all those things for which men are esteemed, being often forced, in order to maintain the state, to act contrary to fidelity, friendship, humanity, and religion. Therefore it is necessary for him to have a mind ready to turn itself accordingly as the winds and variations of fortune force it, yet, as I have said above, not to diverge from the good if he can avoid doing so, but, if compelled, then to know how to set about it.

For this reason a prince ought to take care that he never lets anything slip from his lips that is not replete with the above-named five qualities, that he may appear to him who sees and hears him altogether merciful, faithful, humane, upright, and religious. There is nothing more necessary to appear to have than this last quality, inasmuch as men judge generally more by the eye than by the hand, because it belongs to everybody to see you, to few to come in touch with you. Every one sees what you appear to be, few really know what you are, and those few dare not oppose themselves to the opinion of the many, who have the majesty of the state to defend them; and in the actions of all men, and especially of princes, which it is not prudent to challenge, one judges by the result.

For that reason, let a prince have the credit of conquering and holding his state, the means will always be considered honest, and he will be praised by everybody; because the vulgar are always taken by what a thing seems to be and by what comes of it; and in the world there are only the vulgar, for the few find a place there only when the many have no ground to rest on.

One prince of the present time, whom it is not well to name, never preaches anything else but peace and good faith, and to both he is most hostile, and either, if he had kept it, would have deprived him of reputation and kingdom many a time.

XIX — THAT ONE SHOULD AVOID BEING DESPISED AND HATED

Now, concerning the characteristics of which mention is made above, I have spoken of the more important ones, the others I wish to discuss briefly under this generality, that the prince must consider, as has been in part said before, how to avoid those things which will make him hated or contemptible; and as often as he shall have succeeded he will have fulfilled his part, and he need not fear any danger in other reproaches.

It makes him hated above all things, as I have said, to be rapacious, and to be a violator of the property and women of his subjects, from both of which he must abstain. And when neither their property nor their honor is touched, the majority of men live content, and he has only to contend with the ambition of a few, whom he can curb with ease in many ways.

It makes him contemptible to be considered fickle, frivolous, effeminate, mean-spirited, irresolute, from all of which a prince should guard himself as from a rock; and he should endeavour to show in his actions greatness, courage, gravity, and fortitude; and in his private dealings with his subjects let him show that his judgments are irrevocable, and maintain himself in such reputation that no one can hope either to deceive him or to get round him.

That prince is highly esteemed who conveys this impression of himself, and he who is highly esteemed is not easily conspired against; for, provided it is well known that he is an excellent man and revered by his people, he can only be attacked with difficulty. For this reason a prince ought to have two fears, one from within, on account of his subjects, the other from without, on account of external powers. From the latter he is defended by being well armed and having good allies, and if he is well armed he will have good friends, and affairs will always remain quiet within when they are quiet without, unless they should have been already disturbed by conspiracy; and even should affairs outside be disturbed, if he has carried out his preparations and has lived as I have said, as long as he does not despair, he will resist every attack, as I said Nabis the Spartan did.

But concerning his subjects, when affairs outside are disturbed he has only to fear that they will conspire secretly, from which a prince can easily secure himself by avoiding being hated and despised, and by keeping the people satisfied with him, which it is most necessary for him to accomplish, as I said above at length. And one of the most efficacious remedies that a prince can have against conspiracies is not to be hated and despised by the people, for he who conspires against a prince always expects to please them by his removal; but when the conspirator can only look forward to offending them, he will not have the courage to take such a course, for the difficulties that confront a conspirator are infinite. And as experience shows, many have been the conspiracies, but few have been successful; because he who conspires cannot act alone, nor can he take a companion except from those whom he believes to be malcontents, and as soon as you have opened your mind to a malcontent you have given him the material with which to content himself, for by denouncing you he can look for every advantage; so that, seeing the gain from this course to be assured, and seeing the other to be doubtful and full of dangers, he must be a very rare friend, or a thoroughly obstinate enemy of the prince, to keep faith with you.

And, to reduce the matter into a small compass, I say that, on the side of the conspirator, there is nothing but fear, jealousy, prospect of punishment to terrify him; but on the side of the prince there is the majesty of the principality, the laws, the protection of friends and the state to defend him; so that, adding to all these things the popular goodwill, it is impossible that any one should be so rash as to conspire. For whereas in general the conspirator has to fear before the execution of his plot, in this case he has also to fear the sequel to the crime; because on account of it he has the people for an enemy, and thus cannot hope for any escape.

Endless examples could be given on this subject, but I will be content with one, brought to pass within the memory of our fathers. Messer Annibale Bentivogli, who was prince in Bologna (grandfather of the present Annibale), having been murdered by the Canneschi, who had conspired against him, not one of his family survived but Messer Giovanni, who was in childhood: immediately after his assassination the people rose and murdered all the Canneschi. This sprung from the popular goodwill which the house of Bentivogli enjoyed in those days in Bologna; which was so great that, although none remained there after the death of Annibale who was able to rule the state, the Bolognese, having information that there was one of the Bentivogli family in Florence, who up to that time had been considered the son of a blacksmith, sent to Florence for him and gave him the government of their city, and it was ruled by him until Messer Giovanni came in due course to the government.

For this reason I consider that a prince ought to reckon conspiracies of little account when his people hold him in esteem; but when it is hostile to him, and bears hatred towards him, he ought to fear everything and everybody. And well-ordered states and wise princes have taken every care not to drive the nobles to desperation, and to keep the people satisfied and contented, for this is one of the most important objects a prince can have.

Among the best ordered and governed kingdoms of our times is France, and in it are found many good institutions on which depend the liberty and security of the king; of these the first is the parliament and its authority, because he who founded the kingdom, knowing the ambition of the nobility and their boldness, considered that a bit to their mouths would be necessary to hold them in; and, on the other side, knowing the hatred of the people, founded in fear, against the nobles, he wished to protect them, yet he was not anxious for this to be the particular care of the king;

therefore, to take away the reproach which he would be liable to from the nobles for favouring the people, and from the people for favouring the nobles, he set up an arbiter, who should be one who could beat down the great and favour the lesser without reproach to the king. Neither could you have a better or a more prudent arrangement, or a greater source of security to the king and kingdom. From this one can draw another important conclusion, that princes ought to leave affairs of reproach to the management of others, and keep those of grace in their own hands. And further, I consider that a prince ought to cherish the nobles, but not so as to make himself hated by the people.

It may appear, perhaps, to some who have examined the lives and deaths of the Roman emperors that many of them would be an example contrary to my opinion, seeing that some of them lived nobly and showed great qualities of soul, nevertheless they have lost their empire or have been killed by subjects who have conspired against them. Wishing, therefore, to answer these objections, I will recall the characters of some of the emperors, and will show that the causes of their ruin were not different to those alleged by me; at the same time I will only submit for consideration those things that are noteworthy to him who studies the affairs of those times.

It seems to me sufficient to take all those emperors who succeeded to the empire from Marcus the philosopher down to Maximinus; they were Marcus and his son Commodus, Pertinax, Julian, Severus and his son Antoninus Caracalla, Macrinus, Heliogabalus, Alexander, and Maximinus.

There is first to note that, whereas in other principalities the ambition of the nobles and the insolence of the people only have to be contended with, the Roman emperors had a third difficulty in having to put up with the cruelty and avarice of their soldiers, a matter so beset with difficulties that it was the ruin of many; for it was a hard thing to give satisfaction both to soldiers and people; because the people loved peace, and for this reason they loved the unaspiring prince, whilst the soldiers loved the warlike prince who was bold, cruel, and rapacious, which qualities they were quite willing he should exercise upon the people, so that they could get double pay and give vent to their own greed and cruelty. Hence it arose that those emperors were always overthrown who, either by birth or training, had no great authority, and most of them, especially those who came new to the principality, recognizing the difficulty of these two opposing humours, were inclined to give satisfaction to the soldiers, caring little about injuring the people. Which course was necessary, because, as princes cannot help being hated by someone, they ought, in the first place, to avoid being hated by every one, and when they cannot compass this, they ought to endeavour with the utmost diligence to avoid the hatred of the most powerful. Therefore, those emperors who through inexperience had need of special favour adhered more readily to the soldiers than to the people; a course which turned out advantageous to them or not, accordingly as the prince knew how to maintain authority over them.

From these causes it arose that Marcus, Pertinax, and Alexander, being all men of modest life, lovers of justice, enemies to cruelty, humane, and benignant, came to a sad end except Marcus; he alone lived and died honoured, because he had succeeded to the throne by hereditary title, and owed nothing either to the soldiers or the people; and afterwards, being possessed of many virtues which made him respected, he always kept both orders in their places whilst he lived, and was neither hated nor despised.

But Pertinax was created emperor against the wishes of the soldiers, who, being accustomed to live licentiously under Commodus, could not endure the honest life to which Pertinax wished to reduce them; thus, having given cause for hatred, to which hatred there was added contempt for his old age, he was overthrown at the very beginning of his administration. And here it should be noted that hatred is acquired as much by good works as by bad ones, therefore, as I said before, a prince wishing to keep his state is very often forced to do evil; for when that body is corrupt whom you think you have need of to maintain yourself—it may be either the people or the soldiers or the nobles—you have to submit to its humours and to gratify them, and then good works will do you harm.

But let us come to Alexander, who was a man of such great goodness, that among the other praises which are accorded him is this, that in the fourteen years he held the empire no one was ever put to death by him unjudged; nevertheless, being considered effeminate and a man who allowed himself to be governed by his mother, he became despised, the army conspired against him, and murdered him.

Turning now to the opposite characters of Commodus, Severus, Antoninus Caracalla, and Maximinus, you will find them all cruel and rapacious-men who, to satisfy their soldiers, did not hesitate to commit every kind of iniquity against the people; and all, except Severus, came to a bad end; but in Severus there was so much valour that, keeping the soldiers friendly, although the people were oppressed by him, he reigned successfully; for his valour made him so much admired in the sight of the soldiers and people that the latter were kept in a way astonished and awed and the former respectful and satisfied. And because the actions of this man, as a new prince, were great, I wish to show briefly that he knew well how to counterfeit the fox and the lion, which natures, as I said above, it is necessary for a prince to imitate.

Knowing the sloth of the Emperor Julian, he persuaded the army in Sclavonia, of which he was captain, that it would be right to go to Rome and avenge the death of Pertinax, who had been killed by the praetorian soldiers; and under this pretext, without appearing to aspire to the throne, he moved the army on Rome, and reached Italy before it was known that he had started. On his arrival at Rome, the Senate, through fear, elected him emperor and killed Julian. After this there remained for Severus, who wished to make himself master of the whole empire, two difficulties; one in Asia, where Niger, head of the Asiatic army, had caused himself to be proclaimed emperor; the other in the west where Albinus was, who also aspired to the throne. And as he considered it dangerous to declare himself hostile to both, he decided to attack Niger and to deceive Albinus. To the latter he wrote that, being elected emperor by the Senate, he was willing to share that dignity with him and sent him the title of Caesar; and, moreover, that the Senate had made Albinus his colleague; which things were accepted by Albinus as true. But after Severus had conquered and killed Niger, and settled oriental affairs, he returned to Rome and complained to the Senate that Albinus, little recognizing the benefits that he had received from him, had by treachery sought to murder him, and for this ingratitude he was compelled to punish him. Afterwards he sought him out in France, and took from him his government and life. He who will, therefore, carefully examine the actions of this man will find him a most valiant lion and a most cunning fox; he will find him feared and respected by every one, and not hated by the army; and it need not be wondered at that he, a new man, was able to hold the empire so well, because his supreme renown always protected him from that hatred which the people might have conceived against him for his violence.

But his son Antoninus was a most eminent man, and had very excellent qualities, which made him admirable in the sight of the people and acceptable to the soldiers, for he was a warlike man, most enduring of fatigue, a despiser of all delicate food and other luxuries, which caused him to be beloved by the armies. Nevertheless, his ferocity and cruelties were so great and so unheard of that, after endless single murders, he killed a large number of the people of Rome and all those of Alexandria. He became hated by the whole world, and also feared by those he had around him, to such an extent that he was murdered in the midst of his army by a centurion. And here it must be noted that such-like deaths, which are deliberately inflicted with a resolved and desperate courage, cannot be avoided by princes, because any one who does not fear to die can inflict them; but a prince may fear them the less because they are very rare; he has only to be careful not to do any grave injury to those whom he employs or has around him in the service of the state. Antoninus had not taken this care, but had contumeliously killed a brother of that centurion, whom also he daily threatened, yet retained in his bodyguard; which, as it turned out, was a rash thing to do, and proved the emperor's ruin.

But let us come to Commodus, to whom it should have been very easy to hold the empire, for, being the son of Marcus, he had inherited it, and he had only to follow in the footsteps of his father to please his people and soldiers; but, being by nature cruel and brutal, he gave himself up to amusing the soldiers and corrupting them, so that he might indulge his rapacity upon the people; on the other hand, not maintaining his dignity, often descending to the theatre to compete with gladiators, and doing other vile things, little worthy of the imperial majesty, he fell into contempt with the soldiers, and being hated by one party and despised by the other, he was conspired against and was killed.

It remains to discuss the character of Maximinus. He was a very warlike man, and the armies, being disgusted with the effeminacy of Alexander, of whom I have already spoken, killed him and elected Maximinus to the throne. This he did not possess for long, for two things made him hated and despised; the one, his having kept sheep in Thrace, which brought him into contempt (it being well known to all, and considered a great indignity by every one), and the other, his having at the accession to his dominions deferred going to Rome and taking possession of the imperial seat; he had also gained a reputation for the utmost ferocity by having, through his prefects in Rome and elsewhere in the empire, practised many cruelties, so that the whole world was moved to anger at the meanness of his birth and to fear at his barbarity. First Africa rebelled, then the Senate with all the people of Rome, and all Italy conspired against him, to which may be added his own army; this latter, besieging Aquileia and meeting with difficulties in taking it, were disgusted with his cruelties, and fearing him less when they found so many against him, murdered him.

I do not wish to discuss Heliogabalus, Macrinus, or Julian, who, being thoroughly contemptible, were quickly wiped out; but I will bring this discourse to a conclusion by saying that princes in our times have this difficulty of giving inordinate satisfaction to their soldiers in a far less degree, because, notwithstanding one has to give them some indulgence, that is soon done; none of these princes have armies that are veterans in the governance and administration of provinces, as were the armies of the Roman Empire; and whereas it was then more necessary to give satisfaction to the soldiers than to the people, it is now more necessary to all princes, except the Turk and the Soldan, to satisfy the people rather the soldiers, because the people are the more powerful.

From the above I have excepted the Turk, who always keeps round him twelve thousand infantry and fifteen thousand cavalry on which depend the security and strength of the kingdom, and it is necessary that, putting aside every consideration for the people, he should keep them his friends. The kingdom of the Soldan is similar; being entirely in the hands of soldiers, it follows again that, without regard to the people, he must keep them his friends. But you must note that the state of the Soldan is unlike all other principalities, for the reason that it is like the Christian pontificate, which cannot be called either an hereditary or a newly formed principality; because the sons of the old prince are not the heirs, but he who is elected to that position by those who have authority, and the sons remain only noblemen. And this being an ancient custom, it cannot be called a new principality, because there are none of those difficulties in it that are met with in new ones; for although the prince is new, the constitution of the state is old, and it is framed so as to receive him as if he were its hereditary lord.

But returning to the subject of our discourse, I say that whoever will consider it will acknowledge that either hatred or contempt has been fatal to the above-named emperors, and it will be recognized also how it happened that, a number of them acting in one way and a number in another, only one in each way came to a happy end and the rest to unhappy ones. Because it would have been useless and dangerous for Pertinax and Alexander, being new princes, to imitate Marcus, who was heir to the principality; and likewise it would have been utterly destructive to Caracalla, Commodus, and Maximinus to have imitated Severus, they not having sufficient valour to enable them to tread in his footsteps. Therefore a prince, new to the principality, cannot imitate the actions of Marcus, nor, again, is it necessary to follow those of Severus, but he ought to take from Severus those parts which are necessary to found his state, and from Marcus those which are proper and glorious to keep a state that may already be stable and firm.

XX — ARE FORTRESSES, AND MANY OTHER THINGS TO WHICH PRINCES OFTEN RESORT, ADVANTAGEOUS OR HURTFUL?

1. Some princes, so as to hold securely the state, have disarmed their subjects; others have kept their subject towns distracted by factions; others have fostered en-

mities against themselves; others have laid themselves out to gain over those whom they distrusted in the beginning of their governments; some have built fortresses; some have overthrown and destroyed them. And although one cannot give a final judgment on all of these things unless one possesses the particulars of those states in which a decision has to be made, nevertheless I will speak as comprehensively as the matter of itself will admit.

2. There never was a new prince who has disarmed his subjects; rather when he has found them disarmed he has always armed them, because, by arming them, those arms become yours, those men who were distrusted become faithful, and those who were faithful are kept so, and your subjects become your adherents. And whereas all subjects cannot be armed, yet when those whom you do arm are benefited, the others can be handled more freely, and this difference in their treatment, which they quite understand, makes the former your dependents, and the latter, considering it to be necessary that those who have the most danger and service should have the most reward, excuse you. But when you disarm them, you at once offend them by showing that you distrust them, either for cowardice or for want of loyalty, and either of these opinions breeds hatred against you. And because you cannot remain unarmed, it follows that you turn to mercenaries, which are of the character already shown; even if they should be good they would not be sufficient to defend you against powerful enemies and distrusted subjects. Therefore, as I have said, a new prince in a new principality has always distributed arms. Histories are full of examples. But when a prince acquires a new state, which he adds as a province to his old one, then it is necessary to disarm the men of that state, except those who have been his adherents in acquiring it; and these again, with time and opportunity, should be rendered soft and effeminate; and matters should be managed in such a way that all the armed men in the state shall be your own soldiers who in your old state were living near you.

3. Our forefathers, and those who were reckoned wise, were accustomed to say that it was necessary to hold Pistoia by factions and Pisa by fortresses; and with this idea they fostered quarrels in some of their tributary towns so as to keep possession of them the more easily. This may have been well enough in those times when Italy was in a way balanced, but I do not believe that it can be accepted as a precept for to-day, because I do not believe that factions can ever be of use; rather it is certain that when the enemy comes upon you in divided cities you are quickly lost, because the weakest party will always assist the outside forces and the other will not be able to resist. The Venetians, moved, as I believe, by the above reasons, fostered the Guelph and Ghibelline factions in their tributary cities; and although they never allowed them to come to bloodshed, yet they nursed these disputes amongst them, so that the citizens, distracted by their differences, should not unite against them. Which, as we saw, did not afterwards turn out as expected, because, after the rout at Vaila, one party at once took courage and seized the state. Such methods argue, therefore, weakness in the prince, because these factions will never be permitted in a vigorous principality; such methods for enabling one the more easily to manage subjects are only useful in times of peace, but if war comes this policy proves fallacious.

4. Without doubt princes become great when they overcome the difficulties and obstacles by which they are confronted, and therefore fortune, especially when she desires to make a new prince great, who has a greater necessity to earn renown than an hereditary one, causes enemies to arise and form designs against him, in order that he may have the opportunity of overcoming them, and by them to mount higher, as by a ladder which his enemies have raised. For this reason many consider that a wise prince, when he has the opportunity, ought with craft to foster some animosity against himself, so that, having crushed it, his renown may rise higher.

5. Princes, especially new ones, have found more fidelity and assistance in those men who in the beginning of their rule were distrusted than among those who in the beginning were trusted. Pandolfo Petrucci, Prince of Siena, ruled his state more by those who had been distrusted than by others. But on this question one cannot speak generally, for it varies so much with the individual; I will only say this, that those men who at the commencement of a princedom have been hostile, if they are of a description to need assistance to support themselves, can always be gained over with the greatest ease, and they will be tightly held to serve the prince with fidelity, inasmuch as they know it to be very necessary for them to cancel by deeds the bad impression which he had formed of them; and thus the prince always extracts more profit from them than from those who, serving him in too much security, may neglect his affairs. And since the matter demands it, I must not fail to warn a prince, who by means of secret favours has acquired a new state, that he must well consider the reasons which induced those to favour him who did so; and if it be not a natural affection towards him, but only discontent with their government, then he will only keep them friendly with great trouble and difficulty, for it will be impossible to satisfy them. And weighing well the reasons for this in those examples which can be taken from ancient and modern affairs, we shall find that it is easier for the prince to make friends of those men who were contented under the former government, and are therefore his enemies, than of those who, being discontented with it, were favourable to him and encouraged him to seize it.

6. It has been a custom with princes, in order to hold their states more securely, to build fortresses that may serve as a bridle and bit to those who might design to work against them, and as a place of refuge from a first attack. I praise this system because it has been made use of formerly. Notwithstanding that, Messer Nicolo Vitelli in our times has been seen to demolish two fortresses in Citta di Castello so that he might keep that state; Guido Ubaldo, Duke of Urbino, on returning to his dominion, whence he had been driven by Cesare Borgia, razed to the foundations all the fortresses in that province, and considered that without them it would be more difficult to lose it; the Bentivogli returning to Bologna came to a similar decision. Fortresses, therefore, are useful or not according to circumstances; if they do you good in one way they injure you in another. And this question can be reasoned thus: the prince who has more to fear from the people than from foreigners ought to build fortresses, but he who has more to fear from foreigners than from the people ought to leave them alone. The castle of Milan, built by Francesco Sforza, has made, and will make, more trouble for the house of Sforza than any other disorder in the state. For this reason the best possible fortress is—not to be hated by the people, because,

although you may hold the fortresses, yet they will not save you if the people hate you, for there will never be wanting foreigners to assist a people who have taken arms against you. It has not been seen in our times that such fortresses have been of use to any prince, unless to the Countess of Forli, when the Count Girolamo, her consort, was killed; for by that means she was able to withstand the popular attack and wait for assistance from Milan, and thus recover her state; and the posture of affairs was such at that time that the foreigners could not assist the people. But fortresses were of little value to her afterwards when Cesare Borgia attacked her, and when the people, her enemy, were allied with foreigners. Therefore, it would have been safer for her, both then and before, not to have been hated by the people than to have had the fortresses. All these things considered then, I shall praise him who builds fortresses as well as him who does not, and I shall blame whoever, trusting in them, cares little about being hated by the people.

XXI — HOW A PRINCE SHOULD CONDUCT HIMSELF SO AS TO GAIN RENOWN

Nothing makes a prince so much esteemed as great enterprises and setting a fine example. We have in our time Ferdinand of Aragon, the present King of Spain. He can almost be called a new prince, because he has risen, by fame and glory, from being an insignificant king to be the foremost king in Christendom; and if you will consider his deeds you will find them all great and some of them extraordinary. In the beginning of his reign he attacked Granada, and this enterprise was the foundation of his dominions. He did this quietly at first and without any fear of hindrance, for he held the minds of the barons of Castile occupied in thinking of the war and not anticipating any innovations; thus they did not perceive that by these means he was acquiring power and authority over them. He was able with the money of the Church and of the people to sustain his armies, and by that long war to lay the foundation for the military skill which has since distinguished him. Further, always using religion as a plea, so as to undertake greater schemes, he devoted himself with pious cruelty to driving out and clearing his kingdom of the Moors; nor could there be a more admirable example, nor one more rare. Under this same cloak he assailed Africa, he came down on Italy, he has finally attacked France; and thus his achievements and designs have always been great, and have kept the minds of his people in suspense and admiration and occupied with the issue of them. And his actions have arisen in such a way, one out of the other, that men have never been given time to work steadily against him.

Again, it much assists a prince to set unusual examples in internal affairs, similar to those which are related of Messer Bernabo da Milano, who, when he had the opportunity, by any one in civil life doing some extraordinary thing, either good or bad, would take some method of rewarding or punishing him, which would be much spoken about. And a prince ought, above all things, always endeavour in every action to gain for himself the reputation of being a great and remarkable man.

A prince is also respected when he is either a true friend or a downright enemy, that is to say, when, without any reservation, he declares himself in favour of one party against the other; which course will always be more advantageous than standing neutral; because if two of your powerful neighbours come to blows, they are of such a character that, if one of them conquers, you have either to fear him or not. In either case it will always be more advantageous for you to declare yourself and to make war strenuously; because, in the first case, if you do not declare yourself, you will invariably fall a prey to the conqueror, to the pleasure and satisfaction of him who has been conquered, and you will have no reasons to offer, nor anything to protect or to shelter you. Because he who conquers does not want doubtful friends who will not aid him in the time of trial; and he who loses will not harbour you because you did not willingly, sword in hand, court his fate.

Antiochus went into Greece, being sent for by the Aetolians to drive out the Romans. He sent envoys to the Achaeans, who were friends of the Romans, exhorting them to remain neutral; and on the other hand the Romans urged them to take up arms. This question came to be discussed in the council of the Achaeans, where the legate of Antiochus urged them to stand neutral. To this the Roman legate answered: "As for that which has been said, that it is better and more advantageous for your state not to interfere in our war, nothing can be more erroneous; because by not interfering you will be left, without favour or consideration, the guerdon of the conqueror." Thus it will always happen that he who is not your friend will demand your neutrality, whilst he who is your friend will entreat you to declare yourself with arms. And irresolute princes, to avoid present dangers, generally follow the neutral path, and are generally ruined. But when a prince declares himself gallantly in favour of one side, if the party with whom he allies himself conquers, although the victor may be powerful and may have him at his mercy, yet he is indebted to him, and there is established a bond of amity; and men are never so shameless as to become a monument of ingratitude by oppressing you. Victories after all are never so complete that the victor must not show some regard, especially to justice. But if he with whom you ally yourself loses, you may be sheltered by him, and whilst he is able he may aid you, and you become companions on a fortune that may rise again.

In the second case, when those who fight are of such a character that you have no anxiety as to who may conquer, so much the more is it greater prudence to be allied, because you assist at the destruction of one by the aid of another who, if he had been wise, would have saved him; and conquering, as it is impossible that he should not do with your assistance, he remains at your discretion. And here it is to be noted that a prince ought to take care never to make an alliance with one more powerful than himself for the purposes of attacking others, unless necessity compels him, as is said above; because if he conquers you are at his discretion, and princes ought to avoid as much as possible being at the discretion of any one. The Venetians joined with France against the Duke of Milan, and this alliance, which caused their ruin, could have been avoided. But when it cannot be avoided, as happened to the Florentines when the Pope and Spain sent armies to attack Lombardy, then in such a case, for the above reasons, the prince ought to favour one of the parties.

Never let any Government imagine that it can choose perfectly safe courses; rather let it expect to have to take very doubtful ones, because it is found in ordinary affairs that one never seeks to avoid one trouble without running into another; but prudence consists in knowing how to distinguish the character of troubles, and for choice to take the lesser evil.

A prince ought also to show himself a patron of ability, and to honour the proficient in every art. At the same time he should encourage his citizens to practise their callings peaceably, both in commerce and agriculture, and in every other following, so that the one should not be deterred from improving his possessions for fear lest they be taken away from him or another from opening up trade for fear of taxes; but the prince ought to offer rewards to whoever wishes to do these things and designs in any way to honour his city or state.

Further, he ought to entertain the people with festivals and spectacles at convenient seasons of the year; and as every city is divided into guilds or into societies, he ought to hold such bodies in esteem, and associate with them sometimes, and show himself an example of courtesy and liberality; nevertheless, always maintaining the majesty of his rank, for this he must never consent to abate in anything.

XXII — CONCERNING THE SECRETARIES OF PRINCES

The choice of servants is of no little importance to a prince, and they are good or not according to the discrimination of the prince. And the first opinion which one forms of a prince, and of his understanding, is by observing the men he has around him; and when they are capable and faithful he may always be considered wise, because he has known how to recognize the capable and to keep them faithful. But when they are otherwise one cannot form a good opinion of him, for the prime error which he made was in choosing them.

There were none who knew Messer Antonio da Venafro as the servant of Pandolfo Petrucci, Prince of Siena, who would not consider Pandolfo to be a very clever man in having Venafro for his servant. Because there are three classes of intellects: one which comprehends by itself; another which appreciates what others comprehended; and a third which neither comprehends by itself nor by the showing of others; the first is the most excellent, the second is good, the third is useless. Therefore, it follows necessarily that, if Pandolfo was not in the first rank, he was in the second, for whenever one has judgment to know good and bad when it is said and done, although he himself may not have the initiative, yet he can recognize the good and the bad in his servant, and the one he can praise and the other correct; thus the servant cannot hope to deceive him, and is kept honest.

But to enable a prince to form an opinion of his servant there is one test which never fails; when you see the servant thinking more of his own interests than of yours, and seeking inwardly his own profit in everything, such a man will never make a good servant, nor will you ever be able to trust him; because he who has the state of another in his hands ought never to think of himself, but always of his prince, and never pay any attention to matters in which the prince is not concerned.

On the other hand, to keep his servant honest the prince ought to study him, honouring him, enriching him, doing him kindnesses, sharing with him the honours and cares; and at the same time let him see that he cannot stand alone, so that many honours may not make him desire more, many riches make him wish for more, and that many cares may make him dread chances. When, therefore, servants, and princes towards servants, are thus disposed, they can trust each other, but when it is otherwise, the end will always be disastrous for either one or the other.

XXIII — HOW FLATTERERS SHOULD BE AVOIDED

I do not wish to leave out an important branch of this subject, for it is a danger from which princes are with difficulty preserved, unless they are very careful and discriminating. It is that of flatterers, of whom courts are full, because men are so self-complacent in their own affairs, and in a way so deceived in them, that they are preserved with difficulty from this pest, and if they wish to defend themselves they run the danger of falling into contempt. Because there is no other way of guarding oneself from flatterers except letting men understand that to tell you the truth does not offend you; but when every one may tell you the truth, respect for you abates.

Therefore a wise prince ought to hold a third course by choosing the wise men in his state, and giving to them only the liberty of speaking the truth to him, and then only of those things of which he inquires, and of none others; but he ought to question them upon everything, and listen to their opinions, and afterwards form his own conclusions. With these councillors, separately and collectively, he ought to carry himself in such a way that each of them should know that, the more freely he shall speak, the more he shall be preferred; outside of these, he should listen to no one, pursue the thing resolved on, and be steadfast in his resolutions. He who does otherwise is either overthrown by flatterers, or is so often changed by varying opinions that he falls into contempt.

I wish on this subject to adduce a modern example. Fra Luca, the man of affairs to Maximilian, the present emperor, speaking of his majesty, said: He consulted with no one, yet never got his own way in anything. This arose because of his following a practice the opposite to the above; for the emperor is a secretive man—he does not communicate his designs to any one, nor does he receive opinions on them. But as in carrying them into effect they become revealed and known, they are at once obstructed by those men whom he has around him, and he, being pliant, is diverted from them. Hence it follows that those things he does one day he undoes the next, and no one ever understands what he wishes or intends to do, and no one can rely on his resolutions.

A prince, therefore, ought always to take counsel, but only when he wishes and not when others wish; he ought rather to discourage every one from offering advice unless he asks it; but, however, he ought to be a constant inquirer, and afterwards a patient listener concerning the things of which he inquired; also, on learning that any one, on any consideration, has not told him the truth, he should let his anger be felt.

And if there are some who think that a prince who conveys an impression of his wisdom is not so through his own ability, but through the good advisers that he has around him, beyond doubt they are deceived, because this is an axiom which never fails: that a prince who is not wise himself will never take good advice, unless by chance he has yielded his affairs entirely to one person who happens to be a very prudent man. In this case indeed he may be well governed, but it would not be for long, because such a governor would in a short time take away his state from him.

But if a prince who is not inexperienced should take counsel from more than one he will never get united counsels, nor will he know how to unite them. Each of the counsellors will think of his own interests, and the prince will not know how to control them or to see through them. And they are not to found otherwise, because men will always prove untrue to you unless they are kept honest by constraint. Therefore it must be inferred that good counsels, whencesoever they come, are born of the wisdom of the prince, and not the wisdom of the prince from good counsels.

XXIV — WHY THE PRINCES OF ITALY HAVE LOST THEIR STATES

The previous suggestions, carefully observed, will enable a new prince to appear well established, and render him at once more secure and fixed in the state than if he had been long seated there. For the actions of a new prince are more narrowly observed than those of an hereditary one, and when they are seen to be able they gain more men and bind far tighter than ancient blood; because men are attracted more by the present than by the past, and when they find the present good they enjoy it and seek no further; they will also make the utmost defence of a prince if he fails them not in other things. Thus it will be a double glory for him to have established a new principality, and adorned and strengthened it with good laws, good arms, good allies, and with a good example; so will it be a double disgrace to him who, born a prince, shall lose his state by want of wisdom.

And if those seigniors are considered who have lost their states in Italy in our times, such as the King of Naples, the Duke of Milan, and others, there will be found in them, firstly, one common defect in regard to arms from the causes which have been discussed at length; in the next place, some one of them will be seen, either to have had the people hostile, or if he has had the people friendly, he has not known how to secure the nobles. In the absence of these defects states that have power enough to keep an army in the field cannot be lost.

Philip of Macedon, not the father of Alexander the Great, but he who was conquered by Titus Quintius, had not much territory compared to the greatness of the Romans and of Greece who attacked him, yet being a warlike man who knew how to attract the people and secure the nobles, he sustained the war against his enemies for many years, and if in the end he lost the dominion of some cities, nevertheless he retained the kingdom.

Therefore, do not let our princes accuse fortune for the loss of their principalities after so many years' possession, but rather their own sloth, because in quiet times they never thought there could be a change (it is a common defect in man not to make any provision in the calm against the tempest), and when afterwards the bad times came they thought of flight and not of defending themselves, and they hoped that the people, disgusted with the insolence of the conquerors, would recall them. This course, when others fail, may be good, but it is very bad to have neglected all other expedients for that, since you would never wish to fall because you trusted to be able to find someone later on to restore you. This again either does not happen, or, if it does, it will not be for your security, because that deliverance is of no avail which does not depend upon yourself; those only are reliable, certain, and durable that depend on yourself and your valour.

XXV — WHAT FORTUNE CAN EFFECT IN HUMAN AFFAIRS AND HOW TO WITHSTAND HER

It is not unknown to me how many men have had, and still have, the opinion that the affairs of the world are in such wise governed by fortune and by God that men with their wisdom cannot direct them and that no one can even help them; and because of this they would have us believe that it is not necessary to labour much in affairs, but to let chance govern them. This opinion has been more credited in our times because of the great changes in affairs which have been seen, and may still be seen, every day, beyond all human conjecture. Sometimes pondering over this, I am in some degree inclined to their opinion. Nevertheless, not to extinguish our free will, I hold it to be true that Fortune is the arbiter of one-half of our actions, but that she still leaves us to direct the other half, or perhaps a little less.

I compare her to one of those raging rivers, which when in flood overflows the plains, sweeping away trees and buildings, bearing away the soil from place to place; everything flies before it, all yield to its violence, without being able in any way to withstand it; and yet, though its nature be such, it does not follow therefore that men, when the weather becomes fair, shall not make provision, both with defences and barriers, in such a manner that, rising again, the waters may pass away by canal, and their force be neither so unrestrained nor so dangerous. So it happens with fortune, who shows her power where valour has not prepared to resist her, and thither she turns her forces where she knows that barriers and defences have not been raised to constrain her.

And if you will consider Italy, which is the seat of these changes, and which has given to them their impulse, you will see it to be an open country without barriers and without any defence. For if it had been defended by proper valour, as are Germany, Spain, and France, either this invasion would not have made the great changes it has made or it would not have come at all. And this I consider enough to say concerning resistance to fortune in general.

But confining myself more to the particular, I say that a prince may be seen happy to-day and ruined to-morrow without having shown any change of disposition or character. This, I believe, arises firstly from causes that have already been discussed at length, namely, that the prince who relies entirely on fortune is lost when it changes. I believe also that he will be successful who directs his actions according to the spirit of the times, and that he whose actions do not accord with the times will not be successful. Because men are seen, in affairs that lead to the end which every man has before him, namely, glory and riches, to get there by various methods; one with caution, another with haste; one by force, another by skill; one by patience, another by its opposite; and each one succeeds in reaching the goal by a different method. One can also see of two cautious men the one attain his end, the other fail; and similarly, two men by different observances are equally successful, the one being cautious, the other impetuous; all this arises from nothing else than whether or not they conform in their methods to the spirit of the times. This follows from what I have said, that two men working differently bring about the same effect, and of two working similarly, one attains his object and the other does not.

Changes in estate also issue from this, for if, to one who governs himself with caution and patience, times and affairs converge in such a way that his administration is successful, his fortune is made; but if times and affairs change, he is ruined if he does not change his course of action. But a man is not often found sufficiently circumspect to know how to accommodate himself to the change, both because he cannot deviate from what nature inclines him to do, and also because, having always prospered by acting in one way, he cannot be persuaded that it is well to leave it; and, therefore, the cautious man, when it is time to turn adventurous, does not know how to do it, hence he is ruined; but had he changed his conduct with the times fortune would not have changed.

Pope Julius the Second went to work impetuously in all his affairs, and found the times and circumstances conform so well to that line of action that he always met with success. Consider his first enterprise against Bologna, Messer Giovanni Bentivogli being still alive. The Venetians were not agreeable to it, nor was the King of Spain, and he had the enterprise still under discussion with the King of France; nevertheless he personally entered upon the expedition with his accustomed boldness and energy, a move which made Spain and the Venetians stand irresolute and passive, the latter from fear, the former from desire to recover the kingdom of Naples; on the other hand, he drew after him the King of France, because that king, having observed the movement, and desiring to make the Pope his friend so as to humble the Venetians, found it impossible to refuse him. Therefore Julius with his impetuous action accomplished what no other pontiff with simple human wisdom could have done; for if he had waited in Rome until he could get away, with his plans arranged and everything fixed, as any other pontiff would have done, he would never have succeeded. Because the King of France would have made a thousand excuses, and the others would have raised a thousand fears.

I will leave his other actions alone, as they were all alike, and they all succeeded, for the shortness of his life did not let him experience the contrary; but if circumstances had arisen which required him to go cautiously, his ruin would have followed, because he would never have deviated from those ways to which nature inclined him.

I conclude, therefore that, fortune being changeful and mankind steadfast in their ways, so long as the two are in agreement men are successful, but unsuccessful when they fall out. For my part I consider that it is better to be adventurous than cautious, because fortune is a woman, and if you wish to keep her under it is necessary to beat and ill-use her; and it is seen that she allows herself to be mastered by the adventurous rather than by those who go to work more coldly. She is, therefore, always, woman-like, a lover of young men, because they are less cautious, more violent, and with more audacity command her.

XXVI — AN EXHORTATION TO LIBERATE ITALY FROM THE BARBARIANS

Having carefully considered the subject of the above discourses, and wondering within myself whether the present times were propitious to a new prince, and whether there were elements that would give an opportunity to a wise and virtuous one to introduce a new order of things which would do honour to him and good to the people of this country, it appears to me that so many things concur to favour a new prince that I never knew a time more fit than the present.

And if, as I said, it was necessary that the people of Israel should be captive so as to make manifest the ability of Moses; that the Persians should be oppressed by the Medes so as to discover the greatness of the soul of Cyrus; and that the Athenians should be dispersed to illustrate the capabilities of Theseus: then at the present time, in order to discover the virtue of an Italian spirit, it was necessary that Italy should be reduced to the extremity that she is now in, that she should be more enslaved than the Hebrews, more oppressed than the Persians, more scattered than the Athenians; without head, without order, beaten, despoiled, torn, overrun; and to have endured every kind of desolation.

Although lately some spark may have been shown by one, which made us think he was ordained by God for our redemption, nevertheless it was afterwards seen, in the height of his career, that fortune rejected him; so that Italy, left as without life, waits for him who shall yet heal her wounds and put an end to the ravaging and plundering of Lombardy, to the swindling and taxing of the kingdom and of Tuscany, and cleanse those sores that for long have festered. It is seen how she entreats God to send someone who shall deliver her from these wrongs and barbarous insolencies. It is seen also that she is ready and willing to follow a banner if only someone will raise it.

Nor is there to be seen at present one in whom she can place more hope than in your illustrious house, with its valour and fortune, favoured by God and by the Church of which it is now the chief, and which could be made the head of this redemption. This will not be difficult if you will recall to yourself the actions and lives of the men I have named. And although they were great and wonderful men, yet they were men, and each one of them had no more opportunity than the present offers, for their enterprises were neither more just nor easier than this, nor was God more their friend than He is yours.

With us there is great justice, because that war is just which is necessary, and arms are hallowed when there is no other hope but in them. Here there is the greatest willingness, and where the willingness is great the difficulties cannot be great if you will only follow those men to whom I have directed your attention. Further than this, how extraordinarily the ways of God have been manifested beyond example: the sea is divided, a cloud has led the way, the rock has poured forth water, it has rained manna, everything has contributed to your greatness; you ought to do the rest. God is not willing to do everything, and thus take away our free will and that share of glory which belongs to us.

And it is not to be wondered at if none of the above-named Italians have been able to accomplish all that is expected from your illustrious house; and if in so many revolutions in Italy, and in so many campaigns, it has always appeared as if military virtue were exhausted, this has happened because the old order of things was not good, and none of us have known how to find a new one. And nothing honours a man more than to establish new laws and new ordinances when he himself was newly risen. Such things when they are well founded and dignified will make him revered and admired, and in Italy there are not wanting opportunities to bring such into use in every form.

Here there is great valour in the limbs whilst it fails in the head. Look attentively at the duels and the hand-to-hand combats, how superior the Italians are in strength, dexterity, and subtlety. But when it comes to armies they do not bear comparison, and this springs entirely from the insufficiency of the leaders, since those who are capable are not obedient, and each one seems to himself to know, there having never been any one so distinguished above the rest, either by valour or fortune, that others would yield to him. Hence it is that for so long a time, and during so much fighting in the past twenty years, whenever there has been an army wholly Italian, it has always given a poor account of itself; the first witness to this is Il Taro, afterwards Allesandria, Capua, Genoa, Vaila, Bologna, Mestri.

If, therefore, your illustrious house wishes to follow these remarkable men who have redeemed their country, it is necessary before all things, as a true foundation for every enterprise, to be provided with your own forces, because there can be no more faithful, truer, or better soldiers. And although singly they are good, altogether they will be much better when they find themselves commanded by their prince, honoured by him, and maintained at his expense. Therefore it is necessary to be prepared with such arms, so that you can be defended against foreigners by Italian valour.

And although Swiss and Spanish infantry may be considered very formidable, nevertheless there is a defect in both, by reason of which a third order would not only be able to oppose them, but might be relied upon to overthrow them. For the Spaniards cannot resist cavalry, and the Switzers are afraid of infantry whenever they encounter them in close combat. Owing to this, as has been and may again be seen, the Spaniards are unable to resist French cavalry, and the Switzers are overthrown by Spanish infantry. And although a complete proof of this latter cannot be shown, nevertheless there was some evidence of it at the battle of Ravenna, when the Spanish infantry were confronted by German battalions, who follow the same tactics as the Swiss; when the Spaniards, by agility of body and with the aid of their shields, got in under the pikes of the Germans and stood out of danger, able to attack, while the Germans stood helpless, and, if the cavalry had not dashed up, all would have been over with them. It is possible, therefore, knowing the defects of both these infantries, to invent a new one, which will resist cavalry and not be afraid of infantry; this need not create a new order of arms, but a variation upon the old. And these are the kind of improvements which confer reputation and power upon a new prince.

This opportunity, therefore, ought not to be allowed to pass for letting Italy at last see her liberator appear. Nor can one express the love with which he would be received in all those provinces which have suffered so much from these foreign scourings, with what thirst for revenge, with what stubborn faith, with what devotion, with what tears. What door would be closed to him? Who would refuse obedience to him? What envy would hinder him? What Italian would refuse him homage? To all of us this barbarous dominion stinks. Let, therefore, your illustrious house take up this charge with that courage and hope with which all just enterprises are undertaken, so that under its standard our native country may be ennobled, and under its auspices may be verified that saying of Petrarch:

Virtu contro al Furore
Prendera l'arme, e fia il combatter corto:
Che l'antico valore
Negli italici cuor non e ancor morto.

Virtue against fury shall advance the fight,
And it i' th' combat soon shall put to flight:
For the old Roman valour is not dead,
Nor in th' Italians' brests extinguished.

Edward Dacre, 1640.

On War (Vom Kriege) by Carl von Clausewitz

VOL. I.

BOOK I: ON THE NATURE OF WAR

CHAPTER I - WHAT IS WAR?

1. INTRODUCTION.

WE propose to consider first the single elements of our subject, then each branch or part, and, last of all, the whole, in all its relations—therefore to advance from the simple to the complex. But it is necessary for us to commence with a glance at the nature of the whole, because it is particularly necessary that in the consideration of any of the parts their relation to the whole should be kept constantly in view.

2. DEFINITION.

We shall not enter into any of the abstruse definitions of War used by publicists. We shall keep to the element of the thing itself, to a duel. War is nothing but a duel on an extensive scale. If we would conceive as a unit the countless number of duels which make up a War, we shall do so best by supposing to ourselves two wrestlers. Each strives by physical force to compel the other to submit to his will: each endeavours to throw his adversary, and thus render him incapable of further resistance.

War therefore is an act of violence intended to compel our opponent to fulfil our will.

Violence arms itself with the inventions of Art and Science in order to contend against violence. Self-imposed restrictions, almost imperceptible and hardly worth mentioning, termed usages of International Law, accompany it without essentially impairing its power. Violence, that is to say, physical force (for there is no moral force without the conception of States and Law), is therefore the MEANS; the compulsory submission of the enemy to our will is the ultimate object. In order to attain this object fully, the enemy must be disarmed, and disarmament becomes therefore the immediate OBJECT of hostilities in theory. It takes the place of the final object, and puts it aside as something we can eliminate from our calculations.

3. UTMOST USE OF FORCE.

Now, philanthropists may easily imagine there is a skilful method of disarming and overcoming an enemy without great bloodshed, and that this is the proper tendency of the Art of War. However plausible this may appear, still it is an error which must be extirpated; for in such dangerous things as War, the errors which proceed from a spirit of benevolence are the worst. As the use of physical power to the utmost extent by no means excludes the co-operation of the intelligence, it follows that he who uses force unsparingly, without reference to the bloodshed involved, must obtain a superiority if his adversary uses less vigour in its application. The former then dictates the law to the latter, and both proceed to extremities to which the only limitations are those imposed by the amount of counter-acting force on each side.

This is the way in which the matter must be viewed and it is to no purpose, it is even against one's own interest, to turn away from the consideration of the real nature of the affair because the horror of its elements excites repugnance.

If the Wars of civilised people are less cruel and destructive than those of savages, the difference arises from the social condition both of States in themselves and in their relations to each other. Out of this social condition and its relations War arises, and by it War is subjected to conditions, is controlled and modified. But these things do not belong to War itself; they are only given conditions; and to introduce into the philosophy of War itself a principle of moderation would be an absurdity.

Two motives lead men to War: instinctive hostility and hostile intention. In our definition of War, we have chosen as its characteristic the latter of these elements, because it is the most general. It is impossible to conceive the passion of hatred of the wildest description, bordering on mere instinct, without combining with it the idea of a hostile intention. On the other hand, hostile intentions may often exist without being accompanied by any, or at all events by any extreme, hostility of feeling. Amongst savages views emanating from the feelings, amongst civilised nations those emanating from the understanding, have the predominance; but this difference arises from attendant circumstances, existing institutions, &c., and, therefore, is not to be found necessarily in all cases, although it prevails in the majority. In short, even the most civilised nations may burn with passionate hatred of each other.

We may see from this what a fallacy it would be to refer the War of a civilised nation entirely to an intelligent act on the part of the Government, and to imagine it as continually freeing itself more and more from all feeling of passion in such a way that at last the physical masses of combatants would no longer be required; in reality, their mere relations would suffice—a kind of algebraic action.

Theory was beginning to drift in this direction until the facts of the last War taught it better. If War is an ACT of force, it belongs necessarily also to the feelings. If it does not originate in the feelings, it REACTS, more or less, upon them, and the extent of this reaction depends not on the degree of civilisation, but upon the importance and duration of the interests involved.

Therefore, if we find civilised nations do not put their prisoners to death, do not devastate towns and countries, this is because their intelligence exercises greater influence on their mode of carrying on War, and has taught them more effectual means of applying force than these rude acts of mere instinct. The invention of gun-powder, the constant progress of improvements in the construction of firearms, are sufficient proofs that the tendency to destroy the adversary which lies at the bottom of the conception of War is in no way changed or modified through the progress of civilisation.

We therefore repeat our proposition, that War is an act of violence pushed to its utmost bounds; as one side dictates the law to the other, there arises a sort of reciprocal action, which logically must lead to an extreme. This is the first recipro-cal action, and the first extreme with which we meet (FIRST RECIPROCAL ACTION).

4. THE AIM IS TO DISARM THE ENEMY.

We have already said that the aim of all action in War is to disarm the enemy, and we shall now show that this, theoretically at least, is indispensable.

If our opponent is to be made to comply with our will, we must place him in a situation which is more oppressive to him than the sacrifice which we demand; but the disadvantages of this position must naturally not be of a transitory nature, at least in appearance, otherwise the enemy, instead of yielding, will hold out, in the prospect of a change for the better. Every change in this position which is produced by a continuation of the War should therefore be a change for the worse. The worst condition in which a belligerent can be placed is that of being completely disarmed. If, therefore, the enemy is to be reduced to submission by an act of War, he must either be positively disarmed or placed in such a position that he is threatened with it. From this it follows that the disarming or overthrow of the enemy, whichever we call it, must always be the aim of Warfare. Now War is always the shock of two hostile bodies in collision, not the action of a living power upon an inanimate mass, because an absolute state of endurance would not be making War; therefore, what we have just said as to the aim of action in War applies to both parties. Here, then, is another case of reciprocal action. As long as the enemy is not defeated, he may defeat me; then I shall be no longer my own master; he will dictate the law to me as I did to him. This is the second reciprocal action, and leads to a second extreme (SECOND RECIPROCAL ACTION).

5. UTMOST EXERTION OF POWERS.

If we desire to defeat the enemy, we must proportion our efforts to his powers of resistance. This is expressed by the product of two factors which cannot be sepa-rated, namely, the sum of available means and the strength of the Will. The sum of the available means may be estimated in a measure, as it depends (although not entirely) upon numbers; but the strength of volition is more difficult to determine, and can only be estimated to a certain extent by the strength of the motives. Granted we have obtained in this way an approximation to the strength of the power to be contended with, we can then take of our own means, and either increase them so as to obtain a preponderance, or, in case we have not the resources to effect this, then do our best by increasing our means as far as possible. But the adversary does the same; therefore, there is a new mutual enhancement, which, in pure conception, must create a fresh effort towards an extreme. This is the third case of reciprocal action, and a third extreme with which we meet (THIRD RECIPROCAL ACTION).

6. MODIFICATION IN THE REALITY.

Thus reasoning in the abstract, the mind cannot stop short of an extreme, because it has to deal with an extreme, with a conflict of forces left to themselves, and obeying no other but their own inner laws. If we should seek to deduce from the pure conception of War an absolute point for the aim which we shall propose and for the means which we shall apply, this constant reciprocal action would involve us in extremes, which would be nothing but a play of ideas produced by an almost invisible train of logical subtleties. If, adhering closely to the absolute, we try to avoid all difficulties by a stroke of the pen, and insist with logical strictness that in every case the extreme must be the object, and the utmost effort must be exerted in that direction, such a stroke of the pen would be a mere paper law, not by any means adapted to the real world.

Even supposing this extreme tension of forces was an absolute which could easily be ascertained, still we must admit that the human mind would hardly submit itself to this kind of logical chimera. There would be in many cases an unnecessary waste of power, which would be in opposition to other principles of statecraft; an effort of Will would be required disproportioned to the proposed object, which therefore it would be impossible to realise, for the human will does not derive its impulse from logical subtleties.

But everything takes a different shape when we pass from abstractions to reality. In the former, everything must be subject to optimism, and we must imagine the one side as well as the other striving after perfection and even attaining it. Will this ever take place in reality? It will if,

(1) War becomes a completely isolated act, which arises suddenly, and is in no way connected with the previous history of the combatant States.

(2) If it is limited to a single solution, or to several simultaneous solutions.

(3) If it contains within itself the solution perfect and complete, free from any reaction upon it, through a calculation beforehand of the political situation which will follow from it.

7. WAR IS NEVER AN ISOLATED ACT.

With regard to the first point, neither of the two opponents is an abstract person to the other, not even as regards that factor in the sum of resistance which does not depend on objective things, viz., the Will. This Will is not an entirely unknown quantity; it indicates what it will be to-morrow by what it is to-day. War does not spring up quite suddenly, it does not spread to the full in a moment; each of the two opponents can, therefore, form an opinion of the other, in a great measure, from what he is and what he does, instead of judging of him according to what he, strictly speaking, should be or should do. But, now, man with his incomplete organisation is always below the line of absolute perfection, and thus these deficiencies, having an influence on both sides, become a modifying principle.

8. WAR DOES NOT CONSIST OF A SINGLE INSTANTANEOUS BLOW.

The second point gives rise to the following considerations:—

If War ended in a single solution, or a number of simultaneous ones, then naturally all the preparations for the same would have a tendency to the extreme, for an omission could not in any way be repaired; the utmost, then, that the world of reality could furnish as a guide for us would be the preparations of the enemy, as far as they are known to us; all the rest would fall into the domain of the abstract. But if the result is made up from several successive acts, then naturally that which precedes with all its phases may be taken as a measure for that which will follow, and in this manner the world of reality again takes the place of the abstract, and thus modifies the effort towards the extreme.

Yet every War would necessarily resolve itself into a single solution, or a sum of simultaneous results, if all the means required for the struggle were raised at once, or could be at once raised; for as one adverse result necessarily diminishes the means, then if all the means have been applied in the first, a second cannot properly be supposed. All hostile acts which might follow would belong essentially to the first, and form, in reality only its duration.

But we have already seen that even in the preparation for War the real world steps into the place of mere abstract conception—a material standard into the place of the hypotheses of an extreme: that therefore in that way both parties, by the influence of the mutual reaction, remain below the line of extreme effort, and therefore all forces are not at once brought forward.

It lies also in the nature of these forces and their application that they cannot all be brought into activity at the same time. These forces are THE ARMIES ACTUALLY ON FOOT, THE COUNTRY, with its superficial extent and its population, AND THE ALLIES.

In point of fact, the country, with its superficial area and the population, besides being the source of all military force, constitutes in itself an integral part of the efficient quantities in War, providing either the theatre of war or exercising a considerable influence on the same.

Now, it is possible to bring all the movable military forces of a country into operation at once, but not all fortresses, rivers, mountains, people, &c.—in short, not the whole country, unless it is so small that it may be completely embraced by the first act of the War. Further, the co-operation of allies does not depend on the Will of the belligerents; and from the nature of the political relations of states to each other, this co-operation is frequently not afforded until after the War has commenced, or it may be increased to restore the balance of power.

That this part of the means of resistance, which cannot at once be brought into activity, in many cases, is a much greater part of the whole than might at first be supposed, and that it often restores the balance of power, seriously affected by the great force of the first decision, will be more fully shown hereafter. Here it is sufficient to show that a complete concentration of all available means in a moment of time is contradictory to the nature of War.

Now this, in itself, furnishes no ground for relaxing our efforts to accumulate strength to gain the first result, because an unfavourable issue is always a disadvantage to which no one would purposely expose himself, and also because the first decision, although not the only one, still will have the more influence on subsequent events, the greater it is in itself.

But the possibility of gaining a later result causes men to take refuge in that expectation, owing to the repugnance in the human mind to making excessive efforts; and therefore forces are not concentrated and measures are not taken for the first decision with that energy which would otherwise be used. Whatever one belligerent omits from weakness, becomes to the other a real objective ground for limiting his own efforts, and thus again, through this reciprocal action, extreme tendencies are brought down to efforts on a limited scale.

9. THE RESULT IN WAR IS NEVER ABSOLUTE.

Lastly, even the final decision of a whole War is not always to be regarded as absolute. The conquered State often sees in it only a passing evil, which may be repaired in after times by means of political combinations. How much this must modify the degree of tension, and the vigour of the efforts made, is evident in itself.

10. THE PROBABILITIES OF REAL LIFE TAKE THE PLACE OF THE CONCEPTIONS OF THE EXTREME AND THE ABSOLUTE.

In this manner, the whole act of War is removed from the rigorous law of forces exerted to the utmost. If the extreme is no longer to be apprehended, and no longer to be sought for, it is left to the judgment to determine the limits for the efforts to be made in place of it, and this can only be done on the data furnished by the facts of the real world by the Laws of Probability. Once the belligerents are no longer mere conceptions, but individual States and Governments, once the War is no longer an ideal, but a definite substantial procedure, then the reality will furnish the data to compute the unknown quantities which are required to be found.

From the character, the measures, the situation of the adversary, and the relations with which he is surrounded, each side will draw conclusions by the law of probability as to the designs of the other, and act accordingly.

11. THE POLITICAL OBJECT NOW REAPPEARS.

Here the question which we had laid aside forces itself again into consideration (see No. 2), viz., the political object of the War. The law of the extreme, the view to disarm the adversary, to overthrow him, has hitherto to a certain extent usurped the place of this end or object. Just as this law loses its force, the political must again come forward. If the whole consideration is a calculation of probability based on definite persons and relations, then the political object, being the original motive, must be an essential factor in the product. The smaller the sacrifice we demand from ours, the smaller, it may be expected, will be the means of resistance which he will employ; but the smaller his preparation, the smaller will ours require to be. Further, the smaller our political object, the less value shall we set upon it, and the more easily shall we be induced to give it up altogether.

Thus, therefore, the political object, as the original motive of the War, will be the standard for determining both the aim of the military force and also the amount of effort to be made. This it cannot be in itself, but it is so in relation to both the belligerent States, because we are concerned with realities, not with mere abstractions. One and the same political object may produce totally different effects upon different people, or even upon the same people at different times; we can, therefore, only admit the political object as the measure, by considering it in its effects upon those masses which it is to move, and consequently the nature of those masses also comes into consideration. It is easy to see that thus the result may be very different according as these masses are animated with a spirit which will infuse vigour into the action or otherwise. It is quite possible for such a state of feeling to exist between two States that a very trifling political motive for War may produce an effect quite disproportionate—in fact, a perfect explosion.

This applies to the efforts which the political object will call forth in the two States, and to the aim which the military action shall prescribe for itself. At times it may itself be that aim, as, for example, the conquest of a province. At other times the political object itself is not suitable for the aim of military action; then such a one must be chosen as will be an equivalent for it, and stand in its place as regards the conclusion of peace. But also, in this, due attention to the peculiar character of the States concerned is always supposed. There are circumstances in which the equivalent must be much greater than the political object, in order to secure the latter. The political object will be so much the more the standard of aim and effort, and have more influence in itself, the more the masses are indifferent, the less that any mutual feeling of hostility prevails in the two States from other causes, and therefore there are cases where the political object almost alone will be decisive.

If the aim of the military action is an equivalent for the political object, that action will in general diminish as the political object diminishes, and in a greater degree the more the political object dominates. Thus it is explained how, without any contradiction in itself, there may be Wars of all degrees of importance and energy, from a War of extermination down to the mere use of an army of observation. This, however, leads to a question of another kind which we have hereafter to develop and answer.

12. A SUSPENSION IN THE ACTION OF WAR UNEXPLAINED BY ANYTHING SAID AS YET.

However insignificant the political claims mutually advanced, however weak the means put forth, however small the aim to which military action is directed, can this action be suspended even for a moment? This is a question which penetrates deeply into the nature of the subject.

Every transaction requires for its accomplishment a certain time which we call its duration. This may be longer or shorter, according as the person acting throws more or less despatch into his movements.

About this more or less we shall not trouble ourselves here. Each person acts in his own fashion; but the slow person does not protract the thing because he wishes to spend more time about it, but because by his nature he requires more time, and if he made more haste would not do the thing so well. This time, therefore, depends on subjective causes, and belongs to the length, so called, of the action.

If we allow now to every action in War this, its length, then we must assume, at first sight at least, that any expenditure of time beyond this length, that is, every suspension of hostile action, appears an absurdity; with respect to this it must not be forgotten that we now speak not of the progress of one or other of the two opponents, but of the general progress of the whole action of the War.

13. THERE IS ONLY ONE CAUSE WHICH CAN SUSPEND THE ACTION, AND THIS SEEMS TO BE ONLY POSSIBLE ON ONE SIDE IN ANY CASE.

If two parties have armed themselves for strife, then a feeling of animosity must have moved them to it; as long now as they continue armed, that is, do not come to terms of peace, this feeling must exist; and it can only be brought to a standstill by either side by one single motive alone, which is, THAT HE WAITS FOR A MORE FAVOURABLE MOMENT FOR ACTION. Now, at first sight, it appears that this motive can never exist except on one side, because it, eo ipso, must be prejudicial to the other. If the one has an interest in acting, then the other must have an interest in waiting.

A complete equilibrium of forces can never produce a suspension of action, for during this suspension he who has the positive object (that is, the assailant) must continue progressing; for if we should imagine an equilibrium in this way, that he who has the positive object, therefore the strongest motive, can at the same time only command the lesser means, so that the equation is made up by the product of the motive and the power, then we must say, if no alteration in this condition of equilibrium is to be expected, the two parties must make peace; but if an alteration is to be expected, then it can only be favourable to one side, and therefore the other has a manifest interest to act without delay. We see that the conception of an equilibrium cannot explain a suspension of arms, but that it ends in the question of the EXPECTATION OF A MORE FAVOURABLE MOMENT.

Let us suppose, therefore, that one of two States has a positive object, as, for instance, the conquest of one of the enemy's provinces—which is to be utilised in the settlement of peace. After this conquest, his political object is accomplished, the necessity for action ceases, and for him a pause ensues. If the adversary is also contented with this solution, he will make peace; if not, he must act. Now, if we suppose that in four weeks he will be in a better condition to act, then he has sufficient grounds for putting off the time of action.

But from that moment the logical course for the enemy appears to be to act that he may not give the conquered party THE DESIRED time. Of course, in this mode of reasoning a complete insight into the state of circumstances on both sides is supposed.

14. THUS A CONTINUANCE OF ACTION WILL ENSUE WHICH WILL ADVANCE TOWARDS A CLIMAX.

If this unbroken continuity of hostile operations really existed, the effect would be that everything would again be driven towards the extreme; for, irrespective of the effect of such incessant activity in inflaming the feelings, and infusing into the whole a greater degree of passion, a greater elementary force, there would also follow from this continuance of action a stricter continuity, a closer connection between cause and effect, and thus every single action would become of more importance, and consequently more replete with danger.

But we know that the course of action in War has seldom or never this unbroken continuity, and that there have been many Wars in which action occupied by far the smallest portion of time employed, the whole of the rest being consumed in inaction. It is impossible that this should be always an anomaly; suspension of action in War must therefore be possible, that is no contradiction in itself. We now proceed to show how this is.

15. HERE, THEREFORE, THE PRINCIPLE OF POLARITY IS BROUGHT INTO REQUISITION.

As we have supposed the interests of one Commander to be always antagonistic to those of the other, we have assumed a true POLARITY. We reserve a fuller explanation of this for another chapter, merely making the following observation on it at present.

The principle of polarity is only valid when it can be conceived in one and the same thing, where the positive and its opposite the negative completely destroy each other. In a battle both sides strive to conquer; that is true polarity, for the victory of the one side destroys that of the other. But when we speak of two different things which have a common relation external to themselves, then it is not the things but their relations which have the polarity.

16. ATTACK AND DEFENCE ARE THINGS DIFFERING IN KIND AND OF UNEQUAL FORCE. POLARITY IS, THEREFORE, NOT APPLICABLE TO THEM.

If there was only one form of War, to wit, the attack of the enemy, therefore no defence; or, in other words, if the attack was distinguished from the defence merely by the positive motive, which the one has and the other has not, but the methods of each were precisely one and the same: then in this sort of fight every advantage gained on the one side would be a corresponding disadvantage on the other, and true polarity would exist.

But action in War is divided into two forms, attack and defence, which, as we shall hereafter explain more particularly, are very different and of unequal strength. Polarity therefore lies in that to which both bear a relation, in the decision, but not in the attack or defence itself.

If the one Commander wishes the solution put off, the other must wish to hasten it, but only by the same form of action. If it is A's interest not to attack his enemy at present, but four weeks hence, then it is B's interest to be attacked, not four weeks hence, but at the present moment. This is the direct antagonism of interests, but it by no means follows that it would be for B's interest to attack A at once. That is plainly something totally different.

17. THE EFFECT OF POLARITY IS OFTEN DESTROYED BY THE SUPERIORITY OF THE DEFENCE OVER THE ATTACK, AND THUS THE SUSPENSION OF ACTION IN WAR IS EXPLAINED.

If the form of defence is stronger than that of offence, as we shall hereafter show, the question arises, Is the advantage of a deferred decision as great on the one side as the advantage of the defensive form on the other? If it is not, then it cannot by its counter-weight over-balance the latter, and thus influence the progress of the action of the War. We see, therefore, that the impulsive force existing in the polarity of interests may be lost in the difference between the strength of the offensive and the defensive, and thereby become ineffectual.

If, therefore, that side for which the present is favourable, is too weak to be able to dispense with the advantage of the defensive, he must put up with the unfavourable prospects which the future holds out; for it may still be better to fight a defensive battle in the unpromising future than to assume the offensive or make peace at present. Now, being convinced that the superiority of the defensive (rightly understood) is very great, and much greater than may appear at first sight, we conceive that the greater number of those periods of inaction which occur in war are thus explained without involving any contradiction. The weaker the motives to action are, the more will those motives be absorbed and neutralised by this difference between attack and defence, the more frequently, therefore, will action in warfare be stopped, as indeed experience teaches.

18 A SECOND GROUND CONSISTS IN THE IMPERFECT KNOWLEDGE OF CIRCUMSTANCES.

But there is still another cause which may stop action in War, viz., an incomplete view of the situation. Each Commander can only fully know his own position; that of his opponent can only be known to him by reports, which are uncertain; he may, therefore, form a wrong judgment with respect to it upon data of this description, and, in consequence of that error, he may suppose that the power of taking the initiative rests with his adversary when it lies really with himself. This want of perfect insight might certainly just as often occasion an untimely action as untimely inaction, and hence it would in itself no more contribute to delay than to accelerate action in War. Still, it must always be regarded as one of the natural causes which may bring action in War to a standstill without involving a contradiction. But if we reflect how much more we are inclined and induced to estimate the power of our opponents too high than too low, because it lies in human nature to do so, we shall admit that our imperfect insight into facts in general must contribute very much to delay action in War, and to modify the application of the principles pending our conduct.

The possibility of a standstill brings into the action of War a new modification, inasmuch as it dilutes that action with the element of time, checks the influence or sense of danger in its course, and increases the means of reinstating a lost balance of force. The greater the tension of feelings from which the War springs, the greater therefore the energy with which it is carried on, so much the shorter will be the periods of inaction; on the other hand, the weaker the principle of warlike activity, the longer will be these periods: for powerful motives increase the force of the will, and this, as we know, is always a factor in the product of force.

19. FREQUENT PERIODS OF INACTION IN WAR REMOVE IT FURTHER FROM THE ABSOLUTE, AND MAKE IT STILL MORE A CALCULATION OF PROBABILITIES.

But the slower the action proceeds in War, the more frequent and longer the periods of inaction, so much the more easily can an error be repaired; therefore, so much the bolder a General will be in his calculations, so much the more readily will he keep them below the line of the absolute, and build everything upon probabilities and conjecture. Thus, according as the course of the War is more or less slow, more or less time will be allowed for that which the nature of a concrete case particularly requires, calculation of probability based on given circumstances.

20. THEREFORE, THE ELEMENT OF CHANCE ONLY IS WANTING TO MAKE OF WAR A GAME, AND IN THAT ELEMENT IT IS LEAST OF ALL DEFICIENT.

We see from the foregoing how much the objective nature of War makes it a calculation of probabilities; now there is only one single element still wanting to make it a game, and that element it certainly is not without: it is chance. There is no human affair which stands so constantly and so generally in close connection with chance as War. But together with chance, the accidental, and along with it good luck, occupy a great place in War.

21. WAR IS A GAME BOTH OBJECTIVELY AND SUBJECTIVELY.

If we now take a look at the subjective nature of War, that is to say, at those conditions under which it is carried on, it will appear to us still more like a game. Primarily the element in which the operations of War are carried on is danger; but which of all the moral qualities is the first in danger? COURAGE. Now certainly courage is quite compatible with prudent calculation, but still they are things of quite a different kind, essentially different qualities of the mind; on the other hand, daring reliance on good fortune, boldness, rashness, are only expressions of courage, and all these propensities of the mind look for the fortuitous (or accidental), because it is their element.

We see, therefore, how, from the commencement, the absolute, the mathematical as it is called, nowhere finds any sure basis in the calculations in the Art of War; and that from the outset there is a play of possibilities, probabilities, good and bad luck, which spreads about with all the coarse and fine threads of its web, and makes War of all branches of human activity the most like a gambling game.

22. HOW THIS ACCORDS BEST WITH THE HUMAN MIND IN GENERAL.

Although our intellect always feels itself urged towards clearness and certainty, still our mind often feels itself attracted by uncertainty. Instead of threading its way with the understanding along the narrow path of philosophical investigations and logical conclusions, in order, almost unconscious of itself, to arrive in spaces where it feels itself a stranger, and where it seems to part from all well-known objects, it prefers to remain with the imagination in the realms of chance and luck. Instead of living yonder on poor necessity, it revels here in the wealth of possibilities; animated thereby, courage then takes wings to itself, and daring and danger make the element into which it launches itself as a fearless swimmer plunges into the stream.

Shall theory leave it here, and move on, self-satisfied with absolute conclusions and rules? Then it is of no practical use. Theory must also take into account the human element; it must accord a place to courage, to boldness, even to rashness. The Art of War has to deal with living and with moral forces, the consequence of which is that it can never attain the absolute and positive. There is therefore everywhere a margin for the accidental, and just as much in the greatest things as in the smallest. As there is room for this accidental on the one hand, so on the other there must be courage and self-reliance in proportion to the room available. If these qualities are forthcoming in a high degree, the margin left may likewise be great. Courage and self-reliance are, therefore, principles quite essential to War; consequently, theory must only set up such rules as allow ample scope for all degrees and varieties of these necessary and noblest of military virtues. In daring there may still be wisdom, and prudence as well, only they are estimated by a different standard of value.

23. WAR IS ALWAYS A SERIOUS MEANS FOR A SERIOUS OBJECT. ITS MORE PARTICULAR DEFINITION.

Such is War; such the Commander who conducts it; such the theory which rules it. But War is no pastime; no mere passion for venturing and winning; no work of a free enthusiasm: it is a serious means for a serious object. All that appearance which it wears from the varying hues of fortune, all that it assimilates into itself of the oscillations of passion, of courage, of imagination, of enthusiasm, are only particular properties of this means.

The War of a community—of whole Nations, and particularly of civilised Nations—always starts from a political condition, and is called forth by a political motive. It is, therefore, a political act. Now if it was a perfect, unrestrained, and absolute expression of force, as we had to deduct it from its mere conception, then the moment it is called forth by policy it would step into the place of policy, and as something quite independent of it would set it aside, and only follow its own laws, just as a mine at the moment of explosion cannot be guided into any other direction than that which has been given to it by preparatory arrangements. This is how the thing has really been viewed hitherto, whenever a want of harmony between policy and the conduct of a War has led to theoretical distinctions of the kind. But it is not so, and the idea is radically false. War in the real world, as we have already seen, is not an extreme thing which expends itself at one single discharge; it is the operation of powers which do not develop themselves completely in the same manner and in the same measure, but which at one time expand sufficiently to overcome the resistance opposed by inertia or friction, while at another they are too weak to produce an effect; it is therefore, in a certain measure, a pulsation of violent force more or less vehement, consequently making its discharges and exhausting its powers more or less quickly—in other words, conducting more or less quickly to the aim, but always lasting long enough to admit of influence being exerted on it in its course, so as to give it this or that direction, in short, to be subject to the will of a guiding intelligence., if we reflect that War has its root in a political object, then naturally this original motive which called it into existence should also continue the first and highest consideration in its conduct. Still, the political object is no despotic lawgiver on that account; it must accommodate itself to the nature of the means, and though changes in these means may involve modification in the political objective, the latter always retains a prior right to consideration. Policy, therefore, is interwoven with the whole action of War, and must exercise a continuous influence upon it, as far as the nature of the forces liberated by it will permit.

24. WAR IS A MERE CONTINUATION OF POLICY BY OTHER MEANS.

We see, therefore, that War is not merely a political act, but also a real political instrument, a continuation of political commerce, a carrying out of the same by other means. All beyond this which is strictly peculiar to War relates merely to the peculiar nature of the means which it uses. That the tendencies and views of policy shall not be incompatible with these means, the Art of War in general and the Commander in each particular case may demand, and this claim is truly not a trifling one. But however powerfully this may react on political views in particular cases, still it must always be regarded as only a modification of them; for the political view is the object, War is the means, and the means must always include the object in our conception.

25. DIVERSITY IN THE NATURE OF WARS.

The greater and the more powerful the motives of a War, the more it affects the whole existence of a people. The more violent the excitement which precedes the War, by so much the nearer will the War approach to its abstract form, so much the more will it be directed to the destruction of the enemy, so much the nearer will the military and political ends coincide, so much the more purely military and less political the War appears to be; but the weaker the motives and the tensions, so much the less will the natural direction of the military element—that is, force—be coincident with the direction which the political element indicates; so much the more must, therefore, the War become diverted from its natural direction, the political object diverge from the aim of an ideal War, and the War appear to become political.

But, that the reader may not form any false conceptions, we must here observe that by this natural tendency of War we only mean the philosophical, the strictly logical, and by no means the tendency of forces actually engaged in conflict, by which would be supposed to be included all the emotions and passions of the combatants. No doubt in some cases these also might be excited to such a degree as to be with difficulty restrained and confined to the political road; but in most cases such a contradiction will not arise, because by the existence of such strenuous exertions a great plan in harmony therewith would be implied. If the plan is directed only upon a small object, then the impulses of feeling amongst the masses will be also so weak that these masses will require to be stimulated rather than repressed.

26. THEY MAY ALL BE REGARDED AS POLITICAL ACTS.

Returning now to the main subject, although it is true that in one kind of War the political element seems almost to disappear, whilst in another kind it occupies a very prominent place, we may still affirm that the one is as political as the other; for if we regard the State policy as the intelligence of the personified State, then amongst all the constellations in the political sky whose movements it has to compute, those must be included which arise when the nature of its relations imposes the necessity of a great War. It is only if we understand by policy not a true appreciation of affairs in general, but the conventional conception of a cautious, subtle, also dishonest craftiness, averse from violence, that the latter kind of War may belong more to policy than the first.

27. INFLUENCE OF THIS VIEW ON THE RIGHT UNDERSTANDING OF MILITARY HISTORY, AND ON THE FOUNDATIONS OF THEORY.

We see, therefore, in the first place, that under all circumstances War is to be regarded not as an independent thing, but as a political instrument; and it is only by taking this point of view that we can avoid finding ourselves in opposition to all military history. This is the only means of unlocking the great book and making it intelligible. Secondly, this view shows us how Wars must differ in character according to the nature of the motives and circumstances from which they proceed.

Now, the first, the grandest, and most decisive act of judgment which the Statesman and General exercises is rightly to understand in this respect the War in which he engages, not to take it for something, or to wish to make of it something, which by the nature of its relations it is impossible for it to be. This is, therefore, the first, the most comprehensive, of all strategical questions. We shall enter into this more fully in treating of the plan of a War.

For the present we content ourselves with having brought the subject up to this point, and having thereby fixed the chief point of view from which War and its theory are to be studied.

28. RESULT FOR THEORY.

War is, therefore, not only chameleon-like in character, because it changes its colour in some degree in each particular case, but it is also, as a whole, in relation to the predominant tendencies which are in it, a wonderful trinity, composed of the original violence of its elements, hatred and animosity, which may be looked upon as blind instinct; of the play of probabilities and chance, which make it a free activity of the soul; and of the subordinate nature of a political instrument, by which it belongs purely to the reason.

The first of these three phases concerns more the people the second, more the General and his Army; the third, more the Government. The passions which break forth in War must already have a latent existence in the peoples. The range which the display of courage and talents shall get in the realm of probabilities and of chance depends on the particular characteristics of the General and his Army, but the political objects belong to the Government alone.

These three tendencies, which appear like so many different law-givers, are deeply rooted in the nature of the subject, and at the same time variable in degree. A theory which would leave any one of them out of account, or set up any arbitrary relation between them, would immediately become involved in such a contradiction with the reality, that it might be regarded as destroyed at once by that alone.

The problem is, therefore, that theory shall keep itself poised in a manner between these three tendencies, as between three points of attraction.

The way in which alone this difficult problem can be solved we shall examine in the book on the "Theory of War." In every case the conception of War, as here defined, will be the first ray of light which shows us the true foundation of theory, and which first separates the great masses and allows us to distinguish them from one another.

CHAPTER II - END AND MEANS IN WAR

HAVING in the foregoing chapter ascertained the complicated and variable nature of War, we shall now occupy ourselves in examining into the influence which this nature has upon the end and means in War.

If we ask, first of all, for the object upon which the whole effort of War is to be directed, in order that it may suffice for the attainment of the political object, we shall find that it is just as variable as are the political object and the particular circumstances of the War.

If, in the next place, we keep once more to the pure conception of War, then we must say that the political object properly lies out of its province, for if War is an act of violence to compel the enemy to fulfil our will, then in every case all depends on our overthrowing the enemy, that is, disarming him, and on that alone. This object, developed from abstract conceptions, but which is also the one aimed at in a great many cases in reality, we shall, in the first place, examine in this reality.

In connection with the plan of a campaign we shall hereafter examine more closely into the meaning of disarming a nation, but here we must at once draw a distinction between three things, which, as three general objects, comprise everything else within them. They are the MILITARY POWER, THE COUNTRY, and THE WILL OF THE ENEMY.

The military power must be destroyed, that is, reduced to such a state as not to be able to prosecute the War. This is the sense in which we wish to be understood hereafter, whenever we use the expression "destruction of the enemy's military power."

The country must be conquered, for out of the country a new military force may be formed.

But even when both these things are done, still the War, that is, the hostile feeling and action of hostile agencies, cannot be considered as at an end as long as the will of the enemy is not subdued also; that is, its Government and its Allies must be forced into signing a peace, or the people into submission; for whilst we are in full occupation of the country, the War may break out afresh, either in the interior or through assistance given by Allies. No doubt, this may also take place after a peace, but that shows nothing more than that every War does not carry in itself the elements for a complete decision and final settlement.

But even if this is the case, still with the conclusion of peace a number of sparks are always extinguished which would have smouldered on quietly, and the excitement of the passions abates, because all those whose minds are disposed to peace, of which in all nations and under all circumstances there is always a great number, turn themselves away completely from the road to resistance. Whatever may take place subsequently, we must always look upon the object as attained, and the business of War as ended, by a peace.

As protection of the country is the primary object for which the military force exists, therefore the natural order is, that first of all this force should be destroyed, then the country subdued; and through the effect of these two results, as well as the position we then hold, the enemy should be forced to make peace. Generally the destruction of the enemy's force is done by degrees, and in just the same measure the conquest of the country follows immediately. The two likewise usually react upon each other, because the loss of provinces occasions a diminution of military force. But this order is by no means necessary, and on that account it also does not always take place. The enemy's Army, before it is sensibly weakened, may retreat to the opposite side of the country, or even quite outside of it. In this case, therefore, the greater part or the whole of the country is conquered.

But this object of War in the abstract, this final means of attaining the political object in which all others are combined, the DISARMING THE ENEMY, is rarely attained in practice and is not a condition necessary to peace. Therefore it can in no wise be set up in theory as a law. There are innumerable instances of treaties in which peace has been settled before either party could be looked upon as disarmed; indeed, even before the balance of power had undergone any sensible alteration. Nay, further, if we look at the case in the concrete, then we must say that in a whole class of cases, the idea of a complete defeat of the enemy would be a mere imaginative flight, especially when the enemy is considerably superior.

The reason why the object deduced from the conception of War is not adapted in general to real War lies in the difference between the two, which is discussed in the preceding chapter. If it was as pure theory gives it, then a War between two States of very unequal military strength would appear an absurdity; therefore impossible. At most, the inequality between the physical forces might be such that it could be balanced by the moral forces, and that would not go far with our present social condition in Europe. Therefore, if we have seen Wars take place between States of very unequal power, that has been the case because there is a wide difference between War in reality and its original conception.

There are two considerations which as motives may practically take the place of inability to continue the contest. The first is the improbability, the second is the excessive price, of success.

According to what we have seen in the foregoing chapter, War must always set itself free from the strict law of logical necessity, and seek aid from the calculation of probabilities; and as this is so much the more the case, the more the War has a bias that way, from the circumstances out of which it has arisen—the smaller its motives are, and the excitement it has raised—so it is also conceivable how out of this calculation of probabilities even motives to peace may arise. War does not, therefore, always require to be fought out until one party is overthrown; and we may suppose that, when the motives and passions are slight, a weak probability will suffice to move that side to which it is unfavourable to give way. Now, were the other side convinced of this beforehand, it is natural that he would strive for this probability only, instead of first wasting time and effort in the attempt to achieve the total destruction of the enemy's Army.

Still more general in its influence on the resolution to peace is the consideration of the expenditure of force already made, and further required. As War is no act of blind passion, but is dominated by the political object, therefore the value of that object determines the measure of the sacrifices by which it is to be purchased. This will be the case, not only as regards extent, but also as regards duration. As soon, therefore, as the required outlay becomes so great that the political object is no longer equal in value, the object must be given up, and peace will be the result.

We see, therefore, that in Wars where one side cannot completely disarm the other, the motives to peace on both sides will rise or fall on each side according to the probability of future success and the required outlay. If these motives were equally strong on both sides, they would meet in the centre of their political difference. Where they are strong on one side, they might be weak on the other. If their amount is only sufficient, peace will follow, but naturally to the advantage of that side which has the weakest motive for its conclusion. We purposely pass over here the difference which the POSITIVE and NEGATIVE character of the political end must necessarily produce practically; for although that is, as we shall hereafter show, of the highest importance, still we are obliged to keep here to a more general point of view, because the original political views in the course of the War change very much, and at last may become totally different, JUST BECAUSE THEY ARE DETERMINED BY RESULTS AND PROBABLE EVENTS.

Now comes the question how to influence the probability of success. In the first place, naturally by the same means which we use when the object is the subjugation of the enemy, by the destruction of his military force and the conquest of his provinces; but these two means are not exactly of the same import here as they would be in reference to that object. If we attack the enemy's Army, it is a very different thing whether we intend to follow up the first blow with a succession of others, until the whole force is destroyed, or whether we mean to content ourselves with a victory to shake the enemy's feeling of security, to convince him of our superiority, and to instill into him a feeling of apprehension about the future. If this is our object, we only go so far in the destruction of his forces as is sufficient. In like manner, the conquest, of the enemy's provinces is quite a different measure if the object is not the destruction of the enemy's Army. In the latter case the destruction of the Army is the real effectual action, and the taking of the provinces only a consequence of it; to take them before the Army had been defeated would always be looked upon only as a necessary evil. On the other hand, if our views are not directed upon the complete destruction of the enemy's force, and if we are sure that the enemy does not seek but fears to bring matters to a bloody decision, the taking possession of a weak or defenceless province is an advantage in itself, and if this advantage is of sufficient importance to make the enemy apprehensive about the general result, then it may also be regarded as a shorter road to peace.

But now we come upon a peculiar means of influencing the probability of the result without destroying the enemy's Army, namely, upon the expeditions which have a direct connection with political views. If there are any enterprises which are particularly likely to break up the enemy's alliances or make them inoperative, to gain new alliances for ourselves, to raise political powers in our own favour, then it is easy to conceive how much these may increase the probability of success, and become a shorter way towards our object than the routing of the enemy's forces.

The second question is how to act upon the enemy's expenditure in strength, that is, to raise the price of success.

The enemy's outlay in strength lies in the WEAR AND TEAR of his forces, consequently in the DESTRUCTION of them on our part, and in the LOSS of PROVINCES, consequently the CONQUEST of them by us.

Here, again, on account of the various significations of these means, so likewise it will be found that neither of them will be identical in its signification in all cases if the objects are different. The smallness in general of this difference must not cause us perplexity, for in reality the weakest motives, the finest shades of difference, often decide in favour of this or that method of applying force. Our only business here is to show that, certain conditions being supposed, the possibility of attaining our purpose in different ways is no contradiction, absurdity, nor even error.

Besides these two means, there are three other peculiar ways of directly increasing the waste of the enemy's force. The first is INVASION, that is THE OCCUPATION OF THE ENEMY'S TERRITORY, NOT WITH A VIEW TO KEEPING IT, but in order to levy contributions upon it, or to devastate it.

The immediate object here is neither the conquest of the enemy's territory nor the defeat of his armed force, but merely to DO HIM DAMAGE IN A GENERAL WAY. The second way is to select for the object of our enterprises those points at which we can do the enemy most harm. Nothing is easier to conceive than two different directions in which our force may be employed, the first of which is to be preferred if our object is to defeat the enemy's Army, while the other is more advantageous if the defeat of the enemy is out of the question. According to the usual mode of speaking, we should say that the first is primarily military, the other more political. But if we take our view from the highest point, both are equally military, and neither the one nor the other can be eligible unless it suits the circumstances of the case. The third, by far the most important, from the great number of cases which it embraces, is the WEARING OUT of the enemy. We choose this expression not only to explain our meaning in few words, but because it represents the thing exactly, and is not so figurative as may at first appear. The idea of wearing out in a struggle amounts in practice to A GRADUAL EXHAUSTION OF THE PHYSICAL POWERS AND OF THE WILL BY THE LONG CONTINUANCE OF EXERTION.

Now, if we want to overcome the enemy by the duration of the contest, we must content ourselves with as small objects as possible, for it is in the nature of the thing that a great end requires a greater expenditure of force than a small one; but the smallest object that we can propose to ourselves is simple passive resistance, that is a combat without any positive view. In this way, therefore, our means attain their greatest relative value, and therefore the result is best secured. How far now can this negative mode of proceeding be carried? Plainly not to absolute passivity, for mere endurance would not be fighting; and the defensive is an activity by which so much of the enemy's power must be destroyed that he must give up his object. That alone is what we aim at in each single act, and therein consists the negative nature of our object.

No doubt this negative object in its single act is not so effective as the positive object in the same direction would be, supposing it successful; but there is this difference in its favour, that it succeeds more easily than the positive, and therefore it holds out greater certainty of success; what is wanting in the efficacy of its single act must be gained through time, that is, through the duration of the contest, and therefore this negative intention, which constitutes the principle of the pure defensive, is also the natural means of overcoming the enemy by the duration of the combat, that is of wearing him out.

Here lies the origin of that difference of OFFENSIVE and DEFENSIVE, the influence of which prevails throughout the whole province of War. We cannot at present pursue this subject further than to observe that from this negative intention are to be deduced all the advantages and all the stronger forms of combat which are on the side of the Defensive, and in which that philosophical-dynamic law which exists between the greatness and the certainty of success is realised. We shall resume the consideration of all this hereafter.

If then the negative purpose, that is the concentration of all the means into a state of pure resistance, affords a superiority in the contest, and if this advantage is sufficient to BALANCE whatever superiority in numbers the adversary may have, then the mere DURATION of the contest will suffice gradually to bring the loss of force on the part of the adversary to a point at which the political object can no longer be an equivalent, a point at which, therefore, he must give up the contest. We see then that this class of means, the wearing out of the enemy, includes the great number of cases in which the weaker resists the stronger.

Frederick the Great, during the Seven Years' War, was never strong enough to overthrow the Austrian monarchy; and if he had tried to do so after the fashion of Charles the Twelfth, he would inevitably have had to succumb himself. But after his skilful application of the system of husbanding his resources had shown the powers allied against him, through a seven years' struggle, that the actual expenditure of strength far exceeded what they had at first anticipated, they made peace.

We see then that there are many ways to one's object in War; that the complete subjugation of the enemy is not essential in every case; that the destruction of the enemy's military force, the conquest of the enemy's provinces, the mere occupation of them, the mere invasion of them—enterprises which are aimed directly at political objects—lastly, a passive expectation of the enemy's blow, are all means which, each in itself, may be used to force the enemy's will according as the peculiar circumstances of the case lead us to expect more from the one or the other. We could still add to these a whole category of shorter methods of gaining the end, which might be called arguments ad hominem. What branch of human affairs is there in which these sparks of individual spirit have not made their appearance, surmounting all formal considerations? And least of all can they fail to appear in War, where the personal character of the combatants plays such an important part, both in the cabinet and in the field. We limit ourselves to pointing this out, as it would be pedantry to attempt to reduce such influences into classes. Including these, we may say that the number of possible ways of reaching the object rises to infinity.

To avoid under-estimating these different short roads to one's purpose, either estimating them only as rare exceptions, or holding the difference which they cause in the conduct of War as insignificant, we must bear in mind the diversity of political objects which may cause a War—measure at a glance the distance which there is between a death struggle for political existence and a War which a forced or tottering alliance makes a matter of disagreeable duty. Between the two innumerable gradations occur in practice. If we reject one of these gradations in theory, we might with equal right reject the whole, which would be tantamount to shutting the real world completely out of sight.

These are the circumstances in general connected with the aim which we have to pursue in War; let us now turn to the means.

There is only one single means, it is the FIGHT. However diversified this may be in form, however widely it may differ from a rough vent of hatred and animosity in a hand-to-hand encounter, whatever number of things may introduce themselves which are not actual fighting, still it is always implied in the conception of War that all the effects manifested have their roots in the combat.

That this must always be so in the greatest diversity and complication of the reality is proved in a very simple manner. All that takes place in War takes place through armed forces, but where the forces of War, i.e., armed men, are applied, there the idea of fighting must of necessity be at the foundation.

All, therefore, that relates to forces of War—all that is connected with their creation, maintenance, and application—belongs to military activity.

Creation and maintenance are obviously only the means, whilst application is the object.

The contest in War is not a contest of individual against individual, but an organised whole, consisting of manifold parts; in this great whole we may distinguish units of two kinds, the one determined by the subject, the other by the object. In an Army the mass of combatants ranges itself always into an order of new units, which again form members of a higher order. The combat of each of these members forms, therefore, also a more or less distinct unit. Further, the motive of the fight; therefore its object forms its unit.

Now, to each of these units which we distinguish in the contest we attach the name of combat.

If the idea of combat lies at the foundation of every application of armed power, then also the application of armed force in general is nothing more than the determining and arranging a certain number of combats.

Every activity in War, therefore, necessarily relates to the combat either directly or indirectly. The soldier is levied, clothed, armed, exercised, he sleeps, eats, drinks, and marches, all MERELY TO FIGHT AT THE RIGHT TIME AND PLACE.

If, therefore, all the threads of military activity terminate in the combat, we shall grasp them all when we settle the order of the combats. Only from this order and its execution proceed the effects, never directly from the conditions preceding them. Now, in the combat all the action is directed to the DESTRUCTION of the enemy, or rather of HIS FIGHTING POWERS, for this lies in the conception of combat. The destruction of the enemy's fighting power is, therefore, always the means to attain the object of the combat.

This object may likewise be the mere destruction of the enemy's armed force; but that is not by any means necessary, and it may be something quite different. Whenever, for instance, as we have shown, the defeat of the enemy is not the only means to attain the political object, whenever there are other objects which may be pursued as the aim in a War, then it follows of itself that such other objects may become the object of particular acts of Warfare, and therefore also the object of combats.

But even those combats which, as subordinate acts, are in the strict sense devoted to the destruction of the enemy's fighting force need not have that destruction itself as their first object.

If we think of the manifold parts of a great armed force, of the number of circumstances which come into activity when it is employed, then it is clear that the combat of such a force must also require a manifold organisation, a subordinating of parts and formation. There may and must naturally arise for particular parts a number of objects which are not themselves the destruction of the enemy's armed force, and which, while they certainly contribute to increase that destruction, do so only in an indirect manner. If a battalion is ordered to drive the enemy from a rising ground, or a bridge, &c., then properly the occupation of any such locality is the real object, the destruction of the enemy's armed force which takes place only the means or secondary matter. If the enemy can be driven away merely by a demonstration, the object is attained all the same; but this hill or bridge is, in point of fact, only required as a means of increasing the gross amount of loss inflicted on the enemy's armed force. It is the case on the field of battle, much more must it be so on the whole theatre of war, where not only one Army is opposed to another, but one State, one Nation, one whole country to another. Here the number of possible relations, and consequently possible combinations, is much greater, the diversity of measures increased, and by the gradation of objects, each subordinate to another the first means employed is further apart from the ultimate object.

It is therefore for many reasons possible that the object of a combat is not the destruction of the enemy's force, that is, of the force immediately opposed to us, but that this only appears as a means. But in all such cases it is no longer a question of complete destruction, for the combat is here nothing else but a measure of strength—has in itself no value except only that of the present result, that is, of its decision.

But a measuring of strength may be effected in cases where the opposing sides are very unequal by a mere comparative estimate. In such cases no fighting will take place, and the weaker will immediately give way.

If the object of a combat is not always the destruction of the enemy's forces therein engaged—and if its object can often be attained as well without the combat taking place at all, by merely making a resolve to fight, and by the circumstances to which this resolution gives rise—then that explains how a whole campaign may be carried on with great activity without the actual combat playing any notable part in it.

That this may be so military history proves by a hundred examples. How many of those cases can be justified, that is, without involving a contradiction and whether some of the celebrities who rose out of them would stand criticism, we shall leave undecided, for all we have to do with the matter is to show the possibility of such a course of events in War.

We have only one means in War—the battle; but this means, by the infinite variety of paths in which it may be applied, leads us into all the different ways which the multiplicity of objects allows of, so that we seem to have gained nothing; but that is not the case, for from this unity of means proceeds a thread which assists the study of the subject, as it runs through the whole web of military activity and holds it together.

But we have considered the destruction of the enemy's force as one of the objects which maybe pursued in War, and left undecided what relative importance should be given to it amongst other objects. In certain cases it will depend on circumstances, and as a general question we have left its value undetermined. We are once more brought back upon it, and we shall be able to get an insight into the value which must necessarily be accorded to it.

The combat is the single activity in War; in the combat the destruction of the enemy opposed to us is the means to the end; it is so even when the combat does not actually take place, because in that case there lies at the root of the decision the supposition at all events that this destruction is to be regarded as beyond doubt. It follows, therefore, that the destruction of the enemy's military force is the foundation-stone of all action in War, the great support of all combinations, which rest upon it like the arch on its abutments. All action, therefore, takes place on the supposition that if the solution by force of arms which lies at its foundation should be realised, it will be a favourable one. The decision by arms is, for all operations in War, great and small, what cash payment is in bill transactions. However remote from each other these relations, however seldom the realisation may take place, still it can never entirely fail to occur.

If the decision by arms lies at the foundation of all combinations, then it follows that the enemy can defeat each of them by gaining a victory on the field, not merely in the one on which our combination directly depends, but also in any other encounter, if it is only important enough; for every important decision by arms—that is, destruction of the enemy's forces—reacts upon all preceding it, because, like a liquid element, they tend to bring themselves to a level.

Thus, the destruction of the enemy's armed force appears, therefore, always as the superior and more effectual means, to which all others must give way.

It is, however, only when there is a supposed equality in all other conditions that we can ascribe to the destruction of the enemy's armed force the greater efficacy. It would, therefore, be a great mistake to draw the conclusion that a blind dash must always gain the victory over skill and caution. An unskilful attack would lead to the destruction of our own and not of the enemy's force, and therefore is not what is here meant. The superior efficacy belongs not to the MEANS but to the END, and we are only comparing the effect of one realised purpose with the other.

If we speak of the destruction of the enemy's armed force, we must expressly point out that nothing obliges us to confine this idea to the mere physical force; on the contrary, the moral is necessarily implied as well, because both in fact are interwoven with each other, even in the most minute details, and therefore cannot be separated. But it is just in connection with the inevitable effect which has been referred to, of a great act of destruction (a great victory) upon all other decisions by arms, that this moral element is most fluid, if we may use that expression, and therefore distributes itself the most easily through all the parts.

Against the far superior worth which the destruction of the enemy's armed force has over all other means stands the expense and risk of this means, and it is only to avoid these that any other means are taken. That these must be costly stands to reason, for the waste of our own military forces must, ceteris paribus, always be greater the more our aim is directed upon the destruction of the enemy's power.

The danger lies in this, that the greater efficacy which we seek recoils on ourselves, and therefore has worse consequences in case we fail of success.

Other methods are, therefore, less costly when they succeed, less dangerous when they fail; but in this is necessarily lodged the condition that they are only opposed to similar ones, that is, that the enemy acts on the same principle; for if the enemy should choose the way of a great decision by arms, OUR MEANS MUST ON THAT ACCOUNT BE CHANGED AGAINST OUR WILL, IN ORDER TO CORRESPOND WITH HIS. Then all depends on the issue of the act of destruction; but of course it is evident that, ceteris paribus, in this act we must be at a disadvantage in all respects because our views and our means had been directed in part upon other objects, which is not the case with the enemy. Two different objects of which one is not part, the other exclude each other, and therefore a force which may be applicable for the one may not serve for the other. If, therefore, one of two belligerents is determined to seek the great decision by arms, then he has a high probability of success, as soon as he is certain his opponent will not take that way, but follows a different object; and every one who sets before himself any such other aim only does so in a reasonable manner, provided he acts on the supposition that his adversary has as little intention as he has of resorting to the great decision by arms.

But what we have here said of another direction of views and forces relates only to other POSITIVE OBJECTS, which we may propose to ourselves in War, besides the destruction of the enemy's force, not by any means to the pure defensive, which may be adopted with a view thereby to exhaust the enemy's forces. In the pure defensive the positive object is wanting, and therefore, while on the defensive, our forces cannot at the same time be directed on other objects; they can only be employed to defeat the intentions of the enemy.

We have now to consider the opposite of the destruction of the enemy's armed force, that is to say, the preservation of our own. These two efforts always go together, as they mutually act and react on each other; they are integral parts of one and the same view, and we have only to ascertain what effect is produced when one or the other has the predominance. The endeavour to destroy the enemy's force has a positive object, and leads to positive results, of which the final aim is the conquest of the enemy. The preservation of our own forces has a negative object, leads therefore to the defeat of the enemy's intentions, that is to pure resistance, of which the final aim can be nothing more than to prolong the duration of the contest, so that the enemy shall exhaust himself in it.

The effort with a positive object calls into existence the act of destruction; the effort with the negative object awaits it.

How far this state of expectation should and may be carried we shall enter into more particularly in the theory of attack and defence, at the origin of which we again find ourselves. Here we shall content ourselves with saying that the awaiting must be no absolute endurance, and that in the action bound up with it the destruction of the enemy's armed force engaged in this conflict may be the aim just as well as anything else. It would therefore be a great error in the fundamental idea to suppose that the consequence of the negative course is that we are precluded from choosing the destruction of the enemy's military force as our object, and must prefer a bloodless solution. The advantage which the negative effort gives may certainly lead to that, but only at the risk of its not being the most advisable method, as that question is dependent on totally different conditions, resting not with ourselves but with our opponents. This other bloodless way cannot, therefore, be looked upon at all as the natural means of satisfying our great anxiety to spare our forces; on the contrary, when circumstances are not favourable, it would be the means of completely ruining them. Very many Generals have fallen into this error, and been ruined by it. The only necessary effect resulting from the superiority of the negative effort is the delay of the decision, so that the party acting takes refuge in that way, as it were, in the expectation of the decisive moment. The consequence of that is generally THE POSTPONEMENT OF THE ACTION as much as possible in time, and also in space, in so far as space is in connection with it. If the moment has arrived in which this can no longer be done without ruinous disadvantage, then the advantage of the negative must be considered as exhausted, and then comes forward unchanged the effort for the destruction of the enemy's force, which was kept back by a counterpoise, but never discarded.

We have seen, therefore, in the foregoing reflections, that there are many ways to the aim, that is, to the attainment of the political object; but that the only means is the combat, and that consequently everything is subject to a supreme law: which is the DECISION BY ARMS; that where this is really demanded by one, it is a redress which cannot be refused by the other; that, therefore, a belligerent who takes any other way must make sure that his opponent will not take this means of redress, or his cause may be lost in that supreme court; hence therefore the destruction of the enemy's armed force, amongst all the objects which can be pursued in War, appears always as the one which overrules all others.

What may be achieved by combinations of another kind in War we shall only learn in the sequel, and naturally only by degrees. We content ourselves here with acknowledging in general their possibility, as something pointing to the difference between the reality and the conception, and to the influence of particular circumstances. But we could not avoid showing at once that the BLOODY SOLUTION OF THE CRISIS, the effort for the destruction of the enemy's force, is the firstborn son of War. If when political objects are unimportant, motives weak, the excitement of forces small, a cautious commander tries in all kinds of ways, without great crises and bloody solutions, to twist himself skilfully into a peace through the characteristic weaknesses of his enemy in the field and in the Cabinet, we have no right to find fault with him, if the premises on which he acts are well founded and justified by success; still we must require him to remember that he only travels on forbidden tracks, where the God of War may surprise him; that he ought always to keep his eye on the enemy, in order that he may not have to defend himself with a dress rapier if the enemy takes up a sharp sword.

The consequences of the nature of War, how ends and means act in it, how in the modifications of reality it deviates sometimes more, sometimes less, from its strict original conception, fluctuating backwards and forwards, yet always remaining under that strict conception as under a supreme law: all this we must retain before us, and bear constantly in mind in the consideration of each of the succeeding subjects, if we would rightly comprehend their true relations and proper importance, and not become involved incessantly in the most glaring contradictions with the reality, and at last with our own selves.

CHAPTER III - THE GENIUS FOR WAR

EVERY special calling in life, if it is to be followed with success, requires peculiar qualifications of understanding and soul. Where these are of a high order, and manifest themselves by extraordinary achievements, the mind to which they belong is termed GENIUS.

We know very well that this word is used in many significations which are very different both in extent and nature, and that with many of these significations it is a very difficult task to define the essence of Genius; but as we neither profess to be philosopher nor grammarian, we must be allowed to keep to the meaning usual in ordinary language, and to understand by "genius" a very high mental capacity for certain employments.

We wish to stop for a moment over this faculty and dignity of the mind, in order to vindicate its title, and to explain more fully the meaning of the conception. But we shall not dwell on that (genius) which has obtained its title through a very great talent, on genius properly so called, that is a conception which has no defined limits. What we have to do is to bring under consideration every common tendency of the powers of the mind and soul towards the business of War, the whole of which common tendencies we may look upon as the ESSENCE OF MILITARY GENIUS. We say "common," for just therein consists military genius, that it is not one single quality bearing upon War, as, for instance, courage, while other qualities of mind and soul are wanting or have a direction which is unserviceable for War, but that it is AN HARMONIOUS ASSOCIATION OF POWERS, in which one or other may predominate, but none must be in opposition.

242

If every combatant required to be more or less endowed with military genius, then our armies would be very weak; for as it implies a peculiar bent of the intelligent powers, therefore it can only rarely be found where the mental powers of a people are called into requisition and trained in many different ways. The fewer the employments followed by a Nation, the more that of arms predominates, so much the more prevalent will military genius also be found. But this merely applies to its prevalence, by no means to its degree, for that depends on the general state of intellectual culture in the country. If we look at a wild, warlike race, then we find a warlike spirit in individuals much more common than in a civilised people; for in the former almost every warrior possesses it, whilst in the civilised whole, masses are only carried away by it from necessity, never by inclination. But amongst uncivilised people we never find a really great General, and very seldom what we can properly call a military genius, because that requires a development of the intelligent powers which cannot be found in an uncivilised state. That a civilised people may also have a warlike tendency and development is a matter of course; and the more this is general, the more frequently also will military spirit be found in individuals in their armies. Now as this coincides in such case with the higher degree of civilisation, therefore from such nations have issued forth the most brilliant military exploits, as the Romans and the French have exemplified. The greatest names in these and in all other nations that have been renowned in War belong strictly to epochs of higher culture.

From this we may infer how great a share the intelligent powers have in superior military genius. We shall now look more closely into this point.

War is the province of danger, and therefore courage above all things is the first quality of a warrior.

Courage is of two kinds: first, physical courage, or courage in presence of danger to the person; and next, moral courage, or courage before responsibility, whether it be before the judgment-seat of external authority, or of the inner power, the conscience. We only speak here of the first.

Courage before danger to the person, again, is of two kinds. First, it may be indifference to danger, whether proceeding from the organism of the individual, contempt of death, or habit: in any of these cases it is to be regarded as a permanent condition.

Secondly, courage may proceed from positive motives, such as personal pride, patriotism, enthusiasm of any kind. In this case courage is not so much a normal condition as an impulse.

We may conceive that the two kinds act differently. The first kind is more certain, because it has become a second nature, never forsakes the man; the second often leads him farther. In the first there is more of firmness, in the second, of boldness. The first leaves the judgment cooler, the second raises its power at times, but often bewilders it. The two combined make up the most perfect kind of courage.

War is the province of physical exertion and suffering. In order not to be completely overcome by them, a certain strength of body and mind is required, which, either natural or acquired, produces indifference to them. With these qualifications, under the guidance of simply a sound understanding, a man is at once a proper instrument for War; and these are the qualifications so generally to be met with amongst wild and half-civilised tribes. If we go further in the demands which War makes on it, then we find the powers of the understanding predominating. War is the province of uncertainty: three-fourths of those things upon which action in War must be calculated, are hidden more or less in the clouds of great uncertainty. Here, then, above all a fine and penetrating mind is called for, to search out the truth by the tact of its judgment.

An average intellect may, at one time, perhaps hit upon this truth by accident; an extraordinary courage, at another, may compensate for the want of this tact; but in the majority of cases the average result will always bring to light the deficient understanding.

War is the province of chance. In no sphere of human activity is such a margin to be left for this intruder, because none is so much in constant contact with him on all sides. He increases the uncertainty of every circumstance, and deranges the course of events.

From this uncertainty of all intelligence and suppositions, this continual interposition of chance, the actor in War constantly finds things different from his expectations; and this cannot fail to have an influence on his plans, or at least on the presumptions connected with these plans. If this influence is so great as to render the pre-determined plan completely nugatory, then, as a rule, a new one must be substituted in its place; but at the moment the necessary data are often wanting for this, because in the course of action circumstances press for immediate decision, and allow no time to look about for fresh data, often not enough for mature consideration.

But it more often happens that the correction of one premise, and the knowledge of chance events which have arisen, are not sufficient to overthrow our plans completely, but only suffice to produce hesitation. Our knowledge of circumstances has increased, but our uncertainty, instead of having diminished, has only increased. The reason of this is, that we do not gain all our experience at once, but by degrees; thus our determinations continue to be assailed incessantly by fresh experience; and the mind, if we may use the expression, must always be "under arms."

Now, if it is to get safely through this perpetual conflict with the unexpected, two qualities are indispensable: in the first place an intellect which, even in the midst of this intense obscurity, is not without some traces of inner light, which lead to the truth, and then the courage to follow this faint light. The first is figuratively expressed by the French phrase coup d'oeil. The other is resolution. As the battle is the feature in War to which attention was originally chiefly directed, and as time and space are important elements in it, more particularly when cavalry with their rapid decisions were the chief arm, the idea of rapid and correct decision related in the first instance to the estimation of these two elements, and to denote the idea an expression was adopted which actually only points to a correct judgment by eye. Many teachers of the Art of War then gave this limited signification as the definition of coup d'oeil. But it is undeniable that all able decisions formed in the moment of action soon came to be understood by the expression, as, for instance, the hitting upon the right point of attack, &c. It is, therefore, not only the physical, but more frequently the mental eye which is meant in coup d'oeil. Naturally, the expression, like the thing, is always more in its place in the field of tactics: still, it must not be wanting in strategy, inasmuch as in it rapid decisions are often necessary. If we strip this conception of that which the expression has given it of the over-figurative and restricted, then it amounts simply to the rapid discovery of a truth which to the ordinary mind is either not visible at all or only becomes so after long examination and reflection.

Resolution is an act of courage in single instances, and if it becomes a characteristic trait, it is a habit of the mind. But here we do not mean courage in face of bodily danger, but in face of responsibility, therefore, to a certain extent against moral danger. This has been often called courage d'esprit, on the ground that it springs from the understanding; nevertheless, it is no act of the understanding on that account; it is an act of feeling. Mere intelligence is still not courage, for we often see the cleverest people devoid of resolution. The mind must, therefore, first awaken the feeling of courage, and then be guided and supported by it, because in momentary emergencies the man is swayed more by his feelings than his thoughts.

We have assigned to resolution the office of removing the torments of doubt, and the dangers of delay, when there are no sufficient motives for guidance. Through the unscrupulous use of language which is prevalent, this term is often applied to the mere propensity to daring, to bravery, boldness, or temerity. But, when there are *sufficient motives* in the man, let them be objective or subjective, true or false, we have no right to speak of his resolution; for, when we do so, we put ourselves in his place, and we throw into the scale doubts which did not exist with him.

Here there is no question of anything but of strength and weakness. We are not pedantic enough to dispute with the use of language about this little misapplication, our observation is only intended to remove wrong objections.

This resolution now, which overcomes the state of doubting, can only be called forth by the intellect, and, in fact, by a peculiar tendency of the same. We maintain that the mere union of a superior understanding and the necessary feelings are not sufficient to make up resolution. There are persons who possess the keenest perception for the most difficult problems, who are also not fearful of responsibility, and yet in cases of difficulty cannot come to a resolution. Their courage and their sagacity operate independently of each other, do not give each other a hand, and on that account do not produce resolution as a result. The forerunner of resolution is an act of the mind making evident the necessity of venturing, and thus influencing the will. This quite peculiar direction of the mind, which conquers every other fear in man by the fear of wavering or doubting, is what makes up resolution in strong minds; therefore, in our opinion, men who have little intelligence can never be resolute. They may act without hesitation under perplexing circumstances, but then they act without reflection. Now, of course, when a man acts without reflection he cannot be at variance with himself by doubts, and such a mode of action may now and then lead to the right point; but we say now as before, it is the average result which indicates the existence of military genius. Should our assertion appear extraordinary to any one, because he knows many a resolute hussar officer who is no deep thinker, we must remind him that the question here is about a peculiar direction of the mind, and not about great thinking powers.

We believe, therefore, that resolution is indebted to a special direction of the mind for its existence, a direction which belongs to a strong head rather than to a brilliant one. In corroboration of this genealogy of resolution we may add that there have been many instances of men who have shown the greatest resolution in an inferior rank, and have lost it in a higher position. While, on the one hand, they are obliged to resolve, on the other they see the dangers of a wrong decision, and as they are surrounded with things new to them, their understanding loses its original force, and they become only the more timid the more they become aware of the danger of the irresolution into which they have fallen, and the more they have formerly been in the habit of acting on the spur of the moment.

From the coup d'oeil and resolution we are naturally to speak of its kindred quality, PRESENCE OF MIND, which in a region of the unexpected like War must act a great part, for it is indeed nothing but a great conquest over the unexpected. As we admire presence of mind in a pithy answer to anything said unexpectedly, so we admire it in a ready expedient on sudden danger. Neither the answer nor the expedient need be in themselves extraordinary, if they only hit the point; for that which as the result of mature reflection would be nothing unusual, therefore insignificant in its impression on us, may as an instantaneous act of the mind produce a pleasing impression. The expression "presence of mind" certainly denotes very fitly the readiness and rapidity of the help rendered by the mind.

Whether this noble quality of a man is to be ascribed more to the peculiarity of his mind or to the equanimity of his feelings, depends on the nature of the case, although neither of the two can be entirely wanting. A telling repartee bespeaks rather a ready wit, a ready expedient on sudden danger implies more particularly a well-balanced mind.

If we take a general view of the four elements composing the atmosphere in which War moves, of DANGER, PHYSICAL EFFORT, UNCERTAINTY, and CHANCE, it is easy to conceive that a great force of mind and understanding is requisite to be able to make way with safety and success amongst such opposing elements, a force which, according to the different modifications arising out of circumstances, we find termed by military writers and annalists as ENERGY, FIRMNESS, STAUNCHNESS, STRENGTH OF MIND AND CHARACTER. All these manifestations of the heroic nature might be regarded as one and the same power of volition, modified according to circumstances; but nearly related as these things are to each other, still they are not one and the same, and it is desirable for us to distinguish here a little more closely at least the action of the powers of the soul in relation to them.

In the first place, to make the conception clear, it is essential to observe that the weight, burden, resistance, or whatever it may be called, by which that force of the soul in the General is brought to light, is only in a very small measure the enemy's activity, the enemy's resistance, the enemy's action directly. The enemy's activity only affects the General directly in the first place in relation to his person, without disturbing his action as Commander. If the enemy, instead of two hours, resists for four, the Commander instead of two hours is four hours in danger; this is a quantity which plainly diminishes the higher the rank of the Commander. What is it for one in the post of Commander-in-Chief? It is nothing.

Secondly, although the opposition offered by the enemy has a direct effect on the Commander through the loss of means arising from prolonged resistance, and the responsibility connected with that loss, and his force of will is first tested and called forth by these anxious considerations, still we maintain that this is not the heaviest burden by far which he has to bear, because he has only himself to settle with. All the other effects of the enemy's resistance act directly upon the combatants under his command, and through them react upon him.

As long as his men full of good courage fight with zeal and spirit, it is seldom necessary for the Chief to show great energy of purpose in the pursuit of his object. But as soon as difficulties arise—and that must always happen when great results are at stake—then things no longer move on of themselves like a well-oiled machine, the machine itself then begins to offer resistance, and to overcome this the Commander must have a great force of will. By this resistance we must not exactly suppose disobedience and murmurs, although these are frequent enough with particular individuals; it is the whole feeling of the dissolution of all physical and moral power, it is the heartrending sight of the bloody sacrifice which the Commander has to contend with in himself, and then in all others who directly or indirectly transfer to him their impressions, feelings, anxieties, and desires. As the forces in one individual after another become prostrated, and can no longer be excited and supported by an effort of his own will, the whole inertia of the mass gradually rests its weight on the Will of the Commander: by the spark in his breast, by the light of his spirit, the spark of purpose, the light of hope, must be kindled afresh in others: in so far only as he is equal to this, he stands above the masses and continues to be their master; whenever that influence ceases, and his own spirit is no longer strong enough to revive the spirit of all others, the masses drawing him down with them sink into the lower region of animal nature, which shrinks from danger and knows not shame. These are the weights which the courage and intelligent faculties of the military Commander have to overcome if he is to make his name illustrious. They increase with the masses, and therefore, if the forces in question are to continue equal to the burden, they must rise in proportion to the height of the station.

Energy in action expresses the strength of the motive through which the action is excited, let the motive have its origin in a conviction of the understanding, or in an impulse. But the latter can hardly ever be wanting where great force is to show itself.

Of all the noble feelings which fill the human heart in the exciting tumult of battle, none, we must admit, are so powerful and constant as the soul's thirst for honour and renown, which the German language treats so unfairly and tends to depreciate by the unworthy associations in the words Ehrgeiz (greed of honour) and Ruhmsucht (hankering after glory). No doubt it is just in War that the abuse of these proud aspirations of the soul must bring upon the human race the most shocking outrages, but by their origin they are certainly to be counted amongst the noblest feelings which belong to human nature, and in War they are the vivifying principle which gives the enormous body a spirit. Although other feelings may be more general in their influence, and many of them—such as love of country, fanaticism, revenge, enthusiasm of every kind—may seem to stand higher, the thirst for honour and renown still remains indispensable. Those other feelings may rouse the great masses in general, and excite them more powerfully, but they do not give the Leader a desire to will more than others, which is an essential requisite in his position if he is to make himself distinguished in it. They do not, like a thirst for honour, make the military act specially the property of the Leader, which he strives to turn to the best account; where he ploughs with toil, sows with care, that he may reap plentifully. It is through these aspirations we have been speaking of in Commanders, from the highest to the lowest, this sort of energy, this spirit of emulation, these incentives, that the action of armies is chiefly animated and made successful. And now as to that which specially concerns the head of all, we ask, Has there ever been a great Commander destitute of the love of honour, or is such a character even conceivable?

FIRMNESS denotes the resistance of the will in relation to the force of a single blow, STAUNCHNESS in relation to a continuance of blows. Close as is the analogy between the two, and often as the one is used in place of the other, still there is a notable difference between them which cannot be mistaken, inasmuch as firmness against a single powerful impression may have its root in the mere strength of a feeling, but staunchness must be supported rather by the understanding, for the greater the duration of an action the more systematic deliberation is connected with it, and from this staunchness partly derives its power.

If we now turn to STRENGTH OF MIND OR SOUL, then the first question is, What are we to understand thereby?

Plainly it is not vehement expressions of feeling, nor easily excited passions, for that would be contrary to all the usage of language, but the power of listening to reason in the midst of the most intense excitement, in the storm of the most violent passions. Should this power depend on strength of understanding alone? We doubt it. The fact that there are men of the greatest intellect who cannot command themselves certainly proves nothing to the contrary, for we might say that it perhaps requires an understanding of a powerful rather than of a comprehensive nature; but we believe we shall be nearer the truth if we assume that the power of submitting oneself to the control of the understanding, even in moments of the most violent excitement of the feelings, that power which we call SELF-COMMAND, has its root in the heart itself. It is, in point of fact, another feeling, which in strong minds balances the excited passions without destroying them; and it is only through this equilibrium that the mastery of the understanding is secured. This counterpoise is nothing but a sense of the dignity of man, that noblest pride, that deeply-seated desire of the soul always to act as a being endued with understanding and reason. We may therefore say that a strong mind is one which does not lose its balance even under the most violent excitement.

If we cast a glance at the variety to be observed in the human character in respect to feeling, we find, first, some people who have very little excitability, who are called phlegmatic or indolent.

Secondly, some very excitable, but whose feelings still never overstep certain limits, and who are therefore known as men full of feeling, but sober-minded.

Thirdly, those who are very easily roused, whose feelings blaze up quickly and violently like gunpowder, but do not last.

Fourthly, and lastly, those who cannot be moved by slight causes, and who generally are not to be roused suddenly, but only gradually; but whose feelings become very powerful and are much more lasting. These are men with strong passions, lying deep and latent.

This difference of character lies probably close on the confines of the physical powers which move the human organism, and belongs to that amphibious organisation which we call the nervous system, which appears to be partly material, partly spiritual. With our weak philosophy, we shall not proceed further in this mysterious field. But it is important for us to spend a moment over the effects which these different natures have on, action in War, and to see how far a great strength of mind is to be expected from them.

Indolent men cannot easily be thrown out of their equanimity, but we cannot certainly say there is strength of mind where there is a want of all manifestation of power.

At the same time, it is not to be denied that such men have a certain peculiar aptitude for War, on account of their constant equanimity. They often want the positive motive to action, impulse, and consequently activity, but they are not apt to throw things into disorder.

The peculiarity of the second class is that they are easily excited to act on trifling grounds, but in great matters they are easily overwhelmed. Men of this kind show great activity in helping an unfortunate individual, but by the distress of a whole Nation they are only inclined to despond, not roused to action.

Such people are not deficient in either activity or equanimity in War; but they will never accomplish anything great unless a great intellectual force furnishes the motive, and it is very seldom that a strong, independent mind is combined with such a character.

Excitable, inflammable feelings are in themselves little suited for practical life, and therefore they are not very fit for War. They have certainly the advantage of strong impulses, but that cannot long sustain them. At the same time, if the excitability in such men takes the direction of courage, or a sense of honour, they may often be very useful in inferior positions in War, because the action in War over which commanders in inferior positions have control is generally of shorter duration. Here one courageous resolution, one effervescence of the forces of the soul, will often suffice. A brave attack, a soul-stirring hurrah, is the work of a few moments, whilst a brave contest on the battle-field is the work of a day, and a campaign the work of a year.

Owing to the rapid movement of their feelings, it is doubly difficult for men of this description to preserve equilibrium of the mind; therefore they frequently lose head, and that is the worst phase in their nature as respects the conduct of War. But it would be contrary to experience to maintain that very excitable spirits can never preserve a steady equilibrium—that is to say, that they cannot do so even under the strongest excitement. Why should they not have the sentiment of self-respect, for, as a rule, they are men of a noble nature? This feeling is seldom wanting in them, but it has not time to produce an effect. After an outburst they suffer most from a feeling of inward humiliation. If through education, self-observance, and experience of life, they have learned, sooner or later, the means of being on their guard, so that at the moment of powerful excitement they are conscious betimes of the counteracting force within their own breasts, then even such men may have great strength of mind.

Lastly, those who are difficult to move, but on that account susceptible of very deep feelings, men who stand in the same relation to the preceding as red heat to a flame, are the best adapted by means of their Titanic strength to roll away the enormous masses by which we may figuratively represent the difficulties which beset command in War. The effect of their feelings is like the movement of a great body, slower, but more irresistible.

Although such men are not so likely to be suddenly surprised by their feelings and carried away so as to be afterwards ashamed of themselves, like the preceding, still it would be contrary to experience to believe that they can never lose their equanimity, or be overcome by blind passion; on the contrary, this must always happen whenever the noble pride of self-control is wanting, or as often as it has not sufficient weight. We see examples of this most frequently in men of noble minds belonging to savage nations, where the low degree of mental cultivation favours always the dominance of the passions. But even amongst the most civilised classes in civilised States, life is full of examples of this kind—of men carried away by the violence of their passions, like the poacher of old chained to the stag in the forest.

We therefore say once more a strong mind is not one that is merely susceptible of strong excitement, but one which can maintain its serenity under the most powerful excitement, so that, in spite of the storm in the breast, the perception and judgment can act with perfect freedom, like the needle of the compass in the storm-tossed ship.

By the term *strength of character*, or simply *character*, is denoted tenacity of conviction, let it be the result of our own or of others' views, and whether they are principles, opinions, momentary inspirations, or any kind of emanations of the understanding; but this kind of firmness certainly cannot manifest itself if the views themselves are subject to frequent change. This frequent change need not be the consequence of external influences; it may proceed from the continuous activity of our own mind, in which case it indicates a characteristic unsteadiness of mind. Evidently we should not say of a man who changes his views every moment, however much the motives of change may originate with himself, that he has character. Only those men, therefore, can be said to have this quality whose conviction is very constant, either because it is deeply rooted and clear in itself, little liable to alteration, or because, as in the case of indolent men, there is a want of mental activity, and therefore a want of motives to change; or lastly, because an explicit act of the will, derived from an imperative maxim of the understanding, refuses any change of opinion up to a certain point.

Now in War, owing to the many and powerful impressions to which the mind is exposed, and in the uncertainty of all knowledge and of all science, more things occur to distract a man from the road he has entered upon, to make him doubt himself and others, than in any other human activity.

The harrowing sight of danger and suffering easily leads to the feelings gaining ascendency over the conviction of the understanding; and in the twilight which surrounds everything a deep clear view is so difficult that a change of opinion is more conceivable and more pardonable. It is, at all times, only conjecture or guesses at truth which we have to act upon. This is why differences of opinion are nowhere so great as in War, and the stream of impressions acting counter to one's own convictions never ceases to flow. Even the greatest impassibility of mind is hardly proof against them, because the impressions are powerful in their nature, and always act at the same time upon the feelings.

When the discernment is clear and deep, none but general principles and views of action from a high standpoint can be the result; and on these principles the opinion in each particular case immediately under consideration lies, as it were, at anchor. But to keep to these results of bygone reflection, in opposition to the stream of opinions and phenomena which the present brings with it, is just the difficulty. Between the particular case and the principle there is often a wide space which cannot always be traversed on a visible chain of conclusions, and where a certain faith in self is necessary and a certain amount of scepticism is serviceable. Here often nothing else will help us but an imperative maxim which, independent of reflection, at once controls it: that maxim is, in all doubtful cases to adhere to the first opinion, and not to give it up until a clear conviction forces us to do so. We must firmly believe in the superior authority of well-tried maxims, and under the dazzling influence of momentary events not forget that their value is of an inferior stamp. By this preference which in doubtful cases we give to first convictions, by adherence to the same our actions acquire that stability and consistency which make up what is called character.

It is easy to see how essential a well-balanced mind is to strength of character; therefore men of strong minds generally have a great deal of character.

Force of character leads us to a spurious variety of it—OBSTINACY.

It is often very difficult in concrete cases to say where the one ends and the other begins; on the other hand, it does not seem difficult to determine the difference in idea.

Obstinacy is no fault of the understanding; we use the term as denoting a resistance against our better judgment, and it would be inconsistent to charge that to the understanding, as the understanding is the power of judgment. Obstinacy is A FAULT OF THE FEELINGS or heart. This inflexibility of will, this impatience of contradiction, have their origin only in a particular kind of egotism, which sets above every other pleasure that of governing both self and others by its own mind alone. We should call it a kind of vanity, were it not decidedly something better. Vanity is satisfied with mere show, but obstinacy rests upon the enjoyment of the thing.

We say, therefore, force of character degenerates into obstinacy whenever the resistance to opposing judgments proceeds not from better convictions or a reliance upon a trustworthy maxim, but from a feeling of opposition. If this definition, as we have already admitted, is of little assistance practically, still it will prevent obstinacy from being considered merely force of character intensified, whilst it is something essentially different—something which certainly lies close to it and is cognate to it, but is at the same time so little an intensification of it that there are very obstinate men who from want of understanding have very little force of character.

Having in these high attributes of a great military Commander made ourselves acquainted with those qualities in which heart and head co-operate, we now come to a speciality of military activity which perhaps may be looked upon as the most marked if it is not the most important, and which only makes a demand on the power of the mind without regard to the forces of feelings. It is the connection which exists between War and country or ground.

This connection is, in the first place, a permanent condition of War, for it is impossible to imagine our organised Armies effecting any operation otherwise than in some given space; it is, secondly, of the most decisive importance, because it modifies, at times completely alters, the action of all forces; thirdly, while on the one hand it often concerns the most minute features of locality, on the other it may apply to immense tracts of country.

In this manner a great peculiarity is given to the effect of this connection of War with country and ground. If we think of other occupations of man which have a relation to these objects, on horticulture, agriculture, on building houses and hydraulic works, on mining, on the chase, and forestry, they are all confined within very limited spaces which may be soon explored with sufficient exactness. But the Commander in War must commit the business he has in hand to a corresponding space which his eye cannot survey, which the keenest zeal cannot always explore, and with which, owing to the constant changes taking place, he can also seldom become properly acquainted. Certainly the enemy generally is in the same situation; still, in the first place, the difficulty, although common to both, is not the less a difficulty, and he who by talent and practice overcomes it will have a great advantage on his side; secondly, this equality of the difficulty on both sides is merely an abstract supposition which is rarely realised in the particular case, as one of the two opponents (the defensive) usually knows much more of the locality than his adversary.

This very peculiar difficulty must be overcome by a natural mental gift of a special kind which is known by the—too restricted—term of Orisinn sense of locality. It is the power of quickly forming a correct geometrical idea of any portion of country, and consequently of being able to find one's place in it exactly at any time. This is plainly an act of the imagination. The perception no doubt is formed partly by means of the physical eye, partly by the mind, which fills up what is wanting with ideas derived from knowledge and experience, and out of the fragments visible to the physical eye forms a whole; but that this whole should present itself vividly to the reason, should become a picture, a mentally drawn map, that this picture should be fixed, that the details should never again separate themselves—all that can only be effected by the mental faculty which we call imagination. If some great poet or painter should feel hurt that we require from his goddess such an office; if he shrugs his shoulders at the notion that a sharp gamekeeper must necessarily excel in imagination, we readily grant that we only speak here of imagination in a limited sense, of its service in a really menial capacity. But, however slight this service, still it must be the work of that natural gift, for if that gift is wanting, it would be difficult to imagine things plainly in all the completeness of the visible. That a good memory is a great assistance we freely allow, but whether memory is to be considered as an independent faculty of the mind in this case, or whether it is just that power of imagination which here fixes these things better on the memory, we leave undecided, as in many respects it seems difficult upon the whole to conceive these two mental powers apart from each other.

That practice and mental acuteness have much to do with it is not to be denied. Puysegur, the celebrated Quartermaster-General of the famous Luxemburg, used to say that he had very little confidence in himself in this respect at first, because if he had to fetch the parole from a distance he always lost his way.

It is natural that scope for the exercise of this talent should increase along with rank. If the hussar and rifleman in command of a patrol must know well all the highways and byways, and if for that a few marks, a few limited powers of observation, are sufficient, the Chief of an Army must make himself familiar with the general geographical features of a province and of a country; must always have vividly before his eyes the direction of the roads, rivers, and hills, without at the same time being able to dispense with the narrower "sense of locality" Orisinn. No doubt, information of various kinds as to objects in general, maps, books, memoirs, and for details the assistance of his Staff, are a great help to him; but it is nevertheless certain that if he has himself a talent for forming an ideal picture of a country quickly and distinctly, it lends to his action an easier and firmer step, saves him from a certain mental helplessness, and makes him less dependent on others.

If this talent then is to be ascribed to imagination, it is also almost the only service which military activity requires from that erratic goddess, whose influence is more hurtful than useful in other respects.

We think we have now passed in review those manifestations of the powers of mind and soul which military activity requires from human nature. Everywhere intellect appears as an essential co-operative force; and thus we can understand how the work of War, although so plain and simple in its effects, can never be conducted with distinguished success by people without distinguished powers of the understanding.

When we have reached this view, then we need no longer look upon such a natural idea as the turning an enemy's position, which has been done a thousand times, and a hundred other similar conceptions, as the result of a great effort of genius.

Certainly one is accustomed to regard the plain honest soldier as the very opposite of the man of reflection, full of inventions and ideas, or of the brilliant spirit shining in the ornaments of refined education of every kind. This antithesis is also by no means devoid of truth; but it does not show that the efficiency of the soldier consists only in his courage, and that there is no particular energy and capacity of the brain required in addition to make a man merely what is called a true soldier. We must again repeat that there is nothing more common than to hear of men losing their energy on being raised to a higher position, to which they do not feel themselves equal; but we must also remind our readers that we are speaking of pre-eminent services, of such as give renown in the branch of activity to which they belong. Each grade of command in War therefore forms its own stratum of requisite capacity of fame and honour.

An immense space lies between a General—that is, one at the head of a whole War, or of a theatre of War—and his Second in Command, for the simple reason that the latter is in more immediate subordination to a superior authority and supervision, consequently is restricted to a more limited sphere of independent thought. This is why common opinion sees no room for the exercise of high talent except in high places, and looks upon an ordinary capacity as sufficient for all beneath: this is why people are rather inclined to look upon a subordinate General grown grey in the service, and in whom constant discharge of routine duties has produced a decided poverty of mind, as a man of failing intellect, and, with all respect for his bravery, to laugh at his simplicity. It is not our object to gain for these brave men a better lot—that would contribute nothing to their efficiency, and little to their happiness; we only wish to represent things as they are, and to expose the error of believing that a mere bravo without intellect can make himself distinguished in War.

As we consider distinguished talents requisite for those who are to attain distinction, even in inferior positions, it naturally follows that we think highly of those who fill with renown the place of Second in Command of an Army; and their seeming simplicity of character as compared with a polyhistor, with ready men of business, or with councillors of state, must not lead us astray as to the superior nature of their intellectual activity. It happens sometimes that men import the fame gained in an inferior position into a higher one, without in reality deserving it in the new position; and then if they are not much employed, and therefore not much exposed to the risk of showing their weak points, the judgment does not distinguish very exactly what degree of fame is really due to them; and thus such men are often the occasion of too low an estimate being formed of the characteristics required to shine in certain situations.

For each station, from the lowest upwards, to render distinguished services in War, there must be a particular genius. But the title of genius, history and the judgment of posterity only confer, in general, on those minds which have shone in the highest rank, that of Commanders-in-Chief. The reason is that here, in point of fact, the demand on the reasoning and intellectual powers generally is much greater.

To conduct a whole War, or its great acts, which we call campaigns, to a successful termination, there must be an intimate knowledge of State policy in its higher relations. The conduct of the War and the policy of the State here coincide, and the General becomes at the same time the Statesman.

We do not give Charles XII. the name of a great genius, because he could not make the power of his sword subservient to a higher judgment and philosophy—could not attain by it to a glorious object. We do not give that title to Henry IV. (of France), because he did not live long enough to set at rest the relations of different States by his military activity, and to occupy himself in that higher field where noble feelings and a chivalrous disposition have less to do in mastering the enemy than in overcoming internal dissension.

In order that the reader may appreciate all that must be comprehended and judged of correctly at a glance by a General, we refer to the first chapter. We say the General becomes a Statesman, but he must not cease to be the General. He takes into view all the relations of the State on the one hand; on the other, he must know exactly what he can do with the means at his disposal.

As the diversity, and undefined limits, of all the circumstances bring a great number of factors into consideration in War, as the most of these factors can only be estimated according to probability, therefore, if the Chief of an Army does not bring to bear upon them a mind with an intuitive perception of the truth, a confusion of ideas and views must take place, in the midst of which the judgment will become bewildered. In this sense, Buonaparte was right when he said that many of the questions which come before a General for decision would make problems for a mathematical calculation not unworthy of the powers of Newton or Euler.

What is here required from the higher powers of the mind is a sense of unity, and a judgment raised to such a compass as to give the mind an extraordinary faculty of vision which in its range allays and sets aside a thousand dim notions which an ordinary understanding could only bring to light with great effort, and over which it would exhaust itself. But this higher activity of the mind, this glance of genius, would still not become matter of history if the qualities of temperament and character of which we have treated did not give it their support.

Truth alone is but a weak motive of action with men, and hence there is always a great difference between knowing and action, between science and art. The man receives the strongest impulse to action through the feelings, and the most powerful succour, if we may use the expression, through those faculties of heart and mind which we have considered under the terms of resolution, firmness, perseverance, and force of character.

If, however, this elevated condition of heart and mind in the General did not manifest itself in the general effects resulting from it, and could only be accepted on trust and faith, then it would rarely become matter of history.

All that becomes known of the course of events in War is usually very simple, and has a great sameness in appearance; no one on the mere relation of such events perceives the difficulties connected with them which had to be overcome. It is only now and again, in the memoirs of Generals or of those in their confidence, or by reason of some special historical inquiry directed to a particular circumstance, that a portion of the many threads composing the whole web is brought to light. The reflections, mental doubts, and conflicts which precede the execution of great acts are purposely concealed because they affect political interests, or the recollection of them is accidentally lost because they have been looked upon as mere scaffolding which had to be removed on the completion of the building.

If, now, in conclusion, without venturing upon a closer definition of the higher powers of the soul, we should admit a distinction in the intelligent faculties themselves according to the common ideas established by language, and ask ourselves what kind of mind comes closest to military genius, then a look at the subject as well as at experience will tell us that searching rather than inventive minds, comprehensive minds rather than such as have a special bent, cool rather than fiery heads, are those to which in time of War we should prefer to trust the welfare of our women and children, the honour and the safety of our fatherland.

CHAPTER IV - OF DANGER IN WAR

USUALLY before we have learnt what danger really is, we form an idea of it which is rather attractive than repulsive. In the intoxication of enthusiasm, to fall upon the enemy at the charge—who cares then about bullets and men falling? To throw oneself, blinded by excitement for a moment, against cold death, uncertain whether we or another shall escape him, and all this close to the golden gate of victory, close to the rich fruit which ambition thirsts for—can this be difficult? It will not be difficult, and still less will it appear so. But such moments, which, however, are not the work of a single pulse-beat, as is supposed, but rather like doctors' draughts, must be taken diluted and spoilt by mixture with time—such moments, we say, are but few.

Let us accompany the novice to the battle-field. As we approach, the thunder of the cannon becoming plainer and plainer is soon followed by the howling of shot, which attracts the attention of the inexperienced. Balls begin to strike the ground close to us, before and behind. We hasten to the hill where stands the General and his numerous Staff. Here the close striking of the cannon balls and the bursting of shells is so frequent that the seriousness of life makes itself visible through the youthful picture of imagination. Suddenly some one known to us falls—a shell strikes amongst the crowd and causes some involuntary movements—we begin to feel that we are no longer perfectly at ease and collected; even the bravest is at least to some degree confused. Now, a step farther into the battle which is raging before us like a scene in a theatre, we get to the nearest General of Division; here ball follows ball, and the noise of our own guns increases the confusion. From the General of Division to the Brigadier. He, a man of acknowledged bravery, keeps carefully behind a rising ground, a house, or a tree—a sure sign of increasing danger. Grape rattles on the roofs of the houses and in the fields; cannon balls howl over us, and plough the air in all directions, and soon there is a frequent whistling of musket balls. A step farther towards the troops, to that sturdy infantry which for hours has maintained its firmness under this heavy fire; here the air is filled with the hissing of balls which announce their proximity by a short sharp noise as they pass within an inch of the ear, the head, or the breast.

To add to all this, compassion strikes the beating heart with pity at the sight of the maimed and fallen. The young soldier cannot reach any of these different strata of danger without feeling that the light of reason does not move here in the same medium, that it is not refracted in the same manner as in speculative contemplation. Indeed, he must be a very extraordinary man who, under these impressions for the first time, does not lose the power of making any instantaneous decisions. It is true that habit soon blunts such impressions; in half in hour we begin to be more or less indifferent to all that is going on around us: but an ordinary character never attains to complete coolness and the natural elasticity of mind; and so we perceive that here again ordinary qualities will not suffice—a thing which gains truth, the wider the sphere of activity which is to be filled. Enthusiastic, stoical, natural bravery, great ambition, or also long familiarity with danger—much of all this there must be if all the effects produced in this resistant medium are not to fall far short of that which in the student's chamber may appear only the ordinary standard.

Danger in War belongs to its friction; a correct idea of its influence is necessary for truth of perception, and therefore it is brought under notice here.

CHAPTER V - OF BODILY EXERTION IN WAR

IF no one were allowed to pass an opinion on the events of War, except at a moment when he is benumbed by frost, sinking from heat and thirst, or dying with hunger and fatigue, we should certainly have fewer judgments correct *objectively; but they would be so, *subjectively*, at least; that is, they would contain in themselves the exact relation between the person giving the judgment and the object. We can perceive this by observing how modestly subdued, even spiritless and desponding, is the opinion passed upon the results of untoward events by those who have been eye-witnesses, but especially if they have been parties concerned. This is, according to our view, a criterion of the influence which bodily fatigue exercises, and of the allowance to be made for it in matters of opinion.

Amongst the many things in War for which no tariff can be fixed, bodily effort may be specially reckoned. Provided there is no waste, it is a coefficient of all the forces, and no one can tell exactly to what extent it may be carried. But what is remarkable is, that just as only a strong arm enables the archer to stretch the bowstring to the utmost extent, so also in War it is only by means of a great directing spirit that we can expect the full power latent in the troops to be developed. For it is one thing if an Army, in consequence of great misfortunes, surrounded with danger, falls all to pieces like a wall that has been thrown down, and can only find safety in the utmost exertion of its bodily strength; it is another thing entirely when a victorious Army, drawn on by proud feelings only, is conducted at the will of its Chief. The same effort which in the one case might at most excite our pity must in the other call forth our admiration, because it is much more difficult to sustain.

By this comes to light for the inexperienced eye one of those things which put fetters in the dark, as it were, on the action of the mind, and wear out in secret the powers of the soul.

Although here the question is strictly only respecting the extreme effort required by a Commander from his Army, by a leader from his followers, therefore of the spirit to demand it and of the art of getting it, still the personal physical exertion of Generals and of the Chief Commander must not be overlooked. Having brought the analysis of War conscientiously up to this point, we could not but take account also of the weight of this small remaining residue.

We have spoken here of bodily effort, chiefly because, like danger, it belongs to the fundamental causes of friction, and because its indefinite quantity makes it like an elastic body, the friction of which is well known to be difficult to calculate.

To check the abuse of these considerations, of such a survey of things which aggravate the difficulties of War, nature has given our judgment a guide in our sensibilities, just as an individual cannot with advantage refer to his personal deficiencies if he is insulted and ill-treated, but may well do so if he has successfully repelled the affront, or has fully revenged it, so no Commander or Army will lessen the impression of a disgraceful defeat by depicting the danger, the distress, the exertions, things which would immensely enhance the glory of a victory. Thus our feeling, which after all is only a higher kind of judgment, forbids us to do what seems an act of justice to which our judgment would be inclined.

CHAPTER VI - INFORMATION IN WAR

By the word "information" we denote all the knowledge which we have of the enemy and his country; therefore, in fact, the foundation of all our ideas and actions. Let us just consider the nature of this foundation, its want of trustworthiness, its changefulness, and we shall soon feel what a dangerous edifice War is, how easily it may fall to pieces and bury us in its ruins. For although it is a maxim in all books that we should trust only certain information, that we must be always suspicious, that is only a miserable book comfort, belonging to that description of knowledge in which writers of systems and compendiums take refuge for want of anything better to say.

Great part of the information obtained in War is contradictory, a still greater part is false, and by far the greatest part is of a doubtful character. What is required of an officer is a certain power of discrimination, which only knowledge of men and things and good judgment can give. The law of probability must be his guide. This is not a trifling difficulty even in respect of the first plans, which can be formed in the chamber outside the real sphere of War, but it is enormously increased when in the thick of War itself one report follows hard upon the heels of another; it is then fortunate if these reports in contradicting each other show a certain balance of probability, and thus themselves call forth a scrutiny. It is much worse for the inexperienced when accident does not render him this service, but one report supports another, confirms it, magnifies it, finishes off the picture with fresh touches of colour, until necessity in urgent haste forces from us a resolution which will soon be discovered to be folly, all those reports having been lies, exaggerations, errors, &c. &c. In a few words, most reports are false, and the timidity of men acts as a multiplier of lies and untruths. As a general rule, every one is more inclined to lend credence to the bad than the good. Every one is inclined to magnify the bad in some measure, and although the alarms which are thus propagated like the waves of the sea subside into themselves, still, like them, without any apparent cause they rise again. Firm in reliance on his own better convictions, the Chief must stand like a rock against which the sea breaks its fury in vain. The role is not easy; he who is not by nature of a buoyant disposition, or trained by experience in War, and matured in judgment, may let it be his rule to do violence to his own natural conviction by inclining from the side of fear to that of hope; only by that means will he be able to preserve his balance. This difficulty of seeing things correctly, which is one of the greatest sources of friction in War, makes things appear quite different from what was expected. The impression of the senses is stronger than the force of the ideas resulting from methodical reflection, and this goes so far that no important undertaking was ever yet carried out without the Commander having to subdue new doubts in himself at the time of commencing the execution of his work. Ordinary men who follow the suggestions of others become, therefore, generally undecided on the spot; they think that they have found circumstances different from what they had expected, and this view gains strength by their again yielding to the suggestions of others. But even the man who has made his own plans, when he comes to see things with his own eyes will often think he has done wrong. Firm reliance on self must make him proof against the seeming pressure of the moment; his first conviction will in the end prove true, when the foreground scenery which fate has pushed on to the stage of War, with its accompaniments of terrific objects, is drawn aside and the horizon extended. This is one of the great chasms which separate CONCEPTION from EXECUTION.

CHAPTER VII - FRICTION IN WAR

As long as we have no personal knowledge of War, we cannot conceive where those difficulties lie of which so much is said, and what that genius and those extraordinary mental powers required in a General have really to do. All appears so simple, all the requisite branches of knowledge appear so plain, all the combinations so unimportant, that in comparison with them the easiest problem in higher mathematics impresses us with a certain scientific dignity. But if we have seen War, all becomes intelligible; and still, after all, it is extremely difficult to describe what it is which brings about this change, to specify this invisible and completely efficient factor.

Everything is very simple in War, but the simplest thing is difficult. These difficulties accumulate and produce a friction which no man can imagine exactly who has not seen War, Suppose now a traveller, who towards evening expects to accomplish the two stages at the end of his day's journey, four or five leagues, with posthorses, on the high road—it is nothing. He arrives now at the last station but one, finds no horses, or very bad ones; then a hilly country, bad roads; it is a dark night, and he is glad when, after a great deal of trouble, he reaches the next station, and finds there some miserable accommodation. So in War, through the influence of an infinity of petty circumstances, which cannot properly be described on paper, things disappoint us, and we fall short of the mark. A powerful iron will overcomes this friction; it crushes the obstacles, but certainly the machine along with them. We shall often meet with this result. Like an obelisk towards which the principal streets of a town converge, the strong will of a proud spirit stands prominent and commanding in the middle of the Art of War.

Friction is the only conception which in a general way corresponds to that which distinguishes real War from War on paper. The military machine, the Army and all belonging to it, is in fact simple, and appears on this account easy to manage. But let us reflect that no part of it is in one piece, that it is composed entirely of individuals, each of which keeps up its own friction in all directions. Theoretically all sounds very well: the commander of a battalion is responsible for the execution of the order given; and as the battalion by its discipline is glued together into one piece, and the chief must be a man of acknowledged zeal, the beam turns on an iron pin with little friction. But it is not so in reality, and all that is exaggerated and false in such a conception manifests itself at once in War. The battalion always remains composed of a number of men, of whom, if chance so wills, the most insignificant is able to occasion delay and even irregularity. The danger which War brings with it, the bodily exertions which it requires, augment this evil so much that they may be regarded as the greatest causes of it.

This enormous friction, which is not concentrated, as in mechanics, at a few points, is therefore everywhere brought into contact with chance, and thus incidents take place upon which it was impossible to calculate, their chief origin being chance. As an instance of one such chance: the weather. Here the fog prevents the enemy from being discovered in time, a battery from firing at the right moment, a report from reaching the General; there the rain prevents a battalion from arriving at the right time, because instead of for three it had to march perhaps eight hours; the cavalry from charging effectively because it is stuck fast in heavy ground.

These are only a few incidents of detail by way of elucidation, that the reader may be able to follow the author, for whole volumes might be written on these difficulties. To avoid this, and still to give a clear conception of the host of small difficulties to be contended with in War, we might go on heaping up illustrations, if we were not afraid of being tiresome. But those who have already comprehended us will permit us to add a few more.

Activity in War is movement in a resistant medium. Just as a man immersed in water is unable to perform with ease and regularity the most natural and simplest movement, that of walking, so in War, with ordinary powers, one cannot keep even the line of mediocrity. This is the reason that the correct theorist is like a swimming master, who teaches on dry land movements which are required in the water, which must appear grotesque and ludicrous to those who forget about the water. This is also why theorists, who have never plunged in themselves, or who cannot deduce any generalities from their experience, are unpractical and even absurd, because they only teach what every one knows—how to walk.

Further, every War is rich in particular facts, while at the same time each is an unexplored sea, full of rocks which the General may have a suspicion of, but which he has never seen with his eye, and round which, moreover, he must steer in the night. If a contrary wind also springs up, that is, if any great accidental event declares itself adverse to him, then the most consummate skill, presence of mind, and energy are required, whilst to those who only look on from a distance all seems to proceed with the utmost ease. The knowledge of this friction is a chief part of that so often talked of, experience in War, which is required in a good General. Certainly he is not the best General in whose mind it assumes the greatest dimensions, who is the most over-awed by it (this includes that class of over-anxious Generals, of whom there are so many amongst the experienced); but a General must be aware of it that he may overcome it, where that is possible, and that he may not expect a degree of precision in results which is impossible on account of this very friction. Besides, it can never be learnt theoretically; and if it could, there would still be wanting that experience of judgment which is called tact, and which is always more necessary in a field full of innumerable small and diversified objects than in great and decisive cases, when one's own judgment may be aided by consultation with others. Just as the man of the world, through tact of judgment which has become habit, speaks, acts, and moves only as suits the occasion, so the officer experienced in War will always, in great and small matters, at every pulsation of War as we may say, decide and determine suitably to the occasion. Through this experience and practice the idea comes to his mind of itself that so and so will not suit. And thus he will not easily place himself in a position by which he is compromised, which, if it often occurs in War, shakes all the foundations of confidence and becomes extremely dangerous.

It is therefore this friction, or what is so termed here, which makes that which appears easy in War difficult in reality. As we proceed, we shall often meet with this subject again, and it will hereafter become plain that besides experience and a strong will, there are still many other rare qualities of the mind required to make a man a consummate General.

CHAPTER VIII - CONCLUDING REMARKS, BOOK I

THOSE things which as elements meet together in the atmosphere of War and make it a resistant medium for every activity we have designated under the terms danger, bodily effort (exertion), information, and friction. In their impedient effects they may therefore be comprehended again in the collective notion of a general friction. Now is there, then, no kind of oil which is capable of diminishing this friction? Only one, and that one is not always available at the will of the Commander or his Army. It is the habituation of an Army to War.

Habit gives strength to the body in great exertion, to the mind in great danger, to the judgment against first impressions. By it a valuable circumspection is generally gained throughout every rank, from the hussar and rifleman up to the General of Division, which facilitates the work of the Chief Commander.

As the human eye in a dark room dilates its pupil, draws in the little light that there is, partially distinguishes objects by degrees, and at last knows them quite well, so it is in War with the experienced soldier, whilst the novice is only met by pitch dark night.

Habituation to War no General can give his Army at once, and the camps of manoeuvre (peace exercises) furnish but a weak substitute for it, weak in comparison with real experience in War, but not weak in relation to other Armies in which the training is limited to mere mechanical exercises of routine. So to regulate the exercises in peace time as to include some of these causes of friction, that the judgment, circumspection, even resolution of the separate leaders may be brought into exercise, is of much greater consequence than those believe who do not know the thing by experience. It is of immense importance that the soldier, high or low, whatever rank he has, should not have to encounter in War those things which, when seen for the first time, set him in astonishment and perplexity; if he has only met with them one single time before, even by that he is half acquainted with them. This relates even to bodily fatigues. They should be practised less to accustom the body to them than the mind. In War the young soldier is very apt to regard unusual fatigues as the consequence of faults, mistakes, and embarrassment in the conduct of the whole, and to become distressed and despondent as a consequence. This would not happen if he had been prepared for this beforehand by exercises in peace.

Another less comprehensive but still very important means of gaining habituation to War in time of peace is to invite into the service officers of foreign armies who have had experience in War. Peace seldom reigns over all Europe, and never in all quarters of the world. A State which has been long at peace should, therefore, always seek to procure some officers who have done good service at the different scenes of Warfare, or to send there some of its own, that they may get a lesson in War.

However small the number of officers of this description may appear in proportion to the mass, still their influence is very sensibly felt. Their experience, the bent of their genius, the stamp of their character, influence their subordinates and comrades; and besides that, if they cannot be placed in positions of superior command, they may always be regarded as men acquainted with the country, who may be questioned on many special occasions.

BOOK II: ON THE THEORY OF WAR

CHAPTER I - BRANCHES OF THE ART OF WAR

WAR in its literal meaning is fighting, for fighting alone is the efficient principle in the manifold activity which in a wide sense is called War. But fighting is a trial of strength of the moral and physical forces by means of the latter. That the moral cannot be omitted is evident of itself, for the condition of the mind has always the most decisive influence on the forces employed in War.

The necessity of fighting very soon led men to special inventions to turn the advantage in it in their own favour: in consequence of these the mode of fighting has undergone great alterations; but in whatever way it is conducted its conception remains unaltered, and fighting is that which constitutes War.

The inventions have been from the first weapons and equipments for the individual combatants. These have to be provided and the use of them learnt before the War begins. They are made suitable to the nature of the fighting, consequently are ruled by it; but plainly the activity engaged in these appliances is a different thing from the fight itself; it is only the preparation for the combat, not the conduct of the same. That arming and equipping are not essential to the conception of fighting is plain, because mere wrestling is also fighting.

Fighting has determined everything appertaining to arms and equipment, and these in turn modify the mode of fighting; there is, therefore, a reciprocity of action between the two.

Nevertheless, the fight itself remains still an entirely special activity, more particularly because it moves in an entirely special element, namely, in the element of danger.

If, then, there is anywhere a necessity for drawing a line between two different activities, it is here; and in order to see clearly the importance of this idea, we need only just to call to mind how often eminent personal fitness in one field has turned out nothing but the most useless pedantry in the other.

It is also in no way difficult to separate in idea the one activity from the other, if we look at the combatant forces fully armed and equipped as a given means, the profitable use of which requires nothing more than a knowledge of their general results.

The Art of War is therefore, in its proper sense, the art of making use of the given means in fighting, and we cannot give it a better name than the "Conduct of War." On the other hand, in a wider sense all activities which have their existence on account of War, therefore the whole creation of troops, that is levying them, arming, equipping, and exercising them, belong to the Art of War.

To make a sound theory it is most essential to separate these two activities, for it is easy to see that if every act of War is to begin with the preparation of military forces, and to presuppose forces so organised as a primary condition for conducting War, that theory will only be applicable in the few cases to which the force available happens to be exactly suited. If, on the other hand, we wish to have a theory which shall suit most cases, and will not be wholly useless in any case, it must be founded on those means which are in most general use, and in respect to these only on the actual results springing from them.

The conduct of War is, therefore, the formation and conduct of the fighting. If this fighting was a single act, there would be no necessity for any further subdivision, but the fight is composed of a greater or less number of single acts, complete in themselves, which we call combats, as we have shown in the first chapter of the first book, and which form new units. From this arises the totally different activities, that of the *formation* and *conduct* of these single combats in themselves, and the combination of them with one another, with a view to the ultimate object of the War. The first is called TACTICS, the other STRATEGY.

This division into tactics and strategy is now in almost general use, and every one knows tolerably well under which head to place any single fact, without knowing very distinctly the grounds on which the classification is founded. But when such divisions are blindly adhered to in practice, they must have some deep root. We have searched for this root, and we might say that it is just the usage of the majority which has brought us to it. On the other hand, we look upon the arbitrary, unnatural definitions of these conceptions sought to be established by some writers as not in accordance with the general usage of the terms.

According to our classification, therefore, tactics is the theory of *the use of military forces in combat*. Strategy is the theory of *the use of combats for the object of the war*.

The way in which the conception of a single, or independent combat, is more closely determined, the conditions to which this unit is attached, we shall only be able to explain clearly when we consider the combat; we must content ourselves for the present with saying that in relation to space, therefore in combats taking place at the same time, the unit reaches just as far as *personal command* reaches; but in regard to time, and therefore in relation to combats which follow each other in close succession, it reaches to the moment when the crisis which takes place in every combat is entirely passed.

That doubtful cases may occur, cases, for instance, in which several combats may perhaps be regarded also as a single one, will not overthrow the ground of distinction we have adopted, for the same is the case with all grounds of distinction of real things which are differentiated by a gradually diminishing scale. There may, therefore, certainly be acts of activity in War which, without any alteration in the point of view, may just as well be counted strategic as tactical; for example, very extended positions resembling a chain of posts, the preparations for the passage of a river at several points, &c.

Our classification reaches and covers only the USE OF THE MILITARY FORCE. But now there are in War a number of activities which are subservient to it, and still are quite different from it; sometimes closely allied, sometimes less near in their affinity. All these activities relate to the MAINTENANCE OF THE MILITARY FORCE. In the same way as its creation and training precede its use, so its maintenance is always a necessary condition. But, strictly viewed, all activities thus connected with it are always to be regarded only as preparations for fighting; they are certainly nothing more than activities which are very close to the action, so that they run through the hostile act alternate in importance with the use of the forces. We have therefore a right to exclude them as well as the other preparatory activities from the Art of War in its restricted sense, from the conduct of War properly so called; and we are obliged to do so if we would comply with the first principle of all theory, the elimination of all heterogeneous elements. Who would include in the real "conduct of War" the whole litany of subsistence and administration, because it is admitted to stand in constant reciprocal action with the use of the troops, but is something essentially different from it?

We have said, in the third chapter of our first book, that as the fight or combat is the only directly effective activity, therefore the threads of all others, as they end in it, are included in it. By this we meant to say that to all others an object was thereby appointed which, in accordance with the laws peculiar to themselves, they must seek to attain. Here we must go a little closer into this subject.

The subjects which constitute the activities outside of the combat are of various kinds.

The one part belongs, in one respect, to the combat itself, is identical with it, whilst it serves in another respect for the maintenance of the military force. The other part belongs purely to the subsistence, and has only, in consequence of the reciprocal action, a limited influence on the combats by its results. The subjects which in one respect belong to the fighting itself are MARCHES, CAMPS, and CANTONMENTS, for they suppose so many different situations of troops, and where troops are supposed there the idea of the combat must always be present.

The other subjects, which only belong to the maintenance, are SUBSISTENCE, CARE OF THE SICK, the SUPPLY AND REPAIR OF ARMS AND EQUIPMENT.

Marches are quite identical with the use of the troops. The act of marching in the combat, generally called manoeuvring, certainly does not necessarily include the use of weapons, but it is so completely and necessarily combined with it that it forms an integral part of that which we call a combat. But the march outside the combat is nothing but the execution of a strategic measure. By the strategic plan is settled WHEN, WHERE, and WITH WHAT FORCES a battle is to be delivered—and to carry that into execution the march is the only means.

The march outside of the combat is therefore an instrument of strategy, but not on that account exclusively a subject of strategy, for as the armed force which executes it may be involved in a possible combat at any moment, therefore its execution stands also under tactical as well as strategic rules. If we prescribe to a column its route on a particular side of a river or of a branch of a mountain, then that is a strategic measure, for it contains the intention of fighting on that particular side of the hill or river in preference to the other, in case a combat should be necessary during the march.

But if a column, instead of following the road through a valley, marches along the parallel ridge of heights, or for the convenience of marching divides itself into several columns, then these are tactical arrangements, for they relate to the manner in which we shall use the troops in the anticipated combat.

The particular order of march is in constant relation with readiness for combat, is therefore tactical in its nature, for it is nothing more than the first or preliminary disposition for the battle which may possibly take place.

As the march is the instrument by which strategy apportions its active elements, the combats, but these last often only appear by their results and not in the details of their real course, it could not fail to happen that in theory the instrument has often been substituted for the efficient principle. Thus we hear of a decisive skilful march, allusion being thereby made to those combat-combinations to which these marches led. This substitution of ideas is too natural and conciseness of expression too desirable to call for alteration, but still it is only a condensed chain of ideas in regard to which we must never omit to bear in mind the full meaning, if we would avoid falling into error.

We fall into an error of this description if we attribute to strategical combinations a power independent of tactical results. We read of marches and manoeuvres combined, the object attained, and at the same time not a word about combat, from which the conclusion is drawn that there are means in War of conquering an enemy without fighting. The prolific nature of this error we cannot show until hereafter.

But although a march can be regarded absolutely as an integral part of the combat, still there are in it certain relations which do not belong to the combat, and therefore are neither tactical nor strategic. To these belong all arrangements which concern only the accommodation of the troops, the construction of bridges, roads, &c. These are only conditions; under many circumstances they are in very close connection, and may almost identify themselves with the troops, as in building a bridge in presence of the enemy; but in themselves they are always activities, the theory of which does not form part of the theory of the conduct of War.

Camps, by which we mean every disposition of troops in concentrated, therefore in battle order, in contradistinction to cantonments or quarters, are a state of rest, therefore of restoration; but they are at the same time also the strategic appointment of a battle on the spot, chosen; and by the manner in which they are taken up they contain the fundamental lines of the battle, a condition from which every defensive battle starts; they are therefore essential parts of both strategy and tactics.

Cantonments take the place of camps for the better refreshment of the troops. They are therefore, like camps, strategic subjects as regards position and extent; tactical subjects as regards internal organisation, with a view to readiness to fight.

The occupation of camps and cantonments no doubt usually combines with the recuperation of the troops another object also, for example, the covering a district of country, the holding a position; but it can very well be only the first. We remind our readers that strategy may follow a great diversity of objects, for everything which appears an advantage may be the object of a combat, and the preservation of the instrument with which War is made must necessarily very often become the object of its partial combinations.

If, therefore, in such a case strategy ministers only to the maintenance of the troops, we are not on that account out of the field of strategy, for we are still engaged with the use of the military force, because every disposition of that force upon any point Whatever of the theatre of War is such a use.

But if the maintenance of the troops in camp or quarters calls forth activities which are no employment of the armed force, such as the construction of huts, pitching of tents, subsistence and sanitary services in camps or quarters, then such belong neither to strategy nor tactics.

Even entrenchments, the site and preparation of which are plainly part of the order of battle, therefore tactical subjects, do not belong to the theory of the conduct of War so far as respects the execution of their construction the knowledge and skill required for such work being, in point of fact, qualities inherent in the nature of an organised Army; the theory of the combat takes them for granted.

Amongst the subjects which belong to the mere keeping up of an armed force, because none of the parts are identified with the combat, the victualling of the troops themselves comes first, as it must be done almost daily and for each individual. Thus it is that it completely permeates military action in the parts constituting strategy—we say parts constituting strategy, because during a battle the subsistence of troops will rarely have any influence in modifying the plan, although the thing is conceivable enough. The care for the subsistence of the troops comes therefore into reciprocal action chiefly with strategy, and there is nothing more common than for the leading strategic features of a campaign and War to be traced out in connection with a view to this supply. But however frequent and however important these views of supply may be, the subsistence of the troops always remains a completely different activity from the use of the troops, and the former has only an influence on the latter by its results.

The other branches of administrative activity which we have mentioned stand much farther apart from the use of the troops. The care of sick and wounded, highly important as it is for the good of an Army, directly affects it only in a small portion of the individuals composing it, and therefore has only a weak and indirect influence upon the use of the rest. The completing and replacing articles of arms and equipment, except so far as by the organism of the forces it constitutes a continuous activity inherent in them—takes place only periodically, and therefore seldom affects strategic plans.

We must, however, here guard ourselves against a mistake. In certain cases these subjects may be really of decisive importance. The distance of hospitals and depôts of munitions may very easily be imagined as the sole cause of very important strategic decisions. We do not wish either to contest that point or to throw it into the shade. But we are at present occupied not with the particular facts of a concrete case, but with abstract theory; and our assertion therefore is that such an influence is too rare to give the theory of sanitary measures and the supply of munitions and arms an importance in theory of the conduct of War such as to make it worth while to include in the theory of the conduct of War the consideration of the different ways and systems which the above theories may furnish, in the same way as is certainly necessary in regard to victualling troops.

If we have clearly understood the results of our reflections, then the activities belonging to War divide themselves into two principal classes, into such as are only "preparations for War" and into the "War itself." This division must therefore also be made in theory.

The knowledge and applications of skill in the preparations for War are engaged in the creation, discipline, and maintenance of all the military forces; what general names should be given to them we do not enter into, but we see that artillery, fortification, elementary tactics, as they are called, the whole organisation and administration of the various armed forces, and all such things are included. But the theory of War itself occupies itself with the use of these prepared means for the object of the war. It needs of the first only the results, that is, the knowledge of the principal properties of the means taken in hand for use. This we call "The Art of War" in a limited sense, or "Theory of the Conduct of War," or "Theory of the Employment of Armed Forces," all of them denoting for us the same thing.

The present theory will therefore treat the combat as the real contest, marches, camps, and cantonments as circumstances which are more or less identical with it. The subsistence of the troops will only come into consideration like OTHER GIVEN CIRCUMSTANCES in respect of its results, not as an activity belonging to the combat.

The Art of War thus viewed in its limited sense divides itself again into tactics and strategy. The former occupies itself with the form of the separate combat, the latter with its use. Both connect themselves with the circumstances of marches, camps, cantonments only through the combat, and these circumstances are tactical or strategic according as they relate to the form or to the signification of the battle.

No doubt there will be many readers who will consider superfluous this careful separation of two things lying so close together as tactics and strategy, because it has no direct effect on the conduct itself of War. We admit, certainly that it would be pedantry to look for direct effects on the field of battle from a theoretical distinction.

But the first business of every theory is to clear up conceptions and ideas which have been jumbled together, and, we may say, entangled and confused; and only when a right understanding is established, as to names and conceptions, can we hope to progress with clearness and facility, and be certain that author and reader will always see things from the same point of view. Tactics and strategy are two activities mutually permeating each other in time and space, at the same time essentially different activities, the inner laws and mutual relations of which cannot be intelligible at all to the mind until a clear conception of the nature of each activity is established.

He to whom all this is nothing, must either repudiate all theoretical consideration, OR HIS UNDERSTANDING HAS NOT AS YET BEEN PAINED by the confused and perplexing ideas resting on no fixed point of view, leading to no satisfactory result, sometimes dull, sometimes fantastic, sometimes floating in vague generalities, which we are often obliged to hear and read on the conduct of War, owing to the spirit of scientific investigation having hitherto been little directed to these subjects.

CHAPTER II - ON THE THEORY OF WAR

1. THE FIRST CONCEPTION OF THE "ART OF WAR" WAS MERELY THE PREPARATION OF THE ARMED FORCES.

FORMERLY by the term "Art of War," or "Science of War," nothing was understood but the totality of those branches of knowledge and those appliances of skill occupied with material things. The pattern and preparation and the mode of using arms, the construction of fortifications and entrenchments, the organism of an army and the mechanism of its movements, were the subject; these branches of knowledge and skill above referred to, and the end and aim of them all was the establishment of an armed force fit for use in War. All this concerned merely things belonging to the material world and a one-sided activity only, and it was in fact nothing but an activity advancing by gradations from the lower occupations to a finer kind of mechanical art. The relation of all this to War itself was very much the same as the relation of the art of the sword cutler to the art of using the sword. The employment in the moment of danger and in a state of constant reciprocal action of the particular energies of mind and spirit in the direction proposed to them was not yet even mooted.

2. TRUE WAR FIRST APPEARS IN THE ART OF SIEGES.

In the art of sieges we first perceive a certain degree of guidance of the combat, something of the action of the intellectual faculties upon the material forces placed under their control, but generally only so far that it very soon embodied itself again in new material forms, such as approaches, trenches, counter-approaches, batteries, &c., and every step which this action of the higher faculties took was marked by some such result; it was only the thread that was required on which to string these material inventions in order. As the intellect can hardly manifest itself in this kind of War, except in such things, so therefore nearly all that was necessary was done in that way.

3. THEN TACTICS TRIED TO FIND ITS WAY IN THE SAME DIRECTION.

Afterwards tactics attempted to give to the mechanism of its joints the character of a general disposition, built upon the peculiar properties of the instrument, which character leads indeed to the battle-field, but instead of leading to the free activity of mind, leads to an Army made like an automaton by its rigid formations and orders of battle, which, movable only by the word of command, is intended to unwind its activities like a piece of clockwork.

4. THE REAL CONDUCT OF WAR ONLY MADE ITS APPEARANCE INCIDENTALLY AND INCOGNITO.

The conduct of War properly so called, that is, a use of the prepared means adapted to the most special requirements, was not considered as any suitable subject for theory, but one which should be left to natural talents alone. By degrees, as War passed from the hand-to-hand encounters of the middle ages into a more regular and systematic form, stray reflections on this point also forced themselves into men's minds, but they mostly appeared only incidentally in memoirs and narratives, and in a certain measure incognito.

5. REFLECTIONS ON MILITARY EVENTS BROUGHT ABOUT THE WANT OF A THEORY.

As contemplation on War continually increased, and its history every day assumed more of a critical character, the urgent want appeared of the support of fixed maxims and rules, in order that in the controversies naturally arising about military events the war of opinions might be brought to some one point. This whirl of opinions, which neither revolved on any central pivot nor according to any appreciable laws, could not but be very distasteful to people's minds.

6. ENDEAVOURS TO ESTABLISH A POSITIVE THEORY.

There arose, therefore, an endeavour to establish maxims, rules, and even systems for the conduct of War. By this the attainment of a positive object was proposed, without taking into view the endless difficulties which the conduct of War presents in that respect. The conduct of War, as we have shown, has no definite limits in any direction, while every system has the circumscribing nature of a synthesis, from which results an irreconcileable opposition between such a theory and practice.

7. LIMITATION TO MATERIAL OBJECTS.

Writers on theory felt the difficulty of the subject soon enough, and thought themselves entitled to get rid of it by directing their maxims and systems only upon material things and a one-sided activity. Their aim was to reach results, as in the science for the preparation for War, entirely certain and positive, and therefore only to take into consideration that which could be made matter of calculation.

8. SUPERIORITY OF NUMBERS.

The superiority in numbers being a material condition, it was chosen from amongst all the factors required to produce victory, because it could be brought under mathematical laws through combinations of time and space. It was thought possible to leave out of sight all other circumstances, by supposing them to be equal on each side, and therefore to neutralise one another. This would have been very well if it had been done to gain a preliminary knowledge of this one factor, according to its relations, but to make it a rule for ever to consider superiority of numbers as the sole law; to see the whole secret of the Art of War in the formula, IN A CERTAIN TIME, AT A CERTAIN POINT, TO BRING UP SUPERIOR MASSES—was a restriction overruled by the force of realities.

9. VICTUALLING OF TROOPS.

By one theoretical school an attempt was made to systematise another material element also, by making the subsistence of troops, according to a previously established organism of the Army, the supreme legislator in the higher conduct of War. In this way certainly they arrived at definite figures, but at figures which rested on a number of arbitrary calculations, and which therefore could not stand the test of practical application.

10. BASE.

An ingenious author tried to concentrate in a single conception, that of a BASE, a whole host of objects amongst which sundry relations even with immaterial forces found their way in as well. The list comprised the subsistence of the troops, the keeping them complete in numbers and equipment, the security of communications with the home country, lastly, the security of retreat in case it became necessary; and, first of all, he proposed to substitute this conception of a base for all these things; then for the base itself to substitute its own length (extent); and, last of all, to substitute the angle formed by the army with this base: all this was done to obtain a pure geometrical result utterly useless. This last is, in fact, unavoidable, if we reflect that none of these substitutions could be made without violating truth and leaving out some of the things contained in the original conception. The idea of a base is a real necessity for strategy, and to have conceived it is meritorious; but to make such a use of it as we have depicted is completely inadmissible, and could not but lead to partial conclusions which have forced these theorists into a direction opposed to common sense, namely, to a belief in the decisive effect of the enveloping form of attack.

11. INTERIOR LINES.

As a reaction against this false direction, another geometrical principle, that of the so-called interior lines, was then elevated to the throne. Although this principle rests on a sound foundation, on the truth that the combat is the only effectual means in War, still it is, just on account of its purely geometrical nature, nothing but another case of one-sided theory which can never gain ascendency in the real world.

12. ALL THESE ATTEMPTS ARE OPEN TO OBJECTION.

All these attempts at theory are only to be considered in their analytical part as progress in the province of truth, but in their synthetical part, in their precepts and rules, they are quite unserviceable.

They strive after determinate quantities, whilst in War all is undetermined, and the calculation has always to be made with varying quantities.

They direct the attention only upon material forces, while the whole military action is penetrated throughout by intelligent forces and their effects.

They only pay regard to activity on one side, whilst War is a constant state of reciprocal action, the effects of which are mutual.

13. AS A RULE THEY EXCLUDE GENIUS.

All that was not attainable by such miserable philosophy, the offspring of partial views, lay outside the precincts of science—and was the field of genius, which RAISES ITSELF ABOVE RULES.

Pity the warrior who is contented to crawl about in this beggardom of rules, which are too bad for genius, over which it can set itself superior, over which it can perchance make merry! What genius does must be the best of all rules, and theory cannot do better than to show how and why it is so.

Pity the theory which sets itself in opposition to the mind! It cannot repair this contradiction by any humility, and the humbler it is so much the sooner will ridicule and contempt drive it out of real life.

14. THE DIFFICULTY OF THEORY AS SOON AS MORAL QUANTITIES COME INTO CONSIDERATION.

Every theory becomes infinitely more difficult from the moment that it touches on the province of moral quantities. Architecture and painting know quite well what they are about as long as they have only to do with matter; there is no dispute about mechanical or optical construction. But as soon as the moral activities begin their work, as soon as moral impressions and feelings are produced, the whole set of rules dissolves into vague ideas.

The science of medicine is chiefly engaged with bodily phenomena only; its business is with the animal organism, which, liable to perpetual change, is never exactly the same for two moments. This makes its practice very difficult, and places the judgment of the physician above his science; but how much more difficult is the case if a moral effect is added, and how much higher must we place the physician of the mind?

15. THE MORAL QUANTITIES MUST NOT BE EXCLUDED IN WAR.

But now the activity in War is never directed solely against matter; it is always at the same time directed against the intelligent force which gives life to this matter, and to separate the two from each other is impossible.

But the intelligent forces are only visible to the inner eye, and this is different in each person, and often different in the same person at different times.

As danger is the general element in which everything moves in War, it is also chiefly by courage, the feeling of one's own power, that the judgment is differently influenced. It is to a certain extent the crystalline lens through which all appearances pass before reaching the understanding.

And yet we cannot doubt that these things acquire a certain objective value simply through experience.

Every one knows the moral effect of a surprise, of an attack in flank or rear. Every one thinks less of the enemy's courage as soon as he turns his back, and ventures much more in pursuit than when pursued. Every one judges of the enemy's General by his reputed talents, by his age and experience, and shapes his course accordingly. Every one casts a scrutinising glance at the spirit and feeling of his own and the enemy's troops. All these and similar effects in the province of the moral nature of man have established themselves by experience, are perpetually recurring, and therefore warrant our reckoning them as real quantities of their kind. What could we do with any theory which should leave them out of consideration?

Certainly experience is an indispensable title for these truths. With psychological and philosophical sophistries no theory, no General, should meddle.

16. PRINCIPAL DIFFICULTY OF A THEORY FOR THE CONDUCT OF WAR.

In order to comprehend clearly the difficulty of the proposition which is contained in a theory for the conduct of War, and thence to deduce the necessary characteristics of such a theory, we must take a closer view of the chief particulars which make up the nature of activity in War.

17. FIRST SPECIALITY.—MORAL FORCES AND THEIR EFFECTS. (HOSTILE FEELING.)

The first of these specialities consists in the moral forces and effects.

The combat is, in its origin, the expression of HOSTILE FEELING, but in our great combats, which we call Wars, the hostile feeling frequently resolves itself into merely a hostile VIEW, and there is usually no innate hostile feeling residing in individual against individual. Nevertheless, the combat never passes off without such feelings being brought into activity. National hatred, which is seldom wanting in our Wars, is a substitute for personal hostility in the breast of individual opposed to individual. But where this also is wanting, and at first no animosity of feeling subsists, a hostile feeling is kindled by the combat itself; for an act of violence which any one commits upon us by order of his superior, will excite in us a desire to retaliate and be revenged on him, sooner than on the superior power at whose command the act was done. This is human, or animal if we will; still it is so. We are very apt to regard the combat in theory as an abstract trial of strength, without any participation on the part of the feelings, and that is one of the thousand errors which theorists deliberately commit, because they do not see its consequences.

Besides that excitation of feelings naturally arising from the combat itself, there are others also which do not essentially belong to it, but which, on account of their relationship, easily unite with it—ambition, love of power, enthusiasm of every kind, &c. &c.

18. THE IMPRESSIONS OF DANGER. (COURAGE.)

Finally, the combat begets the element of danger, in which all the activities of War must live and move, like the bird in the air or the fish in the water. But the influences of danger all pass into the feelings, either directly—that is, instinctively—or through the medium of the understanding. The effect in the first case would be a desire to escape from the danger, and, if that cannot be done, fright and anxiety. If this effect does not take place, then it is COURAGE, which is a counterpoise to that instinct. Courage is, however, by no means an act of the understanding, but likewise a feeling, like fear; the latter looks to the physical preservation, courage to the moral preservation. Courage, then, is a nobler instinct. But because it is so, it will not allow itself to be used as a lifeless instrument, which produces its effects exactly according to prescribed measure. Courage is therefore no mere counterpoise to danger in order to neutralise the latter in its effects, but a peculiar power in itself.

19. EXTENT OF THE INFLUENCE OF DANGER.

But to estimate exactly the influence of danger upon the principal actors in War, we must not limit its sphere to the physical danger of the moment. It dominates over the actor, not only by threatening him, but also by threatening all entrusted to him, not only at the moment in which it is actually present, but also through the imagination at all other moments, which have a connection with the present; lastly, not only directly by itself, but also indirectly by the responsibility which makes it bear with tenfold weight on the mind of the chief actor. Who could advise, or resolve upon a great battle, without feeling his mind more or less wrought up, or perplexed by, the danger and responsibility which such a great act of decision carries in itself? We may say that action in War, in so far as it is real action, not a mere condition, is never out of the sphere of danger.

20. OTHER POWERS OF FEELING.

If we look upon these affections which are excited by hostility and danger as peculiarly belonging to War, we do not, therefore, exclude from it all others accompanying man in his life's journey. They will also find room here frequently enough. Certainly we may say that many a petty action of the passions is silenced in this serious business of life; but that holds good only in respect to those acting in a lower sphere, who, hurried on from one state of danger and exertion to another, lose sight of the rest of the things of life, BECOME UNUSED TO DECEIT, because it is of no avail with death, and so attain to that soldierly simplicity of character which has always been the best representative of the military profession. In higher regions it is otherwise, for the higher a man's rank, the more he must look around him; then arise interests on every side, and a manifold activity of the passions of good and bad. Envy and generosity, pride and humility, fierceness and tenderness, all may appear as active powers in this great drama.

21. PECULIARITY OF MIND

The peculiar characteristics of mind in the chief actor have, as well as those of the feelings, a high importance. From an imaginative, flighty, inexperienced head, and from a calm, sagacious understanding, different things are to be expected.

22. FROM THE DIVERSITY IN MENTAL INDIVIDUALITIES ARISES THE DIVERSITY OF WAYS LEADING TO THE END.

It is this great diversity in mental individuality, the influence of which is to be supposed as chiefly felt in the higher ranks, because it increases as we progress upwards, which chiefly produces the diversity of ways leading to the end noticed by us in the first book, and which gives, to the play of probabilities and chance, such an unequal share in determining the course of events.

23. SECOND PECULIARITY.—LIVING REACTION.

The second peculiarity in War is the living reaction, and the reciprocal action resulting therefrom. We do not here speak of the difficulty of estimating that reaction, for that is included in the difficulty before mentioned, of treating the moral powers as quantities; but of this, that reciprocal action, by its nature, opposes anything like a regular plan. The effect which any measure produces upon the enemy is the most distinct of all the data which action affords; but every theory must keep to classes (or groups) of phenomena, and can never take up the really individual case in itself: that must everywhere be left to judgment and talent. It is therefore natural that in a business such as War, which in its plan—built upon general circumstances—is so often thwarted by unexpected and singular accidents, more must generally be left to talent; and less use can be made of a THEORETICAL GUIDE than in any other.

24. THIRD PECULIARITY.—UNCERTAINTY OF ALL DATA.

Lastly, the great uncertainty of all data in War is a peculiar difficulty, because all action must, to a certain extent, be planned in a mere twilight, which in addition not unfrequently—like the effect of a fog or moonshine—gives to things exaggerated dimensions and an unnatural appearance.

What this feeble light leaves indistinct to the sight talent must discover, or must be left to chance. It is therefore again talent, or the favour of fortune, on which reliance must be placed, for want of objective knowledge.

25. POSITIVE THEORY IS IMPOSSIBLE.

With materials of this kind we can only say to ourselves that it is a sheer impossibility to construct for the Art of War a theory which, like a scaffolding, shall ensure to the chief actor an external support on all sides. In all those cases in which he is thrown upon his talent he would find himself away from this scaffolding of theory and in opposition to it, and, however many-sided it might be framed, the same result would ensue of which we spoke when we said that talent and genius act beyond the law, and theory is in opposition to reality.

26. MEANS LEFT BY WHICH A THEORY IS POSSIBLE (THE DIFFICULTIES ARE NOT EVERYWHERE EQUALLY GREAT).

Two means present themselves of getting out of this difficulty. In the first place, what we have said of the nature of military action in general does not apply in the same manner to the action of every one, whatever may be his standing. In the lower ranks the spirit of self-sacrifice is called more into request, but the difficulties which the understanding and judgment meet with are infinitely less. The field of occurrences is more confined. Ends and means are fewer in number. Data more distinct; mostly also contained in the actually visible. But the higher we ascend the more the difficulties increase, until in the Commander-in-Chief they reach their climax, so that with him almost everything must be left to genius.

Further, according to a division of the subject in AGREEMENT WITH ITS NATURE, the difficulties are not everywhere the same, but diminish the more results manifest themselves in the material world, and increase the more they pass into the moral, and become motives which influence the will. Therefore it is easier to determine, by theoretical rules, the order and conduct of a battle, than the use to be made of the battle itself. Yonder physical weapons clash with each other, and although mind is not wanting therein, matter must have its rights. But in the effects to be produced by battles when the material results become motives, we have only to do with the moral nature. In a word, it is easier to make a theory for TACTICS than for STRATEGY.

27. THEORY MUST BE OF THE NATURE OF OBSERVATIONS NOT OF DOCTRINE.

The second opening for the possibility of a theory lies in the point of view that it does not necessarily require to be a DIRECTION for action. As a general rule, whenever an ACTIVITY is for the most part occupied with the same objects over and over again, with the same ends and means, although there may be trifling alterations and a corresponding number of varieties of combination, such things are capable of becoming a subject of study for the reasoning faculties. But such study is just the most essential part of every THEORY, and has a peculiar title to that name. It is an analytical investigation of the subject that leads to an exact knowledge; and if brought to bear on the results of experience, which in our case would be military history, to a thorough familiarity with it. The nearer theory attains the latter object, so much the more it passes over from the objective form of knowledge into the subjective one of skill in action; and so much the more, therefore, it will prove itself effective when circumstances allow of no other decision but that of personal talents; it will show its effects in that talent itself. If theory investigates the subjects which constitute War; if it separates more distinctly that which at first sight seems amalgamated; if it explains fully the properties of the means; if it shows their probable effects; if it makes evident the nature of objects; if it brings to bear all over the field of War the light of essentially critical investigation—then it has fulfilled the chief duties of its province. It becomes then a guide to him who wishes to make himself acquainted with War from books; it lights up the whole road for him, facilitates his progress, educates his judgment, and shields him from error.

If a man of expertness spends half his life in the endeavour to clear up an obscure subject thoroughly, he will probably know more about it than a person who seeks to master it in a short time. Theory is instituted that each person in succession may not have to go through the same labour of clearing the ground and toiling through his subject, but may find the thing in order, and light admitted on it. It should educate the mind of the future leader in War, or rather guide him in his self-instruction, but not accompany him to the field of battle; just as a sensible tutor forms and enlightens the opening mind of a youth without, therefore, keeping him in leading strings all through his life.

If maxims and rules result of themselves from the considerations which theory institutes, if the truth accretes itself into that form of crystal, then theory will not oppose this natural law of the mind; it will rather, if the arch ends in such a key-stone, bring it prominently out; but so does this, only in order to satisfy the philosophical law of reason, in order to show distinctly the point to which the lines all converge, not in order to form out of it an algebraical formula for use upon the battle-field; for even these maxims and rules serve more to determine in the reflecting mind the leading outline of its habitual movements than as landmarks indicating to it the way in the act of execution.

28. BY THIS POINT OF VIEW THEORY BECOMES POSSIBLE, AND CEASES TO BE IN CONTRADICTION TO PRACTICE.

Taking this point of view, there is a possibility afforded of a satisfactory, that is, of a useful, theory of the conduct of War, never coming into opposition with the reality, and it will only depend on rational treatment to bring it so far into harmony with action that between theory and practice there shall no longer be that absurd difference which an unreasonable theory, in defiance of common sense, has often produced, but which, just as often, narrow-mindedness and ignorance have used as a pretext for giving way to their natural incapacity.

29. THEORY THEREFORE CONSIDERS THE NATURE OF ENDS AND MEANS—ENDS AND MEANS IN TACTICS.

Theory has therefore to consider the nature of the means and ends.

In tactics the means are the disciplined armed forces which are to carry on the contest. The object is victory. The precise definition of this conception can be better explained hereafter in the consideration of the combat. Here we content ourselves by denoting the retirement of the enemy from the field of battle as the sign of victory. By means of this victory strategy gains the object for which it appointed the combat, and which constitutes its special signification. This signification has certainly some influence on the nature of the victory. A victory which is intended to weaken the enemy's armed forces is a different thing from one which is designed only to put us in possession of a position. The signification of a combat may therefore have a sensible influence on the preparation and conduct of it, consequently will be also a subject of consideration in tactics.

30. CIRCUMSTANCES WHICH ALWAYS ATTEND THE APPLICATION OF THE MEANS.

As there are certain circumstances which attend the combat throughout, and have more or less influence upon its result, therefore these must be taken into consideration in the application of the armed forces.

These circumstances are the locality of the combat (ground), the time of day, and the weather.

31. LOCALITY.

The locality, which we prefer leaving for solution, under the head of "Country and Ground," might, strictly speaking, be without any influence at all if the combat took place on a completely level and uncultivated plain.

In a country of steppes such a case may occur, but in the cultivated countries of Europe it is almost an imaginary idea. Therefore a combat between civilised nations, in which country and ground have no influence, is hardly conceivable.

32. TIME OF DAY.

The time of day influences the combat by the difference between day and night; but the influence naturally extends further than merely to the limits of these divisions, as every combat has a certain duration, and great battles last for several hours. In the preparations for a great battle, it makes an essential difference whether it begins in the morning or the evening. At the same time, certainly many battles may be fought in which the question of the time of day is quite immaterial, and in the generality of cases its influence is only trifling.

33. WEATHER.

Still more rarely has the weather any decisive influence, and it is mostly only by fogs that it plays a part.

34. END AND MEANS IN STRATEGY.

Strategy has in the first instance only the victory, that is, the tactical result, as a means to its object, and ultimately those things which lead directly to peace. The application of its means to this object is at the same time attended by circumstances which have an influence thereon more or less.

35. CIRCUMSTANCES WHICH ATTEND THE APPLICATION OF THE MEANS OF STRATEGY.

These circumstances are country and ground, the former including the territory and inhabitants of the whole theatre of war; next the time of the day, and the time of the year as well; lastly, the weather, particularly any unusual state of the same, severe frost, &c.

36. THESE FORM NEW MEANS.

By bringing these things into combination with the results of a combat, strategy gives this result—and therefore the combat—a special signification, places before it a particular object. But when this object is not that which leads directly to peace, therefore a subordinate one, it is only to be looked upon as a means; and therefore in strategy we may look upon the results of combats or victories, in all their different significations, as means. The conquest of a position is such a result of a combat applied to ground. But not only are the different combats with special objects to be considered as means, but also every higher aim which we may have in view in the combination of battles directed on a common object is to be regarded as a means. A winter campaign is a combination of this kind applied to the season.

There remain, therefore, as objects, only those things which may be supposed as leading DIRECTLY to peace, Theory investigates all these ends and means according to the nature of their effects and their mutual relations.

37. STRATEGY DEDUCES ONLY FROM EXPERIENCE THE ENDS AND MEANS TO BE EXAMINED.

The first question is, How does strategy arrive at a complete list of these things? If there is to be a philosophical inquiry leading to an absolute result, it would become entangled in all those difficulties which the logical necessity of the conduct of War and its theory exclude. It therefore turns to experience, and directs its attention on those combinations which military history can furnish. In this manner, no doubt, nothing more than a limited theory can be obtained, which only suits circumstances such as are presented in history. But this incompleteness is unavoidable, because in any case theory must either have deduced from, or have compared with, history what it advances with respect to things. Besides, this incompleteness in every case is more theoretical than real.

One great advantage of this method is that theory cannot lose itself in abstruse disquisitions, subtleties, and chimeras, but must always remain practical.

38. HOW FAR THE ANALYSIS OF THE MEANS SHOULD BE CARRIED.

Another question is, How far should theory go in its analysis of the means? Evidently only so far as the elements in a separate form present themselves for consideration in practice. The range and effect of different weapons is very important to tactics; their construction, although these effects result from it, is a matter of indifference; for the conduct of War is not making powder and cannon out of a given quantity of charcoal, sulphur, and saltpetre, of copper and tin: the given quantities for the conduct of War are arms in a finished state and their effects. Strategy makes use of maps without troubling itself about triangulations; it does not inquire how the country is subdivided into departments and provinces, and how the people are educated and governed, in order to attain the best military results; but it takes things as it finds them in the community of European States, and observes where very different conditions have a notable influence on War.

39. GREAT SIMPLIFICATION OF THE KNOWLEDGE REQUIRED.

That in this manner the number of subjects for theory is much simplified, and the knowledge requisite for the conduct of War much reduced, is easy to perceive. The very great mass of knowledge and appliances of skill which minister to the action of War in general, and which are necessary before an army fully equipped can take the field, unite in a few great results before they are able to reach, in actual War, the final goal of their activity; just as the streams of a country unite themselves in rivers before they fall into the sea. Only those activities emptying themselves directly into the sea of War have to be studied by him who is to conduct its operations.

40. THIS EXPLAINS THE RAPID GROWTH OF GREAT GENERALS, AND WHY A GENERAL IS NOT A MAN OF LEARNING.

This result of our considerations is in fact so necessary, any other would have made us distrustful of their accuracy. Only thus is explained how so often men have made their appearance with great success in War, and indeed in the higher ranks even in supreme Command, whose pursuits had been previously of a totally different nature; indeed how, as a rule, the most distinguished Generals have never risen from the very learned or really erudite class of officers, but have been mostly men who, from the circumstances of their position, could not have attained to any great amount of knowledge. On that account those who have considered it necessary or even beneficial to commence the education of a future General by instruction in all details have always been ridiculed as absurd pedants. It would be easy to show the injurious tendency of such a course, because the human mind is trained by the knowledge imparted to it and the direction given to its ideas. Only what is great can make it great; the little can only make it little, if the mind itself does not reject it as something repugnant.

41. FORMER CONTRADICTIONS.

Because this simplicity of knowledge requisite in War was not attended to, but that knowledge was always jumbled up with the whole impedimenta of subordinate sciences and arts, therefore the palpable opposition to the events of real life which resulted could not be solved otherwise than by ascribing it all to genius, which requires no theory and for which no theory could be prescribed.

42. ON THIS ACCOUNT ALL USE OF KNOWLEDGE WAS DENIED, AND EVERYTHING ASCRIBED TO NATURAL TALENTS.

People with whom common sense had the upper hand felt sensible of the immense distance remaining to be filled up between a genius of the highest order and a learned pedant; and they became in a manner free-thinkers, rejected all belief in theory, and affirmed the conduct of War to be a natural function of man, which he performs more or less well according as he has brought with him into the world more or less talent in that direction. It cannot be denied that these were nearer to the truth than those who placed a value on false knowledge: at the same time it may easily be seen that such a view is itself but an exaggeration. No activity of the human understanding is possible without a certain stock of ideas; but these are, for the greater part at least, not innate but acquired, and constitute his knowledge. The only question therefore is, of what kind should these ideas be; and we think we have answered it if we say that they should be directed on those things which man has directly to deal with in War.

43. THE KNOWLEDGE MUST BE MADE SUITABLE TO THE POSITION.

Inside this field itself of military activity, the knowledge required must be different according to the station of the Commander. It will be directed on smaller and more circumscribed objects if he holds an inferior, upon greater and more comprehensive ones if he holds a higher situation. There are Field Marshals who would not have shone at the head of a cavalry regiment, and vice versa.

44. THE KNOWLEDGE IN WAR IS VERY SIMPLE, BUT NOT, AT THE SAME TIME, VERY EASY.

But although the knowledge in War is simple, that is to say directed to so few subjects, and taking up those only in their final results, the art of execution is not, on that account, easy. Of the difficulties to which activity in War is subject generally, we have already spoken in the first book; we here omit those things which can only be overcome by courage, and maintain also that the activity of mind, is only simple, and easy in inferior stations, but increases in difficulty with increase of rank, and in the highest position, in that of Commander-in-Chief, is to be reckoned among the most difficult which there is for the human mind.

45. OF THE NATURE OF THIS KNOWLEDGE.

The Commander of an Army neither requires to be a learned explorer of history nor a publicist, but he must be well versed in the higher affairs of State; he must know, and be able to judge correctly of traditional tendencies, interests at stake, the immediate questions at issue, and the characters of leading persons; he need not be a close observer of men, a sharp dissector of human character, but he must know the character, the feelings, the habits, the peculiar faults and inclinations of those whom he is to command. He need not understand anything about the make of a carriage, or the harness of a battery horse, but he must know how to calculate exactly the march of a column, under different circumstances, according to the time it requires. These are matters the knowledge of which cannot be forced out by an apparatus of scientific formula and machinery: they are only to be gained by the exercise of an accurate judgment in the observation of things and of men, aided by a special talent for the apprehension of both.

The necessary knowledge for a high position in military action is therefore distinguished by this, that by observation, therefore by study and reflection, it is only to be attained through a special talent which as an intellectual instinct understands how to extract from the phenomena of life only the essence or spirit, as bees do the honey from the flowers; and that it is also to be gained by experience of life as well as by study and reflection. Life will never bring forth a Newton or an Euler by its rich teachings, but it may bring forth great calculators in War, such as Conde' or Frederick.

It is therefore not necessary that, in order to vindicate the intellectual dignity of military activity, we should resort to untruth and silly pedantry. There never has been a great and distinguished Commander of contracted mind, but very numerous are the instances of men who, after serving with the greatest distinction in inferior positions, remained below mediocrity in the highest, from insufficiency of intellectual capacity. That even amongst those holding the post of Commander-in-Chief there may be a difference according to the degree of their plenitude of power is a matter of course.

46. SCIENCE MUST BECOME ART.

Now we have yet to consider one condition which is more necessary for the knowledge of the conduct of War than for any other, which is, that it must pass completely into the mind and almost completely cease to be something objective. In almost all other arts and occupations of life the active agent can make use of truths which he has only learnt once, and in the spirit and sense of which he no longer lives, and which he extracts from dusty books. Even truths which he has in hand and uses daily may continue something external to himself, If the architect takes up a pen to settle the strength of a pier by a complicated calculation, the truth found as a result is no emanation from his own mind. He had first to find the data with labour, and then to submit these to an operation of the mind, the rule for which he did not discover, the necessity of which he is perhaps at the moment only partly conscious of, but which he applies, for the most part, as if by mechanical dexterity. But it is never so in War. The moral reaction, the ever-changeful form of things, makes it necessary for the chief actor to carry in himself the whole mental apparatus of his knowledge, that anywhere and at every pulse-beat he may be capable of giving the requisite decision from himself. Knowledge must, by this complete assimilation with his own mind and life, be converted into real power. This is the reason why everything seems so easy with men distinguished in War, and why everything is ascribed to natural talent. We say natural talent, in order thereby to distinguish it from that which is formed and matured by observation and study.

We think that by these reflections we have explained the problem of a theory of the conduct of War; and pointed out the way to its solution.

Of the two fields into which we have divided the conduct of War, tactics and strategy, the theory of the latter contains unquestionably, as before observed, the greatest difficulties, because the first is almost limited to a circumscribed field of objects, but the latter, in the direction of objects leading directly to peace, opens to itself an unlimited field of possibilities. Since for the most part the Commander-in-Chief has only to keep these objects steadily in view, therefore the part of strategy in which he moves is also that which is particularly subject to this difficulty.

Theory, therefore, especially where it comprehends the highest services, will stop much sooner in strategy than in tactics at the simple consideration of things, and content itself to assist the Commander to that insight into things which, blended with his whole thought, makes his course easier and surer, never forces him into opposition with himself in order to obey an objective truth.

CHAPTER III - ART OR SCIENCE OF WAR

1.—USAGE STILL UNSETTLED

(POWER AND KNOWLEDGE. SCIENCE WHEN MERE KNOWING; ART, WHEN DOING, IS THE OBJECT.)

THE choice between these terms seems to be still unsettled, and no one seems to know rightly on what grounds it should be decided, and yet the thing is simple. We have already said elsewhere that "knowing" is something different from "doing." The two are so different that they should not easily be mistaken the one for the other. The "doing" cannot properly stand in any book, and therefore also Art should never be the title of a book. But because we have once accustomed ourselves to combine in conception, under the name of theory of Art, or simply Art, the branches of knowledge (which may be separately pure sciences) necessary for the practice of an Art, therefore it is consistent to continue this ground of distinction, and to call everything Art when the object is to carry out the "doing" (being able), as for example, Art of building; Science, when merely knowledge is the object; as Science of mathematics, of astronomy. That in every Art certain complete sciences may be included is intelligible of itself, and should not perplex us. But still it is worth observing that there is also no science without a mixture of Art. In mathematics, for instance, the use of figures and of algebra is an Art, but that is only one amongst many instances. The reason is, that however plain and palpable the difference is between knowledge and power in the composite results of human knowledge, yet it is difficult to trace out their line of separation in man himself.

2. DIFFICULTY OF SEPARATING PERCEPTION FROM JUDGMENT. (ART OF WAR.)

All thinking is indeed Art. Where the logician draws the line, where the premises stop which are the result of cognition—where judgment begins, there Art begins. But more than this even the perception of the mind is judgment again, and consequently Art; and at last, even the perception by the senses as well. In a word, if it is impossible to imagine a human being possessing merely the faculty of cognition, devoid of judgment or the reverse, so also Art and Science can never be completely separated from each other. The more these subtle elements of light embody themselves in the outward forms of the world, so much the more separate appear their domains; and now once more, where the object is creation and production, there is the province of Art; where the object is investigation and knowledge Science holds sway.—After all this it results of itself that it is more fitting to say Art of War than Science of War.

So much for this, because we cannot do without these conceptions. But now we come forward with the assertion that War is neither an Art nor a Science in the real signification, and that it is just the setting out from that starting-point of ideas which has led to a wrong direction being taken, which has caused War to be put on a par with other arts and sciences, and has led to a number of erroneous analogies.

This has indeed been felt before now, and on that it was maintained that War is a handicraft; but there was more lost than gained by that, for a handicraft is only an inferior art, and as such is also subject to definite and rigid laws. In reality the Art of War did go on for some time in the spirit of a handicraft—we allude to the times of the Condottieri—but then it received that direction, not from intrinsic but from external causes; and military history shows how little it was at that time in accordance with the nature of the thing.

3. WAR IS PART OF THE INTERCOURSE OF THE HUMAN RACE.

We say therefore War belongs not to the province of Arts and Sciences, but to the province of social life. It is a conflict of great interests which is settled by bloodshed, and only in that is it different from others. It would be better, instead of comparing it with any Art, to liken it to business competition, which is also a conflict of human interests and activities; and it is still more like State policy, which again, on its part, may be looked upon as a kind of business competition on a great scale. Besides, State policy is the womb in which War is developed, in which its outlines lie hidden in a rudimentary state, like the qualities of living creatures in their germs.

4. DIFFERENCE.

The essential difference consists in this, that War is no activity of the will, which exerts itself upon inanimate matter like the mechanical Arts; or upon a living but still passive and yielding subject, like the human mind and the human feelings in the ideal Arts, but against a living and reacting force. How little the categories of Arts and Sciences are applicable to such an activity strikes us at once; and we can understand at the same time how that constant seeking and striving after laws like those which may be developed out of the dead material world could not but lead to constant errors. And yet it is just the mechanical Arts that some people would imitate in the Art of War. The imitation of the ideal Arts was quite out of the question, because these themselves dispense too much with laws and rules, and those hitherto tried, always acknowledged as insufficient and one-sided, are perpetually undermined and washed away by the current of opinions, feelings, and customs.

Whether such a conflict of the living, as takes place and is settled in War, is subject to general laws, and whether these are capable of indicating a useful line of action, will be partly investigated in this book; but so much is evident in itself, that this, like every other subject which does not surpass our powers of understanding, may be lighted up, and be made more or less plain in its inner relations by an inquiring mind, and that alone is sufficient to realise the idea of a THEORY.

CHAPTER IV - METHODICISM

IN order to explain ourselves clearly as to the conception of method, and method of action, which play such an important part in War, we must be allowed to cast a hasty glance at the logical hierarchy through which, as through regularly constituted official functionaries, the world of action is governed.

LAW, in the widest sense strictly applying to perception as well as action, has plainly something subjective and arbitrary in its literal meaning, and expresses just that on which we and those things external to us are dependent. As a subject of cognition, LAW is the relation of things and their effects to one another; as a subject of the will, it is a motive of action, and is then equivalent to COMMAND or PROHIBITION.

PRINCIPLE is likewise such a law for action, except that it has not the formal definite meaning, but is only the spirit and sense of law in order to leave the judgment more freedom of application when the diversity of the real world cannot be laid hold of under the definite form of a law. As the judgment must of itself suggest the cases in which the principle is not applicable, the latter therefore becomes in that way a real aid or guiding star for the person acting.

Principle is OBJECTIVE when it is the result of objective truth, and consequently of equal value for all men; it is SUBJECTIVE, and then generally called MAXIM if there are subjective relations in it, and if it therefore has a certain value only for the person himself who makes it.

RULE is frequently taken in the sense of LAW, and then means the same as Principle, for we say "no rule without exceptions," but we do not say "no law without exceptions," a sign that with RULE we retain to ourselves more freedom of application.

In another meaning RULE is the means used of discerning a recondite truth in a particular sign lying close at hand, in order to attach to this particular sign the law of action directed upon the whole truth. Of this kind are all the rules of games of play, all abridged processes in mathematics, &c.

DIRECTIONS and INSTRUCTIONS are determinations of action which have an influence upon a number of minor circumstances too numerous and unimportant for general laws.

Lastly, METHOD, MODE OF ACTING, is an always recurring proceeding selected out of several possible ones; and METHODICISM (METHODISMUS) is that which is determined by methods instead of by general principles or particular prescriptions. By this the cases which are placed under such methods must necessarily be supposed alike in their essential parts. As they cannot all be this, then the point is that at least as many as possible should be; in other words, that Method should be calculated on the most probable cases. Methodicism is therefore not founded on determined particular premises, but on the average probability of cases one with another; and its ultimate tendency is to set up an average truth, the constant and uniform, application of which soon acquires something of the nature of a mechanical appliance, which in the end does that which is right almost unwittingly.

The conception of law in relation to perception is not necessary for the conduct of War, because the complex phenomena of War are not so regular, and the regular are not so complex, that we should gain anything more by this conception than by the simple truth. And where a simple conception and language is sufficient, to resort to the complex becomes affected and pedantic. The conception of law in relation to action cannot be used in the theory of the conduct of War, because owing to the variableness and diversity of the phenomena there is in it no determination of such a general nature as to deserve the name of law.

But principles, rules, prescriptions, and methods are conceptions indispensable to a theory of the conduct of War, in so far as that theory leads to positive doctrines, because in doctrines the truth can only crystallise itself in such forms.

As tactics is the branch of the conduct of War in which theory can attain the nearest to positive doctrine, therefore these conceptions will appear in it most frequently.

Not to use cavalry against unbroken infantry except in some case of special emergency, only to use firearms within effective range in the combat, to spare the forces as much as possible for the final struggle—these are tactical principles. None of them can be applied absolutely in every case, but they must always be present to the mind of the Chief, in order that the benefit of the truth contained in them may not be lost in cases where that truth can be of advantage.

If from the unusual cooking by an enemy's camp his movement is inferred, if the intentional exposure of troops in a combat indicates a false attack, then this way of discerning the truth is called rule, because from a single visible circumstance that conclusion is drawn which corresponds with the same.

If it is a rule to attack the enemy with renewed vigour, as soon as he begins to limber up his artillery in the combat, then on this particular fact depends a course of action which is aimed at the general situation of the enemy as inferred from the above fact, namely, that he is about to give up the fight, that he is commencing to draw off his troops, and is neither capable of making a serious stand while thus drawing off nor of making his retreat gradually in good order.

REGULATIONS and METHODS bring preparatory theories into the conduct of War, in so far as disciplined troops are inoculated with them as active principles. The whole body of instructions for formations, drill, and field service are regulations and methods: in the drill instructions the first predominate, in the field service instructions the latter. To these things the real conduct of War attaches itself; it takes them over, therefore, as given modes of proceeding, and as such they must appear in the theory of the conduct of War.

But for those activities retaining freedom in the employment of these forces there cannot be regulations, that is, definite instructions, because they would do away with freedom of action. Methods, on the other hand, as a general way of executing duties as they arise, calculated, as we have said, on an average of probability, or as a dominating influence of principles and rules carried through to application, may certainly appear in the theory of the conduct of War, provided only they are not represented as something different from what they are, not as the absolute and necessary modes of action (systems), but as the best of general forms which may be used as shorter ways in place of a particular disposition for the occasion, at discretion.

But the frequent application of methods will be seen to be most essential and unavoidable in the conduct of War, if we reflect how much action proceeds on mere conjecture, or in complete uncertainty, because one side is prevented from learning all the circumstances which influence the dispositions of the other, or because, even if these circumstances which influence the decisions of the one were really known, there is not, owing to their extent and the dispositions they would entail, sufficient time for the other to carry out all necessary counteracting measures—that therefore measures in War must always be calculated on a certain number of possibilities; if we reflect how numberless are the trifling things belonging to any single event, and which therefore should be taken into account along with it, and that therefore there is no other means to suppose the one counteracted by the other, and to base our arrangements only upon what is of a general nature and probable; if we reflect lastly that, owing to the increasing number of officers as we descend the scale of rank, less must be left to the true discernment and ripe judgment of individuals the lower the sphere of action, and that when we reach those ranks where we can look for no other notions but those which the regulations of the service and experience afford, we must help them with the methodic forms bordering on those regulations. This will serve both as a support to their judgment and a barrier against those extravagant and erroneous views which are so especially to be dreaded in a sphere where experience is so costly.

Besides this absolute need of method in action, we must also acknowledge that it has a positive advantage, which is that, through the constant repetition of a formal exercise, a readiness, precision, and firmness is attained in the movement of troops which diminishes the natural friction, and makes the machine move easier.

Method will therefore be the more generally used, become the more indispensable, the farther down the scale of rank the position of the active agent; and on the other hand, its use will diminish upwards, until in the highest position it quite disappears. For this reason it is more in its place in tactics than in strategy.

War in its highest aspects consists not of an infinite number of little events, the diversities in which compensate each other, and which therefore by a better or worse method are better or worse governed, but of separate great decisive events which must be dealt with separately. It is not like a field of stalks, which, without any regard to the particular form of each stalk, will be mowed better or worse, according as the mowing instrument is good or bad, but rather as a group of large trees, to which the axe must be laid with judgment, according to the particular form and inclination of each separate trunk.

How high up in military activity the admissibility of method in action reaches naturally determines itself, not according to actual rank, but according to things; and it affects the highest positions in a less degree, only because these positions have the most comprehensive subjects of activity. A constant order of battle, a constant formation of advance guards and outposts, are methods by which a General ties not only his subordinates' hands, but also his own in certain cases. Certainly they may have been devised by himself, and may be applied by him according to circumstances, but they may also be a subject of theory, in so far as they are based on the general properties of troops and weapons. On the other hand, any method by which definite plans for wars or campaigns are to be given out all ready made as if from a machine are absolutely worthless.

As long as there exists no theory which can be sustained, that is, no enlightened treatise on the conduct of War, method in action cannot but encroach beyond its proper limits in high places, for men employed in these spheres of activity have not always had the opportunity of educating themselves, through study and through contact with the higher interests. In the impracticable and inconsistent disquisitions of theorists and critics they cannot find their way, their sound common sense rejects them, and as they bring with them no knowledge but that derived from experience, therefore in those cases which admit of, and require, a free individual treatment they readily make use of the means which experience gives them—that is, an imitation of the particular methods practised by great Generals, by which a method of action then arises of itself. If we see Frederick the Great's Generals always making their appearance in the so-called oblique order of battle, the Generals of the French Revolution always using turning movements with a long, extended line of battle, and Buonaparte's lieutenants rushing to the attack with the bloody energy of concentrated masses, then we recognise in the recurrence of the mode of proceeding evidently an adopted method, and see therefore that method of action can reach up to regions bordering on the highest. Should an improved theory facilitate the study of the conduct of War, form the mind and judgment of men who are rising to the highest commands, then also method in action will no longer reach so far, and so much of it as is to be considered indispensable will then at least be formed from theory itself, and not take place out of mere imitation. However pre-eminently a great Commander does things, there is always something subjective in the way he does them; and if he has a certain manner, a large share of his individuality is contained in it which does not always accord with the individuality of the person who copies his manner.

At the same time, it would neither be possible nor right to banish subjective methodicism or manner completely from the conduct of War: it is rather to be regarded as a manifestation of that influence which the general character of a War has upon its separate events, and to which satisfaction can only be done in that way if theory is not able to foresee this general character and include it in its considerations. What is more natural than that the War of the French Revolution had its own way of doing things? and what theory could ever have included that peculiar method? The evil is only that such a manner originating in a special case easily outlives itself, because it continues whilst circumstances imperceptibly change. This is what theory should prevent by lucid and rational criticism. When in the year 1806 the Prussian Generals, Prince Louis at Saalfeld, Tauentzien on the Dornberg near Jena, Grawert before and Ruechel behind Kappellendorf, all threw themselves into the open jaws of destruction in the oblique order of Frederick the Great, and managed to ruin Hohenlohe's Army in a way that no Army was ever ruined, even on the field of battle, all this was done through a manner which had outlived its day, together with the most downright stupidity to which methodicism ever led.

CHAPTER V - CRITICISM

THE influence of theoretical principles upon real life is produced more through criticism than through doctrine, for as criticism is an application of abstract truth to real events, therefore it not only brings truth of this description nearer to life, but also accustoms the understanding more to such truths by the constant repetition of their application. We therefore think it necessary to fix the point of view for criticism next to that for theory.

From the simple narration of an historical occurrence which places events in chronological order, or at most only touches on their more immediate causes, we separate the CRITICAL.

In this CRITICAL three different operations of the mind may be observed.

First, the historical investigation and determining of doubtful facts. This is properly historical research, and has nothing in common with theory.

Secondly, the tracing of effects to causes. This is the REAL CRITICAL INQUIRY; it is indispensable to theory, for everything which in theory is to be established, supported, or even merely explained, by experience can only be settled in this way.

Thirdly, the testing of the means employed. This is criticism, properly speaking, in which praise and censure is contained. This is where theory helps history, or rather, the teaching to be derived from it.

In these two last strictly critical parts of historical study, all depends on tracing things to their primary elements, that is to say, up to undoubted truths, and not, as is so often done, resting half-way, that is, on some arbitrary assumption or supposition.

As respects the tracing of effect to cause, that is often attended with the insuperable difficulty that the real causes are not known. In none of the relations of life does this so frequently happen as in War, where events are seldom fully known, and still less motives, as the latter have been, perhaps purposely, concealed by the chief actor, or have been of such a transient and accidental character that they have been lost for history. For this reason critical narration must generally proceed hand in hand with historical investigation, and still such a want of connection between cause and effect will often present itself, that it does not seem justifiable to consider effects as the necessary results of known causes. Here, therefore must occur, that is, historical results which cannot be made use of for teaching. All that theory can demand is that the investigation should be rigidly conducted up to that point, and there leave off without drawing conclusions. A real evil springs up only if the known is made perforce to suffice as an explanation of effects, and thus a false importance is ascribed to it.

Besides this difficulty, critical inquiry also meets with another great and intrinsic one, which is that the progress of events in War seldom proceeds from one simple cause, but from several in common, and that it therefore is not sufficient to follow up a series of events to their origin in a candid and impartial spirit, but that it is then also necessary to apportion to each contributing cause its due weight. This leads, therefore, to a closer investigation of their nature, and thus a critical investigation may lead into what is the proper field of theory.

The critical CONSIDERATION, that is, the testing of the means, leads to the question, Which are the effects peculiar to the means applied, and whether these effects were comprehended in the plans of the person directing?

The effects peculiar to the means lead to the investigation of their nature, and thus again into the field of theory.

We have already seen that in criticism all depends upon attaining to positive truth; therefore, that we must not stop at arbitrary propositions which are not allowed by others, and to which other perhaps equally arbitrary assertions may again be opposed, so that there is no end to pros and cons; the whole is without result, and therefore without instruction.

We have seen that both the search for causes and the examination of means lead into the field of theory; that is, into the field of universal truth, which does not proceed solely from the case immediately under examination. If there is a theory which can be used, then the critical consideration will appeal to the proofs there afforded, and the examination may there stop. But where no such theoretical truth is to be found, the inquiry must be pushed up to the original elements. If this necessity occurs often, it must lead the historian (according to a common expression) into a labyrinth of details. He then has his hands full, and it is impossible for him to stop to give the requisite attention everywhere; the consequence is, that in order to set bounds to his investigation, he adopts some arbitrary assumptions which, if they do not appear so to him, do so to others, as they are not evident in themselves or capable of proof.

A sound theory is therefore an essential foundation for criticism, and it is impossible for it, without the assistance of a sensible theory, to attain to that point at which it commences chiefly to be instructive, that is, where it becomes demonstration, both convincing and sans re'plique.

But it would be a visionary hope to believe in the possibility of a theory applicable to every abstract truth, leaving nothing for criticism to do but to place the case under its appropriate law: it would be ridiculous pedantry to lay down as a rule for criticism that it must always halt and turn round on reaching the boundaries of sacred theory. The same spirit of analytical inquiry which is the origin of theory must also guide the critic in his work; and it can and must therefore happen that he strays beyond the boundaries of the province of theory and elucidates those points with which he is more particularly concerned. It is more likely, on the contrary, that criticism would completely fail in its object if it degenerated into a mechanical application of theory. All positive results of theoretical inquiry, all principles, rules, and methods, are the more wanting in generality and positive truth the more they become positive doctrine. They exist to offer themselves for use as required, and it must always be left for judgment to decide whether they are suitable or not. Such results of theory must never be used in criticism as rules or norms for a standard, but in the same way as the person acting should use them, that is, merely as aids to judgment. If it is an acknowledged principle in tactics that in the usual order of battle cavalry should be placed behind infantry, not in line with it, still it would be folly on this account to condemn every deviation from this principle. Criticism must investigate the grounds of the deviation, and it is only in case these are insufficient that it has a right to appeal to principles laid down in theory. If it is further established in theory that a divided attack diminishes the probability of success, still it would be just as unreasonable, whenever there is a divided attack and an unsuccessful issue, to regard the latter as the result of the former, without further investigation into the connection between the two, as where a divided attack is successful to infer from it the fallacy of that theoretical principle. The spirit of investigation which belongs to criticism cannot allow either. Criticism therefore supports itself chiefly on the results of the analytical investigation of theory; what has been made out and determined by theory does not require to be demonstrated over again by criticism, and it is so determined by theory that criticism may find it ready demonstrated.

This office of criticism, of examining the effect produced by certain causes, and whether a means applied has answered its object, will be easy enough if cause and effect, means and end, are all near together.

If an Army is surprised, and therefore cannot make a regular and intelligent use of its powers and resources, then the effect of the surprise is not doubtful.—If theory has determined that in a battle the convergent form of attack is calculated to produce greater but less certain results, then the question is whether he who employs that convergent form had in view chiefly that greatness of result as his object; if so, the proper means were chosen. But if by this form he intended to make the result more certain, and that expectation was founded not on some exceptional circumstances (in this case), but on the general nature of the convergent form, as has happened a hundred times, then he mistook the nature of the means and committed an error.

Here the work of military investigation and criticism is easy, and it will always be so when confined to the immediate effects and objects. This can be done quite at option, if we abstract the connection of the parts with the whole, and only look at things in that relation.

But in War, as generally in the world, there is a connection between everything which belongs to a whole; and therefore, however small a cause may be in itself, its effects reach to the end of the act of warfare, and modify or influence the final result in some degree, let that degree be ever so small. In the same manner every means must be felt up to the ultimate object.

We can therefore trace the effects of a cause as long as events are worth noticing, and in the same way we must not stop at the testing of a means for the immediate object, but test also this object as a means to a higher one, and thus ascend the series of facts in succession, until we come to one so absolutely necessary in its nature as to require no examination or proof. In many cases, particularly in what concerns great and decisive measures, the investigation must be carried to the final aim, to that which leads immediately to peace.

It is evident that in thus ascending, at every new station which we reach a new point of view for the judgment is attained, so that the same means which appeared advisable at one station, when looked at from the next above it may have to be rejected.

The search for the causes of events and the comparison of means with ends must always go hand in hand in the critical review of an act, for the investigation of causes leads us first to the discovery of those things which are worth examining.

This following of the clue up and down is attended with considerable difficulty, for the farther from an event the cause lies which we are looking for, the greater must be the number of other causes which must at the same time be kept in view and allowed for in reference to the share which they have in the course of events, and then eliminated, because the higher the importance of a fact the greater will be the number of separate forces and circumstances by which it is conditioned. If we have unravelled the causes of a battle being lost, we have certainly also ascertained a part of the causes of the consequences which this defeat has upon the whole War, but only a part, because the effects of other causes, more or less according to circumstances, will flow into the final result.

The same multiplicity of circumstances is presented also in the examination of the means the higher our point of view, for the higher the object is situated, the greater must be the number of means employed to reach it. The ultimate object of the War is the object aimed at by all the Armies simultaneously, and it is therefore necessary that the consideration should embrace all that each has done or could have done.

It is obvious that this may sometimes lead to a wide field of inquiry, in which it is easy to wander and lose the way, and in which this difficulty prevails—that a number of assumptions or suppositions must be made about a variety of things which do not actually appear, but which in all probability did take place, and therefore cannot possibly be left out of consideration.

When Buonaparte, in 1797, at the head of the Army of Italy, advanced from the Tagliamento against the Archduke Charles, he did so with a view to force that General to a decisive action before the reinforcements expected from the Rhine had reached him. If we look, only at the immediate object, the means were well chosen and justified by the result, for the Archduke was so inferior in numbers that he only made a show of resistance on the Tagliamento, and when he saw his adversary so strong and resolute, yielded ground, and left open the passages, of the Norican Alps. Now to what use could Buonaparte turn this fortunate event? To penetrate into the heart of the Austrian empire itself, to facilitate the advance of the Rhine Armies under Moreau and Hoche, and open communication with them? This was the view taken by Buonaparte, and from this point of view he was right. But now, if criticism places itself at a higher point of view—namely, that of the French Directory, which body could see and know that the Armies on the Rhine could not commence the campaign for six weeks, then the advance of Buonaparte over the Norican Alps can only be regarded as an extremely hazardous measure; for if the Austrians had drawn largely on their Rhine Armies to reinforce their Army in Styria, so as to enable the Archduke to fall upon the Army of Italy, not only would that Army have been routed, but the whole campaign lost. This consideration, which attracted the serious attention of Buonaparte at Villach, no doubt induced him to sign the armistice of Leoben with so much readiness.

If criticism takes a still higher position, and if it knows that the Austrians had no reserves between the Army of the Archduke Charles and Vienna, then we see that Vienna became threatened by the advance of the Army of Italy.

Supposing that Buonaparte knew that the capital was thus uncovered, and knew that he still retained the same superiority in numbers over the Archduke as he had in Styria, then his advance against the heart of the Austrian States was no longer without purpose, and its value depended on the value which the Austrians might place on preserving their capital. If that was so great that, rather than lose it, they would accept the conditions of peace which Buonaparte was ready to offer them, it became an object of the first importance to threaten Vienna. If Buonaparte had any reason to know this, then criticism may stop there, but if this point was only problematical, then criticism must take a still higher position, and ask what would have followed if the Austrians had resolved to abandon Vienna and retire farther into the vast dominions still left to them. But it is easy to see that this question cannot be answered without bringing into the consideration the probable movements of the Rhine Armies on both sides. Through the decided superiority of numbers on the side of the French—130,000 to 80,000—there could be little doubt of the result; but then next arises the question, What use would the Directory make of a victory; whether they would follow up their success to the opposite frontiers of the Austrian monarchy, therefore to the complete breaking up or overthrow of that power, or whether they would be satisfied with the conquest of a considerable portion to serve as a security for peace? The probable result in each case must be estimated, in order to come to a conclusion as to the probable determination of the Directory. Supposing the result of these considerations to be that the French forces were much too weak for the complete subjugation of the Austrian monarchy, so that the attempt might completely reverse the respective positions of the contending Armies, and that even the conquest and occupation of a considerable district of country would place the French Army in strategic relations to which they were not equal, then that result must naturally influence the estimate of the position of the Army of Italy, and compel it to lower its expectations. And this, it was no doubt which influenced Buonaparte, although fully aware of the helpless condition of the Archduke, still to sign the peace of Campo Formio, which imposed no greater sacrifices on the Austrians than the loss of provinces which, even if the campaign took the most favourable turn for them, they could not have reconquered. But the French could not have reckoned on even the moderate treaty of Campo Formio, and therefore it could not have been their object in making their bold advance if two considerations had not presented themselves to their view, the first of which consisted in the question, what degree of value the Austrians would attach to each of the above-mentioned results; whether, notwithstanding the probability of a satisfactory result in either of these cases, would it be worth while to make the sacrifices inseparable from a continuance of the War, when they could be spared those sacrifices by a peace on terms not too humiliating? The second consideration is the question whether the Austrian Government, instead of seriously weighing the possible results of a resistance pushed to extremities, would not prove completely disheartened by the impression of their present reverses.

The consideration which forms the subject of the first is no idle piece of subtle argument, but a consideration of such decidedly practical importance that it comes up whenever the plan of pushing War to the utmost extremity is mooted, and by its weight in most cases restrains the execution of such plans.

The second consideration is of equal importance, for we do not make War with an abstraction but with a reality, which we must always keep in view, and we may be sure that it was not overlooked by the bold Buonaparte—that is, that he was keenly alive to the terror which the appearance of his sword inspired. It was reliance on that which led him to Moscow. There it led him into a scrape. The terror of him had been weakened by the gigantic struggles in which he had been engaged; in the year 1797 it was still fresh, and the secret of a resistance pushed to extremities had not been discovered; nevertheless even in 1797 his boldness might have led to a negative result if, as already said, he had not with a sort of presentiment avoided it by signing the moderate peace of Campo Formio.

We must now bring these considerations to a close—they will suffice to show the wide sphere, the diversity and embarrassing nature of the subjects embraced in a critical examination carried to the fullest extent, that is, to those measures of a great and decisive class which must necessarily be included. It follows from them that besides a theoretical acquaintance with the subject, natural talent must also have a great influence on the value of critical examinations, for it rests chiefly with the latter to throw the requisite light on the interrelations of things, and to distinguish from amongst the endless connections of events those which are really essential.

But talent is also called into requisition in another way. Critical examination is not merely the appreciation of those means which have been actually employed, but also of all possible means, which therefore must be suggested in the first place— that is, must be discovered; and the use of any particular means is not fairly open to censure until a better is pointed out. Now, however small the number of possible combinations may be in most cases, still it must be admitted that to point out those which have not been used is not a mere analysis of actual things, but a spontaneous creation which cannot be prescribed, and depends on the fertility of genius.

We are far from seeing a field for great genius in a case which admits only of the application of a few simple combinations, and we think it exceedingly ridiculous to hold up, as is often done, the turning of a position as an invention showing the highest genius; still nevertheless this creative self-activity on the part of the critic is necessary, and it is one of the points which essentially determine the value of critical examination.

When Buonaparte on 30th July, 1796, determined to raise the siege of Mantua, in order to march with his whole force against the enemy, advancing in separate columns to the relief of the place, and to beat them in detail, this appeared the surest way to the attainment of brilliant victories. These victories actually followed, and were afterwards again repeated on a still more brilliant scale on the attempt to relieve the fortress being again renewed. We hear only one opinion on these achievements, that of unmixed admiration.

At the same time, Buonaparte could not have adopted this course on the 30th July without quite giving up the idea of the siege of Mantua, because it was impossible to save the siege train, and it could not be replaced by another in this campaign. In fact, the siege was converted into a blockade, and the town, which if the siege had continued must have very shortly fallen, held out for six months in spite of Buonaparte's victories in the open field.

Criticism has generally regarded this as an evil that was unavoidable, because critics have not been able to suggest any better course. Resistance to a relieving Army within lines of circumvallation had fallen into such disrepute and contempt that it appears to have entirely escaped consideration as a means. And yet in the reign of Louis XIV. that measure was so often used with success that we can only attribute to the force of fashion the fact that a hundred years later it never occurred to any one even to propose such a measure. If the practicability of such a plan had ever been entertained for a moment, a closer consideration of circumstances would have shown that 40,000 of the best infantry in the world under Buonaparte, behind strong lines of circumvallation round Mantua, had so little to fear from the 50,000 men coming to the relief under Wurmser, that it was very unlikely that any attempt even would be made upon their lines. We shall not seek here to establish this point, but we believe enough has been said to show that this means was one which had a right to a share of consideration. Whether Buonaparte himself ever thought of such a plan we leave undecided; neither in his memoirs nor in other sources is there any trace to be found of his having done so; in no critical works has it been touched upon, the measure being one which the mind had lost sight of. The merit of resuscitating the idea of this means is not great, for it suggests itself at once to any one who breaks loose from the trammels of fashion. Still it is necessary that it should suggest itself for us to bring it into consideration and compare it with the means which Buonaparte employed. Whatever may be the result of the comparison, it is one which should not be omitted by criticism.

When Buonaparte, in February, 1814, after gaining the battles at Etoges, Champ-Aubert, and Montmirail, left Bluecher's Army, and turning upon

Schwartzenberg, beat his troops at Montereau and Mormant, every one was filled with admiration, because Buonaparte, by thus throwing his concentrated force first upon one opponent, then upon another, made a brilliant use of the mistakes which his adversaries had committed in dividing their forces. If these brilliant strokes in different directions failed to save him, it was generally considered to be no fault of his, at least. No one has yet asked the question, What would have been the result if, instead of turning from Bluecher upon Schwartzenberg, he had tried another blow at Bluecher, and pursued him to the Rhine? We are convinced that it would have completely changed the course of the campaign, and that the Army of the Allies, instead of marching to Paris, would have retired behind the Rhine. We do not ask others to share our conviction, but no one who understands the thing will doubt, at the mere mention of this alternative course, that it is one which should not be overlooked in criticism.

In this case the means of comparison lie much more on the surface than in the foregoing, but they have been equally overlooked, because one-sided views have prevailed, and there has been no freedom of judgment.

From the necessity of pointing out a better means which might have been used in place of those which are condemned has arisen the form of criticism almost exclusively in use, which contents itself with pointing out the better means without demonstrating in what the superiority consists. The consequence is that some are not convinced, that others start up and do the same thing, and that thus discussion arises which is without any fixed basis for the argument. Military literature abounds with matter of this sort.

The demonstration we require is always necessary when the superiority of the means propounded is not so evident as to leave no room for doubt, and it consists in the examination of each of the means on its own merits, and then of its comparison with the object desired. When once the thing is traced back to a simple truth, controversy must cease, or at all events a new result is obtained, whilst by the other plan the pros and cons go on for ever consuming each other.

Should we, for example, not rest content with assertion in the case before mentioned, and wish to prove that the persistent pursuit of Bluecher would have been more advantageous than the turning on Schwartzenberg, we should support the arguments on the following simple truths:

1. In general it is more advantageous to continue our blows in one and the same direction, because there is a loss of time in striking in different directions; and at a point where the moral power is already shaken by considerable losses there is the more reason to expect fresh successes, therefore in that way no part of the preponderance already gained is left idle.

2. Because Bluecher, although weaker than Schwartzenberg, was, on account of his enterprising spirit, the more important adversary; in him, therefore, lay the centre of attraction which drew the others along in the same direction.

3. Because the losses which Bluecher had sustained almost amounted to a defeat, which gave Buonaparte such a preponderance over him as to make his retreat to the Rhine almost certain, and at the same time no reserves of any consequence awaited him there.

296

4. Because there was no other result which would be so terrific in its aspects, would appear to the imagination in such gigantic proportions, an immense advantage in dealing with a Staff so weak and irresolute as that of Schwartzenberg notoriously was at this time. What had happened to the Crown Prince of Wartemberg at Montereau, and to Count Wittgenstein at Mormant, Prince Schwartzenberg must have known well enough; but all the untoward events on Bluecher's distant and separate line from the Marne to the Rhine would only reach him by the avalanche of rumour. The desperate movements which Buonaparte made upon Vitry at the end of March, to see what the Allies would do if he threatened to turn them strategically, were evidently done on the principle of working on their fears; but it was done under far different circumstances, in consequence of his defeat at Laon and Arcis, and because Bluecher, with 100,000 men, was then in communication with Schwartzenberg.

There are people, no doubt, who will not be convinced on these arguments, but at all events they cannot retort by saying, that "whilst Buonaparte threatened Schwartzenberg's base by advancing to the Rhine, Schwartzenberg at the same time threatened Buonaparte's communications with Paris," because we have shown by the reasons above given that Schwartzenberg would never have thought of marching on Paris.

With respect to the example quoted by us from the campaign of 1796, we should say: Buonaparte looked upon the plan he adopted as the surest means of beating the Austrians; but admitting that it was so, still the object to be attained was only an empty victory, which could have hardly any sensible influence on the fall of Mantua. The way which we should have chosen would, in our opinion, have been much more certain to prevent the relief of Mantua; but even if we place ourselves in the position of the French General and assume that it was not so, and look upon the certainty of success to have been less, the question then amounts to a choice between a more certain but less useful, and therefore less important, victory on the one hand, and a somewhat less probable but far more decisive and important victory, on the other hand. Presented in this form, boldness must have declared for the second solution, which is the reverse of what took place, when the thing was only superficially viewed. Buonaparte certainly was anything but deficient in boldness, and we may be sure that he did not see the whole case and its consequences as fully and clearly as we can at the present time.

Naturally the critic, in treating of the means, must often appeal to military history, as experience is of more value in the Art of War than all philosophical truth. But this exemplification from history is subject to certain conditions, of which we shall treat in a special chapter and unfortunately these conditions are so seldom regarded that reference to history generally only serves to increase the confusion of ideas.

We have still a most important subject to consider, which is, How far criticism in passing judgments on particular events is permitted, or in duty bound, to make use of its wider view of things, and therefore also of that which is shown by results; or when and where it should leave out of sight these things in order to place itself, as far as possible, in the exact position of the chief actor?

If criticism dispenses praise or censure, it should seek to place itself as nearly as possible at the same point of view as the person acting, that is to say, to collect all he knew and all the motives on which he acted, and, on the other hand, to leave out of the consideration all that the person acting could not or did not know, and above all, the result. But this is only an object to aim at, which can never be reached because the state of circumstances from which an event proceeded can never be placed before the eye of the critic exactly as it lay before the eye of the person acting. A number of inferior circumstances, which must have influenced the result, are completely lost to sight, and many a subjective motive has never come to light.

The latter can only be learnt from the memoirs of the chief actor, or from his intimate friends; and in such things of this kind are often treated of in a very desultory manner, or purposely misrepresented. Criticism must, therefore, always forego much which was present in the minds of those whose acts are criticised.

On the other hand, it is much more difficult to leave out of sight that which criticism knows in excess. This is only easy as regards accidental circumstances, that is, circumstances which have been mixed up, but are in no way necessarily related. But it is very difficult, and, in fact, can never be completely done with regard to things really essential.

Let us take first, the result. If it has not proceeded from accidental circumstances, it is almost impossible that the knowledge of it should not have an effect on the judgment passed on events which have preceded it, for we see these things in the light of this result, and it is to a certain extent by it that we first become acquainted with them and appreciate them. Military history, with all its events, is a source of instruction for criticism itself, and it is only natural that criticism should throw that light on things which it has itself obtained from the consideration of the whole. If therefore it might wish in some cases to leave the result out of the consideration, it would be impossible to do so completely.

But it is not only in relation to the result, that is, with what takes place at the last, that this embarrassment arises; the same occurs in relation to preceding events, therefore with the data which furnished the motives to action. Criticism has before it, in most cases, more information on this point than the principal in the transaction. Now it may seem easy to dismiss from the consideration everything of this nature, but it is not so easy as we may think. The knowledge of preceding and concurrent events is founded not only on certain information, but on a number of conjectures and suppositions; indeed, there is hardly any of the information respecting things not purely accidental which has not been preceded by suppositions or conjectures destined to take the place of certain information in case such should never be supplied. Now is it conceivable that criticism in after times, which has before it as facts all the preceding and concurrent circumstances, should not allow itself to be thereby influenced when it asks itself the question, What portion of the circumstances, which at the moment of action were unknown, would it have held to be probable? We maintain that in this case, as in the case of the results, and for the same reason, it is impossible to disregard all these things completely.

If therefore the critic wishes to bestow praise or blame upon any single act, he can only succeed to a certain degree in placing himself in the position of the person whose act he has under review. In many cases he can do so sufficiently near for any practical purpose, but in many instances it is the very reverse, and this fact should never be overlooked.

But it is neither necessary nor desirable that criticism should completely identify itself with the person acting. In War, as in all matters of skill, there is a certain natural aptitude required which is called talent. This may be great or small. In the first case it may easily be superior to that of the critic, for what critic can pretend to the skill of a Frederick or a Buonaparte? Therefore, if criticism is not to abstain altogether from offering an opinion where eminent talent is concerned, it must be allowed to make use of the advantage which its enlarged horizon affords. Criticism must not, therefore, treat the solution of a problem by a great General like a sum in arithmetic; it is only through the results and through the exact coincidences of events that it can recognise with admiration how much is due to the exercise of genius, and that it first learns the essential combination which the glance of that genius devised.

But for every, even the smallest, act of genius it is necessary that criticism should take a higher point of view, so that, having at command many objective grounds of decision, it may be as little subjective as possible, and that the critic may not take the limited scope of his own mind as a standard.

This elevated position of criticism, its praise and blame pronounced with a full knowledge of all the circumstances, has in itself nothing which hurts our feelings; it only does so if the critic pushes himself forward, and speaks in a tone as if all the wisdom which he has obtained by an exhaustive examination of the event under consideration were really his own talent. Palpable as is this deception, it is one which people may easily fall into through vanity, and one which is naturally distasteful to others. It very often happens that although the critic has no such arrogant pretensions, they are imputed to him by the reader because he has not expressly disclaimed them, and then follows immediately a charge of a want of the power of critical judgment.

If therefore a critic points out an error made by a Frederick or a Buonaparte, that does not mean that he who makes the criticism would not have committed the same error; he may even be ready to grant that had he been in the place of these great Generals he might have made much greater mistakes; he merely sees this error from the chain of events, and he thinks that it should not have escaped the sagacity of the General.

This is, therefore, an opinion formed through the connection of events, and therefore through the RESULT. But there is another quite different effect of the result itself upon the judgment, that is if it is used quite alone as an example for or against the soundness of a measure. This may be called JUDGMENT ACCORDING TO THE RESULT. Such a judgment appears at first sight inadmissible, and yet it is not.

When Buonaparte marched to Moscow in 1812, all depended upon whether the taking of the capital, and the events which preceded the capture, would force the Emperor Alexander to make peace, as he had been compelled to do after the battle of Friedland in 1807, and the Emperor Francis in 1805 and 1809 after Austerlitz and

Wagram; for if Buonaparte did not obtain a peace at Moscow, there was no alternative but to return—that is, there was nothing for him but a strategic defeat. We shall leave out of the question what he did to get to Moscow, and whether in his advance he did not miss many opportunities of bringing the Emperor Alexander to peace; we shall also exclude all consideration of the disastrous circumstances which attended his retreat, and which perhaps had their origin in the general conduct of the campaign. Still the question remains the same, for however much more brilliant the course of the campaign up to Moscow might have been, still there was always an uncertainty whether the Emperor Alexander would be intimidated into making peace; and then, even if a retreat did not contain in itself the seeds of such disasters as did in fact occur, still it could never be anything else than a great strategic defeat. If the Emperor Alexander agreed to a peace which was disadvantageous to him, the campaign of 1812 would have ranked with those of Austerlitz, Friedland, and Wagram. But these campaigns also, if they had not led to peace, would in all probability have ended in similar catastrophes. Whatever, therefore, of genius, skill, and energy the Conqueror of the World applied to the task, this last question addressed to fate remained always the same. Shall we then discard the campaigns of 1805, 1807, 1809, and say on account of the campaign of 1812 that they were acts of imprudence; that the results were against the nature of things, and that in 1812 strategic justice at last found vent for itself in opposition to blind chance? That would be an unwarrantable conclusion, a most arbitrary judgment, a case only half proved, because no human, eye can trace the thread of the necessary connection of events up to the determination of the conquered Princes.

Still less can we say the campaign of 1812 merited the same success as the others, and that the reason why it turned out otherwise lies in something unnatural, for we cannot regard the firmness of Alexander as something unpredictable.

What can be more natural than to say that in the years 1805, 1807, 1809, Buonaparte judged his opponents correctly, and that in 1812 he erred in that point? On the former occasions, therefore, he was right, in the latter wrong, and in both cases we judge by the RESULT.

All action in War, as we have already said, is directed on probable, not on certain, results. Whatever is wanting in certainty must always be left to fate, or chance, call it which you will. We may demand that what is so left should be as little as possible, but only in relation to the particular case—that is, as little as is possible in this one case, but not that the case in which the least is left to chance is always to be preferred. That would be an enormous error, as follows from all our theoretical views. There are cases in which the greatest daring is the greatest wisdom.

Now in everything which is left to chance by the chief actor, his personal merit, and therefore his responsibility as well, seems to be completely set aside; nevertheless we cannot suppress an inward feeling of satisfaction whenever expectation realises itself, and if it disappoints us our mind is dissatisfied; and more than this of right and wrong should not be meant by the judgment which we form from the mere result, or rather that we find there.

Nevertheless, it cannot be denied that the satisfaction which our mind experiences at success, the pain caused by failure, proceed from a sort of mysterious feeling; we suppose between that success ascribed to good fortune and the genius of the chief a fine connecting thread, invisible to the mind's eye, and the supposition gives pleasure. What tends to confirm this idea is that our sympathy increases, becomes more decided, if the successes and defeats of the principal actor are often repeated. Thus it becomes intelligible how good luck in War assumes a much nobler nature than good luck at play. In general, when a fortunate warrior does not otherwise lessen our interest in his behalf, we have a pleasure in accompanying him in his career.

Criticism, therefore, after having weighed all that comes within the sphere of human reason and conviction, will let the result speak for that part where the deep mysterious relations are not disclosed in any visible form, and will protect this silent sentence of a higher authority from the noise of crude opinions on the one hand, while on the other it prevents the gross abuse which might be made of this last tribunal.

This verdict of the result must therefore always bring forth that which human sagacity cannot discover; and it will be chiefly as regards the intellectual powers and operations that it will be called into requisition, partly because they can be estimated with the least certainty, partly because their close connection with the will is favourable to their exercising over it an important influence. When fear or bravery precipitates the decision, there is nothing objective intervening between them for our consideration, and consequently nothing by which sagacity and calculation might have met the probable result.

We must now be allowed to make a few observations on the instrument of criticism, that is, the language which it uses, because that is to a certain extent connected with the action in War; for the critical examination is nothing more than the deliberation which should precede action in War. We therefore think it very essential that the language used in criticism should have the same character as that which deliberation in War must have, for otherwise it would cease to be practical, and criticism could gain no admittance in actual life.

We have said in our observations on the theory of the conduct of War that it should educate the mind of the Commander for War, or that its teaching should guide his education; also that it is not intended to furnish him with positive doctrines and systems which he can use like mental appliances. But if the construction of scientific formulae is never required, or even allowable, in War to aid the decision on the case presented, if truth does not appear there in a systematic shape, if it is not found in an indirect way, but directly by the natural perception of the mind, then it must be the same also in a critical review.

It is true as we have seen that, wherever complete demonstration of the nature of things would be too tedious, criticism must support itself on those truths which theory has established on the point. But, just as in War the actor obeys these theoretical truths rather because his mind is imbued with them than because he regards them as objective inflexible laws, so criticism must also make use of them, not as an external law or an algebraic formula, of which fresh proof is not required each time they are applied, but it must always throw a light on this proof itself, leaving only to theory the more minute and circumstantial proof. Thus it avoids a mysterious, unintelligible phraseology, and makes its progress in plain language, that is, with a clear and always visible chain of ideas.

Certainly this cannot always be completely attained, but it must always be the aim in critical expositions. Such expositions must use complicated forms of science as sparingly as possible, and never resort to the construction of scientific aids as of a truth apparatus of its own, but always be guided by the natural and unbiassed impressions of the mind.

But this pious endeavour, if we may use the expression, has unfortunately seldom hitherto presided over critical examinations: the most of them have rather been emanations of a species of vanity—a wish to make a display of ideas.

The first evil which we constantly stumble upon is a lame, totally inadmissible application of certain one-sided systems as of a formal code of laws. But it is never difficult to show the one-sidedness of such systems, and this only requires to be done once to throw discredit for ever on critical judgments which are based on them. We have here to deal with a definite subject, and as the number of possible systems after all can be but small, therefore also they are themselves the lesser evil.

Much greater is the evil which lies in the pompous retinue of technical terms—scientific expressions and metaphors, which these systems carry in their train, and which like a rabble-like the baggage of an Army broken away from its Chief—hang about in all directions. Any critic who has not adopted a system, either because he has not found one to please him, or because he has not yet been able to make himself master of one, will at least occasionally make use of a piece of one, as one would use a ruler, to show the blunders committed by a General. The most of them are incapable of reasoning without using as a help here and there some shreds of scientific military theory. The smallest of these fragments, consisting in mere scientific words and metaphors, are often nothing more than ornamental flourishes of critical narration. Now it is in the nature of things that all technical and scientific expressions which belong to a system lose their propriety, if they ever had any, as soon as they are distorted, and used as general axioms, or as small crystalline talismans, which have more power of demonstration than simple speech.

Thus it has come to pass that our theoretical and critical books, instead of being straightforward, intelligible dissertations, in which the author always knows at least what he says and the reader what he reads, are brimful of these technical terms, which form dark points of interference where author and reader part company. But frequently they are something worse, being nothing but hollow shells without any kernel. The author himself has no clear perception of what he means, contents himself with vague ideas, which if expressed in plain language would be unsatisfactory even to himself.

A third fault in criticism is the MISUSE of HISTORICAL EXAMPLES, and a display of great reading or learning. What the history of the Art of War is we have already said, and we shall further explain our views on examples and on military history in general in special chapters. One fact merely touched upon in a very cursory manner may be used to support the most opposite views, and three or four such facts of the most heterogeneous description, brought together out of the most distant lands and remote times and heaped up, generally distract and bewilder the judgment and understanding without demonstrating anything; for when exposed to the light they turn out to be only trumpery rubbish, made use of to show off the author's learning.

But what can be gained for practical life by such obscure, partly false, confused arbitrary conceptions? So little is gained that theory on account of them has always been a true antithesis of practice, and frequently a subject of ridicule to those whose soldierly qualities in the field are above question.

But it is impossible that this could have been the case, if theory in simple language, and by natural treatment of those things which constitute the Art of making War, had merely sought to establish just so much as admits of being established; if, avoiding all false pretensions and irrelevant display of scientific forms and historical parallels, it had kept close to the subject, and gone hand in hand with those who must conduct affairs in the field by their own natural genius.

CHAPTER VI - ON EXAMPLES

EXAMPLES from history make everything clear, and furnish the best description of proof in the empirical sciences. This applies with more force to the Art of War than to any other. General Scharnhorst, whose handbook is the best ever written on actual War, pronounces historical examples to be of the first importance, and makes an admirable use of them himself. Had he survived the War in which he fell, the fourth part of his revised treatise on artillery would have given a still greater proof of the observing and enlightened spirit in which he sifted matters of experience.

But such use of historical examples is rarely made by theoretical writers; the way in which they more commonly make use of them is rather calculated to leave the mind unsatisfied, as well as to offend the understanding. We therefore think it important to bring specially into view the use and abuse of historical examples.

Unquestionably the branches of knowledge which lie at the foundation of the Art of War come under the denomination of empirical sciences; for although they are derived in a great measure from the nature of things, still we can only learn this very nature itself for the most part from experience; and besides that, the practical application is modified by so many circumstances that the effects can never be completely learnt from the mere nature of the means.

The effects of gunpowder, that great agent in our military activity, were only learnt by experience, and up to this hour experiments are continually in progress in order to investigate them more fully. That an iron ball to which powder has given a velocity of 1000 feet in a second, smashes every living thing which it touches in its course is intelligible in itself; experience is not required to tell us that; but in producing this effect how many hundred circumstances are concerned, some of which can only be learnt by experience! And the physical is not the only effect which we have to study, it is the moral which we are in search of, and that can only be ascertained by experience; and there is no other way of learning and appreciating it but by experience. In the middle ages, when firearms were first invented, their effect, owing to their rude make, was materially but trifling compared to what it now is, but their effect morally was much greater. One must have witnessed the firmness of one of those masses taught and led by Buonaparte, under the heaviest and most un-intermittent cannonade, in order to understand what troops, hardened by long prac-practice in the field of danger, can do, when by a career of victory they have reached the noble principle of demanding from themselves their utmost efforts. In pure conception no one would believe it. On the other hand, it is well known that there are troops in the service of European Powers at the present moment who would easily be dispersed by a few cannon shots.

But no empirical science, consequently also no theory of the Art of War, can always corroborate its truths by historical proof; it would also be, in some measure, difficult to support experience by single facts. If any means is once found effica-cious in War, it is repeated; one nation copies another, the thing becomes the fashion, and in this manner it comes into use, supported by experience, and takes its place in theory, which contents itself with appealing to experience in general in or-der to show its origin, but not as a verification of its truth.

But it is quite otherwise if experience is to be used in order to overthrow some means in use, to confirm what is doubtful, or introduce something new; then partic-ular examples from history must be quoted as proofs.

Now, if we consider closely the use of historical proofs, four points of view readily present themselves for the purpose.

First, they may be used merely as an EXPLANATION of an idea. In every ab-stract consideration it is very easy to be misunderstood, or not to be intelligible at all: when an author is afraid of this, an exemplification from history serves to throw the light which is wanted on his idea, and to ensure his being intelligible to his read-er.

Secondly, it may serve as an APPLICATION of an idea, because by means of an example there is an opportunity of showing the action of those minor circum-stances which cannot all be comprehended and explained in any general expression of an idea; for in that consists, indeed, the difference between theory and experi-ence. Both these cases belong to examples properly speaking, the two following belong to historical proofs.

Thirdly, a historical fact may be referred to particularly, in order to support what one has advanced. This is in all cases sufficient, if we have ONLY to prove the *possibility* of a fact or effect.

Lastly, in the fourth place, from the circumstantial detail of a historical event, and by collecting together several of them, we may deduce some theory, which therefore has its true *proof* in this testimony itself.

For the first of these purposes all that is generally required is a cursory notice of the case, as it is only used partially. Historical correctness is a secondary consid-eration; a case invented might also serve the purpose as well, only historical ones are always to be preferred, because they bring the idea which they illustrate nearer to practical life.

The second use supposes a more circumstantial relation of events, but historical authenticity is again of secondary importance, and in respect to this point the same is to be said as in the first case.

For the third purpose the mere quotation of an undoubted fact is generally sufficient. If it is asserted that fortified positions may fulfil their object under certain conditions, it is only necessary to mention the position of Bunzelwitz in support of the assertion.

But if, through the narrative of a case in history, an abstract truth is to be demonstrated, then everything in the case bearing on the demonstration must be analysed in the most searching and complete manner; it must, to a certain extent, develop itself carefully before the eyes of the reader. The less effectually this is done the weaker will be the proof, and the more necessary it will be to supply the demonstrative proof which is wanting in the single case by a number of cases, because we have a right to suppose that the more minute details which we are unable to give neutralise each other in their effects in a certain number of cases.

If we want to show by example derived from experience that cavalry are better placed behind than in a line with infantry; that it is very hazardous without a decided preponderance of numbers to attempt an enveloping movement, with widely separated columns, either on a field of battle or in the theatre of war—that is, either tactically or strategically—then in the first of these cases it would not be sufficient to specify some lost battles in which the cavalry was on the flanks and some gained in which the cavalry was in rear of the infantry; and in the tatter of these cases it is not sufficient to refer to the battles of Rivoli and Wagram, to the attack of the Austrians on the theatre of war in Italy, in 1796, or of the French upon the German theatre of war in the same year. The way in which these orders of battle or plans of attack essentially contributed to disastrous issues in those particular cases must be shown by closely tracing out circumstances and occurrences. Then it will appear how far such forms or measures are to be condemned, a point which it is very necessary to show, for a total condemnation would be inconsistent with truth.

It has been already said that when a circumstantial detail of facts is impossible, the demonstrative power which is deficient may to a certain extent be supplied by the number of cases quoted; but this is a very dangerous method of getting out of the difficulty, and one which has been much abused. Instead of one well-explained example, three or four are just touched upon, and thus a show is made of strong evidence. But there are matters where a whole dozen of cases brought forward would prove nothing, if, for instance, they are facts of frequent occurrence, and therefore a dozen other cases with an opposite result might just as easily be brought forward. If any one will instance a dozen lost battles in which the side beaten attacked in separate converging columns, we can instance a dozen that have been gained in which the same order was adopted. It is evident that in this way no result is to be obtained.

Upon carefully considering these different points, it will be seen how easily examples may be misapplied.

An occurrence which, instead of being carefully analysed in all its parts, is superficially noticed, is like an object seen at a great distance, presenting the same appearance on each side, and in which the details of its parts cannot be distinguished. Such examples have, in reality, served to support the most contradictory opinions. To some Daun's campaigns are models of prudence and skill. To others, they are nothing but examples of timidity and want of resolution. Buonaparte's passage across the Noric Alps in 1797 may be made to appear the noblest resolution, but also as an act of sheer temerity. His strategic defeat in 1812 may be represented as the consequence either of an excess, or of a deficiency, of energy. All these opinions have been broached, and it is easy to see that they might very well arise, because each person takes a different view of the connection of events. At the same time these antagonistic opinions cannot be reconciled with each other, and therefore one of the two must be wrong.

Much as we are obliged to the worthy Feuquieres for the numerous examples introduced in his memoirs—partly because a number of historical incidents have thus been preserved which might otherwise have been lost, and partly because he was one of the first to bring theoretical, that is, abstract, ideas into connection with the practical in war, in so far that the cases brought forward may be regarded as intended to exemplify and confirm what is theoretically asserted—yet, in the opinion of an impartial reader, he will hardly be allowed to have attained the object he proposed to himself, that of proving theoretical principles by historical examples. For although he sometimes relates occurrences with great minuteness, still he falls short very often of showing that the deductions drawn necessarily proceed from the inner relations of these events.

Another evil which comes from the superficial notice of historical events, is that some readers are either wholly ignorant of the events, or cannot call them to remembrance sufficiently to be able to grasp the author's meaning, so that there is no alternative between either accepting blindly what is said, or remaining unconvinced.

It is extremely difficult to put together or unfold historical events before the eyes of a reader in such a way as is necessary, in order to be able to use them as proofs; for the writer very often wants the means, and can neither afford the time nor the requisite space; but we maintain that, when the object is to establish a new or doubtful opinion, one single example, thoroughly analysed, is far more instructive than ten which are superficially treated. The great mischief of these superficial representations is not that the writer puts his story forward as a proof when it has only a false title, but that he has not made himself properly acquainted with the subject, and that from this sort of slovenly, shallow treatment of history, a hundred false views and attempts at the construction of theories arise, which would never have made their appearance if the writer had looked upon it as his duty to deduce from the strict connection of events everything new which he brought to market, and sought to prove from history.

When we are convinced of these difficulties in the use of historical examples, and at the same time of the necessity (of making use of such examples), then we shall also come to the conclusion that the latest military history is naturally the best field from which to draw them, inasmuch as it alone is sufficiently authentic and detailed.

In ancient times, circumstances connected with War, as well as the method of carrying it on, were different; therefore its events are of less use to us either theoretically or practically; in addition to which, military history, like every other, naturally loses in the course of time a number of small traits and lineaments originally to be seen, loses in colour and life, like a worn-out or darkened picture; so that perhaps at last only the large masses and leading features remain, which thus acquire undue proportions.

If we look at the present state of warfare, we should say that the Wars since that of the Austrian succession are almost the only ones which, at least as far as armament, have still a considerable similarity to the present, and which, notwithstanding the many important changes which have taken place both great and small, are still capable of affording much instruction. It is quite otherwise with the War of the Spanish succession, as the use of fire-arms had not then so far advanced towards perfection, and cavalry still continued the most important arm. The farther we go back, the less useful becomes military history, as it gets so much the more meagre and barren of detail. The most useless of all is that of the old world.

But this uselessness is not altogether absolute, it relates only to those subjects which depend on a knowledge of minute details, or on those things in which the method of conducting war has changed. Although we know very little about the tactics in the battles between the Swiss and the Austrians, the Burgundians and French, still we find in them unmistakable evidence that they were the first in which the superiority of a good infantry over the best cavalry was, displayed. A general glance at the time of the Condottieri teaches us how the whole method of conducting War is dependent on the instrument used; for at no period have the forces used in War had so much the characteristics of a special instrument, and been a class so totally distinct from the rest of the national community. The memorable way in which the Romans in the second Punic War attacked the Carthaginan possessions in Spain and Africa, while Hannibal still maintained himself in Italy, is a most instructive subject to study, as the general relations of the States and Armies concerned in this indirect act of defence are sufficiently well known.

But the more things descend into particulars and deviate in character from the most general relations, the less we can look for examples and lessons of experience from very remote periods, for we have neither the means of judging properly of corresponding events, nor can we apply them to our completely different method of War.

Unfortunately, however, it has always been the fashion with historical writers to talk about ancient times. We shall not say how far vanity and charlatanism may have had a share in this, but in general we fail to discover any honest intention and earnest endeavour to instruct and convince, and we can therefore only look upon such quotations and references as embellishments to fill up gaps and hide defects.

It would be an immense service to teach the Art of War entirely by historical examples, as Feuquieres proposed to do; but it would be full work for the whole life of a man, if we reflect that he who undertakes it must first qualify himself for the task by a long personal experience in actual War.

Whoever, stirred by ambition, undertakes such a task, let him prepare himself for his pious undertaking as for a long pilgrimage; let him give up his time, spare no sacrifice, fear no temporal rank or power, and rise above all feelings of personal vanity, of false shame, in order, according to the French code, to speak THE TRUTH, THE WHOLE TRUTH, AND NOTHING BUT THE TRUTH.

BOOK III: OF STRATEGY IN GENERAL

CHAPTER I - STRATEGY

IN the second chapter of the second book, Strategy has been defined as "the employment of the battle as the means towards the attainment of the object of the War." Properly speaking it has to do with nothing but the battle, but its theory must include in this consideration the instrument of this real activity—the armed force—in itself and in its principal relations, for the battle is fought by it, and shows its effects upon it in turn. It must be well acquainted with the battle itself as far as relates to its possible results, and those mental and moral powers which are the most important in the use of the same.

Strategy is the employment of the battle to gain the end of the War; it must therefore give an aim to the whole military action, which must be in accordance with the object of the War; in other words, Strategy forms the plan of the War, and to this end it links together the series of acts which are to lead to the final decision, that, is to say, it makes the plans for the separate campaigns and regulates the combats to be fought in each. As these are all things which to a great extent can only be determined on conjectures some of which turn out incorrect, while a number of other arrangements pertaining to details cannot be made at all beforehand, it follows, as a matter of course, that Strategy must go with the Army to the field in order to arrange particulars on the spot, and to make the modifications in the general plan, which incessantly become necessary in War. Strategy can therefore never take its hand from the work for a moment.

That this, however, has not always been the view taken is evident from the former custom of keeping Strategy in the cabinet and not with the Army, a thing only allowable if the cabinet is so near to the Army that it can be taken for the chief head-quarters of the Army.

Theory will therefore attend on Strategy in the determination of its plans, or, as we may more properly say, it will throw a light on things in themselves, and on their relations to each other, and bring out prominently the little that there is of principle or rule.

If we recall to mind from the first chapter how many things of the highest importance War touches upon, we may conceive that a consideration of all requires a rare grasp of mind.

A Prince or General who knows exactly how to organise his War according to his object and means, who does neither too little nor too much, gives by that the greatest proof of his genius. But the effects of this talent are exhibited not so much by the invention of new modes of action, which might strike the eye immediately, as in the successful final result of the whole. It is the exact fulfilment of silent suppositions, it is the noiseless harmony of the whole action which we should admire, and which only makes itself known in the total result. Inquirer who, tracing back from the final result, does not perceive the signs of that harmony is one who is apt to seek for genius where it is not, and where it cannot be found.

The means and forms which Strategy uses are in fact so extremely simple, so well known by their constant repetition, that it only appears ridiculous to sound common sense when it hears critics so frequently speaking of them with high-flown emphasis. Turning a flank, which has been done a thousand times, is regarded here as a proof of the most brilliant genius, there as a proof of the most profound penetration, indeed even of the most comprehensive knowledge. Can there be in the book-world more absurd productions?

It is still more ridiculous if, in addition to this, we reflect that the same critic, in accordance with prevalent opinion, excludes all moral forces from theory, and will not allow it to be concerned with anything but the material forces, so that all must be confined to a few mathematical relations of equilibrium and preponderance, of time and space, and a few lines and angles. If it were nothing more than this, then out of such a miserable business there would not be a scientific problem for even a schoolboy.

But let us admit: there is no question here about scientific formulas and problems; the relations of material things are all very simple; the right comprehension of the moral forces which come into play is more difficult. Still, even in respect to them, it is only in the highest branches of Strategy that moral complications and a great diversity of quantities and relations are to be looked for, only at that point where Strategy borders on political science, or rather where the two become one, and there, as we have before observed, they have more influence on the "how much" and "how little" is to be done than on the form of execution. Where the latter is the principal question, as in the single acts both great and small in War, the moral quantities are already reduced to a very small number.

Thus, then, in Strategy everything is very simple, but not on that account very easy. Once it is determined from the relations of the State what should and may be done by War, then the way to it is easy to find; but to follow that way straightforward, to carry out the plan without being obliged to deviate from it a thousand times by a thousand varying influences, requires, besides great strength of character, great clearness and steadiness of mind, and out of a thousand men who are remarkable, some for mind, others for penetration, others again for boldness or strength of will, perhaps not one will combine in himself all those qualities which are required to raise a man above mediocrity in the career of a general.

It may sound strange, but for all who know War in this respect it is a fact beyond doubt, that much more strength of will is required to make an important decision in Strategy than in tactics. In the latter we are hurried on with the moment; a Commander feels himself borne along in a strong current, against which he durst not contend without the most destructive consequences, he suppresses the rising fears, and boldly ventures further. In Strategy, where all goes on at a slower rate, there is more room allowed for our own apprehensions and those of others, for objections and remonstrances, consequently also for unseasonable regrets; and as we do not see things in Strategy as we do at least half of them in tactics, with the living eye, but everything must be conjectured and assumed, the convictions produced are less powerful. The consequence is that most Generals, when they should act, remain stuck fast in bewildering doubts.

Now let us cast a glance at history—upon Frederick the Great's campaign of 1760, celebrated for its fine marches and manoeuvres: a perfect masterpiece of Strategic skill as critics tell us. Is there really anything to drive us out of our wits with admiration in the King's first trying to turn Daun's right flank, then his left, then again his right, &c.? Are we to see profound wisdom in this? No, that we cannot, if we are to decide naturally and without affectation. What we rather admire above all is the sagacity of the King in this respect, that while pursuing a great object with very limited means, he undertook nothing beyond his powers, and JUST ENOUGH to gain his object. This sagacity of the General is visible not only in this campaign, but throughout all the three Wars of the Great King!

To bring Silesia into the safe harbour of a well-guaranteed peace was his object.

At the head of a small State, which was like other States in most things, and only ahead of them in some branches of administration; he could not be an Alexander, and, as Charles XII, he would only, like him, have broken his head. We find, therefore, in the whole of his conduct of War, a controlled power, always well balanced, and never wanting in energy, which in the most critical moments rises to astonishing deeds, and the next moment oscillates quietly on again in subordination to the play of the most subtle political influences. Neither vanity, thirst for glory, nor vengeance could make him deviate from his course, and this course alone it is which brought him to a fortunate termination of the contest.

These few words do but scant justice to this phase of the genius of the great General; the eyes must be fixed carefully on the extraordinary issue of the struggle, and the causes which brought about that issue must be traced out, in order thoroughly to understand that nothing but the King's penetrating eye brought him safely out of all his dangers.

Another feature relates to the difficulty of execution. Marches to turn a flank, right or left, are easily combined; the idea of keeping a small force always well concentrated to be able to meet the enemy on equal terms at any point, to multiply a force by rapid movement, is as easily conceived as expressed; the mere contrivance in these points, therefore, cannot excite our admiration, and with respect to such simple things, there is nothing further than to admit that they are simple.

But let a General try to do these things like Frederick the Great. Long afterwards authors, who were eyewitnesses, have spoken of the danger, indeed of the imprudence, of the King's camps, and doubtless, at the time he pitched them, the danger appeared three times as great as afterwards.

It was the same with his marches, under the eyes, nay, often under the cannon of the enemy's Army; these camps were taken up, these marches made, not from want of prudence, but because in Daun's system, in his mode of drawing up his Army, in the responsibility which pressed upon him, and in his character, Frederick found that security which justified his camps and marches. But it required the King's boldness, determination, and strength of will to see things in this light, and not to be led astray and intimidated by the danger of which thirty years after people still wrote and spoke. Few Generals in this situation would have believed these simple strategic means to be practicable.

Again, another difficulty in execution lay in this, that the King's Army in this campaign was constantly in motion. Twice it marched by wretched cross-roads, from the Elbe into Silesia, in rear of Daun and pursued by Lascy (beginning of July, beginning of August). It required to be always ready for battle, and its marches had to be organised with a degree of skill which necessarily called forth a proportionate amount of exertion. Although attended and delayed by thousands of waggons, still its subsistence was extremely difficult. In Silesia, for eight days before the battle of Leignitz, it had constantly to march, defiling alternately right and left in front of the enemy:—this costs great fatigue, and entails great privations.

Is it to be supposed that all this could have been done without producing great friction in the machine? Can the mind of a Commander elaborate such movements with the same ease as the hand of a land surveyor uses the astrolabe? Does not the sight of the sufferings of their hungry, thirsty comrades pierce the hearts of the Commander and his Generals a thousand times? Must not the murmurs and doubts which these cause reach his ear? Has an ordinary man the courage to demand such sacrifices, and would not such efforts most certainly demoralise the Army, break up the bands of discipline, and, in short, undermine its military virtue, if firm reliance on the greatness and infallibility of the Commander did not compensate for all? Here, therefore, it is that we should pay respect; it is these miracles of execution which we should admire. But it is impossible to realise all this in its full force without a foretaste of it by experience. He who only knows War from books or the drill-ground cannot realise the whole effect of this counterpoise in action; WE BEG HIM, THEREFORE, TO ACCEPT FROM US ON FAITH AND TRUST ALL THAT HE IS UNABLE TO SUPPLY FROM ANY PERSONAL EXPERIENCES OF HIS OWN.

OBSERVATION

In an earlier manuscript of the second book are the following passages endorsed by the author himself to be used for the first Chapter of the second Book: the projected revision of that chapter not having been made, the passages referred to are introduced here in full.

By the mere assemblage of armed forces at a particular point, a battle there becomes possible, but does not always take place. Is that possibility now to be regarded as a reality and therefore an effective thing? Certainly, it is so by its results, and these effects, whatever they may be, can never fail.

1. POSSIBLE COMBATS ARE ON ACCOUNT OF THEIR RESULTS TO BE LOOKED UPON AS REAL ONES.

If a detachment is sent away to cut off the retreat of a flying enemy, and the enemy surrenders in consequence without further resistance, still it is through the combat which is offered to him by this detachment sent after him that he is brought to his decision.

If a part of our Army occupies an enemy's province which was undefended, and thus deprives the enemy of very considerable means of keeping up the strength of his Army, it is entirely through the battle which our detached body gives the enemy to expect, in case he seeks to recover the lost province, that we remain in possession of the same.

In both cases, therefore, the mere possibility of a battle has produced results, and is therefore to be classed amongst actual events. Suppose that in these cases the enemy has opposed our troops with others superior in force, and thus forced ours to give up their object without a combat, then certainly our plan has failed, but the battle which we offered at (either of) those points has not on that account been without effect, for it attracted the enemy's forces to that point. And in case our whole undertaking has done us harm, it cannot be said that these positions, these possible battles, have been attended with no results; their effects, then, are similar to those of a lost battle.

In this manner we see that the destruction of the enemy's military forces, the overthrow of the enemy's power, is only to be done through the effect of a battle, whether it be that it actually takes place, or that it is merely offered, and not accepted.

2. TWOFOLD OBJECT OF THE COMBAT.

But these effects are of two kinds, direct and indirect they are of the latter, if other things intrude themselves and become the object of the combat—things which cannot be regarded as the destruction of enemy's force, but only leading up to it, certainly by a circuitous road, but with so much the greater effect. The possession of provinces, towns, fortresses, roads, bridges, magazines, &c., may be the IMMEDIATE object of a battle, but never the ultimate one. Things of this description can never be, looked upon otherwise than as means of gaining greater superiority, so as at last to offer battle to the enemy in such a way that it will be impossible for him to accept it. Therefore all these things must only be regarded as intermediate links, steps, as it were, leading up to the effectual principle, but never as that principle itself.

3. EXAMPLE.

In 1814, by the capture of Buonaparte's capital the object of the War was attained. The political divisions which had their roots in Paris came into active operation, and an enormous split left the power of the Emperor to collapse of itself. Nevertheless the point of view from which we must look at all this is, that through these causes the forces and defensive means of Buonaparte were suddenly very much diminished, the superiority of the Allies, therefore, just in the same measure increased, and any further resistance then became IMPOSSIBLE. It was this impossibility which produced the peace with France. If we suppose the forces of the Allies at that moment diminished to a like extent through external causes;—if the superiority vanishes, then at the same time vanishes also all the effect and importance of the taking of Paris.

We have gone through this chain of argument in order to show that this is the natural and only true view of the thing from which it derives its importance. It leads always back to the question, What at any given moment of the War or campaign will be the probable result of the great or small combats which the two sides might offer to each other? In the consideration of a plan for a campaign, this question only is decisive as to the measures which are to be taken all through from the very commencement.

4. WHEN THIS VIEW IS NOT TAKEN, THEN A FALSE VALUE IS GIVEN TO OTHER THINGS.

If we do not accustom ourselves to look upon War, and the single campaigns in a War, as a chain which is all composed of battles strung together, one of which always brings on another; if we adopt the idea that the taking of a certain geographical point, the occupation of an undefended province, is in itself anything; then we are very likely to regard it as an acquisition which we may retain; and if we look at it so, and not as a term in the whole series of events, we do not ask ourselves whether this possession may not lead to greater disadvantages hereafter. How often we find this mistake recurring in military history.

We might say that, just as in commerce the merchant cannot set apart and place in security gains from one single transaction by itself, so in War a single advantage cannot be separated from the result of the whole. Just as the former must always operate with the whole bulk of his means, just so in War, only the sum total will decide on the advantage or disadvantage of each item.

If the mind's eye is always directed upon the series of combats, so far as they can be seen beforehand, then it is always looking in the right direction, and thereby the motion of the force acquires that rapidity, that is to say, willing and doing acquire that energy which is suitable to the matter, and which is not to be thwarted or turned aside by extraneous influences.

CHAPTER II - ELEMENTS OF STRATEGY

THE causes which condition the use of the combat in Strategy may be easily divided into elements of different kinds, such as the moral, physical, mathematical, geographical and statistical elements.

The first class includes all that can be called forth by moral qualities and effects; to the second belong the whole mass of the military force, its organisation, the proportion of the three arms, &c. &c.; to the third, the angle of the lines of operation, the concentric and eccentric movements in as far as their geometrical nature has any value in the calculation; to the fourth, the influences of country, such as commanding points, hills, rivers, woods, roads, &c. &c.; lastly, to the fifth, all the means of supply. The separation of these things once for all in the mind does good in giving clearness and helping us to estimate at once, at a higher or lower value, the different classes as we pass onwards. For, in considering them separately, many lose of themselves their borrowed importance; one feels, for instance, quite plainly that the value of a base of operations, even if we look at nothing in it but its relative position to the line of operations, depends much less in that simple form on the geometrical element of the angle which they form with one another, than on the nature of the roads and the country through which they pass.

But to treat upon Strategy according to these elements would be the most unfortunate idea that could be conceived, for these elements are generally manifold, and intimately connected with each other in every single operation of War. We should lose ourselves in the most soulless analysis, and as if in a horrid dream, we should be for ever trying in vain to build up an arch to connect this base of abstractions with facts belonging to the real world. Heaven preserve every theorist from such an undertaking! We shall keep to the world of things in their totality, and not pursue our analysis further than is necessary from time to time to give distinctness to the idea which we wish to impart, and which has come to us, not by a speculative investigation, but through the impression made by the realities of War in their entirety.

CHAPTER III - MORAL FORCES

WE must return again to this subject, which is touched upon in the third chapter of the second book, because the moral forces are amongst the most important subjects in War. They form the spirit which permeates the whole being of War. These forces fasten themselves soonest and with the greatest affinity on to the Will which puts in motion and guides the whole mass of powers, uniting with it as it were in one stream, because this is a moral force itself. Unfortunately they will escape from all book-analysis, for they will neither be brought into numbers nor into classes, and require to be both seen and felt.

The spirit and other moral qualities which animate an Army, a General, or Governments, public opinion in provinces in which a War is raging, the moral effect of a victory or of a defeat, are things which in themselves vary very much in their nature, and which also, according as they stand with regard to our object and our relations, may have an influence in different ways.

Although little or nothing can be said about these things in books, still they belong to the theory of the Art of War, as much as everything else which constitutes War. For I must here once more repeat that it is a miserable philosophy if, according to the old plan, we establish rules and principles wholly regardless of all moral forces, and then, as soon as these forces make their appearance, we begin to count exceptions which we thereby establish as it were theoretically, that is, make into rules; or if we resort to an appeal to genius, which is above all rules, thus giving out by implication, not only that rules were only made for fools, but also that they themselves are no better than folly.

Even if the theory of the Art of War does no more in reality than recall these things to remembrance, showing the necessity of allowing to the moral forces their full value, and of always taking them into consideration, by so doing it extends its borders over the region of immaterial forces, and by establishing that point of view, condemns beforehand every one who would endeavour to justify himself before its judgment seat by the mere physical relations of forces.

Further out of regard to all other so-called rules, theory cannot banish the moral forces beyond its frontier, because the effects of the physical forces and the moral are completely fused, and are not to be decomposed like a metal alloy by a chemical process. In every rule relating to the physical forces, theory must present to the mind at the same time the share which the moral powers will have in it, if it would not be led to categorical propositions, at one time too timid and contracted, at another too dogmatical and wide. Even the most matter-of-fact theories have, without knowing it, strayed over into this moral kingdom; for, as an example, the effects of a victory cannot in any way be explained without taking into consideration the moral impressions. And therefore the most of the subjects which we shall go through in this book are composed half of physical, half of moral causes and effects, and we might say the physical are almost no more than the wooden handle, whilst the moral are the noble metal, the real bright-polished weapon.

The value of the moral powers, and their frequently incredible influence, are best exemplified by history, and this is the most generous and the purest nourishment which the mind of the General can extract from it.—At the same time it is to be observed, that it is less demonstrations, critical examinations, and learned treatises, than sentiments, general impressions, and single flashing sparks of truth, which yield the seeds of knowledge that are to fertilise the mind.

We might go through the most important moral phenomena in War, and with all the care of a diligent professor try what we could impart about each, either good or bad. But as in such a method one slides too much into the commonplace and trite, whilst real mind quickly makes its escape in analysis, the end is that one gets imperceptibly to the relation of things which everybody knows. We prefer, therefore, to remain here more than usually incomplete and rhapsodical, content to have drawn attention to the importance of the subject in a general way, and to have pointed out the spirit in which the views given in this book have been conceived.

CHAPTER IV - THE CHIEF MORAL POWERS

THESE are The Talents of the Commander; The Military Virtue of the Army; Its National feeling. Which of these is the most important no one can tell in a general way, for it is very difficult to say anything in general of their strength, and still more difficult to compare the strength of one with that of another. The best plan is not to undervalue any of them, a fault which human judgment is prone to, sometimes on one side, sometimes on another, in its whimsical oscillations. It is better to satisfy ourselves of the undeniable efficacy of these three things by sufficient evidence from history.

It is true, however, that in modern times the Armies of European states have arrived very much at a par as regards discipline and fitness for service, and that the conduct of War has—as philosophers would say—naturally developed itself, thereby become a method, common as it were to all Armies, so that even from Commanders there is nothing further to be expected in the way of application of special means of Art, in the limited sense (such as Frederick the Second's oblique order). Hence it cannot be denied that, as matters now stand, greater scope is afforded for the influence of National spirit and habituation of an army to War. A long peace may again alter all this.

The national spirit of an Army (enthusiasm, fanatical zeal, faith, opinion) displays itself most in mountain warfare, where every one down to the common soldier is left to himself. On this account, a mountainous country is the best campaigning ground for popular levies.

Expertness of an Army through training, and that well-tempered courage which holds the ranks together as if they had been cast in a mould, show their superiority in an open country.

The talent of a General has most room to display itself in a closely intersected, undulating country. In mountains he has too little command over the separate parts, and the direction of all is beyond his powers; in open plains it is simple and does not exceed those powers.

According to these undeniable elective affinities, plans should be regulated.

CHAPTER V - MILITARY VIRTUE OF AN ARMY

THIS is distinguished from mere bravery, and still more from enthusiasm for the business of War. The first is certainly a necessary constituent part of it, but in the same way as bravery, which is a natural gift in some men, may arise in a soldier as a part of an Army from habit and custom, so with him it must also have a different direction from that which it has with others. It must lose that impulse to unbridled activity and exercise of force which is its characteristic in the individual, and submit itself to demands of a higher kind, to obedience, order, rule, and method. Enthusiasm for the profession gives life and greater fire to the military virtue of an Army, but does not necessarily constitute a part of it.

War is a special business, and however general its relations may be, and even if all the male population of a country, capable of bearing arms, exercise this calling, still it always continues to be different and separate from the other pursuits which occupy the life of man.—To be imbued with a sense of the spirit and nature of this business, to make use of, to rouse, to assimilate into the system the powers which should be active in it, to penetrate completely into the nature of the business with the understanding, through exercise to gain confidence and expertness in it, to be completely given up to it, to pass out of the man into the part which it is assigned to us to play in War, that is the military virtue of an Army in the individual.

However much pains may be taken to combine the soldier and the citizen in one and the same individual, whatever may be done to nationalise Wars, and however much we may imagine times have changed since the days of the old Condottieri, never will it be possible to do away with the individuality of the business; and if that cannot be done, then those who belong to it, as long as they belong to it, will always look upon themselves as a kind of guild, in the regulations, laws and customs in which the "Spirit of War" by preference finds its expression. And so it is in fact. Even with the most decided inclination to look at War from the highest point of view, it would be very wrong to look down upon this corporate spirit (e'sprit de corps) which may and should exist more or less in every Army. This corporate spirit forms the bond of union between the natural forces which are active in that which we have called military virtue. The crystals of military virtue have a greater affinity for the spirit of a corporate body than for anything else.

An Army which preserves its usual formations under the heaviest fire, which is never shaken by imaginary fears, and in the face of real danger disputes the ground inch by inch, which, proud in the feeling of its victories, never loses its sense of obedience, its respect for and confidence in its leaders, even under the depressing effects of defeat; an Army with all its physical powers, inured to privations and fatigue by exercise, like the muscles of an athlete; an Army which looks upon all its toils as the means to victory, not as a curse which hovers over its standards, and which is always reminded of its duties and virtues by the short catechism of one idea, namely the HONOUR OF ITS ARMS;—Such an Army is imbued with the true military spirit.

Soldiers may fight bravely like the Vendeans, and do great things like the Swiss, the Americans, or Spaniards, without displaying this military virtue. A Commander may also be successful at the head of standing Armies, like Eugene and Marlborough, without enjoying the benefit of its assistance; we must not, therefore, say that a successful War without it cannot be imagined; and we draw especial attention to that point, in order the more to individualise the conception which is here brought forward, that the idea may not dissolve into a generalisation and that it may not be thought that military virtue is in the end everything. It is not so. Military virtue in an Army is a definite moral power which may be supposed wanting, and the influence of which may therefore be estimated—like any instrument the power of which may be calculated.

Having thus characterised it, we proceed to consider what can be predicated of its influence, and what are the means of gaining its assistance.

Military virtue is for the parts, what the genius of the Commander is for the whole. The General can only guide the whole, not each separate part, and where he cannot guide the part, there military virtue must be its leader. A General is chosen by the reputation of his superior talents, the chief leaders of large masses after careful probation; but this probation diminishes as we descend the scale of rank, and in just the same measure we may reckon less and less upon individual talents; but what is wanting in this respect military virtue should supply. The natural qualities of a warlike people play just this part: BRAVERY, APTITUDE, POWERS OF ENDURANCE and ENTHUSIASM.

These properties may therefore supply the place of military virtue, and vice versa, from which the following may be deduced:

1. Military virtue is a quality of standing Armies only, but they require it the most. In national risings its place is supplied by natural qualities, which develop themselves there more rapidly.

2. Standing Armies opposed to standing Armies, can more easily dispense with it, than a standing Army opposed to a national insurrection, for in that case, the troops are more scattered, and the divisions left more to themselves. But where an Army can be kept concentrated, the genius of the General takes a greater place, and supplies what is wanting in the spirit of the Army. Therefore generally military virtue becomes more necessary the more the theatre of operations and other circumstances make the War complicated, and cause the forces to be scattered.

From these truths the only lesson to be derived is this, that if an Army is deficient in this quality, every endeavour should be made to simplify the operations of the War as much as possible, or to introduce double efficiency in the organisation of the Army in some other respect, and not to expect from the mere name of a standing Army, that which only the veritable thing itself can give.

The military virtue of an Army is, therefore, one of the most important moral powers in War, and where it is wanting, we either see its place supplied by one of the others, such as the great superiority of generalship or popular enthusiasm, or we find the results not commensurate with the exertions made.—How much that is great, this spirit, this sterling worth of an army, this refining of ore into the polished metal, has already done, we see in the history of the Macedonians under Alexander, the Roman legions under Cesar, the Spanish infantry under Alexander Farnese, the Swedes under Gustavus Adolphus and Charles XII, the Prussians under Frederick the Great, and the French under Buonapartc. We must purposely shut our eyes against all historical proof, if we do not admit, that the astonishing successes of these Generals and their greatness in situations of extreme difficulty, were only possible with Armies possessing this virtue.

This spirit can only be generated from two sources, and only by these two conjointly; the first is a succession of campaigns and great victories; the other is, an activity of the Army carried sometimes to the highest pitch. Only by these, does the soldier learn to know his powers. The more a General is in the habit of demanding from his troops, the surer he will be that his demands will be answered. The soldier is as proud of overcoming toil, as he is of surmounting danger. Therefore it is only in the soil of incessant activity and exertion that the germ will thrive, but also only in the sunshine of victory. Once it becomes a STRONG TREE, it will stand against the fiercest storms of misfortune and defeat, and even against the indolent inactivity of peace, at least for a time. It can therefore only be created in War, and under great Generals, but no doubt it may last at least for several generations, even under Generals of moderate capacity, and through considerable periods of peace.

With this generous and noble spirit of union in a line of veteran troops, covered with scars and thoroughly inured to War, we must not compare the self-esteem and vanity of a standing Army, held together merely by the glue of service-regulations and a drill book; a certain plodding earnestness and strict discipline may keep up military virtue for a long time, but can never create it; these things therefore have a certain value, but must not be over-rated. Order, smartness, good will, also a certain degree of pride and high feeling, are qualities of an Army formed in time of peace which are to be prized, but cannot stand alone. The whole retains the whole, and as with glass too quickly cooled, a single crack breaks the whole mass. Above all, the highest spirit in the world changes only too easily at the first check into depression, and one might say into a kind of rhodomontade of alarm, the French sauve que peut.—Such an Army can only achieve something through its leader, never by itself. It must be led with double caution, until by degrees, in victory and hardships, the strength grows into the full armour. Beware then of confusing the SPIRIT of an Army with its temper.

CHAPTER VI - BOLDNESS

THE place and part which boldness takes in the dynamic system of powers, where it stands opposed to Foresight and prudence, has been stated in the chapter on the certainty of the result in order thereby to show, that theory has no right to restrict it by virtue of its legislative power.

But this noble impulse, with which the human soul raises itself above the most formidable dangers, is to be regarded as an active principle peculiarly belonging to War. In fact, in what branch of human activity should boldness have a right of citizenship if not in War?

From the transport-driver and the drummer up to the General, it is the noblest of virtues, the true steel which gives the weapon its edge and brilliancy.

Let us admit in fact it has in War even its own prerogatives. Over and above the result of the calculation of space, time, and quantity, we must allow a certain percentage which boldness derives from the weakness of others, whenever it gains the mastery. It is therefore, virtually, a creative power. This is not difficult to demonstrate philosophically. As often as boldness encounters hesitation, the probability of the result is of necessity in its favour, because the very state of hesitation implies a loss of equilibrium already. It is only when it encounters cautious foresight—which we may say is just as bold, at all events just as strong and powerful as itself—that it is at a disadvantage; such cases, however, rarely occur. Out of the whole multitude of prudent men in the world, the great majority are so from timidity.

Amongst large masses, boldness is a force, the special cultivation of which can never be to the detriment of other forces, because the great mass is bound to a higher will by the frame-work and joints of the order of battle and of the service, and therefore is guided by an intelligent power which is extraneous. Boldness is therefore here only like a spring held down until its action is required.

The higher the rank the more necessary it is that boldness should be accompanied by a reflective mind, that it may not be a mere blind outburst of passion to no purpose; for with increase of rank it becomes always less a matter of self-sacrifice and more a matter of the preservation of others, and the good of the whole. Where regulations of the service, as a kind of second nature, prescribe for the masses, reflection must be the guide of the General, and in his case individual boldness in action may easily become a fault. Still, at the same time, it is a fine failing, and must not be looked at in the same light as any other. Happy the Army in which an untimely boldness frequently manifests itself; it is an exuberant growth which shows a rich soil. Even foolhardiness, that is boldness without an object, is not to be despised; in point of fact it is the same energy of feeling, only exercised as a kind of passion without any co-operation of the intelligent faculties. It is only when it strikes at the root of obedience, when it treats with contempt the orders of superior authority, that it must be repressed as a dangerous evil, not on its own account but on account of the act of disobedience, for there is nothing in War which is of GREATER IMPORTANCE THAN OBEDIENCE.

The reader will readily agree with us that, supposing an equal degree of discernment to be forthcoming in a certain number of cases, a thousand times as many of them will end in disaster through over-anxiety as through boldness.

One would suppose it natural that the interposition of a reasonable object should stimulate boldness, and therefore lessen its intrinsic merit, and yet the reverse is the case in reality.

The intervention of lucid thought or the general supremacy of mind deprives the emotional forces of a great part of their power. On that account BOLDNESS BECOMES OF RARER OCCURRENCE THE HIGHER WE ASCEND THE SCALE OF RANK, for whether the discernment and the understanding do or do not increase with these ranks still the Commanders, in their several stations as they rise, are pressed upon more and more severely by objective things, by relations and claims from without, so that they become the more perplexed the lower the degree of their individual intelligence. This so far as regards War is the chief foundation of the truth of the French proverb:—

"Tel brille au second qui s' e'clipse an premier."

Almost all the Generals who are represented in history as merely having attained to mediocrity, and as wanting in decision when in supreme command, are men celebrated in their antecedent career for their boldness and decision.

In those motives to bold action which arise from the pressure of necessity we must make a distinction. Necessity has its degrees of intensity. If it lies near at hand, if the person acting is in the pursuit of his object driven into great dangers in order to escape others equally great, then we can only admire his resolution, which still has also its value. If a young man to show his skill in horsemanship leaps across a deep cleft, then he is bold; if he makes the same leap pursued by a troop of head-chopping Janissaries he is only resolute. But the farther off the necessity from the point of action, the greater the number of relations intervening which the mind has to traverse; in order to realise them, by so much the less does necessity take from boldness in action. If Frederick the Great, in the year 1756, saw that War was inevitable, and that he could only escape destruction by being beforehand with his enemies, it became necessary for him to commence the War himself, but at the same time it was certainly very bold: for few men in his position would have made up their minds to do so.

Although Strategy is only the province of Generals-in-Chief or Commanders in the higher positions, still boldness in all the other branches of an Army is as little a matter of indifference to it as their other military virtues. With an Army belonging to a bold race, and in which the spirit of boldness has been always nourished, very different things may be undertaken than with one in which this virtue, is unknown; for that reason we have considered it in connection with an Army. But our subject is specially the boldness of the General, and yet we have not much to say about it after having described this military virtue in a general way to the best of our ability.

The higher we rise in a position of command, the more of the mind, understanding, and penetration predominate in activity, the more therefore is boldness, which is a property of the feelings, kept in subjection, and for that reason we find it so rarely in the highest positions, but then, so much the more should it be admired. Boldness, directed by an overruling intelligence, is the stamp of the hero: this boldness does not consist in venturing directly against the nature of things, in a downright contempt of the laws of probability, but, if a choice is once made, in the rigorous adherence to that higher calculation which genius, the tact of judgment, has gone over with the speed of lightning. The more boldness lends wings to the mind and the discernment, so much the farther they will reach in their flight, so much the more comprehensive will be the view, the more exact the result, but certainly always only in the sense that with greater objects greater dangers are connected. The ordinary man, not to speak of the weak and irresolute, arrives at an exact result so far as such is possible without ocular demonstration, at most after diligent reflection in his chamber, at a distance from danger and responsibility. Let danger and responsibility draw close round him in every direction, then he loses the power of comprehensive vision, and if he retains this in any measure by the influence of others, still he will lose his power of DECISION, because in that point no one can help him.

We think then that it is impossible to imagine a distinguished General without boldness, that is to say, that no man can become one who is not born with this power of the soul, and we therefore look upon it as the first requisite for such a career. How much of this inborn power, developed and moderated through education and the circumstances of life, is left when the man has attained a high position, is the second question. The greater this power still is, the stronger will genius be on the wing, the higher will be its flight. The risks become always greater, but the purpose grows with them. Whether its lines proceed out of and get their direction from a distant necessity, or whether they converge to the keystone of a building which ambition has planned, whether Frederick or Alexander acts, is much the same as regards the critical view. If the one excites the imagination more because it is bolder, the other pleases the understanding most, because it has in it more absolute necessity.

We have still to advert to one very important circumstance.

The spirit of boldness can exist in an Army, either because it is in the people, or because it has been generated in a successful War conducted by able Generals. In the latter case it must of course be dispensed with at the commencement.

Now in our days there is hardly any other means of educating the spirit of a people in this respect, except by War, and that too under bold Generals. By it alone can that effeminacy of feeling be counteracted, that propensity to seek for the enjoyment of comfort, which cause degeneracy in a people rising in prosperity and immersed in an extremely busy commerce.

A Nation can hope to have a strong position in the political world only if its character and practice in actual War mutually support each other in constant reciprocal action.

CHAPTER VII - PERSEVERANCE

THE reader expects to hear of angles and lines, and finds, instead of these citizens of the scientific world, only people out of common life, such as he meets with every day in the street. And yet the author cannot make up his mind to become a hair's breadth more mathematical than the subject seems to him to require, and he is not alarmed at the surprise which the reader may show.

In War more than anywhere else in the world things happen differently to what we had expected, and look differently when near, to what they did at a distance. With what serenity the architect can watch his work gradually rising and growing into his plan. The doctor although much more at the mercy of mysterious agencies and chances than the architect, still knows enough of the forms and effects of his means. In War, on the other hand, the Commander of an immense whole finds himself in a constant whirlpool of false and true information, of mistakes committed through fear, through negligence, through precipitation, of contraventions of his authority, either from mistaken or correct motives, from ill will, true or false sense of duty, indolence or exhaustion, of accidents which no mortal could have foreseen. In short, he is the victim of a hundred thousand impressions, of which the most have an intimidating, the fewest an encouraging tendency. By long experience in War, the tact is acquired of readily appreciating the value of these incidents; high courage and stability of character stand proof against them, as the rock resists the beating of the waves. He who would yield to these impressions would never carry out an undertaking, and on that account PERSEVERANCE in the proposed object, as long as there is no decided reason against it, is a most necessary counterpoise. Further, there is hardly any celebrated enterprise in War which was not achieved by endless exertion, pains, and privations; and as here the weakness of the physical and moral man is ever disposed to yield, only an immense force of will, which manifests itself in perseverance admired by present and future generations, can conduct to our goal.

CHAPTER VIII - SUPERIORITY OF NUMBERS

THIS is in tactics, as well as in Strategy, the most general principle of victory, and shall be examined by us first in its generality, for which we may be permitted the following exposition:

Strategy fixes the point where, the time when, and the numerical force with which the battle is to be fought. By this triple determination it has therefore a very essential influence on the issue of the combat. If tactics has fought the battle, if the result is over, let it be victory or defeat, Strategy makes such use of it as can be made in accordance with the great object of the War. This object is naturally often a very distant one, seldom does it lie quite close at hand. A series of other objects subordinate themselves to it as means. These objects, which are at the same time means to a higher purpose, may be practically of various kinds; even the ultimate aim of the whole War may be a different one in every case. We shall make ourselves acquainted with these things according as we come to know the separate objects which they come, in contact with; and it is not our intention here to embrace the whole subject by a complete enumeration of them, even if that were possible. We therefore let the employment of the battle stand over for the present.

Even those things through which Strategy has an influence on the issue of the combat, inasmuch as it establishes the same, to a certain extent decrees them, are not so simple that they can be embraced in one single view. For as Strategy appoints time, place and force, it can do so in practice in many ways, each of which influences in a different manner the result of the combat as well as its consequences. Therefore we shall only get acquainted with this also by degrees, that is, through the subjects which more closely determine the application.

If we strip the combat of all modifications which it may undergo according to its immediate purpose and the circumstances from which it proceeds, lastly if we set aside the valour of the troops, because that is a given quantity, then there remains only the bare conception of the combat, that is a combat without form, in which we distinguish nothing but the number of the combatants.

This number will therefore determine victory. Now from the number of things above deducted to get to this point, it is shown that the superiority in numbers in a battle is only one of the factors employed to produce victory that therefore so far from having with the superiority in number obtained all, or even only the principal thing, we have perhaps got very little by it, according as the other circumstances which co-operate happen to vary.

But this superiority has degrees, it may be imagined as twofold, threefold or fourfold, and every one sees, that by increasing in this way, it must (at last) overpower everything else.

In such an aspect we grant, that the superiority in numbers is the most important factor in the result a combat, only it must be sufficiently great to be a counterpoise to all the other co-operating circumstances. The direct result of this is, that the greatest possible number of troops should be brought into action at the decisive point.

Whether the troops thus brought are sufficient or not, we have then done in this respect all that our means allowed. This is the first principle in Strategy, therefore in general as now stated, it is just as well suited for Greeks and Persians, or for Englishmen and Mahrattas, as for French and Germans. But we shall take a glance at our relations in Europe, as respects War, in order to arrive at some more definite idea on this subject.

Here we find Armies much more alike in equipment, organisation, and practical skill of every kind. There only remains a difference in the military virtue of Armies, and in the talent of Generals which may fluctuate with time from side to side. If we go through the military history of modern Europe, we find no example of a Marathon.

Frederick the Great beat 80,000 Austrians at Leuthen with about 30,000 men, and at Rosbach with 25,000 some 50,000 allies; these are however the only instances of victories gained against an enemy double, or more than double in numbers. Charles XII, in the battle of Narva, we cannot well quote, for the Russians were at that time hardly to be regarded as Europeans, also the principal circumstances, even of the battle, are too little known. Buonaparte had at Dresden 120,000 against 220,000, therefore not the double. At Kollin, Frederick the Great did not succeed, with 30,000 against 50,000 Austrians, neither did Buonaparte in the desperate battle of Leipsic, where he was 160,000 strong, against 280,000.

From this we may infer, that it is very difficult in the present state of Europe, for the most talented General to gain a victory over an enemy double his strength. Now if we see double numbers prove such a weight in the scale against the greatest Generals, we may be sure, that in ordinary cases, in small as well as great combats, an important superiority of numbers, but which need not be over two to one, will be sufficient to ensure the victory, however disadvantageous other circumstances may be. Certainly, we may imagine a defile which even tenfold would not suffice to force, but in such a case it can be no question of a battle at all.

We think, therefore, that under our conditions, as well as in all similar ones, the superiority at the decisive point is a matter of capital importance, and that this subject, in the generality of cases, is decidedly the most important of all. The strength at the decisive point depends on the absolute strength of the Army, and on skill in making use of it.

The first rule is therefore to enter the field with an Army as strong as possible. This sounds very like a commonplace, but still it is really not so.

In order to show that for a long time the strength of forces was by no means regarded as a chief point, we need only observe, that in most, and even in the most detailed histories of the Wars in the eighteenth century, the strength of the Armies is either not given at all, or only incidentally, and in no case is any special value laid upon it. Tempelhof in his history of the Seven Years' War is the earliest writer who gives it regularly, but at the same time he does it only very superficially.

Even Massenbach, in his manifold critical observations on the Prussian campaigns of 1793-94 in the Vosges, talks a great deal about hills and valleys, roads and footpaths, but does not say a syllable about mutual strength.

Another proof lies in a wonderful notion which haunted the heads of many critical historians, according to which there was a certain size of an Army which was the best, a normal strength, beyond which the forces in excess were burdensome rather than serviceable.

Lastly, there are a number of instances to be found, in which all the available forces were not really brought into the battle, or into the War, because the superiority of numbers was not considered to have that importance which in the nature of things belongs to it.

If we are thoroughly penetrated with the conviction that with a considerable superiority of numbers everything possible is to be effected, then it cannot fail that this clear conviction reacts on the preparations for the War, so as to make us appear in the field with as many troops as possible, and either to give us ourselves the superiority, or at least to guard against the enemy obtaining it. So much for what concerns the absolute force with which the War is to be conducted.

The measure of this absolute force is determined by the Government; and although with this determination the real action of War commences, and it forms an essential part of the Strategy of the War, still in most cases the General who is to command these forces in the War must regard their absolute strength as a given quantity, whether it be that he has had no voice in fixing it, or that circumstances prevented a sufficient expansion being given to it.

There remains nothing, therefore, where an absolute superiority is not attainable, but to produce a relative one at the decisive point, by making skilful use of what we have.

The calculation of space and time appears as the most essential thing to this end—and this has caused that subject to be regarded as one which embraces nearly the whole art of using military forces. Indeed, some have gone so far as to ascribe to great strategists and tacticians a mental organ peculiarly adapted to this point.

But the calculation of time and space, although it lies universally at the foundation of Strategy, and is to a certain extent its daily bread, is still neither the most difficult, nor the most decisive one.

If we take an unprejudiced glance at military history, we shall find that the instances in which mistakes in such a calculation have proved the cause of serious losses are very rare, at least in Strategy. But if the conception of a skilful combination of time and space is fully to account for every instance of a resolute and active Commander beating several separate opponents with one and the same army (Frederick the Great, Buonaparte), then we perplex ourselves unnecessarily with conventional language. For the sake of clearness and the profitable use of conceptions, it is necessary that things should always be called by their right names.

The right appreciation of their opponents (Daun, Schwartzenberg), the audacity to leave for a short space of time a small force only before them, energy in forced marches, boldness in sudden attacks, the intensified activity which great souls acquire in the moment of danger, these are the grounds of such victories; and what have these to do with the ability to make an exact calculation of two such simple things as time and space?

But even this ricochetting play of forces, "when the victories at Rosbach and Montmirail give the impulse to victories at Leuthen and Montereau," to which great Generals on the defensive have often trusted, is still, if we would be clear and exact, only a rare occurrence in history.

Much more frequently the relative superiority—that is, the skilful assemblage of superior forces at the decisive point—has its foundation in the right appreciation of those points, in the judicious direction which by that means has been given to the forces from the very first, and in the resolution required to sacrifice the unimportant to the advantage of the important—that is, to keep the forces concentrated in an overpowering mass. In this, Frederick the Great and Buonaparte are particularly characteristic.

We think we have now allotted to the superiority in numbers the importance which belongs to it; it is to be regarded as the fundamental idea, always to be aimed at before all and as far as possible.

But to regard it on this account as a necessary condition of victory would be a complete misconception of our exposition; in the conclusion to be drawn from it there lies nothing more than the value which should attach to numerical strength in the combat. If that strength is made as great as possible, then the maxim is satisfied; a review of the total relations must then decide whether or not the combat is to be avoided for want of sufficient force.

CHAPTER IX - THE SURPRISE

FROM the subject of the foregoing chapter, the general endeavour to attain a relative superiority, there follows another endeavour which must consequently be just as general in its nature: this is the SURPRISE of the enemy. It lies more or less at the foundation of all undertakings, for without it the preponderance at the decisive point is not properly conceivable.

The surprise is, therefore, not only the means to the attainment of numerical superiority; but it is also to be regarded as a substantive principle in itself, on account of its moral effect. When it is successful in a high degree, confusion and broken courage in the enemy's ranks are the consequences; and of the degree to which these multiply a success, there are examples enough, great and small. We are not now speaking of the particular surprise which belongs to the attack, but of the endeavour by measures generally, and especially by the distribution of forces, to surprise the enemy, which can be imagined just as well in the defensive, and which in the tactical defence particularly is a chief point.

We say, surprise lies at the foundation of all undertakings without exception, only in very different degrees according to the nature of the undertaking and other circumstances.

This difference, indeed, originates in the properties or peculiarities of the Army and its Commander, in those even of the Government.

Secrecy and rapidity are the two factors in this product and these suppose in the Government and the Commander-in-Chief great energy, and on the part of the

Army a high sense of military duty. With effeminacy and loose principles it is in vain to calculate upon a surprise. But so general, indeed so indispensable, as is this endeavour, and true as it is that it is never wholly unproductive of effect, still it is not the less true that it seldom succeeds to a REMARKABLE degree, and this follows from the nature of the idea itself. We should form an erroneous conception if we believed that by this means chiefly there is much to be attained in War. In idea it promises a great deal; in the execution it generally sticks fast by the friction of the whole machine.

In tactics the surprise is much more at home, for the very natural reason that all times and spaces are on a smaller scale. It will, therefore, in Strategy be the more feasible in proportion as the measures lie nearer to the province of tactics, and more difficult the higher up they lie towards the province of policy.

The preparations for a War usually occupy several months; the assembly of an Army at its principal positions requires generally the formation of depôts and magazines, and long marches, the object of which can be guessed soon enough.

It therefore rarely happens that one State surprises another by a War, or by the direction which it gives the mass of its forces. In the seventeenth and eighteenth centuries, when War turned very much upon sieges, it was a frequent aim, and quite a peculiar and important chapter in the Art of War, to invest a strong place unexpectedly, but even that only rarely succeeded.

On the other hand, with things which can be done in a day or two, a surprise is much more conceivable, and, therefore, also it is often not difficult thus to gain a march upon the enemy, and thereby a position, a point of country, a road, &c. But it is evident that what surprise gains in this way in easy execution, it loses in the efficacy, as the greater the efficacy the greater always the difficulty of execution. Whoever thinks that with such surprises on a small scale, he may connect great results—as, for example, the gain of a battle, the capture of an important magazine—believes in something which it is certainly very possible to imagine, but for which there is no warrant in history; for there are upon the whole very few instances where anything great has resulted from such surprises; from which we may justly conclude that inherent difficulties lie in the way of their success.

Certainly, whoever would consult history on such points must not depend on sundry battle steeds of historical critics, on their wise dicta and self-complacent terminology, but look at facts with his own eyes. There is, for instance, a certain day in the campaign in Silesia, 1761, which, in this respect, has attained a kind of notoriety. It is the 22nd July, on which Frederick the Great gained on Laudon the march to Nossen, near Neisse, by which, as is said, the junction of the Austrian and Russian armies in Upper Silesia became impossible, and, therefore, a period of four weeks was gained by the King. Whoever reads over this occurrence carefully in the principal histories, and considers it impartially, will, in the march of the 22nd July, never find this importance; and generally in the whole of the fashionable logic on this subject, he will see nothing but contradictions; but in the proceedings of Laudon, in this renowned period of manoeuvres, much that is unaccountable. How could one, with a thirst for truth, and clear conviction, accept such historical evidence?

When we promise ourselves great effects in a campaign from the principle of surprising, we think upon great activity, rapid resolutions, and forced marches, as the means of producing them; but that these things, even when forthcoming in a very high degree, will not always produce the desired effect, we see in examples given by Generals, who may be allowed to have had the greatest talent in the use of these means, Frederick the Great and Buonaparte. The first when he left Dresden so suddenly in July 1760, and falling upon Lascy, then turned against Dresden, gained nothing by the whole of that intermezzo, but rather placed his affairs in a condition notably worse, as the fortress Glatz fell in the meantime.

In 1813, Buonaparte turned suddenly from Dresden twice against Bluecher, to say nothing of his incursion into Bohemia from Upper Lusatia, and both times without in the least attaining his object. They were blows in the air which only cost him time and force, and might have placed him in a dangerous position in Dresden.

Therefore, even in this field, a surprise does not necessarily meet with great success through the mere activity, energy, and resolution of the Commander; it must be favoured by other circumstances. But we by no means deny that there can be success; we only connect with it a necessity of favourable circumstances, which, certainly do not occur very frequently, and which the Commander can seldom bring about himself.

Just those two Generals afford each a striking illustration of this. We take first Buonaparte in his famous enterprise against Bluecher's Army in February 1814, when it was separated from the Grand Army, and descending the Marne. It would not be easy to find a two days' march to surprise the enemy productive of greater results than this; Bluecher's Army, extended over a distance of three days' march, was beaten in detail, and suffered a loss nearly equal to that of defeat in a great battle. This was completely the effect of a surprise, for if Bluecher had thought of such a near possibility of an attack from Buonaparte he would have organised his march quite differently. To this mistake of Bluecher's the result is to be attributed. Buonaparte did not know all these circumstances, and so there was a piece of good fortune that mixed itself up in his favour.

It is the same with the battle of Liegnitz, 1760. Frederick the Great gained this fine victory through altering during the night a position which he had just before taken up. Laudon was through this completely surprised, and lost 70 pieces of artillery and 10,000 men. Although Frederick the Great had at this time adopted the principle of moving backwards and forwards in order to make a battle impossible, or at least to disconcert the enemy's plans, still the alteration of position on the night of the 14-15 was not made exactly with that intention, but as the King himself says, because the position of the 14th did not please him. Here, therefore, also chance was hard at work; without this happy conjunction of the attack and the change of position in the night, and the difficult nature of the country, the result would not have been the same.

Also in the higher and highest province of Strategy there are some instances of surprises fruitful in results. We shall only cite the brilliant marches of the Great Elector against the Swedes from Franconia to Pomerania and from the Mark (Brandenburg) to the Pregel in 1757, and the celebrated passage of the Alps by

Buonaparte, 1800. In the latter case an Army gave up its whole theatre of war by a capitulation, and in 1757 another Army was very near giving up its theatre of war and itself as well. Lastly, as an instance of a War wholly unexpected, we may bring forward the invasion of Silesia by Frederick the Great. Great and powerful are here the results everywhere, but such events are not common in history if we do not confuse with them cases in which a State, for want of activity and energy (Saxony 1756, and Russia, 1812), has not completed its preparations in time.

Now there still remains an observation which concerns the essence of the thing. A surprise can only be effected by that party which gives the law to the other; and he who is in the right gives the law. If we surprise the adversary by a wrong measure, then instead of reaping good results, we may have to bear a sound blow in return; in any case the adversary need not trouble himself much about our surprise, he has in our mistake the means of turning off the evil. As the offensive includes in itself much more positive action than the defensive, so the surprise is certainly more in its place with the assailant, but by no means invariably, as we shall hereafter see. Mutual surprises by the offensive and defensive may therefore meet, and then that one will have the advantage who has hit the nail on the head the best.

So should it be, but practical life does not keep to this line so exactly, and that for a very simple reason. The moral effects which attend a surprise often convert the worst case into a good one for the side they favour, and do not allow the other to make any regular determination. We have here in view more than anywhere else not only the chief Commander, but each single one, because a surprise has the effect in particular of greatly loosening unity, so that the individuality of each separate leader easily comes to light.

Much depends here on the general relation in which the two parties stand to each other. If the one side through a general moral superiority can intimidate and outdo the other, then he can make use of the surprise with more success, and even reap good fruit where properly he should come to ruin.

CHAPTER X - STRATAGEM

STRATAGEM implies a concealed intention, and therefore is opposed to straightforward dealing, in the same way as wit is the opposite of direct proof. It has therefore nothing in common with means of persuasion, of self-interest, of force, but a great deal to do with deceit, because that likewise conceals its object. It is itself a deceit as well when it is done, but still it differs from what is commonly called deceit, in this respect that there is no direct breach of word. The deceiver by stratagem leaves it to the person himself whom he is deceiving to commit the errors of understanding which at last, flowing into ONE result, suddenly change the nature of things in his eyes. We may therefore say, as nit is a sleight of hand with ideas and conceptions, so stratagem is a sleight of hand with actions.

At first sight it appears as if Strategy had not improperly derived its name from stratagem; and that, with all the real and apparent changes which the whole character of War has undergone since the time of the Greeks, this term still points to its real nature.

If we leave to tactics the actual delivery of the blow, the battle itself, and look upon Strategy as the art of using this means with skill, then besides the forces of the character, such as burning ambition which always presses like a spring, a strong will which hardly bends &c. &c., there seems no subjective quality so suited to guide and inspire strategic activity as stratagem. The general tendency to surprise, treated of in the foregoing chapter, points to this conclusion, for there is a degree of stratagem, be it ever so small, which lies at the foundation of every attempt to surprise.

But however much we feel a desire to see the actors in War outdo each other in hidden activity, readiness, and stratagem, still we must admit that these qualities show themselves but little in history, and have rarely been able to work their way to the surface from amongst the mass of relations and circumstances.

The explanation of this is obvious, and it is almost identical with the subject matter of the preceding chapter.

Strategy knows no other activity than the regulating of combat with the measures which relate to it. It has no concern, like ordinary life, with transactions which consist merely of words—that is, in expressions, declarations, &c. But these, which are very inexpensive, are chiefly the means with which the wily one takes in those he practises upon.

That which there is like it in War, plans and orders given merely as make-believers, false reports sent on purpose to the enemy—is usually of so little effect in the strategic field that it is only resorted to in particular cases which offer of themselves, therefore cannot be regarded as spontaneous action which emanates from the leader.

But such measures as carrying out the arrangements for a battle, so far as to impose upon the enemy, require a considerable expenditure of time and power; of course, the greater the impression to be made, the greater the expenditure in these respects. And as this is usually not given for the purpose, very few demonstrations, so-called, in Strategy, effect the object for which they are designed. In fact, it is dangerous to detach large forces for any length of time merely for a trick, because there is always the risk of its being done in vain, and then these forces are wanted at the decisive point.

The chief actor in War is always thoroughly sensible of this sober truth, and therefore he has no desire to play at tricks of agility. The bitter earnestness of necessity presses so fully into direct action that there is no room for that game. In a word, the pieces on the strategical chess-board want that mobility which is the element of stratagem and subtility.

The conclusion which we draw, is that a correct and penetrating eye is a more necessary and more useful quality for a General than craftiness, although that also does no harm if it does not exist at the expense of necessary qualities of the heart, which is only too often the case.

But the weaker the forces become which are under the command of Strategy, so much the more they become adapted for stratagem, so that to the quite feeble and little, for whom no prudence, no sagacity is any longer sufficient at the point where all art seems to forsake him, stratagem offers itself as a last resource. The more helpless his situation, the more everything presses towards one single, desperate blow, the more readily stratagem comes to the aid of his boldness. Let loose from all further calculations, freed from all concern for the future, boldness and stratagem intensify each other, and thus collect at one point an infinitesimal glimmering of hope into a single ray, which may likewise serve to kindle a flame.

CHAPTER XI - ASSEMBLY OF FORCES IN SPACE

THE best Strategy is ALWAYS TO BE VERY STRONG, first generally then at the decisive point. Therefore, apart from the energy which creates the Army, a work which is not always done by the General, there is no more imperative and no simpler law for Strategy than to KEEP THE FORCES CONCENTRATED.—No portion is to be separated from the main body unless called away by some urgent necessity. On this maxim we stand firm, and look upon it as a guide to be depended upon. What are the reasonable grounds on which a detachment of forces may be made we shall learn by degrees. Then we shall also see that this principle cannot have the same general effects in every War, but that these are different according to the means and end.

It seems incredible, and yet it has happened a hundred times, that troops have been divided and separated merely through a mysterious feeling of conventional manner, without any clear perception of the reason.

If the concentration of the whole force is acknowledged as the norm, and every division and separation as an exception which must be justified, then not only will that folly be completely avoided, but also many an erroneous ground for separating troops will be barred admission.

CHAPTER XII - ASSEMBLY OF FORCES IN TIME

WE have here to deal with a conception which in real life diffuses many kinds of illusory light. A clear definition and development of the idea is therefore necessary, and we hope to be allowed a short analysis.

War is the shock of two opposing forces in collision with each other, from which it follows as a matter of course that the stronger not only destroys the other, but carries it forward with it in its movement. This fundamentally admits of no successive action of powers, but makes the simultaneous application of all forces intended for the shock appear as a primordial law of War.

So it is in reality, but only so far as the struggle resembles also in practice a mechanical shock, but when it consists in a lasting, mutual action of destructive forces, then we can certainly imagine a successive action of forces. This is the case in tactics, principally because firearms form the basis of all tactics, but also for other reasons as well. If in a fire combat 1000 men are opposed to 500, then the gross loss is calculated from the amount of the enemy's force and our own; 1000 men fire twice as many shots as 500, but more shots will take effect on the 1000 than on the 500 because it is assumed that they stand in closer order than the other. If we were to suppose the number of hits to be double, then the losses on each side would be equal. From the 500 there would be for example 200 disabled, and out of the body of 1000 likewise the same; now if the 500 had kept another body of equal number quite out of fire, then both sides would have 800 effective men; but of these, on the one side there would be 500 men quite fresh, fully supplied with ammunition, and in their full vigour; on the other side only 800 all alike shaken in their order, in want of sufficient ammunition and weakened in physical force. The assumption that the 1000 men merely on account of their greater number would lose twice as many as 500 would have lost in their place, is certainly not correct; therefore the greater loss which the side suffers that has placed the half of its force in reserve, must be regarded as a disadvantage in that original formation; further it must be admitted, that in the generality of cases the 1000 men would have the advantage at the first commencement of being able to drive their opponent out of his position and force him to a retrograde movement; now, whether these two advantages are a counterpoise to the disadvantage of finding ourselves with 800 men to a certain extent disorganised by the combat, opposed to an enemy who is not materially weaker in numbers and who has 500 quite fresh troops, is one that cannot be decided by pursuing an analysis further, we must here rely upon experience, and there will scarcely be an officer experienced in War who will not in the generality of cases assign the advantage to that side which has the fresh troops.

In this way it becomes evident how the employment of too many forces in combat may be disadvantageous; for whatever advantages the superiority may give in the first moment, we may have to pay dearly for in the next.

But this danger only endures as long as the disorder, the state of confusion and weakness lasts, in a word, up to the crisis which every combat brings with it even for the conqueror. Within the duration of this relaxed state of exhaustion, the appearance of a proportionate number of fresh troops is decisive.

But when this disordering effect of victory stops, and therefore only the moral superiority remains which every victory gives, then it is no longer possible for fresh troops to restore the combat, they would only be carried along in the general movement; a beaten Army cannot be brought back to victory a day after by means of a strong reserve. Here we find ourselves at the source of a highly material difference between tactics and strategy.

The tactical results, the results within the four corners of the battle, and before its close, lie for the most part within the limits of that period of disorder and weakness. But the strategic result, that is to say, the result of the total combat, of the victories realised, let them be small or great, lies completely (beyond) outside of that period. It is only when the results of partial combats have bound themselves together into an independent whole, that the strategic result appears, but then, the state of crisis is over, the forces have resumed their original form, and are now only weakened to the extent of those actually destroyed (placed hors de combat).

The consequence of this difference is, that tactics can make a continued use of forces, Strategy only a simultaneous one.

If I cannot, in tactics, decide all by the first success, if I have to fear the next moment, it follows of itself that I employ only so much of my force for the success of the first moment as appears sufficient for that object, and keep the rest beyond the reach of fire or conflict of any kind, in order to be able to oppose fresh troops to fresh, or with such to overcome those that are exhausted. But it is not so in Strategy. Partly, as we have just shown, it has not so much reason to fear a reaction after a success realised, because with that success the crisis stops; partly all the forces strategically employed are not necessarily weakened. Only so much of them as have been tactically in conflict with the enemy's force, that is, engaged in partial combat, are weakened by it; consequently, only so much as was unavoidably necessary, but by no means all which was strategically in conflict with the enemy, unless tactics has expended them unnecessarily. Corps which, on account of the general superiority in numbers, have either been little or not at all engaged, whose presence alone has assisted in the result, are after the decision the same as they were before, and for new enterprises as efficient as if they had been entirely inactive. How greatly such corps which thus constitute our excess may contribute to the total success is evident in itself; indeed, it is not difficult to see how they may even diminish considerably the loss of the forces engaged in tactical, conflict on our side.

If, therefore, in Strategy the loss does not increase with the number of the troops employed, but is often diminished by it, and if, as a natural consequence, the decision in our favor is, by that means, the more certain, then it follows naturally that in Strategy we can never employ too many forces, and consequently also that they must be applied simultaneously to the immediate purpose.

But we must vindicate this proposition upon another ground. We have hitherto only spoken of the combat itself; it is the real activity in War, but men, time, and space, which appear as the elements of this activity, must, at the same time, be kept in view, and the results of their influence brought into consideration also.

Fatigue, exertion, and privation constitute in War a special principle of destruction, not essentially belonging to contest, but more or less inseparably bound up with it, and certainly one which especially belongs to Strategy. They no doubt exist in tactics as well, and perhaps there in the highest degree; but as the duration of the tactical acts is shorter, therefore the small effects of exertion and privation on them can come but little into consideration. But in Strategy on the other hand, where time and space, are on a larger scale, their influence is not only always very considerable, but often quite decisive. It is not at all uncommon for a victorious Army to lose many more by sickness than on the field of battle.

If, therefore, we look at this sphere of destruction in Strategy in the same manner as we have considered that of fire and close combat in tactics, then we may well imagine that everything which comes within its vortex will, at the end of the campaign or of any other strategic period, be reduced to a state of weakness, which makes the arrival of a fresh force decisive. We might therefore conclude that there is a motive in the one case as well as the other to strive for the first success with as few forces as possible, in order to keep up this fresh force for the last.

In order to estimate exactly this conclusion, which, in many cases in practice, will have a great appearance of truth, we must direct our attention to the separate ideas which it contains. In the first place, we must not confuse the notion of reinforcement with that of fresh unused troops. There are few campaigns at the end of which an increase of force is not earnestly desired by the conqueror as well as the conquered, and indeed should appear decisive; but that is not the point here, for that increase of force could not be necessary if the force had been so much larger at the first. But it would be contrary to all experience to suppose that an Army coming fresh into the field is to be esteemed higher in point of moral value than an Army already in the field, just as a tactical reserve is more to be esteemed than a body of troops which has been already severely handled in the fight. Just as much as an unfortunate campaign lowers the courage and moral powers of an Army, a successful one raises these elements in their value. In the generality of cases, therefore, these influences are compensated, and then there remains over and above as clear gain the habituation to War. We should besides look more here to successful than to unsuccessful campaigns, because when the greater probability of the latter may be seen beforehand, without doubt forces are wanted, and, therefore, the reserving a portion for future use is out of the question.

This point being settled, then the question is, Do the losses which a force sustains through fatigues and privations increase in proportion to the size of the force, as is the case in a combat? And to that we answer "No."

The fatigues of War result in a great measure from the dangers with which every moment of the act of War is more or less impregnated. To encounter these dangers at all points, to proceed onwards with security in the execution of one's plans, gives employment to a multitude of agencies which make up the tactical and strategic service of the Army. This service is more difficult the weaker an Army is, and easier as its numerical superiority over that of the enemy increases. Who can doubt this? A campaign against a much weaker enemy will therefore cost smaller efforts than against one just as strong or stronger.

So much for the fatigues. It is somewhat different with the privations; they consist chiefly of two things, the want of food, and the want of shelter for the troops, either in quarters or in suitable camps. Both these wants will no doubt be greater in proportion as the number of men on one spot is greater. But does not the superiority in force afford also the best means of spreading out and finding more room, and therefore more means of subsistence and shelter?

If Buonaparte, in his invasion of Russia in 1812, concentrated his Army in great masses upon one single road in a manner never heard of before, and thus caused privations equally unparalleled, we must ascribe it to his maxim THAT IT IS IMPOSSIBLE TO BE TOO STRONG AT THE DECISIVE POINT. Whether in this instance he did not strain the principle too far is a question which would be out of place here; but it is certain that, if he had made a point of avoiding the distress which was by that means brought about, he had only to advance on a greater breadth of front. Room was not wanted for the purpose in Russia, and in very few cases can it be wanted. Therefore, from this no ground can be deduced to prove that the simultaneous employment of very superior forces must produce greater weakening. But now, supposing that in spite of the general relief afforded by setting apart a portion of the Army, wind and weather and the toils of War had produced a diminution even on the part which as a spare force had been reserved for later use, still we must take a comprehensive general view of the whole, and therefore ask, Will this diminution of force suffice to counterbalance the gain in forces, which we, through our superiority in numbers, may be able to make in more ways than one?

But there still remains a most important point to be noticed. In a partial combat, the force required to obtain a great result can be approximately estimated without much difficulty, and, consequently, we can form an idea of what is superfluous. In Strategy this may be said to be impossible, because the strategic result has no such well-defined object and no such circumscribed limits as the tactical. Thus what can be looked upon in tactics as an excess of power, must be regarded in Strategy as a means to give expansion to success, if opportunity offers for it; with the magnitude of the success the gain in force increases at the same time, and in this way the superiority of numbers may soon reach a point which the most careful economy of forces could never have attained.

By means of his enormous numerical superiority, Buonaparte was enabled to reach Moscow in 1812, and to take that central capital. Had he by means of this superiority succeeded in completely defeating the Russian Army, he would, in all probability, have concluded a peace in Moscow which in any other way was much less attainable. This example is used to explain the idea, not to prove it, which would require a circumstantial demonstration, for which this is not the place.

All these reflections bear merely upon the idea of a successive employment of forces, and not upon the conception of a reserve properly so called, which they, no doubt, come in contact with throughout, but which, as we shall see in the following chapter, is connected with some other considerations.

What we desire to establish here is, that if in tactics the military force through the mere duration of actual employment suffers a diminution of power, if time, therefore, appears as a factor in the result, this is not the case in Strategy in a material degree. The destructive effects which are also produced upon the forces in Strategy by time, are partly diminished through their mass, partly made good in other ways, and, therefore, in Strategy it cannot be an object to make time an ally on its own account by bringing troops successively into action.

We say on "its own account," for the influence which time, on account of other circumstances which it brings about but which are different from itself can have, indeed must necessarily have, for one of the two parties, is quite another thing, is anything but indifferent or unimportant, and will be the subject of consideration hereafter.

The rule which we have been seeking to set forth is, therefore, that all forces which are available and destined for a strategic object should be SIMULTANEOUSLY applied to it; and this application will be so much the more complete the more everything is compressed into one act and into one movement.

But still there is in Strategy a renewal of effort and a persistent action which, as a chief means towards the ultimate success, is more particularly not to be overlooked, it is the CONTINUAL DEVELOPMENT OF NEW FORCES. This is also the subject of another chapter, and we only refer to it here in order to prevent the reader from having something in view of which we have not been speaking.

We now turn to a subject very closely connected with our present considerations, which must be settled before full light can be thrown on the whole, we mean the STRATEGIC RESERVE.

CHAPTER XIII - STRATEGIC RESERVE

A RESERVE has two objects which are very distinct from each other, namely, first, the prolongation and renewal of the combat, and secondly, for use in case of unforeseen events. The first object implies the utility of a successive application of forces, and on that account cannot occur in Strategy. Cases in which a corps is sent to succour a point which is supposed to be about to fall are plainly to be placed in the category of the second object, as the resistance which has to be offered here could not have been sufficiently foreseen. But a corps which is destined expressly to prolong the combat, and with that object in view is placed in rear, would be only a corps placed out of reach of fire, but under the command and at the disposition of the General Commanding in the action, and accordingly would be a tactical and not a strategic reserve.

But the necessity for a force ready for unforeseen events may also take place in Strategy, and consequently there may also be a strategic reserve, but only where unforeseen events are imaginable. In tactics, where the enemy's measures are generally first ascertained by direct sight, and where they may be concealed by every wood, every fold of undulating ground, we must naturally always be alive, more or less, to the possibility of unforeseen events, in order to strengthen, subsequently, those points which appear too weak, and, in fact, to modify generally the disposition of our troops, so as to make it correspond better to that of the enemy.

Such cases must also happen in Strategy, because the strategic act is directly linked to the tactical. In Strategy also many a measure is first adopted in consequence of what is actually seen, or in consequence of uncertain reports arriving from day to day, or even from hour to hour, and lastly, from the actual results of the combats it is, therefore, an essential condition of strategic command that, according to the degree of uncertainty, forces must be kept in reserve against future contingencies.

In the defensive generally, but particularly in the defence of certain obstacles of ground, like rivers, hills, &c., such contingencies, as is well known, happen constantly.

But this uncertainty diminishes in proportion as the strategic activity has less of the tactical character, and ceases almost altogether in those regions where it borders on politics.

The direction in which the enemy leads his columns to the combat can be perceived by actual sight only; where he intends to pass a river is learnt from a few preparations which are made shortly before; the line by which he proposes to invade our country is usually announced by all the newspapers before a pistol shot has been fired. The greater the nature of the measure the less it will take the enemy by surprise. Time and space are so considerable, the circumstances out of which the action proceeds so public and little susceptible of alteration, that the coming event is either made known in good time, or can be discovered with reasonable certainty.

On the other hand the use of a reserve in this province of Strategy, even if one were available, will always be less efficacious the more the measure has a tendency towards being one of a general nature.

We have seen that the decision of a partial combat is nothing in itself, but that all partial combats only find their complete solution in the decision of the total combat.

But even this decision of the total combat has only a relative meaning of many different gradations, according as the force over which the victory has been gained forms a more or less great and important part of the whole. The lost battle of a corps may be repaired by the victory of the Army. Even the lost battle of an Army may not only be counterbalanced by the gain of a more important one, but converted into a fortunate event (the two days of Kulm, August 29 and 30, 1813). No one can doubt this; but it is just as clear that the weight of each victory (the successful issue of each total combat) is so much the more substantial the more important the part conquered, and that therefore the possibility of repairing the loss by subsequent events diminishes in the same proportion. In another place we shall have to examine this more in detail; it suffices for the present to have drawn attention to the indubitable existence of this progression.

If we now add lastly to these two considerations the third, which is, that if the persistent use of forces in tactics always shifts the great result to the end of the whole act, law of the simultaneous use of the forces in Strategy, on the contrary, lets the principal result (which need not be the final one) take place almost always at the commencement of the great (or whole) act, then in these three results we have grounds sufficient to find strategic reserves always more superfluous, always more useless, always more dangerous, the more general their destination.

The point where the idea of a strategic reserve begins to become inconsistent is not difficult to determine: it lies in the SUPREME DECISION. Employment must be given to all the forces within the space of the supreme decision, and every reserve (active force available) which is only intended for use after that decision is opposed to common sense.

If, therefore, tactics has in its reserves the means of not only meeting unforeseen dispositions on the part of the enemy, but also of repairing that which never can be foreseen, the result of the combat, should that be unfortunate; Strategy on the other hand must, at least as far as relates to the capital result, renounce the use of these means. As A rule, it can only repair the losses sustained at one point by advantages gained at another, in a few cases by moving troops from one point to another; the idea of preparing for such reverses by placing forces in reserve beforehand, can never be entertained in Strategy.

We have pointed out as an absurdity the idea of a strategic reserve which is not to co-operate in the capital result, and as it is so beyond a doubt, we should not have been led into such an analysis as we have made in these two chapters, were it not that, in the disguise of other ideas, it looks like something better, and frequently makes its appearance. One person sees in it the acme of strategic sagacity and foresight; another rejects it, and with it the idea of any reserve, consequently even of a tactical one. This confusion of ideas is transferred to real life, and if we would see a memorable instance of it we have only to call to mind that Prussia in 1806 left a reserve of 20,000 men cantoned in the Mark, under Prince Eugene of Wurtemberg, which could not possibly reach the Saale in time to be of any use, and that another force Of 25,000 men belonging to this power remained in East and South Prussia, destined only to be put on a war-footing afterwards as a reserve.

After these examples we cannot be accused of having been fighting with windmills.

CHAPTER XIV - ECONOMY OF FORCES

THE road of reason, as we have said, seldom allows itself to be reduced to a mathematical line by principles and opinions. There remains always a certain margin. But it is the same in all the practical arts of life. For the lines of beauty there are no abscissae and ordinates; circles and ellipses are not described by means of their algebraical formulae. The actor in War therefore soon finds he must trust himself to the delicate tact of judgment which, founded on natural quickness of perception, and educated by reflection, almost unconsciously seizes upon the right; he soon finds that at one time he must simplify the law (by reducing it) to some prominent characteristic points which form his rules; that at another the adopted method must become the staff on which he leans.

As one of these simplified characteristic points as a mental appliance, we look upon the principle of watching continually over the co-operation of all forces, or in other words, of keeping constantly in view that no part of them should ever be idle. Whoever has forces where the enemy does not give them sufficient employment, whoever has part of his forces on the march—that is, allows them to lie dead—while the enemy's are fighting, he is a bad manager of his forces. In this sense there is a waste of forces, which is even worse than their employment to no purpose. If there must be action, then the first point is that all parts act, because the most purposeless activity still keeps employed and destroys a portion of the enemy's force, whilst troops completely inactive are for the moment quite neutralised. Unmistakably this idea is bound up with the principles contained in the last three chapters, it is the same truth, but seen from a somewhat more comprehensive point of view and condensed into a single conception.

CHAPTER XV - GEOMETRICAL ELEMENT

THE length to which the geometrical element or form in the disposition of military force in War can become a predominant principle, we see in the art of fortification, where geometry looks after the great and the little. Also in tactics it plays a great part. It is the basis of elementary tactics, or of the theory of moving troops; but in field fortification, as well as in the theory of positions, and of their attack, its angles and lines rule like law givers who have to decide the contest. Many things here were at one time misapplied, and others were mere fribbles; still, however, in the tactics of the present day, in which in every combat the aim is to surround the enemy, the geometrical element has attained anew a great importance in a very simple, but constantly recurring application. Nevertheless, in tactics, where all is more movable, where the moral forces, individual traits, and chance are more influential than in a war of sieges, the geometrical element can never attain to the same degree of supremacy as in the latter. But less still is its influence in Strategy; certainly here, also, form in the disposition of troops, the shape of countries and states is of great importance; but the geometrical element is not decisive, as in fortification, and not nearly so important as in tactics.—The manner in which this influence exhibits itself, can only be shown by degrees at those places where it makes its appearance, and deserves notice. Here we wish more to direct attention to the difference which there is between tactics and Strategy in relation to it.

In tactics time and space quickly dwindle to their absolute minimum. If a body of troops is attacked in flank and rear by the enemy, it soon gets to a point where retreat no longer remains; such a position is very close to an absolute impossibility of continuing the fight; it must therefore extricate itself from it, or avoid getting into it. This gives to all combinations aiming at this from the first commencement a great efficiency, which chiefly consists in the disquietude which it causes the enemy as to consequences. This is why the geometrical disposition of the forces is such an important factor in the tactical product.

In Strategy this is only faintly reflected, on account of the greater space and time. We do not fire from one theatre of war upon another; and often weeks and months must pass before a strategic movement designed to surround the enemy can be executed. Further, the distances are so great that the probability of hitting the right point at last, even with the best arrangements, is but small.

In Strategy therefore the scope for such combinations, that is for those resting on the geometrical element, is much smaller, and for the same reason the effect of an advantage once actually gained at any point is much greater. Such advantage has time to bring all its effects to maturity before it is disturbed, or quite neutralised therein, by any counteracting apprehensions. We therefore do not hesitate to regard as an established truth, that in Strategy more depends on the number and the magnitude of the victorious combats, than on the form of the great lines by which they are connected.

A view just the reverse has been a favourite theme of modern theory, because a greater importance was supposed to be thus given to Strategy, and, as the higher functions of the mind were seen in Strategy, it was thought by that means to ennoble War, and, as it was said—through a new substitution of ideas—to make it more scientific. We hold it to be one of the principal uses of a complete theory openly to expose such vagaries, and as the geometrical element is the fundamental idea from which theory usually proceeds, therefore we have expressly brought out this point in strong relief.

CHAPTER XVI - ON THE SUSPENSION OF THE ACT IN WARFARE

IF one considers War as an act of mutual destruction, we must of necessity imagine both parties as making some progress; but at the same time, as regards the existing moment, we must almost as necessarily suppose the one party in a state of expectation, and only the other actually advancing, for circumstances can never be actually the same on both sides, or continue so. In time a change must ensue, from which it follows that the present moment is more favourable to one side than the other. Now if we suppose that both commanders have a full knowledge of this circumstance, then the one has a motive for action, which at the same time is a motive for the other to wait; therefore, according to this it cannot be for the interest of both at the same time to advance, nor can waiting be for the interest of both at the same time. This opposition of interest as regards the object is not deduced here from the principle of general polarity, and therefore is not in opposition to the argument in the fifth chapter of the second book; it depends on the fact that here in reality the same thing is at once an incentive or motive to both commanders, namely the probability of improving or impairing their position by future action.

But even if we suppose the possibility of a perfect equality of circumstances in this respect, or if we take into account that through imperfect knowledge of their mutual position such an equality may appear to the two Commanders to subsist, still the difference of political objects does away with this possibility of suspension. One of the parties must of necessity be assumed politically to be the aggressor, because no War could take place from defensive intentions on both sides. But the aggressor has the positive object, the defender merely a negative one. To the first then belongs the positive action, for it is only by that means that he can attain the positive object; therefore, in cases where both parties are in precisely similar circumstances, the aggressor is called upon to act by virtue of his positive object.

Therefore, from this point of view, a suspension in the act of Warfare, strictly speaking, is in contradiction with the nature of the thing; because two Armies, being two incompatible elements, should destroy one another unremittingly, just as fire and water can never put themselves in equilibrium, but act and react upon one another, until one quite disappears. What would be said of two wrestlers who remained clasped round each other for hours without making a movement. Action in War, therefore, like that of a clock which is wound up, should go on running down in regular motion.—But wild as is the nature of War it still wears the chains of human weakness, and the contradiction we see here, viz., that man seeks and creates dangers which he fears at the same time will astonish no one.

If we cast a glance at military history in general, we find so much the opposite of an incessant advance towards the aim, that STANDING STILL and DOING NOTHING is quite plainly the NORMAL CONDITION of an Army in the midst of War, ACTING, the EXCEPTION. This must almost raise a doubt as to the correctness of our conception. But if military history leads to this conclusion when viewed in the mass the latest series of campaigns redeems our position. The War of the French Revolution shows too plainly its reality, and only proves too clearly its necessity. In these operations, and especially in the campaigns of Buonaparte, the conduct of War attained to that unlimited degree of energy which we have represented as the natural law of the element. This degree is therefore possible, and if it is possible then it is necessary.

How could any one in fact justify in the eyes of reason the expenditure of forces in War, if acting was not the object? The baker only heats his oven if he has bread to put into it; the horse is only yoked to the carriage if we mean to drive; why then make the enormous effort of a War if we look for nothing else by it but like efforts on the part of the enemy?

So much in justification of the general principle; now as to its modifications, as far as they lie in the nature of the thing and are independent of special cases.

There are three causes to be noticed here, which appear as innate counterpoises and prevent the over-rapid or uncontrollable movement of the wheel-work.

The first, which produces a constant tendency to delay, and is thereby a retarding principle, is the natural timidity and want of resolution in the human mind, a kind of inertia in the moral world, but which is produced not by attractive, but by repellent forces, that is to say, by dread of danger and responsibility.

In the burning element of War, ordinary natures appear to become heavier; the impulsion given must therefore be stronger and more frequently repeated if the motion is to be a continuous one. The mere idea of the object for which arms have been taken up is seldom sufficient to overcome this resistant force, and if a warlike enterprising spirit is not at the head, who feels himself in War in his natural element, as much as a fish in the ocean, or if there is not the pressure from above of some great responsibility, then standing still will be the order of the day, and progress will be the exception.

The second cause is the imperfection of human perception and judgment, which is greater in War than anywhere, because a person hardly knows exactly his own position from one moment to another, and can only conjecture on slight grounds that of the enemy, which is purposely concealed; this often gives rise to the case of both parties looking upon one and the same object as advantageous for them, while in reality the interest of one must preponderate; thus then each may think he acts wisely by waiting another moment, as we have already said in the fifth chapter of the second book.

The third cause which catches hold, like a ratchet wheel in machinery, from time to time producing a complete standstill, is the greater strength of the defensive form. A may feel too weak to attack B, from which it does not follow that B is strong enough for an attack on A. The addition of strength, which the defensive gives is not merely lost by assuming the offensive, but also passes to the enemy just as, figuratively expressed, the difference of a + b and a - b is equal to 2b. Therefore it may so happen that both parties, at one and the same time, not only feel themselves too weak to attack, but also are so in reality.

Thus even in the midst of the act of War itself, anxious sagacity and the apprehension of too great danger find vantage ground, by means of which they can exert their power, and tame the elementary impetuosity of War.

However, at the same time these causes without an exaggeration of their effect, would hardly explain the long states of inactivity which took place in military operations, in former times, in Wars undertaken about interests of no great importance, and in which inactivity consumed nine-tenths of the time that the troops remained under arms. This feature in these Wars, is to be traced principally to the influence which the demands of the one party, and the condition, and feeling of the other, exercised over the conduct of the operations, as has been already observed in the chapter on the essence and object of War.

These things may obtain such a preponderating influence as to make of War a half-and-half affair. A War is often nothing more than an armed neutrality, or a menacing attitude to support negotiations or an attempt to gain some small advantage by small exertions, and then to wait the tide of circumstances, or a disagreeable treaty obligation, which is fulfilled in the most niggardly way possible.

In all these cases in which the impulse given by interest is slight, and the principle of hostility feeble, in which there is no desire to do much, and also not much to dread from the enemy; in short, where no powerful motives press and drive, cabinets will not risk much in the game; hence this tame mode of carrying on War, in which the hostile spirit of real War is laid in irons.

The more War becomes in this manner devitalised so much the more its theory becomes destitute of the necessary firm pivots and buttresses for its reasoning; the necessary is constantly diminishing, the accidental constantly increasing.

Nevertheless in this kind of Warfare, there is also a certain shrewdness, indeed, its action is perhaps more diversified, and more extensive than in the other. Hazard played with realeaux of gold seems changed into a game of commerce with groschen. And on this field, where the conduct of War spins out the time with a number of small flourishes, with skirmishes at outposts, half in earnest half in jest, with long dispositions which end in nothing with positions and marches, which afterwards are designated as skilful only because their infinitesimally small causes are lost, and common sense can make nothing of them, here on this very field many theorists find the real Art of War at home: in these feints, parades, half and quarter thrusts of former Wars, they find the aim of all theory, the supremacy of mind over matter, and modern Wars appear to them mere savage fisticuffs, from which nothing is to be learnt, and which must be regarded as mere retrograde steps towards barbarism. This opinion is as frivolous as the objects to which it relates. Where great forces and great passions are wanting, it is certainly easier for a practised dexterity to show its game; but is then the command of great forces, not in itself a higher exercise of the intelligent faculties? Is then that kind of conventional sword-exercise not comprised in and belonging to the other mode of conducting War? Does it not bear the same relation to it as the motions upon a ship to the motion of the ship itself? Truly it can take place only under the tacit condition that the adversary does no better. And can we tell, how long he may choose to respect those conditions? Has not then the French Revolution fallen upon us in the midst of the fancied security of our old system of War, and driven us from Chalons to Moscow? And did not Frederick the Great in like manner surprise the Austrians reposing in their ancient habits of War, and make their monarchy tremble? Woe to the cabinet which, with a shilly-shally policy, and a routine-ridden military system, meets with an adversary who, like the rude element, knows no other law than that of his intrinsic force. Every deficiency in energy and exertion is then a weight in the scales in favour of the enemy; it is not so easy then to change from the fencing posture into that of an athlete, and a slight blow is often sufficient to knock down the whole.

The result of all the causes now adduced is, that the hostile action of a campaign does not progress by a continuous, but by an intermittent movement, and that, therefore, between the separate bloody acts, there is a period of watching, during which both parties fall into the defensive, and also that usually a higher object causes the principle of aggression to predominate on one side, and thus leaves it in general in an advancing position, by which then its proceedings become modified in some degree.

CHAPTER XVII - ON THE CHARACTER OF MODERN WAR

THE attention which must be paid to the character of War as it is now made, has a great influence upon all plans, especially on strategic ones.

Since all methods formerly usual were upset by Buonaparte's luck and boldness, and first-rate Powers almost wiped out at a blow; since the Spaniards by their stubborn resistance have shown what the general arming of a nation and insurgent measures on a great scale can effect, in spite of weakness and porousness of individual parts; since Russia, by the campaign of 1812 has taught us, first, that an Empire of great dimensions is not to be conquered (which might have been easily known before), secondly, that the probability of final success does not in all cases diminish in the same measure as battles, capitals, and provinces are lost (which was formerly an incontrovertible principle with all diplomatists, and therefore made them always ready to enter at once into some bad temporary peace), but that a nation is often strongest in the heart of its country, if the enemy's offensive power has exhausted itself, and with what enormous force the defensive then springs over to the offensive; further, since Prussia (1813) has shown that sudden efforts may add to an Army sixfold by means of the militia, and that this militia is just as fit for service abroad as in its own country;—since all these events have shown what an enormous factor the heart and sentiments of a Nation may be in the product of its political and military strength, in fine, since governments have found out all these additional aids, it is not to be expected that they will let them lie idle in future Wars, whether it be that danger threatens their own existence, or that restless ambition drives them on.

That a War which is waged with the whole weight of the national power on each side must be organised differently in principle to those where everything is calculated according to the relations of standing Armies to each other, it is easy to perceive. Standing Armies once resembled fleets, the land force the sea force in their relations to the remainder of the State, and from that the Art of War on shore had in it something of naval tactics, which it has now quite lost.

CHAPTER XVIII - TENSION AND REST

The Dynamic Law of War

WE have seen in the sixteenth chapter of this book, how, in most campaigns, much more time used to be spent in standing still and inaction than in activity.

Now, although, as observed in the preceding chapter we see quite a different character in the present form of War, still it is certain that real action will always be interrupted more or less by long pauses; and this leads to the necessity of our examining more closely the nature of these two phases of War.

If there is a suspension of action in War, that is, if neither party wills something positive, there is rest, and consequently equilibrium, but certainly an equilibrium in the largest signification, in which not only the moral and physical war-forces, but all relations and interests, come into calculation. As soon as ever one of the two parties proposes to himself a new positive object, and commences active steps towards it, even if it is only by preparations, and as soon as the adversary opposes this, there is a tension of powers; this lasts until the decision takes place—that is, until one party either gives up his object or the other has conceded it to him.

This decision—the foundation of which lies always in the combat—combinations which are made on each side—is followed by a movement in one or other direction.

When this movement has exhausted itself, either in the difficulties which had to be mastered, in overcoming its own internal friction, or through new resistant forces prepared by the acts of the enemy, then either a state of rest takes place or a new tension with a decision, and then a new movement, in most cases in the opposite direction.

This speculative distinction between equilibrium, tension, and motion is more essential for practical action than may at first sight appear.

In a state of rest and of equilibrium a varied kind of activity may prevail on one side that results from opportunity, and does not aim at a great alteration. Such an activity may contain important combats—even pitched battles—but yet it is still of quite a different nature, and on that account generally different in its effects.

If a state of tension exists, the effects of the decision are always greater partly because a greater force of will and a greater pressure of circumstances manifest themselves therein; partly because everything has been prepared and arranged for a great movement. The decision in such cases resembles the effect of a mine well closed and tamped, whilst an event in itself perhaps just as great, in a state of rest, is more or less like a mass of powder puffed away in the open air.

At the same time, as a matter of course, the state of tension must be imagined in different degrees of intensity, and it may therefore approach gradually by many steps towards the state of rest, so that at the last there is a very slight difference between them.

Now the real use which we derive from these reflections is the conclusion that every measure which is taken during a state of tension is more important and more prolific in results than the same measure could be in a state of equilibrium, and that this importance increases immensely in the highest degrees of tension.

The cannonade of Valmy, September 20, 1792, decided more than the battle of Hochkirch, October 14, 1758.

In a tract of country which the enemy abandons to us because he cannot defend it, we can settle ourselves differently from what we should do if the retreat of the enemy was only made with the view to a decision under more favourable circumstances. Again, a strategic attack in course of execution, a faulty position, a single false march, may be decisive in its consequence; whilst in a state of equilibrium such errors must be of a very glaring kind, even to excite the activity of the enemy in a general way.

Most bygone Wars, as we have already said, consisted, so far as regards the greater part of the time, in this state of equilibrium, or at least in such short tensions with long intervals between them, and weak in their effects, that the events to which they gave rise were seldom great successes, often they were theatrical exhibitions, got up in honour of a royal birthday (Hochkirch), often a mere satisfying of the honour of the arms (Kunersdorf), or the personal vanity of the commander (Freiberg).

That a Commander should thoroughly understand these states, that he should have the tact to act in the spirit of them, we hold to be a great requisite, and we have had experience in the campaign of 1806 how far it is sometimes wanting. In that tremendous tension, when everything pressed on towards a supreme decision, and that alone with all its consequences should have occupied the whole soul of the Commander, measures were proposed and even partly carried out (such as the reconnaissance towards Franconia), which at the most might have given a kind of gentle play of oscillation within a state of equilibrium. Over these blundering schemes and views, absorbing the activity of the Army, the really necessary means, which could alone save, were lost sight of.

But this speculative distinction which we have made is also necessary for our further progress in the construction of our theory, because all that we have to say on the relation of attack and defence, and on the completion of this double-sided act, concerns the state of the crisis in which the forces are placed during the tension and motion, and because all the activity which can take place during the condition of equilibrium can only be regarded and treated as a corollary; for that crisis is the real War and this state of equilibrium only its reflection.

BOOK IV: THE COMBAT

CHAPTER I - INTRODUCTORY

HAVING in the foregoing book examined the subjects which may be regarded as the efficient elements of War, we shall now turn our attention to the combat as the real activity in Warfare, which, by its physical and moral effects, embraces sometimes more simply, sometimes in a more complex manner, the object of the whole campaign. In this activity and in its effects these elements must therefore, reappear.

The formation of the combat is tactical in its nature; we only glance at it here in a general way in order to get acquainted with it in its aspect as a whole. In practice the minor or more immediate objects give every combat a characteristic form; these minor objects we shall not discuss until hereafter. But these peculiarities are in comparison to the general characteristics of a combat mostly only insignificant, so that most combats are very like one another, and, therefore, in order to avoid repeating that which is general at every stage, we are compelled to look into it here, before taking up the subject of its more special application.

In the first place, therefore, we shall give in the next chapter, in a few words, the characteristics of the modern battle in its tactical course, because that lies at the foundation of our conceptions of what the battle really is.

CHAPTER II - CHARACTER OF THE MODERN BATTLE

ACCORDING to the notion we have formed of tactics and strategy, it follows, as a matter of course, that if the nature of the former is changed, that change must have an influence on the latter. If tactical facts in one case are entirely different from those in another, then the strategic, must be so also, if they are to continue consistent and reasonable. It is therefore important to characterise a general action in its modern form before we advance with the study of its employment in strategy.

What do we do now usually in a great battle? We place ourselves quietly in great masses arranged contiguous to and behind one another. We deploy relatively only a small portion of the whole, and let it wring itself out in a fire-combat which lasts for several hours, only interrupted now and again, and removed hither and thither by separate small shocks from charges with the bayonet and cavalry attacks. When this line has gradually exhausted part of its warlike ardour in this manner and there remains nothing more than the cinders, it is withdrawn and replaced by another.

In this manner the battle on a modified principle burns slowly away like wet powder, and if the veil of night commands it to stop, because neither party can any longer see, and neither chooses to run the risk of blind chance, then an account is taken by each side respectively of the masses remaining, which can be called still effective, that is, which have not yet quite collapsed like extinct volcanoes; account is taken of the ground gained or lost, and of how stands the security of the rear; these results with the special impressions as to bravery and cowardice, ability and stupidity, which are thought to have been observed in ourselves and in the enemy are collected into one single total impression, out of which there springs the resolution to quit the field or to renew the combat on the morrow.

This description, which is not intended as a finished picture of a modern battle, but only to give its general tone, suits for the offensive and defensive, and the special traits which are given, by the object proposed, the country, &c. &c., may be introduced into it, without materially altering the conception.

But modern battles are not so by accident; they are so because the parties find themselves nearly on a level as regards military organisation and the knowledge of the Art of War, and because the warlike element inflamed by great national interests has broken through artificial limits and now flows in its natural channel. Under these two conditions, battles will always preserve this character.

This general idea of the modern battle will be useful to us in the sequel in more places than one, if we want to estimate the value of the particular co-efficients of strength, country, &c. &c. It is only for general, great, and decisive combats, and such as come near to them that this description stands good; inferior ones have changed their character also in the same direction but less than great ones. The proof of this belongs to tactics; we shall, however, have an opportunity hereafter of making this subject plainer by giving a few particulars.

CHAPTER III - THE COMBAT IN GENERAL

THE Combat is the real warlike activity, everything else is only its auxiliary; let us therefore take an attentive look at its nature.

Combat means fighting, and in this the destruction or conquest of the enemy is the object, and the enemy, in the particular combat, is the armed force which stands opposed to us.

This is the simple idea; we shall return to it, but before we can do that we must insert a series of others.

If we suppose the State and its military force as a unit, then the most natural idea is to imagine the War also as one great combat, and in the simple relations of savage nations it is also not much otherwise. But our Wars are made up of a number of great and small simultaneous or consecutive combats, and this severance of the activity into so many separate actions is owing to the great multiplicity of the relations out of which War arises with us.

In point of fact, the ultimate object of our Wars, the political one, is not always quite a simple one; and even were it so, still the action is bound up with such a number of conditions and considerations to be taken into account, that the object can no longer be attained by one single great act but only through a number of greater or smaller acts which are bound up into a whole; each of these separate acts is therefore a part of a whole, and has consequently a special object by which it is bound to this whole.

We have already said that every strategic act can be referred to the idea of a combat, because it is an employment of the military force, and at the root of that there always lies the idea of fighting. We may therefore reduce every military activity in the province of Strategy to the unit of single combats, and occupy ourselves with the object of these only; we shall get acquainted with these special objects by degrees as we come to speak of the causes which produce them; here we content ourselves with saying that every combat, great or small, has its own peculiar object in subordination to the main object. If this is the case then, the destruction and conquest of the enemy is only to be regarded as the means of gaining this object; as it unquestionably is.

But this result is true only in its form, and important only on account of the connection which the ideas have between themselves, and we have only sought it out to get rid of it at once.

What is overcoming the enemy? Invariably the destruction of his military force, whether it be by death, or wounds, or any means; whether it be completely or only to such a degree that he can no longer continue the contest; therefore as long as we set aside all special objects of combats, we may look upon the complete or partial destruction of the enemy as the only object of all combats.

Now we maintain that in the majority of cases, and especially in great battles, the special object by which the battle is individualised and bound up with the great whole is only a weak modification of that general object, or an ancillary object bound up with it, important enough to individualise the battle, but always insignificant in comparison with that general object; so that if that ancillary object alone should be obtained, only an unimportant part of the purpose of the combat is fulfilled. If this assertion is correct, then we see that the idea, according to which the destruction of the enemy's force is only the means, and something else always the object, can only be true in form, but, that it would lead to false conclusions if we did not recollect that this destruction of the enemy's force is comprised in that object, and that this object is only a weak modification of it. Forgetfulness of this led to completely false views before the Wars of the last period, and created tendencies as well as fragments of systems, in which theory thought it raised itself so much the more above handicraft, the less it supposed itself to stand in need of the use of the real instrument, that is the destruction of the enemy's force.

Certainly such a system could not have arisen unless supported by other false suppositions, and unless in place of the destruction of the enemy, other things had been substituted to which an efficacy was ascribed which did not rightly belong to them. We shall attack these falsehoods whenever occasion requires, but we could not treat of the combat without claiming for it the real importance and value which belong to it, and giving warning against the errors to which merely formal truth might lead.

But now how shall we manage to show that in most cases, and in those of most importance, the destruction of the enemy's Army is the chief thing? How shall we manage to combat that extremely subtle idea, which supposes it possible, through the use of a special artificial form, to effect by a small direct destruction of the enemy's forces a much greater destruction indirectly, or by means of small but extremely well-directed blows to produce such paralysation of the enemy's forces, such a command over the enemy's will, that this mode of proceeding is to be viewed as a great shortening of the road? Undoubtedly a victory at one point may be of more value than at another. Undoubtedly there is a scientific arrangement of battles amongst themselves, even in Strategy, which is in fact nothing but the Art of thus arranging them. To deny that is not our intention, but we assert that the direct destruction of the enemy's forces is everywhere predominant; we contend here for the overruling importance of this destructive principle and nothing else.

We must, however, call to mind that we are now engaged with Strategy, not with tactics, therefore we do not speak of the means which the former may have of destroying at a small expense a large body of the enemy's forces, but under direct destruction we understand the tactical results, and that, therefore, our assertion is that only great tactical results can lead to great strategical ones, or, as we have already once before more distinctly expressed it, THE TACTICAL SUCCESSES are of paramount importance in the conduct of War.

The proof of this assertion seems to us simple enough, it lies in the time which every complicated (artificial) combination requires. The question whether a simple attack, or one more carefully prepared, i.e., more artificial, will produce greater effects, may undoubtedly be decided in favour of the latter as long as the enemy is assumed to remain quite passive. But every carefully combined attack requires time for its preparation, and if a counter-stroke by the enemy intervenes, our whole design may be upset. Now if the enemy should decide upon some simple attack, which can be executed in a shorter time, then he gains the initiative, and destroys the effect of the great plan. Therefore, together with the expediency of a complicated attack we must consider all the dangers which we run during its preparation, and should only adopt it if there is no reason to fear that the enemy will disconcert our scheme. Whenever this is the case we must ourselves choose the simpler, i.e., quicker way, and lower our views in this sense as far as the character, the relations of the enemy, and other circumstances may render necessary. If we quit the weak impressions of abstract ideas and descend to the region of practical life, then it is evident that a bold, courageous, resolute enemy will not let us have time for wide-reaching skilful combinations, and it is just against such a one we should require skill the most. By this it appears to us that the advantage of simple and direct results over those that are complicated is conclusively shown.

Our opinion is not on that account that the simple blow is the best, but that we must not lift the arm too far for the time given to strike, and that this condition will always lead more to direct conflict the more warlike our opponent is. Therefore, far from making it our aim to gain upon the enemy by complicated plans, we must rather seek to be beforehand with him by greater simplicity in our designs.

If we seek for the lowest foundation-stones of these converse propositions we find that in the one it is ability, in the other, courage. Now, there is something very attractive in the notion that a moderate degree of courage joined to great ability will produce greater effects than moderate ability with great courage. But unless we suppose these elements in a disproportionate relation, not logical, we have no right to assign to ability this advantage over courage in a field which is called danger, and which must be regarded as the true domain of courage.

After this abstract view we shall only add that experience, very far from leading to a different conclusion, is rather the sole cause which has impelled us in this direction, and given rise to such reflections.

Whoever reads history with a mind free from prejudice cannot fail to arrive at a conviction that of all military virtues, energy in the conduct of operations has always contributed the most to the glory and success of arms.

How we make good our principle of regarding the destruction of the enemy's force as the principal object, not only in the War as a whole but also in each separate combat, and how that principle suits all the forms and conditions necessarily demanded by the relations out of which War springs, the sequel will show. For the present all that we desire is to uphold its general importance, and with this result we return again to the combat.

CHAPTER IV - THE COMBAT IN GENERAL (CONTINUATION)

IN the last chapter we showed the destruction of the enemy as the true object of the combat, and we have sought to prove by a special consideration of the point, that this is true in the majority of cases, and in respect to the most important battles, because the destruction of the enemy's Army is always the preponderating object in War. The other objects which may be mixed up with this destruction of the enemy's force, and may have more or less influence, we shall describe generally in the next chapter, and become better acquainted with by degrees afterwards; here we divest the combat of them entirely, and look upon the destruction of the enemy as the complete and sufficient object of any combat.

What are we now to understand by destruction of the enemy's Army? A diminution of it relatively greater than that on our own side. If we have a great superiority in numbers over the enemy, then naturally the same absolute amount of loss on both sides is for us a smaller one than for him, and consequently may be regarded in itself as an advantage. As we are here considering the combat as divested of all (other) objects, we must also exclude from our consideration the case in which the combat is used only indirectly for a greater destruction of the enemy's force; consequently also, only that direct gain which has been made in the mutual process of destruction, is to be regarded as the object, for this is an absolute gain, which runs through the whole campaign, and at the end of it will always appear as pure profit. But every other kind of victory over our opponent will either have its motive in other objects, which we have completely excluded here, or it will only yield a temporary relative advantage. An example will make this plain.

If by a skilful disposition we have reduced our opponent to such a dilemma, that he cannot continue the combat without danger, and after some resistance he retires, then we may say, that we have conquered him at that point; but if in this victory we have expended just as many forces as the enemy, then in closing the account of the campaign, there is no gain remaining from this victory, if such a result can be called a victory. Therefore the overcoming the enemy, that is, placing him in such a position that he must give up the fight, counts for nothing in itself, and for that reason cannot come under the definition of object. There remains, therefore, as we have said, nothing over except the direct gain which we have made in the process of destruction; but to this belong not only the losses which have taken place in the course of the combat, but also those which, after the withdrawal of the conquered part, take place as direct consequences of the same.

Now it is known by experience, that the losses in physical forces in the course of a battle seldom present a great difference between victor and vanquished respectively, often none at all, sometimes even one bearing an inverse relation to the result, and that the most decisive losses on the side of the vanquished only commence with the retreat, that is, those which the conqueror does not share with him. The weak remains of battalions already in disorder are cut down by cavalry, exhausted men strew the ground, disabled guns and broken caissons are abandoned, others in the bad state of the roads cannot be removed quickly enough, and are captured by the enemy's troops, during the night numbers lose their way, and fall defenceless into the enemy's hands, and thus the victory mostly gains bodily substance after it is already decided. Here would be a paradox, if it did not solve itself in the following manner.

The loss in physical force is not the only one which the two sides suffer in the course of the combat; the moral forces also are shaken, broken, and go to ruin. It is not only the loss in men, horses and guns, but in order, courage, confidence, cohesion and plan, which come into consideration when it is a question whether the fight can be still continued or not. It is principally the moral forces which decide here, and in all cases in which the conqueror has lost as heavily as the conquered, it is these alone.

The comparative relation of the physical losses is difficult to estimate in a battle, but not so the relation of the moral ones. Two things principally make it known. The one is the loss of the ground on which the fight has taken place, the other the superiority of the enemy's. The more our reserves have diminished as compared with those of the enemy, the more force we have used to maintain the equilibrium; in this at once, an evident proof of the moral superiority of the enemy is given which seldom fails to stir up in the soul of the Commander a certain bitterness of feeling, and a sort of contempt for his own troops. But the principal thing is, that men who have been engaged for a long continuance of time are more or less like burnt-out cinders; their ammunition is consumed; they have melted away to a certain extent; physical and moral energies are exhausted, perhaps their courage is broken as well. Such a force, irrespective of the diminution in its number, if viewed as an organic whole, is very different from what it was before the combat; and thus it is that the loss of moral force may be measured by the reserves that have been used as if it were on a foot-rule.

Lost ground and want of fresh reserves, are, therefore, usually the principal causes which determine a retreat; but at the same time we by no means exclude or desire to throw in the shade other reasons, which may lie in the interdependence of parts of the Army, in the general plan, &c.

Every combat is therefore the bloody and destructive measuring of the strength of forces, physical and moral; whoever at the close has the greatest amount of both left is the conqueror.

In the combat the loss of moral force is the chief cause of the decision; after that is given, this loss continues to increase until it reaches its culminating-point at the close of the whole act. This then is the opportunity the victor should seize to reap his harvest by the utmost possible restrictions of his enemy's forces, the real object of engaging in the combat. On the beaten side, the loss of all order and control often makes the prolongation of resistance by individual units, by the further punishment they are certain to suffer, more injurious than useful to the whole. The spirit of the mass is broken; the original excitement about losing or winning, through which danger was forgotten, is spent, and to the majority danger now appears no longer an appeal to their courage, but rather the endurance of a cruel punishment. Thus the instrument in the first moment of the enemy's victory is weakened and blunted, and therefore no longer fit to repay danger by danger.

This period, however, passes; the moral forces of the conquered will recover by degrees, order will be restored, courage will revive, and in the majority of cases there remains only a small part of the superiority obtained, often none at all. In some cases, even, although rarely, the spirit of revenge and intensified hostility may bring about an opposite result. On the other hand, whatever is gained in killed, wounded, prisoners, and guns captured can never disappear from the account.

The losses in a battle consist more in killed and wounded; those after the battle, more in artillery taken and prisoners. The first the conqueror shares with the conquered, more or less, but the second not; and for that reason they usually only take place on one side of the conflict, at least, they are considerably in excess on one side.

Artillery and prisoners are therefore at all times regarded as the true trophies of victory, as well as its measure, because through these things its extent is declared beyond a doubt. Even the degree of moral superiority may be better judged of by them than by any other relation, especially if the number of killed and wounded is compared therewith; and here arises a new power increasing the moral effects.

We have said that the moral forces, beaten to the ground in the battle and in the immediately succeeding movements, recover themselves gradually, and often bear no traces of injury; this is the case with small divisions of the whole, less frequently with large divisions; it may, however, also be the case with the main Army, but seldom or never in the State or Government to which the Army belongs. These estimate the situation more impartially, and from a more elevated point of view, and recognise in the number of trophies taken by the enemy, and their relation to the number of killed and wounded, only too easily and well, the measure of their own weakness and inefficiency.

In point of fact, the lost balance of moral power must not be treated lightly because it has no absolute value, and because it does not of necessity appear in all cases in the amount of the results at the final close; it may become of such excessive weight as to bring down everything with an irresistible force. On that account it may often become a great aim of the operations of which we shall speak elsewhere. Here we have still to examine some of its fundamental relations.

The moral effect of a victory increases, not merely in proportion to the extent of the forces engaged, but in a progressive ratio—that is to say, not only in extent, but also in its intensity. In a beaten detachment order is easily restored. As a single frozen limb is easily revived by the rest of the body, so the courage of a defeated detachment is easily raised again by the courage of the rest of the Army as soon as it rejoins it. If, therefore, the effects of a small victory are not completely done away with, still they are partly lost to the enemy. This is not the case if the Army itself sustains a great defeat; then one with the other fall together. A great fire attains quite a different heat from several small ones.

Another relation which determines the moral value of a victory is the numerical relation of the forces which have been in conflict with each other. To beat many with few is not only a double success, but shows also a greater, especially a more general superiority, which the conquered must always be fearful of encountering again. At the same time this influence is in reality hardly observable in such a case. In the moment of real action, the notions of the actual strength of the enemy are generally so uncertain, the estimate of our own commonly so incorrect, that the party superior in numbers either does not admit the disproportion, or is very far from admitting the full truth, owing to which, he evades almost entirely the moral disadvantages which would spring from it. It is only hereafter in history that the truth, long suppressed through ignorance, vanity, or a wise discretion, makes its appearance, and then it certainly casts a lustre on the Army and its Leader, but it can then do nothing more by its moral influence for events long past.

If prisoners and captured guns are those things by which the victory principally gains substance, its true crystallisations, then the plan of the battle should have those things specially in view; the destruction of the enemy by death and wounds appears here merely as a means to an end.

How far this may influence the dispositions in the battle is not an affair of Strategy, but the decision to fight the battle is in intimate connection with it, as is shown by the direction given to our forces, and their general grouping, whether we threaten the enemy's flank or rear, or he threatens ours. On this point, the number of prisoners and captured guns depends very much, and it is a point which, in many cases, tactics alone cannot satisfy, particularly if the strategic relations are too much in opposition to it.

The risk of having to fight on two sides, and the still more dangerous position of having no line of retreat left open, paralyse the movements and the power of resistance; further, in case of defeat, they increase the loss, often raising it to its extreme point, that is, to destruction. Therefore, the rear being endangered makes defeat more probable, and, at the same time, more decisive.

From this arises, in the whole conduct of the War, especially in great and small combats, a perfect instinct to secure our own line of retreat and to seize that of the enemy; this follows from the conception of victory, which, as we have seen, is something beyond mere slaughter.

In this effort we see, therefore, the first immediate purpose in the combat, and one which is quite universal. No combat is imaginable in which this effort, either in its double or single form, does not go hand in hand with the plain and simple stroke of force. Even the smallest troop will not throw itself upon its enemy without thinking of its line of retreat, and, in most cases, it will have an eye upon that of the enemy also.

We should have to digress to show how often this instinct is prevented from going the direct road, how often it must yield to the difficulties arising from more important considerations: we shall, therefore, rest contented with affirming it to be a general natural law of the combat.

It is, therefore, active; presses everywhere with its natural weight, and so becomes the pivot on which almost all tactical and strategic manoeuvres turn.

If we now take a look at the conception of victory as a whole, we find in it three elements:—

1. The greater loss of the enemy in physical power.
2. In moral power.
3. His open avowal of this by the relinquishment of his intentions.

The returns made up on each side of losses in killed and wounded, are never exact, seldom truthful, and in most cases, full of intentional misrepresentations. Even the statement of the number of trophies is seldom to be quite depended on; consequently, when it is not considerable it may also cast a doubt even on the reality of the victory. Of the loss in moral forces there is no reliable measure, except in the trophies: therefore, in many cases, the giving up the contest is the only real evidence of the victory. It is, therefore, to be regarded as a confession of inferiority—as the lowering of the flag, by which, in this particular instance, right and superiority are conceded to the enemy, and this degree of humiliation and disgrace, which, however, must be distinguished from all the other moral consequences of the loss of equilibrium, is an essential part of the victory. It is this part alone which acts upon the public opinion outside the Army, upon the people and the Government in both belligerent States, and upon all others in any way concerned.

But renouncement of the general object is not quite identical with quitting the field of battle, even when the battle has been very obstinate and long kept up; no one says of advanced posts, when they retire after an obstinate combat, that they have given up their object; even in combats aimed at the destruction of the enemy's Army, the retreat from the battlefield is not always to be regarded as a relinquishment of this aim, as for instance, in retreats planned beforehand, in which the ground is disputed foot by foot; all this belongs to that part of our subject where we shall speak of the separate object of the combat; here we only wish to draw attention to the fact that in most cases the giving up of the object is very difficult to distinguish from the retirement from the battlefield, and that the impression produced by the latter, both in and out of the Army, is not to be treated lightly.

For Generals and Armies whose reputation is not made, this is in itself one of the difficulties in many operations, justified by circumstances when a succession of combats, each ending in retreat, may appear as a succession of defeats, without being so in reality, and when that appearance may exercise a very depressing influence. It is impossible for the retreating General by making known his real intentions to prevent the moral effect spreading to the public and his troops, for to do that with effect he must disclose his plans completely, which of course would run counter to his principal interests to too great a degree.

In order to draw attention to the special importance of this conception of victory we shall only refer to the battle of Soor, the trophies from which were not important (a few thousand prisoners and twenty guns), and where Frederick proclaimed his victory by remaining for five days after on the field of battle, although his retreat into Silesia had been previously determined on, and was a measure natural to his whole situation. According to his own account, he thought he would hashasten a peace by the moral effect of his victory. Now although a couple of other successes were likewise required, namely, the battle at Katholisch Hennersdorf, in Lusatia, and the battle of Kesseldorf, before this peace took place, still we cannot say that the moral effect of the battle of Soor was nil.

If it is chiefly the moral force which is shaken by defeat, and if the number of trophies reaped by the enemy mounts up to an unusual height, then the lost combat becomes a rout, but this is not the necessary consequence of every victory. A rout only sets in when the moral force of the defeated is very severely shaken then there often ensues a complete incapability of further resistance, and the whole action consists of giving way, that is of flight.

Jena and Belle Alliance were routs, but not so Borodino.

Although without pedantry we can here give no single line of separation, because the difference between the things is one of degrees, yet still the retention of the conception is essential as a central point to give clearness to our theoretical ideas and it is a want in our terminology that for a victory over the enemy tantamount to a rout, and a conquest of the enemy only tantamount to a simple victory, there is only one and the same word to use.

CHAPTER V - ON THE SIGNIFICATION OF THE COMBAT

HAVING in the preceding chapter examined the combat in its absolute form, as the miniature picture of the whole War, we now turn to the relations which it bears to the other parts of the great whole. First we inquire what is more precisely the signification of a combat.

As War is nothing else but a mutual process of destruction, then the most natural answer in conception, and perhaps also in reality, appears to be that all the powers of each party unite in one great volume and all results in one great shock of these masses. There is certainly much truth in this idea, and it seems to be very advisable that we should adhere to it and should on that account look upon small combats at first only as necessary loss, like the shavings from a carpenter's plane. Still, however, the thing cannot be settled so easily.

That a multiplication of combats should arise from a fractioning of forces is a matter of course, and the more immediate objects of separate combats will therefore come before us in the subject of a fractioning of forces; but these objects, and together with them, the whole mass of combats may in a general way be brought under certain classes, and the knowledge of these classes will contribute to make our observations more intelligible.

Destruction of the enemy's military forces is in reality the object of all combats; but other objects may be joined thereto, and these other objects may be at the same time predominant; we must therefore draw a distinction between those in which the destruction of the enemy's forces is the principal object, and those in which it is more the means. The destruction of the enemy's force, the possession of a place or the possession of some object may be the general motive for a combat, and it may be either one of these alone or several together, in which case however usually one is the principal motive. Now the two principal forms of War, the offensive and defensive, of which we shall shortly speak, do not modify the first of these motives, but they certainly do modify the other two, and therefore if we arrange them in a scheme they would appear thus:—

OFFENSIVE. DEFENSIVE

1. Destruction of enemy's force 1. Destruction of enemy's force.
2. Conquest of a place. 2. Defence of a place.
3. Conquest of some object. 3. Defence of some object.

These motives, however, do not seem to embrace completely the whole of the subject, if we recollect that there are reconnaissances and demonstrations, in which plainly none of these three points is the object of the combat. In reality we must, therefore, on this account be allowed a fourth class. Strictly speaking, in reconnaissances in which we wish the enemy to show himself, in alarms by which we wish to wear him out, in demonstrations by which we wish to prevent his leaving some point or to draw him off to another, the objects are all such as can only be attained indirectly and UNDER THE PRETEXT OF ONE OF THE THREE OBJECTS SPECIFIED IN THE TABLE, usually of the second; for the enemy whose aim is to reconnoitre must draw up his force as if he really intended to attack and defeat us, or drive us off, &c. &c. But this pretended object is not the real one, and our present question is only as to the latter; therefore, we must to the above three objects of the offensive further add a fourth, which is to lead the enemy to make a false conclusion. That offensive means are conceivable in connection with this object, lies in the nature of the thing.

On the other hand we must observe that the defence of a place may be of two kinds, either absolute, if as a general question the point is not to be given up, or relative if it is only required for a certain time. The latter happens perpetually in the combats of advanced posts and rear guards.

That the nature of these different intentions of a combat must have an essential influence on the dispositions which are its preliminaries, is a thing clear in itself. We act differently if our object is merely to drive an enemy's post out of its place from what we should if our object was to beat him completely; differently, if we mean to defend a place to the last extremity from what we should do if our design is only to detain the enemy for a certain time. In the first case we trouble ourselves little about the line of retreat, in the latter it is the principal point, &c.

But these reflections belong properly to tactics, and are only introduced here by way of example for the sake of greater clearness. What Strategy has to say on the different objects of the combat will appear in the chapters which touch upon these objects. Here we have only a few general observations to make, first, that the importance of the object decreases nearly in the order as they stand above, therefore, that the first of these objects must always predominate in the great battle; lastly, that the two last in a defensive battle are in reality such as yield no fruit, they are, that is to say, purely negative, and can, therefore, only be serviceable, indirectly, by facilitating something else which is positive. IT IS, THEREFORE, A BAD SIGN OF THE STRATEGIC SITUATION IF BATTLES OF THIS KIND BECOME TOO FREQUENT.

CHAPTER VI - DURATION OF THE COMBAT

IF we consider the combat no longer in itself but in relation to the other forces of War, then its duration acquires a special importance.

This duration is to be regarded to a certain extent as a second subordinate success. For the conqueror the combat can never be finished too quickly, for the vanquished it can never last too long. A speedy victory indicates a higher power of victory, a tardy decision is, on the side of the defeated, some compensation for the loss.

This is in general true, but it acquires a practical importance in its application to those combats, the object of which is a relative defence.

Here the whole success often lies in the mere duration. This is the reason why we have included it amongst the strategic elements.

The duration of a combat is necessarily bound up with its essential relations. These relations are, absolute magnitude of force, relation of force and of the different arms mutually, and nature of the country. Twenty thousand men do not wear themselves out upon one another as quickly as two thousand: we cannot resist an enemy double or three times our strength as long as one of the same strength; a cavalry combat is decided sooner than an infantry combat; and a combat between infantry only, quicker than if there is artillery as well; in hills and forests we cannot advance as quickly as on a level country; all this is clear enough.

From this it follows, therefore, that strength, relation of the three arms, and position, must be considered if the combat is to fulfil an object by its duration; but to set up this rule was of less importance to us in our present considerations than to connect with it at once the chief results which experience gives us on the subject.

Even the resistance of an ordinary Division of 8000 to 10,000 men of all arms even opposed to an enemy considerably superior in numbers, will last several hours, if the advantages of country are not too preponderating, and if the enemy is only a little, or not at all, superior in numbers, the combat will last half a day. A Corps of three or four Divisions will prolong it to double the time; an Army of 80,000 or 100,000 to three or four times. Therefore the masses may be left to themselves for that length of time, and no separate combat takes place if within that time other forces can be brought up, whose co-operation mingles then at once into one stream with the results of the combat which has taken place.

These calculations are the result of experience; but it is important to us at the same time to characterise more particularly the moment of the decision, and consequently the termination.

CHAPTER VII - DECISION OF THE COMBAT

No battle is decided in a single moment, although in every battle there arise moments of crisis, on which the result depends. The loss of a battle is, therefore, a gradual falling of the scale. But there is in every combat a point of time when it may be regarded as decided, in such a way that the renewal of the fight would be a new battle, not a continuation of the old one. To have a clear notion on this point of time, is very important, in order to be able to decide whether, with the prompt assistance of reinforcements, the combat can again be resumed with advantage.

Often in combats which are beyond restoration new forces are sacrificed in vain; often through neglect the decision has not been seized when it might easily have been secured. Here are two examples, which could not be more to the point:

When the Prince of Hohenlohe, in 1806, at Jena, with 35,000 men opposed to from 60,000 to 70,000, under Buonaparte, had accepted battle, and lost it—but lost it in such a way that the 35,000 might be regarded as dissolved—General Ruchel undertook to renew the fight with about 12,000; the consequence was that in a moment his force was scattered in like manner.

On the other hand, on the same day at Auerstadt, the Prussians maintained a combat with 25,000, against Davoust, who had 28,000, until mid-day, without success, it is true, but still without the force being reduced to a state of dissolution without even greater loss than the enemy, who was very deficient in cavalry;—but they neglected to use the reserve of 18,000, under General Kalkreuth, to restore the battle which, under these circumstances, it would have been impossible to lose.

Each combat is a whole in which the partial combats combine themselves into one total result. In this total result lies the decision of the combat. This success need not be exactly a victory such as we have denoted in the sixth chapter, for often the preparations for that have not been made, often there is no opportunity if the enemy gives way too soon, and in most cases the decision, even when the resistance has been obstinate, takes place before such a degree of success is attained as would completely satisfy the idea of a victory.

We therefore ask, Which is commonly the moment of the decision, that is to say, that moment when a fresh, effective, of course not disproportionate, force, can no longer turn a disadvantageous battle?

If we pass over false attacks, which in accordance with their nature are properly without decision, then,

1. If the possession of a movable object was the object of the combat, the loss of the same is always the decision.

2. If the possession of ground was the object of the combat, then the decision generally lies in its loss. Still not always, only if this ground is of peculiar strength,

ground which is easy to pass over, however important it may be in other respects, can be re-taken without much danger.

3. But in all other cases, when these two circumstances have not already decided the combat, therefore, particularly in case the destruction of the enemy's force is the principal object, the decision is reached at that moment when the conqueror ceases to feel himself in a state of disintegration, that is, of unserviceableness to a certain extent, when therefore, there is no further advantage in using the successive efforts spoken of in the twelfth chapter of the third book. On this ground we have given the strategic unity of the battle its place here.

A battle, therefore, in which the assailant has not lost his condition of order and perfect efficiency at all, or, at least, only in a small part of his force, whilst the opposing forces are, more or less, disorganised throughout, is also not to be retrieved; and just as little if the enemy has recovered his efficiency.

The smaller, therefore, that part of a force is which has really been engaged, the greater that portion which as reserve has contributed to the result only by its presence. So much the less will any new force of the enemy wrest again the victory from our hands, and that Commander who carries out to the furthest with his Army the principle of conducting the combat with the greatest economy of forces, and making the most of the moral effect of strong reserves, goes the surest way to victory. We must allow that the French, in modern times, especially when led by Buonaparte, have shown a thorough mastery in this.

Further, the moment when the crisis-stage of the combat ceases with the conqueror, and his original state of order is restored, takes place sooner the smaller the unit he controls. A picket of cavalry pursuing an enemy at full gallop will in a few minutes resume its proper order, and the crisis ceases. A whole regiment of cavalry requires a longer time. It lasts still longer with infantry, if extended in single lines of skirmishers, and longer again with Divisions of all arms, when it happens by chance that one part has taken one direction and another part another direction, and the combat has therefore caused a loss of the order of formation, which usually becomes still worse from no part knowing exactly where the other is. Thus, therefore, the point of time when the conqueror has collected the instruments he has been using, and which are mixed up and partly out of order, the moment when he has in some measure rearranged them and put them in their proper places, and thus brought the battle-workshop into a little order, this moment, we say, is always later, the greater the total force.

Again, this moment comes later if night overtakes the conqueror in the crisis, and, lastly, it comes later still if the country is broken and thickly wooded. But with regard to these two points, we must observe that night is also a great means of protection, and it is only seldom that circumstances favour the expectation of a successful result from a night attack, as on March 10, 1814, at Laon, where York against Marmont gives us an example completely in place here. In the same way a wooded and broken country will afford protection against a reaction to those who are engaged in the long crisis of victory. Both, therefore, the night as well as the wooded and broken country are obstacles which make the renewal of the same battle more difficult instead of facilitating it.

Hitherto, we have considered assistance arriving for the losing side as a mere increase of force, therefore, as a reinforcement coming up directly from the rear, which is the most usual case. But the case is quite different if these fresh forces come upon the enemy in flank or rear.

On the effect of flank or rear attacks so far as they belong to Strategy, we shall speak in another place: such a one as we have here in view, intended for the restoration of the combat, belongs chiefly to tactics, and is only mentioned because we are here speaking of tactical results, our ideas, therefore, must trench upon the province of tactics.

By directing a force against the enemy's flank and rear its efficacy may be much intensified; but this is so far from being a necessary result always that the efficacy may, on the other hand, be just as much weakened. The circumstances under which the combat has taken place decide upon this part of the plan as well as upon every other, without our being able to enter thereupon here. But, at the same time, there are in it two things of importance for our subject: first, FLANK AND REAR ATTACKS HAVE, AS A RULE, A MORE FAVOURABLE EFFECT ON THE CONSEQUENCES OF THE DECISION THAN UPON THE DECISION ITSELF. Now as concerns the retrieving a battle, the first thing to be arrived at above all is a favourable decision and not magnitude of success. In this view one would therefore think that a force which comes to re-establish our combat is of less assistance if it falls upon the enemy in flank and rear, therefore separated from us, than if it joins itself to us directly; certainly, cases are not wanting where it is so, but we must say that the majority are on the other side, and they are so on account of the second point which is here important to us.

This second point IS THE MORAL EFFECT OF THE SURPRISE, WHICH, AS A RULE, A REINFORCEMENT COMING UP TO RE-ESTABLISH A COMBAT HAS GENERALLY IN ITS FAVOUR. Now the effect of a surprise is always heightened if it takes place in the flank or rear, and an enemy completely engaged in the crisis of victory in his extended and scattered order, is less in a state to counteract it. Who does not feel that an attack in flank or rear, which at the commencement of the battle, when the forces are concentrated and prepared for such an event would be of little importance, gains quite another weight in the last moment of the combat.

We must, therefore, at once admit that in most cases a reinforcement coming up on the flank or rear of the enemy will be more efficacious, will be like the same weight at the end of a longer lever, and therefore that under these circumstances, we may undertake to restore the battle with the same force which employed in a direct attack would be quite insufficient. Here results almost defy calculation, because the moral forces gain completely the ascendency. This is therefore the right field for boldness and daring.

The eye must, therefore, be directed on all these objects, all these moments of co-operating forces must be taken into consideration, when we have to decide in doubtful cases whether or not it is still possible to restore a combat which has taken an unfavourable turn.

If the combat is to be regarded as not yet ended, then the new contest which is opened by the arrival of assistance fuses into the former; therefore they flow together into one common result, and the first disadvantage vanishes completely out of the calculation. But this is not the case if the combat was already decided; then there are two results separate from each other. Now if the assistance which arrives is only of a relative strength, that is, if it is not in itself alone a match for the enemy, then a favourable result is hardly to be expected from this second combat: but if it is so strong that it can undertake the second combat without regard to the first, then it may be able by a favourable issue to compensate or even overbalance the first combat, but never to make it disappear altogether from the account.

At the battle of Kunersdorf, Frederick the Great at the first onset carried the left of the Russian position, and took seventy pieces of artillery; at the end of the battle both were lost again, and the whole result of the first combat was wiped out of the account. Had it been possible to stop at the first success, and to put off the second part of the battle to the coming day, then, even if the King had lost it, the advantages of the first would always have been a set off to the second.

But when a battle proceeding disadvantageously is arrested and turned before its conclusion, its minus result on our side not only disappears from the account, but also becomes the foundation of a greater victory. If, for instance, we picture to ourselves exactly the tactical course of the battle, we may easily see that until it is finally concluded all successes in partial combats are only decisions in suspense, which by the capital decision may not only be destroyed, but changed into the opposite. The more our forces have suffered, the more the enemy will have expended on his side; the greater, therefore, will be the crisis for the enemy, and the more the superiority of our fresh troops will tell. If now the total result turns in our favour, if we wrest from the enemy the field of battle and recover all the trophies again, then all the forces which he has sacrificed in obtaining them become sheer gain for us, and our former defeat becomes a stepping-stone to a greater triumph. The most brilliant feats which with victory the enemy would have so highly prized that the loss of forces which they cost would have been disregarded, leave nothing now behind but regret at the sacrifice entailed. Such is the alteration which the magic of victory and the curse of defeat produces in the specific weight of the same elements.

Therefore, even if we are decidedly superior in strength, and are able to repay the enemy his victory by a greater still, it is always better to forestall the conclusion of a disadvantageous combat, if it is of proportionate importance, so as to turn its course rather than to deliver a second battle.

Field-Marshal Daun attempted in the year 1760 to come to the assistance of General Laudon at Leignitz, whilst the battle lasted; but when he failed, he did not attack the King next day, although he did not want for means to do so.

For these reasons serious combats of advance guards which precede a battle are to be looked upon only as necessary evils, and when not necessary they are to be avoided.

We have still another conclusion to examine.

If on a regular pitched battle, the decision has gone against one, this does not constitute a motive for determining on a new one. The determination for this new one must proceed from other relations. This conclusion, however, is opposed by a moral force, which we must take into account: it is the feeling of rage and revenge. From the oldest Field-Marshal to the youngest drummer-boy this feeling is general, and, therefore, troops are never in better spirits for fighting than when they have to wipe out a stain. This is, however, only on the supposition that the beaten portion is not too great in proportion to the whole, because otherwise the above feeling is lost in that of powerlessness.

There is therefore a very natural tendency to use this moral force to repair the disaster on the spot, and on that account chiefly to seek another battle if other circumstances permit. It then lies in the nature of the case that this second battle must be an offensive one.

In the catalogue of battles of second-rate importance there are many examples to be found of such retaliatory battles; but great battles have generally too many other determining causes to be brought on by this weaker motive.

Such a feeling must undoubtedly have led the noble Bluecher with his third Corps to the field of battle on February 14, 1814, when the other two had been beaten three days before at Montmirail. Had he known that he would have come upon Buonaparte in person, then, naturally, preponderating reasons would have determined him to put off his revenge to another day: but he hoped to revenge himself on Marmont, and instead of gaining the reward of his desire for honourable satisfaction, he suffered the penalty of his erroneous calculation.

On the duration of the combat and the moment of its decision depend the distances from each other at which those masses should be placed which are intended to fight IN CONJUNCTION WITH each other. This disposition would be a tactical arrangement in so far as it relates to one and the same battle; it can, however, only be regarded as such, provided the position of the troops is so compact that two separate combats cannot be imagined, and consequently that the space which the whole occupies can be regarded strategically as a mere point. But in War, cases frequently occur where even those forces intended to fight IN UNISON must be so far separated from each other that while their union for one common combat certainly remains the principal object, still the occurrence of separate combats remains possible. Such a disposition is therefore strategic.

Dispositions of this kind are: marches in separate masses and columns, the formation of advance guards, and flanking columns, also the grouping of reserves intended to serve as supports for more than one strategic point; the concentration of several Corps from widely extended cantonments, &c. &c. We can see that the necessity for these arrangements may constantly arise, and may consider them something like the small change in the strategic economy, whilst the capital battles, and all that rank with them are the gold and silver pieces.

CHAPTER VIII - MUTUAL UNDERSTANDING AS TO A BATTLE

NO battle can take place unless by mutual consent; and in this idea, which constitutes the whole basis of a duel, is the root of a certain phraseology used by historical writers, which leads to many indefinite and false conceptions.

According to the view of the writers to whom we refer, it has frequently happened that one Commander has offered battle to the other, and the latter has not accepted it.

But the battle is a very modified duel, and its foundation is not merely in the mutual wish to fight, that is in consent, but in the objects which are bound up with the battle: these belong always to a greater whole, and that so much the more, as even the whole war considered as a "combat-unit" has political objects and conditions which belong to a higher standpoint. The mere desire to conquer each other therefore falls into quite a subordinate relation, or rather it ceases completely to be anything of itself, and only becomes the nerve which conveys the impulse of action from the higher will.

Amongst the ancients, and then again during the early period of standing Armies, the expression that we had offered battle to the enemy in vain, had more sense in it than it has now. By the ancients everything was constituted with a view to measuring each other's strength in the open field free from anything in the nature of a hindrance, and the whole Art of War consisted in the organisation, and formation of the Army, that is in the order of battle.

Now as their Armies regularly entrenched themselves in their camps, therefore the position in a camp was regarded as something unassailable, and a battle did not become possible until the enemy left his camp, and placed himself in a practicable country, as it were entered the lists.

If therefore we hear about Hannibal having offered battle to Fabius in vain, that tells us nothing more as regards the latter than that a battle was not part of his plan, and in itself neither proves the physical nor moral superiority of Hannibal; but with respect to him the expression is still correct enough in the sense that Hannibal really wished a battle.

In the early period of modern Armies, the relations were similar in great combats and battles. That is to say, great masses were brought into action, and managed throughout it by means of an order of battle, which like a great helpless whole required a more or less level plain and was neither suited to attack, nor yet to defence in a broken, close or even mountainous country. The defender therefore had here also to some extent the means of avoiding battle. These relations although gradually becoming modified, continued until the first Silesian War, and it was not until the Seven Years' War that attacks on an enemy posted in a difficult country gradually became feasible, and of ordinary occurrence: ground did not certainly cease to be a principle of strength to those making use of its aid, but it was no longer a charmed circle, which shut out the natural forces of War.

During the past thirty years War has perfected itself much more in this respect, and there is no longer anything which stands in the way of a General who is in earnest about a decision by means of battle; he can seek out his enemy, and attack him: if he does not do so he cannot take credit for having wished to fight, and the expression he offered a battle which his opponent did not accept, therefore now means nothing more than that he did not find circumstances advantageous enough for a battle, an admission which the above expression does not suit, but which it only strives to throw a veil over.

It is true the defensive side can no longer refuse a battle, yet he may still avoid it by giving up his position, and the role with which that position was connected: this is however half a victory for the offensive side, and an acknowledgment of his superiority for the present.

This idea in connection with the cartel of defiance can therefore no longer be made use of in order by such rhodomontade to qualify the inaction of him whose part it is to advance, that is, the offensive. The defender who as long as he does not give way, must have the credit of willing the battle, may certainly say, he has offered it if he is not attacked, if that is not understood of itself.

But on the other hand, he who now wishes to, and can retreat cannot easily be forced to give battle. Now as the advantages to the aggressor from this retreat are often not sufficient, and a substantial victory is a matter of urgent necessity for him, in that way the few means which there are to compel such an opponent also to give battle are often sought for and applied with particular skill.

The principal means for this are—first SURROUNDING the enemy so as to make his retreat impossible, or at least so difficult that it is better for him to accept battle; and, secondly, SURPRISING him. This last way, for which there was a motive formerly in the extreme difficulty of all movements, has become in modern times very inefficacious.

From the pliability and manoeuvring capabilities of troops in the present day, one does not hesitate to commence a retreat even in sight of the enemy, and only some special obstacles in the nature of the country can cause serious difficulties in the operation.

As an example of this kind the battle of Neresheim may be given, fought by the Archduke Charles with Moreau in the Rauhe Alp, August 11, 1796, merely with a view to facilitate his retreat, although we freely confess we have never been able quite to understand the argument of the renowned general and author himself in this case.

The battle of Rosbach is another example, if we suppose the commander of the allied army had not really the intention of attacking Frederick the Great.

Of the battle of Soor, the King himself says that it was only fought because a retreat in the presence of the enemy appeared to him a critical operation; at the same time the King has also given other reasons for the battle.

On the whole, regular night surprises excepted, such cases will always be of rare occurrence, and those in which an enemy is compelled to fight by being practically surrounded, will happen mostly to single corps only, like Mortier's at Durrenstein 1809, and Vandamme at Kulm, 1813.

CHAPTER IX - THE BATTLE

WHAT is a battle? A conflict of the main body, but not an unimportant one about a secondary object, not a mere attempt which is given up when we see betimes that our object is hardly within our reach: it is a conflict waged with all our forces for the attainment of a decisive victory.

Minor objects may also be mixed up with the principal object, and it will take many different tones of colour from the circumstances out of which it originates, for a battle belongs also to a greater whole of which it is only a part, but because the essence of War is conflict, and the battle is the conflict of the main Armies, it is always to be regarded as the real centre of gravity of the War, and therefore its distinguishing character is, that unlike all other encounters, it is arranged for, and undertaken with the sole purpose of obtaining a decisive victory.

This has an influence on the MANNER OF ITS DECISION, on the EFFECT OF THE VICTORY CONTAINED IN IT, and determines THE VALUE WHICH THEORY IS TO ASSIGN TO IT AS A MEANS TO AN END.

On that account we make it the subject of our special consideration, and at this stage before we enter upon the special ends which may be bound up with it, but which do not essentially alter its character if it really deserves to be termed a battle.

If a battle takes place principally on its own account, the elements of its decision must be contained in itself; in other words, victory must be striven for as long as a possibility or hope remains. It must not, therefore, be given up on account of secondary circumstances, but only and alone in the event of the forces appearing completely insufficient.

Now how is that precise moment to be described?

If a certain artificial formation and cohesion of an Army is the principal condition under which the bravery of the troops can gain a victory, as was the case during a great part of the period of the modern Art of War, THEN THE BREAKING UP OF THIS FORMATION is the decision. A beaten wing which is put out of joint decides the fate of all that was connected with it. If as was the case at another time the essence of the defence consists in an intimate alliance of the Army with the ground on which it fights and its obstacles, so that Army and position are only one, then the CONQUEST of AN ESSENTIAL POINT in this position is the decision. It is said the key of the position is lost, it cannot therefore be defended any further; the battle cannot be continued. In both cases the beaten Armies are very much like the broken strings of an instrument which cannot do their work.

That geometrical as well as this geographical principle which had a tendency to place an Army in a state of crystallising tension which did not allow of the available powers being made use of up to the last man, have at least so far lost their influence that they no longer predominate. Armies are still led into battle in a certain order, but that order is no longer of decisive importance; obstacles of ground are also still turned to account to strengthen a position, but they are no longer the only support.

We attempted in the second chapter of this book to take a general view of the nature of the modern battle. According to our conception of it, the order of battle is only a disposition of the forces suitable to the convenient use of them, and the course of the battle a mutual slow wearing away of these forces upon one another, to see which will have soonest exhausted his adversary.

The resolution therefore to give up the fight arises, in a battle more than in any other combat, from the relation of the fresh reserves remaining available; for only these still retain all their moral vigour, and the cinders of the battered, knocked-about battalions, already burnt out in the destroying element, must not be placed on a level with them; also lost ground as we have elsewhere said, is a standard of lost moral force; it therefore comes also into account, but more as a sign of loss suffered than for the loss itself, and the number of fresh reserves is always the chief point to be looked at by both Commanders.

In general, an action inclines in one direction from the very commencement, but in a manner little observable. This direction is also frequently given in a very decided manner by the arrangements which have been made previously, and then it shows a want of discernment in that General who commences battle under these unfavourable circumstances without being aware of them. Even when this does not occur it lies in the nature of things that the course of a battle resembles rather a slow disturbance of equilibrium which commences soon, but as we have said almost imperceptibly at first, and then with each moment of time becomes stronger and more visible, than an oscillating to and fro, as those who are misled by mendacious descriptions usually suppose.

But whether it happens that the balance is for a long time little disturbed, or that even after it has been lost on one side it rights itself again, and is then lost on the other side, it is certain at all events that in most instances the defeated General foresees his fate long before he retreats, and that cases in which some critical event acts with unexpected force upon the course of the whole have their existence mostly in the colouring with which every one depicts his lost battle.

We can only here appeal to the decision of unprejudiced men of experience, who will, we are sure, assent to what we have said, and answer for us to such of our readers as do not know War from their own experience. To develop the necessity of this course from the nature of the thing would lead us too far into the province of tactics, to which this branch of the subject belongs; we are here only concerned with its results.

If we say that the defeated General foresees the unfavourable result usually some time before he makes up his mind to give up the battle, we admit that there are also instances to the contrary, because otherwise we should maintain a proposition contradictory in itself. If at the moment of each decisive tendency of a battle it should be considered as lost, then also no further forces should be used to give it a turn, and consequently this decisive tendency could not precede the retreat by any length of time. Certainly there are instances of battles which after having taken a decided turn to one side have still ended in favour of the other; but they are rare, not usual; these exceptional cases, however, are reckoned upon by every General against whom fortune declares itself, and he must reckon upon them as long as there remains a possibility of a turn of fortune. He hopes by stronger efforts, by raising the remaining moral forces, by surpassing himself, or also by some fortunate chance that the next moment will bring a change, and pursues this as far as his courage and his judgment can agree. We shall have something more to say on this subject, but before that we must show what are the signs of the scales turning.

The result of the whole combat consists in the sum total of the results of all partial combats; but these results of separate combats are settled by different considerations.

First by the pure moral power in the mind of the leading officers. If a General of Division has seen his battalions forced to succumb, it will have an influence on his demeanour and his reports, and these again will have an influence on the measures of the Commander-in-Chief; therefore even those unsuccessful partial combats which to all appearance are retrieved, are not lost in their results, and the impressions from them sum themselves up in the mind of the Commander without much trouble, and even against his will.

Secondly, by the quicker melting away of our troops, which can be easily estimated in the slow and relatively little tumultuary course of our battles.

Thirdly, by lost ground.

All these things serve for the eye of the General as a compass to tell the course of the battle in which he is embarked. If whole batteries have been lost and none of the enemy's taken; if battalions have been overthrown by the enemy's cavalry, whilst those of the enemy everywhere present impenetrable masses; if the line of fire from his order of battle wavers involuntarily from one point to another; if fruitless efforts have been made to gain certain points, and the assaulting battalions each, time been scattered by well-directed volleys of grape and case;—if our artillery begins to reply feebly to that of the enemy—if the battalions under fire diminish unusually, fast, because with the wounded crowds of unwounded men go to the rear;—if single Divisions have been cut off and made prisoners through the disruption of the plan of the battle;—if the line of retreat begins to be endangered: the Commander may tell very well in which direction he is going with his battle. The longer this direction continues, the more decided it becomes, so much the more difficult will be the turning, so much the nearer the moment when he must give up the battle. We shall now make some observations on this moment.

We have already said more than once that the final decision is ruled mostly by the relative number of the fresh reserves remaining at the last; that Commander who sees his adversary is decidedly superior to him in this respect makes up his mind to retreat. It is the characteristic of modern battles that all mischances and losses which take place in the course of the same can be retrieved by fresh forces, because the arrangement of the modern order of battle, and the way in which troops are brought into action, allow of their use almost generally, and in each position. So long, therefore, as that Commander against whom the issue seems to declare itself still retains a superiority in reserve force, he will not give up the day. But from the moment that his reserves begin to become weaker than his enemy's, the decision may be regarded as settled, and what he now does depends partly on special circumstances, partly on the degree of courage and perseverance which he personally possesses, and which may degenerate into foolish obstinacy. How a Commander can attain to the power of estimating correctly the still remaining reserves on both sides is an affair of skilful practical genius, which does not in any way belong to this place; we keep ourselves to the result as it forms itself in his mind. But this conclusion is still not the moment of decision properly, for a motive which only arises gradually does not answer to that, but is only a general motive towards resolution, and the resolution itself requires still some special immediate causes. Of these there are two chief ones which constantly recur, that is, the danger of retreat, and the arrival of night.

If the retreat with every new step which the battle takes in its course becomes constantly in greater danger, and if the reserves are so much diminished that they are no longer adequate to get breathing room, then there is nothing left but to submit to fate, and by a well-conducted retreat to save what, by a longer delay ending in flight and disaster, would be lost.

But night as a rule puts an end to all battles, because a night combat holds out no hope of advantage except under particular circumstances; and as night is better suited for a retreat than the day, so, therefore, the Commander who must look at the retreat as a thing inevitable, or as most probable, will prefer to make use of the night for his purpose.

That there are, besides the above two usual and chief causes, yet many others also, which are less or more individual and not to be overlooked, is a matter of course; for the more a battle tends towards a complete upset of equilibrium the more sensible is the influence of each partial result in hastening the turn. Thus the loss of a battery, a successful charge of a couple of regiments of cavalry, may call into life the resolution to retreat already ripening.

As a conclusion to this subject, we must dwell for a moment on the point at which the courage of the Commander engages in a sort of conflict with his reason.

If, on the one hand the overbearing pride of a victorious conqueror, if the inflexible will of a naturally obstinate spirit, if the strenuous resistance of noble feelings will not yield the battlefield, where they must leave their honour, yet on the other hand, reason counsels not to give up everything, not to risk the last upon the game, but to retain as much over as is necessary for an orderly retreat. However highly we must esteem courage and firmness in War, and however little prospect there is of victory to him who cannot resolve to seek it by the exertion of all his power, still there is a point beyond which perseverance can only be termed desperate folly, and therefore can meet with no approbation from any critic. In the most celebrated of all battles, that of Belle-Alliance, Buonaparte used his last reserve in an effort to retrieve a battle which was past being retrieved. He spent his last farthing, and then, as a beggar, abandoned both the battle-field and his crown.

CHAPTER X - EFFECTS OF VICTORY (continuation)

. ACCORDING to the point from which our view is taken, we may feel as much astonished at the extraordinary results of some great battles as at the want of results in others. We shall dwell for a moment on the nature of the effect of a great victory.

Three things may easily be distinguished here: the effect upon the instrument itself, that is, upon the Generals and their Armies; the effect upon the States interested in the War; and the particular result of these effects as manifested in the subsequent course of the campaign.

If we only think of the trifling difference which there usually is between victor and vanquished in killed, wounded, prisoners, and artillery lost on the field of battle itself, the consequences which are developed out of this insignificant point seem often quite incomprehensible, and yet, usually, everything only happens quite naturally.

We have already said in the seventh chapter that the magnitude of a victory increases not merely in the same measure as the vanquished forces increase in number, but in a higher ratio. The moral effects resulting from the issue of a great battle are greater on the side of the conquered than on that of the conqueror: they lead to greater losses in physical force, which then in turn react on the moral element, and so they go on mutually supporting and intensifying each other. On this moral effect we must therefore lay special weight. It takes an opposite direction on the one side from that on the other; as it undermines the energies of the conquered so it elevates the powers and energy of the conqueror. But its chief effect is upon the vanquished, because here it is the direct cause of fresh losses, and besides it is homogeneous in nature with danger, with the fatigues, the hardships, and generally with all those embarrassing circumstances by which War is surrounded, therefore enters into league with them and increases by their help, whilst with the conqueror all these things are like weights which give a higher swing to his courage. It is therefore found, that the vanquished sinks much further below the original line of equilibrium than the conqueror raises himself above it; on this account, if we speak of the effects of victory we allude more particularly to those which manifest themselves in the army. If this effect is more powerful in an important combat than in a smaller one, so again it is much more powerful in a great battle than in a minor one. The great battle takes place for the sake of itself, for the sake of the victory which it is to give, and which is sought for with the utmost effort. Here on this spot, in this very hour, to conquer the enemy is the purpose in which the plan of the War with all its threads converges, in which all distant hopes, all dim glimmerings of the future meet, fate steps in before us to give an answer to the bold question.—This is the state of mental tension not only of the Commander but of his whole Army down to the lowest waggon-driver, no doubt in decreasing strength but also in decreasing importance.

According to the nature of the thing, a great battle has never at any time been an unprepared, unexpected, blind routine service, but a grand act, which, partly of itself and partly from the aim of the Commander, stands out from amongst the mass of ordinary efforts, sufficiently to raise the tension of all minds to a higher degree. But the higher this tension with respect to the issue, the more powerful must be the effect of that issue.

Again, the moral effect of victory in our battles is greater than it was in the earlier ones of modern military history. If the former are as we have depicted them, a real struggle of forces to the utmost, then the sum total of all these forces, of the physical as well as the moral, must decide more than certain special dispositions or mere chance.

A single fault committed may be repaired next time; from good fortune and chance we can hope for more favour on another occasion; but the sum total of moral and physical powers cannot be so quickly altered, and, therefore, what the award of a victory has decided appears of much greater importance for all futurity. Very probably, of all concerned in battles, whether in or out of the Army, very few have given a thought to this difference, but the course of the battle itself impresses on the minds of all present in it such a conviction, and the relation of this course in public documents, however much it may be coloured by twisting particular circumstances, shows also, more or less, to the world at large that the causes were more of a general than of a particular nature.

He who has not been present at the loss of a great battle will have difficulty in forming for himself a living or quite true idea of it, and the abstract notions of this or that small untoward affair will never come up to the perfect conception of a lost battle. Let us stop a moment at the picture.

The first thing which overpowers the imagination—and we may indeed say, also the understanding—is the diminution of the masses; then the loss of ground, which takes place always, more or less, and, therefore, on the side of the assailant also, if he is not fortunate; then the rupture of the original formation, the jumbling together of troops, the risks of retreat, which, with few exceptions may always be seen sometimes in a less sometimes in a greater degree; next the retreat, the most part of which commences at night, or, at least, goes on throughout the night. On this first march we must at once leave behind, a number of men completely worn out and scattered about, often just the bravest, who have been foremost in the fight who held out the longest: the feeling of being conquered, which only seized the superior officers on the battlefield, now spreads through all ranks, even down to the common soldiers, aggravated by the horrible idea of being obliged to leave in the enemy's hands so many brave comrades, who but a moment since were of such value to us in the battle, and aggravated by a rising distrust of the chief, to whom, more or less, every subordinate attributes as a fault the fruitless efforts he has made; and this feeling of being conquered is no ideal picture over which one might become master; it is an evident truth that the enemy is superior to us; a truth of which the causes might have been so latent before that they were not to be discovered, but which, in the issue, comes out clear and palpable, or which was also, perhaps, before suspected, but which in the want of any certainty, we had to oppose by the hope of chance, reliance on good fortune, Providence or a bold attitude. Now, all this has proved insufficient, and the bitter truth meets us harsh and imperious.

All these feelings are widely different from a panic, which in an army fortified by military virtue never, and in any other, only exceptionally, follows the loss of a battle. They must arise even in the best of Armies, and although long habituation to War and victory together with great confidence in a Commander may modify them a little here and there, they are never entirely wanting in the first moment. They are not the pure consequences of lost trophies; these are usually lost at a later period, and the loss of them does not become generally known so quickly; they will therefore not fail to appear even when the scale turns in the slowest and most gradual manner, and they constitute that effect of a victory upon which we can always count in every case.

We have already said that the number of trophies intensifies this effect.

It is evident that an Army in this condition, looked at as an instrument, is weakened! How can we expect that when reduced to such a degree that, as we said before, it finds new enemies in all the ordinary difficulties of making War, it will be able to recover by fresh efforts what has been lost! Before the battle there was a real or assumed equilibrium between the two sides; this is lost, and, therefore, some external assistance is requisite to restore it; every new effort without such external support can only lead to fresh losses.

Thus, therefore, the most moderate victory of the chief Army must tend to cause a constant sinking of the scale on the opponent's side, until new external circumstances bring about a change. If these are not near, if the conqueror is an eager opponent, who, thirsting for glory, pursues great aims, then a first-rate Commander, and in the beaten Army a true military spirit, hardened by many campaigns are required, in order to stop the swollen stream of prosperity from bursting all bounds, and to moderate its course by small but reiterated acts of resistance, until the force of victory has spent itself at the goal of its career.

And now as to the effect of defeat beyond the Army, upon the Nation and Government! It is the sudden collapse of hopes stretched to the utmost, the downfall of all self-reliance. In place of these extinct forces, fear, with its destructive properties of expansion, rushes into the vacuum left, and completes the prostration. It is a real shock upon the nerves, which one of the two athletes receives from the electric spark of victory. And that effect, however different in its degrees, is never completely wanting. Instead of every one hastening with a spirit of determination to aid in repairing the disaster, every one fears that his efforts will only be in vain, and stops, hesitating with himself, when he should rush forward; or in despondency he lets his arm drop, leaving everything to fate.

The consequence which this effect of victory brings forth in the course of the War itself depend in part on the character and talent of the victorious General, but more on the circumstances from which the victory proceeds, and to which it leads. Without boldness and an enterprising spirit on the part of the leader, the most brilliant victory will lead to no great success, and its force exhausts itself all the sooner on circumstances, if these offer a strong and stubborn opposition to it. How very differently from Daun, Frederick the Great would have used the victory at Kollin; and what different consequences France, in place of Prussia, might have given a battle of Leuthen!

The conditions which allow us to expect great results from a great victory we shall learn when we come to the subjects with which they are connected; then it will be possible to explain the disproportion which appears at first sight between the magnitude of a victory and its results, and which is only too readily attributed to a want of energy on the part of the conqueror. Here, where we have to do with the great battle in itself, we shall merely say that the effects now depicted never fail to attend a victory, that they mount up with the intensive strength of the victory— mount up more the more the whole strength of the Army has been concentrated in it, the more the whole military power of the Nation is contained in that Army, and the State in that military power.

But then the question may be asked, Can theory accept this effect of victory as absolutely necessary?—must it not rather endeavour to find out counteracting means capable of neutralising these effects? It seems quite natural to answer this question in the affirmative; but heaven defend us from taking that wrong course of most theories, out of which is begotten a mutually devouring Pro et Contra.

Certainly that effect is perfectly necessary, for it has its foundation in the nature of things, and it exists, even if we find means to struggle against it; just as the motion of a cannon ball is always in the direction of the terrestrial, although when fired from east to west part of the general velocity is destroyed by this opposite motion.

All War supposes human weakness, and against that it is directed.

Therefore, if hereafter in another place we examine what is to be done after the loss of a great battle, if we bring under review the resources which still remain, even in the most desperate cases, if we should express a belief in the possibility of retrieving all, even in such a case; it must not be supposed we mean thereby that the effects of such a defeat can by degrees be completely wiped out, for the forces and means used to repair the disaster might have been applied to the realisation of some positive object; and this applies both to the moral and physical forces.

Another question is, whether, through the loss of a great battle, forces are not perhaps roused into existence, which otherwise would never have come to life. This case is certainly conceivable, and it is what has actually occurred with many Nations. But to produce this intensified reaction is beyond the province of military art, which can only take account of it where it might be assumed as a possibility.

If there are cases in which the fruits of a victory appear rather of a destructive nature in consequence of the reaction of the forces which it had the effect of rousing into activity—cases which certainly are very exceptional—then it must the more surely be granted, that there is a difference in the effects which one and the same victory may produce according to the character of the people or state, which has been conquered.

CHAPTER XI - THE USE OF THE BATTLE (continued)

WHATEVER form the conduct of War may take in particular cases, and whatever we may have to admit in the sequel as necessary respecting it: we have only to refer to the conception of War to be convinced of what follows:

1. The destruction of the enemy's military force, is the leading principle of War, and for the whole chapter of positive action the direct way to the object.

2. This destruction of the enemy's force, must be principally effected by means of battle.

3. Only great and general battles can produce great results.

4. The results will be greatest when combats unite themselves in one great battle.

5. It is only in a great battle that the General-in-Chief commands in person, and it is in the nature of things, that he should place more confidence in himself than in his subordinates.

From these truths a double law follows, the parts of which mutually support each other; namely, that the destruction of the enemy's military force is to be sought for principally by great battles, and their results; and that the chief object of great battles must be the destruction of the enemy's military force.

No doubt the annihilation-principle is to be found more or less in other means—granted there are instances in which through favourable circumstances in a minor combat, the destruction of the enemy's forces has been disproportionately great (Maxen), and on the other hand in a battle, the taking or holding a single post may be predominant in importance as an object—but as a general rule it remains a paramount truth, that battles are only fought with a view to the destruction of the enemy's Army, and that this destruction can only be effected by their means.

The battle may therefore be regarded as War concentrated, as the centre of effort of the whole War or campaign. As the sun's rays unite in the focus of the concave mirror in a perfect image, and in the fulness of their heat; to the forces and circumstances of War, unite in a focus in the great battle for one concentrated utmost effort.

The very assemblage of forces in one great whole, which takes place more or less in all Wars, indicates an intention to strike a decisive blow with this whole, either voluntarily as assailant, or constrained by the opposite party as defender. When this great blow does not follow, then some modifying, and retarding motives have attached themselves to the original motive of hostility, and have weakened, altered or completely checked the movement. But also, even in this condition of mutual inaction which has been the key-note in so many Wars, the idea of a possible battle serves always for both parties as a point of direction, a distant focus in the construction of their plans. The more War is War in earnest, the more it is a venting of animosity and hostility, a mutual struggle to overpower, so much the more will all activities join deadly contest, and also the more prominent in importance becomes the battle.

In general, when the object aimed at is of a great and positive nature, one therefore in which the interests of the enemy are deeply concerned, the battle offers itself as the most natural means; it is, therefore, also the best as we shall show more plainly hereafter: and, as a rule, when it is evaded from aversion to the great decision, punishment follows.

The positive object belong to the offensive, and therefore the battle is also more particularly his means. But without examining the conception of offensive and defensive more minutely here, we must still observe that, even for the defender in most cases, there is no other effectual means with which to meet the exigencies of his situation, to solve the problem presented to him.

The battle is the bloodiest way of solution. True, it is not merely reciprocal slaughter, and its effect is more a killing of the enemy's courage than of the enemy's soldiers, as we shall see more plainly in the next chapter—but still blood is always its price, and slaughter its character as well as name; from this the humanity in the General's mind recoils with horror.

But the soul of the man trembles still more at the thought of the decision to be given with one single blow. IN ONE POINT of space and time all action is here pressed together, and at such a moment there is stirred up within us a dim feeling as if in this narrow space all our forces could not develop themselves and come into activity, as if we had already gained much by mere time, although this time owes us nothing at all. This is all mere illusion, but even as illusion it is something, and the same weakness which seizes upon the man in every other momentous decision may well be felt more powerfully by the General, when he must stake interests of such enormous weight upon one venture.

Thus, then, Statesmen and Generals have at all times endeavoured to avoid the decisive battle, seeking either to attain their aim without it, or dropping that aim unperceived. Writers on history and theory have then busied themselves to discover in some other feature in these campaigns not only an equivalent for the decision by battle which has been avoided, but even a higher art. In this way, in the present age, it came very near to this, that a battle in the economy of War was looked upon as an evil, rendered necessary through some error committed, a morbid paroxysm to which a regular prudent system of War would never lead: only those Generals were to deserve laurels who knew how to carry on War without spilling blood, and the theory of War—a real business for Brahmins—was to be specially directed to teaching this.

Contemporary history has destroyed this illusion, but no one can guarantee that it will not sooner or later reproduce itself, and lead those at the head of affairs to perversities which please man's weakness, and therefore have the greater affinity for his nature. Perhaps, by-and-by, Buonaparte's campaigns and battles will be looked upon as mere acts of barbarism and stupidity, and we shall once more turn with satisfaction and confidence to the dress-sword of obsolete and musty institutions and forms. If theory gives a caution against this, then it renders a real service to those who listen to its warning voice. MAY WE SUCCEED IN LENDING A HAND TO THOSE WHO IN OUR DEAR NATIVE LAND ARE CALLED UPON TO SPEAK WITH AUTHORITY ON THESE MATTERS, THAT WE MAY BE THEIR GUIDE INTO THIS FIELD OF INQUIRY, AND EXCITE THEM TO MAKE A CANDID EXAMINATION OF THE SUBJECT.

Not only the conception of War but experience also leads us to look for a great decision only in a great battle. From time immemorial, only great victories have led to great successes on the offensive side in the absolute form, on the defensive side in a manner more or less satisfactory. Even Buonaparte would not have seen the day of Ulm, unique in its kind, if he had shrunk from shedding blood; it is rather to be regarded as only a second crop from the victorious events in his preceding campaigns. It is not only bold, rash, and presumptuous Generals who have sought to complete their work by the great venture of a decisive battle, but also fortunate ones as well; and we may rest satisfied with the answer which they have thus given to this vast question.

Let us not hear of Generals who conquer without bloodshed. If a bloody slaughter is a horrible sight, then that is a ground for paying more respect to War, but not for making the sword we wear blunter and blunter by degrees from feelings of humanity, until some one steps in with one that is sharp and lops off the arm from our body.

We look upon a great battle as a principal decision, but certainly not as the only one necessary for a War or a campaign. Instances of a great battle deciding a whole campaign, have been frequent only in modern times, those which have decided a whole War, belong to the class of rare exceptions.

A decision which is brought about by a great battle depends naturally not on the battle itself, that is on the mass of combatants engaged in it, and on the intensity of the victory, but also on a number of other relations between the military forces opposed to each other, and between the States to which these forces belong. But at the same time that the principal mass of the force available is brought to the great duel, a great decision is also brought on, the extent of which may perhaps be foreseen in many respects, though not in all, and which although not the only one, still is the FIRST decision, and as such, has an influence on those which succeed. Therefore a deliberately planned great battle, according to its relations, is more or less, but always in some degree, to be regarded as the leading means and central point of the whole system. The more a General takes the field in the true spirit of War as well as of every contest, with the feeling and the idea, that is the conviction, that he must and will conquer, the more he will strive to throw every weight into the scale in the first battle, hope and strive to win everything by it. Buonaparte hardly ever entered upon a War without thinking of conquering his enemy at once in the first battle, and Frederick the Great, although in a more limited sphere, and with interests of less magnitude at stake, thought the same when, at the head of a small Army, he sought to disengage his rear from the Russians or the Federal Imperial Army.

The decision which is given by the great battle, depends, we have said, partly on the battle itself, that is on the number of troops engaged, and partly on the magnitude of the success.

How the General may increase its importance in respect to the first point is evident in itself and we shall merely observe that according to the importance of the great battle, the number of cases which are decided along with it increases, and that therefore Generals who, confident in themselves have been lovers of great decisions, have always managed to make use of the greater part of their troops in it without neglecting on that account essential points elsewhere.

As regards the consequences or speaking more correctly the effectiveness of a victory, that depends chiefly on four points:

1. On the tactical form adopted as the order of battle.
2. On the nature of the country.
3. On the relative proportions of the three arms.
4. On the relative strength of the two Armies.

A battle with parallel fronts and without any action against a flank will seldom yield as great success as one in which the defeated Army has been turned, or compelled to change front more or less. In a broken or hilly country the successes are likewise smaller, because the power of the blow is everywhere less.

If the cavalry of the vanquished is equal or superior to that of the victor, then the effects of the pursuit are diminished, and by that great part of the results of victory are lost.

Finally it is easy to understand that if superior numbers are on the side of the conqueror, and he uses his advantage in that respect to turn the flank of his adversary, or compel him to change front, greater results will follow than if the conqueror had been weaker in numbers than the vanquished. The battle of Leuthen may certainly be quoted as a practical refutation of this principle, but we beg permission for once to say what we otherwise do not like, NO RULE WITHOUT AN EXCEPTION.

In all these ways, therefore, the Commander has the means of giving his battle a decisive character; certainly he thus exposes himself to an increased amount of danger, but his whole line of action is subject to that dynamic law of the moral world.

There is then nothing in War which can be put in comparison with the great battle in point of importance, AND THE ACME OF STRATEGIC ABILITY IS DISPLAYED IN THE PROVISION OF MEANS FOR THIS GREAT EVENT, IN THE SKILFUL DETERMINATION OF PLACE AND TIME, AND DIRECTION OF TROOPS, AND ITS THE GOOD USE MADE OF SUCCESS.

But it does not follow from the importance of these things that they must be of a very complicated and recondite nature; all is here rather simple, the art of combination by no means great; but there is great need of quickness in judging of circumstances, need of energy, steady resolution, a youthful spirit of enterprise—heroic qualities, to which we shall often have to refer. There is, therefore, but little wanted here of that which can be taught by books and there is much that, if it can be taught at all, must come to the General through some other medium than printer's type.

The impulse towards a great battle, the voluntary, sure progress to it, must proceed from a feeling of innate power and a clear sense of the necessity; in other words, it must proceed from inborn courage and from perceptions sharpened by contact with the higher interests of life.

Great examples are the best teachers, but it is certainly a misfortune if a cloud of theoretical prejudices comes between, for even the sunbeam is refracted and tinted by the clouds. To destroy such prejudices, which many a time rise and spread themselves like a miasma, is an imperative duty of theory, for the misbegotten offspring of human reason can also be in turn destroyed by pure reason.

CHAPTER XII - STRATEGIC MEANS OF UTILISING VICTORY

THE more difficult part, viz., that of perfectly preparing the victory, is a silent service of which the merit belongs to Strategy and yet for which it is hardly sufficiently commended. It appears brilliant and full of renown by turning to good account a victory gained.

What may be the special object of a battle, how it is connected with the whole system of a War, whither the career of victory may lead according to the nature of circumstances, where its culminating-point lies—all these are things which we shall not enter upon until hereafter. But under any conceivable circumstances the fact holds good, that without a pursuit no victory can have a great effect, and that, however short the career of victory may be, it must always lead beyond the first steps in pursuit; and in order to avoid the frequent repetition of this, we shall now dwell for a moment on this necessary supplement of victory in general.

The pursuit of a beaten Army commences at the moment that Army, giving up the combat, leaves its position; all previous movements in one direction and another belong not to that but to the progress of the battle itself. Usually victory at the moment here described, even if it is certain, is still as yet small and weak in its proportions, and would not rank as an event of any great positive advantage if not completed by a pursuit on the first day. Then it is mostly, as we have before said, that the trophies which give substance to the victory begin to be gathered up. Of this pursuit we shall speak in the next place.

Usually both sides come into action with their physical powers considerably deteriorated, for the movements immediately preceding have generally the character of very urgent circumstances. The efforts which the forging out of a great combat costs, complete the exhaustion; from this it follows that the victorious party is very little less disorganised and out of his original formation than the vanquished, and therefore requires time to reform, to collect stragglers, and issue fresh ammunition to those who are without. All these things place the conqueror himself in the state of crisis of which we have already spoken. If now the defeated force is only a detached portion of the enemy's Army, or if it has otherwise to expect a considerable reinforcement, then the conqueror may easily run into the obvious danger of having to pay dear for his victory, and this consideration, in such a case, very soon puts an end to pursuit, or at least restricts it materially. Even when a strong accession of force by the enemy is not to be feared, the conqueror finds in the above circumstances a powerful check to the vivacity of his pursuit. There is no reason to fear that the victory will be snatched away, but adverse combats are still possible, and may diminish the advantages which up to the present have been gained. Moreover, at this moment the whole weight of all that is sensuous in an Army, its wants and weaknesses, are dependent on the will of the Commander. All the thousands under his command require rest and refreshment, and long to see a stop put to toil and danger for the present; only a few, forming an exception, can see and feel beyond the present moment, it is only amongst this little number that there is sufficient mental vigour to think, after what is absolutely necessary at the moment has been done, upon those results which at such a moment only appear to the rest as mere embellishments of victory—as a luxury of triumph. But all these thousands have a voice in the council of the General, for through the various steps of the military hierarchy these interests of the sensuous creature have their sure conductor into the heart of the Commander. He himself, through mental and bodily fatigue, is more or less weakened in his natural activity, and thus it happens then that, mostly from these causes, purely incidental to human nature, less is done than might have been done, and that generally what is done is to be ascribed entirely to the THIRST FOR GLORY, the energy, indeed also the HARD-HEARTEDNESS of the General-in-Chief. It is only thus we can explain the hesitating manner in which many Generals follow up a victory which superior numbers have given them. The first pursuit of the enemy we limit in general to the extent of the first day, including the night following the victory. At the end of that period the necessity of rest ourselves prescribes a halt in any case.

This first pursuit has different natural degrees.

The first is, if cavalry alone are employed; in that case it amounts usually more to alarming and watching than to pressing the enemy in reality, because the smallest obstacle of ground is generally sufficient to check the pursuit. Useful as cavalry may be against single bodies of broken demoralised troops, still when opposed to the bulk of the beaten Army it becomes again only the auxiliary arm, because the troops in retreat can employ fresh reserves to cover the movement, and, therefore, at the next trifling obstacle of ground, by combining all arms they can make a stand with success. The only exception to this is in the case of an army in actual flight in a complete state of dissolution.

The second degree is, if the pursuit is made by a strong advance-guard composed of all arms, the greater part consisting naturally of cavalry. Such a pursuit generally drives the enemy as far as the nearest strong position for his rear-guard, or the next position affording space for his Army. Neither can usually be found at once, and, therefore, the pursuit can be carried further; generally, however, it does not extend beyond the distance of one or at most a couple of leagues, because otherwise the advance-guard would not feel itself sufficiently supported. The third and most vigorous degree is when the victorious Army itself continues to advance as far as its physical powers can endure. In this case the beaten Army will generally quit such ordinary positions as a country usually offers on the mere show of an attack, or of an intention to turn its flank; and the rear-guard will be still less likely to engage in an obstinate resistance.

In all three cases the night, if it sets in before the conclusion of the whole act, usually puts an end to it, and the few instances in which this has not taken place, and the pursuit has been continued throughout the night, must be regarded as pursuits in an exceptionally vigorous form.

If we reflect that in fighting by night everything must be, more or less, abandoned to chance, and that at the conclusion of a battle the regular cohesion and order of things in an army must inevitably be disturbed, we may easily conceive the reluctance of both Generals to carrying on their business under such disadvantageous conditions. If a complete dissolution of the vanquished Army, or a rare superiority of the victorious Army in military virtue does not ensure success, everything would in a manner be given up to fate, which can never be for the interest of any one, even of the most fool-hardy General. As a rule, therefore, night puts an end to pursuit, even when the battle has only been decided shortly before darkness sets in. This allows the conquered either time for rest and to rally immediately, or, if he retreats during the night it gives him a march in advance. After this break the conquered is decidedly in a better condition; much of that which had been thrown into confusion has been brought again into order, ammunition has been renewed, the whole has been put into a fresh formation. Whatever further encounter now takes place with the enemy is a new battle not a continuation of the old, and although it may be far from promising absolute success, still it is a fresh combat, and not merely a gathering up of the debris by the victor.

When, therefore, the conqueror can continue the pursuit itself throughout the night, if only with a strong advance-guard composed of all arms of the service, the effect of the victory is immensely increased, of this the battles of Leuthen and La Belle Alliance are examples.

The whole action of this pursuit is mainly tactical, and we only dwell upon it here in order to make plain the difference which through it may be produced in the effect of a victory.

This first pursuit, as far as the nearest stopping-point, belongs as a right to every conqueror, and is hardly in any way connected with his further plans and combinations. These may considerably diminish the positive results of a victory gained with the main body of the Army, but they cannot make this first use of it impossible; at least cases of that kind, if conceivable at all, must be so uncommon that they should have no appreciable influence on theory. And here certainly we must say that the example afforded by modern Wars opens up quite a new field for energy. In preceding Wars, resting on a narrower basis, and altogether more circumscribed in their scope, there were many unnecessary conventional restrictions in various ways, but particularly in this point. THE CONCEPTION, HONOUR OF VICTORY seemed to Generals so much by far the chief thing that they thought the less of the complete destruction of the enemy's military force, as in point of fact that destruction of force appeared to them only as one of the many means in War, not by any means as the principal, much less as the only means; so that they the more readily put the sword in its sheath the moment the enemy had lowered his. Nothing seemed more natural to them than to stop the combat as soon as the decision was obtained, and to regard all further carnage as unnecessary cruelty. Even if this false philosophy did not determine their resolutions entirely, still it was a point of view by which representations of the exhaustion of all powers, and physical impossibility of continuing the struggle, obtained readier evidence and greater weight. Certainly the sparing one's own instrument of victory is a vital question if we only possess this one, and foresee that soon the time may arrive when it will not be sufficient for all that remains to be done, for every continuation of the offensive must lead ultimately to complete exhaustion. But this calculation was still so far false, as the further loss of forces by a continuance of the pursuit could bear no proportion to that which the enemy must suffer. That view, therefore, again could only exist because the military forces were not considered the vital factor. And so we find that in former Wars real heroes only—such as Charles XII., Marlborough, Eugene, Frederick the Great—added a vigorous pursuit to their victories when they were decisive enough, and that other Generals usually contented themselves with the possession of the field of battle. In modern times the greater energy infused into the conduct of Wars through the greater importance of the circumstances from which they have proceeded has thrown down these conventional barriers; the pursuit has become an all-important business for the conqueror; trophies have on that account multiplied in extent, and if there are cases also in modern Warfare in which this has not been the case, still they belong to the list of exceptions, and are to be accounted for by peculiar circumstances.

At Gorschen and Bautzen nothing but the superiority of the allied cavalry prevented a complete rout, at Gross Beeren and Dennewitz the ill-will of Bernadotte, the Crown Prince of Sweden; at Laon the enfeebled personal condition of Bluecher, who was then seventy years old and at the moment confined to a dark room owing to an injury to his eyes.

But Borodino is also an illustration to the point here, and we cannot resist saying a few more words about it, partly because we do not consider the circumstances are explained simply by attaching blame to Buonaparte, partly because it might appear as if this, and with it a great number of similar cases, belonged to that class which we have designated as so extremely rare, cases in which the general relations seize and fetter the General at the very beginning of the battle. French authors in particular, and great admirers of Buonaparte (Vaudancourt, Chambray, Se'gur), have blamed him decidedly because he did not drive the Russian Army completely off the field, and use his last reserves to scatter it, because then what was only a lost battle would have been a complete rout. We should be obliged to diverge too far to describe circumstantially the mutual situation of the two Armies; but this much is evident, that when Buonaparte passed the Niemen with his Army the same corps which afterwards fought at Borodino numbered 300,000 men, of whom now only 120,000 remained, he might therefore well be apprehensive that he would not have enough left to march upon Moscow, the point on which everything seemed to depend. The victory which he had just gained gave him nearly a certainty of taking that capital, for that the Russians would be in a condition to fight a second battle within eight days seemed in the highest degree improbable; and in Moscow he hoped to find peace. No doubt the complete dispersion of the Russian Army would have made this peace much more certain; but still the first consideration was to get to Moscow, that is, to get there with a force with which he should appear dictator over the capital, and through that over the Empire and the Government. The force which he brought with him to Moscow was no longer sufficient for that, as shown in the sequel, but it would have been still less so if, in scattering the Russian Army, he had scattered his own at the same time. Buonaparte was thoroughly alive to all this, and in our eyes he stands completely justified. But on that account this case is still not to be reckoned amongst those in which, through the general relations, the General is interdicted from following up his victory, for there never was in his case any question of mere pursuit. The victory was decided at four o'clock in the afternoon, but the Russians still occupied the greater part of the field of battle; they were not yet disposed to give up the ground, and if the attack had been renewed, they would still have offered a most determined resistance, which would have undoubtedly ended in their complete defeat, but would have cost the conqueror much further bloodshed. We must therefore reckon the Battle of Borodino as amongst battles, like Bautzen, left unfinished. At Bautzen the vanquished preferred to quit the field sooner; at Borodino the conqueror preferred to content himself with a half victory, not because the decision appeared doubtful, but because he was not rich enough to pay for the whole.

Returning now to our subject, the deduction from our reflections in relation to the first stage of pursuit is, that the energy thrown into it chiefly determines the value of the victory; that this pursuit is a second act of the victory, in many cases more important also than the first, and that strategy, whilst here approaching tactics to receive from it the harvest of success, exercises the first act of her authority by demanding this completion of the victory.

But further, the effects of victory are very seldom found to stop with this first pursuit; now first begins the real career to which victory lent velocity. This course is conditioned as we have already said, by other relations of which it is not yet time to speak. But we must here mention, what there is of a general character in the pursuit in order to avoid repetition when the subject occurs again.

In the further stages of pursuit, again, we can distinguish three degrees: the simple pursuit, a hard pursuit, and a parallel march to intercept.

The simple FOLLOWING or PURSUING causes the enemy to continue his retreat, until he thinks he can risk another battle. It will therefore in its effect suffice to exhaust the advantages gained, and besides that, all that the enemy cannot carry with him, sick, wounded, and disabled from fatigue, quantities of baggage, and carriages of all kinds, will fall into our hands, but this mere following does not tend to heighten the disorder in the enemy's Army, an effect which is produced by the two following causes.

If, for instance, instead of contenting ourselves with taking up every day the camp the enemy has just vacated, occupying just as much of the country as he chooses to abandon, we make our arrangements so as every day to encroach further, and accordingly with our advance-guard organised for the purpose, attack his rear-guard every time it attempts to halt, then such a course will hasten his retreat, and consequently tend to increase his disorganisation.—This it will principally effect by the character of continuous flight, which his retreat will thus assume. Nothing has such a depressing influence on the soldier, as the sound of the enemy's cannon afresh at the moment when, after a forced march he seeks some rest; if this excitement is continued from day to day for some time, it may lead to a complete rout. There lies in it a constant admission of being obliged to obey the law of the enemy, and of being unfit for any resistance, and the consciousness of this cannot do otherwise than weaken the moral of an Army in a high degree. The effect of pressing the enemy in this way attains a maximum when it drives the enemy to make night marches. If the conqueror scares away the discomfited opponent at sunset from a camp which has just been taken up either for the main body of the Army, or for the rear-guard, the conquered must either make a night march, or alter his position in the night, retiring further away, which is much the same thing; the victorious party can on the other hand pass the night in quiet.

The arrangement of marches, and the choice of positions depend in this case also upon so many other things, especially on the supply of the Army, on strong natural obstacles in the country, on large towns, &c. &c., that it would be ridiculous pedantry to attempt to show by a geometrical analysis how the pursuer, being able to impose his laws on the retreating enemy, can compel him to march at night while he takes his rest. But nevertheless it is true and practicable that marches in pursuit may be so planned as to have this tendency, and that the efficacy of the pursuit is very much enchanced thereby. If this is seldom attended to in the execution, it is because such a procedure is more difficult for the pursuing Army, than a regular adherence to ordinary marches in the daytime. To start in good time in the morning, to encamp at mid-day, to occupy the rest of the day in providing for the ordinary wants of the Army, and to use the night for repose, is a much more convenient method than to regulate one's movements exactly according to those of the enemy, therefore to determine nothing till the last moment, to start on the march, sometimes in the morning, sometimes in the evening, to be always for several hours in the presence of the enemy, and exchanging cannon shots with him, and keeping up skirmishing fire, to plan manoeuvres to turn him, in short, to make the whole outlay of tactical means which such a course renders necessary. All that naturally bears with a heavy weight on the pursuing Army, and in War, where there are so many burdens to be borne, men are always inclined to strip off those which do not seem absolutely necessary. These observations are true, whether applied to a whole Army or as in the more usual case, to a strong advance-guard. For the reasons just mentioned, this second method of pursuit, this continued pressing of the enemy pursued is rather a rare occurrence; even Buonaparte in his Russian campaign, 1812, practised it but little, for the reasons here apparent, that the difficulties and hardships of this campaign, already threatened his Army with destruction before it could reach its object; on the other hand, the French in their other campaigns have distinguished themselves by their energy in this point also.

Lastly, the third and most effectual form of pursuit is, the parallel march to the immediate object of the retreat.

Every defeated Army will naturally have behind it, at a greater or less distance, some point, the attainment of which is the first purpose in view, whether it be that failing in this its further retreat might be compromised, as in the case of a defile, or that it is important for the point itself to reach it before the enemy, as in the case of a great city, magazines, &c., or, lastly, that the Army at this point will gain new powers of defence, such as a strong position, or junction with other corps.

Now if the conqueror directs his march on this point by a lateral road, it is evident how that may quicken the retreat of the beaten Army in a destructive manner, convert it into hurry, perhaps into flight. The conquered has only three ways to counteract this: the first is to throw himself in front of the enemy, in order by an unexpected attack to gain that probability of success which is lost to him in general from his position; this plainly supposes an enterprising bold General, and an excellent Army, beaten but not utterly defeated; therefore, it can only be employed by a beaten Army in very few cases.

The second way is hastening the retreat; but this is just what the conqueror wants, and it easily leads to immoderate efforts on the part of the troops, by which enormous losses are sustained, in stragglers, broken guns, and carriages of all kinds.

The third way is to make a detour, and get round the nearest point of interception, to march with more ease at a greater distance from the enemy, and thus to render the haste required less damaging. This last way is the worst of all, it generally turns out like a new debt contracted by an insolvent debtor, and leads to greater embarrassment. There are cases in which this course is advisable; others where there is nothing else left; also instances in which it has been successful; but upon the whole it is certainly true that its adoption is usually influenced less by a clear persuasion of its being the surest way of attaining the aim than by another inadmissible motive—this motive is the dread of encountering the enemy. Woe to the Commander who gives in to this! However much the moral of his Army may have deteriorated, and however well founded may be his apprehensions of being at a disadvantage in any conflict with the enemy, the evil will only be made worse by too anxiously avoiding every possible risk of collision. Buonaparte in 1813 would never have brought over the Rhine with him the 30,000 or 40,000 men who remained after the battle of Hanau, if he had avoided that battle and tried to pass the Rhine at Mannheim or Coblenz. It is just by means of small combats carefully prepared and executed, and in which the defeated army being on the defensive, has always the assistance of the ground—it is just by these that the moral strength of the Army can first be resuscitated.

The beneficial effect of the smallest successes is incredible; but with most Generals the adoption of this plan implies great self-command. The other way, that of evading all encounter, appears at first so much easier, that there is a natural preference for its adoption. It is therefore usually just this system of evasion which best, promotes the view of the pursuer, and often ends with the complete downfall of the pursued; we must, however, recollect here that we are speaking of a whole Army, not of a single Division, which, having been cut off, is seeking to join the main Army by making a de'tour; in such a case circumstances are different, and success is not uncommon. But there is one condition requisite to the success of this race of two Corps for an object, which is that a Division of the pursuing army should follow by the same road which the pursued has taken, in order to pick up stragglers, and keep up the impression which the presence of the enemy never fails to make. Bluecher neglected this in his, in other respects unexceptionable, pursuit after La Belle Alliance.

Such marches tell upon the pursuer as well as the pursued, and they are not advisable if the enemy's Army rallies itself upon another considerable one; if it has a distinguished General at its head, and if its destruction is not already well prepared. But when this means can be adopted, it acts also like a great mechanical power. The losses of the beaten Army from sickness and fatigue are on such a disproportionate scale, the spirit of the Army is so weakened and lowered by the constant solicitude about impending ruin, that at last anything like a well organised stand is out of the question; every day thousands of prisoners fall into the enemy's hands without striking a blow. In such a season of complete good fortune, the conqueror need not hesitate about dividing his forces in order to draw into the vortex of destruction everything within reach of his Army, to cut off detachments, to take fortresses unprepared for defence, to occupy large towns, &c. &c. He may do anything until a new state of things arises, and the more he ventures in this way the longer will it be before that change will take place. There is no want of examples of brilliant results from grand decisive victories, and of great and vigorous pursuits in the wars of Buonaparte. We need only quote Jena 1806, Ratisbonne 1809, Leipsic 1813, and Belle- Alliance 1815.

CHAPTER XIII - RETREAT AFTER A LOST BATTLE

IN a lost battle the power of an Army is broken, the moral to a greater degree than the physical. A second battle unless fresh favourable circumstances come into play, would lead to a complete defeat, perhaps, to destruction. This is a military axiom. According to the usual course the retreat is continued up to that point where the equilibrium of forces is restored, either by reinforcements, or by the protection of strong fortresses, or by great defensive positions afforded by the country, or by a separation of the enemy's force. The magnitude of the losses sustained, the extent of the defeat, but still more the character of the enemy, will bring nearer or put off the instant of this equilibrium. How many instances may be found of a beaten Army rallied again at a short distance, without its circumstances having altered in any way since the battle. The cause of this may be traced to the moral weakness of the adversary, or to the preponderance gained in the battle not having been sufficient to make lasting impression.

To profit by this weakness or mistake of the enemy, not to yield one inch breadth more than the pressure of circumstances demands, but above all things, in order to keep up the moral forces to as advantageous a point as possible, a slow retreat, offering incessant resistance, and bold courageous counterstrokes, whenever the enemy seeks to gain any excessive advantages, are absolutely necessary. Retreats of great Generals and of Armies inured to War have always resembled the retreat of a wounded lion, such is, undoubtedly, also the best theory.

It is true that at the moment of quitting a dangerous position we have often seen trifling formalities observed which caused a waste of time, and were, therefore, attended with danger, whilst in such cases everything depends on getting out of the place speedily. Practised Generals reckon this maxim a very important one. But such cases must not be confounded with a general retreat after a lost battle. Whoever then thinks by a few rapid marches to gain a start, and more easily to recover a firm standing, commits a great error. The first movements should be as small as possible, and it is a maxim in general not to suffer ourselves to be dictated to by the enemy. This maxim cannot be followed without bloody fighting with the enemy at our heels, but the gain is worth the sacrifice; without it we get into an accelerated pace which soon turns into a headlong rush, and costs merely in stragglers more men than rear-guard combats, and besides that extinguishes the last remnants of the spirit of resistance.

A strong rear-guard composed of picked troops, commanded by the bravest General, and supported by the whole Army at critical moments, a careful utilisation of ground, strong ambuscades wherever the boldness of the enemy's advance-guard, and the ground, afford opportunity; in short, the preparation and the system of regular small battles,—these are the means of following this principle.

The difficulties of a retreat are naturally greater or less according as the battle has been fought under more or less favourable circumstances, and according as it has been more or less obstinately contested. The battle of Jena and La Belle-Alliance show how impossible anything like a regular retreat may become, if the last man is used up against a powerful enemy.

Now and again it has been suggested to divide for the purpose of retreating, therefore to retreat in separate divisions or even eccentrically. Such a separation as is made merely for convenience, and along with which concentrated action continues possible and is kept in view, is not what we now refer to; any other kind is extremely dangerous, contrary to the nature of the thing, and therefore a great error. Every lost battle is a principle of weakness and disorganisation; and the first and immediate desideratum is to concentrate, and in concentration to recover order, courage, and confidence. The idea of harassing the enemy by separate corps on both flanks at the moment when he is following up his victory, is a perfect anomaly; a faint-hearted pedant might be overawed by his enemy in that manner, and for such a case it may answer; but where we are not sure of this failing in our opponent it is better let alone. If the strategic relations after a battle require that we should cover ourselves right and left by detachments, so much must be done, as from circumstances is unavoidable, but this fractioning must always be regarded as an evil, and we are seldom in a state to commence it the day after the battle itself.

If Frederick the Great after the battle of Kollin, and the raising of the siege of Prague retreated in three columns that was done not out of choice, but because the position of his forces, and the necessity of covering Saxony, left him no alternative, Buonaparte after the battle of Brienne, sent Marmont back to the Aube, whilst he himself passed the Seine, and turned towards Troyes; but that this did not end in disaster, was solely owing to the circumstance that the Allies, instead of pursuing divided their forces in like manner, turning with the one part (Bluecher) towards the Marne, while with the other (Schwartzenberg), from fear of being too weak, they advanced with exaggerated caution.

CHAPTER XIV - NIGHT FIGHTING

THE manner of conducting a combat at night, and what concerns the details of its course, is a tactical subject; we only examine it here so far as in its totality it appears as a special strategic means.

Fundamentally every night attack is only a more vehement form of surprise. Now at the first look of the thing such an attack appears quite pre-eminently advantageous, for we suppose the enemy to be taken by surprise, the assailant naturally to be prepared for everything which can happen. What an inequality! Imagination paints to itself a picture of the most complete confusion on the one side, and on the other side the assailant only occupied in reaping the fruits of his advantage. Hence the constant creation of schemes for night attacks by those who have not to lead them, and have no responsibility, whilst these attacks seldom take place in reality.

These ideal schemes are all based on the hypothesis that the assailant knows the arrangements of the defender because they have been made and announced beforehand, and could not escape notice in his reconnaissances, and inquiries; that on the other hand, the measures of the assailant, being only taken at the moment of execution, cannot be known to the enemy. But the last of these is not always quite the case, and still less is the first. If we are not so near the enemy as to have him completely under our eye, as the Austrians had Frederick the Great before the battle of Hochkirch (1758), then all that we know of his position must always be imperfect, as it is obtained by reconnaissances, patrols, information from prisoners, and spies, sources on which no firm reliance can be placed because intelligence thus obtained is always more or less of an old date, and the position of the enemy may have been altered in the meantime. Moreover, with the tactics and mode of encampment of former times it was much easier than it is now to examine the position of the enemy. A line of tents is much easier to distinguish than a line of huts or a bivouac; and an encampment on a line of front, fully and regularly drawn out, also easier than one of Divisions formed in columns, the mode often used at present. We may have the ground on which a Division bivouacs in that manner completely under our eye, and yet not be able to arrive at any accurate idea.

But the position again is not all that we want to know the measures which the defender may take in the course of the combat are just as important, and do not by any means consist in mere random shots. These measures also make night attacks more difficult in modern Wars than formerly, because they have in these campaigns an advantage over those already taken. In our combats the position of the defender is more temporary than definitive, and on that account the defender is better able to surprise his adversary with unexpected blows, than he could formerly.

Therefore what the assailant knows of the defensive previous to a night attack, is seldom or never sufficient to supply the want of direct observation.

But the defender has on his side another small advantage as well, which is that he is more at home than the assailant, on the ground which forms his position, and therefore, like the inhabitant of a room, will find his way about it in the dark with more ease than a stranger. He knows better where to find each part of his force, and therefore can more readily get at it than is the case with his adversary.

From this it follows, that the assailant in a combat at night feels the want of his eyes just as much as the defender, and that therefore, only particular reasons can make a night attack advisable.

Now these reasons arise mostly in connection with subordinate parts of an Army, rarely with the Army itself; it follows that a night attack also as a rule can only take place with secondary combats, and seldom with great battles.

We may attack a portion of the enemy's Army with a very superior force, consequently enveloping it with a view either to take the whole, or to inflict very severe loss on it by an unequal combat, provided that other circumstances are in our favour. But such a scheme can never succeed except by a great surprise, because no fractional part of the enemy's Army would engage in such an unequal combat, but would retire instead. But a surprise on an important scale except in rare instances in a very close country, can only be effected at night. If therefore we wish to gain such an advantage as this from the faulty disposition of a portion of the enemy's Army, then we must make use of the night, at all events, to finish the preliminary part even if the combat itself should not open till towards daybreak. This is therefore what takes place in all the little enterprises by night against outposts, and other small bodies, the main point being invariably through superior numbers, and getting round his position, to entangle him unexpectedly in such a disadvantageous combat, that he cannot disengage himself without great loss.

The larger the body attacked the more difficult the undertaking, because a strong force has greater resources within itself to maintain the fight long enough for help to arrive.

On that account the whole of the enemy's Army can never in ordinary cases be the object of such an attack for although it has no assistance to expect from any quarter outside itself, still, it contains within itself sufficient means of repelling attacks from several sides particularly in our day, when every one from the commencement is prepared for this very usual form of attack. Whether the enemy can attack us on several sides with success depends generally on conditions quite different from that of its being done unexpectedly; without entering here into the nature of these conditions, we confine ourselves to observing, that with turning an enemy, great results, as well as great dangers are connected; that therefore, if we set aside special circumstances, nothing justifies it but a great superiority, just such as we should use against a fractional part of the enemy's Army.

But the turning and surrounding a small fraction of the enemy, and particularly in the darkness of night, is also more practicable for this reason, that whatever we stake upon it, and however superior the force used may be, still probably it constitutes only a limited portion of our Army, and we can sooner stake that than the whole on the risk of a great venture. Besides, the greater part or perhaps the whole serves as a support and rallying-point for the portion risked, which again very much diminishes the danger of the enterprise.

Not only the risk, but the difficulty of execution as well confines night enterprises to small bodies. As surprise is the real essence of them so also stealthy approach is the chief condition of execution: but this is more easily done with small bodies than with large, and for the columns of a whole Army is seldom practicable. For this reason such enterprises are in general only directed against single outposts, and can only be feasible against greater bodies if they are without sufficient outposts, like Frederick the Great at Hochkirch. This will happen seldomer in future to Armies themselves than to minor divisions.

In recent times, when War has been carried on with so much more rapidity and vigour, it has in consequence often happened that Armies have encamped very close to each other, without having a very strong system of outposts, because those circumstances have generally occurred just at the crisis which precedes a great decision.

But then at such times the readiness for battle on both sides is also more perfect; on the other hand, in former Wars it was a frequent practice for armies to take up camps in sight of each other, when they had no other object but that of mutually holding each other in check, consequently for a longer period. How often Frederick the Great stood for weeks so near to the Austrians, that the two might have exchanged cannon shots with each other.

But these practices, certainly more favourable to night attacks, have been discontinued in later days; and armies being now no longer in regard to subsistence and requirements for encampment, such independent bodies complete in themselves, find it necessary to keep usually a day's march between themselves and the enemy. If we now keep in view especially the night attack of an army, it follows that sufficient motives for it can seldom occur, and that they fall under one or other of the following classes.

1. An unusual degree of carelessness or audacity which very rarely occurs, and when it does is compensated for by a great superiority in moral force.

2. A panic in the enemy's army, or generally such a degree of superiority in moral force on our side, that this is sufficient to supply the place of guidance in action.

3. Cutting through an enemy's army of superior force, which keeps us enveloped, because in this all depends on surprise, and the object of merely making a passage by force, allows a much greater concentration of forces.

4. Finally, in desperate cases, when our forces have such a disproportion to the enemy's, that we see no possibility of success, except through extraordinary daring.

But in all these cases there is still the condition that the enemy's army is under our eyes, and protected by no advance-guard.

As for the rest, most night combats are so conducted as to end with daylight, so that only the approach and the first attack are made under cover of darkness, because the assailant in that manner can better profit by the consequences of the state of confusion into which he throws his adversary; and combats of this description which do not commence until daybreak, in which the night therefore is only made use of to approach, are not to be counted as night combats.

Battle Studies: Ancient and Modern Battle by Ardant Du Picq

PART ONE: ANCIENT BATTLE

INTRODUCTION

Battle is the final objective of armies and man is the fundamental instrument in battle. Nothing can wisely be prescribed in an army—its personnel, organization, discipline and tactics, things which are connected like the fingers of a hand—without exact knowledge of the fundamental instrument, man, and his state of mind, his morale, at the instant of combat.

It often happens that those who discuss war, taking the weapon for the starting point, assume unhesitatingly that the man called to serve it will always use it as contemplated and ordered by the regulations. But such a being, throwing off his variable nature to become an impassive pawn, an abstract unit in the combinations of battle, is a creature born of the musings of the library, and not a real man. Man is flesh and blood; he is body and soul. And, strong as the soul often is, it can not dominate the body to the point where there will not be a revolt of the flesh and mental perturbation in the face of destruction.

The human heart, to quote Marshal de Saxe, is then the starting point in all matters pertaining to war.

Let us study the heart, not in modern battle, complicated and not readily grasped, but in ancient battle. For, although nowhere explained in detail, ancient battle was simple and clear.

Centuries have not changed human nature. Passions, instincts, among them the most powerful one of self-preservation, may be manifested in various ways according to the time, the place, the character and temperament of the race. Thus in our times we can admire, under the same conditions of danger, emotion and anguish, the calmness of the English, the dash of the French, and that inertia of the Russians which is called tenacity. But at bottom there is always found the same man. It is this man that we see disposed of by the experts, by the masters, when they organize and discipline, when they order detailed combat methods and take general dispositions for action. The best masters are those who know man best, the man of today and the man of history. This knowledge naturally comes from a study of formations and achievements in ancient war.

The development of this work leads us to make such an analysis, and from a study of combat we may learn to know man.

Let us go even back of ancient battle, to primeval struggle. In progressing from the savage to our times we shall get a better grasp of life.

And shall we then know as much as the masters? No more than one is a painter by having seen the methods of painting. But we shall better understand these able men and the great examples they have left behind them.

We shall learn from them to distrust mathematics and material dynamics as applied to battle principles. We shall learn to beware of the illusions drawn from the range and the maneuver field.

There, experience is with the calm, settled, unfatigued, attentive, obedient soldier, with an intelligent and tractable man-instrument in short, and not with the nervous, easily swayed, moved, troubled, distrait, excited, restless being, not even under self-control, who is the fighting man from general to private. There are strong men, exceptions, but they are rare.

These illusions, nevertheless, stubborn and persistent, always repair the very next day the most damaging injuries inflicted on them by experience. Their least dangerous effect is to lead to prescribing the impractical, as if ordering the impractical were not really an attack on discipline, and did not result in disconcerting officers and men by the unexpected and by surprise at the contrast between battle and the theories of peacetime training.

Battle, of course, always furnishes surprises. But it furnishes less in proportion as good sense and the recognition of truth have had their effect on the training of the fighting man, and are disseminated in the ranks. Let us then study man in battle, for it is he who really fights.

CHAPTER I - MAN IN PRIMITIVE AND ANCIENT COMBAT

Man does not enter battle to fight, but for victory. He does everything that he can to avoid the first and obtain the second.

War between savage tribes, between Arabs, even today, is a war of ambush by small groups of men of which each one, at the moment of surprise, chooses, not his adversary, but his victim, and is an assassin. Because the arms are similar on both sides, the only way of giving the advantage to one side is by surprise. A man surprised, needs an instant to collect his thoughts and defend himself; during this instant he is killed if he does not run away.

The surprised adversary does not defend himself, he tries to flee. Face to face or body to body combat with primitive arms, ax or dagger, so terrible among enemies without defensive arms, is very rare. It can take place only between enemies mutually surprised and without a chance of safety for any one except in victory. And still ... in case of mutual surprise, there is another chance of safety; that of falling back, of flight on the part of one or the other; and that chance is often seized. Here is an example, and if it does not concern savages at all, but soldiers of our days, the fact is none the less significant. It was observed by a man of warlike temperament who has related what he saw with his own eyes, although he was a forced spectator, held to the spot by a wound.

During the Crimean War, on a day of heavy fighting, two detachments of soldiers, A and B, coming around one of the mounds of earth that covered the country and meeting unexpectedly face to face, at ten paces, stopped thunderstruck. Then, forgetting their rifles, they threw stones and withdrew. Neither of the two groups had a decided leader to lead it to the front, and neither of the two dared to shoot first for fear that the other would at the same time bring his own arm to his shoulder. They were too near to hope to escape, or so they thought at least, although in reality, reciprocal firing, at such short ranges, is almost always too high. The man who would fire sees himself already killed by the return fire. He throws stones, and not with great force, to avoid using his rifle, to distract the enemy, to occupy the time, until flight offers him some chance of escaping at point-blank range.

This agreeable state of affairs did not last long, a minute perhaps. The appearance of a troop B on one flank determined the flight of A, and then the opposing group fired.

Surely, the affair is ridiculous and laughable.

Let us see, however. In a thick forest, a lion and a tiger meet face to face at a turn in the trail. They stop at once, rearing and ready to spring. They measure each other with their eyes, there is a rumbling in their throats. The claws move convulsively, the hair stands up. With tails lashing the ground, and necks stretched, ears flattened, lips turned up, they show their formidable fangs in that terrible threatening grimace of fear characteristic of felines.

Unseen, I shudder.

The situation is disagreeable for both: movement ahead means the death of a beast. Of which? Of both perhaps.

Slowly, quite slowly, one leg, bent for the leap, bending still, moves a few inches to the rear. Gently, quite gently, a fore paw follows the movement. After a stop, slowly, quite slowly, the other legs do the same, and both beasts, insensibly, little by little, and always facing, withdraw, up to the moment where their mutual withdrawal has created between them an interval greater than can be traversed in a bound. Lion and tiger turn their backs slowly and, without ceasing to observe, walk freely. They resume without haste their natural gaits, with that sovereign dignity characteristic of great seigneurs. I have ceased to shudder, but I do not laugh.

There is no more to laugh at in man in battle, because he has in his hands a weapon more terrible than the fangs and claws of lion or tiger, the rifle, which instantly, without possible defense, sends one from life into death. It is evident that no one close to his enemy is in a hurry to arm himself, to put into action a force which may kill him. He is not anxious to light the fuse that is to blow up the enemy, and himself at the same time.

Who has not observed like instances between dogs, between dog and cat, cat and cat?

In the Polish War of 1831, two Russian and two Polish regiments of cavalry charged each other. They went with the same dash to meet one another. When close enough to recognize faces, these cavalrymen slackened their gait and both turned their backs. The Russians and Poles, at this terrible moment, recognized each other as brothers, and rather than spill fraternal blood, they extricated themselves from a combat as if it were a crime. That is the version of an eyewitness and narrator, a Polish officer.

What do you think of cavalry troops so moved by brotherly love?

But let us resume:

When people become more numerous, and when the surprise of an entire population occupying a vast space is no longer possible, when a sort of public conscience has been cultivated within society, one is warned beforehand. War is formally declared. Surprise is no longer the whole of war, but it remains one of the means in war, the best means, even today. Man can no longer kill his enemy without defense. He has forewarned him. He must expect to find him standing and in numbers. He must fight; but he wishes to conquer with as little risk as possible. He employs the iron shod mace against the staff, arrows against the mace, the shield against arrows, the shield and cuirass against the shield alone, the long lance against the short lance, the tempered sword against the iron sword, the armed chariot against man on foot, and so on.

Man taxes his ingenuity to be able to kill without running the risk of being killed. His bravery is born of his strength and it is not absolute. Before a stronger he flees without shame. The instinct of self-preservation is so powerful that he does not feel disgraced in obeying it, although, thanks to the defensive power of arms and armor he can fight at close quarters. Can you expect him to act in any other way? Man must test himself before acknowledging a stronger. But once the stronger is recognized, no one will face him.

Individual strength and valor were supreme in primitive combats, so much so that when its heroes were killed, the nation was conquered. As a result of a mutual and tacit understanding, combatants often stopped fighting to watch with awe and anxiety two champions struggling. Whole peoples often placed their fate in the hands of the champions who took up the task and who alone fought. This was perfectly natural. They counted their champion a superman, and no man can stand against the superman.

But intelligence rebels against the dominance of force. No one can stand against an Achilles, but no Achilles can withstand ten enemies who, uniting their efforts, act in concert. This is the reason for tactics, which prescribe beforehand proper means of organization and action to give unanimity to effort, and for discipline which insures united efforts in spite of the innate weakness of combatants.

In the beginning man battled against man, each one for himself, like a beast that hunts to kill, yet flees from that which would kill him. But now prescriptions of discipline and tactics insure unity between leader and soldier, between the men themselves. Besides the intellectual progress, is there a moral progress? To secure unity in combat, to make tactical dispositions in order to render it practically possible, we must be able to count on the devotion of all. This elevates all combatants to the level of the champions of primitive combat. Esprit appears, flight is a disgrace, for one is no longer alone in combat. There is a legion, and he who gives way quits his commanders and his companions. In all respects the combatant is worth more.

So reason shows us the strength of wisely united effort; discipline makes it possible.

Will the result be terrible fights, conflicts of extermination? No! Collective man, a disciplined body of troops formed in tactical battle order, is invincible against an undisciplined body of troops. But against a similarly disciplined body, he becomes again primitive man. He flees before a greater force of destruction when he recognizes it or when he foresees it. Nothing is changed in the heart of man. Discipline keeps enemies face to face a little longer, but cannot supplant the instinct of self-preservation and the sense of fear that goes with it.

Fear!...

There are officers and soldiers who do not know it, but they are people of rare grit. The mass shudders; because you cannot suppress the flesh. This trembling must be taken into account in all organization, discipline, arrangements, movements, maneuvers, mode of action. All these are affected by the human weakness of the soldier which causes him to magnify the strength of the enemy.

This faltering is studied in ancient combat. It is seen that of nations apt in war, the strongest have been those who, not only best have understood the general conduct of war, but who have taken human weakness into greatest account and taken the best guarantees against it. It is notable that the most warlike peoples are not always those in which military institutions and combat methods are the best or the most rational.

And indeed, in warlike nations there is a good dose of vanity. They only take into account courage in their tactics. One might say that they do not desire to acknowledge weakness.

The Gaul, a fool in war, used barbarian tactics. After the first surprise, he was always beaten by the Greeks and Romans.

The Greek, a warrior, but also a politician, had tactics far superior to those of the Gauls and the Asiatics.

The Roman, a politician above all, with whom war was only a means, wanted perfect means. He had no illusions. He took into account human weakness and he discovered the legion.

But this is merely affirming what should be demonstrated.

CHAPTER II - KNOWLEDGE OF MAN-MADE ROMAN TACTICS - THE SUCCESSES OF HANNIBAL AND CAESAR

Greek tactics developed the phalanx; Roman tactics, the legion; the tactics of the barbarians employed the square phalanx, wedge or lozenge.

The mechanism of these various formations is explained in all elementary books. Polybius enters into a mechanical discussion when he contrasts the phalanx and the legion. (Book 18.)

The Greeks were, in intellectual civilization, superior to the Romans, consequently their tactics ought to have been far more rational. But such was not the case. Greek tactics proceeded from mathematical reasoning; Roman tactics from a profound knowledge of man's heart. Naturally the Greeks did not neglect morale nor the Romans mechanics, but their primary, considerations were diverse.

What formation obtained the maximum effort from the Greek army?

What methods caused the soldiers of a Roman army to fight most effectively?

The first question admits of discussion. The Roman solved the second.

The Roman was not essentially brave. He did not produce any warrior of the type of Alexander. It is acknowledged that the valorous impetuosity of the barbarians, Gauls, Cimbri, Teutons, made him tremble. But to the glorious courage of the Greeks, to the natural bravery of the Gauls he opposed a strict sense of duty, secured by a terrible discipline in the masses. It was inspired in the officers by a sentiment of the strongest patriotism.

The discipline of the Greeks was secured by exercises and rewards; the discipline of the Romans was secured also by the fear of death. They put to death with the club; they decimated their cowardly or traitorous units.

In order to conquer enemies that terrified his men, a Roman general heightened their morale, not by enthusiasm but by anger. He made the life of his soldiers miserable by excessive work and privations. He stretched the force of discipline to the point where, at a critical instant, it must break or expend itself on the enemy. Under similar circumstances, a Greek general caused Tyrtaeus to sing. It would have been curious to see two such forces opposed.

But discipline alone does not constitute superior tactics. Man in battle, I repeat, is a being in whom the instinct of self-preservation dominates, at certain moments, all other sentiments. Discipline has for its aim the domination of that instinct by a greater terror. But it cannot dominate it completely. I do not deny the glorious examples where discipline and devotion have elevated man above himself. But if these examples are glorious, it is because they are rare; if they are admired, it is because they are considered exceptions, and the exception proves the rule.

The determination of that instant where man loses his reasoning power and becomes instinctive is the crowning achievement in the science of combat. In general, here was the strength of the Roman tactics. In particular cases such successful determination makes Hannibals and Caesars.

Combat took place between masses in more or less deep formation commanded and supervised by leaders with a definite mission. The combat between masses was a series of individual conflicts, juxtaposed, with the front rank man alone fighting. If he fell, if he was wounded or worn out, he was replaced by the man of the second rank who had watched and guarded his flanks. This procedure continued up to the last rank. Man is always physically and morally fatigued in a hand-to-hand tournament where he employs all his energy.

These contests generally lasted but a short time. With like morale, the least fatigued always won.

During this engagement of the first two ranks, the one fighting, the other watching close at hand, the men of the rear ranks waited inactive at two paces distance for their turn in the combat, which would come only when their predecessors were killed, wounded or exhausted. They were impressed by the violent fluctuations of the struggle of the first rank. They heard the clashes of the blows and distinguished, perhaps, those that sank into the flesh. They saw the wounded, the exhausted crawl through the intervals to go to the rear. Passive spectators of danger, they were forced to await its terrible approach. These men were subjected to the poignant emotions of combat without being supported by the animation of the struggle. They were thus placed under the moral pressure of the greatest of anxieties. Often they could not stand it until their turn came; they gave way.

The best tactics, the best dispositions were those that made easiest a succession of efforts by assuring the relief by ranks of units in action, actually engaging only the necessary units and keeping the rest as a support or reserve outside of the immediate sphere of moral tension. The superiority of the Romans lay in such tactics and in the terrible discipline which prepared and assured the execution. By their resistance against fatigue which rude and continual tasks gave them and by the renewal of combatants in combat, they secured greater continuity of effort than any others.

The Gauls did not reason. Seeing only the inflexible line, they bound themselves together, thus rendering relief impracticable. They believed, as did the Greeks, in the power of the mass and impulse of deep files, and did not understand that deep files were powerless to push the first ranks forward as they recoiled in the face of death. It is a strange error to believe that the last ranks will go to meet that which made the first ones fall back. On the contrary, the contagion of recoil is so strong that the stopping of the head means the falling back of the rear!

The Greeks, also, certainly had reserves and supports in the second half of their dense ranks. But the idea of mass dominated. They placed these supports and reserves too near, forgetting the essential, man.

The Romans believed in the power of mass, but from the moral point of view only. They did not multiply the files in order to add to the mass, but to give to the combatants the confidence of being aided and relieved. The number of ranks was calculated according to the moral pressure that the last ranks could sustain.

There is a point beyond which man cannot bear the anxiety of combat in the front lines without being engaged. The Romans did not so increase the number of ranks as to bring about this condition. The Greeks did not observe and calculate so well. They sometimes brought the number of files up to thirty-two and their last files, which in their minds, were doubtless their reserves, found themselves forcibly dragged into the material disorder of the first ones.

In the order by maniples in the Roman legion, the best soldiers, those whose courage had been proved by experience in battle, waited stoically, kept in the second and third lines. They were far enough away not to suffer wounds and not to be drawn in by the front line retiring into their intervals. Yet they were near enough to give support when necessary or to finish the job by advancing.

When the three separate and successive maniples of the first cohort were united in order to form the united battle cohort of Marius and of Caesar, the same brain placed the most reliable men in the last lines, i.e., the oldest. The youngest, the most impetuous, were in the first lines. The legion was not increased simply to make numbers or mass. Each had his turn in action, each man in his maniple, each maniple in its cohort, and, when the unit became a cohort, each cohort in the order of battle.

We have seen that the Roman theory dictated a depth of ranks to furnish successive lines of combatants. The genius of the general modified these established formations. If the men were inured to war, well-trained, reliable, tenacious, quick to relieve their file leaders, full of confidence in their general and their own comrades, the general diminished the depth of the files, did away with the lines even, in order to increase the number of immediate combatants by increasing the front. His men having a moral, and sometimes also a physical endurance superior to that of the adversary, the general knew that the last ranks of the latter would not, under pressure, hold sufficiently to relieve the first lines nor to forbid the relief of his own. Hannibal had a part of his infantry, the Africans, armed and drilled in the Roman way; his Spanish infantrymen had the long wind of the Spaniards of today; his Gallic soldiers, tried out by hardship, were in the same way fit for long efforts. Hannibal, strong with the confidence with which he inspired his people, drew up a line less deep by half than the Roman army and at Cannae hemmed in an army which had twice his number and exterminated it. Caesar at Pharsalus, for similar reasons, did not hesitate to decrease his depth. He faced double his strength in the army of Pompey, a Roman army like his own, and crushed it.

We have mentioned Cannae and Pharsalus, we shall study in them the mechanism and the morale of ancient combat, two things which cannot be separated. We cannot find better examples of battle more clearly and more impartially exhibited. This is due in one case to the clear presentation of Polybius, who obtained his information from the fugitives from Cannae, possibly even from some of the conquerors; in the other it is due to the impassive clearness of Caesar in describing the art of war.

CHAPTER III - ANALYSIS OF THE BATTLE OF CANNAE

Recital of Polybius:

"Varro placed the cavalry on the right wing, and rested it on the river; the infantry was deployed near it and on the same line, the maniples drawn close to each other, with smaller intervals than usual, and the maniples presenting more depth than front.

"The cavalry of the allies, on the left wing, completed the line, in front of which were posted the light troops. There were in that army, including the allies, eighty thousand foot and a little more than six thousand horse.

"Meanwhile Hannibal had his slingers and light troops cross the Aufidus and posted them in front of his army. The rest crossed the river at two places. He placed the Iberian and Gallic cavalry on the left wing, next the river and facing the Roman cavalry. He placed on the same line, one half of the African infantry heavily armed, the Iberian and Gallic infantry, the other half of the African infantry, and finally the Numidian cavalry which formed the right wing.

"After he had thus arrayed all his troops upon a single line, he marched to meet the enemy with the Iberian and Gallic infantry moving independently of the main body. As it was joined in a straight line with the rest, on separating, it was formed like the convex face of a crescent. This formation reduced its depth in the center. The intention of the general was to commence the battle with the Iberians and Gauls, and have them supported by the Africans.

396

"The latter infantry was armed like the Roman infantry, having been equipped by Hannibal with arms that had been taken from the Romans in preceding battle. Both Iberians and Gauls had shields; but their swords were quite different. The sword of the former was as fit for thrusting as for cutting while that of the Gauls only cut with the edge, and at a limited distance. These troops were drawn up as follows: the Iberians were in two bodies of troops on the wings, near the Africans; the Gauls in the center. The Gauls were nude; the Iberians in linen shirts of purple color, which to the Romans was an extraordinary and frightening spectacle. The Carthaginian army consisted of ten thousand horse and little more than forty thousand foot.

"Aemilius commanded the right of the Romans, Varro the left; the two consuls of the past year, Servilius and Attilius, were in the center. On the Carthaginian side, Hasdrubal had the left under his orders, Hanno the right, and Hannibal, who had his brother Mago with him, reserved for himself the command of the center. The two armies did not suffer from the glare of the sun when it rose, the one being faced to the South, as I remarked, and the other to the North.

"Action commenced with the light troops, which were in front of both armies. The first engagement gave advantage to neither the one nor the other. Just as soon as the Iberian and Gallic cavalry on the left approached, the conflict became hot. The Romans fought with fury and rather more like barbarians than Romans. This falling back and then returning to the charge was not according to their tactics. Scarcely did they become engaged when they leaped from their horses and each seized his adversary. In the meanwhile the Carthaginians gained the upper hand. The greater number of the Romans remained on the ground after having fought with the greatest valor. The others were pursued along the river and cut to pieces without being able to obtain quarter.

"The heavily armed infantry immediately took the place of the light troops and became engaged. The Iberians and Gauls held firm at first and sustained the shock with vigor; but they soon gave way to the weight of the legions, and, opening the crescent, turned their backs and retreated. The Romans followed them with impetuosity, and broke the Gallic line much more easily because the wings crowded toward the center where the thick of the fighting was. The whole line did not fight at the same time. The action commenced in the center because the Gauls, being drawn up in the form of a crescent, left the wings far behind them, and presented the convex face of the crescent to the Romans. The latter then followed the Gauls and Iberians closely, and crowded towards the center, to the place where the enemy gave way, pushing ahead so forcibly that on both flanks they engaged the heavily armed Africans. The Africans on the right, in swinging about from right to left, found themselves all along the enemy's flank, as well as those on the left which made the swing from left to right. The very circumstances of the action showed them what they had to do. This was what Hannibal had foreseen; that the Romans pursuing the Gauls must be enveloped by the Africans. The Romans then, no longer able to keep their formation were forced to defend themselves man to man and in small groups against those who attacked them on front and flank.

"Aemilius had escaped the carnage on the right wing at the commencement of the battle. Wishing, according to the orders he had given, to be everywhere, and seeing that it was the legionary infantry that would decide the fate of the battle, he pushed his horse through the fray, warded off or killed every one who opposed him, and sought at the same time to reanimate the ardor of the Roman soldiers. Hannibal, who during the entire battle remained in the conflict, did the same in his army.

"The Numidian cavalry on the right wing, without doing or suffering much, was useful on that occasion by its manner of fighting; for, pouncing upon the enemy on all sides, they gave him enough to do so that he might not have time to think of helping his own people. Indeed, when the left wing, where Hasdrubal commanded, had routed almost all the cavalry of the Roman right wing, and a junction had been effected with the Numidians, the auxiliary cavalry did not wait to be attacked but gave way.

"Hasdrubal is said to have done something which proved his prudence and his ability, and which contributed to the success of the battle. As the Numidians were in great number, and as these troops were never more useful than when one was in flight before them, he gave them the fugitives to pursue, and led the Iberian and Gallic cavalry in a charge to aid the African infantry. He pounced on the Romans from the rear, and having bodies of cavalry charge into the mêlée at several places, he gave new strength to the Africans and made the arms drop from the hands of the adversaries. It was then that L. Aemilius, a citizen who during his whole life, as in this last conflict, had nobly fulfilled his duties to his country, finally succumbed, covered with mortal wounds.

"The Romans continued fighting, giving battle to those who were surrounding them. They resisted to the last. But as their numbers diminished more and more, they were finally forced into a smaller circle, and all put to the sword. Attilius and Servilius, two persons of great probity, who had distinguished themselves in the combat as true Romans, were also killed on that occasion.

"While this carnage was taking place in the center, the Numidians pursued the fugitives of the left wing. Most of them were cut down, others were thrown under their horses; some of them escaped to Venusia. Among these was Varro, the Roman general, that abominable man whose administration cost his country so dearly. Thus ended the battle of Cannae, a battle where prodigies of valor were seen on both sides.

"Of the six thousand horse of which the Roman cavalry was composed, only seventy Romans reached Venusia with Varro, and, of the auxiliary cavalry, only three hundred men found shelter in various towns. Ten thousand foot were taken prisoners, but they were not in the battle. Of troops in battle only about three thousand saved themselves in the nearby town; the balance, numbering about twenty thousand, died on the field of honor."

Hannibal lost in that action in the neighborhood of four thousand Gauls, fifteen hundred Iberians and Africans and two hundred horses. Let us analyze:

The light infantry troops were scattered in front of the armies and skirmished without result. The real combat commenced with the attack on the legitimate cavalry of the Roman left wing by the cavalry of Hannibal.

There, says Polybius, the fight grew thickest, the Romans fought with fury and much more like barbarians than like Romans; because this falling back, then returning to the charge was not according to their tactics; scarcely did they become engaged when they leaped from their horses and each seized his adversary, etc., etc.

This means that the Roman cavalry did not habitually fight hand to hand like the infantry. It threw itself in a gallop on the enemy cavalry. When within javelin range, if the enemy's cavalry had not turned in the opposite direction on seeing the Roman cavalry coming, the latter prudently slackened its gait, threw some javelins, and, making an about by platoons, took to the rear for the purpose of repeating the charge. The hostile cavalry did the same, and such an operation might be renewed several times, until one of the two, persuaded that his enemy was going to attack him with a dash, turned in flight and was pursued to the limit.

That day, the fight becoming hot, they became really engaged; the two cavalry bodies closed and man fought man. The fight was forced, however; as there was no giving way on one side or the other, it was necessary actually to attack. There was no space for skirmishing. Closed in by the Aufidus and the legions, the Roman cavalry could not operate (Livy). The Iberian and Gallic cavalry, likewise shut in and double the Roman cavalry, was forced into two lines; it could still less maneuver. This limited front served the Romans, inferior in number, who could thus be attacked only in front, that is by an equal number. It rendered, as we have said, contact inevitable. These two cavalry bodies placed chest to chest had to fight close, had to grapple man to man, and for riders mounted on simple saddle cloths and without stirrup, embarrassed with a shield, a lance, a saber or a sword, to grapple man to man is to grapple together, fall together and fight on foot. That is what happened, as the account of Titus Livius explains it in completing that of Polybius. The same thing happened every time that two ancient cavalry organizations really had to fight, as the battle of the Tecinus showed. This mode of action was all to the advantage of the Romans, who were well-armed and well-trained therein. Note the battle of Tecinus. The Roman light infantry was cut to pieces, but the elite of the Roman cavalry, although surprised and surrounded, fought a-foot and on horse back, inflicted more casualties on the cavalry of Hannibal than they suffered, and brought back from the field their wounded general. The Romans besides were well led by Consul Aemilius, a man of head and heart, who, instead of fleeing when his cavalry was defeated, went himself to die in the ranks of the infantry.

Meanwhile we see thirty to thirty-four hundred Roman cavalrymen nearly exterminated by six to seven thousand Gauls and Iberians who did not lose even two hundred men. Hannibal's entire cavalry lost but two hundred men on that day.

How can that be explained?

Because most of them died without dreaming of selling their lives and because they took to flight during the fight of the first line and were struck with impunity from behind. The words of Polybius: "Most of them remained on the spot after having defended themselves with the utmost valor," were consecrated words before Polybius. The conquered always console themselves with their bravery and conquerors never contradict. Unfortunately, the figures are there. The facts of the battle are found in the account, which sounds no note of desperation. The Gallic and Roman cavalry had each already made a brave effort by attacking each other from the front. This effort was followed by the terrible anxiety of close combat. The Roman cavalrymen, who from behind the combatants on foot were able to see the second Gallic line on horse back, gave ground. Fear very quickly made the disengaged ranks take to their horses, wheel about like a flock of sheep in a stampede, and abandon their comrades and themselves to the mercy of the conquerors.

Yet, these horsemen were brave men, the elite of the army, noble knights, guards of the consuls, volunteers of noble families.

The Roman cavalry defeated, Hasdrubal passed his Gallic and Iberian troopers behind Hannibal's army, to attack the allied cavalry till then engaged by the Numidians. The cavalry of the allies did not await the enemy. It turned its back immediately; pursued to the utmost by the Numidians who were numerous (three thousand), and excellent in pursuit, it was reduced to some three hundred men, without a struggle.

After the skirmishing of the light infantry troops, the foot-soldiers of the line met. Polybius has explained to us how the Roman infantry let itself be enclosed by the two wings of the Carthaginian army and taken in rear by Hasdrubal's cavalry. It is also probable that the Gauls and Iberians, repulsed in the first part of the action and forced to turn their backs, returned, aided by a portion of the light infantry, to the charge upon the apex of the wedge formed by the Romans and completed their encirclement.

But we know, as will be seen further on in examples taken from Caesar, that the ancient cavalryman was powerless against formed infantry, even against the isolated infantryman possessing coolness. The Iberian and Gallic cavalry ought to have found behind the Roman army the reliable triarians penned in, armed, with pikes. It might have held them in check, forced them to give battle, but done them little or no harm as long as the ranks were preserved.

We know that of Hannibal's infantry only twelve thousand at the most were equipped with Roman weapons. We know that his Gallic and Iberian infantry, protected by plain shields, had to fall back, turn, and probably lost in this part of the action very nearly the four thousand men, which the battle cost them.

Let us deduct the ten thousand men that had gone to the attack of Hannibal's camp and the five thousand which the latter must have left there. There remain:

A mass of seventy thousand men surrounded and slaughtered by twenty-eight thousand foot soldiers, or, counting Hasdrubal's cavalry, by thirty-six thousand men, by half their number.

It may be asked how seventy thousand men could have let themselves be slaughtered, without defense, by thirty-six thousand men less well-armed, when each combatant had but one man before him. For in close combat, and especially in so large an envelopment, the number of combatants immediately engaged was the same on each side. Then there were neither guns nor rifles able to pierce the mass by a converging fire and destroy it by the superiority of this fire over diverging fire. Arrows were exhausted in the first period of the action. It seems that, by their mass, the Romans must have presented an insurmountable resistance, and that while permitting the enemy to wear himself out against it, that mass had only to defend itself in order to repel assailants.

But it was wiped out.

In pursuit of the Gauls and Iberians, who certainly were not able, even with like morale, to stand against the superior arms of the legionaries, the center drove all vigorously before it. The wings, in order to support it and not to lose the intervals, followed its movement by a forward oblique march and formed the sides of the salient. The entire Roman army, in wedge order, marched to victory. Suddenly the wings were attacked by the African battalions; the Gauls, the Iberians, who had been in retreat, returned to the fight. The horsemen of Hasdrubal, in the rear, attacked the reserves. Everywhere there was combat, unexpected, unforeseen. At the moment when they believed themselves conquerors, everywhere, in front, to the right, to the left, in the rear, the Roman soldiers heard the furious clamor of combat.

The physical pressure was unimportant. The ranks that they were fighting had not half their own depth. The moral pressure was enormous. Uneasiness, then terror, took hold of them; the first ranks, fatigued or wounded, wanted to retreat; but the last ranks, frightened, withdrew, gave way and whirled into the interior of the wedge. Demoralized and not feeling themselves supported, the ranks engaged followed them, and the routed mass let itself be slaughtered. The weapons fell from their hands, says Polybius.

The analysis of Cannae is ended. Before passing to the recital of Pharsalus, we cannot resist the temptation, though the matter be a little foreign to the subject, to say a few words about the battles of Hannibal.

These battles have a particular character of stubbornness explained by the necessity for overcoming the Roman tenacity. It may be said that to Hannibal victory was not sufficient. He must destroy. Consequently he always tried to cut off all retreat for the enemy. He knew that with Rome, destruction was the only way of finishing the struggle.

He did not believe in the courage of despair in the masses; he believed in terror and he knew the value of surprise in inspiring it.

But it was not the losses of the Romans that was the most surprising thing in these engagements. It was the losses of Hannibal. Who, before Hannibal or after him, has lost as many as the Romans and yet been conqueror? To keep troops in action, until victory comes, with such losses, requires a most powerful hand.

He inspired his people with absolute confidence. Almost always his center, where he put his Gauls, his food for powder, was broken. But that did not seem to disquiet or trouble either him or his men.

It is true that his center was pierced by the Romans who were escaping the pressure of the two Carthaginian wings, that they were in disorder because they had fought and pushed back the Gauls, whom Hannibal knew how to make fight with singular tenacity. They probably felt as though they had escaped from a press, and, happy to be out of it, they thought only of getting further away from the battle and by no means of returning to the flanks or the rear of the enemy. In addition, although nothing is said about it, Hannibal had doubtless taken precautions against their ever returning to the conflict.

All that is probably true. The confidence of the Gallic troops, so broken through, is none the less surprising.

Hannibal, in order to inspire his people with such confidence, had to explain to them before the combat his plan of action, in such a way that treachery could not injure him. He must have warned his troops that the center would be pierced, but that he was not worried about it, because it was a foreseen and prepared affair. His troops, indeed, did not seem to be worried about it.

Let us leave aside his conception of campaigns, his greatest glory in the eyes of all. Hannibal was the greatest general of antiquity by reason of his admirable comprehension of the morale of combat, of the morale of the soldier whether his own or the enemy's. He shows his greatness in this respect in all the different incidents of war, of campaign, of action. His men were not better than the Roman soldiers. They were not as well armed, one-half less in number. Yet he was always the conqueror. He understood the value of morale. He had the absolute confidence of his people. In addition he had the art, in commanding an army, of always securing the advantage of morale.

In Italy he had, it is true, cavalry superior to that of the Romans. But the Romans had a much superior infantry. Had conditions been reversed, he would have changed his methods. The instruments of battle are valuable only if one knows how to use them, and Pompey, we shall see, was beaten at Pharsalus precisely because he had a cavalry superior to that of Caesar.

If Hannibal was vanquished at Zuma, it was because genius cannot accomplish the impossible. Zuma proved again the perfect knowledge of men that Hannibal possessed and his influence over the troops. His third line, the only one where he really had reliable soldiers, was the only one that fought. Beset on all sides, it slew two thousand Romans before it was conquered.

We shall see later what a high state of morale, what desperate fighting, this meant.

CHAPTER IV - ANALYSIS OF THE BATTLE OF PHARSALUS, AND SOME CHARACTERISTIC EXAMPLES

Here is Caesar's account of the battle of Pharsalus.

"As Caesar approached Pompey's camp, he noted that Pompey's army was placed in the following order:

"On the left wing were the 2nd and 3rd Legions which Caesar had sent to Pompey at the commencement of the operation, pursuant to a decree of the Senate, and which Pompey had kept. Scipio occupied the center with the legions from Syria. The legion from Cilicia was placed on the right wing together with the Spanish cohorts of Afranius. Pompey regarded the troops already mentioned as the most reliable of his army. Between them, that is, between the center and the wings, he had distributed the remainder, consisting of one hundred and ten complete cohorts in line. These were made up of forty-five thousand men, two thousand of whom were veterans, previously rewarded for their services, who had come to join him. He had scattered them throughout the whole line of battle. Seven cohorts had been left to guard his camp and the neighboring forts. His right wing rested on a stream with inaccessible banks; and, for that reason, he had placed all his seven thousand cavalry, his archers and his slingers (forty-two hundred men) on the left wing.

"Caesar, keeping his battle order, had placed the 10th Legion on the right wing, and on the left, the 9th, which was much weakened by the combats of Dyrrachium. To the latter he added the 8th in order to form something like a full legion from the two, and ordered them to support one another. He had eighty very completely organized cohorts in line, approximately twenty-two thousand men. Two cohorts had been left to guard the camp. Caesar had entrusted the command of the left wing to Anthony, that of the right to P. Sylla, and of the center to C. Domitius. He placed himself in front of Pompey. But when he saw the disposition of the opposing army, he feared that his right wing was going to be enveloped by Pompey's numerous cavalry. He therefore withdrew immediately from his third line a cohort from each legion (six cohorts), in order to form a fourth line, placed it to receive Pompey's cavalry and showed it what it had to do. Then he explained fully to these cohorts that the success of the day depended on their valor. At the same time he ordered the entire army, and in particular the third line, not to move without his command, reserving to himself authority to give the signal by means of the standard when he thought it opportune.

"Caesar then went through his lines to exhort his men to do well, and seeing them full of ardor, had the signal given.

"Between the two armies there was only enough space to give each the necessary distance for the charge. But Pompey had given his men orders to await the charge without stirring, and to let Caesar's army break its ranks upon them. He did this, they say, on the advice of C. Triarius, as a method of meeting the force of the first dash of Caesar's men. He hoped that their battle order would be broken up and his own soldiers, well disposed in ranks, would have to fight with sword in hand only men in disorder. He thought that this formation would best protect his troops from the force of the fall of heavy javelins. At the same time he hoped that Caesar's soldiers charging at the run would be out of breath and overcome with fatigue at the moment of contact. Pompey's immobility was an error because there is in every one an animation, a natural ardor that is instilled by the onset to the combat. Generals ought not to check but to encourage this ardor. It was for this reason that, in olden times, troops charged with loud shouts, all trumpets sounding, in order to frighten the enemy and encourage themselves.

"In the meanwhile, our soldiers, at the given signal advanced with javelins in hand; but having noticed that Pompey's soldiers were not running towards them, and taught by experience and trained by previous battles, they slowed down and stopped in the midst of their run, in order not to arrive out of breath and worn out. Some moments after, having taken up their run again, they launched their javelins, and immediately afterwards, according to Caesar's order drew their swords. The Pompeians conducted themselves perfectly. They received the darts courageously; they did not stir before the dash of the legions; they preserved their lines, and, having dispatched their javelins, drew their swords.

"At the same time Pompey's entire cavalry dashed from the left wing, as had been ordered, and the mass of his archers ran from all parts of the line. Our cavalry did not await the charge, but fell back a little. Pompey's cavalry became more pressing, and commenced to reform its squadrons and turn our exposed flank. As soon as Caesar saw this intention, he gave the signal to the fourth line of six cohorts. This line started directly and, standards low, they charged the Pompeian cavalry with such vigor and resolution that not a single man stood his ground. All wheeled about and not only withdrew in full flight, but gained the highest mountains as fast as they could. They left the archers and slingers without their defense and protection. These were all killed. At the same time the cohorts moved to the rear of Pompey's left wing, which was still fighting and resisting, and attacked it in rear.

"Meanwhile, Caesar had advanced his third line, which up to this moment had been kept quietly at its post. These fresh troops relieved those that were fatigued. Pompey's men, taken in rear, could no longer hold out and all took to flight.

"Caesar was not in error when he put these cohorts in a fourth line, particularly charged with meeting the cavalry, and urged them to do well, since their effort would bring victory. They repulsed the cavalry. They cut to pieces the slingers and archers. They turned Pompey's left wing, and this decided the day.

"When Pompey saw his cavalry repulsed and that portion of the army upon which he had counted the most seized with terror, he had little confidence in the rest. He quit the battle and galloped to his camp, where, addressing his centurions who were guarding the praetorian gate, he told them in a loud voice heard by the soldiers: 'Guard well the camp and defend it vigorously in case of attack; as for myself, I am going to make the tour of the other gates and assure their defense.'

"That said, he retired to the praetorium, despairing of success and awaiting events.

"After having forced the enemy to flee to his entrenchments Caesar, persuaded that he ought not to give the slightest respite to a terrorized enemy, incited his soldiers to profit by their advantage and attack the camp. Although overcome by the heat, for the struggle was prolonged into the middle of the day, they did not object to greater fatigue and obeyed. The camp was at first well defended by the cohorts on watch and especially by the Thracians and barbarians. The men who had fled from the battle, full of fright and overcome with fatigue, had nearly all thrown their arms and colors away and thought rather more of saving themselves than of defending the camp. Even those who defended the entrenchments were unable long to resist the shower of arrows. Covered with wounds, they abandoned the place, and led by their centurions and tribunes, they took refuge as quickly as they could in the high mountains near the camp.

"Caesar lost in this battle but two hundred soldiers, but nearly thirty of the bravest centurions were killed therein. Of Pompey's army fifteen thousand perished, and more than twenty-four thousand took refuge in the mountains. As Caesar had invested the mountains with entrenchments, they surrendered the following day."

Such is Caesar's account. His action is so clearly shown that there is scarcely any need of comment.

Initially Caesar's formation was in three lines. This was the usual battle order in the Roman armies, without being absolute, however, since Marius fought with two only. But, as we have said, according to the occasion, the genius of the chief decided the battle formation. There is no reason to suppose that Pompey's army was in a different order of battle.

To face that army, twice as large as his, Caesar, if he had had to preserve the disposition of cohorts in ten ranks, would have been able to form but one complete line, the first, and a second, half as numerous, as a reserve. But he knew the bravery of his troops, and he knew the apparent force of deep ranks to be a delusion. He did not hesitate to diminish his depth in order to keep the formation and morale of three-fifths of his troops intact, until the moment of their engagement. In order to be even more sure of the third line of his reserve, and in order to make sure that it would not be carried away by its enthusiasm for action, he paid it most particular attention. Perhaps, the text is doubtful, he kept it at double the usual distance in rear of the fighting lines.

Then, to guard against a turning movement by Pompey's seven thousand cavalry and forty-two hundred slingers and archers, a movement in which Pompey placed the hopes of victory, Caesar posted six cohorts that represented scarcely two thousand men. He had perfect confidence that these two thousand men would make Pompey's cavalry wheel about, and that his one thousand horsemen would then press the action so energetically that Pompey's cavalry would not even think of rallying. It happened so; and the forty-two hundred archers and slingers were slaughtered like sheep by these cohorts, aided, without doubt, by four-hundred foot young and agile, whom Caesar mixed with his thousand horsemen and who remained at this task, leaving the horsemen, whom they had relieved, to pursue the terror-stricken fugitives.

Thus were seven thousand horsemen swept away and forty-two hundred infantrymen slaughtered without a struggle, all demoralized simply by a vigorous demonstration.

The order to await the charge, given by Pompey to his infantry, was judged too severely by Caesar. Caesar certainly was right as a general rule; the enthusiasm of the troops must not be dampened, and the initiative of the attack indeed gives to the assailant a certain moral influence. But with trusted soldiers, duly trained, one can try a stratagem, and the men of Pompey had proven their dependability by awaiting on the spot, without stirring, a vigorous enemy in good order, when they counted on meeting him in disorder and out of breath. Though it may not have led to success, the advice of Triarius was not bad. Even the conduct of Caesar's men proves this. This battle shows the confidence of the soldier in the material rank in ancient combat, as assuring support and mutual assistance.

Notwithstanding the fact the Caesar's soldiers had the initiative in the attack, the first encounter decided nothing. It was a combat on the spot, a struggle of several hours. Forty-five thousand good troops lost scarcely two hundred men in this struggle for, with like arms, courage and ability, Pompey's infantry ought not to have lost in hand-to-hand fighting more than that of Caesar's. These same forty-five thousand men gave way, and, merely between the battle field and their camp, twelve thousand were slaughtered.

Pompey's men had twice the depth of Caesar's ranks, whose attack did not make them fall back a step. On the other hand their mass was unable to repel him, and he was fought on the spot. Pompey had announced to them, says Caesar, that the enemy's army would be turned by his cavalry, and suddenly, when they were fighting bravely, step by step, they heard behind them the shouts of attack by the six cohorts of Caesar, two thousand men.

Does it seem an easy matter for such a force to ward off this menace? No. The wing taken in rear in this way loses ground; more and more the contagion of fear spreads to the rest. Terror is so great that they do not think of re-forming in their camp, which is defended for a moment only by the cohorts on guard. Just as at Cannae, their arms drop from their hands. But for the good conduct of the camp guards which permitted the fugitives to gain the mountains, the twenty-four thousand prisoners of the next day might have been corpses that very day.

Cannae and Pharsalus, are sufficient to illustrate ancient combat. Let us, however, add some other characteristic examples, which we shall select briefly and in chronological order. They will complete our data.

Livy relates that in an action against some of the peoples in the neighborhood of Rome, I do not recall now which, the Romans did not dare to pursue for fear of breaking their ranks.

In a fight against the Hernici, he cites the Roman horsemen, who had not been able to do anything on horseback to break up the enemy, asking the consul for permission to dismount and fight on foot. This is true not only of Roman cavalrymen, for later on we shall see the best riders, the Gauls, the Germans, the Parthanians even, dismounting in order really to fight.

The Volsci, the Latini, the Hernici, etc., combined to fight the Romans; and as the action nears its end, Livy relates: "Finally, the first ranks having fallen, and carnage being all about them, they threw away their arms and started to scatter. The cavalry then dashed forward, with orders not to kill the isolated ones, but to harass the mass with their arrows, annoy it, to delay it, to prevent dispersion in order to permit the infantry to come up and kill."

In Hamilcar's engagement against the mercenaries in revolt, who up to then had always beaten the Carthaginians, the mercenaries endeavored to envelop him. Hamilcar surprised them by a new maneuver and defeated them. He marched in three lines: elephants, cavalry and light infantry, then heavily armed phalanxes. At the approach of the mercenaries who were marching vigorously towards him the two lines formed by the elephants, the cavalry and light infantry, turned about and moved quickly to place themselves on the flanks of the third line. The third line thus exposed met a foe which had thought only of pursuit, and which the surprise put to flight. It thus abandoned itself to the action of the elephants, horses and the light infantry who massacred the fugitives.

Hamilcar killed six thousand men, captured two thousand and lost practically nobody. It was a question as to whether he had lost a single man, since there had been no combat.

In the battle of Lake Trasimenus, the Carthaginians lost fifteen hundred men, nearly all Gauls; the Romans fifteen thousand and fifteen thousand prisoners. The battle raged for three hours.

At Zama, Hannibal had twenty thousand killed, twenty thousand prisoners; the Romans two thousand killed. This was a serious struggle in which Hannibal's third line alone fought. It gave way only under the attack on its rear and flank by the cavalry.

In the battle of Cynoscephalae, between Philip and Flaminius, Philip pressed Flaminius with his phalanx thirty-two deep. Twenty maniples took the phalanx from behind. The battle was lost by Philip. The Romans had seven hundred killed; the Macedonians eighty thousand, and five thousand prisoners.

At Pydna, Aemilius Paulus against Perseus, the phalanx marched without being stopped. But gaps occurred from the resistance that it encountered. Hundreds penetrated into the gaps in the phalanx and killed the men embarrassed with their long pikes. They were effective only when united, abreast, and at shaft's length. There was frightful disorder and butchery; twenty thousand killed, five thousand captured out of forty-four thousand engaged! The historian does not deem it worth while to speak of the Roman losses.

After the battle of Aix against the Teutons, Marius surprised the Teutons from behind. There was frightful carnage; one hundred thousand Teutons and three hundred Romans killed.

In Sulla's battle of Chaeronea against Archelaus, a general of Mithridates, Sulla had about thirty thousand men, Archelaus, one hundred and ten thousand. Archelaus was beaten by being surprised from the rear. The Romans lost fourteen men, and killed their enemies until worn out in pursuit.

The battle of Orchomenus, against Archelaus, was a repetition of Chaeronea.

Caesar states that his cavalry could not fight the Britons without greatly exposing itself, because they pretended flight in order to get the cavalry away from the infantry and then, dashing from their chariots, they fought on foot with advantage.

A little less than two hundred veterans embarked on a boat which they ran aground at night so as not to be taken by superior naval forces. They reached an advantageous position and passed the night. At the break of day, Otacilius dispatched some four hundred horsemen and some infantry from the Alesio garrison against them. They defended themselves bravely; and having killed some, they rejoined Caesar's troops without having lost a single man.

In Macedonia Caesar's rear-guard was caught by Pompey's cavalry at the passage of the Genusus River, the banks of which were quite steep. Caesar opposed Pompey's cavalry five to seven thousand strong, with his cavalry of six hundred to one thousand men, among which he had taken care to intermingle four hundred picked infantrymen. They did their duty so well that, in the combat that followed, they repulsed the enemy, killed many, and fell back upon their own army without the loss of a single man.

In the battle of Thapsus in Africa, against Scipio, Caesar killed ten thousand, lost fifty, and had some wounded.

In the battle under the walls of Munda in Spain, against one of Pompey's sons, Caesar had eighty cohorts and eight thousand horsemen, about forty-eight thousand men. Pompey with thirteen legions had sixty thousand troops of the line, six thousand cavalry, six thousand light infantry, six thousand auxiliaries; in all, about eighty thousand men. The struggle, says the narrator, was valiantly kept up, step by step, sword to sword.

In that battle of exceptional fury, which hung for a long time in the balance, Caesar had one thousand dead, five hundred wounded; Pompey thirty-three thousand dead, and if Munda had not been so near, scarcely two miles away, his losses would have been doubled. The defensive works of Munda were constructed from dead bodies and abandoned arms.

In studying ancient combats, it can be seen that it was almost always an attack from the flank or rear, a surprise action, that won battles, especially against the Romans. It was in this way that their excellent tactics might be confused. Roman tactics were so excellent that a Roman general who was only half as good as his adversary was sure to be victorious. By surprise alone they could be conquered. Note Xanthippe,—Hannibal—the unexpected fighting methods of the Gauls, etc.

Indeed Xenophon says somewhere, "Be it agreeable or terrible, the less anything is foreseen, the more does it cause pleasure or dismay. This is nowhere better illustrated than in war where every surprise strikes terror even to those who are much the stronger."

But very few fighters armed with cuirass and shield were killed in the front lines.

Hannibal in his victories lost almost nobody but Gauls, his cannon-fodder, who fought with poor shields and without armor.

Nearly always driven in, they fought, nevertheless, with a tenacity that they never showed under any other command.

Thucydides characterizes the combat of the lightly armed, by saying: "As a rule, the lightly armed of both sides took to flight."

In combat with closed ranks there was mutual pressure but little loss, the men not being at liberty to strike in their own way and with all their force.

Caesar against the Nervii, saw his men, who in the midst of the action had instinctively closed in mass in order to resist the mass of barbarians, giving way under pressure. He therefore ordered his ranks and files to open, so that his legionaries, closed in mass, paralyzed and forced to give way to a very strong pressure, might be able to kill and consequently demoralize the enemy. And indeed, as soon as a man in the front rank of the Nervii fell under the blows of the legionaries, there was a halt, a falling back. Following an attack from the rear, and a mêlée, the defeat of the Nervii ensued.

CHAPTER V - MORALE IN ANCIENT BATTLE

We now know the morale and mechanism of ancient fighting; the word mêlée employed by the ancients was many times stronger than the idea to be expressed; it meant a crossing of arms, not a confusion of men.

The results of battles, such as losses, suffice to demonstrate this, and an instant of reflection makes us see the error of the word mêlée. In pursuit it was possible to plunge into the midst of the fugitives, but in combat every one had too much need for the next man, for his neighbor, who was guarding his flanks and his back, to let himself be killed out of sheer wantonness by a sure blow from within the ranks of the enemy.

In the confusion of a real mêlée, Caesar at Pharsalus, and Hannibal at Cannae, would have been conquered. Their shallow ranks, penetrated by the enemy, would have had to fight two against one, they would even have been taken in rear in consequence of the breaking of their ranks.

Also has there not been seen, in troops equally reliable and desperate, that mutual weariness which brings about, with tacit accord, falling back for a breathing spell on both sides in order again to take up the battle?

How can this be possible with a mêlée?

With the confusion and medley of combatants, there might be a mutual extermination, but there would not be any victors. How would they recognize each other? Can you conceive two mixed masses of men or groups, where every one occupied in front can be struck with impunity from the side or from behind? That is mutual extermination, where victory belongs only to survivors; for in the mix-up and confusion, no one can flee, no one knows where to flee.

After all, are not the losses we have seen on both sides demonstration that there was no real mêlée?

The word is, therefore, too strong; the imagination of painters' and poets' has created the mêlée.

This is what happened:

At a charging distance troops marched towards the enemy with all the speed compatible with the necessity for fencing and mutual aid. Quite often, the moral impulse, that resolution to go to the end, manifested itself at once in the order and freedom of gait. That impulse alone put to flight a less resolute adversary.

It was customary among good troops to have a clash, but not the blind and headlong onset of the mass; the preoccupation of the rank was very great, as the behavior of Caesar's troops at Pharsalus shows in their slow march, timed by the flutes of Lacedaemonian battalions. At the moment of getting close to the enemy, the dash slackened of its own accord, because the men of the first rank, of necessity and instinctively, assured themselves of the position of their supports, their neighbors in the same line, their comrades in the second, and collected themselves together in order to be more the masters of their movements to strike and parry. There was a contact of man with man; each took the adversary in front of him and attacked him, because by penetrating into the ranks before having struck him down, he risked being wounded in the side by losing his flank supports. Each one then hit his man with his shield, expecting to make him lose his equilibrium, and at the instant he tried to recover himself landed the blow. The men in the second line, back of the intervals necessary for fencing in the first, were ready to protect their sides against any one that advanced between them and were prepared to relieve tired warriors. It was the same in the third line, and so on.

Every one being supported on either side, the first encounter was rarely decisive, and the fencing, the real combat at close quarters, began.

If men of the first line were wounded quickly, if the other ranks were not in a hurry to relieve or replace them, or if there was hesitation, defeat followed. This happened to the Romans in their first encounters with the Gauls. The Gaul, with his shield, parried the first thrust, brought his big iron sword swooping down with fury upon the top of the Roman shield, split it and went after the man. The Romans, already hesitating before the moral impulse of the Gauls, their ferocious yells, their nudeness, an indication of a contempt for wounds, fell then in a greater number than their adversaries and demoralization followed. Soon they accustomed themselves to this valorous but not tenacious spirit of their enemies, and when they had protected the top of their shields with an iron band, they no longer fell, and the roles were changed.

The Gauls, in fact, were unable either to hold their ground against the better arms and the thrusts of the Romans, or against their individual superior tenacity, increased nearly tenfold by the possible relay of eight ranks of the maniple. The maniples were self-renewing. Whereas with the Gauls the duration of the combat was limited to the strength of a single man, on account of the difficulties of close or tumultuous ranks, and the impossibility of replacing losses when they were fighting at close quarters.

If the weapons were nearly alike, preserving ranks and thereby breaking down, driving back and confusing the ranks of the enemy, was to conquer. The man in disordered, broken lines, no longer felt himself supported, but vulnerable everywhere, and he fled. It is true that it is hardly possible to break hostile lines without doing the same with one's own. But the one who breaks through first, has been able to do so only by making the foe fall back before his blows, by killing or wounding. He has thereby raised his courage and that of his neighbor. He knows, he sees where he is marching; whilst the adversary overtaken as a consequence of the retreat or the fall of the troops that were flanking him, is surprised. He sees himself exposed on the flank. He falls back on a line with the rank in rear in order to regain support. But the lines in the rear give way to the retreat of the first. If the withdrawal has a certain duration, terror comes as a result of the blows which drive back and mow down the first line. If, to make room for those pushed back, the last lines turn their backs, there is small chance that they will face the front again. Space has tempted them. They will not return to the fight.

Then by that natural instinct of the soldier to worry, to assure himself of his supports, the contagion of flight spreads from the last ranks to the first. The first, closely engaged, has been held to the fight in the meantime, under pain of immediate death. There is no need to explain what follows; it is butchery. (Caedes).

But to return to combat.

It is evident that the formation of troops in a straight line, drawn close together, existed scarcely an instant. Moreover each group of files formed in action was connected with the next group; the groups, like the individuals, were always concerned about their support. The fight took place along the line of contact of the first ranks of the army, a straight line, broken, curved, and bent in different directions according to the various chances of the action at such or such a point, but always restricting and separating the combatants of the two sides. Once engaged on that line, it was necessary to face the front under pain of immediate death. Naturally and necessarily every one in these first ranks exerted all his energy to defend his life.

At no point did the line become entangled as long as there was fighting, for, general or soldier, the effort of each one was to keep up the continuity of support all along the line, and to break or cut that of the enemy, because victory then followed.

We see then that between men armed with swords, it was possible to have, and there was, if the combat was serious, penetration of one mass into the other, but never confusion, or a jumble of ranks, by the men forming these masses.

Sword to sword combat was the most deadly. It presented the most sudden changes, because it was the one in which the individual valor and dexterity of the combatant had the greatest and most immediate influence. Other methods of combat were simpler.

Let us compare pikes and broadswords.

The close formation of men armed with pikes was irresistible so long as it was maintained. A forest of pikes fifteen to eighteen feet long kept you at a distance. On the other hand it was easy to kill off the cavalry and light infantry about the phalanx, which was an unwieldy mass marching with a measured step, and which a mobile body of troops could always avoid. Openings in the phalanx might be occasioned by marching, by the terrain, by the thousand accidents of struggle, by the individual assault of brave men, by the wounded on the ground creeping under the high held pikes and cutting at the legs of the front rank. Men in the phalanx could scarcely see and even the first two lines hardly had a free position for striking. The men were armed with long lances, useless at close quarters, good only for combat at shaft's length (Polybius). They were struck with impunity by the groups which threw themselves into the intervals. And then, once the enemy was in the body of the phalanx, morale disappeared and it became a mass without order, a flock of panic-stricken sheep falling over each other.

In a mob hard-pressed men prick with their knives those who press them. The contagion of fear changes the direction of the human wave; it bends back upon itself and breaks to escape danger. If, then, the enemy fled before the phalanx there was no mêlée. If he gave way tactically before it and availing himself of gaps penetrated it by groups, still there was no mêlée or mixture of ranks. The wedge entering into a mass does not become intermingled with it.

With a phalanx armed with long pikes against a similar phalanx there was still less confusion. They were able to stand for a long time, if the one did not take the other in flank or in rear by a detached body of troops. In all ancient combat, even in victory achieved by methods which affected the morale, such methods are always effective, for man does not change.

It is unnecessary to repeat that in ancient conflicts, demoralization and flight began in the rear ranks.

We have tried to analyze the fight of infantry of the line because its action alone was decisive in ancient combat. The light infantry of both sides took to flight, as Thucydides states. They returned later to pursue and massacre the vanquished.

In cavalry against cavalry, the moral effect of a mass charging in good order was of the greatest influence. We rarely see two cavalry organizations, neither of which breaks before such reciprocal action. Such action was seen on the Tecinus and at Cannae, engagements cited merely because they are very rare exceptions. And even in these cases there was no shock at full speed, but a halt face to face and then an engagement.

The hurricanes of cavalry of those days were poetic figures. They had no reality. In an encounter at full speed, men and horses would be crushed, and neither men nor horses wished such an encounter. The hands of the cavalrymen reined back, the instinct of men and horses was to slacken, to stop, if the enemy himself did not stop, and to make an about if he continued to advance. And if ever they met, the encounter was so weakened by the hands of the men, the rearing of the horses, the swinging of heads, that it was a face to face stop. Some blows were exchanged with the sword or the lance, but the equilibrium was too unstable, mutual support too uncertain for real sword play. Man felt himself too isolated. The moral pressure was too strong. Although not deadly, the combat lasted but a second, precisely because man felt himself, saw himself, alone and surrounded. The first men, who believed themselves no longer supported, could no longer endure uneasiness: they wheeled about and the rest followed. Unless the enemy had also turned, he then pursued at his pleasure until checked by other cavalry, which pursued him in turn.

There never was an encounter between cavalry and infantry. The cavalry harassed with its arrows, with the lance perhaps, while passing rapidly, but it never attacked.

Close conflict on horseback did not exist. And to be sure, if the horse by adding so much to the mobility of man gave him the means of menacing and charging with swiftness, it permitted him to escape with like rapidity when his menace did not shake the enemy. Man by using the horse, pursuant to his natural inclination and sane reasoning, could do as much damage as possible while risking the least possible. To riders without stirrups or saddle, for whom the throwing of the javelin was a difficult matter (Xenophon), combat was but a succession of reciprocal harassings, demonstrations, menaces, skirmishes with arrows. Each cavalry sought an opportunity to surprise, to intimidate, to avail itself of disorder, and to pursue either the cavalry or the infantry. Then "vae victis;" the sword worked.

Man always has had the greatest fear of being trampled upon by horses. That fear has certainly routed a hundred thousand times more men than the real encounter. This was always more or less avoided by the horse, and no one was knocked down. When two ancient cavalry forces wanted really to fight, were forced to it, they fought on foot (Note the Tecinus, Cannae, examples of Livy). I find but little real fighting on horseback in all antiquity like that of Alexander the Great at the passage of the Granicus. Was even that fighting? His cavalry which traversed a river with steep banks defended by the enemy, lost eighty-five men; the Persian cavalry one thousand; and both were equally well armed!

The fighting of the Middle Ages revived the ancient battles except in science. Cavalrymen attacked each other perhaps more than the ancient cavalry did, for the reason that they were invulnerable: it was not sufficient to throw them down; it was necessary to kill when once they were on the ground. They knew, however, that their fighting on horseback was not important so far as results were concerned, for when they wished really to battle, they fought on foot. (Note the combat of the Thirty, Bayard, etc.)

The victors, arrayed in iron from head to foot, lost no one, the peasants did not count. If the vanquished was taken, he was not massacred, because chivalry had established a fraternity of arms between noblemen, the mounted warriors of different nations, and ransom replaced death.

If we have spoken especially of the infantry fight, it is because it was the most serious. On foot, on horseback, on the bridge of a vessel, at the moment of danger, the same man is always found. Any one who knows him well, deduces from his action in the past what his action will be in the future.

CHAPTER VI - UNDER WHAT CONDITIONS REAL COMBATANTS ARE OBTAINED AND HOW THE FIGHTING OF OUR DAYS, IN ORDER TO BE WELL DONE, REQUIRES THEM TO BE MORE DEPENDABLE THAN IN ANCIENT COMBAT

Let us repeat now, what we said at the beginning of this study. Man does not enter battle to fight, but for victory. He does everything that he can to avoid the first and obtain the second. The continued improvement of all appliances of war has no other goal than the annihilation of the enemy. Absolute bravery, which does not refuse battle even on unequal terms, trusting only to God or to destiny, is not natural in man; it is the result of moral culture. It is infinitely rare, because in the face of danger the animal sense of self-preservation always gains the upper hand. Man calculates his chances, with what errors we are about to see.

Now, man has a horror of death. In the bravest, a great sense of duty, which they alone are capable of understanding and living up to, is paramount. But the mass always cowers at sight of the phantom, death. Discipline is for the purpose of dominating that horror by a still greater horror, that of punishment or disgrace. But there always comes an instant when natural horror gets an upper hand over discipline, and the fighter flees. "Stop, stop, hold out a few minutes, an instant more, and you are victor! You are not even wounded yet,—if you turn your back you are dead!" He does not hear, he cannot hear any more. He is full of fear. How many armies have sworn to conquer or perish? How many have kept their oaths? An oath of sheep to stand up against wolves. History shows, not armies, but firm souls who have fought unto death, and the devotion of Thermopylae is therefore justly immortal.

Here we are again brought to the consideration of essential truths, enunciated by many men, now forgotten or unknown.

To insure success in the rude test of conflict, it is not sufficient to have a mass composed of valiant men like the Gauls or the Germans.

The mass needs, and we give it, leaders who have the firmness and decision of command proceeding from habit and an entire faith in their unquestionable right to command as established by tradition, law and society.

We add good arms. We add methods of fighting suitable to these arms and those of the enemy and which do not overtax the physical and moral forces of man. We add also a rational decentralization that permits the direction and employment of the efforts of all even to the last man.

We animate with passion, a violent desire for independence, a religious fanaticism, national pride, a love of glory, a madness for possession. An iron discipline, which permits no one to escape action, secures the greatest unity from top to bottom, between all the elements, between the commanding officers, between the commanding officers and men, between the soldiers.

Have we then a solid army? Not yet. Unity, that first and supreme force of armies, is sought by enacting severe laws of discipline supported by powerful passions. But to order discipline is not enough. A vigilance from which no one may escape in combat should assure the maintenance of discipline. Discipline itself depends on moral pressure which actuates men to advance from sentiments of fear or pride. But it depends also on surveillance, the mutual supervision of groups of men who know each other well.

A wise organization insures that the personnel of combat groups changes as little as possible, so that comrades in peace time maneuvers shall be comrades in war. From living together, and obeying the same chiefs, from commanding the same men, from sharing fatigue and rest, from coöperation among men who quickly understand each other in the execution of warlike movements, may be bred brotherhood, professional knowledge, sentiment, above all unity. The duty of obedience, the right of imposing discipline and the impossibility of escaping from it, would naturally follow.

And now confidence appears.

It is not that enthusiastic and thoughtless confidence of tumultous or unprepared armies which goes up to the danger point and vanishes rapidly, giving way to a contrary sentiment, which sees treason everywhere. It is that intimate confidence, firm and conscious, which does not forget itself in the heat of action and which alone makes true combatants.

Then we have an army; and it is no longer difficult to explain how men carried away by passions, even men who know how to die without flinching, without turning pale, really strong in the presence of death, but without discipline, without solid organization, are vanquished by others individually less valiant, but firmly, jointly and severally combined.

One loves to picture an armed mob upsetting all obstacles and carried away by a blast of passion.

There is more imagination than truth in that picture. If the struggle depended on individuals, the courageous, impassioned men, composing the mob would have more chance of victory. But in any body of troops, in front of the enemy, every one understands that the task is not the work of one alone, that to complete it requires team work. With his comrades in danger brought together under unknown leaders, he feels the lack of union, and asks himself if he can count on them. A thought of mistrust leads to hesitation. A moment of it will kill the offensive spirit.

Unity and confidence cannot be improvised. They alone can create that mutual trust, that feeling of force which gives courage and daring. Courage, that is the temporary domination of will over instinct, brings about victory.

Unity alone then produces fighters. But, as in everything, there are degrees of unity. Let us see whether modern is in this respect less exacting than ancient combat.

In ancient combat there was danger only at close quarters. If the troops had enough morale (which Asiatic hordes seldom had) to meet the enemy at broadsword's length, there was an engagement. Whoever was that close knew that he would be killed if he turned his back; because, as we have seen, the victors lost but few and the vanquished were exterminated. This simple reasoning held the men and made them fight, if it was but for an instant.

Neglecting the exceptional and very rare circumstances, which may bring two forces together, action today is brought on and fought out from afar. Danger begins at great distances, and it is necessary to advance for a long time under fire which at each step becomes heavier. The vanquished loses prisoners, but often, in dead and in wounded, he does not lose more than the victor.

Ancient combat was fought in groups close together, within a small space, in open ground, in full view of one another, without the deafening noise of present day arms. Men in formation marched into an action that took place on the spot and did not carry them thousands of feet away from the starting point. The surveillance of the leaders was easy, individual weakness was immediately checked. General consternation alone caused flight.

Today fighting is done over immense spaces, along thinly drawn out lines broken every instant by the accidents and the obstacles of the terrain. From the time the action begins, as soon as there are rifle shots, the men spread out as skirmishers or, lost in the inevitable disorder of a rapid march, escape the supervision of their commanding officers. A considerable number conceal themselves; they get away from the engagement and diminish by just so much the material and moral effect and confidence of the brave ones who remain. This can bring about defeat.

But let us look at man himself in ancient combat and in modern. In ancient combat:—I am strong, apt, vigorous, trained, full of calmness, presence of mind; I have good offensive and defensive weapons and trustworthy companions of long standing. They do not let me be overwhelmed without aiding me. I with them, they with me, we are invincible, even invulnerable. We have fought twenty battles and not one of us remained on the field. It is necessary to support each other in time; we see it clearly; we are quick to replace ourselves, to put a fresh combatant in front of a fatigued adversary. We are the legions of Marius, fifty thousand who have held out against the furious avalanches of the Cimbri. We have killed one hundred and forty thousand, taken prisoner sixty thousand, while losing but two or three hundred of our inexperienced soldiers.

Today, as strong, firm, trained, and courageous as I am, I can never say; I shall return. I have no longer to do with men, whom I do not fear, I have to do with fate in the form of iron and lead. Death is in the air, invisible and blind, whispering, whistling. As brave, good, trustworthy, and devoted as my companions may be, they do not shield me. Only,—and this is abstract and less immediately intelligible to all than the material support of ancient combat,—only I imagine that the more numerous we are who run a dangerous risk, the greater is the chance for each to escape therefrom. I also know that, if we have that confidence which none of us should lack in action, we feel, and we are, stronger. We begin more resolutely, are ready to keep up the struggle longer, and therefore finish it more quickly.

We finish it! But in order to finish it, it is necessary to advance, to attack the enemy, and infantryman or troopers, we are naked against iron, naked against lead, which cannot miss at close range. Let us advance in any case, resolutely. Our adversary will not stand at the point-blank range of our rifle, for the attack is never mutual, we are sure of that. We have been told so a thousand times. We have seen it. But what if matters should change now! Suppose the enemy stands at point-blank range! What of that?

How far this is from Roman confidence!

In another place we have shown that in ancient times to retire from action was both a difficult and perilous matter for the soldier. Today the temptation is much stronger, the facility greater and the peril less.

Now, therefore, combat exacts more moral cohesion, greater unity than previously. A last remark on the difficulty of obtaining it will complete the demonstration.

Since the invention of fire arms, the musket, the rifle, the cannon, the distances of mutual aid and support have increased among the different arms.

Besides, the facility of communications of all kinds permits the assembling on a given territory of enormous forces. For these reasons, as we have stated, battle fields have become immense.

Supervision becomes more and more difficult. Direction being more distant tends more often to escape from the supreme commanders and the subordinate leaders. The certain and inevitable disorder, which a body of troops always presents in action, is with the moral effect of modern appliances, becoming greater every day. In the midst of the confusion and the vacillation of firing lines, men and commanding officers often lose each other.

Troops immediately and hotly engaged, such as companies and squads, can maintain themselves only if they are well-organized and serve as supports or rallying points to those out of place. Battles tend to become now, more than they have ever been, the battles of men.

This ought not to be true! Perhaps. But the fact is that it is true.

Not all troops are immediately or hotly engaged in battle. Commanding officers always try to keep in hand, as long as possible, some troops capable of marching, acting at any moment, in any direction. Today, like yesterday, like tomorrow, the decisive action is that of formed troops. Victory belongs to the commander who has known how to keep them in good order, to hold them, and to direct them.

That is incontrovertible.

But commanders can hold out decisive reserves only if the enemy has been forced to commit his.

In troops which do the fighting, the men and the officers closest to them, from corporal to battalion commander, have a more independent action than ever. As it is alone the vigor of that action, more independent than ever of the direction of higher commanders, which leaves in the hands of higher commanders available forces which can be directed at a decisive moment, that action becomes more preponderant than ever. Battles, now more than ever, are battles of men, of captains. They always have been in fact, since in the last analysis the execution belongs to the man in ranks. But the influence of the latter on the final result is greater than formerly. From that comes the maxim of today: The battles of men.

Outside of the regulations on tactics and discipline, there is an evident necessity for combating the hazardous predominance of the action of the soldier over that of the commander. It is necessary to delay as long as possible, that instant which modern conditions tend to hasten—the instant when the soldier gets from under the control of the commander.

This completes the demonstration of the truth stated before: Combat requires today, in order to give the best results, a moral cohesion, a unity more binding than at any other time. It is as true as it is clear, that, if one does not wish bonds to break, one must make them elastic in order to strengthen them.

CHAPTER VII - PURPOSE OF THIS STUDY WHAT WOULD BE NECESSARY TO COMPLETE IT

Any other deductions on this subject must come from the meditations of the reader. To be of value in actual application such deductions should be based upon study of modern combat, and that study cannot be made from the accounts of historians alone.

The latter show the action of troop units only in a general way. Action in detail and the individual action of the soldier remain enveloped in a cloud of dust, in narratives as in reality. Yet these questions must be studied, for the conditions they reveal should be the basis of all fighting methods, past, present and future.

Where can data on these questions be found?

We have very few records portraying action as clearly as the report on the engagement at the Pont de l'Hôpital by Colonel Bugeaud. Such stories in even greater detail, for the smallest detail has its importance, secured from participants and witnesses who knew how to see and knew how to remember, are what is necessary in a study of the battle of today.

The number of killed, the kind and the character of wounds, often tell more than the longest accounts. Sometimes they contradict them. We want to know how man in general and the Frenchman in particular fought yesterday. Under the pressure of danger, impelled by the instinct for self-preservation, did he follow, make light of, or forget the methods prescribed or recommended? Did he fight in the manner imposed upon him, or in that indicated to him by his instinct or by his knowledge of warfare?

When we have the answers to these questions we shall be very near to knowing how he will conduct himself, with and against appliances far more destructive today than those of yesterday. Even now, knowing that man is capable only of a given quantity of terror, knowing that the moral effect of destruction is in proportion to the force applied, we are able to predict that, tomorrow less than ever will studied methods be practicable. Such methods are born of the illusions of the field of fire and are opposed to the teachings of our own experience. Tomorrow, more than ever, will the individual valor of the soldier and of small groups, be predominant. This valor is secured by discipline.

The study of the past alone can give us a true perception of practical methods, and enable us to see how the soldier will inevitably fight tomorrow.

So instructed, so informed, we shall not be confused; because we shall be able to prescribe beforehand such methods of fighting, such organization, such dispositions as are seen to be inevitable. Such prescriptions may even serve to regulate the inevitable. At any rate they will serve to reduce the element of chance by enabling the commanding officer to retain control as long as possible, and by releasing the individual only at the moment when instinct dominates him.

This is the only way to preserve discipline, which has a tendency to go to pieces by tactical disobedience at the moment of greatest necessity.

It should be understood that the prescriptions in question have to do with dispositions before action; with methods of fighting, and not with maneuvers.

Maneuvers are the movements of troops in the theater of action, and they are the swift and ordered movement on the scene of action of tactical units of all sizes. They do not constitute action. Action follows them.

Confusion in many minds between maneuvers and action brings about doubt and mistrust of our regulation drills. These are good, very good as far as they go, inasmuch as they give methods of executing all movements, of taking all possible formations with rapidity and good order.

To change them, to discuss them, does not advance the question one bit. They do not affect the problem of positive action. Its solution lies in the study of what took place yesterday, from which, alone, it is possible to deduce what will happen tomorrow.

This study must be made, and its result set forth. Each leader, whose worth and authority has been tested in war and recognized by armies, has done something of the sort. Of each of these even might be said, "He knew the soldier; he knew how to make use of him."

The Romans, too, had this knowledge. They obtained it from continuous experience and profound reflexion thereon.

Experience is not continuous today. It must be carefully gathered. Study of it should be careful and the results should stimulate reflexion, especially in men of experience. Extremes meet in many things. In ancient times at the point of the pike and sword, armies have conquered similar armies twice their size. Who knows if, in these days of perfected long-range arms of destruction, a small force might not secure, by a happy combination of good sense or genius with morale and appliances, these same heroic victories over a greater force similarly armed?

In spite of the statements of Napoleon I, his assumption that victory is always on the side of the strongest battalions was costly.

PART TWO: MODERN BATTLE

CHAPTER I - GENERAL DISCUSSION

1. Ancient and Modern Battle

I have heard philosophers reproached for studying too exclusively man in general and neglecting the race, the country, the era, so that their studies of him offer little of real social or political value. The opposite criticism can be made of military men of all countries. They are always eager to expound traditional tactics and organization suitable to the particular character of their race, always the bravest of all races. They fail to consider as a factor in the problem, man confronted by danger. Facts are incredibly different from all theories. Perhaps in this time of military reorganization it would not be out of place to make a study of man in battle and of battle itself.

The art of war is subjected to many modifications by industrial and scientific progress. But one thing does not change, the heart of man. In the last analysis, success in battle is a matter of morale. In all matters which pertain to an army, organization, discipline and tactics, the human heart in the supreme moment of battle is the basic factor. It is rarely taken into account; and often strange errors are the result. Witness the carbine, an accurate and long range weapon, which has never given the service expected of it, because it was used mechanically without considering the human heart. We must consider it!

With improvement in weapons, the power of destruction increases, the moral effect of such weapons increases, and courage to face them becomes rarer. Man does not, cannot change. What should increase with the power of material is the strength of organization, the unity of the fighting machine. Yet these are most neglected. A million men at maneuvers are useless, if a sane and reasoned organization does not assure their discipline, and thereby their reliability, that is, their courage in action.

Four brave men who do not know each other will not dare to attack a lion. Four less brave, but knowing each other well, sure of their reliability and consequently of mutual aid, will attack resolutely. There is the science of the organization of armies in a nutshell.

At any time a new invention may assure victory. Granted. But practicable weapons are not invented every day, and nations quickly put themselves on the same footing as regards armament. The determining factor, leaving aside generals of genius, and luck, is the quality of troops, that is, the organization that best assures their esprit, their reliability, their confidence, their unity. Troops, in this sense, means soldiers. Soldiers, no matter how well drilled, who are assembled haphazard into companies and battalions will never have, have never had, that entire unity which is born of mutual acquaintanceship.

In studying ancient battle, we have seen what a terrible thing battle is. We have seen that man will not really fight except under disciplinary pressure. Even before having studied modern battle, we know that the only real armies are those to which a well thought out and rational organization gives unity throughout battle. The destructive power of improved firearms becomes greater. Battle becomes more open, hindering supervision, passing beyond the vision of the commander and even of subordinate officers. In the same degree, unity should be strengthened. The organization which assures unity of the combatants should be better thought out and more rational. The power of arms increases, man and his weaknesses remain the same. What good is an army of two hundred thousand men of whom only one-half really fight, while the other one hundred thousand disappear in a hundred ways? Better to have one hundred thousand who can be counted upon.

The purpose of discipline is to make men fight in spite of themselves. No army is worthy of the name without discipline. There is no army at all without organization, and all organization is defective which neglects any means to strengthen the unity of combatants. Methods cannot be identical. Draconian discipline does not fit our customs. Discipline must be a state of mind, a social institution based on the salient virtues and defects of the nation.

Discipline cannot be secured or created in a day. It is an institution, a tradition. The commander must have confidence in his right to command. He must be accustomed to command and proud to command. This is what strengthens discipline in armies commanded by an aristocracy in certain countries.

The Prussians do not neglect the homogeneity and consequent unity of organization. They recognize its value. Hessian regiments are composed, the first year, of one-third Hessians, two-thirds Prussians, to control the racial tendencies of troops of a recently annexed country; the second year, of two-thirds Hessians, one-third Prussians; the third year, all Hessians with their own officers.

The Americans have shown us what happens in modern battle to large armies without cohesion. With them the lack of discipline and organization has had the inevitable result. Battle has been between hidden skirmishers, at long distance, and has lasted for days, until some faulty movement, perhaps a moral exhaustion, has caused one or the other of the opposing forces to give way.

In this American War, the mêlées of Agincourt are said to have reappeared, which merely means a mêlée of fugitives. But less than ever has there been close combat.

To fight from a distance is instinctive in man. From the first day he has worked to this end, and he continues to do so. It was thought that with long range weapons close combat might return. On the contrary troops keep further off before its effects.

The primitive man, the Arab, is instability incarnate. A breath, a nothing, governs him at each instant in war. The civilized man, in war, which is opposed to civilization, returns naturally to his first instincts.

With the Arab war remains a matter of agility and cunning. Hunting is his principal pastime and the pursuit of wild beasts teaches the pursuit of man. General

Daumas depicts Arabs as cavaliers. What more chivalrous warfare than the night surprise and sack of a camp! Empty words!!

It is commonly said that modern war is the most recondite of things, requiring experts. War, so long as man risks his skin in it, will always be a matter of instinct.

Ancient battle resembled drill. There is no such resemblance in modern battle. This greatly disconcerts both officers and soldiers.

Ancient battles were picnics, for the victors, who lost nobody. Not so today.

Artillery played no part in ancient battle.

The invention of firearms has diminished losses in battle. The improvement of firearms continues to diminish losses. This looks like a paradox. But statistics prove it. Nor is it unreasonable.

Does war become deadlier with the improvement of weapons? Not at all. Man is capable of standing before a certain amount of terror; beyond that he flees from battle. The battle of Pharsalus lasted some four hours. Caesar broke his camp, which is done in the morning; then the formation for battle; then the battle, etc. And he says that his troops were tired, the battle having lasted up to noon. This indicates that he considered it long.

For the middle ages, consult Froissart. The knights in the Battle of the Thirty were armed for battle on foot which they preferred in a serious affair, that is to say in a restricted space. There was a halt, a rest in the combat, when the two parties became exhausted. The Bretons, at this rest, were twenty-five against thirty. The battle had lasted up to exhaustion without loss by the English! Without Montauban the battle would have been terminated by complete and mutual exhaustion and without further losses. For the greater the fatigue, the less strength remained for piercing the armor. Montauban was at the same time felon and hero; felon because he did a thing not permitted by the code of combat; hero, because, if the Bretons had not ably profited by the disorder, he would have been killed when he entered the English formation alone. At the end of the contest the Bretons had four killed, the English eight. Four of the killed were overcome by their armor.

Explain how, under Turenne, men held much longer under fire than today. It is perfectly simple. Man is capable of standing before only a certain amount of terror. Today there must be swallowed in five minutes what took an hour under Turenne. An example will be given.

With the present arms, whose usage is generally known, the instruction of the soldier is of little importance. It does not make the soldier. Take as an example the case of the peasants of the Vendée. Their unity and not individual instruction made them soldiers, whose value could not be denied. Such unity was natural in people of the same village of the same commune, led in battle by their own lords, their own priests, etc.

The greater the perfection of weapons, the more dreadful becomes modern battle, and discipline becomes more difficult to maintain.

The less mobile the troops, the deadlier are battles. Bayonet attacks are not so easily made today, and morale consequently is less affected, man fearing man more than death. Astonishing losses seem to have been suffered without breaking by Turenne's armies. Were the casualty reports submitted by the captains of those days correct?

Frederick liked to say that three men behind the enemy were worth more than fifty in front of him, for moral effect. The field of action today is more extensive than in Frederick's time. Battle is delivered on more accidented terrain, as armies with great mobility do not need any particular terrain to fight on.

The nature of ancient arms required close order. Modern arms require open order, and they are at the same time of such terrible power that against them too often discipline is broken. What is the solution? Have your combatants opened out? Have them well acquainted with each other so as to have unity. Have reserves to threaten with, held with an iron hand.

Modern weapons have a terrible effect and are almost unbearable by the nervous system. Who can say that he has not been frightened in battle? Discipline in battle becomes the more necessary as the ranks become more open, and the material cohesion of the ranks not giving confidence, it must spring from a knowledge of comrades, and a trust in officers, who must always be present and seen. What man today advances with the confidence that rigid discipline and pride in himself gave the Roman soldier, even though the contest is no longer with man but with fate?

Today the artillery is effective at great distances. There is much liberty of movement for the different arms. The apparent liaison between arms is lessened. This has its influence on morale. There is another advantage in reliable troops, in that they can be extended more widely, and will consequently suffer smaller losses and be in better morale for close conflict.

The further off one is, the more difficult it is to judge of the terrain. Consequently the greater is the necessity for scouting, for reconnoitering the terrain by skirmishers. This is something that the Duke of Gramont forgot at Nordlingen, and which is often forgotten; but it constitutes another important reason for the use of skirmishers.

The formation in rank is a disciplinary measure against the weakness of man in the face of danger. This weakness is greater today in that the moral action of weapons is more powerful, and that the material rank has the inherent lack of cohesion of open order. However, open order is necessary to economize losses and permit the use of weapons. Thus today there is greater necessity than ever for the rank, that is for discipline, not for the geometrical rank. It is at the same time more necessary and doubly difficult to attain.

In ancient battle unity existed, at least with the Greeks and the Romans. The soldier was known to his officer and comrades; they saw that he fought.

In modern armies where losses are as great for the victor as for the vanquished, the soldier must more often be replaced. In ancient battle the victor had no losses. Today the soldier is often unknown to his comrades. He is lost in the smoke, the dispersion, the confusion of battle. He seems to fight alone. Unity is no longer insured by mutual surveillance. A man falls, and disappears. Who knows whether it was a bullet or the fear of advancing further that struck him! The ancient combatant was never struck by an invisible weapon and could not fall in this way. The more difficult surveillance, the more necessary becomes the individuality of companies, sections, squads. Not the least of their boasts should be their ability to stand a roll call at all times.

The ancients often avoided hand to hand conflict, so terrible were its consequences. In modern combat, there never is hand to hand conflict if one stands fast.

From day to day close combat tends to disappear. It is replaced by fire action; above all by the moral action of maneuvers. Dispersion brings us back to the necessity for the unity which was an absolute necessity in ancient battle.

Strategy is a game. The first strategist, long before Napoleon, was Horace with his three enemies.

The size of the battle field permits, less than ever, holding units together; the role of the general is much more difficult: many more chances are left to fate. Thus the greater the necessity for the best troops who know best their trade, who are most dependable and of greatest fortitude. To diminish the effect of luck, it is necessary to hold longer, to wait for help from a distance. Battles resolve themselves into battles of soldiers. The final decision is more difficult to obtain. There is a strange similarity in battle at one league to battle at two paces. The value of the soldier is the essential element of success. Let us strengthen the soldier by unity.

Battle has more importance than ever. Communication facilities such as the telegraph, concentration facilities such as the railroad, render more difficult such strategic surprises as Ulm and Jena. The whole forces of a country can thus be united. So united, defeat becomes irreparable, disorganization greater and more rapid.

In modern combat the mêlée really exists more than in ancient battle. This appears paradoxical. It is true nevertheless of the mêlée taken in the sense of a mixed up affair where it is infinitely difficult to see clearly.

Man, in the combat of our days, is a man who, hardly knowing how to swim, is suddenly thrown into the sea.

The good quality of troops will more than ever secure victory.

As to the comparative value of troops with cohesion and of new troops, look at the Zouaves of the Guard or the Grenadiers at Magenta, and the 55th at Solferino.

Nothing should be neglected to make the battle order stronger, man stronger.

2. Moral Elements in Battle

When, in complete security, after dinner, in full physical and moral contentment, men consider war and battle they are animated by a noble ardor that has nothing in common with reality. How many of them, however, even at that moment, would be ready to risk their lives? But oblige them to march for days and weeks to arrive at the battle ground, and on the day of battle oblige them to wait minutes, hours, to deliver it. If they were honest they would testify how much the physical fatigue and the mental anguish that precede action have lowered their morale, how much less eager to fight they are than a month before, when they arose from the table in a generous mood.

Man's heart is as changeable as fortune. Man shrinks back, apprehends danger in any effort in which he does not foresee success. There are some isolated characters of an iron temper, who resist the tendency; but they are carried away by the great majority (Bismarck).

Examples show that if a withdrawal is forced, the army is discouraged and takes flight (Frederick). The brave heart does not change.

Real bravery, inspired by devotion to duty, does not know panic and is always the same. The bravery sprung from hot blood pleases the Frenchman more. He understands it, it appeals to his vanity; it is a characteristic of his nature. But it is passing; it fails him at times, especially when there is nothing for him to gain in doing his duty.

The Turks are full of ardor in the advance. They carry their officers with them. But they retreat with the same facility, abandoning their officers.

Mediocre troops like to be led by their shepherds. Reliable troops like to be directed, with their directors alongside of them or behind. With the former the general must be the leader on horseback; with the latter, the manager.

Warnery did not like officers to head a charge. He thought it useless to have them killed before the others. He did not place them in front and his cavalry was good.

General Leboeuf did not favor the proposed advance into battle with platoon leaders in front of the center of their platoons. The fear exists that the fall of the captain will demoralize the rest. What is the solution? Leboeuf must have known that if the officer is not in front of his command, it will advance less confidently, that, with us, all officers are almost always in advance. Practice is stronger than any theory. Therefore fit theories to it. In column, put the chiefs of platoon on the flank where they can see clearly.

Frightfulness! Witness the Turks in the Polish wars. What gave power to the Turks in their wars with Poland was not so much their real strength as their ferocity. They massacred all who resisted; they massacred without the excuse of resistance. Terror preceded them, breaking down the courage of their enemies. The necessity to win or to submit to extreme peril brought about cowardice and submission, for fear of being conquered.

Turenne said, "You tremble, body...." The instinct of self-preservation can then make the strongest tremble. But they are strong enough to overcome their emotion, the fear of advancing, without even losing their heads or their coolness. Fear with them never becomes terror; it is forgotten in the activities of command. He who does not feel strong enough to keep his heart from ever being gripped by terror, should never think of becoming an officer.

The soldiers themselves have emotion. The sense of duty, discipline, pride, the example of their officers and above all their coolness, sustain them and prevent their fear from becoming terror. Their emotion never allows them to sight, or to more than approximately adjust their fire. Often they fire into the air. Cromwell knew this very well, dependable as his troops were, when he said, "Put your trust in God and aim at their shoe laces."

What is too true is that bravery often does not at all exclude cowardice, horrible devices to secure personal safety, infamous conduct.

The Romans were not mighty men, but men of discipline and obstinacy. We have no idea of the Roman military mind, so entirely different from ours. A Roman general who had as little coolness as we have would have been lost. We have incentives in decorations and medals that would have made a Roman soldier run the gauntlet.

How many men before a lion, have the courage to look him in the face, to think of and put into practice measures of self-defense? In war when terror has seized you, as experience has shown it often does, you are as before a lion. You fly trembling and let yourself be eaten up. Are there so few really brave men among so many soldiers? Alas, yes! Gideon was lucky to find three hundred in thirty thousand.

Napoleon said, "Two Mamelukes held three Frenchmen; but one hundred French cavalry did not fear the same number of Mamelukes; three hundred vanquished the same number; one thousand French beat fifteen hundred Mamelukes. Such was the influence of tactics, order and maneuver." In ordinary language, such was the great moral influence of unity, established by discipline and made possible and effective in battle by organization and mutual support. With unity and sensible formation men of an individual value one-third less beat those who were individually their betters. That is the essential, must be the essential, point in the organization of an army. On reflection, this simple statement of Napoleon's seems to contain the whole of battle morale. Make the enemy believe that support is lacking; isolate; cut off, flank, turn, in a thousand ways make his men believe themselves isolated. Isolate in like manner his squadrons, battalions, brigades and divisions; and victory is yours. If, on account of bad organization, he does not anticipate mutual support, there is no need of such maneuver; the attack is enough.

Some men, such as Orientals, Chinese, Tartars, Mongols do not fear death. They are resigned to it at all times. Why is it that they can not stand before the armies of the western people? It is lack of organization. The instinct of self-preservation which at the last moment dominates them utterly, is not opposed by discipline. We have often seen fanatic eastern peoples, implicitly believing that death in battle means a happy and glorious resurrection, superior in numbers, give way before discipline. If attacked confidently, they are crushed by their own weight. In close combat the dagger is better than the bayonet, but instinct is too strong for such people.

What makes the soldier capable of obedience and direction in action, is the sense of discipline. This includes: respect for and confidence in his chiefs; confidence in his comrades and fear of their reproaches and retaliation if he abandons them in danger; his desire to go where others do without trembling more than they; in a word, the whole of esprit de corps. Organization only can produce these characteristics. Four men equal a lion.

Note the army organizations and tactical formations on paper are always determined from the mechanical point of view, neglecting the essential coefficient, that of morale. They are almost always wrong.

Esprit de corps is secured in war. But war becomes shorter and shorter and more and more violent. Consequently, secure esprit de corps in advance.

Mental acquaintanceship is not enough to make a good organization. A good general esprit is needed. All must work for battle and not merely live, quietly going through with drills without understanding their application. Once a man knows how to use his weapon and obey all commands there is needed only occasional drill to brush up those who have forgotten. Marches and battle maneuvers are what is needed.

The technical training of the soldier is not the most difficult. It is necessary for him to know how to use and take care of his weapon; to know how to move to the right and to the left, forward, to the rear, at command, to charge and to march with full pack. But this does not make the soldier. The Vendeans, who knew little of this, were tough soldiers.

It is absolutely necessary to change the instruction, to reduce it to the necessary minimum and to cut out all the superfluities with which peacetime laborers overload it each year. To know the essential well is better than having some knowledge of a lot of things, many of them useless. Teach this the first year, that the second, but the essential from the beginning! Also instruction should be simple to avoid the mental fatigue of long drills that disgust everybody.

Here is a significant sentence in Colonel Borbstaed's enumeration of the reasons for Prussian victory over the Austrians in 1866, "It was ... because each man, being trained, knew how to act promptly and confidently in all phases of battle." This is a fact.

To be held in a building, at every minute of the day to have every movement, every attitude under a not too intelligent surveillance is indeed to be harried. This incessant surveillance weakens the morale of both the watched and the watcher. What is the reason for this incessant surveillance which has long since exceeded shipboard surveillance? Was not that strict enough?

3. Material and Moral Effect

The effect of an army, of one organization on another, is at the same time material and moral. The material effect of an organization is in its power to destroy, the moral effect in the fear that it inspires.

In battle, two moral forces, even more than two material forces, are in conflict. The stronger conquers. The victor has often lost by fire more than the vanquished. Moral effect does not come entirely from destructive power, real and effective as it may be. It comes, above all, from its presumed, threatening power, present in the form of reserves threatening to renew the battle, of troops that appear on the flank, even of a determined frontal attack.

Material effect is greater as instruments are better (weapons, mounts, etc.), as the men know better how to use them, and as the men are more numerous and stronger, so that in case of success they can carry on longer.

With equal or even inferior power of destruction he will win who has the resolution to advance, who by his formations and maneuvers can continually threaten his adversary with a new phase of material action, who, in a word has the moral ascendancy. Moral effect inspires fear. Fear must be changed to terror in order to vanquish.

When confidence is placed in superiority of material means, valuable as they are against an enemy at a distance, it may be betrayed by the actions of the enemy. If he closes with you in spite of your superiority in means of destruction, the morale of the enemy mounts with the loss of your confidence. His morale dominates yours. You flee. Entrenched troops give way in this manner.

At Pharsalus, Pompey and his army counted on a cavalry corps turning and taking Caesar in the rear. In addition Pompey's army was twice as numerous. Caesar parried the blow, and his enemy, who saw the failure of the means of action he counted on, was demoralized, beaten, lost fifteen thousand men put to the sword (while Caesar lost only two hundred) and as many prisoners.

Even by advancing you affect the morale of the enemy. But your object is to dominate him and make him retreat before your ascendancy, and it is certain that everything that diminishes the enemy's morale adds to your resolution in advancing. Adopt then a formation which permits your destructive agency, your skirmishers, to help you throughout by their material action and to this degree diminish that of the enemy.

Armor, in diminishing the material effect that can be suffered, diminishes the dominating moral effect of fear. It is easy to understand how much armor adds to the moral effect of cavalry action, at the critical moment. You feel that thanks to his armor the enemy will succeed in getting to you.

It is to be noted that when a body actually awaits the attack of another up to bayonet distance (something extraordinarily rare), and the attacking troop does not falter, the first does not defend itself. This is the massacre of ancient battle.

Against unimaginative men, who retain some coolness and consequently the faculty of reasoning in danger, moral effect will be as material effect. The mere act of attack does not completely succeed against such troops. (Witness battles in Spain and Waterloo). It is necessary to destroy them, and we are better at this than they by our aptitude in the use of skirmishers and above all in the mad dash of our cavalry. But the cavalry must not be treated, until it comes to so consider itself, as a precious jewel which must be guarded against injury. There should be little of it, but it must be good.

"Seek and ye shall find" not the ideal but the best method that exists. In maneuvers skirmishers, who have some effect, are returned to ranks to execute fire in two ranks which never killed anybody. Why not put your skirmishers in advance? Why sound trumpet calls which they neither hear nor understand? That they do not is fortunate, for each captain has a different call sounded. Example: at Alma, the retreat, etc.

The great superiority of Roman tactics lay in their constant endeavor to coördinate physical and moral effect. Moral effect passes; finally one sees that the enemy is not so terrible as he appeared to be. Physical effect does not. The Greeks tried to dominate. The Romans preferred to kill, and kill they did. They followed thereby the better method. Their moral effect was aided by their reliable and deadly swords.

What moral force is worth to a nation at war is shown by examples. Pichegru played the traitor; this had great influence at home and we were beaten. Napoleon came back; victory returned with him.

But at that we can do nothing without good troops, not even with a Napoleon. Witness Turenne's army after his death. It remained excellent in spite of conflict between and the inefficiency of its two leaders. Note the defensive retreat across the Rhine; the regiment in Champagne attacked in front by infantry and taken in the rear by cavalry. One of the prettiest feats of the art of war.

In modern battle, which is delivered with combatants so far apart, man has come to have a horror of man. He comes to hand to hand fighting only to defend his body or if forced to it by some fortuitous encounter. More than that! It may be said that he seeks to catch the fugitive only for fear that he will turn and fight.

Guilbert says that shock actions are infinitely rare. Here, infinity is taken in its exact mathematical sense. Guilbert reduces to nothing, by deductions from practical examples, the mathematical theory of the shock of one massed body on another. Indeed the physical impulse is nothing. The moral impulse which estimates the attacker is everything. The moral impulse lies in the perception by the enemy of the resolution that animates you. They say that the battle of Amstetten was the only one in which a line actually waited for the shock of another line charging with the bayonets. Even then the Russians gave way before the moral and not before the physical impulse. They were already disconcerted, wavering, worried, hesitant, vacillating, when the blow fell. They waited long enough to receive bayonet thrusts, even blows with the rifle (in the back, as at Inkermann).

This done, they fled. He who calm and strong of heart awaits his enemy, has all the advantage of fire. But the moral impulse of the assailant demoralizes the assailed. He is frightened; he sets his sight no longer; he does not even aim his piece. His lines are broken without defense, unless indeed his cavalry, waiting halted, horsemen a meter apart and in two ranks, does not break first and destroy all formation.

With good troops on both sides, if an attack is not prepared, there is every reason to believe that it will fail. The attacking troops suffer more, materially, than the defenders. The latter are in better order, fresh, while the assailants are in disorder and already have suffered a loss of morale under a certain amount of punishment. The moral superiority given by the offensive movement may be more than compensated by the good order and integrity of the defenders, when the assailants have suffered losses. The slightest reaction by the defense may demoralize the attack. This is the secret of the success of the British infantry in Spain, and not their fire by rank, which was as ineffective with them as with us.

The more confidence one has in his methods of attack or defense, the more disconcerted he is to see them at some time incapable of stopping the enemy. The effect of the present improved fire arm is still limited, with the present organization and use of riflemen, to point blank ranges. It follows that bayonet charges (where bayonet thrusts never occur), otherwise attacks under fire, will have an increasing value, and that victory will be his who secures most order and determined dash. With these two qualities, too much neglected with us, with willingness, with intelligence enough to keep a firm hold on troops in immediate support, we may hope to take and to hold what we take. Do not then neglect destructive effort before using moral effect. Use skirmishers up to the last moment. Otherwise no attack can succeed. It is true it is haphazard fire, nevertheless it is effective because of its volume.

This moral effect must be a terrible thing. A body advances to meet another. The defender has only to remain calm, ready to aim, each man pitted against a man before him. The attacking body comes within deadly range. Whether or not it halts to fire, it will be a target for the other body which awaits it, calm, ready, sure of its effect. The whole first rank of the assailant falls, smashed. The remainder, little encouraged by their reception, disperse automatically or before the least indication of an advance on them. Is this what happens? Not at all! The moral effect of the assault worries the defenders. They fire in the air if at all. They disperse immediately before the assailants who are even encouraged by this fire now that it is over. It quickens them in order to avoid a second salvo.

It is said by those who fought them in Spain and at Waterloo that the British are capable of the necessary coolness. I doubt it nevertheless. After firing, they made swift attacks. If they had not, they might have fled. Anyhow the English are stolid folks, with little imagination, who try to be logical in all things. The French with their nervous irritability, their lively imagination, are incapable of such a defense.

Anybody who thinks that he could stand under a second fire is a man without any idea of battle. (Prince de Ligne).

Modern history furnishes us with no examples of stonewall troops who can neither be shaken nor driven back, who stand patiently the heaviest fire, yet who retire precipitately when the general orders the retreat. (Bismarck).

Cavalry maneuvers, like those of infantry, are threats. The most threatening win. The formation in ranks is a threat, and more than a threat. A force engaged is out of the hand of its commander. I know, I see what it does, what it is capable of. It acts; I can estimate the effect of its action. But a force in formation is in hand; I know it is there, I see it, feel it. It may be used in any direction. I feel instinctively that it alone can surely reach me, take me on the right, on the left, throw itself into a gap, turn me. It troubles me, threatens me. Where is the threatened blow going to fall?

The formation in ranks is a serious threat, which may at any moment be put into effect. It awes one in a terrible fashion. In the heat of battle, formed troops do more to secure victory than do those actively engaged. This is true, whether such a body actually exists or whether it exists only in the imagination of the enemy. In an indecisive battle, he wins who can show, and merely show, battalions and squadrons in hand. They inspire the fear of the unknown.

From the taking of the entrenchments at Fribourg up to the engagement at the bridge of Arcola, up to Solferino, there occur a multitude of deeds of valor, of positions taken by frontal attack, which deceive every one, generals as well as civilians, and which always cause the same mistakes to be made. It is time to teach these folks that the entrenchments at Fribourg were not won by frontal attack, nor was the bridge of Arcola (see the correspondence of Napoleon I), nor was Solferino.

Lieutenant Hercule took fifty cavalry through Alpon, ten kilometers on the flank of the Austrians at Arcola, and the position that held us up for three days, was evacuated. The evacuation was the result of strategic, if not of tactical, moral effect. General or soldier, man is the same.

Demonstrations should be made at greater or less distance, according to the morale of the enemy. That is to say, battle methods vary with the enemy, and an appropriate method should be employed in each individual case.

We have treated and shall treat only of the infantryman. In ancient as in modern battle, he is the one who suffers most. In ancient battle, if he is defeated, he remains because of his slowness at the mercy of the victor. In modern battle the mounted man moves swiftly through danger, the infantryman has to walk. He even has to halt in danger, often and for long periods of time. He who knows the morale of the infantryman, which is put to the hardest proof, knows the morale of all the combatants.

4. The Theory of Strong Battalions

Today, numbers are considered the essential. Napoleon had this tendency (note his strength reports). The Romans did not pay so much attention to it. What they paid most attention to was to seeing that everybody fought. We assume that all the personnel present with an army, with a division, with a regiment on the day of battle, fights. Right there is the error.

The theory of strong battalions is a shameful theory. It does not reckon on courage but on the amount of human flesh. It is a reflection on the soul. Great and small orators, all who speak of military matters today, talk only of masses. War is waged by enormous masses, etc. In the masses, man as an individual disappears, the number only is seen. Quality is forgotten, and yet today as always, quality alone produces real effect. The Prussians conquered at Sadowa with made soldiers, united, accustomed to discipline. Such soldiers can be made in three or four years now, for the material training of the soldier is not indeed so difficult.

Caesar had legions that he found unseasoned, not yet dependable, which had been formed for nine years.

Austria was beaten because her troops were of poor quality, because they were conscripts.

Our projected organization will give us four hundred thousand good soldiers. But all our reserves will be without cohesion, if they are thrown into this or that organization on the eve of battle. At a distance, numbers of troops without cohesion may be impressive, but close up they are reduced to fifty or twenty-five per cent. who really fight. Wagram was not too well executed. It illustrated desperate efforts that had for once a moral effect on an impressionable enemy. But for once only. Would they succeed again?

The Cimbrians gave an example and man has not changed. Who today is braver than they were? And they did not have to face artillery, nor rifles.

Originally Napoleon found as an instrument, an army with good battle methods, and in his best battles, combat followed these methods. He himself prescribed, at least so they say, for he misrepresented at Saint Helena, the methods used at Wagram, at Eylau, at Waterloo, and engaged enormous masses of infantry which did not give material effect. But it involved a frightful loss of men and a disorder that, after they had once been unleashed, did not permit of the rallying and reemployment that day of the troops engaged. This was a barbaric method, according to the Romans, amateurish, if we may say such a thing of such a man; a method which could not be used against experienced and well trained troops such as d'Erlon's corps at Waterloo. It proved disastrous.

Napoleon looked only at the result to be attained. When his impatience, or perhaps the lack of experience and knowledge in his officers and soldiers, forbade his continued use of real attack tactics, he completely sacrificed the material effect of infantry and even that of cavalry to the moral effect of masses. The personnel of his armies was too changing. In ancient battle victory cost much less than with modern armies, and the same soldiers remained longer in ranks. At the end of his campaigns, when he had soldiers sixty years old, Alexander had lost only seven hundred men by the sword. Napoleon's system is more practicable with the Russians, who naturally group together, mass up, but it is not the most effective. Note the mass formation at Inkermann.

What did Napoleon I do? He reduced the role of man in battle, and depended instead on formed masses. We have not such magnificent material.

Infantry and cavalry masses showed, toward the end of the Empire, a tactical degeneracy resulting from the wearing down of their elements and the consequent lowering of standards of morale and training. But since the allies had recognized and adopted our methods, Napoleon really had a reason for trying something so old that it was new to secure that surprise which will give victory once. It can give victory only once however, tried again surprise will be lacking. This was sort of a desperate method which Napoleon's supremacy allowed him to adopt when he saw his prestige waning.

When misfortune and lack of cannon fodder oppressed him, Napoleon became again the practical man not blinded by his supremacy. His entire good sense, his genius, overcame the madness to conquer at all price, and we have his campaign of 1814.

General Ambert says: "Without military traditions, almost without a command, these confused masses (the American armies of the Civil War) struck as men struck at Agincourt and Crecy." At Agincourt and Crecy, we struck very little, but were struck a lot. These battles were great slaughters of Frenchmen, by English and other Frenchmen, who did not greatly suffer themselves. In what, except in disorder, did the American battles resemble these butcheries with the knife? The Americans were engaged as skirmishers at a distance of leagues. In seeking a resemblance the general has been carried away by the mania for phrase-making.

Victory is always for the strong battalions. This is true. If sixty determined men can rout a battalion, these sixty must be found. Perhaps only as many will be found as the enemy has battalions (Note Gideon's proportion of three hundred to thirty thousand of one to one hundred.) Perhaps it would be far and away better, under these circumstances, to fight at night.

5. Combat Methods

Ancient battle was fought in a confined space. The commander could see his whole force. Seeing clearly, his account should have been clear, although we note that many of these ancient accounts are obscure and incomplete, and that we have to supplement them. In modern battle nobody knows what goes on or what has gone on, except from results. Narrations cannot enter into details of execution.

It is interesting to compare tales of feats of arms, narrated by the victor (so-called) or the vanquished. It is hard to tell which account is truthful, if either. Mere assurance may carry weight. Military politics may dictate a perversion of the facts for disciplinary, moral or political reasons. (Note Sommo-Sierra.)

It is difficult even to determine losses, the leaders are such consummate liars. Why is this?

It is bewildering to read a French account and then a foreign account of the same event, the facts stated are so entirely different. What is the truth? Only results can reveal it, such results as the losses on both sides. They are really instructive if they can be gotten at.

I believe that under Turenne there was not existent to the same degree a national pride which tended to hide unpleasant truths. The troops in contending armies were often of the same nation.

If national vanity and pride were not so touchy about recent occurrences, still passionately debated, numerous lessons might be drawn from our last wars. Who can speak impartially of Waterloo, or Waterloo so much discussed and with such heat, without being ashamed? Had Waterloo been won, it would not have profited us. Napoleon attempted the impossible, which is beyond even genius. After a terrible fight against English firmness and tenacity, a fight in which we were not able to subdue them, the Prussians appear. We would have done no better had they not appeared, but they did, very conveniently to sustain our pride. They were confronted. Then the rout began. It did not begin in the troops facing the Prussians but in those facing the English, who were exhausted perhaps, but not more so than their enemies. This was the moral effect of an attack on their right, when they had rather expected reinforcements to appear. The right conformed to the retrograde movement. And what a movement it was!

Why do not authorities acknowledge facts and try to formulate combat methods that conform to reality? It would reduce a little the disorder that bothers men not warned of it. They jump perhaps from the frying pan into the fire. I have known two colonels, one of them a very brave man, who said, "Let soldiers alone before the enemy. They know what to do better than you do." This is a fine statement of French confidence! That they know better than you what should be done. Especially in a panic, I suppose!

A long time ago the Prince de Ligne justified battle formations, above all the famous oblique formation. Napoleon decided the question. All discussion of formations is pedantry. But there are moral reasons for the power of the depth formation.

The difference between practice and theory is incredible. A general, who has given directions a thousand times on the battle field, when asked for directions, gives this order, "Go there, Colonel." The colonel, a man of good sense, says, "Will you explain, sir? What point do you want me to guide on? How far should I extend? Is there anybody on my right? On my left?" The general says, "Advance on the enemy, sir. It seems to me that that ought to be enough. What does this hesitation mean?" But my dear general, what are your orders? An officer should know where his command is, and the command itself should know. Space is large. If you do not know where to send your troops, and how to direct them, to make them understand where they are to go, to give them guides if necessary, what sort of general are you?

What is our method for occupying a fortified work, or a line? We have none! Why not adopt that of Marshal Saxe? Ask several generals how they would do it. They will not know.

There is always mad impatience for results, without considering the means. A general's ability lies in judging the best moment for attack and in knowing how to prepare for it. We took Melegnano without artillery, without maneuver, but at what a price! At Waterloo the Hougoumont farm held us up all day, cost us dear and disorganized us into a mad mob, until Napoleon finally sent eight mortars to smash and burn the château. This is what should have been done at the commencement of the general attack.

A rational and ordered method of combat, or if not ordered, known to all, is enough to make good troops, if there is discipline be it understood. The Portuguese infantry in the Spanish War, to whom the English had taught their method of combat, almost rivalled the English infantry. Today who has formulated method? Who has a traditional method? Ask the generals. No two will agree.

We have a method, a manner rather, that accords with the national tendency, that of skirmishers in large numbers. But this formation is nowhere formulated. Before a campaign it is decried. Properly so, for it degenerates rapidly into a flock of lost sheep. Consequently troops come to the battle field entirely unused to reality. All the leaders, all the officers, are confused and unoriented. This goes so far that often generals are found who have lost their divisions or brigades; staff officers who have lost their generals and their divisions both; and, although this is more easily understood, many company officers who have lost their commands. This is a serious matter, which might cost us dear in a prolonged war in which the enemy gains experience. Let us hope that experience will lead us, not to change the principle, but to modify and form in a practical way our characteristic battle method of escaping by advancing. The brochure of the Prince of Prussia shows that, without having fought us, the Prussians understand our methods.

There are men such as Marshal Bugeaud who are born warriors in character, mental attitude, intelligence and temperament. They recommend and show by example, such as Colonel Bugeaud's battles in 1815 at the Hospital bridge, tactics entirely appropriate to their national and personal characters. Note Wellington and the Duke of York among the English. But the execution of tactics such as Bugeaud's requires officers who resemble their commanders, at least in courage and decisions. All officers are not of such temper. There is need then of prescribed tactics conforming to the national character, which may serve to guide an ordinary officer without requiring him to have the exceptional ability of a Bugeaud. Such prescribed tactics would serve an officer as the perfectly clear and well defined tactics of the Roman legion served the legion commander. The officer could not neglect them without failing in his duty. Of course they will not make him an exceptional leader. But, except in case of utter incapacity they will keep him from entirely failing in his task, from making absurd mistakes. Nor will they prevent officers of Bugeaud's temper from using their ability. They will on the contrary help them by putting under their command men prepared for the details of battle, which will not then come to them as a surprise.

This method need not be as completely dogmatic as the Roman. Our battle is too varying an affair. But some clearly defined rules, established by experience, would prevent the gross errors of inefficients. (Such as causing skirmishers to fall back when the formed rank fires, and consequently allowing them to carry with them in their retreat, the rank itself.) They would be useful aids to men of coolness and decision.

The laying down of such tactics would answer the many who hold that everything is improvised on the battle field and who find no better improvisation than to leave the soldier to himself. (See above.)

We should try to exercise some control over our soldiers, who advance by flight (note the Vendeans) or escape by advancing, as you like. But if something unexpected surprises them, they flee as precipitately.

Invention is less needed than verification, demonstration and organization of proper methods. To verify; observe better. To demonstrate; try out and describe better. To organize, distribute better, bearing in mind that cohesion means discipline. I do not know who put things that way; but it is truer than ever in this day of invention.

With us very few reason or understand reason, very few are cool. Their effect is negligible in the disorder of the mass; it is lost in numbers. It follows that we above all need a method of combat, sanely thought out in advance. It must be based on the fact that we are not passively obedient instruments, but very nervous and restless people, who wish to finish things quickly and to know in advance where we are going. It must be based on the fact that we are very proud people, but people who would all skulk if we were not seen, and who consequently must always be seen, and act in the presence of our comrades and of the officers who supervise us. From this comes the necessity for organizing the infantry company solidly. It is the infantryman on whom the battle has the most violent effect, for he is always most exposed; it is he therefore who must be the most solidly supported. Unity must be secured by a mutual acquaintanceship of long standing between all elements.

If you only use combat methods that require leaders without fear, of high intelligence, full of good sense, of esprit, you will always make mistakes. Bugeaud's method was the best for him. But it is evident, in his fight at the Hospital bridge that his battalion commanders were useless. If he had not been there, all would have been lost. He alone, omnipresent, was capable of resolute blows that the others could not execute. His system can be summed up in two phrases; always attack even when on the defensive; fire and take cover only when not attacked. His method was rational, considering his mentality and the existing conditions, but in carrying it into execution he judged his officers and soldiers by himself and was deceived. No dogmatic principles can be drawn from his method, nor from any other. Man is always man. He does not always possess ability and resolution. The commander must make his choice of methods, depending on his troops and on himself.

The essential of tactics is: the science of making men fight with their maximum energy. This alone can give an organization with which to fight fear. This has always been true.

We must start here and figure mathematically. Mathematics is the dominant science in war, just as battle is its only purpose. Pride generally causes refusal to acknowledge the truth that fear of being vanquished is basic in war. In the mass, pride, vanity, is responsible for this dissimulation. With the tiny number of absolutely fearless men, what is responsible is their ignorance of a thing they do not feel. There is however, no real basis but this, and all real tactics are based on it. Discipline is a part of tactics, is absolutely at the base of tactics, as the Romans showed. They excelled the Gauls in intelligence, but not in bravery.

To start with: take battalions of four companies, four platoons each, in line or in column. The order of battle may be: two platoons deployed as skirmishers, two companies in reserve, under command of the battalion commander. In obtaining a decision destructive action will come from skirmishers. This action should be directed by battalion commanders, but such direction is not customary. No effect will be secured from skirmishers at six hundred paces. They will never, never, never, be nicely aligned in front of their battalions, calm and collected, after an advance. They will not, even at maneuvers. The battalion commander ought to be advanced enough to direct his skirmishers. The whole battalion, one-half engaged, one-half ready for any effort, ought to remain under his command, under his personal direction as far as possible. In the advance the officers, the soldiers, are content if they are merely directed; but, when the battle becomes hot, they must see their commander, know him to be near. It does not matter even if he is without initiative, incapable of giving an order. His presence creates a belief that direction exists, that orders exist, and that is enough.

When the skirmishers meet with resistance, they fall back to the ranks. It is the role of reserves to support and reinforce the line, and above all, by a swift charge to cut the enemy's line. This then falls back and the skirmishers go forward again, if the advance is resumed. The second line should be in the formation, battalions in line or in column, that hides it best. Cover the infantry troops before their entry into action; cover them as much as possible and by any means; take advantage of the terrain; make them lie down. This is the English method in defense of heights, instanced in Spain and at Waterloo. Only one bugle to each battalion should sound calls. What else is there to be provided for?

Many haughty generals would scream protests like eagles if it were suggested that they take such precautions for second line battalions or first line troops not committed to action. Yet this is merely a sane measure to insure good order without the slightest implication of cowardice.

With breech-loading weapons, the skirmishers on the defensive fire almost always from a prone position. They are made to rise with difficulty, either for retreat or for advance. This renders the defense more tenacious....

CHAPTER II - INFANTRY

1. Masses—Deep Columns.

Study of the effect of columns brings us to the consideration of mass operations in general. Read this singular argument in favor of attacks by battalions in close columns: "A column cannot stop instantly without a command. Suppose your first rank stops at the instant of shock: the twelve ranks of the battalion, coming up successively, would come in contact with it, pushing it forward.... Experiments made have shown that beyond the sixteenth the impulsion of the ranks in rear has no effect on the front, it is completely taken up by the fifteen ranks already massed behind the first.... To make the experiment, march at charging pace and command halt to the front rank without warning the rest. The ranks will precipitate themselves upon each other unless they be very attentive, or unless, anticipating the command, they check themselves unconsciously while marching."

But in a real charge, all your ranks are attentive, restless, anxious about what is taking place at the front and, if the latter halts, if the first line stops, there will be a movement to the rear and not to the front. Take a good battalion, possessed of extraordinary calmness and coolness, thrown full speed on the enemy, at one hundred and twenty steps to the minute. Today it would have to advance under a fire of five shots a minute! At this last desperate moment if the front rank stops, it will not be pushed, according to the theory of successive impulses, it will be upset. The second line will arrive only to fall over the first and so on. There should be a drill ground test to see up to what rank this falling of the pasteboard figures would extend.

Physical impulse is merely a word. If the front rank stops it will let itself fall and be trampled under foot rather than cede to the pressure that pushes it forward. Any one experienced in infantry engagements of today knows that is just what happens. This shows the error of the theory of physical impulse—a theory that continues to dictate as under the Empire (so strong is routine and prejudice) attacks in close column. Such attacks are marked by absolute disorder and lack of leadership. Take a battalion fresh from barracks, in light marching order; intent only on the maneuver to be executed. It marches in close column in good order; its subdivisions are full four paces apart. The non-commissioned officers control the men. But it is true that if the terrain is slightly accidented, if the guide does not march with mathematical precision, the battalion in close column becomes in the twinkling of an eye a flock of sheep. What would happen to a battalion in such a formation, at one hundred paces from the enemy? Nobody will ever see such an instance in these days of the rifle.

If the battalion has marched resolutely, if it is in good order, it is ten to one that the enemy has already withdrawn without waiting any longer. But suppose the enemy does not flinch? Then the man of our days, naked against iron and lead, no longer controls himself. The instinct of preservation controls him absolutely. There are two ways of avoiding or diminishing the danger; they are to flee or to throw one-self upon it. Let us rush upon it. Now, however small the intervals of space and time that separate us from the enemy, instinct shows itself. We rush forward, but ... generally, we rush with prudence, with a tendency to let the most urgent ones, the most intrepid ones, pass on. It is strange, but true, that the nearer we approach the enemy, the less we are closed up. Adieu to the theory of pressure. If the front rank is stopped, those behind fall down rather than push it. Even if this front rank is pushed, it will itself fall down rather than advance. There is nothing to wonder at, it is sheer fact. Any pushing is to the rear. (Battle of Diernstein.)

Today more than ever flight begins in the rear, which is affected quite as much as the front.

Mass attacks are incomprehensible. Not one out of ten was ever carried to completion and none of them could be maintained against counter-attacks. They can be explained only by the lack of confidence of the generals in their troops. Napoleon expressly condemns in his memoirs such attacks. He, therefore, never ordered them. But when good troops were used up, and his generals believed they could not obtain from young troops determined attacks in tactical formation, they came back to the mass formation, which belongs to the infancy of the art, as a desperate resort.

If you use this method of pressing, of pushing, your force will disappear as before a magician's wand.

But the enemy does not stand; the moral pressure of danger that precedes you is too strong for him. Otherwise, those who stood and aimed even with empty rifles, would never see a charge come up to them. The first line of the assailant would be sensible of death and no one would wish to be in the first rank. Therefore, the enemy never merely stands; because if he does, it is you that flee. This always does away with the shock. The enemy entertains no smaller anxiety than yours. When he sees you near, for him also the question is whether to flee or to advance. Two moral impulses are in conflict.

This is the instinctive reasoning of the officer and soldier, "If these men wait for me to close with them, it means death. I will kill, but I will undoubtedly be killed. At the muzzle of the gun-barrel the bullet can not fail to find its mark. But if I can frighten them, they will run away. I can shoot them and bayonet in the back. Let us make a try at it." The trial is made, and one of the two forces, at some stage of the advance, perhaps only at two paces, makes an about and gets the bayonet in the back.

Imagination always sees loaded arms and this fancy is catching.

The shock is a mere term. The de Saxe, the Bugeaud theory: "Close with the bayonet and with fire action at close quarters. That is what kills people and the victor is the one who kills most," is not founded on fact. No enemy awaits you if you are determined, and never, never, never, are two equal determinations opposed to each other. It is well known to everybody, to all nations, that the French have never met any one who resisted a bayonet charge.

The English in Spain, marching resolutely in face of the charges of the French in column, have always defeated them.... The English were not dismayed at the mass. If Napoleon had recalled the defeat of the giants of the Armada by the English vessels, he might not have ordered the use of the d'Erlon column.

Blücher in his instructions to his troops, recalled that the French have never held out before the resolute march of the Prussians in attack column....

Suvaroff used no better tactics. Yet his battalions in Italy drove us at the point of their bayonets.

Each nation in Europe says: "No one stands his ground before a bayonet charge made by us." All are right. The French, no more than others, resist a resolute attack. All are persuaded that their attacks are irresistable; that an advance will frighten the enemy into flight. Whether the bayonet be fixed or in the scabbard makes no difference....

There is an old saying that young troops become uneasy if any one comes upon them in a tumult and in disorder; the old troops, on the contrary, see victory therein. At the commencement of a war, all troops are young. Our impetuosity pushes us to the front like fools ... the enemy flees. If the war lasts, everybody becomes inured. The enemy no longer troubles himself when in front of troops charging in a disordered way, because he knows and feels that they are moved as much by fear as by determination. Good order alone impresses the enemy in an attack, for it indicates real determination. That is why it is necessary to secure good order and retain it to the very last. It is unwise to take the running step prematurely, because you become a flock of sheep and leave so many men behind that you will not reach your objective. The close column is absurd; it turns you in advance into a flock of sheep, where officers and men are jumbled together without mutual support. It is then necessary to march as far as possible in such order as best permits the action of the non-commissioned officers, the action of unity, every one marching in front of eye-witnesses, in the open. On the other hand, in closed columns man marches unobserved and on the slightest pretext he lies down or remains behind. Therefore, it is best always to keep the skirmishers in advance or on the flanks, and never to recall them when in proximity to the enemy. To do so establishes a counter current that carries away your men. Let your skirmishers alone. They are your lost children; they will know best how to take care of themselves.

To sum up: there is no shock of infantry on infantry. There is no physical impulse, no force of mass. There is but a moral impulse. No one denies that this moral impulse is stronger as one feels better supported, that it has greater effect on the enemy as it menaces him with more men. From this it follows that the column is more valuable for the attack than the deployed order.

It might be concluded from this long statement that a moral pressure, which always causes flight when a bold attack is made, would not permit any infantry to hold out against a cavalry charge; never, indeed, against a determined charge. But infantry must resist when it is not possible to flee, and until there is complete demoralization, absolute terror, the infantry appreciates this. Every infantryman knows it is folly to flee before cavalry when the rifle is infallible at point-blank, at least from the rider's point of view. It is true that every really bold charge ought to succeed. But whether man is on foot or on horseback, he is always man. While on foot he has but himself to force; on horseback he must force man and beast to march against the enemy. And mounted, to flee is so easy. (Remark by Varney).

We have seen than in an infantry mass those in rear are powerless to push those in front unless the danger is greater in rear. The cavalry has long understood this. It attacks in a column at double distance rather than at half-distance, in order to avoid the frightful confusion of the mass. And yet, the allurement of mathematical reasoning is such that cavalry officers, especially the Germans, have seriously proposed attacking infantry by deep masses, so that the units in rear might give impulse to those in front. They cite the proverb, "One nail drives the other." What can you say to people who talk such nonsense? Nothing, except, "Attack us always in this way."

Real bayonet attacks occurred in the Crimean war. (Inkermann). They were carried out by a small force against a larger one. The power of mass had no influence in such cases. It was the mass which fell back, turned tail even before the shock. The troops who made the bold charge did nothing but strike and fire at backs. These instances show men unexpectedly finding themselves face to face with the enemy, at a distance at which a man can close fearlessly without falling out on the way breathless. They are chance encounters. Man is not yet demoralized by fire; he must strike or fall back.... Combat at close quarters does not exist. At close quarters occurs the ancient carnage when one force strikes the other in the back.

Columns have absolutely but a moral effect. They are threatening dispositions....

The mass impulse of cavalry has long been discredited. You have given up forming it in deep ranks although cavalry possesses a speed that would bring on more of a push upon the front at a halt than the last ranks of the infantry would bring upon the first. Yet you believe in the mass action of infantry!

As long as the ancient masses marched forward, they did not lose a man and no one lay down to avoid the combat. Dash lasted up to the time of stopping; the run was short in every case. In modern masses, in French masses especially, the march can be continued, but the mass loses while marching under fire. Moral pressure, continually exerted during a long advance, stops one-half of the combatants on the way. Today, above all in France, man protests against such use of his life. The Frenchman wants to fight, to return blow for blow. If he is not allowed to, this is what happens. It happened to Napoleon's masses. Let us take Wagram, where his mass was not repulsed. Out of twenty-two thousand men, three thousand to fifteen hundred reached the position. Certainly the position was not carried by them, but by the material and moral effect of a battery of one hundred pieces, cavalry, etc., etc. Were the nineteen thousand missing men disabled? No. Seven out of twenty-two, a third, an enormous proportion may have been hit. What became of the twelve thousand unaccounted for? They had lain down on the road, had played dummy in order not to go on to the end. In the confused mass of a column of deployed battalions, surveillance, difficult enough in a column at normal distances, is impossible. Nothing is easier than dropping out through inertia; nothing more common.

This thing happens to every body of troops marching forward, under fire, in whatever formation it may be. The number of men falling out in this way, giving up at the least opportunity, is greater as formation is less fixed and the surveillance of officers and comrades more difficult. In a battalion in closed column, this kind of temporary desertion is enormous; one-half of the men drop out on the way. The first platoon is mingled with the fourth. They are really a flock of sheep. No one has control, all being mixed. Even if, in virtue of the first impulse, the position is carried, the disorder is so great that if it is counter-attacked by four men, it is lost.

The condition of morale of such masses is fully described in the battle of Caesar against the Nervii, Marius against the Cimbri.

What better arguments against deep columns could there be than the denials of Napoleon at St. Helena?

2. Skirmishers—Supports—Reserves—Squares

This is singular. The cavalry has definite tactics. Essentially it knows how it fights. The infantry does not.

Our infantry no longer has any battle tactics; the initiative of the soldier rules. The soldiers of the First Empire trusted to the moral and passive action of masses. Today, the soldiers object to the passive action of masses. They fight as skirmishers, or they march to the front as a flock of sheep of which three-fourths seek cover enroute, if the fire is heavy. The first method, although better than the second, is bad unless iron discipline and studied and practical methods of fighting insure maintaining strong reserves. These should be in the hands of the leaders and officers for support purposes, to guard against panics, and to finish by the moral effect of a march on the enemy, of flank menaces, etc., the destructive action of the skirmishers.

Today when the ballistic arm is so deadly, so effective, a unit which closes up in order to fight is a unit in which morale is weakened.

Maneuver is possible only with good organization; otherwise it is no more effective than the passive mass or a rabble in an attack.

In ancient combat, the soldier was controlled by the leader in engagements; now that fighting is open, the soldier cannot be controlled. Often he cannot even be directed. Consequently it is necessary to begin an action at the latest possible moment, and to have the immediate commanders understand what is wanted, what their objectives are, etc.

In the modern engagement, the infantryman gets from under our control by scattering, and we say: a soldier's war. Wrong, wrong. To solve this problem, instead of scattering to the winds, let us increase the number of rallying points by solidifying the companies. From them come battalions; from battalions come regiments.

Action in open order was not possible nor evident under Turenne. The majority of the soldiers that composed the army, were not held near at hand, in formation. They fought badly. There was a general seeking for cover. Note the conduct of the Americans in their late war.

The organization of the legion of Marshal Saxe shows the strength of the tendency toward shock action as opposed to fire action.

The drills, parades and firing at Potsdam were not the tactics of Old Fritz. Frederick's secret was promptitude and rapidity of movement. But they were popularly believed to be his means. People were fond of them, and are yet. The Prussians for all their leaning toward parade, mathematics, etc., ended by adopting the best methods. The Prussians of Jena were taken in themselves by Frederick's methods.

But since then they have been the first to strike out in a practical way, while we, in France, are still laboring at the Potsdam drills.

The greater number of generals who fought in the last wars, under real battle conditions, ask for skirmishers in large units, well supported. Our men have such a strong tendency to place themselves in such units even against the will of their leaders, that they do not fight otherwise.

A number of respectable authors and military men advocate the use of skirmishers in large bodies, as being dictated by certain necessities of war. Ask them to elucidate this mode of action, and you will see that this talk of skirmishers in large bodies is nothing else but an euphemism for absolute disorder. An attempt has been made to fit the theory to the fact. Yet the use of skirmishers in large bodies is absurd with Frenchmen under fire, when the terrain and the sharpness of the action cause the initiative and direction to escape from the commanders, and leave it to the men, to small groups of soldiers.

Arms are for use. The best disposition for material effect in attack or defense is that which permits the easiest and most deadly use of arms. This disposition is the scattered thin line. The whole of the science of combat lies then in the happy, proper combination, of the open order, scattered to secure destructive effect, and a good disposition of troops in formation as supports and reserves, so as to finish by moral effect the action of the advanced troops. The proper combination varies with the enemy, his morale and the terrain. On the other hand, the thin line can have good order only with a severe discipline, a unity which our men attain from pride. Pride exists only among people who know each other well, who have esprit de corps, and company spirit. There is a necessity for an organization that renders unity possible by creating the real individuality of the company.

Self-esteem is unquestionably one of the most powerful motives which moves our men. They do not wish to pass for cowards in the eyes of their comrades. If they march forward they want to distinguish themselves. After every attack, formation (not the formation of the drill ground but that adopted by those rallying to the chief, those marching with him,) no longer exists. This is because of the inherent disorder of every forward march under fire. The bewildered men, even the officers, have no longer the eyes of their comrades or of their commander upon them, sustaining them. Self-esteem no longer impels them, they do not hold out; the least counter-offensive puts them to rout.

The experience of the evening ought always to serve the day following; but as the next day is never identical with the evening before, the counsel of experience can not be applied to the latter. When confused battalions shot at each other some two hundred paces for some time with arms inferior to those of our days, flight commenced at the wings. Therefore, said experience, let us reënforce the wings, and the battalion was placed between two picked companies. But it was found that the combat methods had been transformed. The elite companies were then reassembled into picked corps and the battalion, weaker than ever, no longer had reënforced wings. Perhaps combat in open order predominates, and the companies of light infantrymen being, above all, skirmishers, the battalion again is no longer supported. In our day the use of deployed battalions as skirmishers is no longer possible; and one of the essential reasons for picked companies is the strengthening of the battalion.

The question has been asked; Who saved the French army on the Beresina and at Hanau? The Guard, it is true. But, outside of the picked corps, what was the French army then? Droves, not troops. Abnormal times, abnormal deeds. The Beresina, Hanau, prove nothing today.

With the rapid-firing arms of infantry today, the advantage belongs to the defense which is completed by offensive movements carried out at opportune times.

Fire today is four or five times more rapid even if quite as haphazard as in the days of muzzle loaders. Everybody says that this renders impossible the charges of cavalry against infantry which has not been completely thrown into disorder, demoralized. What then must happen to charges of infantry, which marches while the cavalry charges?

Attacks in deep masses are no longer seen. They are not wise, and never were wise. To advance to the attack with a line of battalions in column, with large intervals and covered by a thick line of skirmishers, when the artillery has prepared the terrain, is very well. People with common sense have never done otherwise. But the thick line of skirmishers is essential. I believe that is the crux of the matter.

But enough of this. It is simple prudence for the artillery to prepare the infantry action by a moment's conversation with the artillery of the enemy infantry. If that infantry is not commanded by an imbecile, as it sometimes is, it will avoid that particular conversation the arguments of which would break it up, although they may not be directed precisely in its direction. All other things being equal, both infantries suffer the same losses in the artillery duel. The proportion does not vary, however complete the artillery preparation.

One infantry must always close with another under rapid fire from troops in position, and such a fire is, today more than ever, to the advantage of the defense. Ten men come towards me; they are at four hundred meters; with the ancient arm, I have time to kill but two before they reach me; with rapid fire, I have time to kill four or five. Morale does not increase with losses. The eight remaining might reach me in the first case; the five or six remaining will certainly not in the second.

If distance be taken, the leader can be seen, the file-closers see, the platoon that follows watches the preceding. Dropping out always exists, but it is less extensive with an open order, the men running more risks of being recognized. Stragglers will be fewer as the companies know each other better, and as the officers and men are more dependable.

It is difficult, if not impossible, to get the French infantry to make use of its fire before charging. If it fires, it will not charge, because it will continue to fire. (Bugeaud's method of firing during the advance is good.) What is needed, then, is skirmishers, who deliver the only effective fire, and troops in formation who push the skirmishers on, in themselves advancing to the attack.

The soldier wants to be occupied, to return shot for shot. Place him in a position to act immediately, individually. Then, whatever he does, you have not wholly lost your authority over him.

Again and again and again, at drill, the officers and non-commissioned officer ought to tell the private: "This is taught you to serve you under such circumstances." Generals, field officers, ought to tell officers the same thing. This alone can make an instructed army like the Roman army. But today, who of us can explain page for page, the use of anything ordered by our tactical regulations except the school of the skirmisher? "Forward," "retreat," and "by the flank," are the only practical movements under fire. But the others should be explained. Explain the position of "carry arms" with the left hand. Explain the ordinary step. Explain firing at command in the school of the battalion. It is well enough for the school of the platoon, because a company can make use thereof, but a battalion never can.

Everything leads to the belief that battle with present arms will be, in the same space of time, more deadly than with ancient ones. The trajectory of the projectile reaching further, the rapidity of firing being four times as great, more men will be put out of commission in less time. While the arm becomes more deadly, man does not change, his morale remains capable of certain efforts and the demands upon it become stronger. Morale is overtaxed; it reaches more rapidly the maximum of tension which throws the soldier to the front or rear. The role of commanders is to maintain morale, to direct those movements which men instinctively execute when heavily engaged and under the pressure of danger.

Napoleon I said that in battle, the role of skirmishers is the most fatiguing and most deadly. This means that under the Empire, as at present, the strongly engaged infantry troops rapidly dissolved into skirmishers. The action was decided by the moral agency of the troops not engaged, held in hand, capable of movement in any direction and acting as a great menace of new danger to the adversary, already shaken by the destructive action of the skirmishers. The same is true today. But the greater force of fire arms requires, more than ever, that they be utilized. The role of the skirmisher becomes preëminently the destructive role; it is forced on every organization seriously engaged by the greater moral pressure of today which causes men to scatter sooner.

Commanders-in-chief imagine formed battalions firing on the enemy and do not include the use of skirmishers in drill. This is an error, for they are necessary in drill and everywhere, etc. The formed rank is more difficult to utilize than ever. General Leboeuf used a very practical movement of going into battle, by platoons, which advance to the battle line in echelon, and can fire, even if they are taken in the very act of the movement. There is always the same dangerous tendency toward mass action even for a battalion in maneuver. This is an error. The principles of maneuver for small units should not be confused with those for great units. Emperor Napoleon did not prescribe skirmishers in flat country. But every officer should be reduced who does not utilize them to some degree.

The role of the skirmisher becomes more and more predominant. He should be so much the more watched and directed as he is used against more deadly arms, and, consequently, is more disposed to escape from all control, from all direction. Yet under such battle conditions formations are proposed which send skirmishers six hundred paces in advance of battalions and which give the battalion commander the mission of watching and directing (with six companies of one hundred and twenty men) troops spread over a space of three hundred paces by five hundred, at a minimum. To advance skirmishers six hundred paces from their battalion and to expect they will remain there is the work of people who have never observed.

Inasmuch as combat by skirmishers tends to predominate and since it becomes more difficult with the increase of danger, there has been a constant effort to bring into the firing line the man who must direct it. Leaders have been seen to spread an entire battalion in front of an infantry brigade or division so that the skirmishers, placed under a single command, might obey a general direction better. This method, scarcely practicable on the drill-ground, and indicating an absolute lack of practical sense, marks the tendency. The authors of new drills go too far in the opposite direction. They give the immediate command of the skirmishers in each battalion to the battalion commander who must at the same time lead his skirmishers and his battalion. This expedient is more practical than the other. It abandons all thought of an impossible general control and places the special direction in the right hands. But the leadership is too distant, the battalion commander has to attend to the participation of his battalion in the line, or in the ensemble of other battalions of the brigade or division, and the particular performance of his skirmishers. The more difficult, confused, the engagement becomes, the more simple and clear ought to be the roles of each one. Skirmishers are in need of a firmer hand than ever to direct and maintain them, so that they may do their part. The battalion commander must be entirely occupied with the role of skirmishers, or with the role of the line. There should be smaller battalions, one-half the number in reserve, one-half as skirmisher battalions. In the latter the men should be employed one-half as skirmishers and one-half held in reserve. The line of skirmishers will then gain steadiness.

Let the battalion commander of the troops of the second line entirely occupy himself with his battalion.

The full battalion of six companies is today too unwieldy for one man. Have battalions of four companies of one hundred men each, which is certainly quite sufficient considering the power of destruction which these four companies place in the hands of one man. He will have difficulty in maintaining and directing these four companies under the operation of increasingly powerful modern appliances. He will have difficulty in watching them, in modern combat, with the greater interval between the men in line that the use of the present arms necessitates. With a unified battalion of six hundred men, I would do better against a battalion of one thousand Prussians, than with a battalion of eight hundred men, two hundred of whom are immediately taken out of my control.

Skirmishers have a destructive effect; formed troops a moral effect. Drill ground maneuvers should prepare for actual battle. In such maneuvers, why, at the decisive moment of an attack, should you lighten the moral anxiety of the foe by ceasing his destruction, by calling back your skirmishers? If the enemy keeps his own skirmishers and marches resolutely behind them, you are lost, for his moral action upon you is augmented by his destructive action against which you have kindly disarmed yourself.

Why do you call back your skirmishers? Is it because your skirmishers hinder the operation of your columns, block bayonet charges? One must never have been in action to advance such a reason. At the last moment, at the supreme moment when one or two hundred meters separate you from the adversary, there is no longer a line. There is a fearless advance, and your skirmishers are your forlorn hope. Let them charge on their own account. Let them be passed or pushed forward by the mass. Do not recall them. Do not order them to execute any maneuver for they are not capable of any, except perhaps, that of falling back and establishing a counter-current which might drag you along. In these moments, everything hangs by a thread. Is it because your skirmishers would prevent you from delivering fire? Do you, then, believe in firing, especially in firing under the pressure of approaching danger, before the enemy? If he is wise, certainly he marches preceded by skirmishers, who kill men in your ranks and who have the confidence of a first success, of having seen your skirmishers disappear before them. These skirmishers will certainly lie down before your unmasked front. In that formation they easily cause you losses, and you are subjected to their destructive effect and to the moral effect of the advance of troops in formation against you. Your ranks become confused; you do not hold the position. There is but one way of holding it, that is to advance, and for that, it is necessary at all costs to avoid firing before moving ahead. Fire opened, no one advances further.

Do you believe in opening and ceasing fire at the will of the commander as on the drill ground? The commencement of fire by a battalion, with the present arms especially, is the beginning of disorder, the moment where the battalion begins to escape from its leader. While drilling even, the battalion commanders, after a little lively drill, after a march, can no longer control the fire.

Do you object that no one ever gets within two hundred meters of the enemy? That a unit attacking from the front never succeeds? So be it! Let us attack from the flank. But a flank is always more or less covered. Men are stationed there, ready for the blow. It will be necessary to pick off these men.

Today, more than ever, no rapid, calm firing is possible except skirmish firing.

The rapidity of firing has reduced six ranks to two ranks. With reliable troops who have no need of the moral support of a second rank behind them, one rank suffices today. At any rate, it is possible to await attack in two ranks.

In prescribing fire at command, in seeking to minimize the role of skirmishers instead of making it predominate, you take sides with the Germans. We are not fitted for that sort of game. If they adopt fire at command, it is just one more reason for our finding another method. We have invented, discovered the skirmisher; he is forced upon us by our men, our arms, etc. He must be organized.

In fire by rank, in battle, men gather into small groups and become confused. The more space they have, the less will be the disorder.

Formed in two ranks, each rank should be still thinner. All the shots of the second line are lost. The men should not touch; they should be far apart. The second rank in firing from position at a supreme moment, ought not to be directly behind the first. The men ought to be echeloned behind the first. There will always be firing from position on any front. It is necessary to make this firing as effective and as easy as possible. I do not wish to challenge the experiences of the target range but I wish to put them to practical use.

It is evident that the present arms are more deadly than the ancient ones; the morale of the troops will therefore be more severely shaken. The influence of the leader should be greater over the combatants, those immediately engaged. If it seems rational, let colonels engage in action, with the battalions of their regiment in two lines. One battalion acts as skirmishers; the other battalion waits, formed ready to aid the first. If you do not wish so to utilize the colonels, put all the battalions of the regiment in the first line, and eventually use them as skirmishers. The thing is inevitable; it will be done in spite of you. Do it yourself at the very first opportunity.

The necessity of replenishing the ammunition supply so quickly used up by the infantry, requires engaging the infantry by units only, which can be relieved by other units after the exhaustion of the ammunition supply. As skirmishers are exhausted quickly, engage entire battalions as skirmishers, assisted by entire battalions as supports or reserves. This is a necessary measure to insure good order. Do not throw into the fight immediately the four companies of the battalion. Up to the crucial moment, the battalion commander ought to guard against throwing every one into the fight.

There is a mania, seen in our maneuver camps, for completely covering a battle front, a defended position, by skirmishers, without the least interval between the skirmishers of different battalions. What will be the result? Initially a waste of men and ammunition. Then, difficulty in replacing them.

Why cover the front everywhere? If you do, then what advantage is there in being able to see from a great distance? Leave large intervals between your deployed companies. We are no longer only one hundred meters from the enemy at the time of firing. Since we are able to see at a great distance we do not risk having the enemy dash into these intervals unexpectedly. Your skirmisher companies at large intervals begin the fight, the killing. While your advance companies move ahead, the battalion commander follows with his formed companies, defilading them as much as possible. He lets them march. If the skirmishers fight at the halt, he supervises them. If the commanding officer wishes to reënforce his line, if he wants to face an enemy who attempts to advance into an interval, if he has any motive for doing it, in a word, he rushes new skirmishers into the interval. Certainly, these companies have more of the forward impulse, more dash, if dash is needed, than the skirmishers already in action. If they pass the first skirmishers, no harm is done. There you have echelons already formed. The skirmishers engaged, seeing aid in front of them, can be launched ahead more easily.

Besides, the companies thrown into this interval are a surprise for the enemy. That is something to be considered, as is the fact that so long as there is fighting at a halt, intervals in the skirmish lines are fit places for enemy bullets. Furthermore, these companies remain in the hands of their leaders. With the present method of reënforcing skirmishers—I am speaking of the practical method of the battlefield, not of theory—a company, starting from behind the skirmishers engaged, without a place in which to deploy, does not find anything better to do than to mingle with the skirmishers. Here it doubles the number of men, but in doing so brings disorder, prevents the control of the commanders and breaks up the regularly constituted groups. While the closing up of intervals to make places for new arrivals is good on the drill ground, or good before or after the combat, it never works during battle.

No prescribed interval will be kept exactly. It will open, it will close, following the fluctuations of the combat. But the onset, during which it can be kept, is not the moment of brisk combat; it is the moment of the engagement, of contact, consequently, of feeling out. It is essential that there remain space in which to advance. Suppose you are on a plain, for in a maneuver one starts from the flat terrain. In extending the new company it will reënforce the wings of the others, the men naturally supporting the flanks of their comrades. The individual intervals will lessen in order to make room for the new company. The company will always have a well determined central group, a rallying point for the others. If the interval has disappeared there is always time to employ the emergency method of doubling the ranks in front; but one must not forget, whatever the course taken, to preserve good order.

We cannot resist closing intervals between battalions; as if we were still in the times of the pikemen when, indeed, it was possible to pass through an interval! To-day, the fighting is done ten times farther away, and the intervals between battalions are not weak joints. They are covered by the fire of the skirmishers, as well covered by fire as the rest of the front, and invisible to the enemy.

Skirmishers and masses are the formations for action of poorly instructed French troops. With instruction and unity there would be skirmishers supported and formation in battalion columns at most.

Troops in close order can have only a moral effect, for the attack, or for a demonstration. If you want to produce a real effect, use musketry. For this it is necessary to form a single line. Formations have purely moral effect. Whoever counts on their material, effective action against reliable, cool troops, is mistaken and is defeated. Skirmishers alone do damage. Picked shots would do more if properly employed.

In attacking a position, start the charge at the latest possible moment, when the leader thinks he can reach the objective not all out of breath. Until then, it has been possible to march in rank, that is under the officers, the rank not being the mathematical line, but the grouping in the hands of the leader, under his eye. With the run comes confusion. Many stop, the fewer as the run is shorter. They lie down on the way and will rejoin only if the attack succeeds, if they join at all. If by running too long the men are obliged to stop in order to breathe and rest, the dash is broken, shattered. At the advance, very few will start. There are ten chances to one of seeing the attack fail, of turning it into a joke, with cries of "Forward with fixed bayonet," but none advancing, except some brave men who will be killed uselessly. The attack vanishes finally before the least demonstration of the foe. An unfortunate shout, a mere nothing, can destroy it.

Absolute rules are foolish, the conduct of every charge being an affair requiring tact. But so regulate by general rules the conduct of an infantry charge that those who commence it too far away can properly be accused of panic. And there is a way. Regulate it as the cavalry charge is regulated, and have a rearguard in each battalion of non-commissioned officers, of most reliable officers, in order to gather together, to follow close upon the charge, at a walk, and to collect all those who have lain down so as not to march or because they were out of breath. This rear-guard might consist of a small platoon of picked shots, such as we need in each battalion. The charge ought to be made at a given distance, else it vanishes, evaporates. The leader who commences it too soon either has no head, or does not want to gain his objective.

The infantry of the line, as opposed to elite commands, should not be kept in support. The least firm, the most impressionable, are thus sent into the road stained with the blood of the strongest. We place them, after a moral anxiety of waiting, face to face with the terrible destruction and mutilation of modern weapons. If antiquity had need of solid troops as supports, we have a greater need of them. Death in ancient combat was not as horrible as in the modern battle where the flesh is mangled, slashed by artillery fire. In ancient combat, except in defeat, the wounded were few in number. This is the reply to those who wish to begin an action by chasseurs, zouaves, etc.

He, general or mere captain, who employs every one in the storming of a position can be sure of seeing it retaken by an organized counter-attack of four men and a corporal.

In order that we may have real supervision and responsibility in units from companies to brigades, the supporting troops ought to be of the same company, the same battalion, the same brigade, as the case may be. Each brigade ought to have its two lines, each battalion its skirmishers, etc.

The system of holding out a reserve as long as possible for independent action when the enemy has used his own, ought to be applied downwards. Each battalion should have its own, each regiment its own, firmly maintained.

There is more need than ever today, for protecting the supporting forces, the reserves. The power of destruction increases, the morale remains the same. The tests of morale, being more violent than previously, ought to be shorter, because the power of morale has not increased. The masses, reserves, the second, the first lines, should be protected and sheltered even more than the skirmishers.

Squares sometimes are broken by cavalry which pursues the skirmishers into the square. Instead of lying down, they rush blindly to their refuge which they render untenable and destroy. No square can hold out against determined troops.... But!

The infantry square is not a thing of mechanics, of mathematical reasoning; it is a thing of morale. A platoon in four ranks, two facing the front, two the rear, its flanks guarded by the extreme files that face to the flank, and conducted, supported by the non-commissioned officers placed in a fifth rank, in the interior of the rectangle, powerful in its compactness and its fire, cannot be dislodged by cavalry. However, this platoon will prefer to form a part of a large square, it will consider itself stronger, because of numbers, and indeed it will be, since the feeling of force pervades this whole force. This feeling is power in war.

People who calculate only according to the fire delivered, according to the destructive power of infantry, would have it fight deployed against cavalry. They do not consider that although supported and maintained, although such a formation seem to prevent flight, the very impetus of the charge, if led resolutely, will break the deployment before the shock arrives. It is clear that if the charge is badly conducted, whether the infantry be solid or not, it will never reach its objective. Why? Moral reasons and no others make the soldier in a square feel himself stronger than when in line. He feels himself watched from behind and has nowhere to flee.

3. Firing

It is easy to misuse breech-loading weapons, such as the rifle. The fashion today is to use small intrenchments, covering battalions. As old as powder. Such shelter is an excellent device on the condition, however, that behind it, a useful fire can be delivered.

Look at these two ranks crouched under the cover of a small trench. Follow the direction of the shots. Even note the trajectory shown by the burst of flame. You will be convinced that, under such conditions, even simple horizontal firing is a fiction. In a second, there will be wild firing on account of the noise, the crowding, the interference of the two ranks. Next everybody tries to get under the best possible cover. Good-by firing.

It is essential to save ammunition, to get all possible efficiency from the arm. Yet the official adoption of fire by rank insures relapsing into useless firing at random. Good shots are wasted, placed where it is impossible for them to fire well.

Since we have a weapon that fires six times more rapidly than the ancient weapon, why not profit by it to cover a given space with six times fewer riflemen than formerly? Riflemen placed at greater intervals, will be less bewildered, will see more clearly, will be better watched (which may seem strange to you), and will consequently deliver a better fire than formerly. Besides, they will expend six times less ammunition. That is the vital point. You must always have ammunition available, that is to say, troops which have not been engaged. Reserves must be held out. This is hard to manage perhaps. It is not so hard to manage, however, as fire by command.

What is the use of fire by rank? By command? It is impracticable against the enemy, except in extraordinary cases. Any attempt at supervision of it is a joke! File firing? The first rank can shoot horizontally, the only thing required; the second rank can fire only into the air. It is useless to fire with our bulky knapsacks interfering so that our men raise the elbow higher than the shoulder. Learn what the field pack can be from the English, Prussians, Austrians, etc.... Could the pack not be thicker and less wide? Have the first rank open; let the second be checkerwise; and let firing against cavalry be the only firing to be executed in line.

One line will be better than two, because it will not be hindered by the one behind it. One kind of fire is practicable and efficient, that of one rank. This is the fire of skirmishers in close formation.

The king's order of June 1st, 1776, reads (p. 28): "Experience in war having proved that three ranks fire standing, and the intention of his majesty being to prescribe only what can be executed in front of the enemy, he orders that in firing, the first man is never to put his knee on the ground, and that the three ranks fire standing at the same time." This same order includes instructions on target practice, etc.

Marshal de Gouvion-Saint Cyr says that conservatively one-fourth of the men who are wounded in an affair are put out of commission by the third rank. This estimate is not high enough if it concerns a unit composed of recruits like those who fought at Lützen and Bautzen. The marshal mentions the astonishment of Napoleon when he saw the great number of men wounded in the hand and forearm. This astonishment of Napoleon's is singular. What ignorance in his marshals not to have explained such wounds! Chief Surgeon Larrey, by observation of the wounds, alone exonerated our soldiers of the accusation of self-inflicted wounds. The observation would have been made sooner, had the wounds heretofore been numerous. That they had not been can be explained only by the fact that while the young soldiers of 1813 kept instinctively close in ranks, up to that time the men must have spaced themselves instinctively, in order to be able to shoot. Or perhaps in 1813, these young men might have been allowed to fire a longer time in order to distract them and keep them in ranks, and not often allowed to act as skirmishers for fear of losing them. Whilst formerly, the fire by rank must have been much rarer and fire action must have given way almost entirely to the use of skirmishers.

Fire by command presupposes an impossible coolness. Had any troops ever possessed it they would have mowed down battalions as one mows down corn stalks. Yet it has been known for a long time, since Frederick, since before Frederick, since the first rifle. Let troops get the range calmly, let them take aim together so that no one disturbs or hinders the other. Have each one see clearly, then, at a signal, let them all fire at once. Who is going to stand against such people? But did they aim in those days? Not so accurately, possibly, but they knew how to shoot waist-high, to shoot at the feet. They knew how to do it. I do not say they did it. If they had done so, there would not have been any need of reminding them of it so often. Note Cromwell's favorite saying, "Aim at their shoe-laces;" that of the officers of the empire, "Aim at the height of the waist." Study of battles, of the expenditure of bullets, show us no such immediate terrible results. If such a means of destruction was so easy to obtain, why did not our illustrious forbears use it and recommend it to us? (Words of de Gouvion-Saint-Cyr.)

Security alone creates calmness under fire.

In minor operations of war, how many captains are capable of tranquilly commanding their fire and maneuvering with calmness?

Here is a singular thing. You hear fire by rank against cavalry seriously recommended in military lectures. Yet not a colonel, not a battalion commander, not a captain, requires this fire to be executed in maneuvers. It is always the soldier who forces the firing. He is ordered to shoot almost before he aims for fear he will shoot without command. Yet he ought to feel that when he is aiming, his finger on the trigger, his shot does not belong to him, but rather to the officer who ought to be able to let him aim for five minutes, if advisable, examining, correcting the positions, etc. He ought, when aiming, always be ready to fire upon the object designated, without ever knowing when it will please his commander to order him to fire.

Fire at command is not practicable in the face of the enemy. If it were, the perfection of its execution would depend on the coolness of the commander and the obedience of the soldier. The soldier is the more easily trained.

The Austrians had fire by command in Italy against cavalry. Did they use it? They fired before the command, an irregular fire, a fire by file, with defective results.

Fire by command is impossible. But why is firing by rank at will impossible, illusory, under the fire of the enemy? Because of the reasons already given and, for this reason: that closed ranks are incompatible with fire-arms, on account of the wounding caused by the latter in ranks. In closed ranks, the two lines touching elbows, a man who falls throws ten men into complete confusion. There is no room for those who drop and, however few fall, the resulting disorder immediately makes of the two ranks a series of small milling groups. If the troops are young, they become a disordered flock before any demonstration. (Caldiero, Duhesme.) If the troops have some steadiness, they of themselves will make space: they will try to make way for the bullets: they will scatter as skirmishers with small intervals. (Note the Grenadier Guards at Magenta.)

With very open ranks, men a pace apart, whoever falls has room, he is noticed by a lesser number, he drags down no one in his fall. The moral impression on his comrades is less. Their courage is less impaired. Besides, with rapid fire everywhere, spaced ranks with no man in front of another, at least permit horizontal fire. Closed ranks permit it hardly in the first rank, whose ears are troubled by the shots from the men behind. When a man has to fire four or five shots a minute, one line is certainly more solid than two, because, while the firing is less by half, it is more than twice as likely to be horizontal fire as in the two-rank formation. Well-sustained fire, even with blank cartridges, would be sufficient to prevent a successful charge. With slow fire, two ranks alone were able to keep up a sufficiently continuous fusillade. With rapid fire, a single line delivers more shots than two with ancient weapons. Such fire, therefore, suffices as a fusillade.

Close ranks, while suitable for marching, do not lend themselves to firing at the halt. Marching, a man likes a comrade at his side. Firing, as if he felt the flesh attracting the lead, he prefers being relatively isolated, with space around him. Breech-loading rifles breed queer ideas. Generals are found who say that rapid firing will bring back fire at command, as if there ever were such a thing. They say it will bring back salvo firing, thus permitting clear vision. As if such a thing were possible! These men have not an atom of common sense.

It is singular to see a man like Guibert, with practical ideas on most things, give a long dissertation to demonstrate that the officers of his time were wrong in aiming at the middle of the body, that is, in firing low. He claims this is ridiculous to one who understands the trajectory of the rifle. These officers were right. They revived the recommendations of Cromwell, because they knew that in combat the soldier naturally fires too high because he does not aim, and because the shape of the rifle, when it is brought to the shoulder, tends to keep the muzzle higher than the breech. Whether that is the reason or something else, the fact is indisputable. It is said that in Prussian drills all the bullets hit the ground at fifty paces. With the arms of that time and the manner of fighting, results would have been magnificent in battle if the bullets had struck fifty paces before the enemy instead of passing over his head.

Yet at Mollwitz, where the Austrians had five thousand men disabled, the Prussians had over four thousand.

Firing with a horizontal sector, if the muzzle be heavy, is more deadly than firing with a vertical sector.

4. Marches. Camps. Night Attacks.

From the fact that infantry ought always to fight in thin formation, scattered, it does not follow that it ought to be kept in that order. Only in column is it possible to maintain the battle order. It is necessary to keep one's men in hand as long as possible, because once engaged, they no longer belong to you.

The disposition in closed mass is not a suitable marching formation, even in a battalion for a short distance. On account of heat, the closed column is intolerable, like an unventilated room. Formation with half-distances is better. (Why? Air, view, etc.)

Such a formation prevents ready entry of the column into battle in case of necessity or surprise. The half-divisions not in the first line are brought up, the arms at the order, and they can furnish either skirmishers or a reserve for the first line which has been deployed as skirmishers.

At Leuctra, Epaminondas diminished, by one-half, the depth of his men; he formed square phalanxes of fifty men to a side. He could have very well dispensed with it, for the Lacedaemonian right was at once thrown into disorder by its own cavalry which was placed in front of that wing. The superior cavalry of Epaminondas overran not only the cavalry but the infantry that was behind it. The infantry of Epaminondas, coming in the wake of his cavalry finished the work. Turning to the right, the left of Epaminondas then took in the flank the Lacedaemonian line. Menaced also in front by the approaching echelons of Epaminondas, this line became demoralized and took to flight. Perhaps this fifty by fifty formation was adopted in order to give, without maneuver, a front of fifty capable of acting in any direction. At Leuctra, it simply acted to the right and took the enemy in the flank and in reverse.

Thick woods are generally passed through in close column. There is never any opening up, with subsequent closing on the far side. The resulting formation is as confused as a flock of sheep.

In a march through mountains, difficult country, a bugler should be on the left, at the orders of an intelligent officer who indicates when the halt seems necessary for discipline in the line. The right responds and if the place has been judged correctly an orderly formation is maintained. Keep in ranks. If one man steps out, others follow. Do not permit men to leave ranks without requiring them to rejoin.

In the rear-guard it is always necessary to have pack mules in an emergency; without this precaution, considerable time may be lost. In certain difficult places time is thus lost every day.

In camp, organize your fatigue parties in advance; send them out in formation and escorted.

Definite and detailed orders ought to be given to the convoy, and the chief baggage-master ought to supervise it, which is rarely the case.

It is a mistake to furnish mules to officers and replace them in case of loss or sickness. The officer overloads the mule and the Government loses more thereby than is generally understood. Convoys are endless owing to overloaded mules and stragglers. If furnished money to buy a mule the officer uses it economically because it is his. If mules are individually furnished to officers instead of money, the officer will care for his beast for the same reason. But it is better to give money only, and the officer, if he is not well cared for on the march has no claim against the Government.

Always, always, take Draconian measures to prevent pillage from commencing. If it begins, it is difficult ever to stop it. A body of infantry is never left alone. There is no reason for calling officers of that arm inapt, when battalions although established in position are not absolutely on the same line, with absolutely equal intervals. Ten moves are made to achieve the exact alignment which the instructions on camp movements prescribe. Yet designating a guiding battalion might answer well enough and still be according to the regulations.

Why are not night attacks more employed today, at least on a grand scale? The great front which armies occupy renders their employment more difficult, and exacts of the troops an extreme aptitude in this kind of surprise tactics (found in the Arabs, Turcos, Spahis), or absolute reliability. There are some men whose knowledge of terrain is wonderful, with an unerring eye for distance, who can find their way through places at night which they have visited only in the day time. Utilizing such material for a system of guides it would be possible to move with certainty. These are simple means, rarely employed, for conducting a body of troops into position on the darkest night. There is, even, a means of assuring at night the fire of a gun upon a given point with as much precision as in plain day.

CHAPTER III - CAVALRY

1. Cavalry and Modern Appliances

They say that cavalry is obsolete; that it can be of no use in battles waged with the weapons of today. Is not infantry affected in the same way?

Examples drawn from the last two wars are not conclusive. In a siege, in a country which is cut off, one does not dare to commit the cavalry, and therefore takes from it its boldness, which is almost its only weapon.

The utility of cavalry has always been doubted. That is because its cost is high. It is little used, just because it does cost. The question of economy is vital in peace times. When we set a high value upon certain men, they are not slow to follow suit, and to guard themselves against being broken. Look at staff officers who are almost never broken (reduced), even when their general himself is.

With new weapons the role of cavalry has certainly changed less than any other, although it is the one which is most worried about. However, cavalry always has the same doctrine: Charge! To start with, cavalry action against cavalry is always the same. Also against infantry. Cavalry knows well enough today, as it has always known, that it can act only against infantry which has been broken. We must leave aside epic legends that are always false, whether they relate to cavalry or infantry. Infantry cannot say as much of its own action against infantry. In this respect there is a complete anarchy of ideas. There is no infantry doctrine.

With the power of modern weapons, which forces you to slow down if it does not stop you, the advance under fire becomes almost impossible. The advantage is with the defensive. This is so evident that only a madman could dispute it. What then is to be done? Halt, to shoot at random and cannonade at long range until ammunition is exhausted? Perhaps. But what is sure, is that such a state of affairs makes maneuver necessary. There is more need than ever for maneuver at a long distance in an attempt to force the enemy to shift, to quit his position. What maneuver is swifter than that of cavalry? Therein is its role.

The extreme perfection of weapons permits only individual action in combat, that is action by scattered forces. At the same time it permits the effective employment of mass action out of range, of maneuvers on the flank or in the rear of the enemy in force imposing enough to frighten him.

Can the cavalry maneuver on the battle field? Why not? It can maneuver rapidly, and above all beyond the range of infantry fire, if not of artillery fire. Maneuver being a threat, of great moral effect, the cavalry general who knows how to use it, can contribute largely to success. He arrests the enemy in movement, doubtful as to what the cavalry is going to attempt. He makes the enemy take some formation that keeps him under artillery fire for a while, above all that of light artillery if the general knows how to use it. He increases the enemy's demoralization and thus is able to rejoin his command.

Rifled cannon and accurate rifles do not change cavalry tactics at all. These weapons of precision, as the word precision indicates, are effective only when all battle conditions, all conditions of aiming, are ideal. If the necessary condition of suitable range is lacking, effect is lacking. Accuracy of fire at a distance is impossible against a troop in movement, and movement is the essence of cavalry action. Rifled weapons fire on them of course, but they fire on everybody.

In short, cavalry is in the same situation as anybody else.

What response is there to this argument? Since weapons have been improved, does not the infantryman have to march under fire to attack a position? Is the cavalryman not of the same flesh? Has he less heart than the infantryman? If one can march under fire, cannot the other gallop under it?

When the cavalryman cannot gallop under fire, the infantryman cannot march under it. Battles will consist of exchanges of rifle shots by concealed men, at long range. The battle will end only when the ammunition is exhausted.

The cavalryman gallops through danger, the infantryman walks. That is why, if he learns, as it is probable he will, to keep at the proper distance, the cavalryman will never see his battle role diminished by the perfection of long range fire. An infantryman will never succeed by himself. The cavalryman will threaten, create diversions, worry, scatter the enemy's fire, often even get to close quarters if he is properly supported. The infantryman will act as usual. But more than ever will he need the aid of cavalry in the attack. He who knows how to use his cavalry with audacity will inevitably be the victor. Even though the cavalryman offers a larger target, long range weapons will paralyze him no more than another.

The most probable effect of artillery of today, will be to increase the scattering in the infantry, and even in the cavalry. The latter can start in skirmisher formation at a distance and close in while advancing, near its objective. It will be more difficult to lead; but this is to the advantage of the Frenchman.

The result of improving the ballistics of the weapon, for the cavalry as for the infantry (there is no reason why it should be otherwise for the cavalry), will be that a man will flee at a greater distance from it, and nothing more.

Since the Empire, the opinion of European armies is that the cavalry has not given the results expected of it.

It has not given great results, for the reason that we and others lacked real cavalry generals. He is, it seems, a phenomenon that is produced only every thousand years, more rarely than a real general of infantry. To be a good general, whether of infantry or cavalry, is an infinitely rare thing, like the good in everything. The profession of a good infantry general is as difficult as, perhaps more difficult than, that of a good cavalry general. Both require calmness. It comes more easily to the cavalryman than to the foot soldier who is much more engaged. Both require a like precision, a judgment of the moral and physical forces of the soldier; and the morale of the infantryman, his constitution, is more tried than is the case with the horseman.

The cavalry general, of necessity, sees less clearly; his vision has its limits. Great cavalry generals are rare. Doubtless Seidlitz could not, in the face of the development of cannon and rifle, repeat his wonders. But there is always room for improvement. I believe there is much room for improvement.

We did not have under the Empire a great cavalry general who knew how to handle masses. The cavalry was used like a blind hammer that strikes heavily and not always accurately. It had immense losses. Like the Gauls, we have a little too much confidence in the "forward, forward, not so many methods." Methods do not hinder the forward movement. They prepare the effect and render it surer and at the same time less costly to the assailant. We have all the Gallic brutality. (Note Marignano, where the force of artillery and the possibility of a turning movement around a village was neglected). What rare things infantry and cavalry generals are!

A leader must combine resolute bravery and impetuosity with prudence and calmness; a difficult matter!

The broken terrain of European fields no longer permits, we are told, the operation of long lines, of great masses of cavalry. I do not regret it. I am struck more with the picturesque effect of these hurricanes of cavalry in the accounts of the Empire than with the results obtained. It does not seem to me that these results were in proportion to the apparent force of the effort and to the real grandeur of the sacrifices. And indeed, these enormous hammers (a usual figure), are hard to handle. They have not the sure direction of a weapon well in hand. If the blow is not true, recovery is impossible, etc. However, the terrain does not today permit the assembling of cavalry in great masses. This compelling reason for new methods renders any other reason superfluous.

Nevertheless, the other reasons given in the ministerial observations of 1868, on the cavalry service, seems to me excellent. The improvement of appliances, the extension of battle fields, the confidence to the infantry and the audacity to the artillery that the immediate support of the cavalry gives, demand that this arm be in eveevery division in sufficient force for efficient action.

I, therefore, think it desirable for a cavalry regiment to be at the disposal of a general commanding a division. Whatever the experiences of instruction centers, they can not change in the least my conviction of the merit of this measure in the field.

2. Cavalry Against Cavalry

Cavalry action, more than that of infantry, is an affair of morale.

Let us study first the morale of the cavalry engagement in single combat. Two riders rush at each other. Are they going to direct their horses front against front? Their horses would collide, both would be forced to their feet, while running the chance of being crushed in the clash or in the fall of their mounts. Each one in the combat counts on his strength, on his skill, on the suppleness of his mount, on his personal courage; he does not want a blind encounter, and he is right. They halt face to face, abreast, to fight man to man; or each passes the other, thrusting with the sabre or lance; or each tries to wound the knee of the adversary and dismount him in this way. But as each is trying to strike the other, he thinks of keeping out of the way himself, he does not want a blind encounter that does away with the combat. The ancient battles, the cavalry engagements, the rare cavalry combats of our days, show us nothing else.

Discipline, while keeping the cavalrymen in the ranks, has not been able to change the instinct of the rider. No more than the isolated man is the rider in the line willing to meet the shock of a clash with the enemy. There is a terrible moral effect in a mass moving forward. If there is no way to escape to the right or to the left, men and horses will avoid the clash by stopping face to face. But only preëminently brave troops, equally seasoned in morale, alike well led and swept along, animated alike, will meet face to face. All these conditions are never found united on either side, so the thing is never seen. Forty-nine times out of fifty, one of the cavalry forces will hesitate, bolt, get into disorder, flee before the fixed purpose of the other. Three quarters of the time this will happen at a distance, before they can see each other's eyes. Often they will get closer. But always, always, the stop, the backward movement, the swerving of horses, the confusion, bring about fear or hesitation. They lessen the shock and turn it into instant flight. The resolute assailant does not have to slacken. He has not been able to overcome or turn the obstacles of horses not yet in flight, in this uproar of an impossible about face executed by routed troops, without being in disorder himself. But this disorder is that of victory, of the advance, and a good cavalry does not trouble itself about it. It rallies in advancing, while the vanquished one has fear at its heels.

On the whole, there are few losses. The engagement, if there is one, is an affair of a second. The proof is that in this action of cavalry against cavalry, the conquered alone loses men, and he loses generally few. The battle against infantry is alone the really deadly struggle. Like numbers of little chasseurs have routed heavy cuirassiers. How could they have done so if the others had not given way before their determination? The essential factor was, and always is, determination.

The cavalry's casualties are always much less than those of the infantry both from fire and from disease. Is it because the cavalry is the aristocratic arm? This explains why in long wars it improves much more than the infantry.

As there are few losses between cavalry and cavalry, so there is little fighting.

Hannibal's Numidians, like the Russian Cossacks, inspired a veritable terror by the incessant alarms they caused. They tired out without fighting and killed by surprise.

Why is the cavalry handled so badly?—It is true that infantry is not used better.—Because its role is one of movement, of morale, of morale and movement so united, that movement alone, often without a charge or shock action of any sort can drive the enemy into retreat, and, if followed closely, into rout. That is a result of the quickness of cavalry. One who knows how to make use of this quickness alone can obtain such results.

All writers on cavalry will tell you that the charge pushed home of two cavalry bodies and the shock at top speed do not exist. Always before the encounter, the weaker runs away, if there is not a face to face check. What becomes then of the MV squared? If this famous MV squared is an empty word, why then crush your horses under giants, forgetting that in the formula besides M there is V squared. In a charge, there is M, there is V squared, there is this and that. There is resolution, and I believe, nothing else that counts!

Cohesion and unity give force to the charge. Alignment is impossible at a fast gait where the most rapid pass the others. Only when the moral effect has been produced should the gait be increased to take advantage of it by falling upon an enemy already in disorder, in the act of fleeing. The cuirassiers charge at a trot. This calm steadiness frightens the enemy into an about face. Then they charge at his back, at a gallop.

They say that at Eckmühl, for every French cuirassier down, fourteen Austrians were struck in the back. Was it because they had no back-plate? It is evident that it was because they offered their backs to the blows.

Jomini speaks of charges at a trot against cavalry at a gallop. He cites Lasalle who used the trot and who, seeing cavalry approach at a gallop, would say: "There are lost men." Jomini insists on the effect of shock. The trot permits that compactness which the gallop breaks up. That may be true. But the effect is moral above all. A troop at the gallop sees a massed squadron coming towards it at a trot. It is surprised at first at such coolness. The material impulse of the gallop is superior; but there are no intervals, no gaps through which to penetrate the line in order to avoid the shock, the shock that overcomes men and horses. These men must be very resolute, as their close ranks do not permit them to escape by about facing. If they move at such a steady gait, it is because their resolution is also firm and they do not feel the need of running away, of diverting themselves by the unchecked speed of the unrestrained gallop, etc.

Galloping men do not reason these things out, but they know them instinctively. They understand that they have before them a moral impulse superior to theirs.

They become uneasy, hesitate. Their hands instinctively turn their horses aside. There is no longer freedom in the attack at a gallop. Some go on to the end, but three-fourths have already tried to avoid the shock. There is complete disorder, demoralization, flight. Then begins the pursuit at a gallop by the men who attacked at the trot.

The charge at a trot exacts of leaders and men complete confidence and steadfastness. It is the experience of battle only that can give this temper to all. But this charge, depending on a moral effect, will not always succeed. It is a question of surprise. Xenophon recommended, in his work on cavalry operations, the use of surprise, the use of the gallop when the trot is customary, and vice-versa. "Because," he says, "agreeable or terrible, the less a thing is foreseen, the more pleasure or fright does it cause. This is nowhere seen better than in war, where every surprise strikes terror even to the strongest."

As a general rule, the gallop is and should be necessary in the charge; it is the winning, intoxicating gait, for men and horses. It is taken up at such a distance as may be necessary to insure its success, whatever it may cost in men and horses. The regulations are correct in prescribing that the charge be started close up. If the troopers waited until the charge was ordered, they would always succeed. I say that strong men, moved by pride or fear, by taking up too soon the charge against a firm enemy, have caused more charges to fail than to succeed. Keeping men in hand until the command "charge," seizing the precise instant for this command, are both difficult. They exact of the energetic leader domination over his men and a keen eye, at a moment when three out of four men no longer see anything, so that good cavalry leaders, squadron leaders in general are very rare. Real charges are just as rare.

Actual shock no longer exists. The moral impulse of one of the adversaries nearly always upsets the other, perhaps far off, perhaps a little nearer. Were this "a little nearer," face to face, one of the two troops would be already defeated before the first saber cut and would disentangle itself for flight. With actual shock, all would be thrown into confusion. A real charge on the one part or the other would cause mutual extermination. In practice the victor scarcely loses any one.

Observation demonstrates that cavalry does not close with cavalry; its deadly combats are those against infantry alone.

Even if a cavalryman waits without flinching, his horse will wish to escape, to shrink before the collision. If man anticipates, so does the horse. Why did Frederick like to see his center closed in for the assault? As the best guarantee against the instincts of man and horse.

The cavalry of Frederick had ordinarily only insignificant losses: a result of determination.

The men want to be distracted from the advancing danger by movement. The cavalrymen who go at the enemy, if left to themselves, would start at a gallop, for fear of not arriving, or of arriving exhausted and material for carnage. The same is true of the Arabs. Note what happened in 1864 to the cavalry of General Martineau. The rapid move relieves anxiety. It is natural to wish to lessen it. But the leaders are there, whom experience, whom regulations order to go slowly, then to accelerate progressively, so as to arrive with the maximum of speed. The procedure should be the walk, then the trot, after that the gallop, then the charge. But it takes a trained eye to estimate distance and the character of the terrain, and, if the enemy approaches, to pick the point where one should meet him. The nearer one approaches, the greater among the troops is the question of morale. The necessity of arriving at the greatest speed is not alone a mechanical question, since indeed one never clashes, it is a moral necessity. It is necessary to seize the moment at which the uneasiness of one's men requires the intoxication of the headlong charging gallop. An instant too late, and a too great anxiety has taken the upper hand and caused the hands of the riders to act on the horses; the start is not free; a number hide by remaining behind. An instant too soon: before arrival the speed has slowed down; the animation, the intoxication of the run, fleeting things, are exhausted. Anxiety takes the upper hand again, the hands act instinctively, and even if the start were unhampered, the arrival is not.

Frederick and Seidlitz were content when they saw the center of the charging squadron three and four ranks deep. It was as if they understood that with this compact center, as the first lines could not escape to the right or left, they were forced to continue straight ahead.

In order to rush like battering-rams, even against infantry, men and horses ought to be watered and fresh (Ponsomby's cavalry at Waterloo). If there is ever contact between cavalry, the shock is so weakened by the hands of the men, the rearing of the horses, the swinging of heads, that both sides come to a halt.

Only the necessity for carrying along the man and the horse at the supreme moment, for distracting them, necessitates the full gallop before attacking the enemy, before having put him to flight.

Charges at the gallop of three or four kilometers, suppose horses of bronze.

Because morale is not studied and because historical accounts are taken too literally, each epoch complains that cavalry forces are no longer seen charging and fighting with the sword, that too much prudence dictates running away instead of clashing with the enemy.

These plaints have been made ever since the Empire, both by the allies, and by us. But this has always been true. Man was never invulnerable. The charging gait has almost always been the trot. Man does not change. Even the combats of cavalry against cavalry today are deadlier than they were in the lamented days of chivalry.

The retreat of the infantry is always more difficult than that of the cavalry; the latter is simple. A cavalry repulsed and coming back in disorder is a foreseen, an ordinary happening; it is going to rally at a distance. It often reappears with advantage. One can almost say, in view of experience, that such is its role. An infantry that is repelled, especially if the action has been a hot one and the cavalry rushes in, is often disorganized for the rest of the day.

Even authors who tell you that two squadrons never collide, tell you continually: "The force of cavalry is in the shock." In the terror of the shock, Yes. In the shock, No! It lies only in determination. It is a mental and not a mechanical condition.

Never give officers and men of the cavalry mathematical demonstrations of the charge. They are good only to shake confidence. Mathematical reasoning shows a mutual collapse that never takes place. Show them the truth. Lasalle with his always victorious charge at a trot guarded against similar reasonings, which might have demonstrated to him mathematically that a charge of cuirassiers at a trot ought to be routed by a charge of hussars at a gallop. He simply told them: "Go resolutely and be sure that you will never find a daredevil determined enough to come to grips with you." It is necessary to be a daredevil in order to go to the end. The Frenchman is one above all. Because he is a good trooper in battle, when his commanders themselves are daredevils he is the best in Europe. (Note the days of the Empire, the remarks of Wellington, a good judge). If moreover, his leaders use a little head work, that never harms anything. The formula of the cavalry is R (Resolution) and R, and always R, and R is greater than all the MV squared in the world.

There is this important element in the pursuit of cavalry by cavalry. The pursued cannot halt without delivering himself up to the pursuer. The pursuer can always see the pursued. If the latter halts and starts to face about the pursuer can fall upon him before he is faced, and take him by surprise. But the pursued does not know how many are pursuing him. If he alone halts two pursuers may rush on him, for they see ahead of them and they naturally attack whoever tries to face about. For with the about face danger again confronts them. The pursuit is often instigated by the fear that the enemy will turn. The material fact that once in flight all together cannot turn again without risking being surprised and overthrown, makes the flight continuous. Even the bravest flee, until sufficient distance between them and the enemy, or some other circumstances such as cover or supporting troops, permits of a rally and a return to the offensive. In this case the pursuit may turn into flight in its turn.

Cavalry is insistent on attacking on an equal front. Because, if with a broader front, the enemy gives way before it, his wings may attack it and make it the pursued instead of the pursuer. The moral effect of resolution is so great that cavalry, breaking and pursuing a more numerous cavalry, is never pursued by the enemy wings. However the idea that one may be taken in rear by forces whom one has left on the flanks in a position to do so, has such an effect that the resolution necessary for an attack under these circumstances is rare.

Why is it that Colonel A—— does not want a depth formation for cavalry, he who believes in pressure of the rear ranks on the first? It is because at heart he is convinced that only the first rank can act in a cavalry charge, and that this rank can receive no impression, no speeding up, from those behind it.

There is debate as to the advantage of one or two ranks for the cavalry. This again is a matter of morale. Leave liberty of choice, and under varying conditions of confidence and morale one or the other will be adopted. There are enough officers for either formation.

It is characteristic of cavalry to advance further than infantry and consequently it exposes its flanks more. It then needs more reserves to cover its flanks and rear than does infantry. It needs reserves to protect and to support the pursuers who are almost always pursued when they return. With cavalry even more than infantry victory belongs to the last reserves held intact. The one with the reserves is always the one who can take the offensive. Tie to that, and no one can stand before you.

With room to maneuver cavalry rallies quickly. In deep columns it cannot.

The engagement of cavalry lasts only a moment. It must be reformed immediately. With a roll call at each reforming, it gets out of hand less than the infantry, which, once engaged, has little respite. There should be a roll call for cavalry, and for infantry after an advance, at each lull. There should be roll calls at drill and in field maneuvers, not that they are necessary but in order to become habituated to them. Then the roll call will not be forgotten on the day of action, when very few think of what ought to be done.

In the confusion and speed of cavalry action, man escapes more easily from surveillance. In our battles his action is increasingly individual and rapid. The cavalryman should not be left too free; that would be dangerous. Frequently in action troops should be reformed and the roll called. It would be an error not to do so. There might be ten to twenty roll calls in a day. The officers, the soldiers, would then have a chance to demand an accounting from each man, and might demand it the next day.

Once in action, and that action lasts, the infantryman of today escapes from the control of his officers. This is due to the disorder inherent in battle, to deployment, to the absence of roll calls, which cannot be held in action. Control, then, can only be in the hands of his comrades. Of modern arms infantry is the one in which there is the greatest need for cohesion.

Cavalry always fights very poorly and very little. This has been true from antiquity, when the cavalryman was of a superior caste to the infantryman, and ought to have been braver.

Anybody advancing, cavalry or infantry, ought to scout and reconnoiter as soon as possible the terrain on which it acts. Condé forgot this at Neerwinden. The 55th forgot it at Solferino. Everybody forgets it. And from the failure to use skirmishers and scouts, come mistakes and disasters.

The cavalry has a rifle for exceptional use. Look out that this exception does not become the rule. Such a tendency has been seen. At the battle of Sicka, the first clash was marred by the lack of dash on the part of a regiment of Chasseurs d'Afrique, which after being sent off at the gallop, halted to shoot. At the second clash General Bugeaud charged at their head to show them how to charge.

A young Colonel of light cavalry, asked carbines for his cavalry. "Why? So that if I want to reconnoiter a village I can sound it from a distance of seven or eight hundred meters without losing anybody." What can you say to a man advancing such ideas? Certainly the carbine makes everybody lose common sense.

The work of light cavalry makes it inevitable that they be captured sometimes. It is impossible to get news of the enemy without approaching him. If one man escapes in a patrol, that is enough. If no one comes back, even that fact is instructive. The cavalry is a priceless object that no leader wants to break. However it is only by breaking it that results can be obtained.

Some authors think of using cavalry as skirmishers, mounted or dismounted. I suppose they advance holding the horse by the bridle? This appears to be to be an absurdity. If the cavalryman fires he will not charge. The African incident cited proves that. It would be better to give the cavalryman two pistols than a carbine.

461

The Americans in their vast country where there is unlimited room, used cavalry wisely in sending it off on distant forays to cut communications, make levies, etc. What their cavalry did as an arm in battle is unknown. The cavalry raids in the American war were part of a war directed against wealth, against public works, against resources. It was war of destruction of riches, not of men. The raiding cavalry had few losses, and inflicted few losses. The cavalry is always the aristocratic arm which loses very lightly, even if it risks all. At least it has the air of risking all, which is something at any rate. It has to have daring and daring is not so common. But the merest infantry engagements in equal numbers costs more than the most brilliant cavalry raid.

3. Cavalry Against Infantry

Cavalry knows how to fight cavalry. But how it fights infantry not one cavalry officer in a thousand knows. Perhaps not one of them knows. Go to it then gaily, with general uncertainty!

A military man, a participant in our great wars, recommends as infallible against infantry in line the charge from the flank, horse following horse. He would have cavalry coming up on the enemy's left, pass along his front and change direction so as to use its arms to the right. This cavalryman is right. Such charges should give excellent results, the only deadly results. The cavalryman can only strike to his right, and in this way each one strikes. Against ancient infantry such charges would have been as valuable as against modern infantry. This officer saw with his own eyes excellent examples of this attack in the wars of the Empire. I do not doubt either the facts he cites or the deductions he makes. But for such charges there must be officers who inspire absolute confidence in their men and dependable and experienced soldiers. There is necessary, in short, an excellent cavalry, seasoned by long wars, and officers and men of very firm resolution. So it is not astonishing that examples of this mode of action are rare. They always will be. They always require a head for the charge, an isolated head, and when he is actually about to strike, he will fall back into the formation. It seems to him that lost in the mass he risks less than when alone. Everybody is willing to charge, but only if all charge together. It is a case of belling the cat.

The attack in column on infantry has a greater moral action than the charge in line. If the first and second squadrons are repulsed, but the infantry sees a third charging through the dust, it will say "When is this going to stop?" And it will be shaken.

An extract from Folard: "Only a capable officer is needed to get the best results from a cavalry which has confidence in its movement, which is known to be good and vigorous, and also is equipped with excellent weapons. Such cavalry will break the strongest battalions, if its leader has sense enough to know its power and courage enough to use this power."

Breaking is not enough, and is a feat that costs more than it is worth if the whole battalion is not killed or taken prisoner, or at least if the cavalry is not immediately followed by other troops, charged with this task.

At Waterloo our cavalry was exhausted fruitlessly, because it acted without artillery or infantry support.

At Krasno, August 14, 1812, Murat, at the head of his cavalry could not break an isolated body of ten thousand Russian infantry which continually held him off by its fire, and retired tranquilly across the plain.

The 72nd was upset by cavalry at Solferino.

From ancient days the lone infantryman has always had the advantage over the lone cavalryman. There is no shadow of a doubt about this in ancient narrations. The cavalryman only fought the cavalryman. He threatened, harassed, troubled the infantryman in the rear, but he did not fight him. He slaughtered him when put to flight by other infantry, or at least he scattered him and the light infantry slaughtered him.

Cavalry is a terrible weapon in the hands of one who knows how to use it. Who can say that Epaminondas could have defeated the Spartans twice without his Thessalonian cavalry.

Eventually rifle and artillery fire deafen the soldier; fatigue overpowers him; he becomes inert; he hears commands no longer. If cavalry unexpectedly appears, he is lost. Cavalry conquers merely by its appearance. (Bismarck or Decker).

Modern cavalry, like ancient cavalry, has a real effect only on troops already broken, on infantry engaged with infantry, on cavalry disorganized by artillery fire or by a frontal demonstration. But against such troops its action is decisive. In such cases its action is certain and gives enormous results. You might fight all day and lose ten thousand men, the enemy might lose as many, but if your cavalry pursues him, it will take thirty thousand prisoners. Its role is less knightly than its reputation and appearance, less so than the role of infantry. It always loses much less than infantry. Its greatest effect is the effect of surprise, and it is thereby that it gets such astonishing results.

What formation should infantry, armed with modern weapons, take to guard against flank attacks by cavalry? If one fires four times as fast, if the fire is better sustained, one needs only a quarter as many men to guard a point against cavalry. Protection might be secured by using small groups, placed the range of a rifle shot apart and flanking each other, left on the flank of the advance. But they must be dependable troops, who will not be worried by what goes on behind them.

4. Armor and Armament

An armored cavalry is clearly required for moral reasons.

Note this with reference to the influence of cuirassiers (armored cavalrymen) on morale. At the battle of Renty, in 1554, Tavannes, a marshal, had with him his company armored in steel. It was the first time that such armor had been seen. Supported by some hundreds of fugitives who had rallied, he threw himself at the head of his company, on a column of two thousand German cavalry who had just thrown both infantry and cavalry into disorder. He chose his time so well that he broke and carried away these two thousand Germans, who fell back and broke the twelve hundred light horsemen who were supporting them. There followed a general flight, and the battle was won.

General Renard says "The decadence of cavalry caused the disappearance of their square formations in battle, which were characteristic in the seventeenth century." It was not the decadence of the cavalry but the abandonment of the cuirass and the perfecting of the infantry weapon to give more rapid fire. When cuirassiers break through they serve as examples, and emulation extends to others, who another time try to break through as they did.

Why cuirassiers? Because they alone, in all history, have charged and do charge to the end.

To charge to the end the cuirassiers need only half the courage of the dragoons, as their armor raises their morale one half. But since the cuirassiers have as much natural courage as the dragoons, for they are all the same men, it is proper to count the more on their action. Shall we have only one kind of cavalry? Which? If all our cavalry could wear the cuirass and at the same time do the fatiguing work of light cavalry, if all our horses could in addition carry the cuirass through such work, I say that there should be only cuirassiers. But I do not understand why the morale given by the cuirass should be lightly done away with, merely to have one cavalry without the cuirass.

A cavalryman armored completely and his horse partially, can charge only at a trot.

On the appearance of fire arms, cavalry, according to General Ambert, an author of the past, covered itself with masses of armor resembling anvils rather than with cuirasses. It was at that time the essential arm. Later as infantry progressed the tactics changed, it needed more mobility. Permanent armies began to be organized by the State. The State thought less of the skin of the individual than of economy and mobility and almost did away with cuirassiers. The cuirass has always given, and today more than ever it will give, confidence to the cavalryman. Courage, dash, and speed have a value beyond that of mere mass. I leave aside mathematical discussions which seem to me to have nothing in common with battle conditions. I would pick to wear the cuirass the best men in the army, big chested, red-blooded, strong limbed, the foot chasseurs. I would organize a regiment of light cuirassiers for each of our divisions. Men and horses, such a cavalry would be much more robust and active than our present cuirassiers. If our armored cavalry is worth more than any other arm by its dash in battle, this cavalry would be worth twice as much. But how would these men of small stature get into the saddle? To this serious objection I answer, "They will arrange it." And this objection, which I do not admit, is the only one that can be made against the organization of a light armored cavalry, an organization that is made imperative by the improvement in weapons. The remainder of those chasseur battalions which furnish cuirassiers, should return to the infantry, which has long demanded them, and hussars and dragoons, dismounted in the necessary number will also be welcomed by the infantry.

As for the thrust, the thrust is deadlier than the cut. You do not have to worry about lifting your arm; you thrust. But it is necessary that the cavalryman be convinced that to parry a vertical cut is folly. This can be done by his officers, by those who have had experience, if there are any such in peace times. This is not easy. But in this respect, as in all others, the advantage lies with the brave. A cavalry charge is a matter of morale above all. It is identical in its methods, its effects, with the infantry charge. All the conditions to be fulfilled in the charge (walk, trot, gallop, charge, etc.) have a reason bearing on morale. These reasons have already been touched on.

Roman discipline and character demand tenacity. The hardening of the men to fatigue, and a good organization, giving mutual support, produced that tenacity, against which the bravest could not stand. The exhausting method of powerful strokes used by the Gauls could not last long against the skillful, terrible and less fatiguing method of fighting by the thrust.

The Sikh cavalrymen of M. Nolan armed with dragoon sabers sharpened by themselves, liked the cut. They knew nothing about methods of swordsmanship; they did not practice. They said "A good saber and a willingness to use it are enough." True, True!

There is always discussion as to the lance or the saber. The lance requires skillful vigorous cavalrymen, good horsemen, very well drilled, very adroit, for the use of the lance is more difficult than that of the straight sword, especially if the sword is not too heavy. Is not this an answer to the question? No matter what is done, no matter what methods are adopted, it must always be remembered that our recruits in war time are sent into squadrons as into battalions, with a hasty and incomplete training. If you give them lances, most of them will just have sticks in their hands, while a straight sword at the end of a strong arm is at the same time simple and terrible. A short trident spear, with three short points just long enough to kill but not only enough to go through the body, would remain in the body of the man and carry him along. It would recoil on the cavalryman who delivered the blow, he would be upset by the blow himself. But the dragoon must be supported by the saddle, and as he had kept hold of the shaft he would be able to disengage the fork which had pierced the body some six inches. No cavalry of equal morale could stand against a cavalry armed with such forked spears.

As between forks and lances, the fork would replace the lance. That is, of course, for beginners in mounted fencing. But the fork! It would be ridiculous, not military!

With the lance one always figures without the horse, whose slightest movement diverts the lance so much. The lance is a weapon frightful even to the mounted man who uses it properly. If he sticks an enemy at the gallop, he is dismounted, torn off by the arm attached to the lance which remains in the body of his enemy.

Cavalry officers and others who seek examples in "Victories and Conquests," in official reports, in "Bazancourt" are too naïve. It is hard to get at the truth. In war, in all things, we take the last example which we have witnessed. And now we want lances, which we do not know how to use, which frighten the cavalryman himself and pluck him from the saddle if he sticks anybody. We want no more cuirasses; we want this and that. We forget that the last example gives only a restricted number of instances relating to the matter in question.

It appears, according to Xenophon, that it was not easy to throw the dart from horseback. He constantly recommends obtaining as many men as possible who know how to throw the dart. He recommends leaning well back to avoid falling from the horse in the charge. In reading Xenophon it is evident that there was much falling from the horse.

It appears that in battle there is as great difficulty in handling the saber as in handling the bayonet. Another difficulty for the cavalryman lies in the handling of the musket. This is seen in the handling of the regulation weapon of the Spahis. There is only one important thing for the cavalryman, to be well seated. Men should be on horseback for hours at a time, every day, from their arrival in the organization. If the selection of those who know something about horses was not neglected in the draft, and if such men were, made cavalrymen, the practical training of the greater number would be much more rapidly concluded. I do not speak of the routine of the stable. Between mounted drills, foot drills might be gone through with in a snappy, free fashion, without rigidity, with daily increasing speed. Such drills would instruct cavalrymen more rapidly than the restricted method employed.

A dragoon horse carries in campaign with one day's food three hundred and eight pounds, without food or forage two hundred and seventy seven pounds. How can such horses carry this and have speed?

Seek the end always, not the means! Make a quarter of your cavalrymen into muleteers, a quarter of your horses into pack animals. You will thus secure, for the remaining three quarters unquestioned vigor. But how will you make up these pack trains? You will have plenty of wounded horses after a week of campaign.

CHAPTER IV - ARTILLERY

If artillery did not have a greater range than the rifle, we could not risk separating it far from its support, as it would have to wait until the enemy was but four or five hundred paces away to fire on him. But the more its range is increased, the further away it can be placed from its support.

The greater the range of artillery, the greater freedom of action from the different arms, which no longer have to be side by side to give mutual support.

The greater the range of artillery, the easier it is to concentrate its fire. Two batteries fifteen hundred meters apart can concentrate on a point twelve hundred meters in front of and between them. Before the range was so long they had to be close together, and the terrain did not always lend itself to this.

Furthermore, do not support a piece by placing infantry just behind or alongside of it, as is done three-quarters of the time at maneuvers. On the contrary hide the infantry to the right or left and far behind, cover it without worrying too much about distance and let the artillery call for help if they think that the piece is in danger of being lost. Why should infantry be placed too close, and consequently have its advance demoralized? This will throw away the greatest advantage that we Frenchmen have in defense, that of defending ourselves by advancing, with morale unimpaired, because we have not suffered heavy losses at a halt. There is always time to run to the defense of artillery. To increase the moral effect advance your supports in formation. Skirmishers can also be swiftly scattered among the batteries. These skirmishers, in the midst of the guns will not have to fear cavalry. Even if they are assailed by infantry it will not be such a terrible thing. The engagement will merely be one between skirmishers, and they will be able to take cover behind the pieces, firing against the enemy who is coming up in the open.

Guibert, I believe, held that artillery should not worry whether it was supported or not; that it should fire up to the last minute, and finally abandon the pieces, which supporting troops might or might not recapture. These supporting troops should not be too close. It is easier to defend pieces, to take them back even, by advancing on an enemy dispersed among them, than to defend them by standing fast after having participated in the losses suffered by the artillery under fire. (Note the English in Spain. The system of having artillery followed by infantry platoons is absurd.)

Artillery in battle has its men grouped around the pieces, stationary assembly points, broadly distributed, each one having its commander and its cannoneers, who are always the same. Thus there is in effect a roll call each time artillery is put into battery. Artillery carries its men with it; they cannot be lost nor can they hide. If the officer is brave, his men rarely desert him. Certainly, in all armies, it is in the artillery that the soldier can best perform his duty.

As General Leboeuf tells us, four batteries of artillery can be maneuvered, not more. That is all right. Here is the thing in a nut-shell. Four battalions is a big enough command for a colonel. A general has eight battalions. He gets orders, "General, do so and so." He orders, "Colonel, do so and so." So that without any maneuvers being laid down for more than four battalions, as many battalions as you like can be maneuvered and drilled.

CHAPTER V - COMMAND, GENERAL STAFF, ADMINISTRATION

There are plenty of carefree generals, who are never worried nor harassed. They do not bother about anything. They say, "I advance. Follow me." The result is an incredible disorder in the advance of columns. If ten raiders should fall on the column with a shout, this disorder would become a rout, a disaster. But these gentlemen never bother with such an eventuality. They are the great men of the day, until the moment that some disaster overwhelms them.

Cavalry is no more difficult to work with than infantry. According to some military authors, a cavalry general ought to have the wisdom of the phoenix. The perfect one should have. So should the perfect infantry general. Man on horseback and man afoot is always the same man. Only, the infantry general rarely has to account for the losses in his command, which may have been due to faulty or improper handling. The cavalry general does have to do this. (We shall lay aside the reasons why.) The infantry general has six chances for real battle to one for the cavalry general. These are the two reasons why, from the beginning of a war, more initiative is found in infantry than in cavalry generals. General Bugeaud might have made a better cavalry general than an infantry general. Why? Because he had immediate decision and firm resolution. There is more need for resolution in the infantryman than in the cavalryman. Why? There are many reasons, which are matters of opinion.

In short, the infantryman is always more tired than the cavalryman. His morale is therefore harder to keep up. I believe therefore that a good infantry general is rarer than one of cavalry. Also, the resolution of an infantry general does not have to last for a moment only; it has to endure for a long, long time.

Good artillery generals are common. They are less concerned with morale than with other things, such as material results. They have less need to bother about the morale of their troops, as combat discipline is always better with them than with the other arms. This is shown elsewhere.

Brigadier generals ought to be in their prescribed places. Very well, but the most of them are not and never have been. They were required to be in place at the battle of Moscow, but, as they were so ordered there, it is evident that they were not habitually in place. They are men; and their rank, it seems to them, ought to diminish rather than increase the risks they have to run. And, then, in actual engagement, where is their prescribed place?

When one occupies a high command there are many things which he does not see. The general-in-chief, even a division commander, can only escape this failing by great activity, moved by strict conscientiousness and aided by clairvoyance. This failing extends to those about him, to his heads of services. These men live well, sleep well; the same must be true of all! They have picked, well-conditioned horses; the roads are excellent! They are never sick; the doctors must be exaggerating sickness! They have attendants and doctors; everybody must be well looked after! Something happens which shows abominable negligence, common enough in war. With a good heart and a full belly they say, "But this is infamous, unheard of! It could not have happened! It is impossible! etc."

Today there is a tendency, whose cause should be sought, on the part of superiors to infringe on the authority of inferiors. This is general. It goes very high and is furthered by the mania for command, inherent in the French character. It results in lessening the authority of subordinate officers in the minds of their soldiers. This is a grave matter, as only the firm authority and prestige of subordinate officers can maintain discipline. The tendency is to oppress subordinates; to want to impose on them, in all things, the views of the superior; not to admit of honest mistakes, and to reprove them as faults; to make everybody, even down to the private, feel that there is only one infallible authority. A colonel, for instance, sets himself up as the sole authority with judgment and intelligence. He thus takes all initiative from subordinate officers, and reduces them to a state of inertia, coming from their lack of confidence in themselves and from fear of being severely reproved. How many generals, before a regiment, think only of showing how much they know! They lessen the authority of the colonel. That is nothing to them. They have asserted their superiority, true or false; that is the essential. With cheeks puffed out, they leave, proud of having attacked discipline.

This firm hand which directs so many things is absent for a moment. All subordinate officers up to this moment have been held with too strong a hand, which has kept them in a position not natural to them. Immediately they are like a horse, always kept on a tight rein, whose rein is loosened or missing. They cannot in an instant recover that confidence in themselves, that has been painstakingly taken away from them without their wishing it. Thus, in such a moment conditions become unsatisfactory, the soldier very quickly feels that the hand that holds him vacillates.

"Ask much, in order to obtain a little," is a false saying, a source of errors, an attack on discipline. One ought to obtain what one asks. It is only necessary to be moderately reasonable and practical.

In following out this matter, one is astonished at the lack of foresight found in three out of four officers. Why? Is there anything so difficult about looking forward a little? Are three-quarters of the officers so stupid? No! It is because their egoism, generally frankly acknowledged, allow them to think only of who is looking at them. They think of their troops by chance perhaps, or because they have to. Their troops are never their preoccupation, consequently they do not think about them at all. A major in command of an organization in Mexico, on his first march in a hot country, started without full canteens, perhaps without canteens at all, without any provision for water, as he might march in France. No officer in his battalion called his attention to the omission, nor was more foresighted than he. In this first march, by an entire lack of foresight in everything, he lost, in dead, half of his command. Was he reduced? No! He was made a lieutenant-colonel.

Officers of the general staff learn to order, not to command. "Sir, I order," a popular phrase, applies to them.

The misfortune is not that there is a general staff, but that it has achieved command. For it always has commanded, in the name of its commanders it is true, and never obeyed, which is its duty. It commands in fact. So be it! But just the same it is not supposed to.

Is it the good quality of staffs or that of combatants that makes the strength of armies? If you want good fighting men, do everything to excite their ambition, to spare them, so that people of intelligence and with a future will not despise the line but will elect to serve in it. It is the line that gives you your high command, the line only, and very rarely the staff. The staff, however, dies infrequently, which is something. Do they say that military science can only be learned in the general staff schools? If you really want to learn to do your work, go to the line.

Today, nobody knows anything unless he knows how to argue and chatter. A peasant knows nothing, he is a being unskilled even in cultivating the soil. But the agriculturist of the office is a farmer emeritus, etc. Is it then believed that there is ability only in the general staff? There is the assurance of the scholar there, of the pedagogue who has never practiced what he preaches. There is book learning, false learning when it treats of military matters. But knowledge of the real trade of a soldier, knowledge of what is possible, knowledge of blows given and received, all these are conspicuously absent.

Slowness of promotion in the general staff as compared to its rapidity in the line might make many men of intelligence, of head and heart, pass the general staff by and enter the line to make their own way. To be in the line would not then be a brevet of imbecility. But today when general staff officers rank the best of the line, the latter are discouraged and rather than submit to this situation, all who feel themselves fitted for advancement want to be on the general staff. So much the better? So much the worse. Selection is only warranted by battle.

How administrative deceits, in politics or elsewhere, falsify the conclusions drawn from a fact!

In the Crimea one hundred per cent. of the French operated upon succumbed, while only twenty-seven per cent. of the English operated upon died. That was attributed to the difference in temperament! The great cause of this discrepancy was the difference in care. Our newspapers followed the self-satisfied and rosy statements given out by our own supply department. They pictured our sick in the Crimea lying in beds and cared for by sisters of charity. The fact is that our soldiers never had sheets, nor mattresses, nor the necessary changes of clothes in the hospitals; that half, three-quarters, lay on mouldy straw, on the ground, under canvass. The fact is, that such were the conditions under which typhus claimed twenty-five to thirty thousand of our sick after the siege; that thousands of pieces of hospital equipment were offered by the English to our Quartermaster General, and that he refused them! Everybody ought to have known that he would! To accept such equipment was to acknowledge that he did not have it. And he ought to have had it. Indeed he did according to the newspapers and the Quartermaster reports. There were twenty-five beds per hospital so that it could be said, "We have beds!" Each hospital had at this time five hundred or more sick.

These people are annoyed if they are called hypocrites. While our soldiers were in hospitals, without anything, so to speak, the English had big, well-ventilated tents, cots, sheets, even night stands with urinals. And our men had not even a cup to drink from! Sick men were cared for in the English hospitals. They might have been in ours, before they died, which they almost always did.

It is true that we had the typhus and the English had not. That was because our men in tents had the same care as in our hospitals, and the English the same care as in their hospitals.

Read the war reports of supply departments and then go unexpectedly to verify them in the hospitals and storehouses. Have them verified by calling up and questioning the heads of departments, but question them conscientiously, without dictating the answers. In the Crimea, in May of the first year, we were no better off than the English who complained so much, Who has dared to say, however, that from the time they entered the hospital to the time that they left it, dead, evacuated, or cured, through fifteen or twenty days of cholera or typhus, our men lay on the same plank, in the same shoes, drawers, shirts and clothing that they brought in with them? They were in a state of living putrefaction that would by itself have killed well men! The newspapers chanted the praises of the admirable French administration. The second winter the English had no sick, a smaller percentage than in London. But to the eternal shame of the French command and administration we lost in peace time, twenty-five to thirty thousand of typhus and more than one thousand frozen to death. Nevertheless, it appeared that we had the most perfect administration in the world, and that our generals, no less than our administration, were full of devoted solicitude to provide all the needs of the soldier. That is an infamous lie, and is known as such, let us hope.

The Americans have given us a good example. The good citizens have gone themselves to see how their soldiers were treated and have provided for them themselves. When, in France, will good citizens lose faith in this best of administrations which is theirs? When will they, confident in themselves, do spontaneously, freely, what their administration cannot and never will be able to do?

The first thing disorganized in an army is the administration. The simplest foresight, the least signs even of order disappear in a retreat. (Note Russia-Vilna).

In the Crimea, and everywhere more or less, the doctor's visit was without benefit to the patient. It was made to keep up his spirits, but could not be followed by care, due to lack of personnel and material. After two or three hours of work, the doctor was exhausted.

In a sane country the field and permanent hospitals ought to be able to handle one-fifth of the strength at least. The hospital personnel of today should be doubled. It is quickly cut down, and it ought to have time, not only to visit the sick, but to care for them, feed them, dose and dress them, etc.

CHAPTER VI - SOCIAL AND MILITARY INSTITUTIONS - NATIONAL CHARACTERISTICS

Man's admiration for the great spectacles of nature is the admiration for force. In the mountains it is mass, a force, that impresses him, strikes him, makes him admire. In the calm sea it is the mysterious and terrible force that he divines, that he feels in that enormous liquid mass; in the angry sea, force again. In the wind, in the storm, in the vast depth of the sky, it is still force that he admires.

All these things astounded man when he was young. He has become old, and he knows them. Astonishment has turned to admiration, but always it is the feeling of a formidable force which compels his admiration. This explains his admiration for the warrior.

The warrior is the ideal of the primitive man, of the savage, of the barbarian. The more people rise in moral civilization, the lower this ideal falls. But with the masses everywhere the warrior still is and for a long time will be the height of their ideals. This is because man loves to admire the force and bravery that are his own attributes. When that force and bravery find other means to assert themselves, or at least when the crowd is shown that war does not furnish the best examples of them, that there are truer and more exalted examples, this ideal will give way to a higher one.

Nations have an equal sovereignty based on their existence as states. They recognize no superior jurisdiction and call on force to decide their differences. Force decides. Whether or not might was right, the weaker bows to necessity until a more successful effort can be made. (Prud'homme). It is easy to understand Gregory VII's ideas on the subject.

In peace, armies are playthings in the hands of princes. If the princes do not know anything about them, which is usually the case, they disorganize them. If they understand them, like the Prince of Prussia, they make their armies strong for war.

The King of Prussia and the Prussian nobility, threatened by democracy, have had to change the passion for equality in their people into a passion for domination over foreign nations. This is easily done, when domination is crowned with success, for man, who is merely the friend of equality is the lover of domination. So that he is easily made to take the shadow for the substance. They have succeeded. They are forced to continue with their system. Otherwise their status as useful members of society would be questioned and they would perish as leaders in war. Peace spells death to a nobility. Consequently nobles do not desire it, and stir up rivalries among peoples, rivalries which alone can justify their existence as leaders in war, and consequently as leaders in peace. This is why the military spirit is dead in France. The past does not live again. In the spiritual as in the physical world, what is dead is dead. Death comes only with the exhaustion of the elements, the conditions which are necessary for life. For these reasons revolutionary wars continued into the war with Prussia. For these reasons if we had been victorious we would have found against us the countries dominated by nobilities, Austria, Russia, England. But with us vanquished, democracy takes up her work in all European countries, protected in the security which victory always gives to victors. This work is slower but surer than the rapid work of war, which, exalting rivalries, halts for a moment the work of democracy within the nations themselves. Democracy then takes up her work with less chance of being deterred by rivalry against us. Thus we are closer to the triumph of democracy than if we had been victors. French democracy rightfully desires to live, and she does not desire to do so at the expense of a sacrifice of national pride. Then, since she will still be surrounded for a long time by societies dominated by the military element, by the nobility, she must have a dependable army. And, as the military spirit is on the wane in France, it must be replaced by having noncommissioned officers and officers well paid. Good pay establishes position in a democracy, and today none turn to the army, because it is too poorly paid. Let us have well paid mercenaries. By giving good pay, good material can be secured, thanks to the old warrior strain in the race. This is the price that must be paid for security.

The soldier of our day is a merchant. So much of my flesh, of my blood, is worth so much. So much of my time, of my affections, etc. It is a noble trade, however, perhaps because man's blood is noble merchandise, the finest that can be dealt in.

M. Guizot says "Get rich!" That may seem cynical to prudes, but it is truly said. Those who deny the sentiment, and talk today so loftily, what do they advise? If not by words, then by example they counsel the same thing; and example is more contagious. Is not private wealth, wealth in general, the avowed ambition sought by all, democrats and others? Let us be rich, that is to say, let us be slaves of the needs that wealth creates.

The Invalides in France, the institutions for pensioners, are superb exhibits of pomp and ostentation. I wish that their founding had been based on ideas of justice and Christianity and not purely on military-political considerations. But the results are disastrous to morality. This collection of weaklings is a school of depravity, where the invalided soldier loses in vice his right to respect.

Some officers want to transform regiments into permanent schools for officers of all ranks, with a two-hour course each day in law, military art, etc. There is little taste for military life in France; such a procedure would lessen it. The leisure of army life attracts three out of four officers, laziness, if you like. But such is the fact. If you make an officer a school-boy all his life he will send his profession to the devil, if he can. And those who are able to do so, will in general be those who have received the best education. An army is an extraordinary thing, but since it is necessary, there should be no astonishment that extraordinary means must be taken to keep it up; such as offering in peace time little work and a great deal of leisure. An officer is a sort of aristocrat, and in France we have no finer ideal of aristocratic life than one of leisure. This is not a proof of the highest ideals, nor of firmness of character. But what is to be done about it?

From the fact that military spirit is lacking in our nation (and officers are with greater difficulty than ever recruited in France) it does not follow that we shall not have to engage in war. Perhaps the contrary is true.

It is not patriotic to say that the military spirit is dead in France? The truth is always patriotic. The military spirit died with the French nobility, perished because it had to perish, because it was exhausted, at the end of its life. That only dies which has no longer the sap of life, and can no longer live. If a thing is merely sick it can return to health. But who can say that of the French nobility? An aristocracy, a nobility that dies, dies always by its own fault; because it no longer performs its duties; because it fails in its task; because its functions are of no more value to the state; because there is no longer any reason for its existence in a society, whose final tendency is to suppress its functions.

After 1789 had threatened our patriotism, the natural desire for self-protection revived the military spirit in the nation and in the army. The Empire developed this movement, changed the defensive military spirit to the offensive, and used it with increasing effect up to 1814 or 1815. The military spirit of the July Restoration was a reminiscence, a relic of the Empire, a form of opposition to government by liberalism instead of democracy. It was really the spirit of opposition and not the military spirit, which is essentially conservative.

There is no military spirit in a democratic society, where there is no aristocracy, no military nobility. A democratic society is antagonistic to the military spirit.

The military spirit was unknown to the Romans. They made no distinction between military and civil duties. I think that the military air dates from the time that the profession of arms became a private profession, from the time of the bravos, the Italian condottieri, who were more terrifying to civilians than to the enemy. When the Romans said "cedant arma togae," they did not refer to civil officials and soldiers; the civil officials were then soldiers in their turn; professional soldiers did not exist. They meant "might gives way to right."

Machiavelli quotes a proverb, "War makes thieves and peace has them hanged" The Spaniards in Mexico, which has been in rebellion for forty years, are more or less thieves. They want to continue to ply the trade. Civil authority exists no longer with them, and they would look on obedience to such an authority as shameful. It is easy to understand the difficulty of organizing a peaceful government in such a country. Half the population would have to hang the other half. The other half does not want to be hanged.

We are a democratic society; we become less and less military. The Prussian, Russian, Austrian aristocracies which alone make the military spirit of those states, feel in our democratic society an example which threatens their existence, as nobility, as aristocracy. They are our enemies and will be until they are wiped, out, until the Russian, Austrian and Prussian states become democratic societies, like ours. It is a matter of time.

The Prussian aristocracy is young. It has not been degenerated by wealth, luxury and servility of the court. The Prussian court is not a court in the luxurious sense of the word. There is the danger.

Meanwhile Machiavellian doctrines not being forbidden to aristocracies, these people appeal to German Jingoism, to German patriotism, to all the passions which move one people who are jealous of another. All this is meant to hide under a patriotic exterior their concern for their own existence as an aristocracy, as a nobility.

The real menace of the day is czarism, stronger than the czars themselves, which calls for a crusade to drive back Russia and the uncultured Slav race.

It is time that we understood the lack of power in mob armies; that we recall to mind the first armies of the revolution that were saved from instant destruction only by the lack of vigor and decision in European cabinets and armies. Look at the examples of revolutionaries of all times, who have all to gain and cannot hope for mercy. Since Spartacus, have they not always been defeated? An army is not really strong unless it is developed from a social institution. Spartacus and his men were certainly terrible individual fighters. They were gladiators used to struggle and death. They were prisoners, barbarian slaves enraged by their loss of liberty, or escaped serfs, all men who could not hope for mercy. What more terrible fighters could be imagined? But discipline, leadership, all was improvised and could not have the firm discipline coming down from the centuries and drawn from the social institutions of the Romans. They were conquered. Time, a long time, is needed to give to leaders the habit of command and confidence in their authority—to the soldiers confidence in their leaders and in their fellows. It is not enough to order discipline. The officers must have the will to enforce it, and its vigorous enforcement must instill subordination in the soldiers. It must make them fear it more than they fear the enemy's blows.

How did Montluc fight, in an aristocratic society? Montluc shows us, tells us. He advanced in the van of the assault, but in bad places he pushed in front of him a soldier whose skin was not worth as much as was his. He had not the slightest doubt or shame about doing this. The soldier did not protest, the propriety of the act was so well established. But you, officers, try that in a democratic army, such as we have commenced to have, such as we shall later have!

In danger the officer is no better than the soldier. The soldier is willing enough to advance, but behind his officer. Also, his comrades' skin is no more precious than is his, they must advance too. This very real concern about equality in danger, which seeks equality only, brings on hesitation and not resolution. Some fools may break their heads in closing in, but the remainder will fire from a distance. Not that this will cause fewer losses, far from it.

Italy will never have a really firm army. The Italians are too civilized, too fine, too democratic in a certain sense of the word. The Spaniards are the same. This may cause laughter, but it is true. The French are indeed worthy sons of their fathers, the Gauls. War, the most solemn act in the life of a nation, the gravest of acts, is a light thing to them. The good Frenchman lets himself be carried away, inflamed by the most ridiculous feats of arms into the wildest enthusiasm. Moreover he interprets the word "honor" in a fashion all his own. An expedition is commenced without sufficient reason, and good Frenchmen, who do not know why the thing is done, disapprove. But presently blood is spilled. Good sense and justice dictate that this spilled blood should taint those responsible for an unjust enterprise. But jingoism says "French blood has been spilled: Honor is at stake!" And millions of gold, which is the unit of labor, millions of men, are sacrificed to a ridiculous high-sounding phrase.

Whence comes this tendency toward war which characterizes above all the good citizen, the populace, who are not called upon personally to participate? The military man is not so easily swayed. Some hope for promotion or pension, but even they are sobered by their sense of duty. It comes from the romance that clothes war and battle, and that has with us ten times more than elsewhere, the power of exciting enthusiasm in the people. It would be a service to humanity and to one's people to dispell this illusion, and to show what battles are. They are buffooneries, and none the less buffooneries because they are made terrible by the spilling of blood. The actors, heroes in the eyes of the crowd, are only poor folk torn between fear, discipline and pride. They play some hours at a game of advance and retreat, without ever meeting, closing with, even seeing closely, the other poor folks, the enemy, who are as fearful as they but who are caught in the same web of circumstance.

What should be considered is how to organize an army in a country in which there is at the same time national and provincial feeling. Such a country is France, where there is no longer any necessity for uniting national and provincial feeling by mixing up the soldiers. In France, will the powerful motif of pride, which comes from the organization of units from particular provinces, be useful? From the fusion of varying elements comes the character of our troops, which is something to be considered. The make-up of the heavy cavalry should be noted. It has perhaps too many Germans and men from the northern provinces.

French sociability creates cohesion in French troops more quickly than could be secured in troops in other nations. Organization and discipline have the same purpose. With a proud people like the French, a rational organization aided by French sociability can often secure desired results without it being necessary to use the coercion of discipline.

Marshal de Gouvion-Saint Cyr said, "Experienced soldiers know and others ought to know that French soldiers once committed to the pursuit of the enemy will not return to their organization that day until forced back into it by the enemy. During this time they must be considered as lost to the rest of the army."

At the beginning of the Empire, officers, trained in the wars of the Revolution by incessant fighting, possessed great firmness. No one would wish to purchase such firmness again at the same price. But in our modern wars the victor often loses more than the vanquished, apart from the temporary loss in prisoners. The losses exceed the resources in good men, and discourage the exhausted, who appear to be very numerous, and those who are skilled in removing themselves from danger. Thus we fall into disorder. The Duke of Fezensac, testifying of other times, shows us the same thing that happens today. Also today we depend only on mass action, and at that game, despite the cleverest strategic handling, we must lose all, and do.

French officers lack firmness but have pride. In the face of danger they lack composure, they are disconcerted, breathless, hesitant, forgetful, unable to think of a way out. They call, "Forward, forward." This is one of the reasons why handling a formation in line is difficult, especially since the African campaigns where much is left to the soldier.

The formation in rank is then an ideal, unobtainable in modern war, but toward which we should strive. But we are getting further away from it. And then, when habit loses its hold, natural instinct resumes its empire. The remedy lies in an organization which will establish cohesion by the mutual acquaintanceship of all. This will make possible mutual surveillance, which has such power over French pride.

It might be said that there are two kinds of war, that in open country, and in the plain, and that of posts garrisoning positions in broken country. In a great war, with no one occupying positions, we should be lost immediately. Marshal Saxe knew us well when he said that the French were best for a war of position. He recognized the lack of stability in the ranks.

On getting within rifle range the rank formation tends to disappear. You hear officers who have been under fire say "When you get near the enemy, the men deploy as skirmishers despite you. The Russians group under fire. Their holding together is the huddling of sheep moved by fear of discipline and of danger." There are then two modes of conduct under fire, the French and the Russian.

The Gauls, seeing the firmness of the Roman formation, chained themselves together, making the first rank unbreakable and tying living to dead. This forbade the virtue they had not divined in the Roman formation, the replacement of wounded and exhausted by fresh men. From this replacement came the firmness which seemed so striking to the Gauls. The rank continually renewed itself.

Why does the Frenchman of today, in singular contrast to the Gaul, scatter under fire? His natural intelligence, his instinct under the pressure of danger causes him to deploy.

His method must be adopted. In view of the impossibility today of the Roman Draconian discipline which put the fear of death behind the soldier, we must adopt the soldier's method and try to put some order into it. How? By French discipline and an organization that permits of it.

Broken, covered country is adapted to our methods. The zouaves at Magenta could not have done so well on another kind of ground.

Above all, with modern weapons, the terrain to be advanced over must be limited in depth.

How much better modern tactics fit the impatient French character! But also how necessary it is to guard against this impatience and to keep supports and reserves under control.

It should be noted that German or Gallic cavalry was always better than Roman cavalry, which could not hold against it, even though certainly better armed. Why was this? Because decision, impetuosity, even blind courage, have more chance with cavalry than with infantry. The defeated cavalry is the least brave cavalry. (A note for our cavalry here!) It was easier for the Gauls to have good cavalry than it is for us, as fire did not bother them in the charge.

The Frenchman has more qualities of the cavalryman than of the infantryman. Yet French infantry appears to be of greater value. Why? Because the use of cavalry on the battlefield requires rare decision and the seizing of the crucial opportunity. If the cavalryman has not been able to show his worth, it is the fault of his leaders. French infantry has always been defeated by English infantry. In cavalry combat the English cavalry has always fled before the French in those terrible cavalry battles that are always flights. Is this because in war man lasts longer in the cavalry and because our cavalrymen were older and more seasoned soldiers than our infantry? This does not apply to us only. If it is true for our cavalrymen, it is also true for the English cavalrymen. The reason is that on the field of battle the role of the infantryman against a firm adversary requires more coolness and nerve than does the role of the cavalryman. It requires the use of tactics based on an understanding of the national characteristics of ourselves and of our enemies. Against the English the confidence in the charge that is implanted in our brains, was completely betrayed. The role of cavalry against cavalry is simpler. The French confidence in the charge makes good fighting cavalry, and the Frenchman is better fitted than any other for this role. Our cavalry charge better than any other. That is the whole thing, on the battle field it is understood. As they move faster than infantry, their dash, which has its limits, is better preserved when they get up to the enemy.

The English have always fled before our cavalry. This proves that, strong enough to hold before the moral impulse of our infantry, they were not strong enough to hold before the stronger impulse of cavalry.

We ought to be much better cavalrymen than infantrymen, because the essential in a cavalryman is a fearless impetuosity. That is for the soldier. The cavalry leader ought to use this trait without hesitation, at the same time taking measures to support it and to guard against its failings. The attack is always, even on the defensive, an evidence of resolution, and gives a moral ascendancy. Its effect is more immediate with cavalry, because the movements of cavalry are more rapid and the moral effect has less time to be modified by reflection. To insure that the French cavalry be the best in Europe, and a really good cavalry, it needs but one thing, to conform to the national temperament, to dare, to dare, and to advance.

One of the singular features of French discipline is that on the road, especially in campaign the methods of punishment for derelictions become illusory, impractical. In 1859 there were twenty-five thousand skulkers in the Army in Italy. The soldier sees this immediately and lack of discipline ensues. If our customs do not permit of Draconian discipline, let us replace that moral coercion by another. Let us insure cohesion by the mutual acquaintanceship of men and officers; let us call French sociability to our aid.

With the Romans discipline was severest and most rigidly enforced in the presence of the enemy. It was enforced by the soldiers themselves. Today, why should not the men in our companies watch discipline and punish themselves. They alone know each other, and the maintenance of discipline is so much to their interest as to encourage them to stop skulking. The twenty-five thousand men who skulked in Italy, all wear the Italian medal. They were discharged with certificates of good conduct. This certificate, in campaign should be awarded by the squad only. In place of that, discipline must be obtained somehow, and it is placed as an additional burden on the officer. He above all has to uphold it. He is treated without regard for his dignity. He is made to do the work of the non-commissioned officer. He is used as fancy dictates.

This cohesion which we hope for in units from squad to company, need not be feared in other armies. It cannot develop to the same point and by the same methods with them as with us. Their make-up is not ours, their character is different. This individuality of squads and companies comes from the make-up of our army and from French sociability.

Is it true that the rations of men and horses are actually insufficient in campaign? This is strange economy! To neglect to increase the soldier's pay five centimes! It would better his fare and prevent making of an officer a trader in vegetables in order to properly feed his men. Yet millions are squandered each year for uniforms, geegaws, shakos, etc!

If a big army is needed, it ought to cost as little as possible. Simplicity in all things! Down with all sorts of plumes! Less amateurs! If superfluous trimmings are not cut down it will be unfortunate! What is the matter with the sailor's uniform? Insignificant and annoying details abound while vital details of proper footgear and instruction, are neglected. The question of clothing for campaign is solved by adopting smocks and greatcoats and by doing away with headquarters companies! This is the height of folly. I suppose it is because our present uniforms need specialists to keep them in condition, and smocks and greatcoats do not!

Image Gallery

A Greek trireme

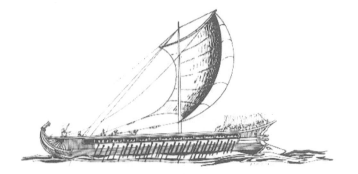

3rd C. sarcophagus depicting a battle between Romans and Goths

1346 Battle of Crécy between the English and French in the Hundred Years' War

Figs. 24 and 25.—Varlet or Squire carrying a Halberd with a thick Blade; and Archer, in Fighting Dress, drawing the String of his Crossbow with a double-handled Winch.—From the Miniatures of the "Jouvencel," and the "Chroniques" of Froissart, Manuscripts of the Fifteenth Century (Imperial Library of Paris).

Crossbowmen at the Martyrdom of St Sebastian.
Detail of a painting from Upper Bavaria, c.1475.

Crossbow by Leonardo da Vinci, c. 1500

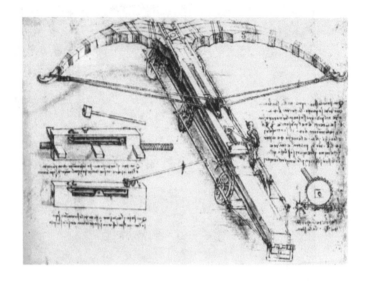

The victory of the Polish-Lithuanian forces over the Muscovites at the Battle of Orsha in 1514

Napoleon in Berlin after defeating Prussian forces at Jena, 1806

Wellington and musketeers at Waterloo, 1815

Made in United States
Troutdale, OR
06/24/2024

20790452R00300